The Author Speaks

The Author Speaks

SELECTED
PW INTERVIEWS
1967–1976

---

by *Publishers Weekly*
Editors and Contributors

R. R. BOWKER COMPANY
New York & London, 1977

Published by R. R. Bowker Company
1180 Avenue of the Americas, New York, N.Y. 10036
Copyright © 1978 by Xerox Corporation
Printed and bound in the United States of America

Library of Congress Cataloging in Publication Data
Main entry under title:

The Author speaks.

  Bibliography: p.
  Includes index.
  1. Authors—Interviews. I. The Publishers' weekly.
PN453.A9   809   77-17517
ISBN 0-8352-1050-2

Contents

Part 2 Mystery and Suspense

Part 3 Biography

Part 4 Autobiography, Letters, Memoirs

Part 5   Current Social Concerns and Social Commentary

Part 6 History and Political Commentary

Foreword

The roots of the book trade begin with authorship—a truism that needs to be restated from time to time only because the trade itself sometimes forgets the chain of its being. *Publishers Weekly*, consciously devoted to the business of the trade, has tried to keep in the forefront of the trade consciousness—and, come to think of it, in the forefront of the publication itself—the fact that authors are warm, breathing creatures, who have observations to make and opinions to state beyond what appear between the covers of their books. The device, "*PW* Interviews," was adopted as the weekly lead-off feature in 1972, to open up the magazine largely to those authors we felt made lively interview subjects, were unhesitant in speaking their minds, willing to field tough questions gracefully, and allowed the magazine, as it were, to lead with a piquant appetizer. As the section became more and more popular—and, thanks to the interviewers, crackled with style and wit—the problem became one of selection. Inundated as we were with requests for interviews from the amiable workhorses of the business—the trade house publicity directors—"*PW* Interviews" could never accommodate more than a fraction of the authors offered for our consideration. It is a measure of the trade's good will that, despite this restraint, the author interview thrives as one of *PW*'s most popular and admired features.

ARNOLD W. EHRLICH

Introduction

Since the beginning of 1967, a regular feature of news reporting in *Publishers Weekly* has been a series of interviews with authors and editors, written by some staff members of the magazine and its contributors. The series was established at that time on a more or less weekly basis coincident with the magazine's shift from its traditional two-column setting and 6¼ × 9¼-inch format to the present three-column setting and 8¼ × 11¼-inch trim size. The regular interviews for several years were called "Authors and Editors" and, beginning in 1972, "*PW* Interviews." These interviews should not be confused with another continuing, though irregularly published feature begun in the 1970s, the "Views on Publishing" series. This deals with book industry people, not authors as such. It is based on questions and answers, quoted and edited, and the articles are much longer than the "*PW* Interviews."

The articles chosen for this volume are taken from those interviews written about authors only. Of the interviews selected, Barbara A. Bannon, senior editor of *PW*, wrote well over a third; John F. Baker, former managing editor, over a fourth; and his predecessor, Roger H. Smith, 16. The rest were written by: Herbert R. Lottman, international editor of *PW*; Jean F. Mercier, children's book editor; Arnold W. Ehrlich, editor-in-chief; his predecessor, Chandler B. Grannis; associate editors Douglas N. Mount, Lila P. Freilicher, Peter Gardner, Daisy G. Maryles, Michael Mok, Alice Payne Hackett, Dan Rustin, Sylvia Auerbach, Albert H. Johnston, and Pamela Bragg; also by a number of contributors: Marcelle Bernstein, Patricia Bosworth, Thomas Chastain, Peter Grosvenor, Joyce Illig, Bernard and Marvin Kalb, Philip Norman, Joan Norris, Stanton Peckham, and John Weisman.

The articles for this collection were selected and arranged by Nada Beth Glick, sponsoring editor, book editorial department, R. R. Bowker.

Interviews have, of course, always been important in *PW*'s reporting, though not on as regular a basis as they have been since 1967. Inspired by the *New Yorker* "Profiles," Mildred C. Smith, editor of *PW*, instituted about 30 years ago an occasional feature called "Take a Bow," mostly about book industry personalities. For many years the seasonal issues devoted to children's books contained interviews and articles by Muriel Fuller about top editors in that field; and the announcements of the Newbery and Caldecott Medals were accompanied by similar pieces about the winning authors and illustrators. Brief author interviews appeared in the "Tips" or "Currents" sections of *PW* occasionally over the 30-year period preceding the 1967 format change. Among the editors who wrote occasional interviews in that era were Eugene Armfield, Mildred C. Smith, Mary Elisabeth Edes Agnew, Peter S. Jennison, Gladys de Silva, and Barbara A. Bannon. The list could be extended back into earlier years.

Bowker acknowledges with gratitude the assistance of interviewers and subjects represented in the pieces offered here.

CHANDLER B. GRANNIS
Consulting Editor
R. R. Bowker Company

1

Novels, Short Stories

Robert Anderson

"I'M WRITING about survival, not death," Robert Anderson said. The well-known playwright, author of "Tea and Sympathy" and a number of other hit plays, sat in Sardi's recently and talked about his first novel, "After," published last month by Random House.

The plot of his somber and moving novel concerns a writer whose wife has just died hideously of cancer. After her death he escapes to their country cottage on Cape Cod, where he becomes involved with a young actress. During their passionate affair he relives his past and weighs the good and bad times of his marriage. By the end of the book the affair is over and the writer is no longer afraid to face life alone.

Since Anderson's first wife died of cancer 15 years ago, many of the book's early readers have been asking whether "After" is in any way autobiographical, and *PW* was no exception. "I think everyone has the right to ask that," the playwright replied. "But if the writer admits it's all fiction the reader feels cheated, and if he admits it's all autobiographical the reader feels embarrassed. I'd rather fill in the background this way. I tell my students that writing is like painting. At first the painter looks back and forth—from his canvas to the bowl of flowers he's painting on the canvas. But finally his total concentration is focused on what is in front of him on the easel, and it may barely resemble the bowl of flowers. The same holds true in writing. The writer draws from memory, imagination and experience, then they melt together and fuse. The best writing, I think, is full of lies that tell the truth.

By Patricia Bosworth. From *Publishers Weekly* 204, no. 2 (July 9, 1973), pp. 16–17. Reprinted by permission of Patricia Bosworth.

"I have always been obsessed with the themes of love and sex and death and marriage," Anderson continued. "What themes are more basic to our existence? I've written about them over and over again—not always successfully as far as the critics are concerned. It's funny about success—the kids I teach always want to hear about my failures. They like to think that being successful can't be artistic. So I tell them about my play 'Silent Night, Lonely Night,' which was a so-called failure—but I loved that play and learned from writing it. Actually, I don't think of any of my plays as failures. Even if some of them haven't had long runs on Broadway, they're still performed all over the world."

How had he got the idea for "After"? "I'd been thinking about a book like this for eight years," Anderson says. "I kept making outlines and notes and drafts. Finally I realized it couldn't be a play—there was so much explicit sex in it, so many interior monologues and so little action."

In between working on the idea behind the book, "which was basically about a man who comes back to life and sex and love after his wife dies," Anderson wrote plays like "You Know I Can't Hear You When the Water's Running" and "I Never Sang for My Father," which became a highly praised motion picture after its Broadway run.

Then, two years ago, he was asked to participate in a symposium, at the University of Rochester's medical school, on death and its effect on those close to it. "Doctors were going to speak theoretically," Anderson said. "I was asked to give a personal account. At first I was reluctant but then I thought: now I'll have a chance to formulate what I really think about death and how I responded when someone close to me became terminally ill. Strangely enough, there is not much information on the subject, perhaps because the whole thing is so painful and mysteriously profound.

"After I made my speech the response was overwhelming. An account of what I'd said was published in newspapers around the country and I received literally thousands of letters of thanks. NBC even asked me to moderate a panel on death—I turned that down. But the experience brought home to me how many people are confused and terrified by the oncoming death of a loved one. They feel guilty, for instance, if they're relieved when death comes. Others don't know how to cope with all the freedom they suddenly have—they may have focused an entire adult existence on caring for an ill member of a family. Anyhow, once I realized what an important theme this was, I began to write my novel. It is a positive book, not a negative one. The main character in my story learns how to feel joy and energy again and enthusiasm—he stops mourning and goes on."

Anderson wrote his novel in the studio a short walk from his country home in Connecticut. As he always does, he rose at 6 A.M. and worked steadily until he completed the first draft, without ever going back to look at it or rewrite chapters along the way. "I do the same thing with my plays—write them straight through without stopping. A neighbor of mine, Arthur Miller, thinks I'm nuts."

Another neighbor, William Styron, couldn't believe Anderson wrote the novel without a contract. "That leaves me under no obligation, with no deadlines. I still respond like a playwright," Anderson says. "None of us is ever *signed* to write a work for the theater—we write our plays and then they're produced or they're not."

Anderson discovered that the actual process of writing a novel was "very different from writing a play. In the novel you must add texture, details—extend scenes, rather than pare them down." However, when he finished the manuscript and Random House accepted "After," he found that "a great editor serves the same function as a great director. Nan Talese, my editor at Random, went over my manuscript in the same way Gadge Kazan went over 'Tea and Sympathy' and other plays of mine."

Anderson first became interested in writing as a student at Harvard. "I'd thought I wanted to be an actor but then a wonderful woman in the theater department there, a director named Phyllis Stohl, who later became my wife, encouraged me to write." He married Phyllis in 1940 before going into the Navy. Between battles at sea he wrote a number of plays which eventually won him a $2000 National Theater Conference grant. In 1945, upon his Navy discharge, he and his wife (who had meanwhile become a play agent for MCA) lived in New York, where Anderson taught at the American Theatre Wing and worked for Theatre Guild on the Air. In one year he adapted 25 classic plays—"everything from Shakespeare to Shaw"—into radio scripts. "That's how I learned to write," he says.

In 1953, after writing 15 unproduced plays, he finished "Tea and Sympathy," about a student in a boys' prep school who falls in love with a professor's wife. It was based in part on Anderson's own experiences at Exeter. "I worked my way through four years—I was a janitor and waited on tables."

After that Anderson wrote consistently for Broadway and the movies. To this day he still loves the "crazy camaraderie" of the theater. He is active with the Dramatists Guild (he is a former president) and continues to encourage young playwrights to write for the stage. "The economics makes it almost impossible for anything to go on Broadway, but regional theater is flourishing; playwrights mustn't be discouraged."

At the moment he and his second wife, actress Teresa Wright, spend most of their time in the country, with side trips to their pied-à-terre in New York. Now Anderson is excited at the prospect of publicizing his book. "Why not? It's mine and I want the novel to be read and enjoyed."

What's next on his agenda? "I never talk about future projects," Anderson says. "It's bad luck and it dissipates your energy." He smiled. "Writing for me is like undoing a dream. And you never talk about a dream until it's over and comes swimming out of your subconscious, do you?"

Michael J. Arlen

FOR MICHAEL J. ARLEN, being the son of a famous writer hasn't helped him at all to become the sort of writer he always wanted to be. "Living in my sort of family I became sophisticated very early," he says. "But it took me a long time to grow up. And I found it very difficult to become a writer. To be a writer you have to have a territory to work from, and for a long time I was unsure of mine."

His books, "Exiles," (1970) and last year's "Passage to Ararat," which won him a National Book Award, were his attempts at defining that territory for himself, and in writing them he felt often that "you have to put yourself on the line." In writing a family memoir, like "Exiles," or seeking out one's ethnic roots, as in "Ararat," he says, "It's important to be spontaneous. It's no good just trying to turn the past into a series of tableaux that you can hold and turn around so as to present them in the best light. You have to proceed by impulse, to become deeply involved yourself—and if there isn't that sort of involvement, why write at all? Why simply join the hubbub? If what I'm writing doesn't matter, deeply, to me, why should it matter to a reader?"

Perhaps because it was so comparatively late (he was nearly 40) before he found his voice professionally, Arlen has an unusually profound sense of vocation, of the importance of communicating the nobility of the human struggle. "What I find lacking so often in writing these days is any feeling of affection," he declares. "Perhaps writers stay away from it because of fear of sentimentality, but it's essential for a writer to feel warmth for his subject. There is something noble in the way people live their lives, the way

By John F. Baker. From *Publishers Weekly* 210, no. 9 (August 30, 1976), pp. 248–249.

they cope, parents with children for instance—it's so doomed, yet the brave, moving attempt goes on."

After his two books of recollection and exploration, and two collections of his very acute writings about television ("The Living Room War" was published in 1969; his new collection, "The View from Highway One," is due next month from his longtime publisher, Farrar, Straus & Giroux), Arlen is working now, for the first time, on a novel. He is spending the summer with his family (several of his own children from a previous marriage and stepchildren from his second) on a ranch in Wyoming, and the novel will have a Western setting. He will not describe it beyond saying that, in accordance with his vision of what is important, it is "about the courage of Americans living an ordinary life."

He muses for a moment on F. Scott Fitzgerald's observation that "there are no second acts in American life," and decides that there is a great deal of truth in it for the writer. "So much energy comes from one's childhood that the temptation is to keep digging into it. But the hardest thing for any writer, as for any person, is to deal truthfully and directly with one's own adult life. It's an area that hardly anyone is exploring today, and only the best—Roth and Updike, for instance—are even trying."

Perhaps as a result of American affluence, Arlen feels, too many young novelists are able to set up shop before they have anything much to say. "They never seem to leave their house, so where on earth do they get their material? And material is so important. One of the things I most admire about Norman Mailer, next to his energy, is his constant attempt, often manic, to get out of the house to seek new material, to experience something new and different. Sensibility is not the problem—Jane Austen would be astonished at the amount of it floating around—but new material is scarce."

As for his writing about TV, Arlen says that is his way of "getting out of the house: it enables me to write simply of ordinary things, after all my heavier efforts at self-exploration." His TV criticism, which helped him to find his feet as a writer, came about almost by accident. "I'd been doing some movie reviews, and William Shawn [*New Yorker* editor] asked if I'd like to try and take a look at TV and write a few pieces. I decided I'd try it, and I've been doing it on and off ever since."

Arlen is not a writer who would be likely to waste his time, and he resents the suggestion, from some writer friends, that he is wasting it by writing about TV—even in the *New Yorker*. "I think that's a great mistake. TV, like it or not, is a central part of American life, and it's a privilege to have the space to comment on it at will. As I tried to say in my introduction to the new book, there's a certain ambiguity about TV in this country. It reflects American life to a certain extent, yet it's also in tension against it. A great deal of it is rubbish, yet it is rubbish that may affect the outlook of millions of people—and to try to explain this ambiguity seems to me entirely interesting and worthwhile.''

His new book contains essays on the Vietnam war as reported on TV, the image of women in TV advertising, the comedy series of Norman Lear, the invasion of British drama on public television, among many other subjects. It also contains a couple of mordantly funny set pieces in which a family is seen having breakfast and enjoying a Thanksgiving dinner, intercut with the subliminal chatter of a quarter-watched TV set. Arlen is delighted that the *PW* interviewer particularly enjoyed these. "Some of my youthful idols were Benchley, Leacock and Perelman," he confesses. "When I started out as a writer I just wanted to do short humorous pieces; I was saved from that by circumstances, but I still like to hit that note when I can.''

But what fascinates Arlen above all about TV, and runs like a constant leitmotif through his writings about it, is the tremendous wealth and power of the TV networks, and the timidity with which they wield that wealth and power. "They really did nothing about Vietnam, for instance, though they could have had an enormous influence on the way we saw the war. People say I'm unrealistic to expect more of them, but I just want to keep pointing out the possibilities and show that they don't *have* to be so limited—and that even on the very limited level on which most TV is created, it still doesn't work.''

Thoughts of TV lead, inevitably, to ponderings on popular culture and what Arlen sees as a growing intellectual inability to seriously criticize its manifestations. "Yes, individual popular songs or movies can be enjoyable, but there's no *duty* to admire them.'' It seems to him that at present "there is a great secret passion play going on in this country between those who think life counts for something and those who think it doesn't, or who don't care. And if you do think it counts for something, why behave so shoddily? All a writer can do is indicate some of these things.''

Now that he feels firmly rooted as a writer ("After 'Ararat' I was able to feel that 'this is where I stand' ''), Arlen can look ahead to two or three more novels he'd like to do when the present one is completed. But although he could never see doing it on a full-time basis, he wants to continue to watch and report on TV—"There's really no one else doing what I'm doing.''

As to his recent National Book Award, he was pleased and proud of it, but would hate to see the awards ceremonies become more obviously commercial or decorative. "This is a reward for demanding effort; it's given out of respect for the best, not necessarily the most salable,'' he says, and adds with a grin: "It's amazing—and, to me, refreshing—to find how wonderfully solitary writers still are, in this media age. That press conference we had for the winners at the Plaza showed how utterly unaccustomed most of us were to even showing our faces in public at all. I'm not exactly a star myself, but there were people there who'd never even spoken into a microphone. And I liked that. The meaning of the occasion comes from a recognition of the quality of what you've done. It doesn't really sell more books, but the recognition makes it a little less hard for you the next time you sit down to write.''

Beryl Bainbridge

BERYL BAINBRIDGE, whose fourth novel, "Sweet William," is just about to be published in America by George Braziller, has received an impressive amount of critical acclaim on both sides of the Atlantic. The hallmark of any Bainbridge novel is a bizarre and often eerie psychological understanding of the tangled relationships possible between the male and the female at all ages. (Her earlier novels published in this country have been "Harriet Said," "The Secret Glass" and "The Bottle Factory Outing.") The new one, "Sweet William," is all of the above and more—a devastatingly funny account of a battle between the sexes in which the woman never has a chance. It is equally wry and biting in its depiction of the clashes between a meddlesome mother and a grown daughter.

Conquering a genuine fear of flying, Miss Bainbridge came to the States briefly to help promote "Sweet William." She has an actress's trained voice and was on the stage in Britain for 10 years, but at times just a trace of a Liverpool accent slips through. That Liverpudlian background is pivotal in her development as a writer and a person.

"My mum and dad met on a Liverpool Number 13 tram," she says. "My mother was lower middle class, my father was working class. I found visiting his family very interesting, but my mother always made clear that her family came from higher up the class structure and that she looked down on his people. My father was a bad-tempered, morose man, but he used to read me Dickens as a child and tell me stories. As a child I adored my mother."

By Barbara A. Bannon. From *Publishers Weekly* 209, no. 11 (March 15, 1976), pp. 6–7.

After her father's death, when she was 17, Beryl Bainbridge began to see him in a different light. "My mother then turned on me as I grew up and began to have other interests of my own. Then I would remember back into the past and be able to understand better what his point of view had been at that time. I could sense that my mother never told me the full story about my father's family, but church records show that I had a Scottish grandpa who spoke Gaelic.

"There were very few people who got on well with my mother," she recalls. "She despised my father. Still, it was always he, the man of the family, who paid the bills from a little tin box kept on the table. Other than this she treated him with contempt. Nevertheless, I was brought up to believe men were privileged creatures. If you did not believe this you were finished romantically for girls of my generation in my part of England." Miss Bainbridge was born "in the middle 30s."

As a child she remembers her mother "buying me little exercise books and sharpening my pencils for me. I was always writing. Reading was encouraged when I was younger, but as I grew older it was frowned upon. I think they locked up the bookcase and threw away the key." Both parents are dead and, she says "all these painful memories about my parents are receding now. I've come to feel about them as if they were the children and I the parent."

This involvement with the past is at the center of Beryl Bainbridge's life. "I like the past and everything to do with it more than anything else," she says and means it. "I'd like to have lived in Victorian times. Women knew where they were then. I'd like to have known what my family was like then."

Divorced from her painter husband, Austin Davies, she lives now with her three children in Camden Town, an inner suburb of London, in a house full of Victorian bric-a-brac, old photos (she collects them) and speaks only slightly facetiously of how delightful it would be to bring back gas lighting throughout the place.

When she left the theater behind to have her first baby, Beryl Bainbridge did what she had always planned to do—she started writing seriously, although not necessarily for publication. An item in a newspaper about two schoolgirls in Australia who had murdered the mother of one of them gave her the impetus for the book that would become "Harriet Said," although only the two evil schoolgirls remained from the real-life plot. "I enjoy plotting very much, making things fit together," she says. "There is something of my own personal past in all of my books, including 'Sweet William,' but I made the girl there a bit more wet and drippy than even I was at that age. I live mostly in my own past and try to stick something out of my own life into the middle of what I am writing."

The dressmaker in "The Secret Glass" was modeled after an elderly aunt on her father's side of the family. But it was in "The Bottle Factory Outing" that she wrote virtually all of the background material out of her own experiences four years ago, actually working in such a bottle factory in London, where the bulk of the workers were imported from Italy and made a little enclave of their own. She remembers her fellow workers with great affection. Everyone was permitted as much wine as he or she wanted to drink, and in the dead of a London winter the employees went home feeling exceedingly good at the end of the day.

There really was a factory outing to Windsor, as in the book, but it was a very tame excursion compared to the one in the novel, which involves a murder. The incident with the horses happened exactly as recounted, however: The Queen's horses were being exercised in Windsor Great Park and the bottlers gave the soldiers wine; the soldiers gave some of the partying factory workers a chance to ride the horses.

In her writing Beryl Bainbridge likes to think about what she is plotting for months, but then she writes very quickly, in about 12–13 weeks. She believes "you should never try to write about anything too long after your experience of it. Little bits of yourself rub off in this kind of writing. I never think of the actual bottle factory any more. I got rid of it by writing about it. It is a sad fact of life that even the most incredibly painful moments in your life you will get over. One should really be able to hang onto feelings, but eventually they do fade off."

There is still another side to Beryl Bainbridge's talents in addition to her writing and her years in the theater. After she and her husband were divorced, she began to resume her own painting again, and her work is selling. The paintings are often another expression of her interest in the past, but a wickedly spoofing one. Two of her best-known subjects have been Napoleon and a British captain of World War I vintage. Napoleon is always dressed in full uniform regalia, but acompanied by a splendid female who seems to be totally unaware of the fact that she is stark naked. The captain ("Dalhousie," Miss Bainbridge has christened him) wears his regimental cap—but nothing else.

Jan Benes

NOT MANY CZECH AUTHORS visit America these days. Jan Benes, whose novel, "Second Breath," based in part upon his own prison camp experiences, has just been published by Orion Press-Grossman Publishers, was one of the last Czech citizens given official permission to leave his country for a trip abroad before the borders were closed a month ago. Mr. Benes was allowed to come to the U.S.A. for the publication of his novel, which has not yet appeared in Czechoslovakia—although publication there has been "pending" for some time.

The 33-year-old writer filed an unprecedented law suit against the Minister of the Interior in Czechoslovakia in 1965 when he was denied a passport without explanation. After collecting more than 300 signatures on a petition against the imprisonment of the Russian writers, Sinyavski and Daniel, he was held 11 months in custody during 1966–67. He was then sentenced to five years in prison in Czechoslovakia. He was pardoned in 1968 by President Novotny, as one of the latter's final acts in office before Dubcek took over.

What Jan Benes wants to be—what he is, in fact—is a writer, not a political figure. He has also been an artist and sculptor, who won a gold medal for toy design at Expo 58 in Brussels; and he has been a taxi driver, a miner and a theater technician. He is part of the plebeian tradition of Czech literature which began to evolve towards the end of the 18th and the beginning of the 19th century.

PW, talking with Mr. Benes during his stay in New York, asked him how he saw his role as a writer. "I feel like one

By Barbara A. Bannon. From *Publishers Weekly* 196, no. 21 (November 24, 1969), pp. 13–15.

who carries dusty mirrors along dusty roads, trying to define reality,'' is the way he put it. "That is the reason why so many of my works have open ends. In the last analysis I prefer a situation where a reader can draw his own final conclusions." The short story form is his preferred medium, and he has adapted several of his stories as television plays.

In recent and past Czech history there have been many instances of writers who managed to keep their talents alive during imprisonment, sometimes for as long as 12 years, and to return to writing again after release. Mr. Benes was not officially permitted to have access to even a pencil with which to write until 10 days before his release from prison, he told *PW*, but he managed to obtain one and put down on toilet paper, the only paper he had, the nucleus of a book that may be published in the U.S. some day under a title roughly equivalent to "Right Here in This Spot." He has another good title in mind for his major work in progress, which says a lot in more ways than one. It is "My Father Didn't Fall for *Anything*."

Access to the works of western writers in translation may not be so easy to come by in Czechoslovakia in the future, but Mr. Benes mentioned as among the Americans with whose work he is quite familiar: J. D. Salinger, John Dos Passos, Arthur Miller, Nelson Algren, Norman Mailer, William Saroyan (one of his special favorites of whom Benes says, "He is from the Caucasus, as is my wife, and he writes exactly what I love to read and what I like to write myself.").

The late Samuel Shellabarger's sweeping historical romance, "Captain from Castile," is so popular that Mr. Benes' 11-year-old copy is getting dog-eared from being loaned out. Many young Czechs know Joseph Heller's "Catch-22" so well that they can recite long passages from it by heart.

Czech publishing differs from American in more ways than just being under state control. Jan Benes told *PW* that any book finally making it to publication in Czechoslovakia has a guaranteed first printing and projected sale of at least 5,000 copies. His that have been published in his own country have had sales of about 16,000 copies each. John Steinbeck's "The Grapes of Wrath" has sold half a million copies in Czechoslovakia and Arthur Miller's plays regularly sell some 25,000 copies. This is in a country where the average worker has to put in several hours of labor to be able to afford the price of a hardcover book.

One of the American writers Jan Benes was able to meet during his stay here was the playwright Arthur Miller. Mr. Miller showed him a copy of the book about a visit to Russia, which he and his wife wrote (*Viking Press*). Purely by coincidence, which neither writer had known about in advance, a large section of the book deals with the Millers' meeting with the Georgian Russian family of Jan Benes' wife.

"Second Breath" is being published in America through a series of quirks of fate. Mr. Benes, his wife and young daughter were in Paris—he, on a small scholarship—when the Russians invaded Czechoslovakia in 1968. Two of his stories and an article had appeared in *Le Figaro Littéraire*. They were still in Paris in October of that year, with funds running low, when Mr. Benes was aided by Michel Gorday of *France Soir*, whose wife, Beverly Gorday, represents Doubleday in Paris. Benes and Gorday had had the shared experience of having been under surveillance in Prague at one time by the same secret police agent. Mme. Gorday referred Jan Benes to a French literary agent, Helena Strassova, whose own background was originally Czech. She was not familiar with Jan Benes' work, but Howard Greenfeld of Orion Press-Grossman Publishers was, and had in fact been trying to make contact with Benes for a year, without success, ever since first hearing about him on a visit to Czechoslovakia and reading one of his stories in a collection of Czech work published by Oxford University Press. Mr. Greenfeld just happened to be visiting Mme. Strassova at the time Jan Benes turned up at her door. The contract with Orion-Grossman for "Second Breath" (and, it is hoped, more books to follow) was signed the next day.

Isabel Bolton

ISABEL BOLTON, at 88, has just begun work on a new novel. Her latest, "The Whirligig of Time," published this spring by Crown, is a haunting portrait of the changing pattern of New York life on a certain social level from the gaslight era of Edith Wharton and Henry James into modern times. "My novel deals with past decades and I have made the attempt to recreate an atmosphere by moving my characters into a past where morals and manners contrast strikingly with those of today," she says.

"I am, myself, dead sick of reading nothing but life between the sheets. Sex has become such a bore. I think, however, that the timidity of any approach to sex which I knew as a girl was real prurience. We were not even allowed to cross our legs at all. That was very foolish. We were too removed and ignorant. Though I have not dealt with sex in 'The Whirligig of Time' by attempting detailed descriptions of sexual love, I have made an attempt to describe with some delicacy how sex was experienced around the turn of the century by many young women who knew little about it when they embarked on their first marital experiences."

That Isabel Bolton is writing at all at the age of 88 is a tribute not only to her intellectual vigor, but to her ability to triumph over extraordinary physical difficulties. She has for many years suffered from severe eye pains caused by low grade arthritis. Although she is in no way blind, she cannot read for more than a minute or two at a time without the onset of pain.

When she is working she begins by simply externalizing her thoughts for two hours every day, dictating to a very

By Barbara A. Bannon. From *Publishers Weekly* 200, no. 1 (July 5, 1971), pp. 7–9.

good secretary. "Then I get her to read back what I've written and we revise it little by little," she says. "This does not make writing as easy as if the ideas could come directly from the end of one's fingers to the typewriter, but I think I have mastered the difficulty. I work very hard on each chapter and when I have finished it, put it into stock. I revise each chapter carefully as I go along but I do not go through any first, second or third drafts of a novel. Something which dominates all of my work is a fear that too many books try to say too much. 'When in doubt, delete' is something I say over and over to myself. I try to bring a good deal of brevity to my writing, and I care a good deal for style. I like to write as good a sentence as I can."

Among the writers whose works Miss Bolton very much admires are Virginia Woolf, Eudora Welty, E. M. Forster, Joyce Carol Oates, Jean Rhys, Ivy Compton-Burnett. "I was always much moved by Flannery O'Connor," she says.

Isabel Bolton's real name is Mary Britton Miller. Her very early childhood was spent in New York, and she remembers playing in the same park that used to be where the armory at Park Avenue and 34th Street now is located and which she describes in her novel. The incident of the tethered bull which escaped in the park one day and which she uses in "The Whirligig of Time" actually occurred.

After the death of her parents, Mary and her brothers and sisters were raised in Massachusetts, first by their grandmother and then by governesses. "I have never had to struggle to make my own money and I seem to know the leisure classes better than any other," she says.

Her identical twin sister died at the age of 14, an experience of which Isabel Bolton wrote movingly in her memoir, "Under Gemini" (*Harcourt, Brace & World*).

After boarding school, she spent two years in Italy and "was more at home there than anywhere else in Europe." She is the author of several volumes of poetry published under her own name of Mary Britton Miller and several collections of verses for children. Her first novel, "In the Days of Thy Youth," was published by Scribners in 1943. Since, as she says, "it made no ripples in the pond," she decided to adopt a pseudonym for her fiction thereafter and chose the name "Isabel Bolton" quite casually one day when having tea with a friend.

"I have had good reviews from good critics but never a big financial success," she says, only slightly wistfully. "I have always been pleased at the literary quality of the reviews I have received." Among those who have been high in their praise of Isabel Bolton's writings are Edmund Wilson and Diana Trilling.

The new novel on which Miss Bolton is now at work takes its impetus from a quotation from the letters of Keats: "Life was a valley of soul-making." It will be, she hopes, a book "with a little philosophy and thought in it—a reflection of the fact that life is a curious business."

"Very few people have seen in their span of life as much as I have seen happen so swiftly," Miss Bolton told *PW*. "To have lived from the gaslight and candlelight era to modern inventions is almost like passing from the Middle Ages to the present. The sound of horses' hooves to me will always be like a perfectly lovely song, and going off for drives was so much more leisurely when I was a child."

Miss Bolton has lived for the past 30 years in a small apartment in New York's Greenwich Village to which she is now closely confined by virtue of her health. Although she can move about physically for only short distances between a sunny back porch overlooking a garden, and the bed-couch from which she dictates her novels, and where she listens to the Library of Congress recordings for those with visual difficulties, she is intensely alive and still exploring an infinite variety of human nuances in her writing. At 88, she is still intellectually curious.

Vance Bourjaily

"FOR ME and perhaps for a number of other writers," Vance Bourjaily was saying over beers at the Plaza Hotel one afternoon last week, "it is no longer possible to do what Faulkner and even O'Hara did: a number of novels all centered in one place. We didn't grow up in the same place where dad and granddad grew up. We left it."

Iowa-based Mr. Bourjaily was in New York in connection with the January 30 publication of his new novel, "The Man Who Knew Kennedy" (*Dial Press*). This book, like his earlier novels, lacks a regional center, he continued. "But if we as writers don't have a place in place, we have a place in time. All my books move through the period of 1933-63. In 1933, I was eleven years old and beginning to take things in. I knew where my sympathies were on issues like Abyssinia and Spain; then came the war and then the post-war period. For so many of us, it seemed that when Kennedy became President, one of our boys had made it, and that we would be able to twist the world the way we wanted to. It seemed that we were finally on our way—in government, in the arts, in business. When history took care of Jack, it took care of us, too—at least for the time being. It was the end of something. Kennedy was succeeded by an old guy."

With that as background, it is not surprising that the views of author Bourjaily and of his novel's first-person narrator, Barney James, are strikingly similar. But, as Mr. Bourjaily pointed out, a novelist puts something of himself in all his characters. "Writers of fiction," he said, "are a lot like actors. We can be several different characters at once. Actually, I'm weaker than Barney James is; he's stronger in his singleness of purpose."

By Roger H. Smith. From *Publishers Weekly* 191, no. 6 (February 6, 1967), pp. 38–39.

Mr. Bourjaily knows a number of people who knew Kennedy, as the novel's protagonist knew him—among them, writers Gore Vidal and Louis Auchincloss, a law professor at the State University of Iowa, where Mr. Bourjaily sometimes teaches in the Writers Workshop, and people in Iowa politics. The novel's title has caused some confusion in bookstores, where instead of going into the displays of fiction, it has been lumped with other nonfiction recollections of the Kennedy years. "It's a novel," Mr. Bourjaily said. "It's got the assassination in it only in the way that a war novel has the war in it."

On November 22, 1963, Mr. Bourjaily was in his studio in North Liberty, Iowa, working on a novel called "Expedition," when his wife came in to report that there were fragments of news on television about the murder of the President in Dallas. "I'm not sure what my immediate reaction was," he said. "I think I typed another paragraph or two before the news really hit me. Later, I decided I had to write a novel about it. In my lifetime, there have been three events when an emotional fix took place: Pearl Harbor, the death of FDR and the assassination of Kennedy. Barney James is a character in 'Expedition,' and I sort of borrowed him to tell the story of 'The Man Who Knew Kennedy.' "

"The Man Who Knew Kennedy" is Mr. Bourjaily's fourth novel—and fifth book—and with its choice by the Literary Guild as its February selection, may mark the author's breakthrough into large hardcover sales, though his work has always sold well in paperback. "In the current publishing scene," Mr. Bourjaily said, "it's hard to tell that you're on the first team until you've had a hardcover success. In my age group of writers, we've all had to prove ourselves over a longer period of time than Hemingway, Fitzgerald or Dos Passos did. I published my first novel 20 years ago. Twenty years after Fitzgerald published his first novel, he was as good as dead.

"It's different, I think, because the whole level of fiction now is so high that it's rare if a novel's sale lasts after the year it is published. I'm grateful to Dial for keeping my earlier books in print; that's helped a lot. It's different because where before maybe six or eight novelists were making a living solely by writing, there now are a hundred or more. And at the same time, if you have a family, you need more money. But you can do it because there are a lot of markets open to writers, and that's part of the difference, too. Before, you made it big or not at all."

Malcolm Braly

MALCOLM BRALY is a large man with a thick mane of graying hair, a wide smile and an infectious laugh. He is not good at armed robbery; he was caught at it, a fact which together with the commission of subsequent minor crimes and parole violations, is the reason he has spent 17 of his 42 years in San Quentin prison.

He *is* good at writing, and his novel, "On the Yard" (*Little, Brown*), may set a new trend or two in the genre of prison fiction. The central "character" in the book, just as it is the central factor in a prisoner's life, is the prison itself, and it is a "character" of many moods. We've come a long way from the "good guys" (cons) *vs*. the "bad guys" (guards and other spear-carriers) in the old George Raft movies.

Mr. Braly is also an editor, recently arrived in book publishing.

He started writing when he was 32, in San Quentin, "looking for a way to accomplish something while I was there," he said the other day in an interview with *PW*. "In prison, you can either paint or write. Every other guy in the joint is writing something." His initial difficulty as a beginning author was that he had no typewriter and, for that matter, did not know how to type. Undeterred, he got a clerical job in the prison, typing file cards, first by the hunt-and-peck system and later with more proficiency. His own writing he did longhand in his cell at night and transcribed his notes in between his official typing chores.

He finished a novel and then had to take another prison clerical job that paid $6 a month in order to raise postage to

By Roger H. Smith. From *Publishers Weekly* 192, no. 14 (October 2, 1967), pp. 16–17.

send the manuscript to New York. He sent it to agent Willis Wing (another San Quentin prisoner-writer was a client of the Wing office). Mr. Wing showed the manuscript to Knox Burger, editor of Fawcett's Gold Medal paperback originals, who didn't publish the book but was generally encouraging. Meanwhile, Mr. Braly had finished a second novel, "The Felony Tank," and this one Gold Medal did publish. It was followed by two more Gold Medal originals: "Shake Him Till He Rattles" (about San Francisco's North Beach) and "It's Cold Out There" (a novel about released convicts trying to adjust to life "outside"; Mr. Braly wrote it after he had been returned from "outside" for his last tour in San Quentin).

A writer in prison, Mr. Braly told *PW*, faces three principal problems: prison officials' attitude toward writers; censorship; and how to get a typewriter. Officials aren't really against writing (it's "recreational") until a writer is published, he said. "They wouldn't bring me down from the work farm to get the scroll the Mystery Writers of America gave me for 'The Felony Tank' because they didn't want me to have the recognition. They held up my second manuscript because they knew it would be published. It had in it a narcotics officer who was addicted—there are some, you know—and I had to take that out. In my third book, I had a scene where a 19-year-old girl was drinking beer—21 is the legal drinking age in California. With a marking pencil, I crossed out 'beer' and wrote in 'Dr. Pepper.' They still objected because you could read 'beer' through the markings. I had to retype seven pages. In prison, the censor is usually the librarian and he doesn't want to stick his neck out. The manuscript that doesn't hurt the prison is the one that is likely to get out of the prison."

During his last four years in San Quentin, Mr. Braly gathered material for "On the Yard" but wrote on it only sporadically. His sentence was five-years-to-life, and he was afraid prison authorities might find out about the book and never let him out. A section of the book, describing a quiet night in a large prison, was published in *Esquire* under a pseudonym and attracted a lot of attention. "Everyone inside knew it had been written by someone in San Quentin. But they never knew who, and I never copped," Mr. Braly said. Knox Burger (the book is dedicated to him) bought "On the Yard" for Fawcett on the basis of 45 pages of notes and then sold it for hardcover publication to Little, Brown.

Mr. Braly was released from prison in April 1965, and came to New York in December 1966 ("I'd never been out of California before"). He arrived at Fawcett during a mild personnel crisis and pitched in, reading manuscripts and writing jacket copy. Before long, he was on the regular payroll. This summer he was named an associate editor of Gold Medal. "The fact that I'm an editor," he says, "surprises me less than the fact that I was a convict."

As an editor at Gold Medal, Mr. Braly occasionally sees a manuscript written by one of his former San Quentin colleagues. ("Every other guy in the joint is writing something.'') One in particular was the cause of some poetic justice. "One guy was writing radio plays in prison, and that made him an 'established writer,' " Mr. Braly said. "He was agented by Wing, but he wouldn't give me Wing's address—I got it out of the files, anyway. He thought it ludicrous that I should try to write. Well, he's back in now, and the other day a manuscript of his came in to Fawcett. When I rejected it, I signed myself 'Editor.' I've had a number of ingratiating letters from him since then."

Hortense Calisher

HORTENSE CALISHER is a New Yorker born and bred, "and obsessed with the place," she says. Perhaps only a New Yorker with the kind of roots she has could have written about the city and its people as she has done in Little, Brown's major new novel, "The New Yorkers."

The focus of the novel is on a remarkable, well-to-do Jewish family, the Mannixes, although many others, Jew and gentile, rich and poor, American and European, are drawn into their story. This is a very different stratum of Jewish life from that dealt with in the so-called "Jewish novel" of recent years. Miss Calisher's own family, Sephardic Jews who came to this country from Germany in the years before the Civil War, and settled first in the South, were, she says, "a clan. The great difference between us and many other Jews is that we knew gentiles always. Part of that comes from our Spanish Jewish heritage. This can get you into trouble with other Jews, who will say, 'You were only Jews by default.' But my father went to Hebrew school and could read Hebrew. Our experience was different but we were no less Jews."

Miss Calisher remembers childhood visits to a great-aunt who lived in the family home on East 79th Street, probably between Lexington and Third, and her book is dedicated to "Hedwig Lichtstern and Joseph Henry Calisher who were married in a house on East Seventy-ninth Street." The Mannixes and the Calishers are not the same family, but for some of the period background Miss Calisher drew on what she had heard "growing up as the youngest of an elderly, anecdotal family who all told stories." Her father and

By Barbara A. Bannon. From *Publishers Weekly* 195, no. 16 (April 21, 1969), pp. 19–20.

grandfather both married younger women late in life. Her grandfather was born in the 18th century and did not marry until he was in his fifties. "I got fascinated young," she told *PW*, about her interest in family history. "I always felt at home in the 1880s. My father, when I knew him best, was reaching seventy, but the 1880s was his time. It never seemed far away. This was the kind of family feeling I knew."

This is a season in which several major works of fiction relate to earlier works by the same author, but the treatment Miss Calisher has accorded the Mannixes and their friends in "The New Yorkers" and in her earlier novel, "False Entry," is intriguingly different. The two books coil back elliptically on one another, with "False Entry," the first published, actually telling more of the Mannix story *after* the events in "The New Yorkers."

"After I finished 'False Entry,' " Miss Calisher told *PW*, "I did not want to drop the Mannix family. I wanted to tell the story of Ruth [the daughter], although I actually had no intention of writing a sequel." After she finished "False Entry," she wrote a page of notes to herself, which she carried around for years, and finally locked away in a safety deposit box.

Every time she thought of going back to the Mannixes again, "another novel intervened," but when she did begin work on "The New Yorkers" finally, she went back once and looked up her notes. Of the two books, Miss Calisher says, "they are like the halves of an apple. You can read either first. I have a very subterranean feeling about my material. I feel it should come from somewhere subliminal."

When she began to write "The New Yorkers" in earnest, she did set down a brief page of notes on when Judge Mannix's beautiful and tragic wife, Mirriam, a pivotal character, was born and married, so that she could refer back to these events with ease, but only once did Miss Calisher actually go back and re-examine what she had written about the the Mannixes and their friends in "The New Yorkers" and in her earlier point of excitement in writing a book like this," she says, "is the way things stay in your head. Whole passages of dialog came flooding out."

A Barnard College graduate, who went through a long rejection slip period involving such magazines as the *Atlantic* and *Harper's* ("Your little story was enjoyed by everyone here, *but* . . ."), Miss Calisher went back to her passion for writing when her youngest child was three. Her first enthusiastic response came from Maggie Cousins and Julian Mueller, then at *Good Housekeeping*. Then the *New Yorker* bought three of her stories and she began to receive letters from editors asking, "When are you going to write a novel?"

It was John Woodman, an editor at Little, Brown, who wrote her the letter that said, "I admire your work so much, I'd like to publish it even if it is only a collection of short stories," and it was to Little, Brown that Miss Calisher went with "In the Absence of Angels."

"If it takes you years to write a novel," she says wryly, "you get lots of publicity. If it only takes one year, you are like a cow who keeps on having calves. If it takes you only a medium number of years, you are chided for being dilatory. Actually, nothing stops you if you're ready."

In addition to her own writing, Miss Calisher teaches at Columbia and City College. "You *can* teach writing," she says, "but I prefer not to. I much prefer to teach literature." Concerning the writing courses she has had to teach, she told *PW*: "First of all, you have to tell them that you cannot tell them anything. What you try to do is to make them read. If someone's going to write, he will want to read like mad on his own. What you do is to expose them to the way writers feel about writing. If they are good, you encourage them like mad, but say nothing in particular. The better it is, the less you say. It is very simple to tell a bad student what is wrong." A really promising young writer, Miss Calisher believes, has his "own insights that are holy."

Arthur A. Cohen

"I NOW THINK of myself as a novelist and bookseller—which, given the present condition of American publishing, seems like the best combination to be in."

Thus Arthur A. Cohen, author and editor of several Jewish theological works, the proprietor of his own rare book dealership specializing in early photographic and avantgarde art materials, former publisher and editor—and novelist whose latest of three, "A Hero in His Time," is just out from Random House.

The joint development of fictional and merchandising gifts is but the newest stage in a career that for nearly 20 years placed Cohen at the heart of the publishing scene during the industry's most dramatic growth period. But his time as a publisher and editor is one he now looks back on without regret, saying simply: "I think I'm fortunate I didn't begin to write fiction until after I grew up."

His creative coming of age has so far produced "The Carpenter Years" (1966), which was generously received ("It didn't deserve as much attention as it got. I examine it from time to time and wonder not that I wrote it, but *why*"), "In the Days of Simon Stern" (1973), a massive fable he himself describes as "saturated with ancient Jewish sources," and now "A Hero in His Time," which is the story of an obscure Russian poet who is incidentally but not essentially Jewish, and of a crucial gesture he makes during a visit to New York.

The book has several difficult and unusual technical effects, and Cohen is proud of the way he has brought them off. For one thing, its entire first half is set in contemporary

By John F. Baker. From *Publishers Weekly* 209, no. 3 (January 19, 1976), pp. 10–12.

Moscow, where hero Yuri Isakoysky edits his journal of folk music and writes his very occasional poems—and Cohen has never been closer to Moscow than Czechoslovakia, which repelled him on a recent visit. To make his Russia as authentic as possible, he read an enormous amount, particularly in the memoirs of Pasternak and Mandelstam (the idea for the book came out of a study he wrote of the latter), talked to friends who had been there, even studied the Baedeker guide to Moscow for distances, street names and numbers and so on.

For another thing, since his hero is a poet, Cohen thought it only fair to create some poetry for him—"As far as I know, this is one of the few attempts to write about a poet, print some of his poems, and also try to characterize him through them." Since the poems, when they occur, are read at a New York gathering by an American translator, they also had to sound as though they were translated from the Russian. Actually, Cohen says, he wrote the poems first—"I felt I had to work out a body of verse before I could clearly define Yuri's character." He wrote about 20—many more than he used—and the one about the poet and his wife who

"lived on and on
as excess.
They lived nowhere"

was, says Cohen, inspired by the story of the Mandelstams, who as poets and therefore superfluous people in Russia, had no right to claim space. "The idea of the poet as excess was at the heart of the book."

As for the book's more political aspects, although on the surface it seems to be a story of a Russian's struggle for freedom of expression, Cohen sees it as being "as much about the way in which American literary politics celebrates and then corrupts its heroes as the way the Russian system does. In many ways the sort of freedom offered the artist here is as brutalizing as the despotism there. What's the real difference between an American poet and a Soviet poet drinking themselves to death? In each case it's because of a sense of being misunderstood by the society. Not that I'm saying it's the same to be a writer in both countries—a bad review in *Literanaya Gazeta* and one would be saying good-bye to life in the capital; a bad review by Anatole Broyard in the *Times* here, and you're assured of the respect of the entire literary community." Cohen grinned wolfishly.

The character of Yasha Tyutychev, an elderly, ugly, eccentric collector of folk songs from the underside of Soviet life, who represents for Yuri the possibilities of freedom, survival and self-respect, is central to the novel—and to Cohen's conception of what fiction should be all about. "We all have models of one kind or another whom we can summon at will to serve as an example to us at vital moments of decision in our lives." Cohen, in fact, has what he calls "an old-fashioned notion that human beings have a moral presence, and that the depiction of such presences is one of the reasons people pay attention to fiction.''

He goes on: ''I don't think serious readers turn to novels for entertainment and recreation as much as in the expectation that *something* will be smuggled in—not so much as a didactic exercise as a moral one. So I feel that by having a hero at all I'm going against the grain of current American fiction. The most important element in a novelist to me is moral energy—one seeks to make ambiguities clear. The business of fiction as I see it is as a mode of clarification—a way of clarifying the problems of reality, of objectifying and examining at a distance the things that baffle one about the ordinary business of living.''

Cohen is not at all interested in linguistic experiment—''ambiguity, for me, is shot through with falsehood; the important thing about language is that it still communicates, and can express moral energy. That's one of the reasons I love a writer like Walker Percy, for instance—his moral energy is so alive, in a period when literature seems obsessed with bravura writing, the exploitation of perversity, exhibitionism, and a concern to shock. It seems to me that the greater the bravura of the writing, the further the writer is likely to be from a moral center, from an establishment of the claims of conscience.''

He is already well into his new novel, whose protagonist will be a sculptor whose creative gift is failing and who, in desperation, becomes involved in the smuggling of pre-Colombian art out of Mexico—''A portrait of an artist as an archetypical man who takes revenge on another culture out of a sense of the profound failure of his own.''

Cohen has now decided that he will work only in fiction in the future as far as the major themes that interest him are concerned—though he will continue to write occasional essays, and would like to publish a collection of such pieces. Random published ''In the Days of Simon Stern'' after his agent offered it around to a number of houses (''It was a very big book, and it was a case of who could do it best'') and James Silberman took it. ''I liked his professionalism, and I don't want to go from publisher to publisher any more, getting things published in different shapes and sizes. I'm at the stage where what I want most is to see a body of work lined up on a shelf, with at least the *look* of a collected edition. And I don't want to have to worry about a publisher, but just to do my work.''

Cohen's own background in publishing dates back to the time when, fresh out of the Jewish Theological Seminary (after the University of Chicago), he met the poet Cecil Hemley and they jointly founded the Noonday Press in 1952. He recalls that its first list was a book of Hemley's poems, an essay by one of his own former teachers, and a Brazilian novel—which fortunately turned out to be Machado de Assis' classic ''Epitaph of a Small Winner,'' which kept the fledgling firm alive for a year. Two years later they split up and Cohen went off on his own to found Meridian Books. This quickly built up a distinguished collection of philosophy, literary criticism and belles-lettres that was one of the early trade paperback lists to catch the public fancy (Kate Simon's "New York: Places and Pleasures," which grew out of a dinner-table suggestion with an advance of $1000, was one of its great successes and became the forerunner to a distinguished series). "We priced resolutely over a dollar," Cohen recalls. "We sewed our books for the first few years, we never printed more than 10,000 copies first time around, and we were instantly successful." He qualifies "successful" by adding that he means "not profit but survival," and goes on: "It was a marvelous time to be in publishing. You could still lose money then, and be prepared to take the loss, yet still keep going. We never made money, but we kept the books in print, and the amount of innovative publishing we could do was remarkable. It has to be *fun* in small publishing like that—once you have to get yourself a budget, and predict the economics for each title, it becomes sheer drudgery."

In the end the process became too precarious and in 1960 Meridian was sold to World. Cohen lingered briefly at the head of his line, but then quit over the issue of editorial independence. Eventually Meridian became merged into the New American Library, still later into the Los Angeles Times–Mirror group. "It is hardly recognizable today, and I have no nostalgia for a corpse." Meanwhile he went to Holt, where for the first three years he was in charge of the religious publishing division, later served as editor-in-chief from 1964–68. When he left them, it was for good. "In solid, durable publishing it's too damn difficult to make any money—now even the small publishers are looking all the time for best sellers."

Since man cannot live by novels alone, Cohen, aided greatly by his photographer–artist–designer wife Elaine Lustig Cohen (the widow of pioneering book and magazine designer Alvin Lustig), has built up over the last few years a successful business in rare books and journals, mostly connected with early photography and early avant-garde art. He publishes his own catalogue for the business, which he calls Ex Libris, and talked to *PW*'s interviewer in an East Side New York apartment lined with his wares—priceless catalogues from early Dada exhibitions, issues of a photography journal edited by Alfred Stieglitz, rare prints by Steichen, Julia Cameron, Man Ray. He shows the interviewer a small pile of roughly printed Russian pamphlets, including first editions of Mayakovsky poems, dating back to the early years of the Revolution. "That little pile is worth $75,000," he notes. He journeys regularly to Europe to pick up material, delights in selling it back to European collectors.

In between the calls from would-be buyers and sellers, and working on his catalogues (the first of which is already something of a collector's item itself), Cohen writes and contemplates writing. He already has the next few novels in his head, makes notes constantly on them, finds that with each one he writes he learns more and more about what can be done in the medium. "As long as he doesn't run out of ideas, the only problem a novelist has is that of dealing with success," he concludes philosophically. "Fortunately," he smiles, "that hasn't been my problem yet."

William B. Decker

WILLIAM B. DECKER is the best darn editor in book publishing who was once a professional cowboy. He is also, unless we are mistaken, the only one.

"All boys want to be cowboys, but they outgrow it," he said the other day. "I never outgrew it. I'm a case of arrested development." A result of Mr. Decker's cowboying is his first published novel, "To Be a Man," issued by Little, Brown.

A native of Virginia, Mr. Decker had as the source of his interest in cowboying the stories that his grandfather told. Grandfather had been a cowboy in Wyoming and was a member of the family that started the Overland Mail (later acquired by Wells Fargo), the first regular mail service through to California. Graduated from high school and with a year to wait to get into the military program he wanted, Mr. Decker went west to Arizona and got a ranch job. When he came out of service in November, 1945, he went back to cowboying, stuck with it until he was injured and then, under the G.I. Bill, enrolled at Stanford University. At Stanford, he got involved in the creative writing program (Wallace Stegner, author of a laudatory quote about "To Be a Man") and coached the polo team. Summer vacations, he worked on ranches. On graduating from Stanford, he cowboyed at ranches in central California and then bought a ranch of his own in Oregon, where he also got into newspaper work.

He sold the ranch in 1959 and headed east to try to find a job in journalism. One of the places where he looked was McGraw-Hill. The interviewer there didn't have a journal-

By Roger H. Smith. From *Publishers Weekly* 192, no. 12 (September 18, 1967), pp. 38–39.

ism job but wondered if Mr. Decker would be interested in book publishing. Within six months, he was advertising manager of the McGraw-Hill trade department, later switching to the editorial side as managing editor. He has been at his present professional address, the Dial Press, where he is a senior editor, since 1965.

How authentic is "To Be a Man"? "I've done everything that's in the book, just the way it's described," Mr. Decker told *PW*. "In one sense, it's a young adult book on how-to-be-a-cowboy. I'd also hope that some of the people I've cowboyed with would read it, though probably they won't. They don't read much, except maybe pulps. Going to a Western movie with them is a gas! The big thing with them is the ritual of the cowboy, and Hollywood never gets it right. They'll sit in the audience and yell something like, 'Hey! He's got his spurs on backwards!' "

Is the cowboy becoming obsolete? "In one sense," Mr. Decker said, "he won't be obsolete as long as people eat meat. What is gone is the 'cowboy myth,' which began with the Civil War and ended with the Great Blizzard of 1888. Cowboying now is basically unchanged since then. The drudgery is the same, but the 'glamor' is gone, if indeed it ever was there."

If "To Be a Man" has any literary ancestors, Mr. Decker continued, they are Conrad, Saint-Exupéry and, in the kind of earthy humor still widely prevalent in the West, Mark Twain. Mr. Decker can get violent on the subjects of the anti-hero and what he takes to be an Eastern Seaboard domination of American fiction. He feels closer to what he calls "an unfashionable kind of writing. In the West," he said, "they still do Mark Twain's jumping frog kind of thing. The kind of writing they really like is yarns. It's oral history. You can hear stories told in the first person that are two generations old."

Has authorship had any effect on his work as an editor? "Now that I'm an author," he said, "I think about all those rejection slips I've written over the last eight years. I wrote and was rejected for years, and that experience can make you sympathetic with the writer who goes out to meet the mailman every day. It makes it harder for you to be as cold-blooded as an editor has to be. My worst days in the office are the ones when I have to write those rejections."

R. F. Delderfield

R. F. DELDERFIELD is one author who turns out to be, in person, exactly the kind of man his novels have led you to expect. The English author of "A Horseman Riding By," "The Green Gauntlet," "The Avenue" and the about-to-be-published "Mr. Sermon" (all *Simon and Schuster* here, *Hodder & Stoughton* in England) is a Devon countryman to the core—although he was born in London and still speaks with the trace of a Cockney accent.

A friendly, kindly man, who made the long trip up from Devon to London to meet an American visitor, he knows perfectly well that the kind of fiction he writes is popular with the general public on both sides of the Atlantic, anathema to the avant-garde, and that it represents an old-fashioned point of view to which he adheres most happily.

"If you do not like what you are writing, you cannot expect other people to do so," he told *PW*. "So much modern literature is about people who haven't any real hope or courage or human dignity. I admire people who stand on their own two feet and fight, people who work and wrestle with their difficulties. And I passionately believe that Britain still has an awful lot to give the world."

The Delderfield story is as fascinating in its own way as any of the three-decker family sagas that are R.F.'s (for Ronald Frederick) specialty. His father was a cattle buyer in London's famous Smithfield Market, a man of decided opinions who supported Lloyd George, the Boers in the Boer War and women's suffrage. He also hero-worshipped Abraham Lincoln and "nearly went mad with joy" when Ronald Frederick was born on Lincoln's birthday. That we have an

By Barbara A. Bannon. From *Publishers Weekly* 197, no. 2 (January 12, 1970), pp. 29–30.

"R. F." Delderfield today instead of "A. L." is due solely to the fact it was Mrs. Delderfield's turn to name one of the four sons.

At age 50 the elder Delderfield decided that he had had enough of city ways and would do what he had always wanted to do—become a newspaper editor. Accordingly, he bought the Exmouth *Chronicle* in the West Country, transported his family there, and became the proprietor of a country weekly. R. F. was then 11.

When Ronald Frederick was 17 his father made another sudden decision, that it was time to turn the paper over to two of his sons. R. F.'s formal education (which had included a good public school near Exmoor) ended, and at 17 he became publisher and editor of the *Chronicle* while another brother took over as printer.

"From a creative writer's point-of-view," he told *PW*, "it was a complete run-around in the department store of life." Bicycling through 36 square miles of Devon countryside, he would cover everything from accidents and weddings to church bazaars and "an inquest on a farm laborer who had just cut his throat."

The Devon country drew many vacationing celebrities and young R. F. started an "In Town This Week" column in the paper, bagging interviews with big names. The first one was George Bernard Shaw, who told him, "I don't believe a word of it, but I admire your cheek," when the young man swore he would be sacked if he couldn't get an interview with the elusive Shaw.

R. F. stayed with the *Chronicle* until the Second World War broke out. "I loved the paper and in 10 years I knew everyone locally, from retired generals to the plumber. It would have been difficult for us to become accepted if it were not for the paper," he says. "You're not really considered a Devonian until you have a grandchild born locally." Mr. Delderfield has one now.

Joining the R.A.F. in wartime, but ineligible for flying because of bad eyesight, he was quickly commissioned on the Air Ministry Staff and traveled many thousands of miles through Belgium and France after D-Day, becoming the first British officer into about 56 towns.

Just as his father had been a Lincoln buff, so R. F. Delderfield has been fascinated by Napoleon since childhood. One of the six books he carried through the war with him was Carlyle's "The French Revolution," and his wartime travels gave him a chance to visit much of the country associated with Napoleon's battles.

It may not be generally known to readers of his novels, but Mr. Delderfield is also the author of serious nonfiction works about Napoleon (some published in the U.S. by Chilton) and has been interviewed on French television about his interest in the French hero.

"My common sense quarrels with my sense of patriotism about Napoleon's projected invasion of England," he says. "Napoleon was primarily an administrator and a lawgiver. Had he won he would have had a common market by 1820. A more just peace ought to have been made with him by England. He wanted to stay in England, you know, and become a country gentleman.''

R. F. Delderfield began writing in army billets during the war, and in the immediate postwar years achieved quite a success as a West End playwright, one of whose comedies, ''A Worm's Eye View,'' ran five-and-a-half years.

Then at age 40, he did what his father before him had done, stopped to take stock of his life and remake it. ''I had a popular image as a playwright, but I wanted to be a novelist,'' he told *PW*. ''What I really wanted to do was to project the English way of life in the tradition of Hardy and Galsworthy.'' His first novel, ''The Dreaming Suburb,'' which became the first half of ''The Avenue,'' took him a year to complete, and dealt, deliberately, with ''the ordinary man next door.''

Before he writes one of his family sagas Mr. Delderfield prepares a detailed map of the territory, county or city, that he will cover, establishing place names, building up details in his own mind about the local flora and fauna. ''I know where I'm going, but I never know how I'm going to get there,'' he says of his long ''three-deckers.'' Sometimes one character takes center stage unexpectedly, while others fade away. Mr. Delderfield constructs careful genealogies for each. ''After the first two or three books in a saga, you have your guidelines,'' he says. ''The first is always the longest to write.''

''I have the most glorious pastures in which to browse,'' Mr. Delderfield says of his preoccupation with English history. It is no accident that the characters in his novels are sometimes subordinate to the historical events surrounding them and what happens to them is dictated by what is happening in the world around them. Thus, a character in the tetralogy on which he is currently working, born in 1883, will be 31 when the First World War breaks out and automatically of an age to be a frontline soldier. The individual Delderfield characters take shape in their author's mind as ''standard-bearers,'' each in a different way for some aspect of the English way of life.

The Delderfields live in Devon in a rebuilt coach house called the Gazebo. It dates originally from about the time of Trafalgar and was remodeled with the help of the architect currently in charge of Exeter cathedral. From its windows ''you can look right across to where the first galley of the Armada was sunk and Boney's invasion fleet would have appeared.'' The view alone would be enough to distract many writers, but 365 days a year R. F. Delderfield writes regularly in the morning and evening, taking the afternoon off for a stroll across the moors with his retriever. He averages 4000 words a day (his record in one day has been 5200) and he is at work now on a tetralogy that will trace the history of transportation in England from early railroad days to modern van lines. It will be, of course, a multi-layered family saga, with its full quota of personal drama and romance. The first head of the clan will be a man who starts as mercenary soldier in India during the height of the British Empire, when the world was regarded as ripe for an Englishman's pickings and England believed it was her duty to colonize the earth. Simon and Schuster plans to publish the novel over here in the fall of 1970, by which time Mr. Delderfield will probably be well away on the writing of volume three, which is entitled "Give Us This Day." Volume two will be "Theirs Was the Kingdom," but it is the title of volume I that really catches the eye. It is "God Is an Englishman."

E. L. Doctorow

E. L. DOCTOROW is already becoming accustomed to being
asked about the characters, real and imaginary, in "Ragtime," his extraordinary new novel from Random House.
And already he is becoming a little impatient with the questions: Did Harry K. Thaw, Stanford White's killer in the
"crime of the century," really watch Harry Houdini stage
an escape from the Tombs? Did Pierpont Morgan really
have a conversation with Henry Ford about reincarnation in
his famous library? Did liberated Emma Goldman really
take society beauty Evelyn Nesbit under her wing?

These are only a few of the happenings in "Ragtime," in
which real people of the first decade of the 20th century in
America interrelate with the cast of a fast-moving but entirely imaginary narrative. For Doctorow, such contemporary
figures are "images of that time," with something of the
power of myth attaching to them, and he is anxious not to
spoil their mystery by being too literal-minded about them.
"As a writer," he says quietly and thoughtfully (and Doctorow thinks carefully about everything he says, no matter
how often he is asked it), "I have learned to trust myself in
the act of writing. These people occurred to me—and specifically *these* people, Morgan, for instance, *not* Andrew Carnegie—because they carried for me the right overtones of
the time."

As to whether they really did some of the things he attributes to them—what is real in his narrative, and what not—
he is as near being playful as one suspects he ever gets,
"What's real and what isn't? I used to know but I've forgotten. Let's just say that 'Ragtime' is a mingling of fact and
invention—a novelist's revenge on an age that celebrates
nonfiction."

By John F. Baker. From *Publishers Weekly* 207, no. 26 (June 30, 1975), pp.
6–7.

Doctorow himself lives in the 1906 house in New Rochelle (just outside New York) where the action of the book begins, and he recalls very specifically its genesis. Sitting in his study looking down at the street, he visualized, suddenly, the people who lived in the house at that time being visited by Harry Houdini—"I don't know why"—and the rest of the book is an elaborate expansion upon that moment, and that idea. He has worked very hard on the book for the past two years, but still looks back on it as a "happy, easy book to write—it didn't fight me."

"Ragtime" is much the most accessible book of the four Doctorow has written, and he is glad of it. "I've always wanted my work to be accessible. Literature, after all, is for people, not some secret society. It probably seems so accessible this time because I was very deliberately concentrating on the narrative element. I wanted a really relentless narrative, full of ongoing energy. I wanted to recover that really marvelous tool for a novelist, the sense of motion. Two or three hundred years ago it was much more common—Defoe had it, Cervantes, more recently Edgar Allan Poe. You have to make sacrifices for it, of course: you lose psychological complexity in your characters, you have to distance yourself from them, and that's an approach that hasn't been characteristic of recent fiction."

And for Doctorow, this dedication to narrative energy worked splendidly for his book. "Once I was under way it generated itself, made its own rules, its own demands, and by the last third of it, it had developed complete inevitability." There are plenty of indications that "Ragtime" is going to be a big success—a BOMC choice, movie rights sold, large printings—and Doctorow, who has previously enjoyed excellent reviews but not overwhelming sales, is delighted at the prospect.

"I shall feel very good if it's a success. It's funny, but all the time you're writing you don't think about that at all, beyond the book being published. Then once it is published, you don't think about anything else but the possibility of its success." But as one who doesn't even relish being interviewed, Doctorow hardly relishes the prospect of literary lionizing. "I don't think I could cope with that. In fact I hope to go right away very soon and get back to work."

Back to work in this case means the completion of a play commissioned by the Yale Repertory Theater, and which, says Doctorow, they hope to perform in the coming season. "Is that a realistic hope?" *PW* asks. Doctorow laughs delightedly. "I see you know a lot about writers? Let's hope it is." He also has a new novel in mind, but nothing is written yet.

Doctorow was in publishing himself for many years before he left five years ago to devote himself to writing (with occasional teaching, currently at Sarah Lawrence). He began as a reader for Columbia Pictures, where for three years "I read just about everything that was published." (His own first novel, "Welcome to Hard Times" was made into a movie.) Thence to New American Library, where he worked his way in five years to senior editor. Finally, in the mid-1960s, he went to Dial Press as editor-in-chief. In his early publishing days, "I just saw it as a means to survival while I continued writing," and he would put in 20-hour days between the office and his typewriter. "Then when I got to Dial I found it very interesting and creative, and I began to neglect my own work because editing and publishing was such fun. Finally I realized I just had to concentrate on my own work."

He looks back fondly on an "enormously satisfying time" at Dial. He was there in the first years after Dell's takeover allowed a great deal of expansion capital. "We were very busy and very ambitious, and it was an exciting period. For a little house we made a lot of noise." He recalls working with Norman Mailer, Vance Bourjaily, James Baldwin, Thomas Berger, Richard Condon, Ann Moody, Larry McMurtry—even one of Abbie Hoffman's first books. "We had a good bit of action with 'Report from Iron Mountain,' if you remember that. And we were ahead of our time—do you know, we commissioned a multivolume Bicentennial history, back in 1966 or '67—and we did probably the first book on 'The Great Comic Book Heroes,' with a terrific introduction by Jules Feiffer."

Although he feels narrative skills are being somewhat neglected by many contemporary novelists, Doctorow doesn't want to be dogmatic about it—or, in fact, about anything. "I don't want my interest in it to appear exclusionary. There's a lot of splendid writing going on. It's a very exciting time for fiction. Literature isn't a horse race after all, and I hate the idea that in this country of 200-million people there's room for only a few writers at a time."

As to whether, with "Ragtime," he has launched a new genre of novel, "maybe we need some new definitions—and I leave that to the critics." He is not likely to be among their number, although he has been asked on occasion. "I think it was Cyril Connolly who said: 'Writers should avoid three things: tennis, sex and reviewing books.' I've accepted a third of this advice."

As a former publisher, Doctorow is overwhelmed at the treatment his new novel has received (Random, almost unprecedentedly, sent out a specially printed gift edition "to friends of the author and publisher" in advance of publication as a mark of its enthusiasm). "As an author, I am prepared to find fault, as a matter of principle, with anything a publisher does. But I must say Random has been tremendous."

In the end, despite all the prepublication praise the book has received, Doctorow appreciated as much as anything what his mother, to whom it is dedicated, said: "She said it was like having a piece of fine lace in your hands, and enjoying the intricacies of the design and pattern. Isn't that great?" He grinned. "Maybe we should print it on the jacket: 'The author's mother writes . . .' "

Lawrence Durrell

INTERVIEWING LAWRENCE DURRELL is an exhilarating experience. The conversation swoops and zooms in all directions. It may begin with a fervent Durrell appreciation of the professionalism of California garbage collectors. Newly arrived in New York from a West Coast visit to his old friend Henry Miller, Mr. Durrell could speak as an expert on the subject of garbage collection because he regularly divides up the compost heap at home in Provence, planting all the tin cans beneath his olive trees with spectacular results in fertility.

Also in California, he met some Topango Canyon hippies and found them "rather sweet, full of good ideas." "I would probably have been a hippie myself 20 years ago," he says, "although I don't go for this drug idea. Mind you, I've smoked a bit of hashish myself in my time, but it didn't give me any better fantasies than I could have on my own steam."

Thoroughly enjoying this, his first visit to America, despite his remembrance of Dylan Thomas' warning to "beware of everything, particularly American hospitality," Mr. Durrell was fascinated by the degree to which he found Dickens' writing "still the best guide to modern America." The first Durrell reaction to any new place "is to do nothing and take it in through your pores. You should treat towns like paintings or books." Gather your own impressions first, Mr. Durrell advises, then you can bother about checking the facts afterwards. Within the realm of future possibilities, he hopes, is a "picaresque travel book about America," after he has had a chance to come back and visit us again as more

By Barbara A. Bannon. From *Publishers Weekly* 193, no. 17 (April 22, 1968), pp. 17–19.

41

of a private individual. Mr. Durrell sees America as still "a relatively unsophisticated place," adding quickly, "You do not have to be sophisticated to have dignity."

Of "The Alexandria Quartet," the baroque volumes that brought him his great fame, he says matter-of-factly, "It was simmering for a long time. You serve the stew when it is ready. You can know everything about a book except what to do with it. Then suddenly *it* knows and everything else is dropped." Although nearly 200 pages of the Quartet were destroyed early on, once Mr. Durrell knew where he was going with it, the individual books were executed rapidly. Now, at long last, the Quartet is about to be made into a film by the same man who performed the prodigious job of transferring Joyce's "Ulysses" to the screen. Anouk Aimée of "A Man and a Woman," will star as the lovely, enigmatic Justine.

The new Durrell novel, "Tunc," and its sequel, "Numquam," the author describes as "more limited in scale, more intense," than "The Alexandria Quartet," adding up to a different use of time, "two sides of a continuum, out of which you get a rectangle." In "Numquam," on which Mr. Durrell expects to go to work this summer, some of the experiences of "Tunc" will be reordered in a different light, with "a big battle" shaping up between forces within Merlin's, the all-powerful international firm that is the background of the metaphysical story.

A fantastic memory bank computer named "Abel" figures largely in "Tunc," and Mr. Durrell says of his use of the computer, "The computer *is* our epoch. We are steadily being modified by it. Men and women are being computerized to the extent that they are losing their sexual differences."

The novel, Lawrence Durrell told *PW*, "is in a bad way everywhere. Poetry on both sides of the water is much healthier than the novel today. It may take 1000 bad artists 'dunging over' the land to produce one flower, and sometimes 100 bad poets may give impetus to one good one. There may be some young man somewhere today with a dirty typescript who has already changed all our lives around by his writing."

In writing "The Alexandria Quartet" Mr. Durrell was doing what he believes he has always tried to do in his writing, "to realize myself." Of the sudden popular success it brought him, he says, "You could have knocked me down with an oleander." Success and money he views as ancillary things, lovely, in a way, but not intrinsically necessary for his own happiness. He says (and you immediately believe him), "I know how to live cheaply and aristocratically, with style." Typical of what he means was an Athens dinner party he once attended at which the host was able to serve only a few bits of bread and salami and water. "After the third round, the water began to taste like gin, and after the seventh, we were all drunk," was Durrell's reaction—and that is style indeed.

Inevitably, somewhere along the line, conversation with Lawrence Durrell turns to his younger brother, Gerald, whose specialty, far from the exotic scenes favored by Lawrence, is the study of animals. "I am the good brother, he's the swine," says Lawrence amiably. "I was thinking of inviting him to join me in New York and then I thought of my room at the Algonquin, all full of anacondas and mongooses, and I wired him 'Don't come.' I used to get fan letters from people who saw Gerald and his ape, Cholmondely, on TV, saying, 'I saw you and your brother on the telly the other day.' He's still being ticked off for the bad ornithology in 'Justine,' while I get letters from sweet old ladies who say, 'now I've bought "The Alexandria Quartet" and I know I'm in for a treat. I just *love* your animal books.' "

James Whitfield Ellison

JAMES WHITFIELD ELLISON, whose third novel, "Master Prim," Little, Brown publishes this month, at one time or another has been involved in several aspects of the book trade. They haven't done his writing any good. They haven't done it any harm, either. The book trade Mr. Ellison takes a rather detached view of the novelist Mr. Ellison.

Since last year, he has been with the Book-of-the-Month Club in what is known as "an executive capacity." The job, as he explained it in a *PW* interview the other day, involves a lot of contact work (i.e., lunches) with publishers regarding possible BOMC selections, some editorial work, some buying ("We're like a big bookstore") and occasional writing for the BOMC *News*, the current issue of which (coincidentally or not) has a rave review by John Hutchens of "Master Prim."

It sounds like a marvelous job, and Mr. Ellison obviously thinks so. "I'm not organized enough to be a full-time professional writer," he said, "and I have to have a job. Book-of-the-Month Club is absolutely informal, devoid of paper-chasing. It's just terribly nice to work with Warren Lynch, Axel Rosin and Harry Scherman."

"Master Prim" comes out on Valentine's Day, which is appropriate. It is a story about how Love, in the persona of a college co-ed on summer vacation, transforms a young chess master (Julian Prim) from an utter boor into a close approximation of a civilized human being. There is a lot of background of big-league chess tournaments, and Mr. Ellison obviously knows that subject, though he says he was never good enough to play chess professionally. The narra-

By Roger H. Smith. From *Publishers Weekly* 193, no. 7 (February 12, 1968), pp. 25–26.

tor of the book wasn't good enough to play chess professionally, either, but at one point the author lets him come close to beating Master Prim.

Mr. Ellison is the son of a bookseller. As a teen-ager, he helped out in his father's store in Lansing, Michigan, which sold mostly old and rare books, and there he would meet publishers' salesmen as they came through, and an occasional author. After graduating from the University of Michigan, he came to New York and went to work, naturally, in bookstores: in his case, Brentano's and Scribner's. He moved on the periphery of the budding Beatnik movement (he is the model, he believes, for a particularly swinish character in Jack Kerouac's "Subterraneans").

After Army service in Korea and another stint in the bookstores, he sold his first novel, "I'm Owen Harrison Harding" (which has some scenes in a bookstore that is clearly the one in Lansing), to Doubleday. Warner Brothers bought the book as a vehicle for Jimmy Dean, who died not long afterward, and Mr. Ellison went to Hollywood himself for two years as a screenwriter at Columbia Pictures.

Since then he has had editorial jobs in paperbacks (Fawcett Gold Medal), hardcovers (Holt and Dutton) and now book clubs. "I've done a lot of different things involving books," he commented.

Would he consider abandoning the book trade for the undiluted life of a novelist? "No," he said happily. "It's like when I play chess. I'm not ruthless enough."

James T. Farrell

THERE MUST BE a moral—about writing, or readers, or reviewers, or publishing—to be drawn somewhere from the enduring literary career of author James T. Farrell.

In the Farrell apartment, on Manhattan's upper East Side, there is a separate bookcase which contains one copy of each of the books he has published since he began writing. The first book, "Young Lonigan," published in 1932, is there. Soon a new book, "Judith and Other Stories," to be published by Doubleday in the fall—will take its place on the shelves. More remarkable than the time span of 41 years between the two books ("Erskine Caldwell is the only other American writer who started to publish when I did and has continued to publish," Mr. Farrell observed in a recent interview) is the fact that the bookcase already contains a total of 46 books, 36 of them novels and short story collections, the remainder books of criticism and essays, poetry, one book on baseball, and one book each of journalism and humor.

This year, too, five of Mr. Farrell's earlier works of fiction will be reprinted in paperback editions: the Studs Lonigan trilogy, "Young Lonigan" (1932), "The Young Manhood of Studs Lonigan" (1934), and "Judgment Day" (1935) in individual volumes by Avon; "A Brand New Life" (1968) by Macfadden; and "Invisible Swords" (1971) by Manor House.

In addition, on February 11, the University of St. Louis Library Association presented to Mr. Farrell its Wilma and Roswell Messing, Jr., Award for "contributions to world literature." Previous recipients of the award include W. H. Auden, Barbara Tuchman, Henry Steele Commager and Jacques Barzun.

By Thomas Chastain. From *Publishers Weekly* 203, no. 7 (February 12, 1973), pp. 30–32. Reprinted by permission of Thomas Chastain.

"I'm grateful and honored," Mr. Farrell says. "I'm not used to receiving awards and I'm especially pleased to receive this one."

James Thomas Farrell, who will be 69 years old on February 27, can look back now over the more than four decades of his writing career and pinpoint probably the most fateful day of his life. "It was on St. Patrick's Day, 1927," he recalls, "that I decided to quit school, educate myself, and try to write." At the time he was attending the University of Chicago in the city where he was born and raised and whose South Side neighborhood, where he grew up, was to color so much of the fiction he would write.

In 1929, his first story appeared in print. "It was a short story called 'Slob,' " Mr. Farrell remembers, "and it appeared in a little magazine, *blues*, which was published in Columbus, Mississippi."

Two years later came the first Farrell novel, "Young Lonigan," and by 1935 he had published four novels and a collection of short stories. Three of the novels, the first, the third, "The Young Manhood of Studs Lonigan," and the fourth, "Judgment Day," were published together, in 1935, as "Studs Lonigan, A Trilogy," and became a landmark in American letters.

Through the remainder of the 1930s and well into the 1940s, James T. Farrell continued to produce either a novel or short story collection, and sometimes one of each, for every year from 1936 through 1947, by which time he had published 18 works of fiction in 15 years. It was during this period that he published the four Danny O'Neill novels, "A World I Never Made," "No Star Is Lost," "Father and Son," and "My Days of Anger," which, with the Studs Lonigan trilogy, were to consolidate his critical reputation. (A fifth Danny O'Neill novel, "The Face of Time," was published later, in 1953, to complete the series.)

Of the Farrell novels published in the 1930s and 1940s, two, "A World I Never Made," and "Barnard Clare," were best sellers, and in 1947 H. L. Mencken, when asked to nominate "the best American novelist," named James T. Farrell as his choice.

Mr. Farrell had by then, of course, become an established literary figure, and knew most of the other leading writers of the time. He says of some of them: Sinclair Lewis ("We were friends. He was a man of generous impulse but he didn't get along well with himself. . . ."); Theodore Dreiser ("We always corresponded. He sent me his last two books to read and asked for my opinion."); Ernest Hemingway ("We were friends for a while in the 1930s . . . I liked everything he wrote up to 'The Snows of Kilimanjaro' . . . ."); Edmund Wilson ("Bunny Wilson never liked my work but I could accept that. I always thought he was an honest man."); Scott Fitzgerald ("Fitzgerald and I never hit it off. . ."); Morley Callaghan ("I first met Morley Callaghan in the 1930s. We've corresponded for the last 10 years . . . I think now he may be the best writer of the lot.").

It was during this period, too, that Mr. Farrell, like many writers of the time, had his Hollywood fling. "I was hired by Twentieth Century–Fox in

1941," he says, "at a thousand dollars a week to write a movie script from a book called 'Common Clay.' But I could never find the guy I was supposed to report to at the studio. I stayed two weeks and came home. The whole thing was goofy." (Later, in the 1950s, Universal Studios made a movie called "Studs," based on Mr. Farrell's Lonigan stories, but he never saw the film and doesn't know who was in it.)

There was no Farrell fiction in 1948, but from 1949 through 1971 he continued to publish, bringing out 18 books of fiction, either novels or short story collections. These Farrell works had their mix of publishers, reviewers and readers. But, despite Mr. Farrell's continuing productivity, it was somewhere within these years that something curious happened: a portion of the public, and even the press, formed the mistaken impression that the author was no longer writing. At least one reviewer stated in a national magazine in 1963, when the novel, "The Silence of History," appeared that James T. Farrell hadn't written anything in 20 years. (Even more curious, during these same years Mr. Farrell was several times nominated for the Nobel Prize for Literature, once by Adlai Stevenson when he was Ambassador to the United Nations.)

Mr. Farrell, reflecting on this perplexing episode in his career, shakes his head and says: "There has been no one period or space of years in which I have been significantly more productive or prolific than during the other years of my long career." But he does speculate that the Studs Lonigan and Danny O'Neill novels, written earlier in his career, may have tended to overshadow the later works.

He takes from his bookcase two of these later novels. The first, "Boardinghouse Blues," published in 1961, he characterizes as "one of the best books I ever published." The other, the 1971 "Invisible Swords," he calls "the single most powerful novel I ever wrote."

Does he feel the critics have neglected him in recent years? He's unwilling to make that statement. Instead, he says mildly: "They probably feel I've had my chance and now it's someone else's turn." (At another point he does mention, however, that when his book, "What Time Collects," came out in 1965, a reviewer wrote: "James T. Farrell is still writing about the Chicago Irish." The author shakes his head again and notes that the book was set in Indianapolis and there were no Irish in it.)

Has the style of his books changed, then, over the years? "I've always tried to write for the long run," he says. He believes this is reflected in his later fiction as well as his early work and feels that, overall, "my writing has been concerned with making characters real." He is, he adds, "satisfied that all my books have had their place and made their impact."

To date, James T. Farrell has published 13 volumes of short stories— "Judith and Other Stories" will be his 14th collection—but unlike most other short story writers, he does not usually try to publish his short fiction anywhere except in book form. ("In 1952," he explains, "I started out to write a series of short stories set around the world. Since that time I have written 50 such stories and over 30 of them have been published in collections.") He describes "Judith," the title story of his new collection, as "an attempt to tell the story of a gifted person (Judith is a pianist) . . . and of a love affair, in a civilized manner, which is not the fashion these days."

Mr. Farrell has lived in New York City since 1932 and in his present East Side apartment since 1969. He still writes every day, although he admits he doesn't work as hard as he once did. He writes more than one draft of every story—the first draft in longhand. "In all my fiction, I try to achieve clarity and the greatest possible simplicity the subject will bear."

He has completed two drafts of the first novel he's written on baseball, a Farrell lifetime passion, a story about the Chicago Black Sox ("I'm still trying to decide what I want to do with it") and "thousands of pages" of a series to which he has given the name "A Universe of Time," made up of numerous "sequences" of intermingled novels and short stories. He sees his last published novel, "Invisible Swords," a story about congenital retardation in a child and the effect it has upon the parents, and the forthcoming "Judith and Other Stories," as part of the projected series.

There must be a moral. . . . Whatever it is, someone other than James T. Farrell will have to draw it; he's too busy with the task he set for himself back on St. Patrick's Day, 1927.

John Fowles

JOHN FOWLES is that rare bird, a novelist whose work is critically admired (in this country, at least) and who at the same time enjoys remarkable sales. People actually seem to *read* his books rather than just talk about them and leave them around for guests to see; and they anxiously await his next. This is a phenomenon to delight any publisher, and Little, Brown's pleasure in having Fowles faithfully on its list is marred only by one cloud: he hates having to publish at all.

This is no mere affectation: It emerges in his work, as an open-ended narrative ambivalence in which, at crucial points, the creator steps away from his creation and dares it, as it were, to continue life on its own. And it emerges just as strongly in conversation. "I love it when a story is still alive," he told *PW* the other day. "Then it's still changeable, still fluid, and you can take it anywhere, do anything with it. Once it's printed, it's set and frozen, like a bronze cast of a sculpture. You can't shape it any more. My whole interest is in the act of writing itself. Being published is a kind of death."

From most writers this would sound extravagant. From Fowles it is entirely believable because, in person as in his stories, he is able to convey you effortlessly into unfamiliar territory. In his work it is done by the extraordinary verisimilitude of his observation, the uncanny accuracy of his dialogue. In face-to-face conversation it is the utter straightforwardness of the man that is most striking. He has a broad, ruddy face that looks younger than his years (48), and his talk moves easily between biographical detail and candid—but rather diffident—self-revelation.

By John F. Baker. From *Publishers Weekly* 206, no. 22 (November 25, 1974), pp. 6–7.

His background is strikingly conventional English middle-class: well-to-do parents, "the usual sort of public school," conscription into the Royal Marines, where he finished his training the day World War II ended ("I remember how relieved we all were, whereas George Orwell regretted all his life that he hadn't fought in World War I: I suppose for his generation it was a form of virility, machismo"), then to Oxford, where he was captivated by the "dreaminess" of the place, and which he still looks back on as his happiest time.

Fowles studied French at Oxford, became fascinated with early French literature, and upon graduation went to teach for a while at the University of Poitiers. Another teaching stint followed, at an expensive boys' school on a Greek island (the background he later used in "The Magus"), from which he and the other masters were all fired when they tried to establish revolutionary changes.

These early years in Europe were of enormous importance to Fowles, and his eyes still light up when he thinks of them. "It was such a thrill to go abroad for our generation," he says. "The war had postponed everything for so long, and when we did go it was like a revelation. People now, who make their first trips as kids or students, can't imagine it. Greece, particularly, was magical then, back before the tourists spoiled it. I walked among the mountains by myself, and whenever you came into a village you were an honored guest. On the hillsides shepherds would be playing their pipes. It was as if nothing had changed for 2000 years."

He started writing in Greece, then returned to England and continued "out of a sense of exile." All through the 1950s he worked on what turned out to be "The Magus"; but meanwhile the idea for "The Collector" came to him—"it seemed more immediately publishable"—and so it came out first. "The Aristos," a collection of aphoristic reflections that is Fowles's least-known book though it is a valuable key to his thinking, followed soon thereafter. "The Magus" finally appeared in 1966, to accelerate Fowles's reputation, and "The French Lieutenant's Woman" three years later consolidated it: a best seller for months, it was one of the most discussed books of its year. Now a book of stories, "The Ebony Tower," has broken what was becoming a long silence: and with a beautiful cover (that gives no indication it is not a novel) and some terrific reviews, it is already edging toward best sellerdom, the first story collection to do so in many years.

It turns out that the collection was never part of Fowles's work in progress at all. He has been working on a long novel ever since "The French Lieutenant's Woman," about which he will say nothing except, cryptically, that it is about "Englishness," and he has no idea when he will be able, reluctantly, to let it go. The "Ebony Tower" stories, he says, came to him quite suddenly, and he dashed off the first drafts of all five of them in a few days, in a burst of activity that saw him writing up to 8000 words a day. "When I'm really on the job, I work very hard, 12 to 16 hours a day," Fowles says. The trouble is that whenever the weather is good he cannot resist being outdoors—gardening, birdwatching or looking for spiders. He is a passionate naturalist and this, as much as anything, is what has kept him living in England.

"It would be impossible to work in Greece in that sun, that light, I could never go indoors. But England is ideal for a writer because the weather just forces you inside so much of the time." He and his wife Elizabeth spend most of their time at their seaside home in Lyme Regis, Dorset (the West Country setting for "The French Lieutenant's Woman" as for the work of Hardy, a Fowles idol) with about a month a year at a flat in Hampstead, London (the setting for "The Collector").

The realization that the "Ebony Tower" stories were variations on a theme only came to Fowles after they were written, he says—and he is amused by the detective work some critics have put in trying to find the links between them. "It wasn't until I'd finished the title story that I was struck by the echoes of the old French tale of Eliduc, and I wrote that in, and the incident of killing the weasel on the road, afterward." In "The Enigma" he returns to a favorite notion, that of the vanished god, "and I've always felt that if God existed he'd probably be very much like a conservative British Member of Parliament, and therefore a man to be avoided." "The Cloud," perhaps the most opaque of the stories, he describes as "a deliberate homage to Katherine Mansfield," and likes to think that there is also a feeling of Joyce's "The Dead," which he thinks of as the finest story of its kind in the English language.

But if the critical efforts to elucidate his work entertain Fowles, he is also delighted by the attention he receives here, and contrasts it bitterly with his standing in his native land. The *New Statesman*, for which Fowles once wrote reviews himself, called "The Ebony Tower" "subpornography," a judgment that seems as incomprehensible to the interviewer as to Fowles himself. "The gist of my English reviewers is that I play too many clever tricks," he says. "I haven't had any really good reviews since 'The Collector.' And they hate to see my success here; they like to talk about American vulgarity, as a way of berating me.

"Reviewing of fiction is in desperate straits in England now," he goes on. "They give it hardly any space, whereas any biography, however bad, gets enormous review space. Any English writer of fiction is really in the same boat. You're much better off here, especially with all the local newspapers that review books, some of them quite well."

He reads little contemporary fiction himself—"I love old books, ancient legends, books about murder trials and such; I'm not a very well-read fellow really"—but when pressed admits to great admiration for Saul Bellow's "Herzog" and Vladimir Nabokov's "Ada."

"The Collector" and "The Magus" were both filmed with some success, but Fowles was not pleased with the way either of them came out—and his happiest memories of Hollywood are of walking around a completely deserted lot at Warner Bros. in the bright sunlight, and of finding his first black widow spider in a garden on Mulholland Drive. "The French Lieutenant's Woman," he says, has been optioned three times, but nobody can lick a script: currently the thinking is for a TV special starring Julie Christie, about which he is less than enthusiastic.

Fowles has always been with the same publishers—Jonathan Cape in London and Little, Brown here, and says this is because he has always been very close to his editors: "I'm always terrified one of them will die or leave." His success has given him what he calls "financial relaxation," but he has carefully arranged his payments so that he is not taxed out of existence in England—like, for instance, Frederick Forsyth. "I could live out of the country, and I've thought of it," Fowles says. "But it's rather an ignominious notion. You should live in the place where you have your inspiration. And although I may hate the English—and not even that, really—I do love the country itself."

After a promotional swing along the Eastern seaboard for "Ebony Tower," Fowles will spend a little time in New Mexico, observing birds and lizards, and will then return to wrestle with his new novel, or perhaps with one of the other fragments still lying around. "There are two early completed novels I may publish one day," he says, "and lots of things I've got a third or half the way through, and put aside to do some more work on."

Little, Brown is hoping it rains a lot in England next year.

Paul Gallico

IN A WARM stone courtyard, beneath a cream parasol, a table bears a bowl of black cherries, a platter of nectarines, figs laid on vine leaves. A dark-haired woman, whose youthful appeal lies in the slight irregularity of her features, the bend of her nose under the straw hat, sips white wine. Beside her, enjoying his after-lunch euphoria, sits Paul Gallico.

He is a big man and his 75 years have not stooped him, nor softened the black of his hair.

He does not look the kind of writer he is. The face is heavily fleshed, big-nosed, Italianate. The mouth is thick, sensual, sardonic. He could be a prosperous businessman, an impresario.

Yet his phenomenal output of books and stories reveal a whimsicality which, if handled less skillfully, would be cloying, and an engagingly naïve quality.

In his work Gallico does not pretend or attempt realism. "We live in a rough, cold world today. But I make a different world when I write: I make it what I think it ought to be." He provides the escape fiction he knows people want, but what matters to him is that the first person to escape is Gallico himself. As he writes he enters another country, another atmosphere, to such an extent that he can hardly bear to pack the book up and send it to the publisher. "I'm very sad for about 10 days, making the transition from all my friends."

So Paul Gallico remains a teller of tales, essentially a romantic. And for such "unfashionable" qualities he has always found a vast market, great financial reward, and the opportunity to live where and as he wishes, which he uti-

By Marcelle Bernstein. From *Publishers Weekly* 203, no. 4 (January 22, 1973), pp. 34–35. Reprinted by permission of Marcelle Bernstein.

lizes to the utmost with a house in Antibes, an apartment in Monte Carlo and a mews cottage in London.

Antibes is Paul Gallico's real home, where he and his English wife Virginia have converted two narrow fishermen's houses high on the ramparts of the town over the harbor. In cool, shuttered rooms there are paintings, brass scales full of heather from the Provençal hills, an old rocking horse in weathered wood.

In his top floor study, Gallico contemplates a goldfish named Ivan Awful Jaundice, which swims opposite his desk, and says that "there is nothing here that I could not write without." Writing, for him, is like "being at a party and saying, 'have you heard the one about?' It's the pleasure of telling a good tale, the logic and neatness of it when you get all the ends to thread up together and it works."

He inherits both his love of storytelling and his long-fingered hands from his musician father, of whom he says, "he was an unexplosive Italian and I adored him." He taught during the day and played in concerts at night. "I can still see him shaving himself with an open razor, very handsome, and saying, 'to be continued tomorrow.' He told me about dragons and adventures, and I was brought up on the fairy books of the Brothers Grimm, in a family whose culture was European, although they emigrated to the United States two years before I was born."

At 10 years old, left alone in a Brussels hotel, Gallico wrote his first story, about a small boy and an Italian workman. It was the escape from loneliness of any only child to "lie in bed at night and see myself in heroic roles: they kept me busy until I fell asleep."

After majoring in English at Columbia University he joined the sports section of the New York *Daily News* and worked there in the 20s and 30s when the heroes of the young were sporting figures and gangsters controlled boxing.

Paul Gallico's first book, "The Snow Goose," was to be his *tour de force*. "After Dunkirk I wanted to write a poem, a song in sympathy." So he created Rhayader, the dark cripple with his bird sanctuary in the marshes, to which a silent girl brings the wounded goose. It was an unashamed tearjerker by a man who says sternly that "emotions are deadly when you are writing. You must never give way to them." Last year "The Snow Goose" made a very auspicious TV debut, starring Richard Harris.

"The Snow Goose" is Gallico's only book to have achieved real critical success. He is no literary lion and all too often critics refer to his charm as "practiced." He does, of course, mind. Although: "I don't think anybody can be more than he is. I can't write like anybody else, and the anybody elses can't write like me." He learned never to envy another writer after bumping into Hemingway at the bar of New York's stylish Stork Club. "My God," said Hemingway, "you're the guy who wrote 'Snow Goose.' I wish I'd written that."

Gallico fingers the flashy golden globe on his desk, an American television film award for "The Snow Goose." "In place of great literary fame, I've got millions of people who care about what I write and who like me. What more do I want?"

Over the years he has achieved a superb professionalism. To feel comfortable he must have a novel "in the works," one "on the runway" and another in the "take-off slot." After two months he has the first draft completed, and by the eighth month the second and final version will be written, "though some go three."

He thoroughly enjoys the whole writing process, even making good badly written material. Gallico will start work soon after nine, dictating slowly with long pauses to think while his American secretary sits patiently. "I might say a line and then 'no, hold that, kill it, let's try it this way.' " He finds this faster than typing himself, which ended 13 years ago when he suffered from pinched nerves resulting from a bent head when typing.

Gallico has a horror of his books being remaindered, which has happened only once since his aim is usually unerring, thanks to the "common touch" on which he so prides himself. It also helps him find plots. Everyone, he believes, has a story—"Go and ask your grocer how he got started." He puts his books together like a casserole. "You take something you've learned, something someone has said, and everything goes into the pot."

One children's book, "Manxmouse," originated with Princess Grace of Monaco, who promised him a mouse when she started ceramic classes. A year later the mouse arrived with her apologies for its broken tail and rabbity ears. "She didn't know I was writing a mouse book until it was delivered to her, bound, illustrated and dedicated."

At the moment Gallico is working on an original screenplay, struggling to bend the dialog into a certain channel. "But the characters won't do it. People are people, and I can't force them to do anything." Names are vital in forming a character, and the blond heroine of the shipwreck book, "Poseidon Adventure," would not work at all until he renamed her Nonnie. "Then she got up off the floor and began to act like a person. I saw her, I felt her."

Many characters originate from people he knows, and he is always amazed if they do not recognize themselves. Ada 'Arris, the Cockney char with a passion for geraniums, is really a London charlady called Katie. The tragic Rhayader of "Snow Goose" is Peter Scott—"his lighthouse, his painting, his sailing ability." Both men were once in love with the same girl figure-skating champion. "The character came from my admiration, turning him into a heroic figure."

Gallico's female characters are not his strong point, the most vivid being the Marquesa in "Love, Let Me Not Hunger." Bloated, bejeweled and totally bald under her wig, she is, claims Gallico with satisfaction: "My old nannie. I hated and loathed her and I've got her to a T."

He is at home in France now. "We live here in the utmost tranquillity and with great delight. I've got everything I want. And now I have a sense of impending extinction. How much longer can I wait? I've reached the life expectancy of this generation. I'm prepared for death, hoping I can go as my father did, who went to sleep and didn't wake up."

Rumer Godden

RUMER GODDEN and her husband are paying their first visit to America for several years—seeing old friends, helping to publicize Miss Godden's new novel about a cloistered order of nuns, "In This House of Brede" (*Viking*) and visiting Washington, D.C. and Baltimore, where Miss Godden is giving two lectures. She has been invited to speak at the Library of Congress on her writing career, and in Baltimore she is inaugurating at the Enoch Pratt Free Library the first Annis Duff lecture on writing for children. The lecture series has been endowed by Viking for 10 years in honor of the firm's long-time children's book editor, now retired.

Miss Godden and her husband are pleasantly informal people. In England they live in Henry James's old home in Rye, which has now been declared a landmark. When *PW* visited them at a New York hotel they were struggling with a flood of telephone calls, but very willing to take time out for tea and a chat. The tea Miss Godden brewed on a small burner and, since there were only two cups on hand, the caller was invited to enjoy a fine China blend—in a champagne glass. Very good it was, too.

The background story on how "In This House of Brede" was written is an interesting one that goes back some years. Miss Godden had discovered in an old library two small pamphlets of French poems on animals and religion. She learned that the author of them was a woman living in a monastery with a cloistered order of nuns South of Paris. In a most unusual move, seldom duplicated, they had accepted her into their enclosure and nursed her back to health after a severe mental breakdown. Miss Godden, who thought the

By Barbara A. Bannon. From *Publishers Weekly* 196, no. 19 (November 10, 1969), pp. 17–20.

poems lovely, visited the abbey—her first experience in such a place—to try to obtain permission to translate some of them into English.

Only one of the French nuns could speak English and, even though they valiantly looked up the English words in a dictionary, they could not make much of Miss Godden's translation. She suggested that they appoint someone in England to act as arbiter on the translation, asking only that the person be a poet.

The French nuns named an English Benedictine nun, who was quite a poet in her own right and a translator of Rilke, and in meeting her Miss Godden made her second visit to such a religious house. The poems eventually appeared in Rumer Godden's beautiful translation as "Prayers from the Ark."

Even then, however, Miss Godden told *PW*, despite her own conversion to Catholicism, she looked on her contacts with the nuns as simply an aspect of her writing, her work. It was not until a girl she knew well became seriously ill while awaiting the birth of a child that Miss Godden's interest in the life of the nuns became more personal. A nun in the English Benedictine house Miss Godden had visited asked if she might write to the girl and did so faithfully every week at a time when the pregnant girl doubted she or her child would come through alive. The girl and her child survived, and a similar incident became the basis of one of the plot elements in "In This House of Brede."

After this more personal encounter with the Benedictines, Miss Godden said she began to look at the nuns with new eyes, and to be in touch with them more regularly. It still did not occur to her, however, to build a novel about them, until one day, one of the cloistered nuns said to her, "I do wish when people write about nuns they would take the trouble to find out what we are really like."

"I thought of 'Black Narcissus,' and blushed," Miss Godden said. That novel, which she still regards as a very good story, "has no spirituality in it," as she sees it today. It was written, she admits candidly, "in a spirit of revenge," wanting to get back at the small group of Anglican nuns to whom she and her sister, Jon, were sent to school after they left India. "We only lasted a term but the nuns were very cruel to my sister," she recalls. Actually, even as she was writing "Black Narcissus," her first novel, she found that the act of writing about nuns was proving a catharsis, and her hatred of the ones she and Jon had encountered was being dissipated.

Once she had decided to write about an order of cloistered nuns living in England today, Miss Godden blocked out the entire story first. Only then did she get down to the detailed research necessary, visiting many individual monasteries, staying in their guest houses, and with the permission of the abbesses, speaking with individual nuns. She promised to ask no personal questions of any of the nuns with whom she spent hours and hours individually. In actual fact, she discovered that they were all quite ready to tell her their personal stories, along with answering questions about their way of life.

"My great worry was not to let slip to one nun what another had said," she told *PW*. "I had to ring in red in my notebook the personal entries." A "very pretty nun who was a lawyer," explained the Benedictine habit to her. An old kitchener reminisced about how they ran the monastery kitchen. One nun drew a plan of an imaginary abbey which Miss Godden tacked up on the wall of her study as she wrote, and this plan became the endpapers of "In This House of Brede."

One of the pivotal plot elements deals with an abbess who, literally, "fiddles the accounts." Although the nuns were not too happy with this idea and pointed out that it would have been an extremely difficult thing to manage in real life, "a nun who should have been a detective story writer" came up with a method of delicate and well-intended embezzlement that Miss Godden used in the book.

The nuns were universally helpful and Miss Godden remembers especially their "extraordinary courtesy. The silence of the cloistered order helps more than anything else," she believes, "because the nuns learn to waste no time in unnecessary words."

When the book was finished a tribunal of three nuns read the manuscript, "going through it with a fine-tooth comb for errors." They had a very few trivial suggestions to make about her depiction of the religious life, Miss Godden recalls, "but they were very hard on my grammar."

"What attracted me to writing about the Benedictines," Miss Godden summed it up, "is that they seem so sane," unlike certain other cloistered orders which she does find "eccentric or exaggerated." The Benedictines try to preserve some individual privacy for their nuns. No nun ever knows what another is doing unless the task requires help. Their mail is private.

The Benedictines, who do not take final vows for at least five-and-a-half years, are trained in psychology as well as in religious matters. Much of the work they carry on—often in voluminous correspondence, or in parlor meetings with visitors—is a kind of counseling.

"They get a lot of near insane cases," Miss Godden said, "and they are not allowed to say one word about what they are told to anyone, but must preserve it in what is almost a secrecy of the confessional." In special cases, with the explicit permission of the one they are counseling, the nuns may consult with *one* other person—perhaps a psychiatrist, a lawyer, a doctor, for professional advice.

Such extraordinary care is taken to screen out girls and women for whom the Benedictine way of life is not suitable, Miss Godden feels, that the cloistered Benedictines have been less touched with defections from their ranks in recent years than many other religious orders. She quoted one abbess as saying, talking about the ferment in the Catholic Church today, "it is more important than ever to insist upon quality not quantity in vocations."

Francine du Plessix Gray

THERE IS A MOMENT in Francine du Plessix Gray's intensely passionate new novel "Lovers and Tyrants" when the narration, which has been in the first person until then, suddenly switches into the third—and for the long last section of the book "me" is transformed into Stephanie. That is also the point, says Ms. Gray, at which the book ceases to be at least partly autobiographical, and becomes entirely fantasy. It is a crucial moment, a dreamlike scene in which the heroine embraces a freedom she knows can only be found "in work, in dreams."

The book has been 12 years in the making, and for much of that time she struggled to come to terms with herself and with what she wanted to create, and fought a losing battle against the compulsion to write it. "It took me years to decide how to do the book and not just create a conventional, polite book about a woman's life," Ms. Gray told *PW* recently as she sat, nervously determined to be frank about herself and her book, in the office of her Simon and Schuster editor. "I think art has to be an irritant, and I wanted to take risks in doing the book, but for a long time I didn't even know how to take risks."

She means artistic risks, of course, for her life has not been without emotional and physical hazard. In many ways it closely resembles that of Stephanie, her heroine. She, too, was born in France, lost her father early in the war, came to the U.S. with her mother in 1941 and saw her struggle with the émigré life while she herself went through the agonies of puberty in a New York girls' school, eventually became a successful journalist, of that versatile kind whose by-line is

By John F. Baker. From *Publishers Weekly* 210, no. 14 (October 4, 1976), pp. 14–15, 18.

equally at home in the *New Yorker*, the *New York Review of Books*, the *New York Times Magazine, Vogue*, even, at one stage, *Cosmopolitan*. She, too, married, raised a family—and wondered: What now?

The genesis of "Lovers and Tyrants" was in some sketches she originally wrote while still at college, then put away for many years while she worked as a reporter (for UPI at first, later for *Réalités* in Paris, then for a time as book editor at *Art in America*). She picked up the work again in 1964, turned the memories of her Paris childhood into a story she called "The Governess" and another sketch, and won a Putnam Creative Writing Award. The *New Yorker* planned to publish them, but as is sometimes the way, left them in galleys there for a year or two. Meanwhile Blanche Knopf, alerted by the award, asked to see them "and anything else I wrote." As a result, Ms. Gray signed with Knopf for a book of short stories, to include the *New Yorker* material; shortly thereafter Blanche Knopf died. "I tried to work out more stories, but I just didn't know how to proceed."

The book lapsed, the 1960s wore on and Ms. Gray (whose studies at college were in religion and philosophy, not literature) became more and more absorbed in the anti-war movement, and with the radical Catholics, including the Berrigans, who participated in it. "It was an exciting time, a time when my life and work were converging; I was consumed by a fascination with the radical church and the peace movement." She wrote for the *New Yorker* and the *NYRB* of the Berrigans, Ivan Illich and others, and in the end the book she actually did with Knopf was "Divine Disobedience," a study of Catholic radicalism which won the National Catholic Book Award in its year (1970).

Then her husband moved to Hawaii for a while to teach and, reluctantly, she went along. As a reporter, however, she found material for another book, "Hawaii: The Sugar-Coated Fortress," which Jason Epstein encouraged, and which Random House published in 1972. "It got good reviews, but went nowhere," she smiles. The urge to expand her childhood stories into a novel that would trace a woman's life out of her own experience was still strong, however she tried to submerge it. She continued her journalistic assignments, traveling, researching far too much, "trying to keep the book at arm's length, yet knowing in the end I'd have to do it, like the sinner who cries: 'Save me, Lord, but not just yet.' "

Two crucial events in her life made further evasion impossible. She went back to France in 1974, saw the French side of her family again after having been out of touch with them all for many years and finally visited her father's grave, just as Stephanie does in the book. "Seeing them, and finally acknowledging that all that part of my life was over, enabled me to face my life so far and seek a new one." On her return she settled with her family into a beach cottage in Nantucket, and found that suddenly she could write of all her childhood with complete freedom—"but now at last I could fictionalize it as I'd never been able to before. Suddenly I was no longer just a recorder of events. I'd exorcized that trauma, and my life was transformed."

Another important experience was the teaching Ms. Gray has recently undertaken at New York's City College, where she has been conducting a course in the New Journalism. "I found a graduate workshop full of women of great gifts, mostly in early middle age, who were trying to be writers and earth mothers at the same time—and in their struggle for an act of creation I recognized my own." She thinks that perhaps this sudden release into a flow of creativity that seems to occur in women around their early 40s may be "the beginning of fear of death, a feeling that life is half over and it's time to start taking risks."

At any rate, the writing of the last parts of the book proceeded apace, as freely fictional as the early parts had been truthful. Its last long section, in which Stephanie takes up with the bisexual hippie Elijah, is, she says, "a fantasy regression to childhood and its complete freedom from responsibility"; and the closing scene, in which Stephanie watches an androgynous figure balancing on the high wire in a circus act in a Las Vegas nightclub, symbolizes for her the essential human balancing act, "striking the balance between personal freedom and the claims of civilization that makes life possible."

It is a balancing act that Ms. Gray sees as being much more difficult for women than for men, and in one important way she thinks of her book as "a study of the different ways in which women can be oppressed." Men, she thinks, are much freer to create their own fates than are women, because women's role in life has been much more clearly defined by society. She has not been at all close to the women's movement, and is touched and pleased at the enthusiastic reaction the book has received from advance readers like Susan Brownmiller and Gail Sheehy. "Living out of town as I do, I don't know many other writers, and I've tended to be wary of radical feminists. But I do like to think the book breaks new ground in talking about women's freedom; it's a bridge between the aesthetic requirements for such freedom and the political requirements, and they're very difficult to reconcile."

The book, incidentally, went to Simon and Schuster rather than to Knopf or Random House largely because of the friendship that grew up between Ms. Gray and S&S editor Alice Mayhew during the anti-Vietnam days. They knew each other slightly at a time they both took part in a demonstration that led to their arrest. "Then we shared a paddy wagon, and found ourselves shouting to each other between jail cells, and since then we've been very close." Ms. Mayhew read the early chapters, heard of the progress of the rest, and last summer said she'd like to publish the book if things could be resolved with Knopf–Random. The ms. went first to Jason Epstein, but at that time it had "about 80 extra pages of theological dialogues, which I love, but which held things up." He demurred at these (they were later cut anyway) and meanwhile Ms. Gray's agent Georges Borchardt arranged for Ms. Mayhew to get the book after all. "She had wanted it all along, and I wanted to work with a woman editor— there were things in the book I felt I could work out better with a woman." She laughed. "When you've been insecure enough to work for 12 years on a book, you need a lot of enthusiasm, and that's what I find I get from S&S."

She's now working on a second novel, which she describes as a "study in friendship," and which involves a group of middle-aged people traveling on a bus through an Iron Curtain country. The writing is coming much easier now—"If doing the second half of 'Lovers' was like learning to walk, this is like learning to fly"—but she is still wary of doing anything too fast. "If 'Lovers' is a success [and considering BOMC has made it a special fall selection, the auguries are sound], I'll be able to take five years or more on the new one without feeling anxious." She'd also like eventually to collect her various pieces of reportage on places and events (the most recent of which was a long piece on Jerusalem in the *New Yorker*) into a book she would call "Everywhere."

And *Rolling Stone* has asked her to do a piece on women and erotic writing, and she's fascinated by the idea. As research she has spent her summer "reading nothing but women writers, everyone from Virginia Woolf on," after having very deliberately abstained from all such reading while she was working on her own book. "It's been the happiest summer of my life," she adds simply.

Gerald Green

AT A SYMPOSIUM at Columbia College not long ago, a panel of authors and critics was debating the question, "Is the Novel Obsolete?" Charged with the task of defending the novel was Gerald Green, a big man and a tough adversary under any circumstances.

When one critic tried to sound the death knell for fiction, claiming that sociological nonfiction would be the novel's undoing, Mr. Green rose to his full elevation, something above six feet, with righteous indignation.

He had read many sociological nonfiction books, he argued and, aside from the statistics, he had found in them nothing new, nothing that could not be found in, say, James T. Farrell on the Irish, Sinclair Lewis on the middle class, or Joseph Conrad on how black Africans regard the white man. Though he conceded that the novel may have lost some of its importance, he believes it is still a thriving, viable medium.

Mr. Green, it would seem, is pretty well sold on the form. Though he has worn many hats on his balding pate—musical comedy librettist, motion picture scenarist, television documentalist, director and producer—he still comes back to the novel when he has something really important or personal to say.

His current book, "To Brooklyn with Love" (*Trident*), is a touchingly sensitive reminiscence about boyhood in Brownsville, the same setting that Mr. Green called up in his most famous novel, "The Last Angry Man" (*Scribners*).

Some of the characters in his new book are carry-overs from the earlier work, the most conspicuous, of course,

By Dan Rustin. From *Publishers Weekly* 193, no. 13 (March 25, 1968), pp. 13–15.

being the doctor–father, still at war with the world and his neighbors in Brownsville.

Mr. Green wrote "To Brooklyn" while he was expatriating for two years in Paris. "It's easy to work over there," the author maintains. "Fewer friends, fewer distractions. When you wake up in the morning the national worries are not on your back. When you're home, the involvement is murderous."

Mr. Green and his family lived in a furnished apartment—"a great view, but tiny and exorbitant, with a kitchen that would have been a disgrace in Brownsville."

He spent five or six months researching and planning his novel (he had brought along for atmosphere several books on the New Deal and a few photostats of the *New York Times* from the year in which the novel is set, 1934). After he felt he had a good grip on his material he began writing— from 8:30 A.M. to 12:30 P.M., five or six days a week, for seven months, his goal set at 3000 words a day.

His two years in Paris produced not only a novel, but an interesting philosophy about the French. The squalor and backwardness of French poverty, he discovered, have no equal in northern Europe. Interestingly, the Parisian blue-collar worker doesn't seem to mind too much, largely because he's drunk most of the time. "I'm not kidding about this," the author says. "The availability of good cheap wine keeps the working man in a semi-stupor all day long. I'm sure he doesn't know what's going on most of the time."

A moody man who can't sit still for long, Gerald Green will finish one project, pack his bags and set out for a completely different place on a completely different assignment. He may wind up in Baja California, as he did for a television documentary with Joseph Wood Krutch, a former professor of his at Columbia. Or he may find himself in Hungary for a film about that country's revolution, 10 years later. This work is part of a commitment to NBC to produce and direct or write two documentaries a year.

He's back home now, in Stamford, Connecticut, working on his next novel, a comic spy story revolving around the literary establishment. Since he's back in the States, his setting, naturally, will be Paris.

Those who have read "To Brooklyn with Love" will be relieved to learn that the tough, scruffy kids who inhabited Longview Avenue grew up okay. The one who is Bushy in the book, a terrifying boy, is today a successful lawyer and customers' man. Another is a successful businessman and a third is a well-known surgeon.

"Had it not been for the depression," Mr. Green explains, "we would have been just lower middle class kids. All finished high school, some went to college. None went to jail."

Though some critics may try to typecast Gerald Green as an urban Jewish writer (and his friend Meyer Levin has kiddingly assigned him to first base on his all-star team of "affirmers" of the religion), Mr. Green recoils at being poured into a mold. He points out that he's got eight novels to his credit, only two of which deal with urban Judaism. What's more, he has in him an Army novel and another with a southwestern setting; then, Brooklyn again.

"The beautiful thing about being a critic," he says, "is that you can be completely arbitrary and defend almost anything by just being brilliant." He charges that critics helped perpetuate formlessness in the arts by writing muddled, hazy, loose-ended reviews. "They didn't do their jobs too well," Mr. Green argues. "I believe that's why movies, plays and novels are without focus today."

About the so-called "Jewish novel," it isn't really such a phenomenon, he feels. To the Jewish community the appeal is obvious; for Gentiles, the setting is something new, different. After the Jewish novel passes its apogee, other "unfamiliar" ethnic backgrounds will move into greater popularity than they have now. First will come those with Negro settings, then, possibly, those about homosexuals. Whatever happens, he's still pretty certain that the novel isn't dead. "As entertainment, as pure storytelling, you'll never be able to kill it with a stick."

Cecelia Holland

CECELIA HOLLAND at 25 has garnered an impressive series of reviews for three very different novels with historical settings: "The Firedrake," "Rakóssy" and the new "The Kings in Winter" (all *Atheneum*). She winces a bit at the term "historical fiction" in connection with her books, since it generally conjures up an image of just the kind of overblown, over-romanticized fiction she does *not* write. Nevertheless, there has never been much question in her mind that history was going to be her field, as either a writer or a teacher.

"I started writing at 13," Miss Holland told *PW* the other day, "because I couldn't get what I wanted to read." The first three chapters of "The Firedrake," which had to do with the Norman invasion, were written while she was still a student at Connecticut College, and were brought to Atheneum's attention by one of her creative writing teachers. The publishing house snapped it up instantly, and Miss Holland gave up the idea of teaching history for that of writing about it, but in fictional form.

Writing about a past period, she says, "beats the devil out of writing modern fiction. In a novel about history you can be more selective in your detail, you can develop a sense of perspective and write on something you know is important."

The Holland style is remarkably spare and lean, and her novels feature battle scenes treated with a realism few women writers have attempted. "What I try to do is to use the most concrete kind of images and very few of them," she says. "I try to keep the pace moving," One of the most

By Barbara A. Bannon. From *Publishers Weekly* 193, no. 6 (February 5, 1968), pp. 27–29.

difficult things in writing fiction with a historical background is to remember that however famous some of your characters may be, "they also had private lives." Miss Holland concentrates hard on trying to write everything "as if you do not know what is going to happen next," so that her readers, no matter how well they may know how the Battle of Hastings or the Danish invasions of Ireland really turned out, accept the outcomes as a matter of suspense for the characters about whom they are reading.

For "The Kings in Winter," which is set in Ireland in the 11th century, Miss Holland went back to the ancient Gaelic chronicles for her source material. They are, she says, "very beautiful and loaded with detail." She also visited Ireland and loved it "although it rained all the time." She is of part Irish descent.

For her next book, which will have to do with the Mongol invasions of Europe, and has a tentative title of "Until the Sun Falls," she is now in Russia and hopes to get as far into what was Mongol territory as Alma-Ata. The Mongols had a secret history (secret in the sense that it was kept hidden while it was being written) and this, too, like so many of the other ancient chronicles, is full of action and such detail that even the color of the horse a rider rode was set down.

"Battle scenes," Miss Holland says, "should be done from one person's viewpoint. After all, people killed each other off individually" (at least in those days). A horsewoman herself, Miss Holland says she "gets perturbed because so many people who write historical fiction do not know anything about horses." Bowmen, such as Muirtagh, hero of "The Kings in Winter," or the Mongol generals who will appear in her next novel, "never rode stallions. A stallion in battle gets hot and fussy and kicks out." Stallions could be war horses for knights, and the maneuvers that the famous white Lippizaner stallions of Vienna still carry out today had their origin in their battle maneuvers of the past. Bowmen, however, like the Gaels of Muirtagh's day or the Mongols of the 12th or 13th century, had to have quieter animals that would permit them to stand up in their stirrups, shoot back while dropping the reins over the horse's head.

It's Miss Holland's aim to continue to write one book a year. Her own favorite period in history is from Rome to the Renaissance. "I suspect it is a span of time a lot closer to our own than many others," she says, "in its dramatic sense of homelessness, its confusion about what was real and what wasn't." It is a span of time that enables her as well to continue to explore in various ways a favorite theme, "how tribes developed into an empire." The forthcoming book on the Mongols will be concerned with "a people who never stopped fighting because they did not understand any other way of life, and of the generation gap that developed when the Mongol empire was becoming an institution."

William Bradford Huie

IT IS NO COINCIDENCE that William Bradford Huie's Delacorte Press novel is entitled "The Klansman" (with a "K") while the famous 1905 Thomas Dixon novel in eulogy of the Klan was "The Clansman." Mr. Huie, a native Alabamian, an outspoken opponent of white supremacy, author of "Three Lives for Mississippi" and factual accounts of the cases of Emmett Till and Ruby McCallum, intends his new novel as a documentary 20th century record of what Klan life is like and what it can do to a man.

Still today, in backwoods areas of the deep South, he says, 16 mm. film versions of the D. W. Griffith movie based on "The Clansman," "The Birth of a Nation," are shown regularly to recruit Klan members. In certain cinematic circles the Griffith film is revered as a classic. Cinema technique aside, Mr. Huie views "The Birth of a Nation" as having done "much more damage in the world than any film ever made," because of its open espousal of Negro racial inferiority and perpetuation of the myth of the brute Negro male out to rape every white woman. He includes in "The Klansman" some quotations from the Dixon novel that give grim testimony to what he means. Ironically, Mr. Huie says, Abraham Lincoln is often cited by the Ku Klux Klan as one of its patron saints because of dire distress he exhibited at the idea of "the assimilation of the Negro into our social and political life as our equal." Some of these Lincoln comments, too, are quoted in the Huie novel.

Mr. Huie was a guest of Delacorte Press at the recent ABA convention, autographing advance unbound copies of his new novel for booksellers in the Dell–Delacorte booth.

By Barbara A. Bannon. From *Publishers Weekly* 191, no. 25 (June 19, 1967), p. 45.

Talking beforehand to a *PW* reporter, he emphasized that although there is a sardonic link between "The Klansman" and "The Clansman," his book is intended first and foremost as an only slightly fictionalized picture of a typical 20th century Klansman. Often, he says, such men make superb soldiers in time of war. (The central figure in his book is a sheriff who has been in time of war a Congressional Medal of Honor winner.) The tragedy is that the "born killer" wanted in wartime can very well turn out to be, in certain circumstances, the same thing in peacetime.

"The Klan," Mr. Huie says, "is not affected as yet by fines and court decrees. The actual number of men who wear sheets is not an indication of its real power. A handful of men who can commit murder with impunity can terrorize a community." The Klansmen, who are willing to do this, hold their power still because of the passive acquiescence of the white power structure in much of the deep South.

Nevertheless, Mr. Huie is not pessimistic about the ultimate future of the South. New industries coming in, young white people who are having, however slowly, to come into contact with young Negroes, all augur well for the future, he believes. There are now more than 300 Negroes in the University of Alabama, and the lower schools are slowly being integrated. "The white kids," Mr. Huie says, "are beginning to wonder what the fuss was all about."

MacKinlay Kantor

MacKINLAY KANTOR, at 71, looks back on over 40 years as a mostly successful, and highly versatile, writer who has written more than 40 books in his time (ranging from the somber Pulitzer Prize-winning novel "Andersonville" to books of verse and juveniles) and says he feels he has been "a very fortunate man."

Kantor, who looks robust and rosy as an old sea dog and has the cheerfully bluff manner of one, was in New York recently to talk about his new novel "Valley Forge," published recently by M. Evans to generally enthusiastic attention. He settled himself at a table in the Algonquin ("I've been staying here for 40 years—I've known the Algonquin longer than the oldest waiter") and reviewed for *PW* a life rich in incident and lively anecdote. He has been in his time a singer, an actor, a screenwriter, a New York City policeman and has flown with the Royal Air Force. He began to write when he was 16 and published his first novel (which he claims was the first ever published by Coward-McCann) when he was 24.

At that time he was a newspaperman in his native Midwest and not exactly prosperous in mid-Depression. The way he recalls it, "One winter I didn't have an overcoat, the next winter my book 'Long Remember' was a Literary Guild choice and I had my first Hollywood contract." That was in 1934, and Mack Kantor suffered no more cold winters thereafter; for one thing, he could afford an overcoat, and for another, in 1936 he moved his family down to Siesta Key in Sarasota, Florida, where he has lived on and off ever since.

By John F. Baker. From *Publishers Weekly* 208, no. 20 (November 17, 1975), pp. 6–7.

A budding literary and screenwriting career was cut short by the war, in which Kantor first flew with the R.A.F. as a correspondent and trained as a gunner on B-17s (he still remembers enough of the art of gun dismemberment so that when the family vacuum cleaner recently failed to function he was able to triumphantly take it apart, fix it and reassemble it). Back in Hollywood after the war he worked on the screenplay for Samuel Goldwyn's Academy Award-winning "The Best Years of Our Lives," adapted from his novel "Glory for Me," then the producer had an idea for a police movie and asked Kantor to do the screenplay. The writer insisted that to do so he must actually serve time as a policeman to know what it was like and so, after a fair amount of string-pulling, Kantor became a city cop for a year or so in 1948—"I had a gun and a badge and everything." As so often happens in Hollywood, however, the movie was never made, though the experience did form the basis for Kantor's novel "Signal Thirty-two."

Ever since "Long Remember," his first big success, Kantor had gone back at intervals to the Civil War for material, and in 1955 his mining of that lode paid off magnificently: "Andersonville," the story of the great camp for Southern prisoners of war, became one of the big best sellers of its year, and won him the Pulitzer Prize. At that time Kantor's editor was the late Donald Friede, then at World; when Friede left to go to Doubleday, he took Kantor with him. The two men worked for some time with General Curtis LeMay, whom Kantor had got to know in the war, to do the controversial Air Force general's autobiography, "Mission with LeMay."

"That should have been a big success, that book," Kantor says regretfully. "We'd hoped it would be a BOMC choice, but LeMay just refused to speak out in it; he didn't want to criticize his superiors at the Defense Department. In the end he said it all in public anyway, but the book was out by then." Shortly thereafter, 10 years ago last summer, Friede died; and Kantor gives the impression that ever since he has felt essentially homeless as a writer.

"After Donald died I got a big offer from Putnam for a novel," he says. "I asked Doubleday to match it, but they wouldn't, so I published with Walter Minton." The book, "Beauty Beast," was not a great success, however, and Kantor moved on again. He published "The Children Sing" with Hawthorn, also without notable success, and a first installment of an autobiography, "I Love You Irene"—dedicated to his wife, with whom he will celebrate a golden wedding anniversary next year—with Doubleday.

As to "Valley Forge," he says: "I knew I should do something about the Bicentennial, and Valley Forge was a dramatic story. I proposed it to Hawthorn, and they paid me a big advance. Then I began to get cold feet. I thought everybody and his dog would be writing Bicentennial novels, and this wasn't really my period anyway. But everyone—Irene, my kids,

Paul Reynolds, my agent—all kept telling me I'd be crazy not to do it.'' Kantor immersed himself in the Library of Congress for detailed research, unearthed some precious, little-known local family histories that gave him much of the flavor of the time and finally, on New Year's Day, 1974, he began to write—on a ship in mid-Pacific.

"I knew I'd never get down to it in Florida, where people keep dropping by all the time," he grins. "So I found a ship, the *Monterey*, leaving L.A. for a long voyage to Hawaii, Australia, New Zealand and the islands of the South Pacific. They set me up in the ship's library, where I had an outlet for my dictaphone''—Kantor dictates all his work, claiming that he has to hear how it *sounds* before he can put it in writing—"and where I could spread out my books. I'd get up at 5 every morning as we sailed across the Pacific and put in hours of dictating before anyone was up.''

He went ashore at the various ports of call, but claims proudly that he never missed a day of work. When he got back in April, the whole of "Valley Forge" was enshrined in a collection of dictabelts, and he only had to polish it.

When he sent the ms. to Hawthorn, however, he got a rude shock. "I guess Charlie Heckelmann [then Hawthorn editor-in-chief] was leery after 'The Children Sing' failed, and he got in some expert assistant to read it. I got back a letter of 16 single-spaced pages telling me what was wrong with it. I've been writing for 45 years and he presumes to tell me how to tell a story!" Kantor snorts. He took it back and Reynolds sent it out; Herbert Katz at Evans gladly took it.

The book is a mosaic of stories, reflections and sketches revolving around the bitter winter that Washington's troops were encamped at Valley Forge; it involves Washington himself, his Martha, the Marquis de Lafayette, and scores of common soldiers and local people. And some of its most touching incidents—a farm boy who brings in his ancient horse to get him into a cavalry squadron, a little black girl who takes Washington something to eat, a truce inspired by the straying of General Howe's pet dog—are, Kantor swears, all true. He worked very hard to get the contemporary language right—"I looked up every word in the OED to make sure it was in use then"—and his editors caught him out only once.

He's not exactly slowing up, despite his age. He has been working on a book about John Tyler, a California insurance tycoon who donated a major ecological award, and plans an autobiographical sequel to "I Love You Irene," which will take the story of their life together up to the late 30s. Nothing more recent than that? He grins. "I don't know who'd be interested." Meanwhile, he plans a vigorous promotion tour for "Valley Forge," and insists, despite the recent ups and downs in his publishing fortunes, that he's been a lucky man. Not long ago, he says, he sent a cable to Kenneth McCormick, who has been an editor at Doubleday about as long as Kantor has been a successful writer, congratulating him on his 45th anniversary with the firm. "Let's do it all over again," Kantor told him.

Elia Kazan

ONE COLD NIGHT last December one of the most unusual parties ever to launch a new novel sprawled all over the stage of an unoccupied Broadway theater. The orchestra seats were covered with the guests' coats, and the large stage was jammed with the guests, who included writers, agents, movie stars, theater people—and a goodly number of publishing-party regulars. There was an almost constant flicker of flashbulbs, and at the heart of it all was a small, intense figure whose many worlds had all come together on-stage that night: author Elia Kazan.

Only in the last few years has he been author Kazan. Before that he was in turn actor Kazan, one of the founding members of the celebrated Group Theatre of the late 30s and early 40s, and cofounder of the "Method"-oriented Actors Studio; theater director Kazan (about 30 plays, including such notable ones as "Death of a Salesman," "Cat on a Hot Tin Roof," "J.B." and "Sweet Bird of Youth"); movie director Kazan (20 movies and two Academy Awards, from "A Tree Grows in Brooklyn" through "Gentleman's Agreement," "A Streetcar Named Desire," "Viva Zapata!" "On the Waterfront," "East of Eden," "Baby Doll," "A Face in the Crowd," "America, America"); and finally to his last—and, he says, his best-loved—career, as best-selling novelist whose "The Arrangement" was a major blockbuster of 1967 and whose "The Understudy," just out from Stein and Day, is already being spoken of as 1975's first big novel.

Kazan's is an intensely theatrical presence. He radiates suppressed energy, he effortlessly focuses attention, he

By John F. Baker. From *Publishers Weekly* 207, no. 2 (January 13, 1975), pp. 10, 19.

thinks swiftly, talks volubly and fast, and somehow manages to avoid coming on like an egomaniac—probably because he would be the first to sense such a thought passing through an interviewer's mind and would be able to crush it with a swift joke: "I also talk a lot too much, as you'll find out," he says within two minutes of meeting *PW*'s reporter at a busy midtown Italian restaurant where, on his second visit, he already seemed like a habitué.

Despite his enormous success with plays and movies, Kazan professes always to have hankered after a literary life. "I've always envied and admired writers, and whatever I chose to do I always put the writer on top. What the writer wanted to say was always more important to me than what the actor or the director wanted to say. I always wanted to write myself, and when I was 55 it suddenly struck me that if I was ever going to make it as a writer, I'd better get going."

This was 10 years ago, a traumatic time for Kazan. He had done a screenplay for "America, America," the story of an emigrant from Turkey to the U.S. in the early years of the century (although Kazan himself was born in Turkey, he actually came here at the age of four, and the story as he wrote it was based on events that happened to his uncle). It was read by Sol Stein, a friend of Kazan's first wife Molly, who thought it read like a novel, and arranged to have it published. It was Stein's first book, and he and Kazan have been very close ever since.

"I was in Turkey working on the movie when it came out, and I remember reading the first reviews, and the thrill I got," Kazan says. Then his wife died and, deeply upset, he flung himself into a round of travel. He went all over the world, "writing all the time—it was as if a dam had burst." Two years later he gave Stein the manuscript of "The Arrangement" and a highly profitable partnership was cemented. Kazan was suddenly a name writer; and apart from what he acknowledges was a misguided attempt to make his own movie of "The Arrangement" ("I shouldn't have done it—you can't really get yourself worked up over the same material twice") and "The Visitors," made two years ago but scarcely seen in this country, he has been busy writing ever since.

He even dabbled in journalism, covering the 1968 Democratic convention for *New York* magazine but doesn't feel this was one of his finest hours. ("I sat next to Norman Mailer, and I've never envied him so much as I did when I saw what he had made out of the same material I had been working on; his pieces were 100 to 1 over mine.") Another novel, "The Assassins," also made the best seller lists two years ago, and now, in "The Understudy," Kazan has drawn on his theater background for the first time.

It had been known for some time that Kazan was working on it and, he says, "I got a lot of offers on it sight unseen." He decided to stay with Sol Stein, however: "Sol is a good editor. He's hungry and he works like hell, and he doesn't just drop a book. And he's a writer himself, and he knows what the problems are.'' He and Stein, Kazan says, fought hard over "The Understudy.'' One of the book's most remarkable passages is about an African safari undertaken by the narrator—and based on two safaris Kazan has made himself. "Sol couldn't see how it worked into the book, and I had to convince him. There were times we've been on the verge of breaking it off but in the end I think fighting the way we do is a sign of health. Indifference is the real killer in the arts.''

It is not a crime of which Kazan is likely ever to stand convicted. His work on stage and screen has always been regarded as strongly felt—sometimes excessively so. He grins acknowledgment of the criticism that his sense of drama has sometimes carried him away. "My wife used to say that if I directed a page of the telephone book it would come out as melodrama,'' he says. And he expresses relief at having broken away from the theater and movie world. "There's always such an atmosphere of hysteria among actors—you never have a moment to think. And now that I'm getting older I enjoy more and more just being by myself, off in the country.'' He maintains an office in New York, but spends most of his time—and does all his writing—at a retreat 60 miles north of the city.

He is full of writing plans, with four books in various stages of preparation, including another novel, which he describes as a sequel to "America, America,'' and a book about directing. "There are no good books about the art of directing in this country—nothing, really, since Stanislavsky and the Russians. I want to do for directing what Somerset Maugham did for writing in 'The Summing Up'—give an idea of the craft of it.''

And despite his avowed relief at getting away from theatrical hysteria, and his determination never again to act as his own producer (as he did on his most recent movies), he still has film plans. One involves a screenplay by Budd Schulberg, who did "On the Waterfront'' and "A Face in the Crowd,'' the other is his own, and "it looks like we'll go ahead with both.'' As to the stage, "I never say never, but I don't ever expect to direct a play again.''

About this time in the interview a gratifying thought strikes Kazan and, as usual with his thoughts, it is instantly expressed. "Hey, this is great. We've been talking all this time and you never asked the questions I nearly always get asked: 'What was James Dean *really* like?' and 'How did you get on with Marlon Brando?' What can you say? It's so far back in my life I hardly remember. I mean, Dean seemed like a nice kid, but just a kid—who wants to look back that far? I want to look ahead, not back; new books, not old movies.''

How does the world of books and publishing strike one who has spent most of his life around greasepaint? He laughs. "There's a lot more of show business in it than I would have expected. I guess I thought it would be more—austere." As on everything, he has his own decided views on current writing. "Too many books are written out of libraries, and by people who just don't have any human feeling for what they're writing about. There've been a lot of books about Bobby Kennedy, for instance, but none has created a living person; he had this open-hearted, generous quality. . . ." What he misses in contemporary novels (and finds in the great writers of the past) is "this feeling of life as change and flux, of people changing and time passing. Sometimes a great biography has that now, like Henri Troyat on Tolstoy." As for the so-called New Journalism, "that wasn't invented by Tom Wolfe or Mailer. Remember Henry Miller's 'Colossus of Maroussi'? That was the beginning of it, his way of evoking not only a place but his relationship to it. One of the great books."

The talk swerves to the subject of critics, on whom Kazan can be impassionedly bitter. "For many of them it's just a subtle ego trip!" he explodes. "There should always be respect for accomplishment, for a man's achievement, but too often there's just meanness and spitefulness. I think of Bill Inge, a suicide, of Hemingway—a great writer in his early work, even though he became pathetic—of John Steinbeck, and the *Times* sniping at him when he won the Nobel, Tennessee Williams, who can't do anything right any more, Arthur Miller. . . . You can't just sneer at such men, they deserve better."

It is time to go. The flow of ideas has been rapid, their expression intense, the changes of mood vivid and dramatic—all in all, the conversation has in retrospect many of the qualities of a Kazan movie. "You got enough?" he inquires solicitously. "I told you I talk too much. It's just like in my books, I put too much in, I keep piling it on. But this one is shorter, I'm working at it."

He moves purposefully through the restaurant, heads turning to follow him as he goes. People may not necessarily recognize him, but he is a Presence and if there's one thing New Yorkers have an instinct for, it's star quality.

Thomas Keneally

THOMAS KENEALLY, at not quite 40, is one of Australia's most distinguished novelists, a prize-winner in his native country several times over. His American publisher is Viking, which has brought out to high critical acclaim such Keneally novels as "Three Cheers for the Paraclete," "A Dutiful Daughter," "The Chant of Jamie Blacksmith" and most recently "Blood Red, Sister Rose," a novel of Joan of Arc that is quite different in its treatment of her from many previous works.

Each of Keneally's eight novels has been very unlike its predecessor and yet each, in its own way, reflects something of his own specifically Catholic, Irish and Australian background. He talked about these three influences on his life during a recent visit to America.

"My grandfather came to Australia from Cork in the 19th century. He had nine kids, the youngest my father. In our class at school in Sydney there were a couple of Italians, a couple of Lebanese, but Australia is an incredibly Irish country and that is what most of us were.

"Our school existed to turn sons of the Irish working class into professionals in order to take jobs away from the Masons, who were viewed as great enemies by the priests and brothers."

Keneally himself spent about seven years studying for the Catholic priesthood. In 1953, when the first whispers of changes that might be coming in the church were beginning to be heard—and two weeks before he was to be ordained—he left the seminary and went home.

"Very few priests left then after ordination," he recalls,

By Barbara A. Bannon. From *Publishers Weekly* 207, no. 12 (March 24, 1975), pp. 8–9.

"although we all knew some scandals about priests that had left and lived with women. I left the seminary because I was physically and mentally exhausted. I had to have a break and time to think things out. When you react in this strong a way, you become liberal in your attitudes at a faster rate than some other Catholics."

Keneally then studied to become a barrister in New South Wales for three years. Writing had always been something of a hobby with him. When he began to be published in *The Bulletin* (which he describes as "something like *The New Yorker*") he achieved his first major break-through and was on his way to a career as a writer. "Just about every writer in Australia cut his teeth there," he says of *The Bulletin*.

"Australian writers have faced an extraordinary dilemma because they have for so long been caught up in the last bastion of publishing imperialism," Keneally says, referring to the power that British publishers can still exercise over books admitted for sale into Australia.

"If you elect to be published from Britain you will certainly have a better chance of being picked up for publication on the international scene, yet your publication date in Britain can come and go without its being even known to your fellow countrymen. If you choose to be published by an Australian publisher you may become well known to your own people but mean nothing to British readers. Australians, in themselves, are great book buyers."

Distances are so vast in Australia that, except for writers' conferences, Australian writers may not be brought together as frequently as their counterparts in other countries, but they have a very active organization behind them in the Australian Society of Authors. This is the group that succeeded last year in forcing through the payment of library royalties for Australian writers.

"The tyranny of physical, geographical distances" hobbles Australians in many of their attitudes towards themselves, Keneally believes. "Western Australians are great talkers about secession from time to time (they have the big mineral rights), and they feel they are looked down upon by the east, and by such cities as Sydney and Melbourne with their trendy suburbs. In Queensland, in the north, the police are convinced local crimes are the work of 'southern criminal elements.'

"There is still roughness around the edges in everything in Australia. Outsiders laugh at us. We can travel the world and dine in embassies, yet people still say we are Yahoos. It's a bit, I suppose, like being a Texan."

The next major project Keneally plans will be an attempt to show what the white man's experiences have been in Australia, somewhat similar, perhaps, to what Günter Grass has done for his native Danzig. It will begin with a kind of "Ship of Fools" leaving Cork in 1800 and carrying the ancestors of those who have become today's Australians, both aristocrats and convicts in the hold. The convicts will include a 27-year-old Dennis

Keneally—whom the author will describe merely as "a figure in the family" when asked about the similar names. "Sydney," he says, "would never have been founded except for the Irish rebellion in the late 18th century. Britain was casting around for new places on which to implant her flag, places that had been charted by Cook in his voyages. They just loaded up the ships with convicts and set sail."

Of his arresting portrait of Joan of Arc in "Blood Red, Sister Rose," Keneally has this to say: "I saw her as a political and revolutionary phenomenon and I wanted to stress this side of her. Even her virginity was political, so that she would not be considered a witch. At a time when if your conscience told you one thing and the church said another, you generally said, 'All right. I was mistaken,' she did not do that. She was like a sister to Martin Luther. The stand she took was not from any intellectual basis but taken intuitively. In an age which was suffering from future shock, when institutions such as chivalry and warfare were not working right, she came along and put a bomb under them. She was an incredible nag, but that works with politicians. As a person, and as a woman, she knew she was trapped in her destiny."

Hans Hellmut Kirst

ONE of postwar Germany's best-selling novelists, Hans Hellmut Kirst, paid his first visit to America this spring. A rugged-looking man, who comes from the same East Prussian farming stock as Alfons Materna, the hero of his new novel, "The Wolves" (*Coward-McCann*), Mr. Kirst talked to *PW* about his writing through an interpreter. Although he speaks only a few words of English, he understands quite a bit more and at one point quickly corrected the interpreter on a slip of the tongue.

In Germany, Mr. Kirst told *PW*, he is still known largely as the author of the Gunner Ashe series of novels, a series he regards as among his lesser work. It was the success of the sardonic "The Officer Factory" and "The Night of the Generals" in America and England and France that brought him international status as a serious writer. For many Germans, these and the other strongly anti-Nazi Kirst novels contain too many "things they do not want to hear about" and Kirst, himself, he believes, is too much the voice of their conscience for comfort.

"My books receive a good critical understanding in America," Mr Kirst said. "It shows in the reviews. I am very happy about the appreciation I get as a storyteller here." Not a joiner by nature, Mr. Kirst belongs to PEN and is the only German member of the Authors' Guild (by invitation).

The key to "The Wolves," Mr. Kirst's new novel, comes from his own boyhood experiences. His father, who had been a prisoner-of-war in Russia during World War I (Kirst was five when he saw his father for the first time), was first a

By Barbara A. Bannon. From *Publishers Weekly* 193, no. 24 (June 10, 1968), p. 26.

farmer, then became a policeman. Every two or three years he was transferred to another part of East Prussia, and the young Kirst lived in many
parts of the country that now is part of Poland. The people in "The
Wolves," he says, are a mixture of many people he met as a young man.
When he decided to write the novel, he suddenly became aware of how
much he remembered. The idea behind "The Wolves" is to show everything that was happening in Germany in microcosm, to use one farm family, the Maternas, as a mirror for the whole German nation. The "terrible
twins" of the novel were three in real life and Hans Hellmut Kirst was one
of them. "Methodical" in his writing, by his own description, he made a
blueprint plan of the village of Maulen, setting of "The Wolves," beforehand to plot his character's whereabouts.

The ritual political murder at the very beginning of the novel which
sparks Alfons Materna's fight against the local Nazis "was not typical,
but it happened frequently" in the years after the First World War in
Germany before the Nazis came to power, Mr. Kirst says. "Then such
murders became legal. In very few cases did the police try to follow up."

"Materna's tragedy," Mr. Kirst believes, "was that he saw everything
that was happening as only a personal tragedy. He did not realize all that
was happening in Germany." Very few Germans were capable of realizing that with World War II their whole way of life would change forever,
Mr. Kirst told *PW*.

Eighteen when he was drafted into the German Army himself, Hans
Hellmut Kirst had been writing even before then. He continued writing
while in the army, "really poor escape literature and romantic plays." It
was only after the war when he began to try to come to terms with "the
stupidity and cruelty" of the Nazi years that his writing became serious.
As a small-town boy in East Prussia, Mr. Kirst says he "had no literature
to turn to and nowhere I could learn to write, no literary models." It was
only after the war that he could read Steinbeck, Hemingway, Mann for
the first time, and another American writer whose work he loves—Raymond Chandler.

Mr. Kirst spent 12 years in the German Army, part of them as a master
sergeant in Poland, France and Russia. Then he was transferred to an
"officer factory" and stayed on there as a teacher of officer candidates
until the end of the war. Of those 12 army years he says, "during all those
years people acted like idiots. One had to do one's duty as 'a good German.' One did not really know one was in a club of murderers. You have
to pay for being involved with criminals."

The next novel on Hans Hellmut Kirst's agenda may shake up the German people more than any he has yet written. It will center on the German
government now in Bonn and will be "much harder" in tone than any of
his previous novels, he says. Up to now, Mr. Kirst told *PW*, he believes
he has been trying to understand and to a certain extent defend the Germans in his writing. Now he is ready to attack what he thinks is wrong in
Germany today. "I feel I can only be as strict and hard as this in writing
about my own country," he says.

Arthur Koestler

IF YOU have to discuss the possible death of the world, the process is undoubtedly improved if it can be done with a glass of scotch to hand. This was what a *PW* reporter found himself doing recently with Arthur Koestler, who has just published his first novel in 19 years, "The Call Girls" (*Random House*). It's a tragicomedy which discusses mankind's chances of survival in the next few decades.

"Just as a little scotch lubricates conversation, so I'm a believer in humor," Koestler said. "The purpose of my novel is deadly serious—to warn mankind of the changes that threaten him; but I have written it with humor because heavy sermons bore people."

The interview took place in his beautiful little house in London's Montpelier Square, just a stone's throw from Harrods. His pretty blond wife Cynthia (20 years his junior)—whom he calls "angel"—poured drinks while two friendly puppies snuffled around. Doomsday seemed light years away.

"I suppose," said Koestler, "you could call me a cheerful pessimist. As long as people can go on discussing intelligent solutions to world problems—the nuclear threat, the poverty gap, overpopulation, pollution and so on—then there is still hope." He sees himself as a bit like Niko, one of the characters in the book—a man with a divided heart. One half of him sees Doomsday, "in the other half he keeps a niche for miracles."

Koestler himself is a small, neat man with iron-gray hair and a face that looks as if it has been eroded by a lot of living. He still speaks in the heavy accent of his native Bu-

By Peter Grosvenor. From *Publishers Weekly* 203, no. 18 (April 30, 1973), pp. 20–22. Reprinted by permission of Peter Grosvenor.

dapest, where he was born in 1905. He studied science, engineering and psychology in Vienna, then became a foreign correspondent. For a while, like so many in the 30s, he saw the Soviet experiment as mankind's only hope.

As a Comintern agent he once betrayed (with anguish) a girl friend to the O.G.P.U. As a war reporter on the Republican side in the Spanish Civil War, he spent three months in a Franco prison in the death cell, six months in a French concentration camp, then six weeks in jail in London as an illegal immigrant on the run from the French Legion. Then he joined the British Army.

"Darkness at Noon," based on the Moscow purges and published in 1940, spelled out his disillusion with the Communists for whom he had once worked. In its impact on leftist intellectuals it racked almost as many consciences as George Orwell's "1984" and "Animal Farm" were to do several years later. His last novel, "The Age of Longing," published in 1954, was also a Cold War novel in which an American girl and a Russian envoy have an affair under the awesome threat of the world awaiting a nuclear catastrophe.

"The Call Girls" of the new book are not quite what they seem from the title. They are in effect intellectual harlots, 12 learned men and women, several of them Nobel Prize winners, ever ready to do their turn on the international conference circuit. With expenses paid (plus honorarium), they will travel anywhere, any time, to display their expert knowledge before moving on to the next symposium—"A perpetuum mobile which circulates hot air," comments one character in the book.

Not that Koestler is as cynical about the symposium circuit as his novel implies. "I have actually organized one myself. I know how full of pretension some of these conferences can be, and how many vanities are paraded; I also know how clever men can be very stupid when their knowledge is too compartmentalized. But these conferences quite often contain people who really do care about the world's problems."

Koestler was asked the question posed by the discussion at the center of the novel: Did he think mankind would survive?

"The problem of overpopulation has been underestimated rather than overestimated," he declared, "and the implosion into the cities—more and more people piling up into less and less space—is equally serious."

The crux of the problem, he felt, was man's emotional immaturity compared with his technological achievements. "But it is very difficult to agree on a precise diagnosis of man's deficiencies. Some see him as a born killer, *homo homicidus*, who needs ritualized outlets for violence on a mass scale such as compulsory all-in wrestling in kindergarten, and war games for adults. Others see mankind as a peaceful individual but a killer when he becomes devoted to a group cause, religion or nation." (Koestler concedes that his own fervent devotion to Communism—until Stalinist excesses cured him—was a classic case of private altruism lending itself to the cause of mass homicide.)

Another popular theory is that there is an evolutionary flaw, or biological malfunction in mankind. The cortex of his recently evolved brain gives him language, logic and reason; but underneath the new brain and lying beyond its control is an old, primitive, emotion-bound brain, compounded of unreason, anxiety and anger. Perhaps the solution, which Koestler has already advocated in a previous nonfiction book, "The Ghost in the Machine," is a new kind of pill to take over where mortality has failed, a sort of mental stabilizer, a synthetic "peace" enzyme slipped into the public water supply.

Koestler also wants to see a much closer study of ESP, in which he is now a convinced believer. "I don't say now, but perhaps in the next decade, advances in ESP will be such that we will know far more how to control our emotions and even involuntary brain processes and project them perhaps into more peaceful channels."

Readers of Koestler's big scientific–philosophical books, like "The Sleepwalkers" and "The Act of Creation," as well as the telepathy and ESP book "The Roots of Coincidence," will have recognized many familiar Koestler themes. "These are ideas I had to expound first as non-fiction. Only when they crystallized still more in the mind was I able to write a novel about them," he said. "I see it as the novelist's duty to point to the sore spot in society, not necessarily to advocate precise solutions."

Like Huxley, Wells and Orwell, Koestler has used the novel as a vehicle for ideas that go to the heart of the human predicament. But the novelist of ideas has not always had a happy time in Britain. "Wells was often derided by the intelligentsia, who thought he was too popular and low-brow. Orwell suffered badly in his lifetime. Huxley achieved intellectual acceptability partly because he came from a distinguished dynasty, partly because he was amusing; it embarrasses the English to be other than funny about serious things."

In "The Call Girls" Koestler has attempted to round up all the major contemporary theories on man's inner psychology and his prospects of survival—including the errors, misconceptions and blind alleys many of these theories embody. This task was also attempted, with wry humor, by Flaubert in his novel "Bouvard et Pecuchet," the story of two French clerks whose experiments in nature are always doomed to disappointment. "Messieurs Bouvard et Pecuchet" are duly acknowledged on the title pages as the inspiration for Koestler's novel.

Koestler has an acute eye for human foibles, as well as a remarkable intellectual grasp. In his novel he writes: "The majority of couples in Niko's age group lived in a state of acute or chronic *misère en deux*. Their marriages were like parcels that had burst open in the mail van, and were precariously held together by bits of string.''

Whether you meet the man or read the book—or ideally do both—you will encounter the same quality: a genuine and compassionate humor.

Jerzy Kosinski

JERZY KOSINSKI is a short, slim, dapper gentleman; a fastidious, thoroughly impatient Polish *émigré* who has lived in the United States since 1957, has published two novels, has won a National Book Award for fiction and has taught English at three American universities.

He is in a hurry ("I am always in a hurry") and he does not think of himself as a writer, though that is what he is known for. ("I only write when I feel like it, which is not very often.") He has no agent, his contracts have no second-book option clauses, he writes his own jacket copy and supplies his own jacket photos. He does not care to talk about his novels—"The Painted Bird," "Steps," "The Devil Tree," "Cockpit," "Blind Date," and "Being There." He keeps a crowded, two-room apartment in mid-Manhattan where we talked to him. He has had it for years, but one suspects that he has never really lived in it. He admits that during those years he has lived in many other places. He was married once, for six years, to an American woman who died of cancer in 1968, but he doesn't care to talk about it. He is incorporated. He is a loner.

He won the National Book Award in 1969 for "Steps." The jury said, "Mr. Kosinski has been a resident of the United States for little more than a decade, but he is already close to being a master of English prose; he writes with brilliant lucidity and vividness. At a time when our culture is plagued with exhibitionism and wanton display, Mr. Kosinski recalls the tradition of high art as a mode of imaginative order."

What is true of his art is also true of his personal style; it

By Douglas N. Mount. From *Publishers Weekly* 199, no. 17 (April 26, 1971), pp. 13–16. Corrected by Jerzy Kosinski, September, 1977.

cannot be characterized as "exhibitionism and wanton display," though he is not without a keen—almost devilish—wit.

He likes best to talk about what he calls his "movement," about language, and about America. The movement, however, is the only thing that really seems to matter to him: the single-minded struggle to avoid restrictions, limits, regimentation.

"I wasn't really coming to the States, I was leaving Eastern Europe. I aimed at three countries: at Argentina, at Brazil and at the United States, in that order. The first two would not take me because I was a social scientist with a Marxist background—Warsaw University, Moscow University—and they felt that a person with my background like that was not the best investment for Latin America. Essentially, I aimed at large, new societies, where I felt I could in some way therefore disregard environment and be disregarded, be left alone. It was a natural reaction for someone who wanted to get out from under the totalitarian system. The formlessness of my life, you see, is the only form I like."

One wall of his apartment is covered with framed photographs, mostly of the Soviet Union, which he took before he came here. In addition to his degrees in social sciences, he very carefully established himself in Eastern Europe as a professional photographer—winning several international prizes and achieving some financial success—before he emigrated, but he did so, he says, so that the Polish authorities would not think that he was leaving for political reasons. He has not exhibited a single picture since, he says, even though he has a complete darkroom in his apartment. "I could take a picture of you and in five minutes you would have it in your hands," he says. "The darkroom is there, but I seldom use it."

"When I came, I did not want to do anything that I had done before. I thought it would be dragging a part of my past into an entirely different place, and one of the reasons I came here was *not* to drag anything from the past. It was not really a matter of leaving the Soviet orbit; it was leaving myself in the Soviet context. I was so much a part of that context, and I did not like myself. I thought that if I changed the frame of reference, it would also change me into something else. It was, therefore, entirely a literary decision."

Did he decide, then, to become a writer? "I did not think in terms of what I wanted to become. I wanted to find out what was within me, what was the force that prompted me to do whatever. In Poland and the USSR, you see, I did not have to provide the frame of reference; it was provided from outside. If anything, I had to counteract it. Half of my life was spent fending off influences from outside, and so not defining myself."

Getting out was not easy. It was, he says hardly "an American Express tour."

"It involved two years of planning and some bureaucratic fraud, and the penalty for capture was approximately 12 to 15 years in prison. That was a high price to pay and in fact I was not willing to pay it. But I had rejected that life to the point where I really could not care less what happened to me, and if I had been caught, I would have removed myself, one way or another. It was both a very practical decision—to get rid of circumstances which I found limiting and painful and unpleasant—and also a metaphysical one, for I was leaving, no matter what. If it worked, I would be leaving and arriving somewhere else. If not, I would be leaving without arriving."

He came to this country, speaking almost no English ("only mixed French–English sociological jargon"), and after a time enrolled at Columbia. While a student there, he published two nonfiction books on collective behavior, his course of study, under the pseudonym Joseph Novak. The first of these was serialized by the *Saturday Evening Post* and condensed by *Reader's Digest*, though apparently neither publication knew anything about the author.

"My former experience had taught me that when you are a student you are not supposed to write books, you are supposed to read them. And what's more, I could hide behind my pen name. I also felt that any book, particularly nonfiction, speaks for itself. I mean, what is there for the author to add, to explain? I knew that the books were sufficiently articulate, but I was not at that time. I did not really have much opportunity to speak to anyone; I was limiting myself to courses and writing. My spoken English was very inferior. I could express myself—this I trusted—but only in writing. I felt that it would be terribly unfair to suddenly become a spokesman for my own books; they had their own voice. Strangely enough, this is the way I feel now, even more so. I think a novel should speak with its own voice, and therefore I never talk about a book."

Later he spoke of these early efforts in English, "This is my way of removing myself from the past by making a nonfiction out of the conditions of my life. Both books deal with collective behavior, the relationship of the individual to the group, all of the oppressive forces which make for the totalitarian society. It was an attempt to turn a major aspect of my growing up into a literary experience, and therefore the natural progression was towards the novel."

That first novel, "The Painted Bird," perhaps his most widely read work, was a contemporary horror story about the grisly pursuit and persecution of a young boy, possibly a Jew or a gypsy, by the Nazis.

"It was a truly novelistic experience," Kosinski insists. "There are those who try to force out of me some sort of confession that this is autobiographical, because there are certain resemblances between the protagonist and myself. They make a serious mistake. If anything, there is no direct connection between historical reality and fiction. Had I believed in such a connection, I could not have written it; I wouldn't have liked it."

He insists that it does not really matter to him. "I don't see myself as a writer, it is part of my movement; I feel like doing it. If I would stop liking it, I would try to find something else to do. I am not committed in any way. I make no promises of any kind. I don't make them to myself. If the movement will carry me through the next novel, fine. If not, then quite likely it will propel me toward something else. I'd have to find out towards what. It is not always easy to find out."

Is the writing, then, incidental to the movement? "It is both a reflection of the movement and a propellant. It also provides a sort of split, in the sense that once in a while you observe yourself, a certain part of yourself is set apart, permanently, almost as a kind of image collector. I notice this very often. I am struck by something, but it is not *I* who is struck by it, it is my new novel which is struck."

He has taught English at Wesleyan, Princeton ("between Bowen and Burgess") and now at the Yale Drama School, where he conducts a course in nonconventional English, the prose of experimental theater, of cabaret, of television, of film, of radio, of lyrics. "And so I can analyze the changes that go on in the American language." He is fascinated by the banality of that language, and one of his novels, "The Devil Tree," is about "that contrived aspect of our reality.

"One of my students said to me the other day, 'To you it may be a cliché, but I experience my clichés very profoundly.' And I think this is exactly what is happening. Look at the language of television, of some of our films, of popular culture. In some ways, we are seeing the death of language altogether. The young don't talk much, you know. They don't trust the language and they distrust the people who use it well.

"In my seminar, I am always astonished by what a struggle it is for them to come out with something which is their own. And they know this, how difficult it is to express oneself, to become direct and honest. And they know that the language does not always help this, that in fact it often torpedoes it. When you confront someone directly, as I often do my students, they become very upset, and once in a while violent. They claim I am manipulating them. But you aim at the primary truth: Why do you get up in the morning? Why don't you kill yourself? What sense is there in doing what you are doing? If you do not do this, you are still a being, but you are not a being *here* any more; you are a being *there*.

"I think this is universal: Once you begin to write in another language, you discover how much freer you are, because the new language disconnects you, and requires from you—because you do not know all the clichés yet—some of your own. Whenever I have to write a letter in Polish or Russian, I spend hours and hours trying to avoid the unavoidable clichés of my growing up. In English, on the other hand, the struggle is shorter, because I'm much more aware of what I am doing, I am much closer to what I really want to say. One is removed from one's Pavlovian restraints, so to speak. The new language has brought for you a new evocative power; it can evoke your imaginary states but not your traumatic states.

"If you were going to offend me right now, you would not traumatize me. You would, had you done it in Polish or Russian. In a way, I am protected. In fact, in some ways one could claim that if literature is in fact externalizing through the symbol, then in some ways, for someone who writes in another language, the literature begins even before he knows it. It applies to speaking too, you know. I couldn't possibly make a speech in public in Polish or Russian, I just couldn't. It happens to me when I am approached by someone who speaks to me suddenly either in Polish or in Russian: my whole manner changes. I get more rigid, my neck is stiffer, I become more European. My tongue is more rigid, my hands not as mobile. I am much more manipulative because I am frightened to say something that is not *exactly* what I want to say. In English, I am not afraid any more." He says this with broad expressive gestures, using his arms, hands, head; moving about the room.

We asked him if he knew other writers, and if he corresponded with them or talked to them about writing.

"Occasionally I do meet other people who write," he replied, "but I think we meet more or less on other levels. What we do is available outside of our relationship, and therefore we never talk about writing or what we write. Americans tend to think about writing as a very specific profession, and therefore they are very professional about it. They like to think you can do it every day. I don't. I do not require a certain solid regimen of writing, whereas a great many writers do.

"It is interesting to me, because of all vocations—well, of all human activities—here is one which requires no place, which requires no paraphernalia, which is freer than any force around you. There is no situation, no setup, that can duplicate the human imagination. If a writer confronts this aspect of himself—and that is obviously what he does—then he is able to transcend every single aspect of human existence. He can transcend himself, he can refashion the world around him, carry it into the most hidden part of his own private universe, which no one else has access to.

"To make an office out of this ability, to institutionalize it, would be for me the most incredible paradox. It would be as if you had the most able bird, who could fly anywhere, who could swim and fly and burrow through the earth, and you had him sit in the Chase Manhattan Bank all day long. What a strange creature that would be. It is an incredible freedom the writer has. It is the freedom to be the maker of the world. No one else knows such a freedom."

"Being There," his shortest novel, is a dark tale of people who speak the language of television, who mouth the clichés of the soap operas, misunderstanding each other completely, and with disastrous consequences. We asked about the future, about the issue of print versus the electronic media, about which so much has been written.

"I don't know where we got this notion that there was once a golden age when everybody read books," he said. "Literature has always been a marginal experience and quite frankly this is the fun of it. If I didn't feel that way I would be making hardware or taking photographs.

"Look, I think humankind moves in some direction, and one has to accept that movement. I don't think we are in any position to alter it. I don't think Western civilization was ever able to alter its own course. Perhaps this is the direction. After all, in terms of the effort needed, the printed word—the symbol—requires a different dimension altogether. If the progress of mankind is toward making the human being 'easier,' making him a composite of external forces, rather than a bastion of human resources—and all the gadgetry around us would indicate that—then this movement would be only natural. I am not going to cry over it. In my new novel I deal with it, but only because it is a trend which confronts me. I am also confronted with my own aging, I am confronted with a changing society. I think the point is to notice them and to deal with them and yet not allow yourself to be seduced by them.

"I often advise my students that if they should all fail at political ideology maybe they should try some fetishes. This presents them with the terrible horror of the cynical European, telling them that if you can't live by a political doctrine, you can certainly do well by a very refined obsession, a good nonexchangeable fetish."

Robert Kotlowitz

THESE DAYS author Robert Kotlowitz occasionally talks to himself while shaving. He stares at his round, pleasant face in the mirror and fantasizes out loud about his novel "Somewhere Else" (*Charterhouse*) selling to Hollywood.

"Then I stop myself because that's not the most important thing. What's really important is that the book have a continuing life of its own," he says.

Since he's been receiving superb reviews from all quarters ever since "Somewhere Else" came out in October, it looks as if he's going to get his wish.

The scope and power of this tale of Jewish life in the 1900s revolves around one family in Lomza, Poland, but the background encompasses the Great War and the rise of Zionism. David Halberstam describes the writing as "ranking with the best of Malamud and Singer."

"I'm pleased," Kotlowitz admitted when he was interviewed recently in his cluttered offices at National Educational Television (NET), where he is editorial director. "I still find it hard to believe I actually completed a work of fiction. My life has been so hectic lately that writing the novel now seems like a long-lost dream." It all began three years ago when as managing editor of *Harper's* magazine he wrote an article for the "Going Home" series.

"It was about Baltimore, where I spent my childhood and where I went to college—Johns Hopkins. Baltimore is a fascinating city sociologically—full of beautiful homes and intellectual stimulus. When I started writing about it memories came swimming back—about my music lessons, about going to the synagogue where my father was head cantor."

By Patricia Bosworth. From *Publishers Weekly* 202, no. 25 (December 18, 1972), pp. 8–9. Reprinted by permission of Patricia Bosworth.

The *Harper's* piece aroused the interest of several publishers and Kotlowitz was subsequently invited on a series of lunches with editors. "All highly enjoyable," he says, "but nobody could convince me I should do another 'Going Home'-type book. Willie Morris was just finishing his book about the south and Bill Moyers was just starting his and Norman Podhoretz was creating a lot of talk with 'Making It.' These were all gifted writers and my friends, and all of them were turning back to write about themselves. I honestly didn't think I had much to add. I've always had a terror that I did not have enough to say. Eventually, Dick Kluger, who was then at Simon and Schuster, and who's now head of Charterhouse, kept at me until it was finally 'put up or shut up.' I think I was working all along—but unaware of it. The germ of a novel was in my head but I was afraid to confront it. I was resisting possible failure."

One Saturday Kotlowitz sat down and started to write—"about my past and about Lomza, the town in Poland from which my father came. My past has always had a kind of mythic glamour for me, because I never knew my relatives. I just heard about them from my father. He told me countless anecdotes about them—little histories, romances, tragedies. But still my uncles and aunts had no faces—I conjured them up. I wrote all that Saturday about my past, and when I finished I realized this was no reminiscence of *my* childhood, this was right out of my father's life.

"I wrote for three Sundays in a row and gave up smoking in the process. What I tried to do was to examine what comes out of an inheritance. I wanted somehow to show how many small and richly textured details make up essentially mundane lives. I wanted to create characters and a place, Lomza, where I've never been in my life. So I created from my father's memories and my imagination. I became obsessed with the book, of course. I was still managing editor of *Harper's*, but my creative energy went into my novel. After a time my colleagues realized how important it was. They found an old photograph of Lomza in the Bettmann Archive and had it framed, and I set it in front of me as I wrote. I wrote every Saturday and Sunday for four hours at a stretch and my wife and kids and even the dog were sympathetic.

"I don't have a study at home—just a makeshift desk in the bedroom. It became a kind of ritual. I'd go in and start writing and then my wife would come in and say she'd forgotten something. Then the kids would come in to ask a question, and finally the dog would curl up at my feet and I'd go to work. I can't describe the creative process—it's so mysterious. Nobody knows what it is but finally it takes hold of you and you let it happen. Sometimes the well runs dry and then you have to wait for it to fill up again.

"After awhile I began to write in my head all the time—at dinner parties—on the street. Once, I remember I was at a baseball game with Willie Morris and our respective kids, and about the third inning my eyes became glazed and I started thinking about the novel again. Willie hit me with what I thought was a spitball but when I opened the little piece of paper he'd scrawled, 'What are you writing now?' ''

Kotlowitz smiled. "I couldn't stop. I'm ruthless about work anyway. I'm a compulsive worker. Near the end I was polishing, polishing—making the prose as supple as possible. I hope the story is as strong as the character of Mendl. I worked hard on both elements."

By the time he'd finished the novel he'd left *Harper's*. "Right after Willie Morris resigned Midge Decter and I did too," he says. Kotlowitz is now New York contributing editor to the *Atlantic Monthly*, "which keeps my hand in with magazines." However, most of his concentration is focused on his work with NET, and he finds that "television is totally different from the printed word. The feedback is instantaneous. The whole money thing is different, too. One documentary show costs as much as *Harper's* magazine budget for the year."

Doris Lessing

DORIS LESSING has been paying her first visit to America and *PW* was fortunate enough to interview her recently. Mrs. Lessing, a highly original writer, with a talent that is not quite like that of anyone else writing in English today, has just had the fifth and final volume in her epic Children of Violence sequence of novels, "The Four-Gated City," published by Knopf.

Reviewers are finding it contains some of her most provocative writing yet—taking positions about psychiatry and mental illness, in particular, and about the future of mankind that are quite outside the mainstream of "popular" opinion. The five novels that make up the Children of Violence all focus in some way on a woman called Martha Quest, whose experiences, from an African girlhood, through marriage and divorce and participation for a time in the Communist Party, are not without certain parallels in Doris Lessing's own life.

Mrs. Lessing was born in Persia, but moved as a child to Southern Rhodesia with her British immigrant parents. She began writing, she told *PW*, when she was 14 or 15, "but everything I wrote for years was rubbish. The only advice I would ever give to a young writer is, 'just go on writing.'"

Her own first published work in book form consisted of two short story collections, "The Grass Is Singing" and "This Was the Old Chief's Country," which dealt with whites and blacks in Africa with great sympathy. A "prohibited immigrant," whom the white supremacist government in Southern Rhodesia today will not let return to that country, although she has both a son and a brother living

By Barbara A. Bannon. From *Publishers Weekly* 195, no. 22 (June 2, 1969), pp. 51–54.

there, Mrs. Lessing has always been an outspoken foe of *apartheid* in any form. "I did not know until I left [for England in 1949] how awful it really was," she says of Rhodesia. "It was such an emotionally heated atmosphere. There was such a tiny minority against white racism. There have always been more whites and blacks in South Africa that fought back than in Rhodesia." The race attitude of the white British settlers in Rhodesia has been worse in many ways than that of the Afrikaners in South Africa, Mrs. Lessing believes. "The English have a capacity for doing the same things other people do and not saying so. It is known as hypocrisy," she says dryly.

"I was a Communist when being one meant that you automatically thought the Soviet Union was a fine place," Mrs. Lessing told us, looking back. "Now it can mean any damn thing you please." (She joined the Party in Britain about three years after coming to England and left in disillusionment a few years later.) "There's one thing about it," she told *PW*, "if you have ever been near any Communist Party you can never be naive about the power structure again. Marxism leaves you with a very skeptical attitude of mind. Actually, I was never so much a Communist as I was in Rhodesia, where there wasn't any Communist Party as such, but there was a great deal of concern about abstract principles."

From the beginning, Mrs. Lessing said, she planned the Children of Violence sequence to consist of five novels. "I had a fairly clear idea of what I wanted to do. Practically all of the things I deal with in the series were there in some degree in the first two novels. [The first, "Martha Quest," was published in 1952.] I think that the part of one's self that writes does not change that much, although your emotional set-up may change."

Mrs. Lessing does not keep notes in her writing. "I can carry an awful lot of things in my head," she said. When she was writing the long multi-level novel, "The Golden Notebook," published in 1962, she "started writing on page one and went straight on to the end." It took about three years. Before going on with each new novel in the Children of Violence sequence she would read back over the others to see that she had the names and dates right, but that was about all. "I did not have some great kind of scheme in mind like 'The Forsyte Saga,' but I knew the project was going to take about 20 years." She summed up: "Lots of people have this kind of feeling about what in life is going to be right for them."

The first four volumes in the Children of Violence sequence and all of her other writing for the last seven years was published by Simon and Schuster. "The Four-Gated City" is being published by Knopf because Doris Lessing is one of the authors who followed her editor, Robert Gottlieb, there. Of Gottlieb, to whom she pays special tribute in a note in the book, she says, simply, "He cares about the books and one's welfare. He puts an immense amount of energy and effort into it."

For herself, Mrs. Lessing says she finds it "physically tiring" being a novelist, and until recently could not have survived on the money from her writing alone. She has done quite a bit of writing for British Granada TV when she needed the money, and has enjoyed it, but would prefer not to have to do this kind of writing in addition to her more serious work. She was one of three TV writers who took turns writing for Granada a series based on Maupassant short stories. "We just dealt the stories out around the table," she recalls. "It was very good discipline, this, for a writer."

One of the things Doris Lessing has consciously tried to do in her own writing is "to write about life as it was lived, to put in the kind of things people really talk about." American literature has much more of this, she believes, but there was a curious gap in this kind of fiction in Britain after H. G. Wells until recently. Mrs. Lessing has no patience with what she calls "Mandarin literature. I find it very hard to identify with anyone in novels by Henry James," she says.

"The Four-Gated City" in many ways takes a somber view of life today and in the not so distant future. "I don't *feel* particularly jolly about the future," Mrs. Lessing told *PW*. "The human race has an infinite capacity for absorbing human suffering.

"You read so many statistics about American violence that one gets a feeling of smugness in Britain, but if you live there, there is a sort of concealed desperation. What is pleasant about London is what is bad for us as a nation, a sort of shrug of the shoulders, a not caring too much."

One of the aspects of "The Four-Gated City" that readers are finding most outside their usual way of thinking lies in the treatment of mental illness. "I'll lay a bet that in the next 10 or 15 years there is going to be an almost total change in the way people look at schizophrenia," Mrs. Lessing said. "Certain classes of people who are now regarded as ill will not be regarded as ill at all." Psychiatrists are in no sense infallible, she insists in the novel, and it is something she feels strongly about personally. We should ask more questions of psychiatrists, she emphasizes, and not be so willing to take everything they say as gospel. When someone is deeply and desperately depressed (a situation with which she deals in important terms in the new novel), they may be depressed for a very good reason. "Depression might be a message from another part of you that you ought not to be living like this, or that you're scared of dying." Instead, "death and depression today have this great smile painted over them."

Sometimes, Mrs. Lessing believes, it is better "to shout and scream and throw glasses. Why not *be* depressed if you feel like it? We are always being told, 'be happy, if it kills you.' Why should one be?"

The relationship between men and women, in and outside of marriage, is a recurrent theme in Doris Lessing's writing. "The relationship between boys and girls today is much less demanding and more relaxed," she believes, "but sometimes I think the only way to deal with the whole sex thing is to get married at 19, have our children, and stay married, not expecting anything more. The only real reason to get married is having children. Otherwise men and women should just live together."

The other aspect of "The Four-Gated City" that is proving especially intriguing and arousing considerable comment is the future Mrs. Lessing foresees in which human beings have developed to a high degree a sense of extra-sensory perception. She is very serious about this. "I think ESP is going on all the time, but it is a convention to pretend it does not happen," she told *PW*. "All my life I have known certain things before they happen, but they tend to be extremely trivial." ESP, she believes, may be for many people, "an atrophied sense" that could be brought back into use again. "All kinds of things are now taken for granted that used to be suspect. Telepathy is now a respectable subject for study."

As for her own work, Mrs. Lessing has already started another novel, which she hopes to finish in about a year. It is to be called "Briefing for a Descent into Hell," and it will be, she said, "a mad, dreamlike book, completely different from anything I have done before."

Doris Lessing is particularly known for her Children of Violence novels, "The Golden Notebook," her reportage and short stories, but there is one of her nonfiction books that has become a classic on a much gentler level. It is "Particularly Cats," an utterly unsentimental, honest statement of affection for cats Mrs. Lessing has known over the years. We are happy to report that Gray Cat, one of the feline heroes of the last part of the book, is still living with Mrs. Lessing. The other, Black Cat, "just walked off one day," but Son of Black Cat lives on.

Ira Levin

IRA LEVIN's rather Mephistophelian-looking beard ante-dates the publication of his novel of modern demonology, "Rosemary's Baby" (*Random House*). You may draw your own conclusions, however, when we tell you that the idea behind the book was six years in developing and Mr. Levin hasn't had his beard *that* long.

He can't remember just what was said that put the idea for a story about a woman pregnant with an unnatural foetus into his head, but Mr. Levin can remember just where he was when he first thought of such a story line. He was attending a serious meeting of the Cycle Society, a group of professional men and women who meet monthly to discuss the significance behind cyclical occurrences in the weather, stock market, etc.

Once he had his basic theme he began to develop it gradually, putting it aside for his work as a playwright and coming back again to add little touches based on his and his wife's experiences as New York City apartment house dwellers (they now live in Connecticut). "We lived in an old apartment house at 82nd and Fifth Avenue," he says, "that had a laundry room kind of like the one in the book. I would never let my wife go down there alone."

As a deliberate contrast to the strong fantasy element in "Rosemary's Baby," Mr. Levin decided to make all of the background details as factual as possible. He kept a pile of newspapers while he was working on the final draft of the book (December, 1965 to August, 1966) and fitted in appropriate references right out of the day's papers as he wrote. He had already decided that "Rosemary's Baby" should be

By Barbara A. Bannon. From *Publishers Weekly* 191, no. 21 (May 22, 1967), p. 19.

born in June, just half a year away from Christmas. By sheer coincidence, when he figured backwards in time to the moment when conception would have to have taken place, he found himself face to face with the actual dates of Pope Paul's visit to New York. The contrast between the Papal visit and what was happening to Rosemary produced some highly effective and quite unexpected drama.

The one hang-up Mr. Levin encountered in writing "Rosemary's Baby" had to do with the ending. He knew the ending he wanted, but it was only when he suddenly realized that Rosemary *must* have the perfectly normal reaction of any mother to her newborn child, a reaction of love and protectiveness, that everything fell into place.

"I don't think any pregnant woman should read it," Mr. Levin says, quite seriously, of "Rosemary's Baby." At one time Random House was toying with the idea of doing some publicity along these lines, but dismissed it as too gimmicky. Mr. Levin means what he says, however. His wife was pregnant during part of the writing of the book, and he wouldn't let her near the manuscript. "Her obstetrician did read it and loved it," he admits. The newest Levin offspring is *not* named Andrew, readers of "Rosemary's Baby" will be happy to know. He is named Nicholas, and references to "the old Nick" are not appreciated.

Mr. Levin will not be involved in the screenplay of "Rosemary's Baby," which will be written by the English-speaking Polish film director and writer, Roman Polansky. Polansky is best known here for his highly acclaimed film, "Knife in the Water." The picture will be produced by Paramount.

Next on Ira Levin's own agenda are plans for the production of a play he has just finished, a melodrama, "Dr. Cook's Garden." Then it's back to another novel, one he began "a hundred years ago," that will be in a different genre entirely from "Rosemary's Baby," but still introducing an element of suspense. He hopes to continue to alternate as a novelist and playwright.

Mr. Levin is very pleased with the Polansky approach to the filming of "Rosemary's Baby." Exterior filming will be done in New York. There has been talk of Warren Beatty for the role of Guy, Rosemary's actor husband, but Mr. Polansky wants, if possible, to find an unknown for the pivotal role of Rosemary. "Polansky showed me how he was going over the book the other day," Mr. Levin told *PW*, in the tone of an author who can hardly believe his good fortune. "He doesn't want to change a thing. All he was doing was cutting out descriptive passages."

Helen MacInnes

IN THE DIMLY LIT foyer of an expensive East Side restaurant in New York, the woman's face seemed familiar. She was dressed in an expensive-looking mink coat, and was clearly waiting for someone—and someone she wouldn't expect to recognize. After all, it was a shadowy world she inhabited, and who knows what this clandestine meeting might bring: an assignment in Brittany, perhaps? A message from Malaga? Possibly someone connected with the Venetian affair, or with some inkling of the Salzburg connection?

She had not been honing her instincts for undercover activities for nothing all these years, however, and she was the first to make a move. She peered through the gloom at the man who had just come in, smiling rather uncertainly: "You must be—" "Of course!" the *PW* interviewer replied with relief. "You're Helen MacInnes!" And so she was.

Seated at a corner table (and Miss MacInnes is the sort of lady who is instinctively escorted to corner tables by *maitre d'*s), and having divested herself of the mink to disclose an equally elegant purple wool dress, she revealed herself in the brighter light to be a woman of a certain age (she is in fact 67), but one whose fair Scottish complexion and trim figure have survived the years better than most women 10 years her junior. She also proved to be voluble and forthright about herself, her 42-year marriage to Gilbert Highet, her work as one of the most successful novelists alive—one of those interview subjects, in fact, who present a problem to the interviewer more because of the volume of the material they supply than out of any reticence or awkwardness.

Miss MacInnes (she retains her maiden name for profes-

By John F. Baker. From *Publishers Weekly* 205, no. 24 (June 17, 1974), pp. 10, 22.

sional purposes) has written 16 novels, from "Above Suspicion" (1941) to "The Snare of the Hunter" (1974). Every one of them has made the best seller lists, though only one ("The Salzburg Connection," published in 1968) made it to the very top. Most of them hover around third or fourth place, which is where "The Snare of the Hunter" is now, and has been for some weeks. Miss MacInnes published her first half-dozen books with Little, Brown, but has been with Harcourt Brace Jovanovich since 1951 and shows no signs of restiveness there. Her productivity has the same regularity as her appearances on the cherished list. Every three or four years, without fail, a new MacInnes appears—usually with a meticulously researched European setting, usually involved with some aspect of the Cold War or the aftermath of World War II—and quite often it is filmed, and always, from her point of view, with disastrous results.

"All the films of my books have been a mess," she declares unequivocally. "They always seem to change all the characters around, and I can never see why; it makes the plots incomprehensible. I've been asked to do the scripts for some of them, but I can't spend all that time in Hollywood, and no one else seems to get them right. Recently I asked my agent to see if they couldn't get whoever it was did the screenplay for Frederick Forsyth's 'The Day of the Jackal.' "

Like Forsyth's book, Miss MacInnes's novels have a sharply contemporary flavor—sometimes startlingly so. "The Snare of the Hunter," for instance, involves a Nobel Prize-winning novelist from behind the Iron Curtain who is living in the West, but was conceived and written before Alexander Solzhenitsyn was exiled to Switzerland. Like many of her books, it came from a careful reading of the newspapers—in this case, dispatches to the *New York Times* about the plight of some Czech writers and a visit to the movie "The Confession." "I began thinking about the men of ideas who have been arrested, and then I thought of the situation of someone who had got out of the country with a lot of names," Miss MacInnes said. "I just took it from there. I wouldn't want to preempt history or to change history. I wouldn't want to do a historical novel for that reason. To fabricate about the dead is an impertinence—my motto has always been 'Don't do to others what you wouldn't want them to do unto you.' "

It's a piece of sound Scottish common sense—as is her description of her working methods: "First you prepare the ground well, then you water it well, then when you plant, the whole thing grows easily, and birds come to nest in it. The characters always come if the basic structure is sound. But you must till the soil carefully first."

For her, "tilling the soil" consists of an almost photographic memory, coupled with an ultra-sensitive eye for detail. She and Highet spend about three months in Europe every second year (most of her books have been set there, with strong emphasis in Austria, Switzerland and northern

Italy) and she feels that "if I went more often, I'd come back too full of impressions." As it is, she implicitly trusts the impressions that remain with her of a place: "If I don't remember it, that means I'm not interested." And she loves to read maps, timetables and guidebooks—all the details that mean a MacInnes reader gets ultimate realism in the background of whatever story he picks up.

She works hard at her writing as well as her research ("Easy writing makes hard reading," she declares firmly) and finds that she learns more about her craft with each new book. Her own literary idols seem unusual until you realize that Miss MacInnes is deeply committed politically. They are Arthur Koestler, George Orwell and Rebecca West. She nearly always seems to find herself writing about Cold War situations—"neither defending it nor attacking it, simply realizing that it exists"—and comments dryly: "For everything I put into my plots, there is always something much more desperate in reality."

The essential MacInnes hero or heroine is someone caught up willy-nilly in international intrigue, and who inevitably determines to see it through to a satisfactory conclusion. This is no mere audience-pleasing on Miss MacInnes's part, but comes from her profound distaste for cynicism and despair—"I can't exist with them at all." And although Highet himself worked for British Intelligence during World War II, she insists she never asked him anything about such work, though some of the details about the Polish Resistance she put into "While Still We Live" (1944) were sufficiently convincing for her to be called to Washington and asked how she knew such things ("It was just common sense," she says comfortably).

Highet, whom she met while they were both students at Glasgow University in the 1920s, beat her into print by many years and was her first (somewhat bemused) critic. She wrote her first book, "Above Suspicion" (1941), in pencil and in longhand. "Gilbert read it and said 'Not bad,' " she recalls. "So I went ahead and typed it, then I sent it off to Gilbert's agent and in four days they accepted it. I think he was rather surprised. Then later on, of course, I got my galleys, and Gilbert told me I had to correct them myself. I was astonished. 'You mean *I* have to do this? But I'm the author!' " She persevered, however, and the book went onto the best seller list, thus establishing a tradition that has never been subsequently broken.

Highet, of course, has long been one of the judges for the Book-of-the-Month Club, which means that his wife's books cannot, in the fitness of things, be considered. "But the Literary Guild has been very good about them," she says. Theirs has been a long and happy marriage ("We were engaged for seven years, because in those days an Oxford don, which Gilbert became, wasn't *allowed* to be married. They finally gave in in 1932, and I think we were the first ever to break that barrier"). They are both keenly musical, and one of their great pleasures is playing piano duets—just as one of Miss MacInnes's greatest regrets, when she feels a new book coming on, is that she has to give up concert-going. With all the Spartan self-denial of a Scottish upbringing she devotes herself whole-heartedly to the job at hand. "You have to concentrate, and you can't do it if you're off at parties and concerts."

Dedicated she may be, but Miss MacInnes is by no means uninhibited. "I have this special war whoop for when I get on the best seller list," she says. "My biggest and loudest one was for Number One, but I got off a good one recently when Gilbert called to tell me I had made Number Three with 'Snare.' The only trouble is, I was in the hairdresser's at the time."

Mary McCarthy

"MY BREATH was taken away by the unfavorable quality of the reviews." The speaker is Mary McCarthy, the setting the art-filled Park Avenue apartment of her brother, Kevin, the noted actor, and the subject the reviews of "Birds of America." Miss McCarthy, a long-time resident of Paris but in New York for a few days during a sultry late June for radio and TV appearances, relaxes on a sofa, lights up a cigarette, and appears smiling and expectant despite the lack of air conditioning. A veteran of many literary engagements, wearing with honor her own wound stripes, nevertheless she waits "for the pain to be drawn."

"What particularly bothered you about the reviews?" *PW* asked.

"The bitchiness," was the prompt answer. "The reviews of 'The Group' were hostile but at least they weren't violent. The quality of reviewing in this country has declined since 'The Group' came out. I'd rather have something like Norman Mailer's perceptive but unfavorable review of 'The Group,' in the *New York Review of Books*, than what I have been getting."

She was particularly annoyed by John Aldridge's criticism of "Birds" in *The Saturday Review*. ("The serenity of the book is so total that one might almost suppose Miss McCarthy has finally developed beyond the point in her career where she felt she had to prove, with all the pounding fists of her being, that she deserves the title of foremost lady intellectual of American letters.")

"But at least that wasn't syndicated," she commented, and proceeded to another gripe—"the sinister case of stand-

By Arnold W. Ehrlich. From *Publishers Weekly* 200, no. 4 (July 26, 1971), pp. 19–21.

ardization of opinion in this country, and the abominable practice of boilerplate reviewing.'' She had been keeping count of her magazine and newspaper reviews, not including syndication, and on the date of the interview her score was ''29 favorable, 24 unfavorable, and 9 middling. But the real power,'' she added with her famous cat grin, ''is reflected in the number of times identical reviews appear over the country. I can't believe there isn't someone intelligent enough in every decent-sized town in this country to write an original review.'' On the other hand, William Hogan, of the *San Francisco Chronicle* had reviewed ''Birds of America'' *three* times—''all favorably.'' Puzzled but obviously pleased grin.

Another ''bitchy'' review that vexed Miss McCarthy was Helen Vendler's in the *New York Times Book Review*. ''Doesn't she have the reputation of trying to destroy famous writers?'' she asked. ''And that caption'' (she meant subhead: ''Mary McCarthy again her own heroine—frozen foods a new villain'')—''that was pretty bitchy, don't you think?''

What was her reaction to V. S. Pritchett's long piece in the *New York Review of Books*, which *PW* interpreted as a velvet-glove putdown, as only a superb English writer can pull off?

''Oh, I don't agree with you at all. Do you really think so? I read it twice. I thought it was favorable and counted it among the favorable category.

''Normally, in London I get better reviews than in America,'' she said, when asked to compare the quality of reviewing in the two countries. ''You know, there's a young French girl who has been doing her thesis on my work. One day she came to me looking very puzzled and said, Did I realize that reviews of my books have always run 60 percent unfavorable? No, I didn't realize it.'' Dazzling smile, radiant self-composure, the stance of a literary warrior knowing it was her turn to get shot down, but tough enough to take it.

We switched to literary chat: What writers did she like or dislike? Her opinions were quick and spontaneous. We start with John Updike. ''I liked the first two books—'The Poorhouse Fair' and 'Rabbit Run.' ''

''How about 'Couples'?''

Grimace.

''Norman Mailer?''

''I liked 'Miami and the Siege of Chicago' and 'Armies of the Night.' I'm anxious to read 'The Prisoner of Sex.' Have you read it? Will I like it?''

(Yes and no.)

''Saul Bellow?''

''Up through 'Herzog.' ''

''Philip Roth?''

''None of it.''

''Malamud?''

"Just the short stories. I think he's a better short-story writer than novelist. But then, many other critics think I'm a better essayist than novelist." Cheshire cat grin.

"Walker Percy?"

"I haven't read him."

"John Fowles?"

Blank stare. Ditto John Barth and Thomas Pynchon.

"Anthony Burgess?"

"Now there's a writer I really like, especially 'The Clockwork Orange.' No, I didn't know there's a movie coming from his book. There should be more people like him around."

"Nabokov?"

"Yes, but 'Ada' was a struggle to finish. I skipped pages, which I rarely do with a writer like Nabokov."

What other writers appeal to her? "Oh, I liked Frank Conroy's 'Stop Time' and do you know a writer named Paul Bailey? You don't? You should. Read 'After Jerusalem' and 'Trespasses.' Alison Lurie is another writer I like—she has a nice *écriture*. And in France, Nathalie Sarraute and Monique Vittig."

As to future writing plans, "a few little things are biting at the edge of my mind," Miss McCarthy said, but there is a long-range plan, a book on "the Gothic," similar in structure to "The Stones of Florence" ("a book I did in good conscience"). "I have seen almost everything Gothic in France," she said, "and it might just turn out that there is some connection between the architecture and politics of that time with the spirit of 'relevance'—God, how I hate that word!—today. I've become so political that unless there is some thread of connection with what's happening today, I don't see any point in doing it."

Another writing project she is eager to undertake, this one for the *New Yorker*, is coverage of the Captain Medina trial, due to get underway in August at Fort MacPherson, Georgia. "This one you do because it has larger overtones."

Would she like to go to China? "Oh, I don't think so," she smiled. "It's not the place where a sensibility like mine can wander. Besides, I don't speak Chinese and they don't speak French."

Miss McCarthy gave *PW* a tour of her brother's apartment, and we admired the collection of contemporary art and the beautifully appointed kitchen. At the door she invited us to visit her in Paris and we went out into the polluted city with a feeling of pleasure after an hour in her company.

James Mills

IN TWO EARLIER nonfiction books, "The Panic in Needle Park" and "The Prosecutor," James Mills has dealt seriously with crime and methods of policing it. His first novel, "Report to the Commissioner" (*Farrar, Straus & Giroux*), takes the matter one step further. It tackles the explosive question of policing the police against a very authentic-seeming New York City background.

Mills, a former *Life* reporter, who now lives in Paris, got his start in journalism as a police reporter for United Press in New York City for two years and has been a police buff ever since. "I had just started," he recalls, "and was very naive and green, when I landed at the scene of a shoot-out in a restaurant on Park Avenue just a few minutes after the police. A hold-up guy had shot and killed a sergeant and two patrolmen had rushed in with enormous courage. One grabbed the hold-up man around the neck. The hold-up guy in turn put his gun up to the other cop's neck. I'll never forget the look on all three faces and the realization they had that any one of them could be dead in the next couple of seconds. It was experiences like this that I had with UP that made all the rest of my life in New York and my previous college years seem small and superficial by comparison and gave me an interest in writing about life-and-death situations. Writing for me is very difficult, very onerous, hard labor. It's not worth suffering through all that unless what comes out of it is something serious. I like frivolity in my life, but not in my writing. Policemen, criminals, lawyers are all part of a subculture that has not one bit of frivolity in it."

The idea for "Report to the Commissioner" came to Mills out of the blue in 1968 when he was in Hollywood inter-

By Barbara A. Bannon. From *Publishers Weekly* 201, no. 21 (May 22, 1972), p. 14.

viewing Robert Evans, the head of Paramount Pictures, for *Life*. "I was driving up Sunset Boulevard one night," he says, "when it just hit me: what would happen if a very naive, idealistic kid, a long-haired young guy with kind of hippie sympathies, suddenly found himself a detective in a very active squad with a lot of tough, older seasoned cops. If anything like that ever happened I imagine his arrival would precipitate quite a furor."

"Report to the Commissioner" is written as if it were an actual confidential report prepared by the Internal Affairs Division of the New York City Police Department, the internal security unit charged with investigating complaints against police officers. All the documents that appear in it reproduce real New York City police documents acquired by Mills through channels he says he "does not choose to disclose."

The portrait of police life and work in New York City that emerges in the novel is, to put it mildly, pretty controversial. Whether or not the kind of fatal confrontation that eventually occurs in the book, between the idealistic young detective, a young undercover policewoman and a black pimp, could take place in real life is something Mills knows his readers will be arguing over. "No professional really likes a book written about his profession by an outsider," he says, "and I know that this book is going to be seen by a lot of people as being very anti-police. It puzzles me that I wrote it like that, because I am personally very pro-police."

As Mills sees it, "people are always amazed to discover that other people they have always thought of as being too physical to be very bright, like policemen or firemen, are human beings. Yet I know policemen who are more intellectual, more compassionate and more exciting than any dozen self-styled 'liberal' editors. The nicest guy I know in the world is a detective named Joe Price. The police department is a society like any other and it has all kinds in it.

"It is in the nature of police work that it cannot be really understood by a layman. Anyone who works in the field of personal danger cannot hope to be understood by the public. To be a law enforcer is quite a lonely job. Good police tend to stick together. All the good detectives I have known had friends who tended to be other detectives."

Mills has a great deal of sympathy for the kind of older detective he portrays in "Report to the Commissioner" as being unable to understand in any way the naive youngster in the squad. "These men who have been detectives for 20 years got on the force when it was still considered quite something to be a policeman," he says, "when candidates for the police force were very carefully scrutinized. They really had to struggle intellectually and physically to make the grade. It is hard to imagine the distress and agony such men are subjected to when they think they see some creepy little jerk getting away with something, and they begin to wonder, 'why have I given my life for this?' All too often the bad guy today winds up back on the corner because the court tossed the case out. The courts in this country today are a joke, and a very sad one. A lot of good cops are retiring early. They are very proud people."

Brian Moore

BRIAN MOORE is a soft-spoken, friendly man who still speaks with a slight brogue, although it is 20 years or more since he left Belfast, Ireland. In those years, first from Canada, now as a resident and soon-to-be citizen of the United States, Mr. Moore has published five novels, all of them greeted by considerable critical acclaim as character studies of depth and compassion: "The Lonely Passion of Judith Hearne," "The Feast of Lupercal," "The Luck of Ginger Coffey," "An Answer from Limbo," "The Emperor of Ice Cream."

His sixth novel, "I Am Mary Dunne," will be published by Viking on June 19, and it promises Mr. Moore a kind of popular sale he has never quite had before, since it has been taken by the Literary Guild as part of a dual selection.

Earlier this spring, Mr. Moore talked with *PW* about his writing and about himself. "I have always been a complete loner wherever I am," he says. "I am not a part of any literary society. I know few writers. One of my problems has been that I never thought of myself as being any particular nationality." As a loner, he is, he says, "naturally leery" of any church or political party, but he is going to become an American citizen because, having lived here several years now (the last three in California), he believes "that if you accept a country's hospitality you owe it to the country to become a citizen."

"The way I write novels is by trying to create a voice," Mr. Moore told *PW*, "to hear that voice and build up a person from it. I try to do it as if I were taking down dictation." He hopes that in the final analysis "I Am Mary Dunne" will turn out to "be written by someone called Mary Dunne."

By Barbara A. Bannon. From *Publishers Weekly* 193, no. 22 (May 27, 1968), pp. 15–17.

"I am very conscious of myself as a listener," Mr. Moore says, "very interested in listening to people's life stories and in what they have to tell me." Only "The Emperor of Ice Cream" among Mr. Moore's novels is in some part autobiographical; the others are not.

Readers and critics will find "I Am Mary Dunne" a tremendous contrast to the first novel Brian Moore wrote 20 years ago, "The Lonely Passion of Judith Hearne." Whereas Judith Hearne was a profoundly moving portrait of a certain type of frustrated Irish Catholic spinster, Mary Dunne is completely a 20th century woman in whose life sexual fulfillment is as important as it was impossible for Judith Hearne.

"Everyone is writing about alienation and problems of identity," Mr. Moore told *PW*. "The tendency since Camus has been to treat them abstractly. Women lose their identity much more than men. In 'I Am Mary Dunne' I was trying to write about what it is like to be a human being in our culture in terms of one ordinary American woman." In one respect, however, Mary Dunne is far from ordinary. She is a beautiful woman, because Mr. Moore believes that "if a woman is pretty it is another mask to hide behind. People do not see what you really are underneath."

In writing "I Am Mary Dunne" Mr. Moore also wanted to deal in some way with a framework of insanity without having to cope with aspects of clinical depression. The product of a medical family, he chose to set Mary's story, with many flashbacks, during a period of one day in which she is suffering acutely from the effects of premenstrual tension that mirror on a lesser level some of the torment a woman might feel if she thought she was losing her mind.

"I try to write a book within a three-year span," Mr. Moore said, "always stopping and doing something else to make enough money for the writing." In recent years he has also done some screen writing, most notably the screen play for the film version of his own novel, "The Luck of Ginger Coffey," which starred Robert Shaw, and was highly praised, and the screen play for the as-yet-unreleased film version of Isaac Bashevis Singer's "The Slave." For years there have been plans to bring "The Lonely Passion of Judith Hearne" to either the stage or the screen, and actresses from Shirley Booth to Katherine Hepburn have been interested. Now Mr. Moore hopes that Irving Kirshner, who directed "Ginger Coffey," can bring "Judith Hearne" to the screen with Deborah Kerr in the starring role. "In writing for the screen you must think in images," Mr. Moore says, "it is a director's medium at present."

Among the other writing with which he has kept himself going between novels have been 10 or 11 short stories and various magazine articles. While Brian Moore was still living in Canada he made the mistake of writing something for *Life* advocating political unity between the United States and Canada. "I nearly got myself killed for it," he says with a reminiscent smile.

Edna O'Brien

EDNA O'BRIEN writes with a cool candor about subjects, sexual and otherwise, which have led to all of her books being banned in her native Ireland. Yet her new novel, "A Pagan Place" (*Knopf*), is a deliberate return to the country Irish setting that was the scene of her two early successes, "The Country Girls" and "The Lonely Girl." This is no coincidence.

A smashing red-haired Irish beauty[. . .] Miss O'Brien proved to be both articulate and friendly on a recent first visit to New York. A divorcée who lives in London with two sons, 14 and 16, she is still so emotionally committed to Ireland that she goes back about once a month to visit her parents in the County Clare village in which she grew up.

"Clare is an enchanting and enchanted place," she says. "I'm interested in the bones and stones of a place." To get really back to a sense of place in an almost atavistic sense is very good for the "lost and fragmented" 1970s person, she believes. It is in this atavistic sense that she writes of Ireland as still essentially "A Pagan Place."

"I wanted to make 'A Pagan Place' a book that would seem to be a piece of life, yet have a mesmerizing quality to the language," she told *PW*. "I hope it reads like a little trip to a lucid hallucination."

The novel, which deals with a girl growing into her teens in a tiny Irish village, "is about the realm of childhood and a state of consciousness," Miss O'Brien says. It happens to be about Clare because that is the place she knows best from her own childhood experiences.

The novel was written "hundreds of times out loud," so

By Barbara A. Bannon. From *Publishers Weekly* 197, no. 21 (May 25, 1970), pp. 21–22.

much so that Miss O'Brien can still quote long stretches of it by heart. Yet the actual writing of the manuscript took her longer than any other book she has written, just about a year.

Country Ireland, she reports, hasn't changed much. "It is still mostly empty and beautiful." There is less domestic surveillance and censorship than there used to be and in Ireland, as everywhere else, the young people have ceased to maintain the values esteemed by their parents. "They are much braver and purer. They want the truth and are searching for it. In some degree the hardest thing to escape is the environment and indoctrination in which you were raised."

Although she jokingly calls herself "just a guilt-ridden Irishwoman," it is manifestly clear in everything she writes that Edna O'Brien managed to escape long ago from the rigid parochialism of Irish Catholicism and Irish country ways. How did she do it, we asked her?

"I think I have a great hunger and curiosity for life and growth," she said. "I have been very lucky in that I have had wonderful access to people who have brought me on." Miss O'Brien went to the national schools in a Clare village where the homes contained only three books: "Gone With the Wind," "Rebecca" and "How Green Was My Valley." They were so precious that they were handed around from house to house in separate pages.

It was a local teacher who first helped to inculcate in her "this love of writing and fairy tales and narrative, the love of legendry" that she still has. "I'm very much against *literature* as such," she says, "but *for* the written word with color and life and air in it."

When she left Clare, Edna O'Brien went up to Dublin and became a pharmacist. The first book she bought on the quais of Dublin was "Introducing James Joyce," with an introduction by T. S. Eliot.

"Reading bits of Joyce," she says, "was the first time in my whole life that I happened on something in a book that was exactly like my own life. I had always been a stranger from what had been my life up to then." She was encouraged in her writing by Paedar O'Donnell of the now defunct Dublin magazine, *The Bell*, who helped many an Irish writer on his way.

"I have managed to be relatively successful and relatively unsuccessful in my writing, which keeps a fine balance between paranoia and fame," she sums it up. None of her writing really worked until after she had married and left Ireland for England, when "something happened and I saw and missed Ireland in a way I had never known myself capable of." The result was "The Country Girls," written in a three-week spasm and later brilliantly filmed with Rita Tushingham and Peter Finch as "The Girl with the Green Eyes."

Nowadays, Miss O'Brien does quite a bit of writing for the films, having adapted Andrea Newman's "Three Into Two Won't Go" for Claire Bloom and Rod Steiger, and having recently finished an adaptation of her own novella, "The Love Object," which stars Jane Fonda.

"I am happier now than I have ever been in my life," she says quite simply, "although I do get suffused with the blackest despair at times. I am very aware of the melancholy of the Irish." If she could have an ideal way of living, it would encompass "three weeks of work, three weeks of loving, one week in a Buddist monastery." And if she had all the money in the world, Edna O'Brien would like nothing better than to sponsor "an uncensorable moving library going through Ireland each week," hopefully bringing to some of the younger people of Ireland the same sense of excitement she has found in words.

Kenzaburo Oë

IN PART because a G.I. gave a teenaged Japanese boy some American paperbacks—Melville and Faulkner—the best-selling novelist in Japan today is also called Japan's first "modern" novelist, one whose literary ancestry is wholly Western. Grove Press will introduce Kenzaburo Oë to American readers on June 10, when it publishes his novel, "A Personal Matter," in a translation by John Nathan. To introduce Mr. Oë to members of the American book trade press, Grove arranged a series of informal interviews with the author in New York, a few weeks before official publication.

Thirty-three years old, Mr. Oë has published eight novels in 10 years. Last fall, the eight were published in a special six-volume edition—an unheard-of honor for a young writer in Japan—and more than 900,000 copies were sold. "A Personal Matter" alone has sold more than 150,000 copies in Japan since it was first published in 1964.

The first American book which young Oë, aged 10, read, was a Japanese translation of "Huckleberry Finn"; it is still his favorite book. (World War II was on then, and his mother told him that if he was challenged about the book, he should say that Mark Twain was a German.) Mr. Oë does not remember the name of his G.I. book benefactor (and doubts that he ever knew it), but the Melville and Faulkner paperbacks confirmed what he had sensed in Mark Twain— "the darkness and the passion," as he described it the other day. "I identified with American writers. They feel uprooted. After the war, we were uprooted, too. My novels and my political essays are about the uprooted of Japan."

By Roger H. Smith. From *Publishers Weekly* 193, no. 23 (June 3, 1968), pp. 55–56.

His interest in American writers has continued. According to his translator, Mr. Oë is a walking encyclopedia of modern American fiction.

Mr. Oë broke into print at the age of 22 with a story in his university newspaper. Editors of big literary magazines saw the story and began clamoring for more. Mr. Oë has been a full-time writer ever since. Each of his early books provoked a "crisis" in the literary community when it appeared, he told *PW*. Attacked by the critics for their "darkness and passion," the books nevertheless sold well. The critics' hostility changed to praise when "A Personal Matter" appeared, and the book won a major prize—"a symbol of my initiation," says Mr. Oë. His most recent novel, "Football in the First Year of Mannen," won the 1967 Tanazaki Prize, named for the author who was in the forefront of those who deplored the Oë style.

Along with Mr. Oë's growing prominence as a writer has come his political development. The period he pines for is 1945–50, when the American Occupation brought to Japan its first heady taste of democracy. It ended abruptly with the Korean War and the suppression of Japan's Communist Party. The experience left Mr. Oë an articulate spokesman for the "uprooted" of Japan's New Left. Not all reacted the same way, of course, and a number of Japanese writers who are Mr. Oë's contemporaries have become ultra-nationalists.

The Bomb is always a poignant issue in Japan. Mr. Oë wrote a book memorializing Hiroshima, and on his U.S. trip went to New Haven to visit another Hiroshima chronicler, John Hersey. Mr. Oë has spoken out against China's nuclear testing and against the U.S. nuclear presence on Okinawa. Although he once, at age 25, interviewed Mao in Shanghai, he now doubts that he could return to China because of his anti-Bomb statements. A part of his political views is the hope for greater communication between Japan and China.

But Mr. Oë wants to be regarded not as a political figure but as a writer. To his translator, John Nathan, Mr. Oë has created a new kind of language in Japanese, as Günter Grass created a new kind of language in German. "There is tremendous excitement in his prose," Mr. Nathan said as the *PW* interview was winding up. "It is violent and wild and headlong—a rush of language, very untraditional. If Faulkner could have read Japanese, he would have been the ideal translator. I can read it accurately, but it requires great craft to translate it."

"He was the first one," said Mr. Oë, smiling at his translator, "who said that my prose was poetic."

Amos Oz

As Israel begins the celebration of its 25th anniversary, it is perhaps an appropriate time to look at the development of Israeli literature during the last quarter-century. At first Israeli writers dealt mostly with army or kibbutz life as it affected the destiny of the nation. The tone was nearly always ideological and nationalistic, leaning toward social realism. However, today's younger generation of Israeli authors are more self-conscious and probing—they concentrate on the individual and treat the future of their country as a comparatively minor theme. And a haunting leitmotiv of guilt and moral anguish pervades the writings of young authors on the subject of the Arabs, especially the Palestinian refugees.

Amos Oz, at 33 one of Israel's more talented and controversial "new" writers, has published three novels, two novellas, a book of stories, and various political, social and literary essays. His work is appearing in England, France, Germany, Spain and South America, as well as in the United States. The first of Mr. Oz's books published here—"My Michael," published by Knopf last May, and recently released in paperback by Lancer—was hailed by critics as one of the finer foreign novels of the past few years. (It was a national bestseller in Israel in 1968.)

American readers will soon get the chance of seeing more of Mr. Oz's range and virtuosity as a novelist. This November Harcourt Brace Jovanovich will publish "Elsewhere, Perhaps," an earlier novel (if the title sounds familiar, it is not due to imitation, but to the fact that the literal translation of the Hebrew title is "Somewhere Else"). This will

By Daisy Maryles. From *Publishers Weekly* 203, no. 21 (May 21, 1973), pp. 16–18.

be followed next spring by a novel just released in Israel, "Touch the Water, Touch the Wind." Harcourt is also planning to publish two novellas, "The Crusaders," which has previously appeared in *Commentary*, and "Late Love." Helen Wolff, Mr. Oz's editor at Harcourt, considers him a writer of tremendous talent who will become a major international literary figure.

It all adds up to a busy publishing career—and one of the paradoxes is that Oz does not even benefit financially from it all. He has been a member of Kibbutz Hulda for the past 17 years, and all his royalties and income are signed over to the kibbutz treasurer. On a recent trip to the United States—Oz's first, occasioned by the fact that he had won a B'nai B'rith Book Award—he talked with *PW* about this arrangement, his writing and his country.

"I am a high school teacher half-time and can devote the rest of my time to writing. The practical arrangement is simple: whatever money I make I give the treasurer. On the other hand, whatever I need in connection with my writing—including 10 days in a hotel in sort of an ivory tower at the other end of the country—all I have to do is ask for the money." He is not the "darling" of the community, and finds himself assigned, like anyone else, to duties like waiter or watchman.

As a novelist he prefers this kind of cloistered life. Mr. Oz feels that in the big city he would never have the opportunity to be so intimately acquainted with 300 people of varying backgrounds. "I know a hell of a lot about the people in Hulda—their family history, secret pains, loves and ambitions. In this respect I am living in the middle of a rushing stream."

Living far away from the centers of literary activity is also his preference. Since Israel is so small, he finds there is "this sweaty kind of intimacy, where everyone knows what everyone else is doing." He is not out of touch with literary trends and dialogue, however, because Israeli writers gather together out of political commitment rather than literary tradition—and Mr. Oz is one of the moral vocal political critics of the Israeli establishment.

He can only write when surrounded by the Hebrew language. "If I hear a foreign language, I lose my musical key. Although I can think in English, when it comes to more serious things my thoughts are only in Hebrew—it's the language in which I dream, love, laugh and cry."

Oz compares modern Hebrew to Elizabethan English, a language in which many things are still possible. "Hebrew is a very old and very new language. It's half solid rock and half sand dunes, with very little in between. Because of the density of time in Israel, a decade can sometimes seem the equivalent of a century anywhere else." In addition, every wave of immigration changes the balance of the language, so that "books written at this time might in 10 or 20 years sound archaic, old-fashioned and even phony." It is because of this peculiarity, according to Mr. Oz, that writing a drama in Hebrew for the Israeli stage is almost impossible. "By the time it's produced, the dialogue is so strange; people don't speak that way anymore—and they don't even remember that they used to speak that way."

Ever since he can remember, Mr. Oz planned to be a writer. "I was five when I learned the alphabet and my father taught me how to type with one finger. The first thing I printed was my name and the subtitle: writer." His parents came to Jerusalem from Russia in the early 1930s, and he grew up in Jerusalem, joining the kibbutz at the age of 16.

"My Michael" is about Hannah Gonen, a young Israeli student of literature, who marries a rather dull geologist, Michael, with whom she finds life unfulfilling. Her monotonous daily routine is sharply contrasted to her fantasy world of violence and sex, involving a pair of Arab twins with whom she had been friendly as a young girl. American reviewers regarded the novel either an extension of the problems of woman in a man's world or as an allegory of the Arab–Israeli conflict. The author disagrees with both assessments.

What surprised Mr. Oz was the fact that few American reviewers paid any attention to the fact that the only Arabs in the novel were the twins, who existed solely in Hannah's imagination. "These twins could be rich oil sheiks in Kuwait. And so I can't agree with the interpretation that the Arabs in the novel are an aspect of Israeli politics."

The book, he said, had two kinds of reception from women: "How dare you? Who are you to know what a woman feels?" and "How on earth did you know?" His answer is based on a deep interest in women and a keen admiration for them. "The entire blend of human experience is reflected in the mind of a woman rather than that of a man." He did not feel that Hannah was typical of Israeli women.

"Fundamentally, I think that many Israeli women are realizing that freedom beyond legal, social and economic aspects is basically a state of mind. Hannah discovers that there is an inner feeling of persecution. It is necessary to liberate oneself from the slavery imposed by the mind."

"Elsewhere, Perhaps" is described by Mr. Oz as a story of the older generations who came as refugees from Germany and Russia and still carry on a "disappointed love affair" with their homelands. "Touch the Water, Touch the Wind" begins in Poland in 1939 and ends in Galilee on the eve of the Six-Day War.

He is reluctant to "award marks among current American writers," and only goes so far as to say that Faulkner and Sherwood Anderson are his favorites. His main criticism of the novels that come out of America and the English-speaking world is that they "are much too witty" for his taste. "People don't talk to each other in your current literature, they exchange punchlines. It's all very amusing, and after a couple of pages I am amazed at the quality of the dialogue—the witticisms and sharpness.

However, I quickly realize that people do not talk like that. The words are all a kind of literary baroque."

Amos Oz is deeply in touch with current Israeli conflicts, and is often a spokesman for his generation. "The young are very aware that the Arab–Israeli conflict is not a Wild West film with the good guys against the bad guys. The Palestinian Arabs have a good case. But that does not lead us to the sort of conclusions typical of American radicals' 'Get out of Vietnam.' There is no question of getting out of Israel.

"The hope of reconciliation with the Arabs is dead among young Israelis. They are more sober, more pessimistic. They have no faith in theories, formulas, or ways out. The most they forecast is a sad, slow, painful process of acceptance."

He points out that the leader of the country is 78 years old; most of the ruling cabinet is composed of senior citizens, many of whom were born in Europe. Even leaders regarded abroad as young—Moshe Dayan and Yigal Allon—are in fact men in their 50s with grandchildren.

The reason for the Sabras' apparent reluctance to enter political life, Mr. Oz explained, is "that the founders succeeded in transplanting to the younger generation a very hostile attitude toward politics altogether." Many of the country's young potential political leaders, therefore, regard it as more dignified to become "a scientist, a scholar, an army officer or a kibbutznik."

As far as Oz is concerned, the most important thing for both sides to do in this conflict is to remove stereotypes. "Many of the Arabs, especially the Palestinians, do not actually have us before their eyes when they fight 'Zionist aggression.' What they fear is an extension of the European oppressors—the white, civilizing, arrogant colonists of their traumatic experience. When we face the Arab, we see the goy, the savage Cossack who is out to make a pogrom."

It is a yawning gulf in communication that Oz can only hope to begin to bridge with the healing power of the writer's art.

Carlene Hatcher Polite

EUROPE has often discovered American writers before America has, or applauded them louder, but if it happened to Henry James and William Faulkner, it doesn't make it anything less of a happy surprise to Detroit-born Carlene Hatcher Polite to have become France's discovery of the year. Her novel "The Flagellants" was largely written in Paris, and published there first under the new Christian Bourgois imprint. It will appear in the United States on June 19 *chez* Farrar, Straus & Giroux.

The author is an attractive 35, tall and poised as a dancer. She has been a dancer, with experience in enough other careers to fill out a lifetime (or a dozen more books). "All my life all I ever wanted secretly to be was a writer," she says. "When I was nine years old the big problem I had with my father was that I borrowed too many books from the public library and he was afraid of having to pay overdue fines. And I'd fall asleep with the light on while reading, which cost him more money." At the age of 12 she had given herself a French-sounding pen name and wrote by candlelight to be more romantic. "They were prose poems," she recalls with a laugh. "I find now they were slightly overwritten, and some people say my style hasn't changed since."

She went east from her Detroit home on a scholarship to Sarah Lawrence, but preferred to study dancing under Martha Graham. "I still can't mention Sarah Lawrence in my parents' home." In New York she danced at YMHA concerts, carried a spear on the Metropolitan Opera stage, did specialty dancing in "The King and I" and "Boyfriend," was a "dark witch" in "Dark of the Moon." This was her

By Herbert R. Lottman. From *Publishers Weekly* 191, no. 24 (June 12, 1967), pp. 20–21. Reprinted by permission of Herbert R. Lottman.

Greenwich Village period—"I lived among the beats, got involved with Zen and breath control. But Martha Graham was a philosophy all by herself, and she was my principal influence at the time."

Despite other endeavors, she felt that only writing fulfilled her. Some of the notes she took in Greenwich Village found their way into "The Flagellants."

After marriage and divorce (she has two daughters), she returned to Detroit, becoming a guest instructor at Wayne State University, teaching modern dance. At Detroit's small Equity Theater she was dancer–actress, business manager, usher, even polished up the handle on the big front door.

Carlene's mother is an international representative for the United Automobile Workers, a board member of NAACP and other civil rights organizations, was a delegate to the Michigan constitutional convention. Under the Kennedy administration Mrs. Hatcher was appointed to the Women's Bureau of the Department of Labor, but declined, preferring to stay home in Detroit. Carlene's father is involved with UAW–Chrysler employee relations. This family influence eventually took Carlene from dancing to what she felt would be more meaningful, politics and civil rights.

In 1962 Carlene Polite worked for the Democratic Party in Michigan, stayed on the permanent staff during the campaign against the revised state constitution, writing political press releases and pamphlets. The voters of the 13th Congressional District of Michigan elected her to the Michigan State Central Committee of the Democratic Party. "But at the same time I continued to write prose poems during coffee breaks." When Governor Romney won the 1962 election the Democrats went broke, and Carlene was out of a job. She joined the Detroit Council for Human Rights and helped organize the state-wide Walk to Freedom to protest the Birmingham bombings and the killing of Medgar Evers. This event brought out a quarter of a million people, as many as the later March on Washington. Martin Luther King, who took part in both, called the Michigan march the demonstration which broke the ground for the national event. Carlene was responsible for the complete organization of the Northern Negro Leadership Conference in November, 1963.

When the Detroit Council closed down Carlene worked at a nightclub to make enough money to pay bills, and enough again to allow her to consider what to do with it. She decided to go to Paris. A French friend asked her what she wanted to see there. She replied in a two-page letter on "what I like." Dominique de Roux, energetic young publisher of the literary magazine L'Herne and adviser to the Presses de la Cité publishing empire, saw the letter and was impressed with her writing talent. He hounded Carlene Polite from that time on, until "The Flagellants" was ready for the presses. By then Monsieur de Roux was editor in chief of the new Presses literary subsidiary, Editions Christian Bourgois.

While working on her novel Carlene also composed an article on rock n' roll which was accepted for Jean-Paul Sartre's magazine Temps Mod-

ernes but never printed because, she learned later, Sartre loved it but Simone de Beauvoir didn't. Then she returned to America, did a public relations stint for a touring Chevrolet auto show, was lured back to Paris by de Roux to get on with that novel. "I lived on soup and hot chocolate all the time I was writing, don't ask me why," she says. "And a lot of the book came from my teen-age notes, the Martha Graham period, and freedom fighter days. In Detroit I had sometimes been taken for a police-woman because I'd sit in a bar writing away in a little notebook."

The novel's publication in France heralded the birth of the new Bourgois publishing house, but was also the occasion for recognition by the French that an American Negro could write something other than a protest novel. "The Flagellants" is the record of a stormy relationship of a couple, Ideal and Jimson, their work, their fights and reconciliation, finally the woman's decision to leave her man. Greenwich Village is the setting for a large part of the story. What it says about the Negro condition comes through in emotional and human terms. "Our love affair," Ideal tells Jimson, "is an irrevocable trauma." Their flagellations are mutual tongue-lashings, a clash which might be compared to "Who's Afraid of Virginia Woolf?" The reader gets as close to the lives of strangers as he is ever likely to. In fact, the reader is flagellated, which may dismay and discourage him, but eventually brings him entirely into the picture.

The first note Carlene Polite wrote to herself before beginning the writing of her novel was "Beat the reader to death." The result is "Theater of Cruelty" in book form. It is also a deeply personal story, partly because it is (partly) Mrs. Polite's own. If Flaubert said he was Madame Bovary, Carlene Polite says: "Jimson (her male protagonist), *c'est moi*."

When the book appeared in France the emphasis was on Paris' discovery of a "captivating" American talent. "She makes us penetrate the black ghetto," wrote *Planète's* reviewer, "and thus reveals the most secret facets of the Negro American soul." "Poetic, tragic, and flashing beauty," was what another critic found. "Naive poetry," said a third. She was compared with James Baldwin, though hers was the language of incantation, the language (said more than one French critic) of Henry Miller. "A born writer" was the general opinion. Farrar, Straus & Giroux purchased U.S. rights, Faber & Faber will do the British edition, and there are pending contracts in Germany, Italy, the Scandinavian countries, and a Dutch edition in progress. Carlene Polite is working on a second novel, while seeking a "nest" in Paris or back home where she can transform her pile of notes into a book. In it she intends to deal with poverty as much as racism. ("I know as many white people who suffer as Negroes," she says.)

To help the freedom fighters, Carlene Polite feels she must first be a good writer, a position which is also that of Ralph Ellison. "I'm of that generation which thought that because we were Negroes we had to write or paint or dance as Negroes," she explains. "To be accepted by white publishers or producers we had to be 'Negroes' in quotes. But I'd rather divide up my writing to do creative literature and editorial protests at separate times. Simone de Beauvior says in 'The Second Sex' that the problem of women is similar to the problem of the Negro. No woman can create literature until she is freed of the cross of second-class citizenship. The French tell me there can't be a real American Negro writer until racism has disappeared.

"My real problem now," she says pensively—then breaking into a smile—"is self-discipline."

Chaim Potok

CHAIM POTOK is the editor of the Jewish Publication Society of America in Philadelphia. He is also the author of one of the most talked about first novels in a long time, Simon and Schuster's "The Chosen," which has a first printing of 20,000, a second printing of 10,000 more and a 70-page excerpt in the April *Ladies' Home Journal.*

"The Chosen" deals with the Williamsburg, Brooklyn world of the ultra-Orthodox Hasidic Jew, and one youth's pilgrimage into the wider world of a more liberal Judaism. Chaim Potok knows the two worlds well first hand. "My father was as close as you could come to being a Hasidic Jew without wearing the special clothes," he says. He, himself, grew up in New York's Bronx, where his father was a businessman, and as a child attended a Hasidic synagogue. "The Hasids," he says, "can be the gentlest people in the world, but two things can arouse them—a serious challenge to the tenets of their faith, and a desire to get so close personally to the rabbi that they will jostle anyone aside to get near him."

Of his own childhood, Mr. Potok says simply, "I cannot remember a time when I was not reading." He knew the Hebrew alphabet at two and by the time he was five was making regular Friday pilgrimages to the local public library, stocking up on reading for the Sabbath weekend. The first sophisticated, adult book he remembers reading was Evelyn Waugh's "Brideshead Revisited" and this intensely Catholic novel of religious conversion became his model from then on as far as the form and structure of his own writing was concerned.

By Barbara A. Bannon. From *Publishers Weekly* 191, no. 14 (April 3, 1967), p. 25.

He was in his last year at Yeshiva University when he faced up to the fact that he, like Danny in "The Chosen," was tormented by a whole host of serious intellectual, philosophical and theological problems. Too often, he felt, the rabbis in the school to whom he brought his questions, could only reply by telling him not to ask the questions in the first place. Disenchanted with Yeshiva's Orthodoxy, he found in the library of a cousin who had married a Jewish seminarian of Conservative persuasion the kind of reading that answered just the questions he, himself, was asking about his faith. Transferring immediately to the Jewish Theological Seminary in New York, he began his own pilgrimage into Conservative Judaism.

In order to really interpret the interior of Jewish religious life Mr. Potok believes you have to be brought up and educated in a very intensely Jewish religious atmosphere. "Yet the more intensive your Jewish education, the less respect you tend to have for the craft of fiction," he says, because all the emphasis instead in your reading is on the Talmud and the Bible.

"There is a criterion for being known as a 'Jewish novelist' today," he thinks, naming some famous names. "It has come to mean someone who is hung up on his Jewishness, who wants to get away from it and cannot."

As for Chaim Potok, himself, he is definitely a practicing, religious Jew, but a Conservative one. He had been working on a novel for many years out of which "The Chosen" was to evolve. The climactic moment that made it possible for him to understand what he really wanted to say about his own beginnings and Judaism occurred, surprisingly enough, at a traveling carnival in Pennsylvania Dutch country. He, his wife, another couple, also Jewish, were lured into trying their hand at a game of chance. They were the only Jews there. Then the proprietor of the game came up. He was an elderly, arthritic Jew, Mr. Potok remembers, and he played upon his Jewishness and that of the Potoks and their friends to up the ante of the game and then, quite blatantly, cheated them. "I felt such rage," Chaim Potok recalls, "that 'one of our own' could do such a thing." The incident so shocked him that he found himself going all the way back in his own life, his own concept of Judaism, reliving the past, to find out what it was that Judaism really meant to him.

"I decided to go all the way back, too, in 'The Chosen,' " he says. "It's my own path I'm following." There will be more novels and they may well explore other aspects of Judaism. "I have," Chaim Potok says, "a very serious commitment to the craft of fiction." This reader of his first novel emphatically agrees with him.

Alain Robbe-Grillet

ALAIN ROBBE-GRILLET, the French writer whose "The Voyeur" (1955) launched the "new novel" or the "antinovel" in contemporary literature, and whose screenplay for "Last Year at Marienbad" had a major effect on the art of filmmaking, is currently in New York. The man who in his 1964 critique, "Towards a New Novel," wrote: "The world is neither significant nor absurd. It just is," is teaching two courses in French at New York University this spring, one on "The New 'New Novel,' " one on "Cinema and Literature." He is also discussing his novels and the films, which he now directs as well as writes, at Columbia University. *PW* interviewed him in the offices of his literary agent, Georges Borchardt, who assisted as translator.

Robbe-Grillet's first impression of American university students compared with those he is used to addressing in France was that the Americans are "more receptive, but perhaps too respectful. French students are more aggressive, more violent and passionate in attacking me." He hopes that as his American students become more used to him, they will fight back more.

M. Robbe-Grillet believes that writing for the screen and writing his kind of novel call for different techniques. He does not think fiction should be transferred to the screen and would never consent to having any of his own novels adapted as a film. For Robbe-Grillet the traditional big, sweeping novel that tells a story, and which flourished in the 19th century in the work of Balzac, for example, no longer has validity or meaning.

"The 'new novel' or the 'new film' acquire their real

By Barbara A. Bannon. From *Publishers Weekly* 201, no. 11 (March 13, 1972), pp. 22–23.

meaning as a sort of constant Passion Play dealing with drives not accepted by society," he says. "As an artist my role is not to submit to the rules of society, but to oppose them. What I am trying to do is to give a meaning to the world not given by the old-fashioned codes of value society imposes on people. I hope my writing is like a love affair between a man and a woman in which each has the impression that everything that is happening is very new and different. My critics are still hoping I will revert to the traditional novel. On the contrary, I am getting farther and farther away from the traditional, to the extent that my new novel, 'Project for a Revolution in New York' (*Grove Press*, spring), while it is set in New York, takes place in a New York I have invented that has nothing to do with the real New York people might expect.

"The modern city secretes myths and New York seems to be the city that secretes the greatest number of myths. Although it is not fundamentally different from Milan or Copenhagen, it is so much bigger that it secretes a kind of super-myth. An element of fear is present in New York more than in any other city. My book deals with a New York way of life as it is imagined in the minds of both New Yorkers and Europeans. It combines many myth elements—blacks, Central Park, fire engines, the police, the subway. What interests me is the importance all these elements have taken on in the minds of people. Each one of these myth elements can be interpreted as sexual or political or both at the same time.

"In New York you are told, 'do not take the subway. You can be raped or killed.' New Yorkers are afraid of this underground Freudian world as contrasted with their great buildings and skyscrapers. Blacks are objects of American mythology in which they become a virility symbol as opposed to impotent whites. There is the myth of white girls being raped by blacks. In addition, there is the political myth of a poor social class seen as a danger to the rich who might be displaced.

"Even revolution has become a myth. This kind of revolution actually has little to do with real revolution. It is born from the sons of the bourgeois. It has gotten to the point where the ideal terrain for revolution is not a poor country, but the richest country in the world, and the richest city, New York, and the richest borough, Manhattan."

Turning to his writing for the screen, Alain Robbe-Grillet defined the traditional, commercial film as being "based on the illusion of the real, in which the filmmaker tries to make his audience believe what it is seeing is reality. In the 'new cinema' what you are shown on the screen is consistently designed as fiction."

His first screenplay, "Last Year at Marienbad" was written in advance of the filming. Now, Robbe-Grillet writes his screen plays as he shoots them. There is very little dialogue and although much of what appears to be happening may look as if the actors are improvising, this is seldom so. With Jean-Louis Trintignant in "L'Homme Qui Ment," Robbe-Grillet did leave him a margin of improvisation. These improvised passages were then rewritten and replayed before the camera.

"The cinema that ages fastest is the realistic film," Robbe-Grillet says. "If you look at a so-called realistic film several years old, how unreal and exaggerated the actors seem. It turns out that what seemed realistic is not so at all. The reason these films seem aged is that all they expressed was an idea of reality as seen in an outdated code of values perhaps 15 years old. This concept of 'realism' merely succeeds in expressing a code of values current at the time."

Summing up his views as both a filmmaker and writer, M. Robbe-Grillet put it this way: "The traditional reader or viewer believes in two different levels of time. He accepts that a film lasts 1 ½ hours or a book may take several hours to read, but that the story may actually span 20 years. The traditionalist will accept incidents he is told may have taken place in the past if they are presented as flashbacks. Many of the people who saw 'Last Year at Marienbad' kept arguing to find out whether one scene was really supposed to have taken place before or after other ones. My concern was simply to present all the scenes I wanted in 1 ½ hours of film. I consider myself a realist of fiction rather than of reality."

Lawrence Sanders

LITERARY HISTORY is full of young writers who zoomed up like rockets with their first book (and of those who burst like rockets, too, and fell back to earth in silence). And people who suddenly decide in middle or late life to write a book, and do it successfully, are not unknown either. A professional magazine writer who toils away, making a solid, unspectacular living for 25 years, then suddenly breaks through into best sellerdom at the age of 50, is not such a common strain.

That, however, is the story of Lawrence Sanders, who burst upon the world six years ago with "The Anderson Tapes," followed it up with the equally successful "The First Deadly Sin" (1973), with "The Tomorrow File" last year, and now with a novel of African intrigue, "The Tangent Objective." In between those known titles have been a couple, "The Pleasures of Helen" and "Love Songs," which he admits did not set booksellers' hearts aflutter but did, he maintains stoutly, earn back their advances with room to spare ("I got driblets of royalties on both" is how he puts it). All these books, which he has been producing steadily at the rate of one a year since his breakthrough, have been published by Putnam.

Sanders does not look unlike a British diplomat, and these days can afford to live like one, dividing his time between New York and Florida. The affluence and the air that goes with it, however, were a long time coming to him. Lunching with *PW* recently in a restaurant not far from Macy's in New York, he recalls early days there as a comparison shopper, checking to make sure that the store's prices were

By John F. Baker. From *Publishers Weekly* 210, no. 5 (August 2, 1976), pp. 44–45.

really competitive with its neighbors'. Then came World War II and the Marines, and after the war began his 25-year training as a writer. "I started doing gag lines for cheesecake magazines right after the war," he says. "Then I branched out to all kinds of other magazines—regular men's magazines, scientific, war, adventure. I learned how to write fast and grab the reader's attention. You *had* to write fast, and if you did it wasn't a bad living. In those days you got about $75 for a story, $100 for a piece of nonfiction—you might have to do a bit of research for the nonfiction. The pieces would be maybe 3500 words and if I was going well I could knock off a story or an article in an evening." His most successful markets turned out to be scientific magazines, and he was an editor on *Mechanix Illustrated* for nine years, the editor of *Science and Mechanics* for four. It was the background he acquired here in the burgeoning art of electronic eavesdropping that led to the idea for "The Anderson Tapes."

"I thought of a plot that could be overheard completely from people's conversations," he says. "Then when I started to write it, I thought: If the cops can hear all this why don't they arrest everyone? It stumped me for a while, then I got the idea that different bits were heard by different eavesdroppers—CIA, FBI, tax guys—and after that it all fell into place." As for his motivation in trying for a novel after years of articles and instantly forgotten stories: "I read a lot, and I would read some new best seller, and I'd think to myself: 'Someone got $100,000 for this. It could have been me—I can do this!'"

At first, when the book was finished, his plans for it were not ambitious. He wrote it with Fawcett's Gold Medal line of original paperback thrillers in mind, and expected $2500 for it. He actually had the ms. wrapped up under his arm and was on his way there when he dropped in to see an editor friend at another house who asked how the book was doing, then added: "Why not try it as hardcover?" So Sanders gave it to his agent, who said he'd try it on Marcia Magill, then editing the Red Mask mystery series at Putnam. "She got it for $3000, but right away Marcia saw something more than just another mystery." Putnam pushed it as a big novel, it climbed the best seller list, went to Dell for $200,000, the movies for $100,000, and suddenly Sanders found that "my whole life changed, at the age of 50."

"Here I was, the kind of guy who took his paycheck to the liquor store and took the balance in cash, and one day I got a check from a movie company for $90,000." Still, he muses, it was probably as well the success came so late. "If I'd been 25, I'd probably have run off buying yachts and chorus girls."

The movie of "The Anderson Tapes" was also a hit, though some critics grumbled that the tapes aspect, which had been clever in the book, simply seemed an unnecessary gimmick in the film; and Sanders's favorite review came from Judith Crist: "She said it would have been best as a radio play, and she was absolutely right." He remains bewildered by filmdom. Rights to "The First Deadly Sin" were bought for a large sum, and he agrees with *PW* that it would make an ideal movie, but somehow nothing has emerged yet. "And I wouldn't want to be involved in that screenplay business—writing by committee. That's an ulcer business."

As if making up for lost time, Sanders has kept working as quickly as he can since. Walter Minton is now his editor ("We work it out face to face") and what he wants above all is for each of his books to be different, so no one can say a book is "a typical Sanders novel." "I know a writer who's been doing the same book over and over for 18 years." Sanders has started a dozen books in the past six years that have never seen the light of day. "At one time I used to send the first 150 pages to my agent and let him decide if it was worth going on. Now I just finish the book, and then I decide myself whether it works."

Sanders is not a widely traveled man, and although his new book is set in Africa he has never been there. "No, it's all research, but I've tried to blend it in so a reader doesn't notice. I don't want to overwhelm anyone with it, as I think Forsyth did in 'The Dogs of War,' which told me altogether more than I ever wanted to know about gun smuggling and the organization of a coup." "The Tangent Objective" in fact has a somewhat similar story, and it is a kind of story Sanders is enthusiastic about. "I'd recommend Africa as a setting for any young novelist. You've got everything—an exotic scene, conflicts, subterfuge, politics, wicked big business. . . ." As for a recent review in the *New York Times*, in which a critic read into the book a deep study of human values, Sanders was genuinely astounded—first of all, that anyone would read his work so carefully, and then that they should be impressed by the depth of his characterization. "I don't take myself seriously, so why should anyone else? I'm writing entertainment—I hope intelligent entertainment, but that's all."

His own most personal book to date has been "The Tomorrow File," at which he worked particularly hard, but which he feels emerged rather ponderous: "I think it demands a lot of its readers—perhaps too much." It secured some good reviews, however, made a reasonable paperback sale, and, says Sanders, brought him a glowing fan letter from science fiction star Robert Heinlein. "If you start off with a big success you build up a following," Sanders muses. "And they'll stay with you through something that doesn't come off."

Since, as Sanders says, he finds himself "afraid to stop writing," his next novel is nearly ready. "It's nearly all dialogue, with a setting of Manhattan theater, about an old ham actor and his son who's in acting school, and the conflict between them. It's not a thriller, and I figure it will sell at least two copies, because my mother said she'd buy a couple."

Sanders thinks thrillers, after the unbridled sex and violence of recent years, are beginning to become more conservative. "I think there's a new hunger for just a good story and traditional characters.'' He remains somewhat baffled by the sort of titles that get put on books these days. ''The idea seems to be to make them sound like nonfiction—'The so-and-so File, or Dossier, or Manifesto, or Plan. Yes, 'Objective,' too. My idea was to call the book 'Black Napoleon,' but they didn't go for that.''

Sanders is proud and delighted to be one of only about 200 people making a good living out of writing fiction in the U.S. today (his own estimate), and sees his late flowering as ''luck, luck, luck.'' But he still cannot quite get used to the vagaries of literary fame, and the sort of fandom it seems to attract.

Once, he recalls, he was approached by someone who breathlessly asked him if he was the author of ''The Anderson Tapes.'' ''I told him yes, and figured he was going to ask me about my writing methods. Actually his next question was: 'Do you type double spaced?' ''

Erich Segal

ERICH SEGAL is a decidedly 20th century Renaissance man. A classicist who teaches graduate and undergraduate courses in Plautus, Terence, Catullus and Greek tragedy at Yale, and writes scholarly books and articles, he is also a Hollywood screen writer who is fast coming into his own, after working on the Beatles' film, "Yellow Submarine"; he is a former varsity track and cross-country runner; and he is the author of a fine Harper & Row first novel, "Love Story." The novel is a Literary Guild choice, has been purchased for reprint by NAL, and is being filmed in color right now with Ali McGraw, Ryan O'Neal and Ray Milland as the leads. Hodder and Stoughton has bought the book in England, Garzanti in Italy; and it has just been made the Dutch equivalent of a B-O-M choice. Oh, yes, Mr. Segal also wrote the lyrics for the movie's "Love Story" theme, with Charles Aznavour doing the music.

As if this wasn't enough, Mr. Segal (who is 32) is off on a quick tour of Yale Clubs to reassure alumni that Old Eli, under what he considers the very able direction of Kingman Brewster, is holding to an intelligent course of action designed to allay student revolts by anticipating points of conflict and applying preventive medicine insofar as possible. He is also about to embark on a cross-country promotion tour for the novel, "Love Story." The way he manages to maintain this back-breaking schedule of work is by running 10 miles every day, and Harper & Row has been requested to make sure there is a good track available for him in each city he visits.

Mr. Segal, exuberant and friendly, finished up his last

By Barbara A. Bannon. From *Publishers Weekly* 197, no. 5 (February 2, 1970), pp. 51–53.

class at Yale the night of January 13. Early the next morning he took a group of book and other press people on a tour to snowy Riverdale, New York, where much of "Love Story" is currently being filmed in a Charles Addams type of old mansion, once occupied by Toscanini, and now owned by the City of New York, which lets it out for special use.

Coming and going, Mr. Segal had quite a bit to say about his writing and teaching. On the set the press had a chance to chat with Ali McGraw and Ryan O'Neal, watch a bit of the filming, and meet with producer Howard Minsky and director Arthur Hiller (whose film credits include "Popi," "The Americanization of Emily" and "The Tiger Makes Out"). It's nice to be able to report that they are all the new breed of film people, articulate and book-oriented. Miss McGraw, a Wellesley graduate who majored in art history and literature, says these days she "likes to read hard more and more." She is particularly fond of Hesse and Krishnamurti, and currently very much "turned on by the East" in her reading tastes. By pure coincidence, she and Erich Segal met some 10 years ago, when he was at Harvard and she was at Wellesley, acting in the only college play she ever appeared in, "Much Ado About Nothing." Harvard student Segal wrote the music for the production.

Ryan O'Neal, who plays the boy in the film, comes out of six years of "Peyton Place" on TV. He is also starring in another film made from a recent book, Hugh Atkinson's "The Games" (*Simon and Schuster*). From Harvard athlete in "Love Story" he goes to the role of Yale Olympics contender in "The Games," the screenplay for which is also Erich Segal's work.

Erich Segal, the Brooklyn-born son of a rabbi, was graduated from Harvard in 1958 as Class Poet and Latin Salutatorian—the only man in Harvard history to receive both honors. "I have a theory," Mr. Segal told the press, "that Jewish teachers of the classics are secular rabbis. Homer, after all, is the nonreligious Bible of western literature." College interest in Greek and Latin goes in cycles and right now Mr. Segal finds "it is coming up again from the nadir."

A writer of the Hasty Pudding Show while he was in Harvard, Mr. Segal worked his way through graduate school there doing play-doctoring, a fact which prompted the William Morris agency to suggest he was good enough to start branching out on his own. He has written an unproduced musical with Richard Rodgers, which led in turn to work ("along with dozens of other writers," he is quick to say) on "Yellow Submarine." After the Beatles' hit, his career as a screenwriter was set, and in addition to "Love Story" and "The Games," he has also written "R.P.M." ("Revs Per Minute"). That's a movie that Stanley Kramer is filming now with Anthony Quinn in the role of a radical college professor in the midst of campus revolt.

Harper & Row, which publishes Mr. Segal's serious classical books, had been wanting him to try his hand at a novel. The first draft of the screen play of "Love Story" came first, and then at the urging of Harper editor Gene Young, the first draft of the novel. "She taught me to write a novel as I went along," Mr. Segal says of Miss Young. He alternated between screenplay and novel, then rewrote both at the same time. The film follows the novel closely. Mr. Segal is well aware that the big hurdle both reader and viewer have to get over, is the first sentence in the book— "What can you say about a twenty-five-year-old girl who died?"—and the opening bit of the movie, in which, even before the credits, it is made clear that Jennie (Ali McGraw) will die.

"It took me two weeks to write the first page of the novel," Mr. Segal says. "I learned on the job." Nevertheless, he views his greatest satisfaction as a writer in being a novelist, "where you can really control your own material" more than a screen writer can.

The very touching wedding scene in the novel in which the two young people take their vows before a Unitarian minister by reciting poetry to each other is based on a real-life wedding of two of his students which Mr. Segal witnessed.

The characters in "Love Story" evolved first in Mr. Segal's mind. He decided to put them together "in a story out of a 1940s movie," that would still reflect the college scene as he himself knew it intimately in the early 1960s before student riots and the furor over Vietnam. Jennie, the pivotal figure in the story, he sees as "a typical smart-assed Radcliffe girl, a lovable bitch." Miss McGraw had some trouble at first by playing her too gently. The four-letter words that are so much a part of Jennie's character are left in the film, but "there is no gratuitous nudity," Mr. Segal says.

" 'Love Story,' " he told *PW*, "is based on what I have observed among my students, living as I do right on campus. It deals with today's personal commitment of one to one and the quest for a permanent relationship which begins much younger than it used to. The old, mindless football game dating is gone. The question of sexual morality is irrelevant, but there is much less 'swinging' among young people now than in the old days."

Students look at professors today with different eyes, too, and Mr. Segal knows it well. "The day of the glib lecturer is over. The teacher himself has to offer some kind of personal involvement to his students," he says. The grueling combination of teaching, writing film plays, continuing as a novelist and writing on classical subjects is one Erich Segal intends to hold to as long as he can. Next year, on a partial sabbatical, he will write on "The Death of Comedy" for Harper & Row. So far, he maintains, the only thing in his life which has suffered is "sleep."

Margaret Shedd

"MALINCHE was a whore, but since everything this woman did was on a grand scale, so too, was her whoring." So begins Margaret Shedd's new novel, "Malinche and Cortes" (*Doubleday*).

Malinche was the Indian woman who became Cortes' mistress, his chief interpreter, mother of his son, and one of the key instruments in the Spanish conquest of Mexico and of the Indian people.

It is this extraordinary role of Malinche as lover, betrayer of her own people and manipulator of great power that Miss Shedd fastens on in her novel. Pocahontas, after all, survives her legends merely as a stiffly painted portrait in Elizabethan court garb. Malinche fades into history, the time and place of her death unknown. Yet the Indians of Mexico named a volcano after her.

Fascinated by "Malinche and Cortes," and wanting to know where in the book fact ends and fiction begins, *PW* interviewed Margaret Shedd recently. She lives part of the year in California, and when in New York, in an apartment hotel with her husband, who represents the Mexican sugar industry, and with an amiable elk hound. This creature has been known to arouse in visitors the same combination of awe and curiosity the first horses imported into the New World by Cortes inspired in the Aztecs.

There are grown children in the family, including a talented dancer–writer daughter, who recently choreographed one of her own short stories, and grandchildren. Miss Shedd began writing while the family was living for several years in British Honduras, and continued during her years in Mexico,

By Barbara A. Bannon. From *Publishers Weekly* 199, no. 9 (March 1, 1971), pp. 21–23.

where she was a director of the Centro Mexicano de Escritores in Mexico City. She has published five novels and her short stories have been anthologized in "Best American Short Story" and "O. Henry" collections.

There is very little in the archives of Mexico on Cortes and Malinche, Miss Shedd told *PW*, although, interestingly enough, what survives of any contemporary Indian references to Malinche is not particularly ugly or cruel. Bernal Diaz, the historian of the conquest of Mexico, mentions her several times, rather sentimentally. One rather touching contemporary reference to the relationship between Cortes and Malinche reads, "He treated her like a wife."

Yet a woman able to remain with Cortes for seven years, going on harrowing campaigns with him, serving as his interpreter and go-between with the Indians he was conquering, must have been made of strong stuff.

"My own attitude towards Malinche is ambivalent," Miss Shedd says. "She was such a violent woman. She had enemies (one of whom, Maldonado, later vilified her). She managed to kill some of her enemies."

The son Malinche bore Cortes was acknowledged by him and taken to be raised in Spain. He served as a soldier, and became part of the retinue of the legitimate son Cortes had after he married a Spanish noblewoman. Both sons were named Martín (a curious but common Spanish custom), and when the foolish legal heir to Cortes became implicated in the first rebellion in the New World against the crown, both suffered sorely. Yet both survived. Malinche later married one of Cortes' captains and bore him a daughter.

The legitimate line founded by Cortes exists in Spain to this day. What happened to the descendants of Malinche and Cortes is not known beyond about the second generation, but Miss Shedd would like some day to try and trace the trail.

It was on her last day in the archives in Seville that Miss Shedd found the most human reference to Malinche in a document in old Spanish set down by scribes. In it, Fernando, the grandson of Malinche and Cortes, appealing to the crown for some favor, dictated, "My grandmother was a great woman."

Cortes, Miss Shedd believes, "was the most noble and manly of the conquistadores. He wrote magnificent letters. Pizarro and some of the others were absolutely vile, going in for atrocities worse than My Lai."

Cortes' will, which Miss Shedd found in Spain, is an extraordinarily open-minded document for its time. In it, the man who had conquered Mexico and destroyed a great Indian civilization, when faced with death, wrote that he was not at all sure that it had been a good thing to make slaves of the Indians.

"I would like some day to write a novel, not pro-black or pro-white, but on the notion of color," Margaret Shedd told *PW*. "In Mexico there is still great consciousness of color. The Mexicans can accept being a pure-blooded Indian like Juarez, or being pure Spanish. It's the mixture of color that is hard for them to accept.

"Yet there is a kind of capacity for friendship in Mexico that is rare, and I believe it comes from the Indians."

Miss Shedd and her husband were once in a serious jeep accident in a remote part of Mexico. They were rescued and treated with immense kindness by the local farmers, all Indians. Miss Shedd (whose mother had died when she was three), hovering between consciousness and unconsciousness, imagined one of the Indian women was her dead mother. The woman fell into the role at once, using it to help her survive.

"I think it takes a special dignity to meet a person's needs like that," she says. Yet when a taxi driver was sent out from the nearest town to take Miss Shedd and her husband to a hospital, the taxi driver ordered one of the rescuing Indians out of the cab when he offered to make the trip and help support Miss Shedd. "The Indian was very dark," she recalls, "and the taxi driver was not."

Much as she loves Mexico, Margaret Shedd has not been back there for two years, since the terrible killing of students and workers by police during the riots at the time of the Olympics.

"I might not be welcomed back," she says candidly. "I have not kept my silence on that subject. These shootings transcended the political. They were aimed directly at the young. The young are our treasures and if you go about shooting them, who's going to be left? The older I get, the more I love the young. The thing I believe in most of all in the world is continuity, and not just a family continuity either. These young people know about it. They are very giving when they know an older person who is not against them. Continuity is giving and taking. The world belongs to all of us, but some of today's young are so much more giving than the rest of us." It's a point of view that seems worth passing on, these days.

Isaac Bashevis Singer

ISAAC BASHEVIS SINGER's new novel, "The Manor" (*Farrar, Straus*) has unusual origins, but then Mr. Singer, as we learned from a conversation with him the other day, is an unusual writer.

A publisher's biography of him states that "although he originally wrote in Hebrew, Mr. Singer long ago adopted Yiddish as his medium of expression." "I will tell you about that," Mr. Singer began in an opening phrase that he used several times in the interview. "Forty years ago, Hebrew was not really a living language. It did not have words for many everyday things like 'saltshaker.' So I switched to Yiddish. Now, because of the State of Israel, Hebrew *is* a living language, more living than Yiddish. But Yiddish is still alive."

Because as a writer he uses a lot of idiom, Mr. Singer presents a translation problem. He was 46 years old before his work was first translated into English. Before that he was an "underground" writer, a fact about which he is philosophical. "I'm accustomed to being known only to Yiddish readers," he said. "I feel that I'm known and not forsaken. It's good enough."

The origins of Mr. Singer as a writer and "The Manor" as a book are in Yiddish journalism. Since 1935, when he arrived in New York from his native Poland, Mr. Singer has been associated as a journalist with the *Jewish Daily Forward*. In 1953–55, every Saturday the paper carried a long installment of the story that is now "The Manor" and will be a subsequent, still-to-be-translated novel. ("The Manor" represents only the first half of the story that the paper published.)

By Roger H. Smith. From *Publishers Weekly* 192, no. 16 (October 16, 1967), pp. 17–18.

"The audience for the *Forward* is shrinking," Mr. Singer commented, "but those who read it—fifty, maybe sixty thousand people—are very attached to it. It is their life. It is really a daily magazine—the news they get from TV—about Jewish life around the world. It is an émigré audience, and for the people reading it the *Forward* is an exercise in nostalgia. When I write my stories for the paper, I put in a lot of description. For my books, I take a lot of this description out."

Mr. Singer's nephew, Joseph Singer, and Elaine Gottlieb, wife of Mr. Singer's late friend and editor, Cecil Hemley, translated "The Manor" into English. "For me," Mr. Singer said, "translation is a collaboration because I have English but I do not trust it because it is not literary English. I will go over the text with the translator 50 times. It is slow. When they translate me into other languages, they use the English text. That is why I worry over the text so much."

First and foremost a storyteller, Mr. Singer in his own reading prefers the "older writers who tell a story" to the "young writers who want to teach a lesson. When a writer tries to teach, there is no story."

With five novels, three collections of stories and a book of memoirs to his credit, Mr. Singer recently has turned to the writing of children's books and will have two new ones (his third and fourth) out this fall: "The Fearsome Inn" (*Scribners*) and "Mazel and Shlimazel" (*Farrar, Straus*). "I enjoy writing for children, and I wonder why I didn't start doing it years ago," he said. "The laws of writing are the same for adults and children, but children are a more critical audience: their taste hasn't been spoiled."

Poland is the setting of most of Mr. Singer's writing, but he has no intention of going back there. "It's destroyed to me. It's a new world which would only mix me up," he said. "You can't go home again—it's certainly true for writers."

Instead, some of Mr. Singer's next work to be published will have American themes and settings. "It's only lately," he said, "that I felt I knew enough about America to write about it. I've just sold a story with an American setting to *Playboy*."

"*Playboy*, Mr. Singer?" asked his surprised visitor.

Mr. Singer shrugged and smiled. "I do what I can do," he said.

Ramona Stewart

NOT THE LEAST fascinating aspect of Ramona Stewart's new novel, "Casey" (*Little, Brown*), is the parallel it offers, straight out of the pages of history, between the situation of the poverty-stricken Irish in New York City between the 1860s and the 1880s and that of the Negroes and Puerto Ricans in big city ghettos today. It was a time when the Irish, fleeing famine at home, were crammed by the thousands into squalid tenements, when "No Irish Need Apply" signs were everywhere, when "native Americans" recoiled in horror from Irish poverty and the inevitable crime it bred. It was also, as "Casey" shows, a time when the Irish in New York City were to rise in a series of the most bloody riots in U.S. history (ironically, many of their victims were Negroes) and then take over political power of the city through Tammany Hall. Estimates of the numbers killed in the draft riots led by the Irish in New York during the Civil War range into the thousands.

PW talked to Miss Stewart the other day about the research she did for "Casey." Every leading character in the novel, with the exception of the clever fancy lady, Claire, is either a real person or based on someone real, Miss Stewart said. McGuire, the early Tammany leader of the novel, who starts Casey on his own rise, is a composite of John Morrissey, later a maverick politician, and a certain Sheriff O'Brien.

Casey, himself, is based on the character of Richard Croker, who, like his fictional counterpart, started life as a New York City fireman (his fire engine, the "Pacific Mutual," was so loaded with weapons for street fighting it was known

By Barbara A. Bannon. From *Publishers Weekly* 193, no. 14 (April 1, 1968), pp. 7–9; and from *Publishers Weekly* 198, no. 7 (August 17, 1970), pp. 17–18.

as the "Arsenal") and who later rose in the echelons of Tammany. Dr. McGlynn, the idealistic Catholic priest of the novel, was a real person, whose church, St. Stephen's, still stands on New York's East 29th Street. After the events depicted in "Casey," he fell into disfavor with the church for his support of the economist, Henry George, was excommunicated, but later reinstated, ending his days in upper New York State. Mme. Rastelle, the high-priced abortionist of "Casey," who specialized in helping out politicians' mistresses, actually existed, as did her husband (his specialty was treating "gentlemen's diseases," and you can see his ads in the back issues of old New York newspapers).

Mme. Rastelle's abortion mill was first located in what is now an electrical repair shop opposite the Cheese of All Nations store on Greenwich Avenue in the Village. Her later place of business, rather unfortunately chosen from the Irish Catholic point of view, was near the new St. Patrick's Cathedral. (Miss Stewart thinks, as nearly as the records can tell, it was located where Best's fashion store stands today on Fifth Avenue.)

Many of the buildings that are still standing on Bleeker Street in New York's Greenwich Village were there when that street was known, as it is in "Casey," as "the street of the mistresses." Where the present Alfred E. Smith housing project stands were once the worst waterfront dives in New York City. The site of the Negro orphanage beset by rioting Irish during the draft riots of the Civil War was about 46th Street and Fifth Avenue. As part of her research for "Casey," Miss Stewart went on walking tours of New York. The bulk of her research was done in the New York Historical Society, in the files of the newspapers of the day (New York had no fewer than seven papers in the late 19th century, some of them scurrilous, all of them remarkably detailed in their coverage of the news) and in the New York Public Library, both the main branch and a small Hudson Street branch in Greenwich Village, which she found rich in New Yorkiana.

The Irish block-voted their way out of poverty via Tammany Hall, Miss Stewart said, imposing on Tammany the sort of tribal hierarchy they had known at home. If they clung to the notion that "a little honest graft" never hurt anyone, they were only doing on their own scale what Boss Tweed, Jim Fiske and the robber barons of the day did among the establishment. However corrupt, the power Tammany gave them, was their lift out of grinding poverty.

The mortality rate in New York City at the time covered by "Casey" was three times that in Dickens' London, Miss Stewart told *PW*. Mindful of the city's recent garbage strike, she informed us that as recently as during Civil War days pigs were scavenging in the streets of the city, while garbage collection contracts were let out again and again on subcontracts until no one was ready to accept any responsibility for handling the actual work.

Insofar as Tammany Hall was concerned, it was only when "Honest John" Kelly (who appears in the final chapters of "Casey") came on the scene that the mantle of religiosity was draped over what had been until then a rather gamey group of politicos. From then on up to Jimmy Walker's heyday, any Tammany man who got a name for women or drink was out. It was a follower of "Honest John" who came to Mme. Rastelle, probably a short time after the period covered by "Casey." There he obtained from her a supply of abortion pills, supposedly for his mistress, and when he got them, promptly turned the now elderly lady over to the police. Her 30 years of protection ended, the Madam went home to her fine mansion and killed herself "in the Roman manner," by permitting herself to bleed to death.

RAMONA STEWART's new novel, "The Possession of Joel Delaney" (*Little, Brown*), has a title which is meant to be taken literally. It deals with "the state of being dominated by, or obsessed with, evil spirits" (American Heritage Dictionary).

In a time in which so much has been written about the occult, Miss Stewart has come up with an aspect of the subject which has not been done to death, and which will be altogether new to most readers. Yet the fascinating thing is that what she is writing about actually exists right now as a very potent influence in the lives of many people living in America in the 1970s. It is Puerto Rican witchcraft and the religion of *Espiritismo*, which Miss Stewart calls "the fastest growing religion in the world today."

Espiritismo involves a worship of spirits of air and water. It exists throughout the Caribbean and South America and in Puerto Rico it has been strongly tinged with *Obeah*, an African magic. It deals in spells, charms, potions, communication with the dead, and it makes bizarre use at times of some of the saints and symbols of Catholicism.

Thus, St. Martin de Porres, an officially canonized black Latin American saint in the Roman Catholic Church, is powerful in *Espiritismo* as the patron saint of the *barrios*. St. Barbara, whose historic existence as a real person is now doubted by the Catholic Church, is alive and well in *Espiritismo* in a black version which represents Shango, the Yoruban African god of thunder. There is even a Saint Judas in *Espiritismo*, and as a notable example of religious eclecticism, the Jewish *mezzuzah* has now become a Puerto Rican charm.

A very considerable amount of this kind of research went into "The Possession of Joel Delaney," and Romona Stewart talked with *PW* about it recently. The idea for the book came from an actual incident she heard of several years ago. A friend of hers, non-Puerto Rican, had fallen in love with a Puerto Rican girl. Gradually he became aware that there was some influence at work over her that he could not understand. He discovered that she was very much in the power of a Puerto Rican "witch woman." Efforts to make the girl see reason were to no avail, and one day she simply vanished into Spanish Harlem and was never seen by the man again.

"There is an awful lot we don't know about the working of the unconscious and the nature of the group unconscious," Miss Stewart says. "In some cultures if you tell a person there is a death curse on him, he will die."

The idea of possession by evil spirits is as old as the cuneiform tablets of Babylon and has existed in every culture and time from ancient China and Africa, through the Middle Ages, down to the 20th century.

"Very weird things do happen," Miss Stewart says, "from the fire dancers of Bali who walk on hot coals to the possessed people in Africa who are found on top of high trees with no idea how they got there. I'm not prepared to say *how* such things happen, but I know they have been reported by reliable witnesses."

Many of the spiritualist ideas of *Espiritismo* were first imported into Brazil in the 19th century, Miss Stewart found in her research. They were brought in by wealthy and cultured people of the upper classes who had been influenced by a European spiritualist named Kardec. These ideas filtered down from the top to the poorest level of society in Brazil and throughout Latin America, where they were influenced by other magic and witchcraft concepts.

Millions of people in Brazil in modern times have watched as a man without medical training performed surgery before cameras, claiming he was being guided through *Espiritismo* by the spirits of a Japanese, a French and a German surgeon. His story as "The Surgeon of the Rusty Knife" was published in this country in 1967 as a chapter in a book entitled "Jesus of the Spirits," published by Stein and Day.

In her research for the new novel Miss Stewart also visited many of the *botanicas* in New York City where the "religious goods" of *Espiritismo* are for sale, and where, sometimes behind the scenes, as she describes in the book, very serious and frightening religious ceremonies take place.

"I would say I had come in to buy a talisman," she told *PW*, "and then try to get talking casually to the proprietor. Some people would refuse to talk, but most of them would show the same feeling anybody in any line of work would have if you were showing an interest in a subject in which they considered themselves to be experts. These people really believe thoroughly in *Espiritismo*."

After delving into the occult to this degree, *PW* wondered how Romona Stewart might react if one day, like the heroine in "The Possession of Joel Delaney," she were to discover that dark forces of witchcraft in which someone honestly believed were at work against her. She thought a minute.

"I would not say it was silly," she said. "I wouldn't dismiss it lightly as just a joke. I would probably try to protect myself as best I could."

Jacqueline Susann

THE ELEVATOR MAN taking a visitor to the 24th story penthouse of Jacqueline Susann and husband Irving Mansfield, overlooking Central Park, had this to contribute: "You're going to a great place. They're real down-to-earth people."

Miss Susann, a bit huskier-voiced than usual after a long bout with bronchitis and double pneumonia, was getting ready to go out on the road for the three-month personal promotion tour she regularly gives each of her books. This time the focus is on the just-published "Once Is Not Enough" (*Morrow*). Mansfield, a former press agent and television producer, whose clients have included Alexander Woollcott, Dorothy Thompson, Fred Allen and Abe Burrows, now acts as her personal manager and has a very important influence on the promotion of the Susann books, behind and in front of the scenes. They met when she was an aspiring TV actress, a career she gave up when they married because "I don't believe in absentee management in marriage," and they have been together 28 years. It is Mansfield who can reel off instantly worldwide sales figures (hardcover and paperback) on "Valley of the Dolls" (between 24- and 27-million) and "The Love Machine" (14-million).

Dancing around the Mansfield apartment was Joseph, the black toy poodle which is the successor to the much-loved Josephine of "Every Night, Josephine" (35,000 copies sold in hard covers, 600,000 in paper). Josephine died in 1970, and her ashes repose in a small gray casket that the Mansfields keep in their kitchen "because that was Josephine's favorite room. She loved to eat."

By Barbara A. Bannon. From *Publishers Weekly* 203, no. 14 (April 2, 1973), pp. 12–14.

Casting its light on the living room scene this day was Morrow's special publication day gift honoring the new Susann novel. Against a blue, simulated book cover backdrop, about the size of an electric heater, shocking pink neon lights blazed out the message, "Once Is Not Enough." Miss Susann thinks that on a night when she can't sleep it may prove soothing to sit up and contemplate this evidence of Morrow's considerable delight at her signing with that house, after Bernard Geis and Simon and Schuster.

Miss Susann is friendly, candid and shrewd. Over the years since "Valley of the Dolls" she has managed to bring down on her head more rage on the part of other writers and certain reviewers and more gratitude on the part of booksellers than almost any other best-selling novelist today.

"How do I view myself as a writer?" she says. "I'm a storyteller. When I wrote 'Every Night, Josephine' I was writing out of love for Josephine and to prove to myself I could write. When I was nine or 10 a schoolteacher predicted, 'Jacqueline should be a writer. She breaks all the rules but it works.'

"When I wrote 'Valley of the Dolls' and my other two novels I was trying to write out of all the experiences I had known or seen happen in New York City, plus what I could add out of my own imagination. My books are not *romans à clef*. I start out with a basic premise and follow it to a logical conclusion. Given the kind of life you live, certain types of characters will always come into your books. It takes me three years to write a book. I suffer. I still cry when things go badly.

"It was Jim Aubrey, then of CBS, who told me, 'Don't read the bad reviews. They will ruin your future writing.' Ever since then Irving has kept all the bad reviews from me, but I know I've had them. It was often, 'Let's get Jackie,' but I've kept my cool. I can say to myself, 'Look, I've written a best seller. They *haven't*.' Then there are all the people who say, 'She's dreadful, but I'm going to imitate her.' "

One of the more explosive personal encounters between Jackie and a critic involved her in a clash with John Simon on a David Frost TV interview program. Simon, who admitted he had read only 30 pages of the Susann novel he was attacking, drew from her: "Little man, who *are* you? I've heard of Simple Simon and Neil Simon, but I've *never* heard of you." The session grew so stormy that a man in the audience jumped up and tried to attack Simon on Jackie's behalf. The Frost episode is still rerun on TV. Every time it is, Miss Susann pockets $320.

Jacqueline Susann is Philadelphia born, the only child of a schoolteacher mother and a well-known portrait painter father, whose bust is prominently displayed in the Mansfield living room. She makes no secret of the fact that she adored her father, and that her relationship with him gave her insight into the much more obsessive, neurotic father fixation of January, the heroine of "Once Is Not Enough."

"There are some girls who just can't make the swinging scene today, and January is one of them," she says. "I'm a product of what my father wanted me to be. I'm very Philadelphia in my thoughts. A Philadelphia girl is much more family oriented. She feels her roots like a New England girl. Philadelphia is a state of mind you can't ever quite escape."

Asked why she has changed hardcover publishers three times, Miss Susann was very frank. "I would have stayed with Bernie Geis for life after 'Josephine' and 'Valley,' " she says, "until I found out he was going bankrupt and hiring other writers who were going to imitate me. It cost me $400,000 to buy my way out of the Geis contract." [Editor's note: Bernard Geis Associates filed bankruptcy proceedings in November of 1971.]

"I went to Simon and Schuster because of Michael Korda," Miss Susann told *PW*. "As an editor he was marvelous, but if I'm out breaking my back in a city promoting my book on 10 TV programs I want enough copies to be there in the stores. I also like to know every minute how I'm doing in sales and reorders."

It is her contention that Simon and Schuster did not give her what she wanted in this respect on "The Love Machine." [A spokesman for Simon and Schuster sees it somewhat differently, however. He told *PW*: "Miss Susann submitted her proposal for her new novel ('Once Is Not Enough') to Simon and Schuster first. It was declined because we felt the financial terms she was seeking were not justified by the commercial expectations of the book. Approximately 290,000 copies of 'The Love Machine' were shipped in this country and another 10,000 in Canada. There were 39,000 returns. Subsequently, 34,000 copies were remaindered. These figures certainly demonstrate there was more than adequate inventory in bookstores throughout the country."]

Miss Susann has had the same paperback publisher from the beginning—Bantam Books—becoming with "The Love Machine" the first big-name author to acquire 100% paperback rights to her work.

"Jackie and Irving are wonderful to deal with," reports Esther Margolis, vice-president of Bantam and director of public relations and publicity. "They've never refused anything I asked them to do. They're real pros." Miss Susann was a pioneer in early morning breakfast-rap sessions with the route men who service the paperback racks.

"I'm maniacally loyal to anybody who is really wonderful to me," Jacqueline Susann says, and all the evidence bears her out. Vince Rivers, then at Hudson's book department, gave her her first autographing party for "Josephine." He's now at Wanamaker's in Philadelphia and he has first bookstore claim on Miss Susann's personal appearances. The "Today" show gets her first on publication date, but radio's Long John Nebel puts her on the day after because he had her on his late night talk show when nobody much else wanted her.

"The only reason I went with Morrow was because of Sherry Arden," Miss Susann told *PW*. [Miss Arden, now a vice-president at Morrow and director of publicity there, met the Mansfields some years ago when she was involved with a TV special investigating the phenomenon of "Valley of the Dolls."]

It was over lunch at "21" with Sherry Arden, Lawrence Hughes, president of Morrow, and James Landis, who was to become her editor there, that Miss Susann announced her decision to go to Morrow. "Let's stop all the bullshit. I'm coming with you," she remembers saying. "Larry Hughes rushed out and came back with three dozen roses and the comment, 'They say when you want a girl, you have to woo her.' "

The love affair between Miss Susann and the booksellers of America goes back a long way. When "Every Night, Josephine" was published, Miss Susann got into the habit of rushing into any bookstore that featured "Josephine" in the window and thanking them profusely. "They were so used to authors coming in with complaints, they really appreciated it," she says.

"I have kept more bookstores from going under. They all tell me that. When a hot book comes along, people come into the bookstores asking 'What else is good?' and the stores sell three of four more books because people have come in to buy mine. It's like having a hit Broadway show that draws people into the next door theaters as well."

According to Morrow, the firm had a 150,000 first printing of "Once Is Not Enough," went back for 25,000 more before publication and by the official March 20 pub date had sold 105,000 books. Jacqueline Susann's own plans after she gets through with the current promotion tour involve a musical based on "Valley of the Dolls," to be called "Helen and the Three Dolls," and a sequel to the first Josephine book, "Good Night Sweet Princess," about the poodle's experiences as a celebrity. She would also like to continue the story of the twins born to Neely in "Valley of the Dolls" in another book of their own.

Tom Tryon

For Tom Tryon, who says, "I fell into acting by accident; I wanted desperately to become a writer," the last six years, in which he made the successful transition between the two worlds, have been pivotal. "Meeting Bob Gottlieb," he says of his editor at Knopf, "changed the whole course of my life." Working with Gottlieb, Tryon has written "The Other," "Harvest Home," "Lady" and the current "Crowned Heads," collecting along the way book club sales, reprint sales, magazine sales and, for "Crowned Heads," not one but two movie sales, with film options on the other two novellas that make up these inter-related tales of Hollywood. "Fedora" will be directed by Billy Wilder; "Bobbitt" by Michael Bennett of "Chorus Line."

Tryon, who has been living for the past two years in New York on Central Park West, is a relaxed interviewee, professional in his approach to his writing, dispassionate in his attitude toward his own Hollywood years.

He grew up in Wethersfield, Connecticut, outside Hartford, one of the oldest towns in the state, with a colonial village green. Tryon fictionalized it as the setting for "Lady," which was written out of his own New England boyhood experiences.

"One night we had a dinner party for some of my parents' old friends in town," he recalls, "and talk turned casually to the fact that there was a white woman in Wethersfield with a black lover. Everyone was quite cool about it and I realized how the town attitudes had changed. In my boyhood such a woman would have been stoned on the green." Delving into his own memories of the past, Tryon introduced this fiction-

By Barbara A. Bannon. From *Publishers Weekly* 210, no. 1 (July 5, 1976), pp. 14–15.

al plot element into "Lady." "There really was a 'Lady' in my life," he says, "my mother's best friend. My brothers and I adored her."

After graduating from Yale, with plans to go to New York to study art in the fall, Tryon got a summer job painting scenery at the Cape Playhouse in Dennis, Massachusetts, then run by Richard Aldrich, to whom the late Gertrude Lawrence was married. The opening production was Shaw's "Caesar and Cleopatra," and Tryon, along with every other available body, was pressed into service as an extra.

"When I came off stage there was a talent scout from RKO, then owned by Howard Hughes, in the audience and he really did try the whole Lana Turner soda fountain discovery bit on me, incredible as it seems," he says.

Guided by Gertrude Lawrence, "who was my great mentor," he went to New York instead, but to study theater and acting, not art. "It was never too difficult, I never starved, I got nice small parts." When he did go out to Hollywood, where he was to stay for some 19 years, starring with great attendant publicity in Otto Preminger's production of Henry Morton Robinson's novel, "The Cardinal," it was to begin a period of his life that would end in great frustration.

Along about 1968 Tryon "was at an ebb in my life, very disappointed in Hollywood. I wanted to get out of acting. Since I was very young I had wanted to write and I was also interested in directing. It seemed to me the best thing to do was to write something and try to get to direct it. I became a recluse, trying to teach myself writing, but I had no way to get feedback on what I was producing." What it was, was the novel that was to become "The Other."

At this time there was a man named D. A. Doran (whose family had been part of the Dorans in the old Doubleday, Doran imprint) in the story department at Paramount. He agreed to read what Tryon had written—and he liked it. "I still remember the day we met in the Polo Lounge in Beverly Hills," Tryon recalls, "and he gave me my first encouragement, telling me he thought the work was about 90% done." Doran arranged to have the work, then in its eighth draft, sent to Bennett Cerf at Random House. Cerf turned it over to "an editor who shall be nameless," says Tryon, "but she had to be one of the most difficult women in the world." Her advice to him was: "Edit the book." His reply: "But that's my problem, I don't know how to." Tryon offered to come to New York to talk with her, to be told, as he recalls it, "Don't do that. I don't want my authors breathing down my neck."

Reclaiming the manuscript, Tryon decided that he had to have an agent and, through a friend, Cynthia Lindsay, who had written books about the movies, was put in touch with Phyllis Jackson.

"Three days after receiving the manuscript Phyllis called me and asked me to hop on a plane for New York because the manuscript was at Knopf, where Bob Gottlieb was very enthusiastic about it. That was in May,

1970. We worked together, Gottlieb and I, for about six weeks. It was mostly a matter of simplifying, paring down. Meeting Gottlieb was a unique experience for me. He was so generous, strict but not crushing, and when he said to me, 'I think you could have a career as a writer,' it was like being in analysis, everything became new and different. The day he took 'The Other,' I started my second novel.''

"Fedora," the first story in "Crowned Heads," was an idea Tryon had been thinking about for four years ever since a photographer friend told him about an extraordinary experience he had had in New York's Metropolitan Museum when a woman came up out of nowhere and began talking to him. It was Greta Garbo. A lot of the scene in the Louvre between Fedora and the young writer is taken from that real-life experience.

"Bobbitt" was the hardest part of "Crowned Heads" to write, Tryon discovered. "It wasn't easy trying to maintain a feeling of lightness and wonder in order to arrive at a happy ending." "Bobbitt" is based on a real person, he says, and his experiences in trying to come to terms with the fantasy world he knew as a child star.

Tryon intends to write more about Hollywood but not until he has produced one or two other novels before returning to that scene. "I get up in the morning and go to the typewriter and type regular as clockwork," he says. "Actors have to have enormous discipline. They are not at all dizzy. Also, I come from New England where if you do not develop good work habits you get whipped."

Tryon did get to be executive producer and screenplay writer on the film version of "The Other," but he looks back on the way the film turned out "with sadness. I had no real control over it." Now Michael Bennett wants him to do the screenplay for "Bobbitt" and he is very keen on the idea, although he admits, "Bob Gottlieb is totally against my having anything to do with Hollywood. He says, 'You got out of the tank, why go back and swim with the sharks?' "

Looking back on his own stay in Hollywood, Tryon sees it this way: "When I got off the plane there in 1955 to star in my first movie, the kind of leading man I was trained to be was already passé. The great ones are dying off today. Now it's all very hyped out there. There's a craziness to today's Hollywood scene that is in many ways lots of fun, but it lacks the old elegance. I miss Hollywood not at all. I'm delighted to be in New York. In Middle America an aura still hangs over you from the silver screen and people want to talk about Hollywood. I'll do it, if they want, but I find it all very boring. Nowadays, if someone comes up to me on the street and says, 'Say, aren't you a movie star?' I say, 'No, I'm not.' But if someone says, 'Hey, I read your new book,' my eyes light up like a Christmas tree and I'll stop and talk gladly."

Leon Uris

DENVER—"This is the very best book I've ever written!" declares Jill Peabody Uris, clutching Leon Uris' big new novel "Trinity," recently out from Doubleday.

She may have a valid claim at that. The book is dedicated to her—"as much a part of these pages as the Irish people"—and to anyone who sees them together they give the impression of a remarkably close husband-and-wife working team.

"That's because I tell her what to do," Uris declares. "That's because photography and writing complement each other," says she, in almost the same breath.

They seem in any case to have resolved a real equality in marriage. She reads, and criticizes, his manuscripts. He criticizes, selects and discards her pictures. Then each makes constructive comments on the other's work. It seems to work: last December their joint by-lines appeared on "Ireland: A Terrible Beauty," a handsome collection of her photography (selected from some 5000 shots), with eloquent text by her husband. And it is clear she has made her contribution to "Trinity" as well.

Denver has seen little of Jill and Leon Uris, although they first met and have lived since their 1970 marriage in nearby Aspen, which they vow they will always call home. Leon, who was first attracted to the skiing, then started acquiring lots at ever-soaring prices, has lived in the old Colorado mining town since 1964, which is just about all Jill's adult life, if not a bit more. "She's a child of the Peace Generation," he says.

Uris had not submitted to a series of author interviews in

By Stanton Peckham. From *Publishers Weekly* 209, no. 13 (March 29, 1976), pp. 6–7. Reprinted by permission of Stanton Peckham.

several years until an old friend, Barbara Taylor, general manager of the Playboy Club in Denver, persuaded them to come to town.She hosted a gala St. Patrick's Day launching party for "Trinity" at the club. The Mayor of Denver was there to present the Urises with a plaque. So was Encyclopaedia Britannica's former president Maurice Mitchell, Chancellor of the University of Denver, which has just taken the Aspen Institute under its wing. So was the dean of Denver novelists, William E. Barrett, another Doubleday author now working on his own novel about Ireland. And so were some 250 others in or around the fringes of the Denver book business. Doubleday representatives were invited guests, and everyone found an autographed copy of "Trinity" at his or her place.

Uris, appearing considerably more mellow than he did back in the days of "Exodus," charmed his audience with a brief and beautifully handled after luncheon talk about himself, Jill, Aspen and "Trinity," but chiefly about Ireland, the similarity in background between the Irish and the Jews in the Middle East, both old peoples now determined to fight in their homelands for justice.

Uris told *PW* later he first became deeply interested in Ireland when they were in London watching events across the way on British television. It was spring 1972, and he thought he saw an opportunity for Jill to do a stint of photojournalism. They spent Easter reconnoitering Ireland, then went back in June and stayed until November. Then they went back again, just to be sure.

Everywhere they went, he says, the Irish were warm-hearted and wonderful to them. When they first went north, Jill, true to her Peace Generation outlook, was inclined to be nervous. But her professional training in photography soon showed through, and eventually when a bomb exploded near them she would grab her camera and demand: "Where is it? Where is it?" Soon she was taking Leon on photographic expeditions that even Uris, an ex-Marine, didn't find too comfortable.

In Belfast, someone asked Uris: "Are you Protestant or Catholic?" "I'm Jewish," Uris told him proudly. But that didn't satisfy the Irishman. "Yes, but are you Protestant-Jewish, or Catholic-Jewish?" Uris found that both sides in Ireland identify with the Israelis.

Almost inordinately pleased to be classified as a Jewish writer, Uris sees no reason why that should restrict his writing to Jewish subjects. After all, he points out, five of his eight novels are on non-Jewish topics. He is primarily a storyteller, and, as he puts it, "You can write Westerns in any part of the world!"

As for actual writing conditions, that's not why he lives in Aspen. "When you start writing, you might as well be in a dark room, as long as it has four walls." The mountain scenery is just out there. In fact, it seems he must hardly notice it, for he refers to "a very good view" of his next-door neighbor's house, which is ugly.

"Trinity" is the fifth Uris novel to be published by Doubleday. One each were brought out by Putnam, Random House and McGraw-Hill. He will probably remain a Doubleday author, at least as long as Kenneth McCormick, his editor, is there. But he is a tough bargainer, too. On his trip to Denver he let it be known that he would not sign copies of "Trinity" in any store that had less than 10 copies of "Ireland: A Terrible Beauty." This automatically limited him to the Scribner bookstore, where he and Jill happily found, and signed, the required 10 copies. ("Trinity" is priced at $10.95; "Ireland" at $24.95.)

With both books out in about the same season, which does Uris prefer writing, fiction or nonfiction? Not admitting it in so many words, he gives the definite impression that fiction is his métier, although acknowledging that "a crash course in history sets up a novel."

So "Ireland" set up "Trinity." The novel, beginning in mid-19th century, ends with the Easter rising in 1916. Why not go on beyond that? Uris cites the quotation in the front of the book, from Eugene O'Neill's "A Moon for the Misbegotten": "There is no present or future—only the past, happening over and over again—now."

This in itself emphasizes his pessimism about Ireland, and it is not arrived at quickly or superficially. "Battle Cry" and "Exodus" were clear in his mind from the beginning, and it was just a matter of getting them on paper. But "Trinity" required much more thought. "This had to come out a day at a time and a page at a time. I had to do a lot more pondering."

Reference books required for the writing of "Trinity" he got from the Denver Public Library, which had also provided for the needs of James Michener in writing "Centennial." But he hasn't been reading recent books about Ireland. Jill read Jimmy Breslin's "World Without End Amen," but was pretty critical of it. "He tried to draw a conclusion from a tiny bit of pertinent matter," she complains. "And he came to a false conclusion."

It may be some time before another Uris novel appears. Leon (and Jill, of course, goes with him) has been campaigning for presidential hopeful Sen. Henry Jackson, and intends to intensify his efforts in New York, Pennsylvania, Ohio and California. That he confidently expects to keep him on the road right up to next November.

Then home to Aspen—and typewriter and camera.

Peter Ustinov

PETER USTINOV lumbers into the Oak Room of the Algonquin Hotel for lunch, stuffed into an expensive, slightly unconventional suit, half-biting his lower lip, his eyes a little squinted, the whole face set in that dog-about-to-be-kicked look that has become his trademark. Successful playwright, actor, director, novelist, essayist, short story writer, mimic, film director and producer, TV star, cartoonist and opera director; winner of two Oscars, three Emmys, a Grammy and a New York Drama Critics "Best Play" Award. A Star.

He sits, orders a drink, and begins to talk. Ostensibly, our meeting is to discuss his new book, a novel called "Krumnagel" (*Little, Brown*). It is about a boorish, Midwestern chief of police who gets into a drunken and violent political argument with a leftwing Scottish shop steward in a London pub. As the Scotsman reaches for a handkerchief to wipe his perpetually running nose, the American picking up on the wrong cue reaches for his gun and shoots his interlocutor dead.

The darkly comic consequences of this encounter, give Mr. Ustinov an opportunity to contrast the American and British systems of justice and to reflect upon the two national mentalities, as he sees them.

But Peter Ustinov can apparently talk knowledgeably about almost anything, and does not talk about any one thing for very long. He is also a superb mimic, a talent which his listeners treasure and which he finds irresistible. During the course of a two-hour lunch, he offered no less than nine separate imitations, including a Turkish lawyer, a Hollywood producer, a famous director, two renowned

By Douglas N. Mount. From *Publishers Weekly* 200, no. 17 (October 25, 1971), pp. 15–17.

British barristers, a Swede, a Dane and customs officials of various nationalities.

He also talked about his book, his work and his life. On "Krumnagel":

"I really haven't got the Agatha Christie kind of mind. I have to drag myself into these things. But I was fascinated by the idea of the two legal systems and how different they are, and I was constantly surprised at how vague the law really is. I visited two different lawyers, both very distinguished, both very famous, and both came to entirely different conclusions about what would happen if this incident had actually occurred. I know nothing about the law really, though I discovered that one of my short stories is included in a collection of great legal fiction!"

On the theater: "I'm not comfortable with the theater. I find the whole process disturbing. I cannot bear the pressure of first nights. For me, it is an intellectual and emotional sport, performing, and I don't think it's any good to perform eight times a week, as you do in New York. I don't think the public is getting its money's worth. You can't keep it up that often; you lose the athletic interest."

The discourse is interrupted by a wizened, smiling old man who approaches our table, arm extended. "Petah," he shouts, "how dare you come to New York without telling me!" It is Leonard Lyons, the café society gossip columnist. Greetings are exchanged, and the columnist moves on to other tables. "I must say, he's got old," says Ustinov, *sotto voce*. "That was a shock. He's table-tottering!" A pause, he wheels the no-neck head to face you, and is off again, this time on the contemporary audience:

"People have changed *enormously*. It's *extraordinary*, what's happened. It's *terrific*, what you can do now. The whole audience has changed. For instance, I had to have lunch the other day with my eldest daughter's . . . well, what used to be called 'intended.' What that means now is that if you call her at eight o'clock in the morning, *he* answers the telephone. The lunch was a *disaster*. He had hair down to his shoulders and was very cool, you know, and I tried to play the father and it was just *awful*. But a few days later, when an interviewer asked him if he would feel overshadowed by a well-known father-in-law—he is a stage director—he said, 'No, I think he's an all right fellow.' "

On film: (He has just written and directed a film, "Hammersmith," starring Richard Burton and Elizabeth Taylor. Though he has not obtained distribution, the project is notable in that the Burtons received no salary, only a percentage of the gross.)

"They're really very similar, film-making and writing. The one thing I like about fiction is that you can get a *voluptuous* sense of a phrase. You can play with it, fawn over it. I like that, that voluptuousness. Film is a hybrid form at the moment. The critics treat it as an art form. But it isn't really an art form, it's a cocktail of artistic sympathies. It is to my mind at its best a poignant and appealing form of journalism set on an artistic base."

On America, and why he doesn't live in it: "I've always been rather frightened of the temptations of America. I've always had the feeling here that, for example, Orson Welles would have had a better career if he had been a Finn. You know, he would have become a sort of a Bergman.

"The artist in America is immediately the victim of *enormous* financial considerations. I don't really want to be a Studebaker. I mean, I'd really rather not be in that race at all. I'd rather make hit-and-run raids. Of course, I also find I'm much freer here than the natives, because it is acknowledged that my loyalties are different, and therefore I am listened to with interest especially on the television."

What are the difficulties, in terms of his own work, of working in America?

"It is very difficult to satirize something that comes 110 percent of the way to meet you."

Gore Vidal

GORE VIDAL, whose new novel "Burr" (*Random House*) has acquired a special pertinence because of the events of Watergate, was interviewed by *PW* recently via trans-Atlantic telephone at his home in Italy. He noted that the same "executive privilege" claim President Nixon is now making with regard to the Watergate tapes was first employed by then President Thomas Jefferson at the time of Aaron Burr's treason trial. Jefferson claimed to have in his possession a letter which proved Burr's treason, but invoked "executive privilege" against releasing it. Chief Justice John Marshall (a cousin of Jefferson's) ruled against him; the letter was submitted to the jury trying Burr, which decided that the evidence for treason in it was insufficient. Burr was acquitted.

"I suppose I started thinking about Burr while I was a kid," Vidal told *PW*. "My Auchincloss stepfather's mother was a descendant of the Burr family. At school everybody told us he was a villain, but at home he was a hero. I was interested and a bit bored. Then I saw a family painting of Burr's beautiful daughter Theodosia, one of the few portraits of her that exist, and that intrigued me.

"After a long and stormy life in contemporary American politics myself I began to think, 'How did we get into this mess?' and about five years ago I started planning the novel. Burr seemed to me like a good center from which to survey the early American political scene, the perfect person to take a sophisticated look at the Republic. It was a very small scene indeed. For 50 years a handful of men—Washington, Jefferson, Madison, Hamilton, the Adamses—ran the

By Barbara A. Bannon. From *Publishers Weekly* 204, no. 18 (October 29, 1973), pp. 12–13.

United States as if it were *their* political machine. Of course the mere mention of George Washington's name affects most of us like a whiff of chloroform, but when I started looking at the footnotes in history books about these men (Washington included), I became convinced that they were very interesting men indeed."

Interesting they are, as Vidal portrays them through Burr's eyes—but men as jealous of their personal ambitions and prerogatives as any 20th century politician. Burr, on the other hand, emerges in the novel as more honorable in his own way than many of his enemies.

A large part of the Vidal novel purports to be excerpts from unpublished Burr memoirs. These are actually Vidal's inventions, although he does weave in many authentic Burr sentences, taken from his letters and a journal he wrote in French for his beloved daughter Theodosia, in which he was extraordinarily candid about his sexual experiences.

"Burr did write a good piece of a history of the Revolution which has vanished," Vidal says. "He had a very good prose style. If he had been less lazy he could have been a very considerable historian."

One of the intriguing sidelights on history included in "Burr" is the suggestion that Martin Van Buren, who went on to become President of the United States, was Aaron Burr's illegitimate son. "Everybody sort of knew about it at the time," Vidal says. "John Quincy Adams's diary practically says it was true. I think it very probably was, and for a curious reason. Van Buren's mother was an older and plainer woman and as a young man Burr was always attracted to older women. Van Buren was a blond version of Burr."

The relevance today of the "executive privilege" issue in "Burr" is "absolutely coincidental," Vidal says. "I was writing the Burr treason trial scenes exactly a year ago, with no idea at all of what was to come."

As Vidal sees President Nixon's claim to executive privilege, "it will be overthrown." He is one of those who believes that the President did have knowledge of Watergate. "In civil court the President is not a sovereign," he says. "He must submit to the law, like any other citizen. The line of argument Nixon's lawyers are using, that he must be impeached first, is one that has never appeared in print or in court before. He can still be President in prison—and personally I hope he will be."

Asked to compare the political climate of the Burr–Jefferson era with that of today, Vidal told *PW*: "This is very tricky. I feel certain storm warnings that people will say my book is a defense of Nixon in that it proves that politicians were dishonest then and connivers at the very beginnings of the Republic. This country has always been pretty tough politically, but not until now did any President try to set himself up above the law to this extent—although Jefferson came pretty close to it with some of his imperialistic land acquisitions.

"Then, too, the men who founded our Republic were so much more intelligent. They could all use the English language so well—not like the near-English computerese our politicians speak today."

Viewers of television will be interested to know that the BBC and Time–Life hope to co-produce a major TV series based upon "Burr." The Vidal novel is also about to become the second one to be singled out by John Leonard in the *New York Times Book Review* for a "The Last Word" comment of his own. Taking personal exception to what the official Sunday *Times* reviewer has to say about the book, Mr. Leonard will plump for it unequivocally as he did once before in the case of Doris Lessing's "The Summer Before the Dark," in contrast to what his reviewer has to say.

Kurt Vonnegut, Jr.

THE TITLE PAGE of Kurt Vonnegut, Jr.'s new novel reads like a billboard: "Slaughterhouse-Five or THE CHILDREN'S CRUSADE A Duty-Dance with Death by Kurt Vonnegut, Jr. A fourth-generation German-American now living in easy circumstances on Cape Cod (and smoking too much), who as an American infantry scout *hors de combat*, as a prisoner of war, witnessed the fire-bombing of Dresden, Germany, 'the Florence of the Elbe,' a long time ago, and survived to tell the tale. This is a novel somewhat in the telegraphic schizophrenic manner of tales of the planet Tralfamadore, where the flying saucers come from. Peace."

To which, having read the book and chatted with its author at *PW* recently, we echo: Peace.

Mr. Vonnegut is a comfortably slouching man who has eased into his middle years under the burden of a droopy moustache and the knowledge that he had a story to tell that was virtually untellable. This is a terribly tired refrain that runs through "Slaughterhouse-Five" like a litany: "So it goes. So it goes." It tells everything its author feels about the thing he has been carrying around in his mind since he was an "American infantry scout" imprisoned with fellow/POW's in a slaughterhouse just beyond the pattern of American fire-bombs that razed Dresden one night toward the end of World War II and killed 135,000 people—more than the number of dead at Hiroshima.

Mr. Vonnegut's marvelously inventive humor, which has won him admiring readers right through the roster of his wacky-sad novels from "Mother Night" and "Cat's Cradle" up to "God Bless You, Mr. Rosewater" and his

By Albert H. Johnston. From *Publishers Weekly* 195, no. 16 (April 21, 1969), pp. 20–21.

newest and saddest, has always carried that overlay of resignation. "So it goes" means what we all know it means. It's significant that Mr. Vonnegut was a *prisoner* during the Dresden holocaust: Weren't the 135,000 dead? Aren't we all? It's no accident that today's college youth, the babies of that war, were the first to latch onto Mr. Vonnegut's sci-fi brand of humor that says life is a space voyage, and man, you'd better hold on and learn to love and be kind—and not believe the lies that send you off into crusades.

Lest that seem impossibly solemn, let us say that Mr. Vonnegut is a man with an easy laugh. He's a big, shaggy, anti-flamboyant fellow whose modesty and candor are wholly a part of his so-it-goes life style. We asked him why, in "Slaughterhouse-Five," he didn't make a Big Scene of the actual fire-bombing of Dresden which his bewildered anti-hero and alter-ego, poor Billy Pilgrim, witnessed, and which so traumatized Billy that he had a breakdown and was never the same again.

Mr. Vonnegut shrugged. We suspect his reply was his way of being kind to us.

He answered, "I don't remember it." To have pressed further, we knew, would have been an unpardonable invasion of his creative privacy. Then Mr. Vonnegut volunteered his heartiest laugh. If we were going to interpret his simple statement, we'd have to do it in retrospect. After all, Mr. Vonnegut was a young soldier in that war; he'd been there—what's more, he'd survived and become part of the historic silence that has since enshrouded the bombing of an "open city"—and his "war novel" has weighed too heavily on him, for too long, to bear anything but laughter. Mr. Vonnegut said, "I guess I wasn't much of a soldier. I went from Private to Pfc. in three years—" and laughed, glanced away, turned back and added pointedly, "with a war on." So it goes.

Mr. Vonnegut lives and does his writing in a big house in West Barnstable on Cape Cod—an old, elm-shaded village, where he has lived for a long time with his wife and six children (three adopted nephews). That parentheses suggests more than a sad family story we had no wish to probe: Mr. Vonnegut is a warm, generous man who takes care of kids—that's the whole thrust of his new novel, when you think about it. The war-babies who are the new generation have thought about it; they're reading Vonnegut today because they know he knows what they only sense—and they like his sardonic humor, the detached wisdom he learned when Billy Pilgrim-Kurt Vonnegut looked on Dresden burning and turned into a pillar of salt.

We asked Mr. Vonnegut what he's writing now—we even asked him, as a matter of curiosity, what *poetry* he might ever have written, and again enjoyed his laughter: he'd been invited to read some of his (unpublished) poems to students not too long ago and was told candidly he's "one of the world's worst poets." We also asked him whether he'll continue to use his trade-mark characters and mythical inventions such as science-fiction

writer Kilgore Trout, Mr. Eliot Rosewater, the fantasy-planet Tralfamadore, the town of Illium.

He's well into a new novel, he said. It's a fun book—"The title is
'Breakfast of Champions,'" Mr. Vonnegut told us, "and I'll be using
Tralfamadore and some of the old characters—I guess." But not Billy
Pilgrim. Billy and Dresden burning are behind him. Mr. Vonnegut in recent years has been visiting campuses; he has spent considerable time at
the University of Iowa's Writer's Workshop. The young dig him, he digs
them. We have a hunch they're on their way to Tralfamadore, laughing it
up all the way—a certain pillar of salt their receding landmark.

Alice Walker

"THE BLACK WOMAN is one of America's greatest heroes. The cruelty of the black man to his wife and family is one of the great tragedies. It has mutilated the spirit and body of the black family and of most black mothers."

The speaker is Alice Walker: young, black, articulate and talented. Her first volume of poetry, "Once," is in a second printing for Harcourt Brace Jovanovich. Her fine first novel, just published by that house, "The Third Life of Grange Copeland," deals directly with this theme of the poor black man's oppression of his family and the unconscious reasons for it.

This is not a theme that finds favor with a lot of black militants, and Miss Walker recognizes that. It does not stop her from believing, however, that "not enough credit has been given to the black woman who has been oppressed beyond recognition. Her men have actually encouraged this oppression and insisted on it."

Alice Walker was born in Eatonton, Georgia, in 1944. She attended Spelman College (an all-black "finishing school" about which she has some highly acid comments), and graduated from Sarah Lawrence, has worked on voter registration in Georgia and on Head Start in Mississippi, and is now writer-in-residence at Tougaloo College in Mississippi. She lives in Jackson, Miss., with her white husband, Mel Leventhal, a member of the NAACP Legal Defense Fund, whom she met while both were active in the voter registration drive in Greenwood, Miss., in 1966. They have one child, Rebecca.

Talking about her own southern background to *PW* re-

By Barbara A. Bannon. From *Publishers Weekly* 198, no. 9 (August 31, 1970), pp. 195–197.

cently, Miss Walker said, "My mother *is* a strong black woman. When I was four she would not take me with her into the fields (the family were tenant farmers) but she persuaded the local first-grade teacher to let me come and sit in class where I was allowed to make chickens out of soap and so on. In a way I had my own Operation Head Start."

In the black schools she had to attend Miss Walker remembers "three or four good teachers." Then she went to Spelman, which she characterizes as "an extremely genteel place dedicated to training black girls to come out like southern whites. You wore patent leather pumps and white gloves. Chapel, sororities, cotillions and debutante balls were big. Every black mother's ideal was to have her daughter marry a medical or law student." (The irony of this is that by quite another route Alice Walker *did* marry a lawyer—a white one.)

Nevertheless, Miss Walker admits that "many wonderful people have come out of Spelman." She would like to write a novel some day about six black women graduating from a college like Spelman and what becomes of them—a sort of black "The Group," perhaps.

It was one of her teachers at Spelman, the white activist Staughton Lynd, who was instrumental in getting her to Sarah Lawrence, where his mother was her don for two years.

At Sarah Lawrence there was plenty of freedom to do or say what you pleased—no obligatory being locked up on the campus at 7 P.M. as Spelman had insisted. What Miss Walker did not like about Sarah Lawrence was the fact that "kids really just talked things to death without any action."

Muriel Rukeyser taught Alice Walker in a poetry course there, and had a profound influence on her (most of the poems in "Once" were written at Sarah Lawrence). From Miss Rukeyser she came to the attention of the agent Monica McCall, who introduced her to Hiram Haydn, now her editor at Harcourt.

Alice Walker Leventhal and her husband are realistic about life for an interracial couple in Jackson, Miss., today. It is not comfortable. It can be dangerous. They expect eventually to live and work in the North, where the NAACP Legal Defense Fund is trying to set up offices in all the bigger cities.

Nevertheless, history of a kind was made recently in this very southern city when the first interracial marriage took place legally and officially and made the front pages of major papers including the *New York Times*. The participants were staff members who work with Mel Leventhal, and he and Alice worked long and hard to help them break through the tangle of red tape and prejudicial bureaucracy to get to the altar.

Irving Wallace

"SOME OF MY READERS may think me presumptuous," said author Irving Wallace, and his large earnest face wrinkled with concern. "You see, I've never tackled a subject of such magnitude before."

He was talking about his upcoming novel, "The Word" (*Simon and Schuster*), which deals with the discovery of a new gospel in the ruins of Ostia Antica, Italy, and the effects this discovery has on the lives of a former nun, an international syndicate of Bible publishers and a radical Dutch minister whose hair is long enough to be braided.

In New York recently, Wallace was squeezing in some interviews before going back to California. Now he paced the confines of his luxurious red velvet suite at the Hotel Plaza. The suite, usually reserved for the Shah of Iran, was so thickly carpeted that all conversation sounded muffled.

"I'm invariably nervous before a book of mine comes out," Wallace confided. "I'm nervous about the reviews. Can you see them? 'Irving Wallace rewrites New Testament.' And I'm worried about my publishers. Will they put big enough ads in the *Times*?"

At this point Dan Green of S&S, who was on the couch opposite him, suppressed a smile. Previous Wallace novels have sold upwards of 70,000,000 in hardcover and paperback. "The Word" 's first printing is to be 60–75,000 copies; it seemed certain there would be a large ad campaign.

Then why worry? "Because, no matter how successful you are, every writer wants to be appreciated," Wallace explained. But, he said, he no longer gets upset when critics pan his work. "I'm a popular novelist who loves to tell sto-

By Patricia Bosworth. From *Publishers Weekly* 201, no. 1 (January 3, 1972), pp. 21–23. Reprinted by permission of Patricia Bosworth.

ries and if the literary establishment can't accept me as I am, that's too bad." However, he admitted not liking comments such as "if you've read one Wallace, you've read'em all."

"Because it's not true! All my books are different." He gave two of his latest novels as examples: "The Man," which was about the first black president (and which will soon be released as an ABC movie starring James Earl Jones), and "The Seven Minutes," which concerns censorship and pornography.

He denied that "The Word" is "quintessential Wallace" because of its heavily researched plot and lively set of characters. " 'The Word' is unlike anything I've ever written," he insisted. "It's the story of one man's search for truth, for meaning in his life. On another level, it's everyman's search for some divine truth, for miracles."

Mr. Wallace has had the idea for a book like "The Word" for over 30 years. The catalyst? "A personal one. Although I'd been raised a Jew and attended synagogue in Kenoshua, Wisconsin, where I grew up, I consider myself agnostic. But I've remained fascinated by the mystique, the influence of Jesus. Did such a man ever exist? We have very little proof. Was he the Messiah? A politician? What was he really like?"

After the Dead Sea Scrolls were discovered, Wallace realized a novel could be written about what happens to the people involved with publicizing and authenticating a similar document—a new gospel perhaps. This gospel, which would be contained on one moldering piece of parchment, would contradict the existing accounts of Christ's life—and even His supposed death.

As he always does, Wallace began by researching his subject thoroughly. First he read and reread the Bible, including the New English Bible because he believes this translation incorporates the most advanced knowledge available to scholars.

Then, from 1963 to 1969, he traveled throughout Europe and the U.S., stopping at key museums to pore over ancient religious manuscripts. He talked to more than 50 experts—from Vatican City prelates and Aramaic scholars at the Louvre, to members of the Yale Divinity School.

Everybody had a different response to his question: "What would happen if a new gospel were discovered which gave a more detailed picture of Christ's life?" Some churchmen refused even to speculate on the subject. Others said it would certainly cause an ecclesiastical revolution. A group of young clergy stressed that the existing gospels needed radicalizing and a 20th century interpretation. They believed that anything that seemed scientifically implausible, like the Immaculate Conception and the Resurrection, should go.

Wallace incorporated these opinions into the story of "The Word." He also drew heavily on discussions with archaeologists and with Nobel Prize winner Dr. William Libby, who invented the radio-carbon device which can authenticate gospel parchment. Side-plot backgrounds were researched with equal diligence. They included locations such as Devil's Island, the Gutenberg Bible factory and a Greek monastery where no women have been allowed for over 2000 years.

Once he completed the research, as well as a detailed outline chapter by chapter, Mr. Wallace began pounding out "The Word" in his isolated Brentwood study. For eight hours a day, six days a week, he typed four separate drafts on his battered old Underwood, the same machine he's had since he was 12. "I use it for good luck," he says.

The most difficult task? "Creating a gospel. It's such an audacious thing to do. I didn't include the whole thing—and I threw entire portions out. Of course I checked with biblical experts to make sure it sounded right." (It does.) In Wallace's version (which he credits to Christ's brother, James) Jesus survives the Crucifixion and lives on for 19 years, finally preaching in Rome.

"The Word" is being published this March. Is he relieved to be finished with the project? "Yes. But I'm already thinking about another novel I want to do, on an even bigger subject." Bigger than God? He nodded emphatically. "No, it's not about man's journey through space, but that's a good guess."

His other plans include a nonfiction book and an assignment to cover the 1972 political conventions for a major newspaper syndicate—"which I can't name because they want to announce it themselves."

Why is he still compelled to write so prodigiously when he doesn't need the money?

"I write because I love to write. It's my consuming passion. After I sold 'The Chapman Report' to the movies, some of my friends said, 'You'll never write another book because now you don't have to.' And I told them, 'You're dead wrong.' I'd been grinding out screenplays for years and hating every minute of it. Now I knew that money was going to give me the freedom to write and write and write. Write books. Write exactly what I wanted. The hungry writer writes what he's told so he can eat."

Wallace paused and the lines in his large earnest face seemed to disappear. He looked younger than his 56 years. "One of my favorite writers, Somerset Maugham, said, 'Writing is an adventure of the soul.' Every time I start a new novel it's a grand adventure. Needless to say, I can't wait to begin again."

Joseph Wambaugh

LOS ANGELES—The arrow points at a doorway marked 208, on the second floor of the Hollenbeck Division police station. The sign below it says "Detectives."

Through the door walks Sgt. Joe Wambaugh, finished with the day watch in Hollenbeck's burglary section. He's a mild-looking man, with short-cropped, thinning hair and an engaging smile. Joe Wambaugh doesn't have a Sgt. Friday syndrome. He doesn't look like a cop, but could pass easily for a clerk or salesman, except for a conspicuous bulge of pistol on his hip and the momentary flash of handcuffs when the vent in his stylish new green sportcoat parts.

Wambaugh is probably the only detective in his division who drives an immense, air-conditioned Imperial. It's one of the few luxuries he has allowed himself as a result of his first novel, "The New Centurions" (*Atlantic–Little, Brown*), which has to date sold over 80,000 copies in bookstores, and perhaps 200,000 more through the Book-of-the-Month Club.

"Aside from the financial security it's given me," says Wambaugh, relaxing over a plate of *carnitas barbacoa* and a bottle of Cervesa Corona at a Mexican hangout on Brooklyn Avenue, a few blocks from the station house, " 'Centurions' has made me a kind of rebel within the department, something I'm not accustomed to being at all.

"I'm embroiled in a conflict with [the office of L.A.P.D.] Chief Ed Davis over whether or not a policeman can publish something without the department's prior approval and consent."

The issue was first raised by Davis's office just before the

By John Weisman. From *Publishers Weekly* 200, no. 8 (August 23, 1971), pp. 33–35. Reprinted by permission of John Weisman.

publication of "The New Centurions." The chief objected strongly to some of the incidents in the book, notably a passage in which one of Wambaugh's protagonists falsifies an arrest report to obtain a conviction. "Liars and perjurers in my department," the chief is reported to have written patriarchally, "are cast out!"

"I think," says Wambaugh, pondering his glass, "that, disregarding the obvious constitutional issue raised by the censorship of a writer, and the problem—a long-standing one, by the way—of whether or not the department 'owns' a cop during his off-duty hours, the problem arose because 'Centurions' depicted cops as human beings, complete with rotten moods and frailties, and not as the robots people are accustomed to seeing on television shows about policemen.

"Police work, after all, isn't a glamorous trade. The cop on the street is resented because he's basically a represser of freedom. And these days, given many situations, he becomes a soldier as well, something that was never intended, and which he wants no part of.

"If a cop has failings—if he falsifies a report, or perjures himself at a trial, or accepts free meals or other things, well, it's human nature to do so. We're all looking for a hustle that works.

"Look, who are cops? They're guys from the community—a real cross-section of L.A. Most of the guys I know just drifted into police work, like I did. The pay is good, it's steady work, the vacations are OK. I have the feeling that a majority of the people who get compulsive about becoming cops get weeded out for one psychological reason or another. So why shouldn't cops be human? And why should people resent their having frailties?"

Joe Wambaugh's four years in Hollenbeck Division supplied him with much of the material for his first novel. Although he's been on the force since 1960, and worked all over L.A., he prefers Hollenbeck to anywhere else. "If I were a single man," he insists, "I'd live here. It's a neighborhood much like the one I grew up in, back in Pittsburgh. When my parents came out here and drove around with me, they really felt at home, even though the racial mixture (Mexican–Japanese–Russian–Jewish) is different from the one they're used to."

Currently awaiting the galleys of his next novel, "The Blue Knight" from Atlantic–Little, Brown, Wambaugh is experiencing some normal nervousness about the book.

"I hope it's all right," he says. "It's about an aging cop named Bumper Morgan, and his last three days after 20 years on the force. He's got to make a decision whether or not to retire. But I think that the book could be about any aging man—a soldier, a plumber—anybody. I just don't think of 'The Blue Knight' as a police book, but about someone who's getting old, and has to face it without love. Bumper's an outsider who, all of a sudden, realizes exactly what the consequences of being an outsider are."

Wambaugh's second novel, like his first, took six months to write. But because of the success of "Centurions," he doesn't have to face the trepidations of rejection slips.

"I sent 'Centurions' to Doubleday, which rejected the manuscript," he recalls. "And then Atlantic–Little, Brown took it. I remember that I got three grand as an advance. I'd never had such a wad of money in my life. My wife and I bought an art store with most of it, and we lost our shirts. Then, with $500 that was left, we went to Mexico, just to blow the cash and have a good time. I got horrendously sick, and we ended up coming back flat broke, two weeks early.

"When we got back, there was a call from the publisher that the Book-of-the-Month Club had bought the book, and would I be willing to accept my percentage of $78,000. Well, I had exactly two dollars in my pocket at that point, so I took the family out, and we celebrated our good fortune at McDonald's."

With the money he's received in royalties, plus cash from the sale of "The New Centurions" to Columbia, where it's being filmed by Richard Fleischer, Wambaugh has probably made as much income as he would in the next 10 years as a cop. He doesn't plan to give up his work, though, because he still thinks of himself as a cop who writes in his spare time, rather than as a writing cop.

"A few things have changed," he admits. "We're going to Hawaii for our vacation this year, because my two kids want to fly somewhere. That beats Mar Vista or Disneyland. And my wife is buying things retail now, instead of waiting for a policeman's discount."

As far as his future with the L.A.P.D. is concerned, Wambaugh plans to stay on the force "if they'll stay with me. They have their ways of making you quit if they think you're a rebel, like giving you the graveyard shift at the Harbor, a 75-mile drive one way, or something like that. I could see the administration being mad if I were giving away secrets, but I'm not: there are no secrets to reveal."

How do his cohorts on the force feel about Wambaugh's success? "I'll tell you," he says, ordering another bottle of Corona in excellent Spanish, "I was always a hustler. I mean, I knew exactly what was going on, and how to hustle it. I've tried them all—even selling suits from a station-wagon in the parking lot of the station.

"When the book finally made the best seller lists, my partner, Dick Kalk, who had just sold 400 copies of it to fellow officers, slammed me on the back and said, 'you old S.O.B., you've finally found a hustle that worked!'"

"I think," says Joe Wambaugh, draining his beer and waving for another round, "that that about says it."

Jerome Weidman

JEROME WEIDMAN is a delight to interview, if you can keep up with the dazzling conversational pace he sets. *PW* talked to Mr. Weidman the other day, and the first thing we found out was that while we wanted to talk about the background of his new publishing novel, "The Center of the Action" (*Random House*), Mr. Weidman kept shying away, to talk about his upcoming books, instead. Persevering mightily, we pressed on, and about an hour-and-a half later we all got down to "The Center."

It is understandable that Mr. Weidman is wary of being quoted too much about "The Center of the Action." It is no secret that he once worked as an assistant to Max Schuster in the early days of Simon and Schuster and there are certain possible fictional parallels in the novel between the beginnings of "Mattlin & Merritt" and the beginnings of Essandess.

Nevertheless, "The Center of the Action" *is* fiction, and Mr. Weidman believes that "whereas any good journalist can move in on a situation and report on it," the test of the novelist is what he lets his imagination add. "Without imagination, what the plate in your memory has recorded won't work," he says of novel-writing. "Total recall won't make a good fictional scene. Your imagination has to push the scene around and get the essence of it." Convincing dialog in a novel, he believes, "is not reporting, it's selecting."

" 'The Center of the Action' could have been written by 20 other guys who lived through the same period of publishing I've lived through," Mr. Weidman told *PW*. "But this is my point of view on what happened—and let the chips fall where they may. You have to be ready to do that or you're in trouble."

By Barbara A. Bannon. From *Publishers Weekly* 196, no. 4 (July 28, 1969), pp. 13–15.

"I began to think about writing 'The Center of the Action' when Dick Simon [Richard Simon of Simon and Schuster] died," Mr. Weidman told us. "He was my big brother from the moment we met, when I was 21 and he was 38. He had an almost incredible warmth. Dick made me feel like a member of his family. He was wonderful to me. He said to me, 'You've never been anywhere but the Bronx and Manhattan, and I think we ought to fall back on the old cliché that travel is broadening.' " Accordingly, Mr. Simon arranged for Simon and Schuster to lend Jerome Weidman, as an advance on a long-term loan basis, $3,000, which freed him and made it possible for him to take a trip around the world. The trip, he says, "changed my life and gave me a whole new perspective."

When his fondness for Dick Simon set Jerome Weidman to work on the novel that became "The Center of the Action," he went to Dick's sister, Betty, and told her what he was planning.

She told him, he says, "If you are going to write about Dick, do any God damn thing you want, but be honest," and this, he believes, he has tried to be. Mr. Weidman's long-time friend and editor at Random House, Bennett Cerf, read the manuscript in an earlier draft, and told him, "This is too close to me. I think you and Jim should work on it." So Jim Silberman of Random House became the editor on the book.

For the record, Mr. Weidman will say only one thing about the villain in "The Center of the Action," and that is that it is *not* the publishing figure a lot of people assume it to be. The book is, finally, a novel, he reminds them.

The next Weidman book after this one will be a collection of short stories called, "Dipping Into Capital." It should be along in six to eight months or so. The title comes from a Washington Irving quote to the effect that, "Memory is to the writer what capital gains is to the banker."

It is the book after this, however, that Mr. Weidman is all enthusiastic about at the moment. It is a novel, "Last Respects," and in part it takes off from a grisly real-life situation, not without its humorously macabre side as Mr. Weidman tells it. It seems that the body of his mother, who died at 90, was lost for some 48 hours between hospital and morgue one Christmas Eve a couple of years ago. It may not *sound* funny, but in Mr. Weidman's hands this part of the novel may very well read like "The Jewish Evelyn Waugh," he sees it as being—reference to Mr. Waugh's "The Loved One."

"I always wanted to write a novel about my mother," Mr. Weidman told *PW*. "She represented something very unique in this country, now vanished. Philip Roth and I have had many discussions about this. His is the first-generation American Jewish mother. Mine represents the immigrant."

Mr. Weidman was born on New York's lower East Side (East 4th Street) 56 years ago, when there were, he says, "two cultures at war with each other, but we did not know it. Everybody over 30 was an immigrant and everybody who was a kid was a first-generation American. I never spoke a word of English until I was five." His father had come from Austria, his mother from Hungary. And when the Jewish mother of those days, kept saying to her kids, "eat, eat," it wasn't the running gag it has become. It had real meaning. "She thought she was saving her children's lives in terms of the Cossacks." What she meant, Mr. Weidman says, was "you eat this, because you may not have bread tomorrow."

"Last Respects" will have as a leading character a woman who is a composite of Jerome Weidman's own mother and two other women he knew as a boy on the East Side. The fictional woman will be "a Jewish lady bootlegger, a stunning, raving beauty like Eva Garbor." It's a whole vanished period of American history, Mr. Weidman points out, but in 1920 when the 18th amendment was passed and Prohibition came in, it was a very serious matter for the religious Jews who needed wine for the Sabbath and other services. "The rum runners used to run their boats right into East 4th Street," Mr. Weidman recalls. As a boy, he says, he often got "25 cents to deliver two bottles to a neighborhood wedding. I was a Boy Scout and I used to signal to the boats by flag. So far as we were concerned, all you were doing was helping the family make a living."

The "Jewish lady bootlegger" in "Last Respects" will make the mistake of falling in love with a gentile rum runner, with tragic results when gang warfare breaks out.

And if you think this is all Mr. Weidman has lined up for the future, you are mistaken. "I am 56," he says, "and I can afford to indulge in certain things. I have long wanted to write a massive work like the "Comédie Humaine' or the 'Music of Time' sequence of Anthony Powell, who is, by the way, the greatest novelist working today." The overall title of Mr. Weidman's major work will be "Irons in the Fire." He has 10 volumes outlined, he says, and is "all ready to go" with the first one, "Talking to Midgets." He estimates that it will take him some 20 years to write the whole sequence of novels. "All my life I have been building up to this big project," he told *PW* in closing. "I want to use five or six central characters throughout and to deal with the movers and shakers of my time and what has made that time."

Jessamyn West

JESSAMYN WEST's new book, "Except for Me and Thee" (*Harcourt, Brace & World*), continues the engaging series of stories about the fictional 19th century Quaker family, the Birdwells, which she began some years ago in "The Friendly Persuasion." It is dedicated to Miss West's own Milhouse Quaker grandparents, who are also the grandparents of her cousin, President Richard M. Nixon.

One of the most pleasantly human portraits of the new President to emerge yet was Jessamyn West's recollections of the California childhood they both shared, which ran as an article in *McCall's* a few months ago. In it she somewhat rashly confessed that she had on occasion served as Richard Nixon's babysitter. Interviewers have been plaguing her for "inside Nixon" stories ever since.

"I am a Democrat, but I don't always vote a straight ticket," Miss West said in a *PW* interview the other day. "I have voted for Richard Nixon—but I won't tell you when." She and her husband, who teaches in the graduate school of education at the University of California, live in the beautiful Napa Valley north of San Francisco. When it comes to politics they are staunch liberals, no admirers of the Max Rafferty concept of education.

The Milhouse–Nixon family feeling is obviously very close. Both Miss West's father and the President's taught Sunday school together, and somehow in between the inaugural parade in Washington last January and that evening's ball the President found time for a special reception just for his relatives-"quite a passel of them on all sides," Miss West recalls.

By Barbara A. Bannon. From *Publishers Weekly* 195, no. 17 (April 28, 1969), pp. 31–32.

The Birdwells of "The Friendly Persuasion" and "Except for Me and Thee" are obviously modeled in some respects on what Miss West knows of her own Quaker ancestry. She has in her possession family letters written before the Revolutionary War, documents that the first Milhouse settlers brought with them from Ireland. By an interesting turn of history, the Milhouses started out in Germany, went to England where they served most militantly in Cromwell's forces, and were rewarded, as many of his troops were, with land in Ireland. It was when William Penn went to Ireland to preach the peace of Quakerism that they converted.

Quaker families and Friends' meeting houses, Miss West points out, had to keep a lot of their own records because Quakers were for a long time outside the law, their marriages, births and deaths not recognized for official records. Miss West is fond of her Irish ancestry, too. Her mother was a MacManaman and she and her husband have visited Ireland and some years ago brought back with them two Irish girls, then 11 and 13, who were raised as their foster daughters in their own Roman Catholic faith.

It was Miss West's mother's Irish spunk (quite a bit of which she has obviously inherited herself) that she attributes with helping to bring her through the most difficult period of her life. As a girl in California she contracted such a severe case of tuberculosis that the sanitarium doctor told her parents to "take her home and let her die among her loved ones." Home she went, but her mother "had no intention of letting any daughter of hers die so easily," and she fought hard for her even though Jessamyn was so ill with adhesions from pleurisy that it was not possible for a lung to be collapsed, one of the few treatments possible for tuberculosis at that time.

Her parents, Jessamyn West remembers, were staunch teetotalers, according to their Quaker heritage. The doctor, however, had prescribed a glass of beer every day as a "tonic" during her illness. Her father reluctantly agreed, but he would only buy the beer if the doctor wrote out a prescription for him saying it was "for medicinal purposes."

Parental love and care and her own determination did pull Jessamyn through tuberculosis eventually. "I knew I was going to get well" she says, "the day I had to go down for X-rays and my mother got out a hat for me that I thought was so terrible I kicked it down the stairs."

For years afterwards, Miss West told *PW*, she was still so haunted by what that siege with tuberculosis was like "that the very word 'consumption' in a sentence used to make me tremble." It was while she was recovering from tuberculosis, however, that she first began to write seriously, although she was keeping notebooks of story ideas as early as 12. "I pasted pictures of writers in albums as other girls pasted pictures of movie stars. Katherine Mansfield was Mary Miles Minter to me and my Rudolph Valentino was John Keats."

"Pieces" began to accumulate, many of them merging into the book that became "The Friendly Persuasion" in 1945. Her first encouragement as a writer came from Mary Lou Aswell, wife of Edward Aswell, who was fiction editor of *Harper's Bazaar*; from Mr. Aswell; from Edward A. Weeks and from John Woodburn.

"The Friendly Persuasion" went on to become a highly acclaimed movie directed by William Wyler and starring Gary Cooper and Dorothy McGuire. Its strong pacifist theme, Miss West believes, put it easily 10 or 15 years ahead of its time and took courage for Hollywood to tackle in those days.

The new book about the Birdwells, "Except for Me and Thee," contains material about the Underground Railroad, through which slaves were smuggled to freedom in the North. "Why has no one ever made a movie about the Underground Railroad?" Miss West wonders. "It was a tremendously exciting time, full of hairbreadth escapes, a time when black and white people were working together and whites were dying so blacks could be free."

Another subject she'd like to see treated in a film is the life of John James Audubon. "Leave the birds out of it, if you want. He was an exciting, handsome, rakish man in his own right." Miss West has worked on film scripts herself. She spent nine months on that for "The Friendly Persuasion."

Miss West has written about the past also in such novels as "The Witchdiggers" and "Leafy Rivers." Others of her books, including "Cress Delahanty" and "A Matter of Time," are contemporary.

"I do not want to be typed as an old Quaker lady or Richard Nixon's babysitter," Miss West told *PW*. "I do not really like writing about the past. I prefer writing about now. I think the most effective writing is writing about your own times." All of her considerable body of short stories are modern in setting.

In her writing, Miss West said, she is "interested in situations where people learn, where life is used to some purpose. I do not think I have ever written about a person who is totally defeated. Even the woman in 'A Matter of Time' who decided to take her own life did what it was her own right to do, when she really had no life left to live. It was a triumph for her. My tendency is to write of people who overcome."

Miss West is perfectly aware, however, "that if you acted as if the whole of life was nothing but Quaker goodness you would be a false writer." The time is coming in her writing, she believes, when she will write more out of her own experience. "The person who wants to be a writer must be willing to stick his neck out and make a fool of himself, to give himself away. These are the very things a person brought up as I was, is brought up not to do." It is time for her, she thinks, "to stick my neck out a little more."

"Perhaps I have been too easily pleased with life because I once thought I could not live long," Miss West said. "I have read that Robert Louis Stevenson and others who have had tuberculosis are in many ways the writers who write optimistically."

John A. Williams

A NOVELIST'S ART is usually to imitate life; when life turns around and imitates his art right back, it can be somewhat unsettling. That's what happened recently, however, to John A. Williams, whose latest novel "The Junior Bachelor Society" came out last month from Doubleday.

His book is an often comical, sometimes dramatic but always affectionate study of a group of blacks returning to a town where they grew up together to honor a football coach who had been an idol to them in their youth and who had helped form their ideals. Yes, there was such an experience in Williams's own life. The town where he grew up (and later went to college and got his first job) was Syracuse, in upstate New York, though it is never so identified in the novel. And there was a man in his life like the coach in the book—"His name was Herbert Johnson, and he was a redcap at the railroad station and a sometime numbers runner, and he knew nothing about athletics, but he was like a surrogate father to a whole bunch of us. He was always there when we needed him, helping keep us out of trouble."

And, only a few weeks before the novel was due to come out, Williams got an invitation from some of his old Syracuse buddies: they were planning to have a little gathering to honor Herbert Johnson, and to get together again, and would he come? "It was the strangest thing. Only a couple of the guys in the group had even read the book at that point, but it happened anyway."

All the men in the fictional group have nicknames, and some of those are real, too, though they don't necessarily apply to their real-life counterparts. Williams's own nick-

By John F. Baker. From *Publishers Weekly* 209, no. 23 (June 7, 1976), pp. 12–13.

name back in Syracuse was Chops. "I guess because I liked pork chops," and a cousin of his is Moon. One of the particularly appealing qualities of the book is its easymoving, slangy dialogue, and Williams is pleased to think that his ear is still good. "I've been teaching school now four years in a row, and that helps me keep up with where it's at." (He has been teaching three courses a week in the New York City university system: Afro-American literature, literature and writing and "a rather loose one" on creative writing, which is *not* his favorite course; when *PW* saw him he was looking forward to no more teaching and a lot of writing, after many years in which he has taught in turn at Sarah Lawrence, Swarthmore, the University of Hawaii and the University of California.)

The book itself came out of Williams's fascination with the idea of human values, and how and when they are implanted. "I tell my students nobody knows where an idea comes from. But I wanted to trace the growth of values, particularly in people for whom growing up was tough." He set the book in Syracuse because that's what he knew: "The sort of values you'd get growing up in the 30s in the South, or in Harlem, would have to be very different from those in a small Northern town."

Life has not been easy for Williams, who is now 50 and was a black writer long before it was a fashionable thing to be. He has had, and still has, his share of frustrations. When he wrote the book by which he has been perhaps best-known to date, "The Man Who Cried I Am," he was, he says, an angry man. But that was nearly 10 years ago, and he says now: "I'm still angry, but you can't just be angry all the time. It all depends on the existence of sane values." He feels now that he has come to terms with life to a certain extent, perhaps mellowed. He lives in Teaneck, New Jersey, just across the river from Manhattan, coaches a Little League baseball team in which his young son plays—and, he says: "Right now I'd accept a headline in the *Teaneck News* for hitting a home run as gladly as I'd accept the accolade for a best-selling book."

Even in his literary career, "I've always had to work very hard," he says, adding with asperity: "After Nelson Algren I'm probably the most often rejected Guggenheim candidate in the country." (Book people still recall that a grant for him to work at the American Academy in Rome was rescinded 15 years ago for no apparent reason; Williams claims it was because, as a black, he was about to marry a white woman, which he later did.) And he has certainly covered all the bases possible to a man making a living by writing. He has been in turn public relations man, newspaper and magazine correspondent, documentary filmmaker, magazine editor, novelist, nonfiction writer, lecturer, publishing executive (with Abelard–Schuman) and, of course, English professor. He has written poetry and short stories, and is one of the most frequently anthologized of contemporary black writers.

But by and large, he feels that, with only occasional exceptions, black writers—particularly novelists—have been neglected by American publishers. "P.E.N. is so concerned with foreign authors and their plight, but how about the plight of black authors here?" he asks. He acknowledges that during what he calls "Harlem Renaissance 2," in the 1960s, there was a big push on black authors and black subjects. "For a while there they were publishing everything, but now it's all just as bad as it was before." Black women writers, he feels—and he cites particularly Toni Morrison, whom he especially admires—have it rather easier, because they get added support from the women's movement.

But, as has become his habit, he works away, and currently has three books in progress. The biggest, an ambitious nonfiction work he calls "The Missing Face of Man," will combine anthropology, archaeology, religion and philosophy in "an attempt to seek out the place of black people in the evolution of Western culture, and their relations to the other major cultures." He sees it as a five-year project involving an enormous amount of travel: "I'll have to go around the world at least twice." He also calls it a labor of love, could certainly use a Guggenheim or some other grant in its preparation, and says one of the chief difficulties is that new discoveries are constantly being made in relevant fields even as he writes.

The other two books, proceeding side by side, are both novels. One is about a black missionary in Africa, who is promised a bishopric on his return to the United States, "but doesn't get much," Williams notes sardonically. The other he expects may cause something of a stir, particularly in literary circles, and even its title is eye-catching: "Photo by Jill Krementz." "It will be a study of a novelist who's really made it, the sort of status that brings, and the effects on other writers when a publisher throws a lot of money into one of those blockbuster books."

Williams says it without rancor, having become philosophical about such things, but leaves little doubt it will be a very personal sort of book.

2

Mystery and Suspense

Adam Diment

ADAM DIMENT, author of "The Dolly, Dolly Spy" (*Dutton*), is an elegantly mod young Englishman who looks made to play the lead in the upcoming film version of his own spy thriller. (The role of "dirty-living, quick-thinking, pot-smoking McAlpine" will be played in fact by David Hemmings, star of "Blow-Up.") Right now, young Mr. Diment—that is his real name and he is 23—is sitting pretty. A prolific, but until recently not notably successful writer, he started putting pen to paper seriously when he was attending—of all improbable things for a Chelsea-based gentleman with Regency and Edwardian tastes in clothes—agricultural college.

Agricultural college gave way fast to a stint as an advertising copywriter and Mr. Diment got the idea of trying his hand at a spy thriller. "I'd read a lot of them, and I thought, 'I'd like a crack at this,' " he told *PW*. First crack out, he hit it big. Within weeks after agent Desmond Elliott had brought "The Dolly, Dolly Spy" to the attention of Michael Joseph, the publisher had signed for three Diment—McAlpine stories. Dutton grabbed up American rights. In Britain, the Sunday *Mirror*, which had never bought a first novel before, made plans for a four-part serialization of the book. Eight foreign language rights have been purchased. Due out next spring is "The Great Spy Race," with "The Bang Bang Birds" to follow.

From a publishing point of view, perhaps the most interesting thing about all of this is the concerted drive Adam Diment and Desmond Elliott are making to promote not only the books Mr. Diment writes, but the young man himself.

By Barbara A. Bannon. From *Publishers Weekly* 192, no. 23 (December 4, 1967), p. 15.

A very lively campaign is under way to sell Diment as a pop personality in the same way pop singers or actors are publicized. There might even be the possibility of a line of Diment–McAlpine men's wear or toiletries in the future.

There is no question that Mr. Diment is eminently publicizable. Candid enough to say, "yes, sure," right off when asked if he, like his hero McAlpine, had ever smoked pot, he prefers not to be quoted too directly on the LSD-acid scene; but he does say he found New York's celebrated East Village dreary, dull and depressing. Much is made in "The Dolly, Dolly Spy" of McAlpine's ability as a pilot. "You might say I fly," Diment told *PW*, "but only on the wings of a dove."

In America until Christmas, he is not overly impressed by New York. Whereas in London the kind of mod gear that Adam Diment prefers is taken for granted, New Yorkers, he has found, boggle provincially at flowered vests and flowing ties. "I know I look slightly abnormal," is the way he puts it, "but in London people laugh in a good-natured way about their fellowmen's eccentricities. Here I feel all the time people are watching each other and particularly me—just waiting for a convenient moment to start the stomping."

The "provincial cities" in America are much more to Adam Diment's taste, particularly Georgetown, Washington, "which looked just like Cheltenham—it even had brick pavements which Cheltenham would have ripped up long ago." Favorite American city so far on the Diment tour has been Cambridge, Massachusetts, "very plainly a young person's town, as London is and New York is not."

The American girls Mr. Diment has seen so far, at least in New York, "do not have the softness of London girls." He approves heartily of American beer, "a far cry from the usual English moan," he admits. When it comes to endorsing products, Mr. Diment is already willing to go on record as saying that, "Budweiser is as nice as anything I have ever drunk." Somebody at the brewery ought to be smart enough to play up that one.

Doris Miles Disney

THE TWO LADIES were obviously old and dear friends. Conversing in gentle, cultivated tones, they sometimes finished each other's sentences, as close companions are wont to do; they had even grown to look somewhat alike. And both wore quietly understated summer frocks; one suspected neither would have been caught dead in a pants suit. Even their names—Doris and Isabelle—sounded reassuringly old-fashioned and genteel. The last thing anyone would have imagined would be that these two ladies have spent the last 30 years or so up to their figurative necks in mayhem, murder, ripoffs and assorted skulduggery.

For Doris is the famous mystery writer Doris Miles Disney, and Isabelle is her friend, editor and mentor Isabelle Taylor, who until her recent retirement was editor of Doubleday's Crime Club and discoverer of Mrs. Disney. Their association began in 1940, when Doris sent a manuscript to the Crime Club. Although Isabelle returned the package, she included a long, encouraging letter and urged Mrs. Disney to try again. For reasons she still can't explain, however, Doris let three years go by before she reworked her story and sent it off again. The result was her first published book, "A Compound for Death," and the beginning of a remarkable literary career—as well as a lifetime working relationship between the two women.

Asked in a recent *PW* interview how and why she had started writing mysteries, Mrs. Disney thought for a moment then answered: "Ego, I guess. I had always loved mysteries but had read a few I thought could certainly be better. When I mentioned one in particular I thought was a flop, my sister suggested I try to do better. So I did."

By Jean F. Mercier. From *Publishers Weekly* 204, no. 7 (August 13, 1973), pp. 24–25. Reprinted by permission of Jean F. Mercier.

Forty-five books and 30 years later, Mrs. Disney was in New York to attend a dinner party in her honor given by her longtime publishers, Doubleday. Except for "The Chandler Policy," printed by Putnam's Red Badge Mysteries in 1971, the Crime Club has produced all Mrs. Disney's novels. A hard-working author, she was producing two suspense books a year during the 1960s.

"Oh, but I've slowed down . . ." said Doris when *PW* mentioned that phenomenal record.

"Yes," said Isabelle. "To about three every two years. . . ."

"Talking of ego," said Doris, "I remember well a reporter on the old *Herald Tribune*. He reviewed my first book and stressed that I was not to be confused with Dorothy Cameron Disney. He made it quite clear that she was the better writer; I was crushed. . . ."

Asked if she had also been confused with Dorothy Salisbury Davis, Mrs. Disney said, "Oh, yes!" And she and Isabelle had a good laugh, remembering one fan letter she got which mentioned two of "her" books. "One was mine," she said. "And the other was Mrs. Davis's."

But despite her talk of her writer's ego, Mrs. Disney has some warm words for her competition. "I adore Josephine Tey, for one," she reported, "and Margaret Millar—she's wonderful. I also enjoy Catherine Aird and Evelyn Berckman, particularly the unusual Berckman plots based on archeology. Of course, the mystery fan can't ever be discussed as one kind of reader. The devotee of Mickey Spillane is totally different from an admirer of Josephine Tey. . . ."

"And of you," said Mrs. Taylor. Which brought the talk to the subject of the new permissiveness in the arts. *PW* inquired whether Doris's stories today contained more sex, violence or plain talk than her books of 15 or 20 years ago. After some reflection, she said she didn't think so, really.

"But Doris," said Isabelle, "would you have written quite such sex scenes in 'Only Couples Need Apply' years ago?" Thinking back over books released by the Crime Club, she added, "I think we would have toned them down, don't you?"

"Well, yes; that's true. When sex was part of the plot in my earlier books, I did make it more implied. And I don't think I would have, even 10 years ago, let my character in 'Miss Bessie Lewis Has Disappeared' say . . ." Doris pasued, looked around to see if anyone was in earshot, then whispered, ". . . bullshit!"

In answer to the question of what her plot ideas stemmed from, Mrs. Disney looked surprised, like the man who confessed he was fascinated by the sight of one-legged midgets. (Asked where he could find them, he answered, "*Find* them! But how does one *avoid* them? They're everywhere!") Like him, she finds her plots everywhere. She got the idea for "Trick or Treat" from the Halloween custom, and devised a plot which had her villain arrive, costumed and masked at a party, and shoot a merrymaker dead. "Should Auld Acquaintance Be Forgot" was born when Doris read a newspaper feature about the plight of lonely widows and invented one of her own. "Do Not Fold, Spindle or Mutilate" is based on the modern business of computer dating and tells what happens when a woman buys the service and is involved with a psychopathic would-be suitor.

Buried newspaper items, bits of overheard conversations, odd sights and sounds are the bedrock upon which Doris has built 45 books which sell between 10,000 and 15,000 copies each in the United States and which have been translated into French, Italian, Swiss, Dutch, German, Swedish, Finnish, Norwegian and Spanish. She has also made use of her early apprenticeship in a Hartford insurance agency, where she once worked as an underwriter-trainee. That experience resulted in the character of Jeff DeMarco, insurance investigator and hero of several of her novels. Her friendship with a postal inspector gave her the know-how to write two books based on the misdeeds of people who tamper with the mails: "Unappointed Rounds" and "Mrs. Meeker's Money."

Mrs. Disney was born in northern Connecticut and spent most of her life in small towns like Farmington and Plainville, near Hartford. One of her neighbors in Plainville was the chief of police; he gave her invaluable technical advice.

Doris lives now in Fredericksburg, Virginia, to be near her daughter Elizabeth, newly married—and because she has found there further grist for her mystery mill. "Miss Bessie Lewis Is Missing" has a Virginia locale, as have other projected works.

Authenticity and believable characters are the *sine qua non* of Disney novels, and they have been popular not only as stories but as movie and TV productions. But neither Mrs. Disney nor Mrs. Taylor has been overjoyed by adaptations of some of these books. Like anxious mothers, they dislike seeing some of their "children" changed. And both agreed that they used to find the old live TV productions much more fun than the modern taped offerings. "It was delightful when something unexpected happened. Speaking of the unexpected, Isabelle," Doris went on, "remember my telling you about my monstrous new electric stove?"

She explained that the stove featured a self-cleaning oven, and the serviceman who told her how to operate it had warned her not to open the door for at least two hours after it had turned itself off. "I said one could probably cremate a body in that oven, and he said, 'Sure, if you cut it up first.'"

PW caught a gleam in her eye, one that was reflected in Isabelle's. It seemed highly likely that some future Doris Miles Disney might feature an unusual way of disposing of a body—involving, perhaps, a hot stove.

Mignon Eberhart

GREAT BRITAIN has its Agatha Christie and Dorothy L. Sayers. And we Americans have our doyenne, Mignon G. Eberhart, one of the few mystery writers who is still collecting four-figure royalties from the paperback reprints of her novels published originally in hardcover (by Doubleday) in the early 1920s.

PW didn't learn that from Mrs. Eberhart during its recent interview with her (she isn't the bragging kind), but from her editor at Random House, Lee Wright. And meeting the author of some 57 novels and innumerable short stories, it seemed hard to believe she was old enough to be publishing over 50 years ago. Though her hair is white, she looks a good 20 years younger than her actual age.

Mrs. Eberhart (she insists on the "Mrs.") married when she was very young and stayed married to Alan Eberhart until his death last February. "Alan was a civil engineer," she explained. "And his work took us to so many places . . . we lived all over the world. While he was busy, I tried my hand at a book and sent it to Doubleday. They published it, and that was the beginning. Then, during the Depression, the writing was a godsend. I was so glad to help out by earning money from books and stories. And I was lucky too that we had traveled so much and had lived in various locales long enough to get authentic details into the stories."

Mrs. Eberhart believes strongly in writing only about places she knows personally. "But one of my books is about Hong Kong ['Message from Hong Kong'], where I had never been, so I researched the city; I also got advice from Bennett Cerf and other sinologists. I read all about jade in a

By Jean F. Mercier. From *Publishers Weekly* 206, no. 12 (September 16, 1974), pp. 10–11. Reprinted by permission of Jean F. Mercier.

beautiful book put out by Gumps of San Francisco. . . . That reminds me of the young man who wanted to be an expert on jade and went to learn from a talented teacher, a very old man. The gentleman put a piece of the stone into the boy's hands and told him to hold it tight. Then he began to talk about philosophy, men, women, the sun and almost everything under it. After an hour, he took back the stone and sent the boy home. The next day, the student returned; the procedure was repeated and so it went, for weeks. The boy was quite frustrated—when would he be told about jade?—but was too polite to interrupt his venerable teacher. Then one day, the old man put a stone into the boy's hands and the student said instantly, 'That's not jade.' "

Mrs. Eberhart feels this is a good example of how a writer learns the craft. "It's like hearing music: listen, listen, listen. And look, observe, see. It's a matter of absorbing, sometimes without conscious effort, like blotting paper."

Her books have been translated into at least 16 languages and Mrs. Eberhart said she thought the stories were popular abroad because people of other nations, other cultures, are intensely curious about Americans. "They want to know what we wear, what we eat, about our priorities and our problems." That curiosity may be one reason but another is the universal appetite for a sound mystery, a puzzle to be solved, which all Mrs. Eberhart's stories offer and which earned her the 1971 Grand Master Award from the Mystery Writers of America, in recognition of her sustained excellence as a suspense writer.

PW asked Mrs. Eberhart about her favorite authors but she hesitated to single out a mere few. "I never miss an Agatha Christie or a Ngaio Marsh—they are old friends, of course. But my real love is for the brotherhood and sisterhood of the genre. And I think I enjoy mysteries and suspense novels for the same reason most fans do—they demand *participation* on the part of the reader. I love mystery writers as a breed, and am so glad to belong.

"I find it incredible that some people still rather sneer at mysteries. A man I know and consider a friend was tactless enough to remark to me that nonfiction—what he called 'serious' literature—was edging out novels and mysteries. So while I don't think of myself as a name-dropper, I found an opportunity to mention the enchanting afternoon I spent cruising the Potomac on the *Sequoia* with President Truman, one of my readers.

"It takes special training and stern discipline to write a convincing mystery," Mrs. Eberhart insists—and currently she finds her work habits the only sure healing agent after her recent bereavement. "I do my stint every day except Saturdays and Sundays. Those days, I reserve for taking care of my house, always have. I am a housewife. Someone has to do it! Even when I have help, I'm glad I'm a woman, who can do her professional work at home. A man writing at home can't bear to hear the vacuum cleaner. A woman can't stand it if she *doesn't* hear it, because then she's distracted by the worry that the house won't be clean.

"I seat myself at the typewriter and hope, and lurk. When an idea appears, I leap on it with all fours and hold it down till I've mastered it. Ideally, I start at the wrong end, the finale. Then I try to develop strong conflicts and use the murder of a catalyst character. I just loathe it when an author has to force a murderer to confess. I always try to evolve jury evidence; it's one of the demands I make on myself: the denouement must be incontrovertible *evidence*, that a district attorney can use. And I want to tell a good story, like a juggler, keep the balls soaring in the air and hope the readers' eyes stay on them; be fair and give clues to the puzzle."

Mrs. Eberhart was reminded of an editor who once asked her opinion of a story by a best-selling author. "I told her, regretfully, that what was presented was not solid evidence but merely supposition." Although the editor never told the other author who had made this observation, the author guessed it was Mrs. Eberhart. "In her next book," she said, "that author invented an ignorant, low, utterly base character whom she named 'Mignon!' "

And the real Mignon loved the joke, as she does all good stories, especially about animals. "Carl Brandt of Brandt and Brandt—they have been my agents ever since I started—used to call me whenever he had a new one. My favorite was about the dog that was an expert poker player but always lost because he wagged his tail whenever he had a good hand."

It seemed clear that Mrs. Eberhart, despite her loss, is still in love with her work and with life. Unlike most men and women of "a certain age," who deplore the habits and attitudes of the young, she is solidly with them. "I believe if I could be born at age 18 now, I'd be quite at home. I have always felt liberated and I am in sympathy with women's demands for equality. But oh, I do believe in marriage. Marriage is forever, or should be.

"And in spite of the movement, there are still so many things a woman can't really do on her own, comfortably: travel, eat in a restaurant, go to the theater. I think I know just one man who wouldn't think I was setting my cap for him if I asked him to escort me to a play, wouldn't feel insulted if I offered to pay my own way." It seemed certain, however, that even such a paragon would not be permitted to intrude upon her working hours. After all, even her most famous fan couldn't get her aboard the *Sequoia* until she had finished her current book.

Dick Francis

WHEN DICK FRANCIS walks into a London hotel lobby, as he did not long ago for an interview with a *PW* editor, you know instantly that this trim, fit-looking chap has to have a sportsman's background. What comes as a surprise, however, is the fact that this former steeplechase jockey of note is so much taller than professional flat racing jockeys in this country, perhaps a shade under 5 feet 10. Mr. Francis began racing at 25 after six years service in the war and left in the 1950s at the top of his career after serving for a time as the Queen Mother's jockey. (She, he says, "is the real horsewoman of the royal family," very knowledgeable in her racing stock.)

In recent years Dick Francis has won considerable acclaim for his series of excellent suspense novels, published over here by Harper and in England by Michael Joseph. They include: "Nerve," "For Kicks," "Odds Against," "Flying Finish" and the new "Blood Sport."

At his peak Mr. Francis rode in about 300-400 races a year. "You're only good for about 10 years," he told *PW*. "That's about all your bones will stand in the way of spills." Even the most expert steeplechase jockey has to expect to take a number of falls, and Mr. Francis doesn't even remember how many times he has broken his collarbone in his career, first as an amateur, then as a professional jockey. In England amateurs and professionals can ride in the same races, and Dick Francis turned professional after about 18 months of steeplechase riding.

His writing career got under way when he was persuaded to start contributing a racing column regularly to the Sunday

By Barbara A. Bannon. From *Publishers Weekly* 193, no. 2 (January 8, 1968), pp. 27–28.

Express, a job he still carries on. He likes everything about it, he says, except being asked to predict the outcome of races.

From the racing column came a publisher's idea for a ghosted autobiography of Mr. Francis as a famous jockey. The ghosting conditions turned out to be so unworkable that Mr. Francis decided he could do better himself and wrote his own autobiographical story of his racing years, "The Sport of Queens," which did quite well in England.

Because he had always liked reading thrillers, Dick Francis thought of this as the next logical step to take in pursuing a writing career. His wife, he says frankly, is of invaluable help as a copyist and sometimes in ironing out the rough spots. When he was plotting "Flying Finish," the novel just before the new "Blood Sport," Mr. Francis, who had been a pilot during the war, arranged to fly to Europe, working his passage tending horses just as the hero in the novel does. He took his wife along, and she became so excited by it that she has now logged over 100 hours as a flyer. Flying will figure again in some of his plots, Mr. Francis is sure, but among his next heroes is going to be a racing newspaperman.

One of the most interesting things about the new "Blood Sport" is its American background, which Mr. Francis handles very convincingly, from Kentucky to Wyoming. He first came to America in 1954 and saw some racing at Belmont and elsewhere. A year or so ago he and his wife came over again and, traveling by Greyhound Bus and Piper Aircraft, visited much of the territory covered in "Blood Sport," including Jackson, Wyoming. In Wyoming Mr. Francis logged eight hours a day riding in the Rockies, the scene of some of the most tense action in the novel. The American parts of "Blood Sport" he took good pains to have carefully vetted by American friends for accuracy before publication.

Although most of the big money in buying racing stock these days rests in America, England and Ireland, Mr. Francis told us, still produce the best blood stock in the world because of the way Gulf Stream, passing nearby, influences the air and the land. There is a direct effect on the bones and blood of the horses bred in this climate, and stock owners from all over the world periodically come back every few racing generations to replenish their breed.

The day we met Dick Francis in London was shortly before British publication of "Blood Sport." There was one thing he wanted to talk about as much as the new book, however, and it's a demonstration of how he still feels about racing. His 17-year-old son, still in school, and even taller than his father, so that he must pare his weight to the bone, had come in third in his first race.

Nicolas Freeling

NICOLAS FREELING, winner of a Mystery Writers of America Edgar for "King of the Rainy Country" (*Harper & Row*) as the best mystery novel of 1966, made a flying trip to New York last month to accept the honor, and was interviewed briefly by *PW*. Since the hero of all but two of his novels is Inspector Van der Valk of the Amsterdam police, and the locale of the stories is usually at least in part Holland, a lot of people take it for granted that Mr. Freeling is Dutch. He is not, although he lived for a number of years in the Netherlands, has a Dutch wife, and may be safely said to be the only MWA-award winner who ever began his career as a mystery writer while serving time in a Dutch jail.

English-born and a British citizen, Mr. Freeling has lived in many parts of Europe both while he was growing up and during the 15 years he traveled around, working in the hotel business. "I was a bit of a beatnik before there were beatniks," he told *PW*. "In the hotel business you can just pack up and go off to a new job like that." The particular area of hotel work in which Mr. Freeling specialized was cooking ("in the kitchen you're away from the customers"). It was after he succumbed to the temptation to pinch some food from the Dutch hotel kitchen in which he was working that he landed in jail.

Bored to distraction with the assigned prison job of wrapping up paper hankies for an airline, he started writing a story on the wrapping papers used and came up with the beginnings of his first Inspector Van der Valk mystery, "Love in Amsterdam." When he got out of jail and started to work on the story in earnest he found that the first 10,000 words he had written in jail could stand virtually untouched.

By Barbara A. Bannon. From *Publishers Weekly* 191, no. 22 (May 29, 1967), p. 25.

The next Freeling novel to appear in this country (*Harper & Row*) will be "The Dresden Green." It is not an Inspector Van der Valk mystery (Mr. Freeling likes to try his hand at something else beside the Van der Valk series every so often), but a powerful story of greed, revenge and retribution, relating in some degree to the World War II bombing of Dresden by British and American planes, in which the civilian population suffered so cruelly. The story, which takes place long after the war, has to do with the rediscovery of a famous emerald ("The Dresden Green") supposedly lost in the bombing.

The Allied bombing of Dresden became "burningly important" to him the more he read about it, Mr. Freeling told *PW*. This concern with moral issues is an interesting part of every Freeling book and crops up in different guises in each of Inspector Van der Valk's cases. Mr. Freeling believes that a moral problem involving interior conflict is at the heart of every good story in the suspense vein. "You must have a moral problem for which you do not know too easily or quickly what the solution will be," he told *PW*. "You do not have a book without a moral issue."

It is precisely because Inspector Van der Valk is a thinking man who sometimes finds a most unpolice-like solution to his crimes (in one book he let a young murderess go, believing she was being punished enough by her own sufferings) that he is such an interesting detective. Curiously enough, the Van der Valk books, while they are published in Holland, are not, despite the undoubted authenticity of their settings, especially popular there.

The Dutch, Mr. Freeling says, "do not like people who go messing about with the conventions. In real life an Inspector Van der Valk would have been drummed off a Dutch police force long ago."

The next specifically Van der Valk book will be called "Strike Out Where Not Applicable." The Inspector's attractive no-nonsense French wife, Arlette, will play a somewhat larger role, assisting in the detection, than she has before. She will even take up horseback riding in the cause of catching the criminal. Arlette, Mr. Freeling finds, is beginning to make herself felt as more of a personality in the series, building up some fans of her own.

Mrs. Freeling, one suspects, plays quite a notable role of her own in the Freeling marriage. The Freelings and their four children now live in Strasbourg, France, because when they were trying to think of some place on the continent in which to locate, Mrs. Freeling put her finger on the map and came up with Strasbourg. They are very happy there.

P. D. James

P. D. JAMES is a British writer of serious fiction in that all of her novels deal with the most personal relationships, often complex and quirky ones, psychologically subtle. She is also a mystery writer in the sense that all six of her novels, published here by Scribners (the most recent is "The Black Tower"), involve a murderer and his (her) victims. The two concepts of writing do not seem at all antagonistic to her.

"Crime writers," she says, "regard themselves as being practitioners of an unappreciated genre. We all feel slightly maligned. What we are writing *is* very 'real fiction' to us."

Two of P. D. James's novels have been awarded Silver Daggers as the best mystery and suspense novels of the year by the British Crime Writers Association, and one was a candidate for an Edgar Award from the Mystery Writers of America, which shows the esteem in which her fellow writers hold her.

The central figure in all six James novels is Scotland Yard's Adam Dalgliesh, who is quite possibly the most intellectual detective of our time. He is, for one thing, a published poet, and when Ms. James introduced us to some of his poetry in her second book it proved to be not at all bad. ("I don't care continue with the inclusion of Dalgliesh's poetry," she confesses. "After all, in England I am published by Faber and Faber, T. S. Eliot's publisher.")

When P. D. James chose Adam Dalgliesh as her detective, however, she "did decide to describe someone who could go on from one book to another, developing as a person." Dalgliesh made his first appearance in "Cover Her Face" in 1962. In successive appearances he has proved

By Barbara A. Bannon. From *Publishers Weekly* 209, no. 1 (January 5, 1976), pp. 8–9.

over and over again that he can combine compassion for human weakness with analytic detective probing. In his fifth novel, "An Unsuitable Job for a Woman," he met a most unusual young Englishwoman named Cordelia Gray, who had fallen heir to a private detective agency and was determined to run it despite hardly any experience. With Dalgliesh's considerably deft behind-the-scenes help she succeeded, and she makes a brief appearance at the beginning of the latest James novel, "The Black Tower." Readers have been rooting for a further development of the romance, but Ms. James says firmly, "He may or may not marry her, or, indeed, anybody. Dalgliesh is intelligent, sensitive, but he can be quite ruthless, and he does not find it easy to establish close personal relationships."

We don't need to worry about Cordelia, however. She is doing very well on her own. Plans are under way for a British television series in which Cordelia Gray will star. P. D. James will be contributing to the scripts.

One final word about Adam Dalgliesh: in "The Black Tower," which deals with a theme not previously encountered in recent detective fiction—murder involving the physically handicapped—Dalgliesh toyed with the idea of resigning from Scotland Yard. Ms. James assures us that he has second thoughts.

Phyllis James was the maiden name of the woman who became on marriage Phyllis James White, herself a hospital administrator and the wife of a doctor. When her husband returned from the war, seriously ill mentally, she turned to a writing career as an additional way of supporting the household, which included two daughters. She chose her unmarried name under which to write, using sexually ambiguous initials. "Because I thought whether I was a man or a woman should not concern people. I wanted simply to be judged as a writer."

Out of her own considerable experience as a hospital administrator and her husband's work as a doctor, P. D. James has gained quite a lot of medical knowledge and this background has often been a key factor in her novels.

After the death of her husband, P. D. James decided to change careers. "I wanted to broaden my horizons," she says, "and the Home Office wanted to broaden its base of recruitment of senior people." Accordingly, she took exams that were highly competitive and somewhat similar to our civil service exams. "We were able to choose the departments in which we were interested the day of the exam" (she chose the criminal department of the Home Office, where she has been for four years now). Among the subjects applicants had to tackle were "writing a précis, eight pages of criticism and arguments dealing with a mixed-up file submitted to a minister, how to conduct a meeting. Anyone who had administrative experience as I did obviously had an advantage."

The Home Secretary's Office in Britain is the oldest of the British departments of state, something of a combination of this country's Departments of the Interior and Justice. P. D. James works in the area of the formulation of criminal law policy. If Britain should ever decide to bring back the death penalty, elaboration of the government's position would fall to the department in which she works.

"We have to be completely apolitical," she says of her work. "Basically, we want to keep as many people out of prison as possible. One of the most important changes in criminal law in Britain in recent years occurred in 1972. It permits defendants who are convicted, at the discretion of the judge, to be sentenced to serve time not in prison but in so many hours of community service. Often, when the right job is found and the individual finds he is doing useful work he really enjoys, he will continue it after the sentence is over. This happened in the case of a boxer who is continuing to work with deprived city boys on his own time."

P. D. James manages her writing in the early mornings and on weekends. It is easy to see that much of the same compassion that Dalgliesh expresses in her books is a direct reflection of her personal attitude in her Home Office work. The two clearly mesh together well.

One type of detective fiction she promises never to inflict on her readers. It is what used to be called the perfect "English country house mystery, in which we encounter the stereotyped English detective hero, a sprig of nobility, who is welcomed by the professional police with gentle fun and suitable awe. The murder usually occurs over the weekend and anyone ill-advised enough to go into the library alone is just asking for a knife in the back. The snow is falling hard enough to keep out the regular police, and the inhabitants of the grange rise to the occasion and prove themselves able to get along without the local authorities and solve everything on their own—led, of course, by that sprig of nobility." P. D. James, it seems, has a healthy respect for the dedicated police officer and a cool eye for the amateur 'tec.

Harry Kemelman

ALTHOUGH Rabbi David Small's congregation is located in a Boston suburb, his followers number in the hundreds of thousands and are residents of almost every country in the world. Indeed his creator, Harry Kemelman, has made Rabbi Small the best known, if not the best loved, rabbi in all of fiction.

Rabbi Small, a shy, scholarly and slightly absentminded young man, is the unlikely detective hero in a series of mysteries which, in addition to containing the usual mix of suspense ingredients, are laced with intellectual dialogues on religion and a careful portrayal of American Jewish life in suburbia. The readers of Kemelman's books observe the use of Talmudic logic in solving "whodunits" and learn about Jewish holidays, keeping kosher, the attitudes of Jews toward birth, marriage and death, and the social and religious responsibilities of a rabbi.

Kemelman's first book, "Friday the Rabbi Slept Late" (*Crown*, 1964), won an Edgar, and the most recent title, "Tuesday the Rabbi Saw Red" (*Arthur Fields*, 1973), appeared for several months on national best-seller charts. All five of the Rabbi Small titles to date received favorable reviews and racked up impressive hardcover sales. They are all now available in paperback from Fawcett, who reports that there are over 5-million books in print, and they have been translated into almost every language except Russian, Chinese and, naturally, the various Arabic languages.

Kemelman recently completed a promotion and publicity tour for the paperback set, his first since he began publishing the Rabbi books. When *PW* met him at New York's St.

By Daisy Maryles. From *Publishers Weekly* 207, no. 17 (April 28, 1975), pp. 8-9.

Regis Hotel, Kemelman had already visited several large cities and had been a guest on numerous talk shows.

Kemelman said he had never planned on writing a detective series with a rabbi as the main character. "My original purpose was to try to explain—via a fictional setting—the Jewish religion." He had been living in a Boston suburb where until the end of World War II he was one of the few resident Jews. Then young Jewish couples began to leave the city for the suburbs, and Kemelman found himself involved with many of them in trying to organize a temple. "I was 40 at the time and when I looked about me I suddenly realized that I was the oldest person there. Here was a completely homogeneous group of people—everyone was about 30 with 1.4 children and earning about the same annual income.

"I began to think what effect suburbia would have on traditional Judaism. These young people were completely separated from their elders and most of them had minimal religious training."

Subsequently, Kemelman wrote a full-length novel, "The Building of a Temple," which examined sociologically "the curious phenomenon of Jews living in a Yankee community, worried about crabgrass, mortgages, etc." He sent his novel to several publishers. "They all said very nice things about the book but turned it down on the grounds that it lacked any real excitement and was too low-keyed."

Kemelman was not a complete unknown as a writer, since several of his short stories had been published in *Ellery Queen's Mystery Magazine* (since collected by Fawcett and published under the title, "Nine Mile Walk"). One editor, Arthur Fields, called Kemelman and asked him to come down and talk. Fields, Kemelman recollected, jokingly suggested that maybe the book would be more interesting if it were written in the style of a detective story. At first Kemelman thought this was just another rejection, but then he began to think more carefully about the idea, and how he could discuss the rabbinate in a suspense setting.

"The principal problem in a murder is where to hide the corpse. It occurred to me that the parking lot in a suburban temple is an ideal spot. The rabbi, just by being in his study in the vicinity of the murder, becomes involved and may even be a suspect. Or he may have to clear a member of his own congregation. What better way to solve a mystery than through the use of talmudic logic?"

After completing his first Rabbi book, Kemelman was not even thinking in terms of a series. "I came up with the first title merely because it sounded interesting. Fields never cared for the title and tried to convince me to change it." Kemelman speaks with great fondness of his editor, who died last year. "My relations with him were not just those of writer to editor—he was my publisher and close friend. I followed him from house to house, with no thought to its possible effect on sales. We worked together very closely—more like a partnership."

Kemelman described how, shortly after Arthur Fields died, his agent Scott Meredith began getting offers to publish subsequent Rabbi books. One publisher called and said, "Look, I know this is gruesome, but I want to be the first to put in a bid for Harry Kemelman." Scott Meredith's answer, the author reports, was: "Yes, it *is* gruesome, but you are the fifth to call."

His new editor is Hillel Black at Morrow. "One reason my agent chose Black was that he wanted to select a house where I would be comfortable, and Scott felt Black would be the sort of person I could work with. So far things seem to be working out." Kemelman is nearly finished with the first draft of the Wednesday installment. No pub date has been scheduled.

His first Rabbi book, Kemelman said, caught on by word of mouth. "Bookstores began calling Crown with orders for "Friday the Rabbit Slept Late" and "Freddy the Rabbit Slept Late" and "Freddy, the Rabbi, Slept Late." Crown, in fact, ran a big ad in the *New York Times*, listing all the titles under which the book was ordered."

With the completion of the second Rabbi book, it was decided to cash in on the first book's popularity and use the same formula for the title: "Saturday the Rabbi Went Hungry." Publisher and author began getting letters from all parts of the country with suggested titles for the rest of the days of the week. "We never used any of the suggestions because they had a point, and mine meant absolutely nothing." *PW* could not help but ask the obvious question: "What are you going to do when you run out of days of the week for your titles?" Answer: "It takes me about two years to write each book, so I have almost four years of work ahead of me—and then there are always Columbus Day, Labor Day, Thanksgiving, etc."

Kemelman does occasionally take breaks from Rabbi Small to write essays, and is currently working on a play. "It deals with women's liberation. In my play the woman, while not considering herself particularly liberated, dares to do the one thing that demonstrates complete equality— she decides to marry beneath her."

Surprised but pleased at the enormous success of his books, Harry Kemelman still can't get accustomed to one reaction. That is being approached by American and Israeli rabbis who tell him how much his books have affected their behavior. It's a curious position for an author of detective stories. But then, Kemelman is no ordinary author, and he does not write ordinary detective stories.

John D. MacDonald

A TELEPHONE CALL caught John D. MacDonald, who has to be near the top of practically anyone's list of the best contemporary American writers in the mystery-suspense genre, in New York en route from Freehold, N.J., to up-state New York and thence to Florida. Mr. MacDonald was headed upstate to spend Christmas with relatives after having covered the murder trial of Dr. Carl A. Coppolino in Freehold (verdict: acquittal) and to rest up before covering the Coppolino murder trial in Florida, now scheduled to start in February.

Mr. MacDonald, needless to say, is at work on a book—maybe two books—about the Coppolino affair, which, to put it mildly, has incited the moral fervor for which Mr. MacDonald is well known by his fans. The job may require two books, Mr. MacDonald told *PW*, because the New Jersey and the Florida cases are quite different: different victims, different courtrooms, different casts of characters, and so on. Whether *two* Coppolino books by Mr. MacDonald are viable commercially is a matter still to be resolved. Publication plans are still up in the air, Mr. MacDonald indicated, but publication will be probably by Doubleday in hardcover, Fawcett in paperback. The working title for one or both books is "No Deadly Medicine," an illusion to the Hippocratic Oath, which Dr. Coppolino may or may not have violated. Also still to be resolved is which will come first: hardcover or paperback publication. One thing certain, however, is that Mr. MacDonald will be in court when Dr. Coppolino's trial begins in Florida: perhaps in Sarasota, where the action was originally brought; perhaps in another

By Roger H. Smith. From *Publishers Weekly* 191, no. 1 (January 2, 1967), p. 21.

part of the state, if the defense is successful in its effort to gain a change of venue. Mr. MacDonald said he rather hoped that the debate on change of venue would take a while, giving him a chance to finish the New Jersey part of his book(s) about the case.

"Even if I never publish a word about the Coppolino case—and that's not likely—just being associated with it as a spectator has given me ideas for at least two novels about the dilemma between personal and professional decisions: if you do one thing, you harm yourself; if you do another thing, you harm your best friend." It's the kind of theme which Mr. MacDonald has been working on for a long time.

Meanwhile, he reported, announcement is imminent on a movie deal involving his hot-selling Travis McGee detective series, published by Fawcett. A television project is in the works for one of his earlier novels, "The Crossroads," which Fawcett will reissue. One of the few full-time novelists with a graduate degree from the Harvard Business School, Mr. MacDonald these days is rarely unoccupied.

Ross Macdonald

VISITING NEW YORK this spring, from his Santa Barbara, California, home, crime novelist Ross Macdonald found himself, purely by chance, standing next to someone in an elevator at the Algonquin, to whom he felt he had to introduce himself. It was Eudora Welty, whose front cover review of his latest novel, "The Underground Man" (*Knopf*) in the *New York Times Book Review*, brought Mr. Macdonald the kind of serious literary acknowledgement he has long deserved.

"It's been a great spring for me," he told *PW* a few minutes after the meeting with Miss Welty. "It's wonderful to make some money for a change ("The Underground Man" has been sold to the movies and the Knopf hardcover edition has now sold about 50,000 copies as of early August). It's even more wonderful to find out that writers whose work you admire like your work; the kind of intelligent response Miss Welty gave me was one of the greatest things ever to happen in my life. I'm a great admirer of her writing, but I had no idea she liked mine until I read her review."

Ross Macdonald (in private life Kenneth Millar) and his Canadian-born wife, the novelist Margaret Millar, have been Santa Barbara residents for more than 20 years and in book after book Mr. Macdonald has been writing about the special California life-style as it is reflected in a tense family situation that almost inevitably leads to violent death. His world-weary and very credible professional, the private detective Lew Archer, is the link between each succeeding case.

"Writing is about 75 percent a good memory for people, and not words," Ross Macdonald says. "Memory is the fac-

By Barbara A. Bannon. From *Publishers Weekly* 200, no. 6 (August 9, 1971), pp. 19–20.

tor in any novelist's work. I'm interested in the span of generations. If I had lived in an earlier era I would probably have written the long, detailed family novel. I used to dote on the 'Forstye Saga' and Mazo de la Roche's 'Jalna' novels. In order to write that kind of novel you have to have a situation in which you can observe three generations. In California you are lucky if you know much at all about your next door neighbor. The average Californian moves every three years. In this country time has speeded up. It is possible now to say certain things in the mystery novel about the flow of generations that could no longer be written in the old triple-decker family novel."

In his own writing, Ross Macdonald is often working on several book ideas at one time "without knowing which I'm finally going to get to first." That keeps me interested. "While completing one book," he says, "I let the others simmer. I keep on changing the plot. I might stick with the main outline—who kills whom—but almost everything else is likely to change. I fill notebooks with ideas, and I may take six to eight months writing about a situation that interests me. My ideas get better as time goes on."

It will come as something of a shock to Ross Macdonald fans to learn that private detective Lew Archer was never really intended as a series character. "I still have to make the decision about him each time," Macdonald says, "although it is 10 years since I've written anything else. Archer has grown older and improved with age. I'm not continuing him for any reason except that it suits me. I'm still finding things to do with him that are new to me as a writer.

"One of the factors that contributes a great deal to Archer's development is that I've gotten to know a great many private detectives. It takes a remarkable man to be this kind of lone wolf. How would you find a good private detective if you needed one? Through a good lawyer or by going to one of the known big agencies. As for what I write about private detectives, I only know what I invent, but the invention has relevance. One young detective came to visit me, proposing that the code by which Lew Archer operates be made a professional code for private detectives."

Mr. Macdonald does a lot of his research by attending trials in California. "The first murder trial I ever attended was a real doozy that permanently shaded my life. One witness fell dead of a heart attack. I got an imaginative sense for the first time of what a murder could mean to a whole range of people."

Insofar as criminal court justice in America is concerned, Mr. Macdonald believes, "in terms of involvement with the law and trials, the more money you have, the more likely you are to get a fair shake." The ideal criminal court judge he describes as one "in love with the law," and he can cite as an example a California judge "willing to stop a murder trial and send the defendant to a mental hospital when he thought that was where he belonged." In terms of his own trial coverage, Ross Macdonald was asked to write about the Charles Manson case. "I thought it was just a dreadful thing to get mixed up in," he told *PW*. "I wrote 'The Underground Man' instead." It would seem to have been a very wise choice.

Ellery Queen

"ELLERY QUEEN," as the trade well knows, is really Frederic Dannay and Manfred B. Lee, first cousins, and long-time collaborators, who on March 10 will see the publication of their 40th anniversary novel, "Cop Out" (*NAL–World*). Not fond of interviews—they have given very few over the years—they consented to meet and talk with *PW* in honor of the anniversary.

The two men play off against each other very well. One is apt to finish a sentence the other has started, and watching them in action is a little like following a fast tennis game. The one question they will not discuss, under any circumstances, is their method of collaboration, which they firmly believe is "nobody's business but our own." A futile opening gambit in this direction from a *PW* reporter drew from Mr. Lee a bark of laughter and the rejoinder, in best Inspector Queen tough guy style, "If that's your angle, sister, you're in big trouble."

An hour later we were all on sufficiently easy terms for this much of an explanation to be given of the Dannay–Lee work plan. "We are both perfectionists. We respect each other's integrity, but we're very different. We work against each other, more as competitors than collaborators, and we fight each other's prerogatives with regard to a finished manuscript." Apparently the fights can sometimes get hot and heavy. When they were in Hollywood at Paramount, both men remember that the entire mimeographing department of the studio, located overhead, used to complain regularly about the noise the two of them generated.

"Forty years ago we came to know what each other's strengths were," Mr. Dannay says. Now, when an argument

By Barbara A. Bannon. From *Publishers Weekly* 195, no. 10 (March 10, 1969), pp. 19–21.

over a book arises, by tacit consent, that member of the team whose strong point of expertise is involved, automatically has the final say on what the outcome will be.

The Ellery Queen collaboration began back in 1929 when the two, who had been close friends since their teen years (their mothers were sisters), decided to enter a detective story contest co-sponsored by the publishing house of Stokes and *McClure's* magazine. Although they won the contest, unofficially, by the time it was over *McClure's* had gone bankrupt, selling out to *Smart Set*, then a magazine aimed at a young women's market. The "Ellery Queen" entry wasn't slanted this way at all, so a Chicago housewife, from whom, presumably, nothing has ever been heard again, was proclaimed winner and Dannay and Lee, although they lost out on the magazine deal, became important Stokes book authors.

The two men think they are pretty close to the top in length of time as living deans of the American detective story, with Rex Stout having published one non-detective story novel, "How Like a God," before them, and Erle Stanley Gardner a close contender. Only Agatha Christie of living detective story writers, still active, has been at it longer than they have as novelists, they believe.

The "Ellery" part of "Ellery Queen" came from a boyhood friend of Frederic Dannay in Elmira, N.Y. "Queen" they just dreamed up, wanting a short mnemonic name. "We were so green in those days," Mr. Lee reminisces, "that we had no idea 'queen' had any homosexual connotations. It was only later we realized that in Hollywood it was taken for granted we were a couple of queers." (They liked the idea of having "Ellery Queen" as both author and detective, because it meant Hollywood, which could make the original author's name pretty small peanuts in giving credits, would let it stand for the lead character.)

For a long time the two men kept their identities secret and worked up a kind of lecture tour vaudeville turn with Colston Leigh in which they would pose mysteries to each other, one supposedly trying to stump the other. They even wore masks for a while to conceal their identities but took those off years ago. For nine years the two wrote the popular "Ellery Queen" radio show, using a format in which guest celebrities were asked to solve the mystery in the last 15 minutes or so, before the actor playing Ellery Queen came on to give the answer. The program was unsponsored at first, paid Lee and Dannay just about "coffee and Danish money," and was in imminent danger of being yanked until one night in Chicago a tube blew just as the solution was about to be given, and the radio station switchboard was jammed with phone calls until 4 A.M. from irate listeners wanting to know how it all turned out.

Looking back at their radio days, the two men, who believe they have often been ahead of time in their use of plot and theme, are especially proud of one show they wrote in about 1950. Except for Ellery and his ever-present secretary–girl friend, Nicky, all the lead characters were Negroes, portrayed as ordinary people. One scene introduced Ellery, Nicky, and a Negro prizefighter stopping off at a tavern together and being refused service because a Negro was sitting down with white people. The network (NBC) blanched, but Mr. Dannay and Lee insisted the scene be kept in and the show ran, uncut.

Looking back at their 40 years as mystery writers, the two see their first books as being "classic mysteries" in keeping with the strictly analytic golden age of the detective story. As "we matured," they say, this began to seem artificial to them and in the next period their stories became much more humanistic, with an emphasis on characterization. Psychiatry as a theme began to involve them, but even in books with a more important theme Ellery Queen has always stuck to the framework of the detective story. Back in the McCarthy era they took "a terrible licking" with their novel, "Glass Village," which emphasized due process of law, and for a time they were both charged with being Communists.

The evolution of the mystery story, as both Lee and Dannay see it, began with the "whodunit," which had a simpler ending. In its second stage the emphasis was on the "howdunit," not so much who was the killer, but how the murder was accomplished. (When they were writing in this vein a doctor friend once invented a new weapon for them in his laboratory.) In its third stage, emphasis in the mystery is on "why the crime was done," the psychology behind it. "We have tried to combine the 'who' and the 'why,' " Dannay and Lee say of their later work. Like a good baseball pitcher, they believe in mixing up their pitches. "Cop Out," their new novel, has a completely contemporary setting and is a one-shot, minus Ellery Queen. Ellery will be back in their next book, which is to be another volume in the excellent series of novels about Wrightsville, a place they see as a kind of microcosm of small town America. The Wrightsville series started with "Calamity Town" and now encompasses several books which the authors like to think of as "a kind of 'Spoon River Anthology' " in a detective story context. Between them, the two men combine big city (Lee) and small town (Dannay) life and they believe something seeps through to their writing from a background each has known personally.

"From the beginning," Mr. Lee says, "we had the feeling that the detective story writer was a second-class citizen and there is no damn reason why he should be. Sure, there's been a lot of trash there, but there has been in general fiction, too."

It was very much because, in addition to their own writing, the Ellery Queen team wanted to elevate the tone and place of other mystery story writers that they started their *Ellery Queen's Mystery Magazine*, now in its 29th year. In that time they have published some 13 or 14 stories by Nobel Prize winners. They believe they published the first short mystery story ever to feature a Negro detective. The magazine, from the beginning, they say, has been "edited by Queen, not farmed out." In all, they estimate, they have introduced more than 320 new mystery writers, many of whom have become leaders in the field. They have published some 36 Pulitzer Prize winners.

Summing up their views on the detective story 40 years after their first book, "The Roman Hat Mystery," was published, Messrs. Dannay and Lee think, "what has happened in the mystery story field is what has happened in every other field of writing, a kind of emancipation as in the theater or the general novel."

Sociologists and psychologists have found that by going back to the old Horatio Alger dime novels of the 1890s they can often obtain a fascinating picture of the life of the times, Mr. Lee and Mr. Dannay say. "The detective story offers that—plus. Whereas serious literature can take a while to catch up with the temper of the times, the detective story often reflects it more immediately and even anticipates what may be happening." The sociologists and psychologists of the future, they think, may well go to today's detective stories for a measure of our own times, and they hope if they do, they will find it in "Ellery Queen."

Donald Westlake

NO AUTHOR has ever been rushed out of *PW's* editorial office with such scant courtesy as Donald Westlake. But don't get us wrong! The reason was that he was so interesting and entertaining to talk to that this *PW* editor waited until the last second to say, "You have to catch the 5:29." Elevator, we meant, because the elevators to the editorial floor stop at 5:30 and after that Donald would have had to be guided on a labyrinthine way to a lower floor.

Donald Westlake gets as much fun out of writing as he does talking about his work. He says he'd far rather "write than work." Writing isn't work, and when it turns out to be work, he hates it. Writing as Donald Westlake, he's turned out about a dozen crime novels since 1960, and very successful they've been. His "God Save the Mark" (*Random*) won the MWA Edgar as the best mystery of 1967. His latest, "The Hot Rock," published last May (*Simon & Schuster*), which the *PW* Forecast called a "typically comic and lively Westlake caper," has been bought by Hal Landers and Bobbie Roberts for movie production. Lee Marvin and Peter Sellers are slated for the cast.

But here's bad news for Westlake crime fans. He told us that "The Hot Rock" will be his last crime novel. (Evidently they're getting to be "work.") He says he's been writing about one a year, a mystery about "an innocent in danger." He feels they're getting to be repetitive, and "not as much fun," as they were at first.

All is not lost, however, as far as crime goes. Like many another mystery writer, Donald writes under pen names as well as his own. As Richard Stark he has created two well-

By Alice Payne Hackett. From *Publishers Weekly* 198, no. 12. (September 21, 1970), pp. 21–23.

known adventure protagonists, Grofield and Parker. Parker started out as a character in paperback originals, eight published by Pocket Books, four by Gold Medal. Now he's about to appear in hardcover—the first to come from Random House this winter. Three Grofield crime novels have been published by Macmillan in hardcover. The next will be published by World this coming winter.

More Richard Stark–Parker stories have been made into movies than any other Westlake books. Strangely enough, Parker, the super-criminal brain, has been played by a white man, a black man, and by a woman. The most successful film was "Point Blank," made from "The Hunter," in which Parker was portrayed by Lee Marvin. Jim Brown played Parker in "The Split," made from "The Seventh." Anna Karina was Parker as a female in "Made in U.S.A.," based upon "The Jugger," which was shown only in France. The fourth Parker movie, made from "The Score," was shown in France as "Mise à Sac."

Although Donald Westlake says he is abandoning the Westlake crime story, he plans to write at least one comic novel a year under his own name. He believes he will always enjoy writing this type of novel best. So far, only two have appeared. "Up Your Banners" (*Macmillan*), which the *PW* reviewer called "humorous and happy," even though it was about a strike in a Brooklyn high school and a black–white confrontation, also had some quite scathing reviews, presumably because the story poked fun at black militants as well as at white conservatives. The second comic novel, published this September 7, is "Adios, Scheherazade" (*Simon & Schuster*), in which Westlake has some fun at the expense of professional writers of pornography. For next year, he's planning "I Gave at the Office," in which TV production tactics are the target of his humor. One incident will be based on an interview his editor at Simon & Schuster, Jonathan Dolger, had on the Mike Wallace show—taped in advance with Mike Wallace not even present. Actually, as some TV watchers will be disillusioned to find out, this is a fairly frequent practice among television interviewers.

Another Westlake goal, despite his enjoyment in writing comic novels, is to write some "straight" serious novels. He is working on one now, which will probably be published by M. Evans. It is a political novel about the first solid, realistic woman candidate for the presidency. The period will be in the near future, covering the months between the New Hampshire primary and the national convention of the party not in power.

We asked Donald Westlake about the role of the agent in the career of a successful popular writer—for one reason, because of the recent comments by Paul Nathan in his *PW* columns about author–publisher–agent difficulties today, and, for another, because Westlake himself had a six-months stint in the Scott Meredith office in 1958–59. Surprisingly, he compared agents to antique dealers in their great variation from good to bad. The good agent, he says, must know the entire scene, including American, foreign, international book rights and movie rights. Many agents, he said, prefer not to handle foreign rights, but he himself, because he has a good agent, derives half his income on books from outside the U.S. Paperback reprint rights, he said, are usually handled by the original hardcover publishers. He believes that many inept people become literary agents because they like to be at least on the fringe of the "glamorous" publishing business, and he thinks that many authors stay with inefficient agents because of long, friendly association. He says they wouldn't stay with indifferent doctors for such a reason.

Elegantly bearded Donald Westlake, one of the most popular crime writers in his 10-year span of publication, has a house in New Jersey, an apartment in New York, a wife and four children, all boys.

Martin Woodhouse

THIS YOUNG MAN with the purposeful air is Dr. Martin Woodhouse, author of Coward-McCann's suspense novel, "Tree Frog," the screeplay of which he is currently writing for Saul David. En route to Hollywood from England he stopped off in New York and revealed himself as a man of aplomb with a flair for Planning Ahead. The aplomb was apparent when he and a *PW* interviewer were summarily asked to leave a rather stuffy midtown hostelry because Dr. Woodhouse was not considered suitably garbed. Moving over to Third Avenue ("much nicer, more like a pub") he began to talk about The Plan.

The son of a doctor and a poet, he decided early on that he would be a writer, and at 19 he was contributing science fiction to the American pulps. Recognizing more sensibly than a number of other young men that you can't really become much of a writer until you're old enough to know quite a bit more about life, he packed it in for Cambridge and medical school, wound up with degrees in both medicine and experimental psychology, served a tour in national service, and got back to the writing again via a British TV series for kiddies, "Supercar," and scripts for the slapstick comedy "Carry On" series of films.

"Supercar," ending just before the era of residuals began (Dr. Woodhouse figures he has lost a quarter of a million dollars since 1960 on the basis of its replaying without the necessity of further payments to the authors), he put in a stint of starving in a garret. "Cheerful girl friends brought me apple pie," he says. Then one day he took a long, hard look at a new British TV series and set out to write a script

By Roger H. Smith. From *Publishers Weekly* 191, no. 5 (January 30, 1967), p. 33.

tailor-made to its needs. The series was "The Avengers," currently flourishing on American screens also, and so successful was the Woodhouse touch that for four years the doctor was lead writer.

Getting a bit tired of TV ("the writer does not have as much control of his material as he would like"), Dr. Woodhouse decided he was really a writer of thrillers by nature and that he would take science as his special thriller gimmick. "Science as a premise for a thriller," he says, "is visually exciting and a better excuse these days for a story line than a bag of jewels or mission z-plans."

First of the Woodhouse science thrillers was "Tree Frog." The next five are blocked out roughly. First one will be "Bush Baby," set in England, Albania, Yugoslavia. The name refers to an automatic recording device, a seismograph for detecting nuclear explosions. All of the Woodhouse books are going to have two-word, four-letter titles patterned after the ones engineers actually apply to such scientific projects. Future titles include "Echo Rose," "Ruby Wasp."

Somewhere on the agenda, however, as Dr. Woodhouse keeps up his scientific reading, is a big, scholarly volume that will treat of the human brain compared with a computer.

3

Biography

Carlos Baker

CARLOS BAKER, who never met Ernest Hemingway, probably knows him better than anyone. The author of the first full-length critical study of Hemingway's work, "Hemingway: The Writer as Artist" (1952), Mr. Baker for the past seven years has been painstakingly reconstructing Hemingway's life, from letters and interviews and the author's own papers, for the first full-length biography. The result, "Ernest Hemingway: A Life Story," will be published by Scribners on April 21 and is the April Book-of-the-Month Club selection.

Sitting one morning last week in the library at Scribners, where among the many books on the shelves were some early Hemingway editions, Mr. Baker talked about the process of reconstructing the life of a major literary figure who, though dead, still seems to many to be contemporary.

First, there were the letters—some 3000 that Hemingway wrote to various people and another 3000 that people wrote to him. "I'm very shy," Mr. Baker said, "but I began approaching people who had Hemingway letters and asked if I could borrow them long enough to have photocopies made, and these meetings led to contacts with other people who had Hemingway letters. Get as many Hemingway letters as possible, lay them end to end and you have the beginning of a biography." Mary Hemingway, the author's widow, helped fill in the other side of the two-way correspondence street by lending Mr. Baker all the letters to Hemingway that she had, and these were shipped to Princeton, where Mr. Baker is Woodrow Wilson Professor of Literature.

Then, there were interviews with Hemingway's friends.

By Roger H. Smith. From *Publishers Weekly* 195, no. 13 (March 31, 1969), pp. 15–17.

"With very few exceptions, Ernest's taste in people was excellent," Mr. Baker said. The biographer had conversations with some people who admired Hemingway extravagantly, like Ivan Wallace and Chub Weaver, who were his hunting companions in Montana, and international sportsmen Thomas Shevlin and Winston Guest, who were generous with their time and their long-distance telephone bills in giving Mr. Baker assistance. He also had conversations with people—particularly women—who did not admire Hemingway. One especially thought that the author disliked all women except Mary—an attitude which Mr. Baker finds hard to accept in light of the fact that Hemingway, in his lifetime, married four times.

And then there were people whose lives had been somehow touched by Hemingway, who heard about Mr. Baker's project and spontaneously communicated with him—for example, a man who at a second-hand store bought a pair of Hemingway's boots that Hemingway had outgrown, wrote him a letter about what fine boots they were and got a letter back. These people communicated, Mr. Baker believes, not because they particularly wanted to be in the book, but because "Ernest passed through their lives like a meteor and they were still brushing the sparks off their lapels." Out of such inspirations, Mr. Baker over seven years built up a world-wide network of Hemingway informants.

With all the letters and data assembled, there remained the task of checking everything for accuracy, since the human mind is fallible. The mass of material was so great that, for the most part, it provided the necessary cross-checks—"edging toward exactitude" is the way Mr. Baker describes this part of the biographer's job.

One thing that comes through in the biography is the great difficulty Hemingway had in writing his stories and his novels, literally spending a whole day's effort sweating out a single paragraph.

In Mr. Baker's view, Hemingway had this great difficulty in writing because, for his best work, he held himself to a very high standard, wanting everything to be so good that it would not need revision. "He talked a lot about revision, but he did very little," Mr. Baker said.

On the other hand, journalism came easy to Hemingway, which was why he scorned it. "Ernest thought that anything that came easy probably wasn't very good," Mr. Baker said. "He also knew when he wasn't living up to his own high standards; with his World War II articles for *Collier's*, he deliberately left good things out because he wanted to use them later in books."

According to Charles Scribner, Hemingway's publisher as well as Mr. Baker's, the Hemingway books sell better every year, for an annual total now of more than a half-million copies. The big sellers are the big books— "Farewell to Arms," "The Sun Also Rises," "For Whom the Bell Tolls," "The Old Man and the Sea." The continued strong sale, Mr. Scribner feels, is because the books are being taught increasingly in colleges and high schools. Mr. Baker, from his Princeton experience, agreed. Today's undergraduates, he said, may experiment with drugs or engage in sit-ins, but they also find an appeal in the life of action and the great outdoors that Hemingway wrote about. They also get interested in the Hemingway literary style. "When I was an undergraduate at Dartmouth," Mr. Baker said, "we all tried to write like Hemingway, and they still do in the colleges today."

Mr. Baker never met Hemingway, in part because he knew Hemingway did not like people digging into his life story, in part because Mr. Baker was looking forward to reading a new Hemingway novel and did not want to interrupt the author. "It may be a blessing that I never met him," Mr. Baker said, "because we might not have liked each other. On the other hand, reconstructing the man only from letters and interviews, I had no exposure to the ambiance of his personality, which everyone said was great. When Ernest came into a room, he had an electrical effect, like a big jungle cat, and he had a wonderful ability to size up situations immediately. But there were other times when he wasn't so good.

"In not knowing him, I missed that. But if I had known him, it would only have been for the last decade of his life, since I didn't even approach him by letter until 1950, and in the last period he was very different from what he had been earlier."

Sybille Bedford

IN SYBILLE BEDFORD'S enormous biography of Aldous
Huxley there is a picture of her, smiling and about 20 years
old, lying on a Riviera beach beside her subject—who was
at that time, the early 1930s, already a major international
literary figure, with most of his best-known novels behind
him. The picture was taken near the beginning of a relationship with Huxley and his family that was to last until his
death in 1963 (ironically, he died at almost exactly the same
hour as President Kennedy was assassinated, and his passing went virtually unremarked). The relationship was one of
unusual closeness between biographer and subject, and it
has produced a biography of unusual detail, insight and
care—as well as length.

It is a biography that has occupied Miss Bedford's every
waking moment for the six years it took her to research and
write it. "I drove myself to it, worked even through the
weekends," she declared recently to a *PW* interviewer. She
even forsook her house in the South of France to live in
London for the duration of the book, so as to be close to
books, sources, Huxley friends. Now that it's all over, she
expected to be relieved, but "actually I feel bereft," she
said rather wistfully. It is a carefully chosen word. In conversation, as in her elegant, patrician writing, Miss Bedford
espouses precision, and this, combined with a sometimes
quirky angle of vision, gives her conversation a tang all its
own. Words, once uttered, are often repeated with relish,
and conventional tag lines are briskly dispensed with (asked
if she was enjoying her American visit, Miss Bedford re-

By John F. Baker. From *Publishers Weekly* 206, no. 25 (December 16,
1974), pp. 6–7.

sponded: "I shouldn't be likely to tell you if I *wasn't* enjoying it, should I?" and the talk moved on rather smartly).

Despite the vast effort involved, she found working on the Huxley book "exhilarating." "Usually one writes for nobody but oneself," she explained. "It doesn't really matter whether you write a novel or not, but on this occasion it was a book hundreds of people *wanted* to appear. So many people loved Aldous, and this feeling was a great stimulus to me."

Miss Bedford said she had thought of eventually doing a book about Huxley almost since she had known him: "When one is young one thinks of so many things as possibilities, without quite realizing what would be involved." Maria, Huxley's first wife, had also suggested it to her, and more recently Huxley's son Matthew had renewed the suggestion. "Frankly, I felt unworthy to the task, and I was worried I'd have too many people on my back." In the end, however, she went ahead—on the firm condition that no one she talked to or wrote to about Huxley was to see any part of the manuscript before the whole was finished.

She started by taping interviews, but gave that up quite early on. "You need to look at people while you're talking to them, not fiddle about with knobs and things," she said firmly, looking at the *PW* interviewer so hard that he glanced guiltily up from his notes. The publishing of "Aldous Huxley" has been a major undertaking on both sides of the Atlantic. In England it was brought out jointly by Chatto & Windus, who as Huxley's lifelong publishers had the rights to his works and letters, and by Collins, Miss Bedford's own publishers. Here it has been done by Harper & Row (Huxley's American publishers) and Knopf, for whom Miss Bedford writes. (Her editor here has always been Robert Gottlieb, and the book was first mooted while he was still at Simon and Schuster. When he went to Knopf, the book went with him.)

As in England, the two houses here are sharing in production costs and in earnings from the book. Knopf, however, like Collins in London, is responsible for its promotion and distribution. It appeared in two volumes in London, several months apart ("They didn't want the books to be too heavy in England"), but here it is in one large volume with considerable avoirdupois ("They seem to *prefer* heavy books here").

Until now, of course, Miss Bedford has been known mostly as a novelist ("A Legacy," "A Compass Error") and as an unusually astute travel writer with an absorption in the legal process ("A Sudden View," "The Trial of Dr. Adams," "The Faces of Justice"). And it was as a novelist that she approached Huxley and his life. "I wanted to give it the maximum dramatic impact without actually dramatizing," she says. "And at the same time I wanted to be scholarly without being pedantic. All my sources are either cited or can be inferred, but I hope it's all readable." As to its length, "I had hoped to be able to compress it, but it just wasn't possible. There were so many themes in Aldous's life. He foresaw all the problems we are living with now: the energy crisis, pollution of the environment, overpopulation, even the possibility of war from the Palestinians."

How about her own life as a novelist, which has been completely put aside during the years of work on "Aldous Huxley"? She smiles her sudden, rather watchful smile. "Actually, Aldous was a strong influence on me, both moral and literary, and his literary influence was very bad. In my youth I was very bookish and full of ideas, and my early work—all unpublished—was very watered-down Huxley; Huxley and soda water perhaps, hardly even soda, really. I suffered through a series of drawn-out and agonizing rejections, and I was 40 before my first book ['A Sudden View'] was published. I took rather a long time to find what I wanted to say."

Now that she has found it, Miss Bedford still feels at odds with her times. "I'd like to get back to a novel, but it's not a climate for novel writing today—not for me. I have a sense of swimming against the stream, of not being understood. There are no general assumptions about social and moral life, and it is therefore very difficult to establish a fabric for a novel, to choose an appropriate setting.

One new book is planned, however, a combination travel book and personal memoir to be called "Euphoria: A Text and Pretext of Travel," in which she wants to show how the quality of travel has changed in recent years, and not, needless to say, for the better. She has no such fierce publishing schedule as the one under which Huxley lived for much of his creative life, and which she recalls with awe. His first contract, with Chatto & Windus in London in 1923, called for two new works of fiction a year for three years, one of which was to be a full-length novel—and it was renewable for a further three years. Later emendations softened it somewhat, but for the first 15 years of his writing life Huxley was always under the gun.

Asked finally to assess his place in literature, Miss Bedford is, as always, forthright and unhesitating. "He was a very great man, but not a great writer. He never made progress, conscious or unconscious, as a writer, but that wasn't what he was interested in. If you want to advance intellectually and spiritually you haven't room for development as a writer. The humanistic quest, the search for the ideal life, occupied Aldous's life. He deliberately chose to make himself the man he became." She pauses, and it is clear that, as usual, her words are selected with great care and precision. "Aldous was the nearest you can come to being a modern-day saint."

Simone Berteaut

FEW BOOKS in recent times have taken off in the blasé literary climate of France the way Henri Charrière's "Papillon" did, or the book which followed it to the top of the best-seller lists later the same year, the equally rugged "Piaf" by Edith Piaf's half-sister Simone Berteaut. Mme. Berteaut shared the singer's intense and disordered life and loves and seemed to have put it all down in the biography to be published by Harper & Row on June 7. Writing about the French edition of "Piaf" in the *New York Review of Books*, Virgil Thomson said it was "told with such impeccable compassion and high spirits . . . so grand, so moving, and so tragic that one is inclined to salute the volume as a great book."

When a woman of 49 who has spent her life in the shadow of a legend sits down to write for the first time and turns out a book which jaded reviewers call "prodigious," "extraordinary," and "hallucinating," you feel that there must be more here than meets the eye; at any rate you want to know how she did it. Madame Berteaut came in to Paris from the country on a recent rainy day to talk about her book. She turned out to be Piaf's double, diminutive, all the bigness in the face, especially the eyes.

"The only things I had written before the book were some poems and songs" she told *PW*. "Then Charles Ronsac, who is my editor at Opera Mundi, asked me if I would be willing to write about life with *la Môme*. Indeed I was tired of the nonsense that was being said about her and I wanted to get the truth on paper—to bring her back to life not as a saint but with the good and the bad. I started writing in small

By Herbert R. Lottman. From *Publishers Weekly* 201, no. 22 (May 29, 1972), pp. 14–15. Reprinted by permission of Herbert R. Lottman.

notebooks and then they gave me a tape recorder. Opera Mundi looked up the old Piaf songs so that I could date the various episodes that I remembered through the songs that accompanied them.''

Obviously this research couldn't help her in the book's remarkable evocation of the early life of the two *gamines*—*la Môme* was 15-1/2 and Simone, Momone, was going on 13 when they teamed up for their life-long partnership. "We had to live, so Edith would sing in the street. How do you do that? When you get on the subway you ask a cop where the police station is. He points to it and you start off in the opposite direction. Edith sang with her hands behind her back so she couldn't pick up the money people threw at her. That was my job. One day we were 'doing the street' near the Champs-Elysées when this man came up to Edith and said she was crazy, she'd ruin her voice that way.

"He gave her a job in his cabaret. She needed a dress for opening night and we both began knitting like crazy but a sleeve was still missing when it was her turn to perform. Maurice Chevalier's wife overheard our panic and loaned her a scarf to cover the bare shoulder. After the first song there was a long silence. Then the applause was deafening.''

When Momone's book became a runaway hit, she says, "Obviously I had stage fright too. There were those 30 seconds of silence before the applause. Now when I hear that the book is going to be translated into languages like Serbo-Croatian, I think: She never sang in those countries when she was alive; now she can tour there through me.''

The book hit French readers with the same hard slap they had from "Papillon"—a hard life told in a hard way, the language recalling Céline. "I don't think anyone can go further in confession," François Mauriac proclaimed in *Le Figaro Littéraire*. "As admirable as Edith Piaf was as a singer, the woman who wrote this book remains on her level." He felt that the reader had to love Piaf in spite of her difficult character.

Simone Berteaut's "Piaf" was also the French public's choice of that season (autumn 1969), with a quick sale of 225,000 of the original Robert Laffont edition, another 50,000 in a Hachette paperback, translations signed up in 15 languages. Sales weren't hurt by the extensive coverage in the popular press, which included a four-part prepublication for which the newsweekly *Express* paid $20,000 (billing it as "a novel by Zola"). They weren't hurt either by the storm of controversy the book was to raise— real in the case of another half-sister of Piaf who demanded seizure and legal proceedings against the book, and of the family of late boxing champion Marcel Cerdan, who asked for suppression of passages concerning Cerdan's relations with Piaf. A flock of possibly imaginary ex-lovers (Yves Montand, among them) of Edith Piaf explained at length in a series of page-length articles in a top circulation daily the way they now felt. (Charles Aznavour and a number of other show business folk willingly submitted affidavits later to say that Piaf's life was essentially as her half-sister said it was.)

Piaf's American days are covered in detail in the book, including the story of the singer's marriage (to Jacques Pills) in St. Patrick's Cathedral, with Marlene Dietrich as a witness. In New York *la Môme* and Momone bought a three-legged table at Bloomingdale's so that Edith could communicate with the spirit of Marcel Cerdan after his death. Simone managed to transmit a great deal of practical advice through the table (the first thing the table said to Piaf was "Eat!"). After that the Bloomingdale table traveled with them everywhere. When Piaf asked Cerdan's spirit to write a song, Simone supplied "Chanson Bleue," introduced by Piaf as "Marcel's song." In memory of both Edith and Marcel, Madame Berteaut's own children, now young adults, were named Edith Marcelle and Marcel Edith.

Madame Berteaut is at work on another book now, the story of her own life up to her 15th year, evoking the poor people's Paris of 1925. She abandoned Paris about a year ago, thinking she would prefer the country. With earnings from her book she bought a house in a small village near Chartres where she lives with a cat, two dogs, four monkeys, and 14 small birds resembling *piafs* as much as possible, although *piaf* is the popular term for the wild sparrows of Paris, and the Berteaut birds are of course in cages. When the weather is bad, as it was this day, Momone feels like one of the caged birds, and she wishes she were living in Paris again.

Joseph Blotner

IN THE MOST LITERAL sense, the massive biography of William Faulkner by Joseph Blotner has been a labor of love. It was born of the strong affection and admiration that show so clearly in the face of the young English professor at the University of Virginia as [in a cherished photograph] he stands beside the great writer who had gone there as a visiting professor in 1957. Now, 17 years later and 11 years after Faulkner's death, it still kindles Blotner's eye as he talks about the man who has been at the center of his life ever since he first knew him.

Random House, which became Faulkner's regular publisher in the early 1930s after a series of rapid shifts at the start of his literary career, has given the 2000-page biography the works—two sturdily produced volumes in a handsome slipcover, weighing (as one awed TV interviewer noted recently, hefting it with difficulty) more than eight pounds. Right from the time that Blotner—inspired by Mark Schorer's exhaustive study of Sinclair Lewis—determined to write the definitive life of Faulkner, he says that he knew he would have to go to Random. "They had been Faulkner's publishers for nearly 30 years, and they had all the archives," he says. "I couldn't think of going anywhere else."

When he told this to his agent, Carol Brandt, he says she saw his point, but advised: "Don't tell them that." Blotner laughs. "She said I should get a big advance, and then spend about three years on the book. I thought maybe five years. In the end it took nearly twice that, in research and writing."

By John F. Baker. From *Publishers Weekly* 205, no. 13 (April 1, 1964), pp. 6–7.

And despite a good advance, Blotner had his worrying times when he saw how long the book was taking. "After all, I had a wife and three children to support." Still, he received a couple of Guggenheim grants and some summer fellowships which enabled him to keep going. "The only trouble was, the first summer fellowship was for Copenhagen. So I had to do my research backwards, beginning with Oslo, where Faulkner went for his Nobel acceptance in 1960, then visiting Gallimard in France and Mondadori in Italy, his European publishers, then to England to check out the Oxford background—all before I ever got down to Mississippi."

When he finally did get to Faulkner's home country, Blotner spent months interviewing, and checking out local records bearing on the Faulkner family—"I read the entire files of the *Oxford Eagle* from 1885 to 1960." Everywhere he went he carried a notebook, and whenever one was filled its contents would be typed up in triplicate—"one would go in the Year file, which I later organized month by month for Faulkner's life, one would go into the Books file, coordinated with the nearest book of his, the third into the Personality file."

With his mountain of material finally accumulated, he began writing in the summer of 1967 and finished the first draft—3500 manuscript pages—late in 1969. He had never told Random House how enormous the project was going to be. "Early on I showed Albert Erskine [who had been Faulkner's editor for much of his time at Random House] a big block of material on the writer's early life. He sat and looked at it for a while, even more taciturn than usual. Then he finally said: 'Well, this is going to be pretty long.' But he never complained. We cut a bit, that's all."

Some critics have complained that Blotner's book is *too* all-inclusive, but he is firm in its defense. "It seemed to me that fate conspired to make all this material available to me," he says. "I felt I had to get it all in." And this resolve was strengthened, he adds, when Richard Ellman, the celebrated Joyce biographer, came to visit him in Virginia and saw some of his material. "He told me: 'I wish I'd had some of this sort of detail on Joyce,' " Blotner says proudly.

In the course of his work Blotner made a number of discoveries about early drafts of various Faulkner works, showing how the novelist worked and reworked his material. Probably the most painful of these came after the book was already in galleys. "A caretaker at the house where Faulkner had lived in Roanoke opened a closet under the stairs, and found a complete early draft of 'Sartoris.' You couldn't ignore it, of course. That sort of discovery is obviously a source of mingled joy and anguish." Galleys were duly revised to reflect the discovery.

Although he had been submerged in Faulkner for so long, "I find I never tire of him," Blotner says. He is discussing a couple of further Faulkner projects with Random House; for one thing, there are a number of unpublished stories. Faulkner himself preferred to forget some of his juvenilia—late in his life. Blotner recalls, he told him, "At this stage I owe more to the name Faulkner than the early Faulkner"—but his biographer isn't so sure. "It's difficult to know what to do with the early work of a great writer. You could easily see it in a different way from the way he did."

About his own place in American literature, Faulkner never had any doubts. Blotner recalls a student at Virginia asking him if he was discouraged about the bad reviews "The Town" had received, and Faulkner replying quietly, "I made up my mind early about the value of my work." He remembers, too, his very first encounter with Faulkner, when he saw him on a train in 1953. "I sent my wife to him with a copy of 'Go Down Moses' for him to autograph. He signed it twice, once on a blank page, and again on the title page, with the date and place. His intuitions were so remarkable—he knew the different meaning and value two such autographs would have."

Faulkner was an intensely private man who could on occasion go through the most remarkable performances (some of them are described in the book) to preserve his privacy. And sometimes the heavy drinking in which he indulged all his life made him a difficult companion (though his worst bouts took place in solitude). He seems always to have been most at ease among friends and neighbors in Oxford, Mississippi, most restive among "lit'ry" folk. Hunting was a particular pleasure, Blotner adds, because then Faulkner was among people who shared his enjoyment—but that too could be marred. He remembers asking Faulkner once whether he had enjoyed a day's hunting, and the writer's reply: "Yes, except that we had some people along who knew they had a Nobel laureate riding with them."

Blotner's own identification with his material was complete. "When I got to the last chapter and had to write about the funeral, I actually got all choked up"—but he was moved to find that Faulkner's brother Jack felt the same way. "There were some things here I didn't know, and which have upset me," he told the biographer. "It's the only study of Bill that's affected me that way."

For a devoted biographer, the knowledge that he knows more about his subject than the subject's own brother is profoundly rewarding. It all helps to contribute to Blotner's current euphoric state, which was probably foreshadowed in a later epigraph Faulkner wrote for him in one of his books. Faulkner had always been particularly keen on flying, and had maintained an aristocratically English persona—both wonderfully combined in the time he spent training for the Royal Air Force in Canada more than 50 years ago. Probably the strangest salutation ever written by a Nobel prize-winning novelist graces Blotner's cherished copy. "Cheeroh," it reads, "and plenty revs!"

Joan Haslip

MAXIMILIAN AND CARLOTA, Emperor and Empress of Mexico, have long been familiar, fascinating, almost irresistible figures to readers and authors alike. But, according to critics, their story has never been told better than in the May Book-of-the-Month Club selection, "The Crown of Mexico," by Joan Haslip (*Holt, Rinehart & Winston*). The author is a happy combination of diligent scholar and warm, compassionate woman, and here undoubtedly is the key to her success. Her feelings for the tragic rulers have moved them from the realm of romantic legend and presented them as human beings, with extraordinary faults and virtues.

Maximilian was Archduke of Austria next in line of succession to the throne when Napoleon III (abetted strongly by Empress Eugenie) offered him and his bride, Carlota, daughter of King Leopold of Belgium, the Mexican empire. The French were eager to protect financial interests in the new world; the Church was anxious to maintain a Catholic bastion there and Franz Josef, Emperor of Austria, wanted to get his handsome, charming, and popular younger brother out of the way. Carlota, only 23 and blazing with ambition, was blind to the difficulties that doomed the adventure from the start. She appealed to Maximilian's sense of *noblesse oblige* and love of the exotic to persuade him to accept the crown. A complex man, he was eager for power but never strong enough to grasp it or use it well. He was infuriatingly dilettantish, absorbed by the pleasures of his fairy-tale castle, Miramar, near Trieste. Carlota was the more anxious to rule and she brushed aside the advice of friends and relatives who opposed the venture.

By Jean F. Mercier. From *Publishers Weekly* 201, no. 6 (June 26, 1972), pp. 28–29. Reprinted by permission of Jean F. Mercier.

Maximilian and Carlota set sail in 1864 for the New World, committed to a rulership that would end with Maximilian's execution by the firing squad of the victorious republican, Juarez—and in the lifelong madness of Carlota.

Asked by *PW* how she became interested in the unlucky royal pair, Miss Haslip explained that "The Crown of Mexico" grew out of a previous work, "The Lonely Empress," a life of Elizabeth, Empress of Austria, who was Maximilian's sister-in-law. "Maximilian and Carlota kept intruding," Miss Haslip recalled. "You might say they *demanded* a biography of their own."

About the staggering amount of research that has obviously gone into the book, she says, "I always do all my own research. Anyone else might just miss that bit of gossip that could reveal so much to me." Miss Haslip kept up this kind of personal attention to detail on Maximilian and Carlota for three-and-a-half years. She went everywhere that they had lived—Belgium, Italy, France and, of course, Mexico. Much of the information she uncovered has never been published before, she believes. She had a tremendous break at home in London one day when a friend called to tell her that Sotheby's famous auction house was putting up "something of interest" on her subject. The "something" turned out to be the private letters of Maximilian and Carlota. Miss Haslip asked for and received the job of cataloging the material and thus came to know the young rulers most intimately. Similarly, she has had access to other unpublished material, including letters from Mlle. Bassompierre, lady-in-waiting to Carlota.

Little poignant touches in the source material appealed to the author, as they will to her readers. She writes graphically of Carlota's condition when she returned to Europe to plead with Napoleon and the Pope for continued support of the crumbling Mexican empire. Arriving in Paris, the Empress sent one of her Mexican attendants out to buy her a hat. Mme. del Barrio, eager for her mistress to look her best, returned with the costliest hat available. It turned out to be too big, too ornate, and only accentuated the look of illness and incipient madness with which Carlota faced society in Napoleon's capital. The Empress Eugenie and other friends and admirers of the formerly beautiful, haughty young Carlota were shocked. Napoleon was more embarrassed by her strangeness than moved, and adamant in his refusal to keep French troops at the disposal of Maximilian.

Miss Haslip's brisk, incisive mind has evaluated all the evidence, old and new, on many aspects of her subjects' lives, and has come to some interesting conclusions. She is convinced, for instance, that Carlota was pregnant with the son of Colonel Van der Smissen, one of Maximilian's officers, when she returned to Europe. The author finds it logical that the vital young Carlota, neglected by her low-sexed and frequently absent husband, had accepted the love of the Colonel. Certainly it is believable that the burden of pregnancy, coupled with her anxiety over the fate of her empire, helped bring on Carlota's insanity. Miss Haslip, in the course of tracking down rumors of this liaison, found in Mexico a portrait of Colonel Van der Smissen in which he strongly resembles the famous French General Maxime Weygand. Weygand was brought up and supported by Carlota's royal Belgian family.

"When I met Monsieur Sabbé, Curator of the Royal Archives in Brussels," says Miss Haslip, "first thing he said to me was, 'I want you to know there isn't a *word* of truth to the gossip that Carlota had a child.' Well," she continued, "*qui s'excuse, s'accuse . . .*"

She also believes that Franz Josef's resentment of his brother Maximilian could have stemmed from rumors, equally persistent, that Maximilian was the illegitimate son of their mother, Archduchess Sophia, by her great friend, the Duke of Reichstadt, son of Napoleon I. The Duke— handsome and charming like Maximilian—died of tuberculosis at the age of 21 while Sophia was carrying Maximilian.

Such details and others, equally provocative, make "The Crown of Mexico" an absorbing retelling of the Mexican fiasco. Miss Haslip has literally lived with her subjects for the years it took her to create their biography and she explains her habitual thoroughness by telling a story on herself.

"When I was in my twenties, I was attempting a novel, the story of an older woman attracted to a young man. I was discouraged; it wouldn't work and finally I tore it up. My friend, Liam O'Flaherty—he wrote 'The Informer' and other marvelous books; he simply has never got the credit he deserves—anyway, he heard of my problems and came to see me. 'Joan!' he said. 'You see that cat of yours? Well, it's got guts, my girl. If you were writing about that cat, you'd have to find out what its guts were like, what makes it act as it does, and it's the same with people. You can't write about people if you don't know what they're like inside.' "

Lesson well learned; it has helped Miss Haslip to create three successful novels and several fine biographies. And it will no doubt be remembered while the author is working on her next, this one about Catherine, Empress of all the Russias. Joan Haslip is off, naturally, to Russia to find out what made Catherine so Great.

The Kalb Brothers

PW: FOR STARTERS, what does Secretary Kissinger think about "Kissinger"?

BK: Even on "Kissinger," Kissinger practices secret diplomacy. The other night, he dropped in—Nancy was with him—on a big party in Washington to promote the book, given by Little, Brown. He was promptly surrounded by reporters: What did *he* think of the book? "Well," he said, serving up an ample portion of anticipated ego, "I haven't had time to read it systematically, but I love the title."

MK: He is—it's hardly a state secret—an extremely sensitive man; the eyes and ears of his staff are on constant alert for any comment on Kissinger. True, he has a professional interest in what's being said about him, but he also has a considerable personal interest. Maybe the more pertinent question is not whether he's read the book—but whether he has asked his staff to memorize it.

PW: Why did you choose to write about Kissinger? The gallery of men around Richard Nixon included a wide choice—Haldeman, Ehrlichman, Mitchell, etc. Why not one of them?

BK: Next question.

PW: Why in fact Kissinger?

BK: What interested us both was the restructuring of U.S. foreign policy. Marvin and I lived abroad for some time: Marvin, for about five years in the Soviet Union, working, first with the U.S. Embassy in Moscow in the late fifties, then as a CBS News correspondent in the early sixties. He's been covering State since 1963, Kissinger and State since 1969. I had spent 15 years or so in Southeast Asia, beginning

By Marvin & Bernard Kalb. From *Publishers Weekly* 206, no. 16 (October 14, 1974), pp. 6–7. Reprinted by permission of Marvin Kalb.

in the mid-fifties—with a lot of that time in Vietnam—first with the *New York Times*, then with CBS News. There was also an opportunity to go along with Nixon on the trip to China in 1972 and to return to Peking the following year. So that U.S. policy has been more than an abstraction; we'd seen its impact, for better or worse, close up, and a look at policy meant a look at Kissinger, and vice versa. He was also the most interesting of the men around the President.

PW: How do you profile Kissinger—swiftly?

BK: A sense of timing, a committed tenacity, endless stamina, other characteristics as well. Pragmatic—a readiness to serve as a gravedigger of ideology, with an emphasis on dealing with what he regards as realities rather than the illusions that have characterized so much of U.S. policy in the past. You'd also have to add a penchant for secrecy, a less than flattering estimate of the bureaucracy, a tendency toward what some see as outright deviousness; in Washington, you can find some people who regard Kissinger, to quote one official who'd rather remain unidentified, as an "unmitigated liar." As amoral, Kissinger is obviously not unaware of these portrayals. He would argue that he is not morally callous. "The preservation of human life and human society are moral values too," was what he emphasized before the Senate Foreign Relations Committee the other day.

PW: Kissinger lately has been running into some pointed criticism. Is it possible that he is heading for a fall?

MK: It's hard to say. In a sense, he has been heading for a fall ever since he came to Washington; to stay on top indefinitely in the power scramble of Washington is a feat beyond even Kissinger's talents. You know, Kissinger is a fatalistic man who recognizes that the days of spectacular diplomacy are gone, and the possibilities of pitfalls and problems are enormous. During the Nixon years, he towered over the men around the President. Now, his image will change, as the Presidency itself changes—away from the intensely controversial Nixon days to the comparatively more normal Ford days. Besides, Kissinger has run into trouble, clearly, with the Pentagon over the future shape of the arms limitation agreements with the Soviet Union; with some senators, who deplore his role in the secret CIA operations in Chile; with some others, who were upset by his handling of the Cyprus situation. He's going to get his lumps, as the saying goes, and he knows it.

PW: Will Kissinger quit?

MK: Well, you know, he threatened to quit once before—last June, in Salzburg, unless he was cleared of allegations that he had played a key role in the initiation of secret wiretaps on thirteen officials and four newsmen. As one of those newsmen, I was obviously very disturbed about those taps. If the criticism of his policies vis-à-vis Chile and Cyprus intensifies, if he feels he may lose his battle with Defense Secretary Schlesinger over arms negotiations with the Russians, if he feels that his integrity is under constant attack and thereby affecting his authority as a negotiator, it would not be surprising to learn one morning that Henry Kissinger had decided that enough is enough.

PW: What would he do if he quit?

MK: I know what he will not do. He will not go back to Harvard. But I don't think the day will ever come when Kissinger hangs up his pin-striped suit. He may, one day, leave his current job—but the job of trying to bring nations together, perhaps as a private international consultant, no. In a surrealistic moment, I can even see Kissinger putting several foreign offices out of business.

PW: Will you write another book on the subject—"Kissinger II"?

MK: That's an idea whose time has not come.

PW: Let's go back to the book we are talking about. How was it collaborating with a brother?

BK: It worked out surprisingly well, particularly when Marvin agreed with me.

PW: Do you see "Kissinger" as a movie or a Broadway musical?

BK: Marvelous. Kissinger playing Kissinger—touring the world. Now if he were to be otherwise occupied, or perhaps to suffer an acute case of stage fright, how about Peter Ustinov? Or Peter Sellers?

MK: It's hard to imagine Kissinger allowing anyone to play Kissinger except himself. My own image is that of a Woody Allen kind of Kissinger, pasting parts of the world together. Others may have a more melancholy image—of perhaps a fiddler on the roof, keeping spirits up, while catastrophe takes place all around him. Kissinger in a way is a mix of both—an alternately brooding and exuberant diplomat, outwardly the optimist, inwardly deeply worried about the state of a nuclear world. There's a line of his: "Each success only buys an admission ticket to a more difficult problem."

BK: Enough. If we keep on talking, we're going to give away the ending of the book.

George R. Marek

GEORGE R. MAREK—scholarly, courtly, elderly, and still with a strong reminder of his native Vienna in his voice—is so much the idealized image of a music critic that it is difficult to imagine that he has spent 20 years as a New York advertising man, and several more as a top executive at RCA. Despite such apparent aberrations, however, music has been a passion throughout his adult life—and it was in his capacity as one of the most skillful of contemporary musical biographers that *PW* recently encountered him.

The latest subject for Marek's examination—and a worshipful one it is in this case—is conductor Arturo Toscanini, who achieved legendary status almost as soon as he appeared on the musical scene, and whose influence on 20th century standards of musical interpretation has remained towering since his death 20 years ago. In a country where only a minute portion of the populace listens regularly to serious music (perhaps about the same number as buys hardcover books, to put it in sad perspective for publishers), Marek discovered that something like 70% of the people had heard of Toscanini and knew he was something to do with music—an astonishing figure when you consider that polls regularly turn up numbers of people who cannot name the current President.

Marek approached the writing of "Toscanini" with some caution, though he had intended to do the book ever since the conductor's death and had also been urged to it by the late Walter Toscanini, Arturo's son. "I was so dazzled by him in life that I wanted to give myself a chance to see him clearly," he says. He had every opportunity to be dazzled

By John F. Baker. From *Publishers Weekly* 207, no. 9 (March 3, 1975), pp. 8–9.

by the conductor in life. He describes in his book how, through the 30s, he and his wife would let their vacations be governed by wherever the Maestro happened to be conducting: at first at Bayreuth and Milan, later, as the Fascism Toscanini hated with all his soul settled over Germany and Italy, in London and New York. He saw him conduct countless times, and in all sorts of conditions—and never did he find him less than revelatory. Not until later did Marek actually come to know Toscanini well, and by that time under the best of all possible circumstances—as head of RCA-Victor's classical music division, ever ready to record anything the Maestro chose to commit to posterity (usually with reluctance, since he disliked recording and, to the despair of record collectors, did most of it in a dead-sounding studio that *he* admired for its clarity).

"He was the only artist I ever knew who was 100 percent artist. He literally cared for nothing but what he was creating. The composers he conducted were gods, and he and his orchestras and singers were there to serve them—and only them. Ego was simply not involved, just a ruthless passion for perfection, a determination that everyone should exert himself to the utmost. I've known many of the great musicians, but his dedication set him apart from anyone I've ever known."

Such singlemindedness, coupled with a fierce temper that emerged whenever he felt a player or singer was not giving his utmost, made for some historic tantrums: broken batons, screams and curses, angry stormings from the podium, refusals to return for encores. Marek has dealt frankly with them and acknowledges that in many ways Toscanini was a difficult man to live with, artistically speaking. On a personal level, however, he was remarkably genial and relaxed, even childlike in many ways. He utterly failed to understand anything mechanical, had a small boy's fascination with trains and airplanes, to the end of his life could not even operate a phonograph properly when he wanted to listen to one of his own or someone else's records.

Marek tells a story that illustrates both Toscanini's fantastic ear (he could write down a full orchestra score from memory after only glancing through it) and the utterly unself-conscious nature of his wrath. It seems that when the RCA engineers had finished taping "Otello" and were playing it back to Toscanini, he noticed a minute slip by one of the players. "At the wrong sound, he screamed like a wounded animal, and the only way we could soothe him was to promise to correct it with a tape splice. Somehow the engineer missed catching the right spot, and when we played it for him again the same mistake was still there. And he screamed in exactly the same way, and the same moment. He didn't shout that we were supposed to have fixed it, or demand why it was still wrong. His was never a *thinking* reaction to a situation. If something gave him pain, musically, he reacted viscerally."

On another occasion he was playing what he had been told was one of his own recordings of a Brahms symphony. "After only a few bars he looked puzzled, then became distraught, and cursed himself for the way in which the music was being played." Then it was realized that it was a recording by another conductor that had been played by mistake. "Toscanini knew there was something wrong, but he was always prepared to believe the worst of himself."

Marek's reign over classical music at RCA, during what music buffs often think of as the golden years of the 1950s, came about as a result of a mingling between his advertising career and his freelance writing. Since the early 1940s he had been writing on music subjects for *Good House-keeping* magazine, and in the course of a visit to the RCA-Victor recording studios on a story he attempted to woo them away from their advertising agency to his own. He roughed out a campaign ("They eventually used it—famous people talking about their favorite musicians, who always happened to be RCA recording artists, of course"), but instead of giving his agency the account, they offered him a job instead—as head of the classical music division.

From that seat he had a good view of the problems of classical record distribution and upon being asked to compare them with those of trade book distribution, his eyes light up. "It's an intensely comparable situation. It all comes down in the end to the problem of how to distribute a quality product to a small audience in a marketplace that postulates high turnover and heavy traffic. Now most of the old-time personal record stores have gone, and nowadays any retailer who wants to stock a tithe of the records being published has to go broke. Do you know who the most successful record dealer in New York is? Korvette!

"There *is* an audience out there for good music, just as there is for trade books. It's probably smaller than we like to think it is, but it's also larger than the cynic thinks it is. The real problem is that it's so difficult to reach. That's the reason why publishers have book clubs, and record companies have record clubs." These days Marek himself is a consultant to the Reader's Digest record operation.

Marek has written studies of Puccini, Richard Strauss, Mendelssohn and, most recently, "Beethoven: Biography of a Genius," which was widely hailed as the best contemporary study of the composer and which got as near as music books ever do to bestsellerdom. "My timing was good, right on Beethoven's bicentennial," Marek says modestly. But he agrees with a sigh that books on musical figures usually don't sell too well. "I'd love to write a book on Schubert, but who would buy it? Sometimes it seems that people who love music just don't read."

Ralph G. Martin

AFTER HIS BEST-SELLING "Jennie: The Life of Lady Randolph Churchill," Ralph G. Martin naturally wanted a subject as dramatic and fascinating for his next book. Thanks to Simon and Schuster, he has more than found it in "The Woman He Loved: The Story of the Duke and Duchess of Windsor," just published.

This is the first time the story of one of the most famous romances in history has been dealt with this impartially, not just from a royal point of view nor just from that of the Duchess herself, although Martin is very sympathetic toward her. He talks about the fascination he found in researching and writing the new book with an enthusiasm that is very winning and should make his promotional appearances on its behalf send people into bookstores in droves.

Martin was well into background reading for the book when he got wind of the fact that two other well-known writers were working way ahead of him on similar Windsor books. Accordingly, he decided to use whatever material he had, not in long book form, but in a two-part magazine piece, and approached the *Ladies' Home Journal* with that in mind. The *Journal* accepted with alacrity (eventually, the *Journal* ran three excerpts from the book, excerpts that were to have legal repercussions in France). Martin began his first-hand research with a trip to Nassau and in time extended it to Palm Beach, London, Paris, Virginia, the French Riviera.

"The timing was just right," he says. "So many of the people who had known the Duke and Duchess were still alive. Yet many of them could not have talked as they did if

By Barbara A. Bannon. From *Publishers Weekly* 206, no. 7 (August 12, 1974), pp. 8–9.

he had been still alive. Very soon it dawned on me that not one of these people who had been so close to the story had been interviewed by another writer and that I really was first, so I went back to Simon and Schuster and said, 'It's going as a book after all.' After that, I worked on it day and night, seven days a week, for about a year."

One of the first contacts Martin made was with Lord Perry Brownlow, a friend so close to the then Prince of Wales that he was the only man Edward would trust to take Wallis Simpson to the South of France for him at a crucial time in the romance. Brownlow was most helpful and passed him on to someone else with a letter of introduction. After that Martin began making contact after contact with members of the Windsor circle, one passing him on to another.

" 'Jennie' was the door opener to everyone," Martin discovered. "Many of these society people could not care less about writers, but virtually all of them had read 'Jennie.' Even the Duchess of Windsor, when I finally met her, had read 'Jennie' and liked it very much."

Martin, who says, "I never depend on anyone else to do my research—another person simply cannot have your own background knowledge," amassed his information simply by sitting down and talking to people. The problem, of course, was that the Duchess was still alive and many people were hesitant about being quoted because of that fact. Martin says he triple-checked each quote.

"My technique in researching a book is to work from the rim to the center," he says. "By the time you get to the center you know the hard questions to ask. The Duchess of Windsor was the last person I wanted to see, and I knew that would be difficult to arrange. I tried to make contact through her friends, making the point that I had talked to so many of them that it would seem ridiculous if some of her own personality did not have a chance to emerge. When I was in London I read in a paper that one of the other American writers supposedly interested in a book about the Windsors had just visited the Duchess in the South of France and came away, defeated, because she wanted a million dollars for an 'authorized' version of their story. I thought, why should she even bother to give me the right time?"

Nevertheless, soon afterwards, word came to Martin that if he could just happen to be on the French Riviera on a certain day the Duchess would be delighted if he could drop by for lunch. It was, of course, the high point of all his work. "She was delightful, witty, in top form all through lunch, and so young looking," he recalls. "I thought that would be all the time I could possibly expect, but after lunch she said, 'Don't you want to ask me some questions?' and we spent the rest of the day talking in her drawing room. There is nothing phoney about this woman. She is a woman deeply interested in other people. You have to see this right away. Men are genuinely drawn to her. When we parted she said, 'Be gentle with your pen.' "

Martin has not yet heard from the Duchess about her personal reaction to the book as a whole. When the *Ladies' Home Journal* sections appeared, dealing not surprisingly with some of the more sensational aspects of the story, including Wallis Simpson's deep love for a South American diplomat before the Prince of Wales, "she hit the roof." Martin admits, and sued to get those issues of the *Journal* containing material from the book banned in France.

"The challenge of the book," Martin sums it up, "was to dig into the mystery of two people who, no matter what they said in the press, kept a great part of themselves to themselves. She really made him her cause. On the other hand, there was probably no man in the world more in love with his wife than he was. When he gave up his throne, he really gave up nothing that meant anything to him. She was the first woman genuinely interested in him as a human being, not just as a celebrity. She knew how to handle this man. She knew how to talk to him about anything. Part of the reason for the attraction was that she was an American. She had a candor and directness he had never known before. She was an American girl who questioned him all the way. That room of his is still the same as he left it on his death. She walks in there every night to say goodnight to him."

No one is predicting anything, least of all Ralph G. Martin, but a quizzical side-note—and a very human one—is the comment by one of Martin's interviewees that the current Prince of Wales, Prince Charles, shows a considerable amount of interest in his great-uncle.

Eileen O'Casey

AS THE JACKET of the forthcoming "Sean" (*Coward, McCann & Geoghegan*) will show, when the young actress, Eileen Carey, married playwright Sean O'Casey in 1927, she was a beautiful, fresh-faced girl of 23. Some 43 years later, she is still a very lovely looking woman, who arrives for an interview in London, where she now lives, slightly husky-voiced from a bad bout of bronchitis, but very attractively dressed in a rosy red pants suit and delicate golden jewelry. The jewelry is the work of Breon, the one surviving O'Casey son, a painter who lives with his wife and children in the artists' colony of St. Ives, Cornwall.

Very pleasant and affable, Eileen O'Casey is just a little wary at first about what an unknown interviewer from America may be going to ask about her completely open and honest memoir of the O'Casey marriage, "Sean." The discovery of mutual friends she and the interviewer share relaxes her considerably and she begins to talk, first about how "Sean" came into being, and then about Sean himself, and their family life.

"So many people had written about Sean who had seen him for only half an hour or so, or for only two or three days—and none had really managed to describe him," she says, "that I very much wanted to write about him myself. I had tried about two chapters when the London publishing firm of W. H. Allen sent a girl to see me to ask me if I would write about my life with Sean. I told her that I had thought about just this kind of writing, but if I pursued it at all the book would have to go to Macmillan [of London], Sean's own publisher. She was a charming young woman. We liked

By Barbara A. Bannon. From *Publishers Weekly* 200, no. 23 (December 6, 1971), pp. 11–13.

each other as people and she told me, 'If you are in any difficulty, just let me know and I will try to help you work it out. Do not worry about our not publishing the book.' "

As it happened, Macmillan of London was decidedly interested, and Alan MacLean of Macmillan suggested J. S. Trewin, an old friend of the O'Casey's, as the perfect choice to edit the book and write an introduction.

"John Trewin's great asset," Eileen O'Casey says, "where he is so good, is that he does not interrupt you at all. He just keeps on reminding you of things you might possibly forget. Sean admired him very much and thought he had great integrity. I began to feel like someone who has to return homework. I would know he was coming on a Tuesday, so I would just have to have the material ready for him. Alan MacLean wanted him not to alter me as myself in what I wrote and I don't think he has.

"No, I was never a person who kept diaries—just appointments—not anything dramatic like, 'I had an emotional day.' I have very good powers of recollection [most actresses do, as Ruth Gordon once pointed out to *PW*], and everything in our lives did work according to the production or rewriting of Sean's plays or the birth of our children.

"There were sections of 'Sean' that were very difficult to write. The death of Niall [the O'Casey's handsome son who died at 20, suddenly and cruelly of leukemia] was the hardest to write about. I suppose that it is really obvious how much I miss Sean, but he had had his life, when he died. His sight was practically gone. Poor Niall was on the threshold of his life. Sean never really recovered from Niall's death. He adored his family. He really loved them. They were everything to him.

"Niall's death had to come into 'Sean.' It was the keynote of our lives. One's never quite the same after something like that. You must live on because the boy, himself, would hate it if you didn't. Sean found it much harder to do than me [although Eileen O'Casey admits she took an overdose of sleeping pills after Niall's death]. Sean was older and people did mourn differently then, after the way in which he was brought up.

"No, none of the children (Niall, Breon, Shivaun) ever lived in the shadow of their father. Sean was particularly unobtrusive as an artist in his own home. He would never mention himself or his own work much to the children. I would get most of that. The children were lucky in going to a modern school where they were encouraged to be themselves. It is always more satisfying to one as a person to be yourself. Shivaun, who is married and has a small son, lives about 20 minutes from me. She is an actress and most recently has just made some marvelous hats for the Bristol production of 'My Fair Lady.' Breon is completely talented in his own right as a painter.

"Isn't it marvelous and extraordinary how Sean's plays are being done so much now in college theaters and other such groups? In the last three years of his life he made more money than we had ever made, and it was some consolation to him that I would be left more comfortable. He did feel that he would be recognized.

"There was never any nonsense about Sean deciding to leave Ireland dramatically. It was simply much easier for Sean to live here in England and to realize that London could offer him more than Dublin could in those days. If only the Abbey Theater had let him have a practicing ground for his plays, but the man just sat there with all these ideas in his mind and no place to experiment in the working theater. So much has been copied from the poor man. He was very far ahead of his time. 'Within the Gates' and 'Cock-a-Doodle-Dandy' have influenced the theater, without full recognition being given to that O'Casey influence.

"I think Sean grew in stature as a person and a playwright under tremendous pressures. For years he had to sit there in his armchair without seeing his plays produced anywhere. I think that is what made him as inventive a writer as he was. He was, by nature, a man who loved people with whom to talk. The prodigious letter-writing he went in for [his letters are subsequently to be published in several volumes] was a substitute for the theater audience he couldn't reach."

One of the most candid sequences in "Sean" deals with Eileen O'Casey's brief lapse back into a sexual liaison with a married American who had been her lover before she met Sean. The incident, and it was hardly more than that, occurred after her marriage with Sean and left her pregnant. In desperation, she tried to get rid of the child and then told O'Casey what had happened. Distraught and anguished, he nevertheless helped her obtain an abortion.

"I do not think it is much good writing a book unless what you do put down is true, otherwise it is very uninteresting," Eileen O'Casey told *PW*. "In my case, I included this incident specifically to try to show what Sean was like, his goodness and kindness to me. Once he loved, he loved completely."

Patrick O'Higgins

FOR PATRICK O'HIGGINS, his former companion, Helena Rubinstein was an empress, a tycoon with eccentricities. "I didn't like her; I adored her," said Mr. O'Higgins when *PW* interviewed him in connection with the publication of his book, "Madame: An Intimate Biography of Helena Rubinstein" (*Viking*). Mr. O'Higgins, who worked for Madame and was her companion for 14 years, told us, "She always fascinated me. She was very old [nearly 80 when they met] and she was very rich and had done it all herself."

From a family face-cream recipe which she brought to Australia from Poland as a young girl, Helena Rubinstein established a cosmetics empire which eventually made her one of the richest women in the world. Mr. O'Higgins told us that she managed to accumulate so many jewels that he had to set up a filing system for them—E for Emeralds, D for Diamonds, etc. Her apartments in New York, Paris and London and her three country homes were lavishly furnished. "She kept hundreds of thousands of dollars in loose cash in safes so that she could go and look at it."

"What irritated me the most about Madame was her inability to live up to the good things that surrounded her. If you live in a grand establishment, why not eat caviar?" Yet, said Mr. O'Higgins, Madame stuck mostly to hamburgers. He attributed this incongruity to the lack of money in her family when she was growing up.

"She had a sense of the theater and realized that she needed jewels to fit her image, but she insisted on doing without taxicabs. In the final analysis I don't think that she ever made a generous gesture, one dictated purely by her

By Lila P. Freilicher. From *Publishers Weekly* 200, no. 7 (August 16, 1971), pp. 23–24.

heart." (A small African statue of which she kept 300 copies was the only gift she gave Mr. O'Higgins in her lifetime, he said.)

Patrick O'Higgins' secret of good living is "to live within your means surrounded by your pretty things." This conclusion he reached long before he met Madame, however. "I was brought up in Paris, and my family was very rich until the crash over here." Surrounding Patrick O'Higgins in his small apartment on East 57th Street in New York, are such objects as an 11th century wooden Chinese princess, a 17th century, hand-carved, Italian chest, a Christian Berard painting, two 100-year-old porcelain gargoyles (family heirlooms) and two Graham Sutherland sketches—one of Madame, the other of Somerset Maugham. The desk on which Mr. O'Higgins had done the writing of "Madame" is an antique Irish kitchen table.

The idea of writing a biography of Helena Rubinstein formed in Mr. O'Higgins' mind when he was editing Madame's autobiography, "My Life for Beauty" (*S&S*). "Every time I tried to make it human she hated it. She didn't want anyone to know what she was really like. Sometimes I think she saw herself as a cross between Joan Crawford and Madame Curie. At that time I decided I would some day write a book of my own about Madame. (She died in 1965.)

Lately, Patrick O'Higgins told us, Madame has been appearing in his dreams. "She tells me she has read the book and says it is 'not strong enough.' She would have looked at it as something to promote her products. I think she would have put up with the descriptions of her flaws if I had told people to buy her cleanser."

His experience working for Madame has changed Patrick O'Higgins' life. He says that it has been for the better. Yet while he worked for her she restricted his advancement. "Basically I was always a writer. But Madame had decided that I was more valuable to her as a companion. I did write all her releases and do her correspondence, but instead of giving me the job of advertising manager which I deserved, she kept me down. However, as a result of my years with her I have written a book, and now I feel I will be writing others."

Eleanor Philby

ELEANOR PHILBY, American wife of the confessed Soviet spy, Kim Philby, impresses as a world-weary lady who, after some pretty battering emotional experiences, would now like to lead her life in peace and quiet. In New York recently, she submitted gracefully but guardedly to a series of interviews set up for her by Ballantine Books in connection with the publication of her story, "The Spy I Married." Talking about "the blue and white Arab town" in Tunisia in which she has been living and working in mosaics ("lovely old bits and pieces fished out of the sea") or her Siamese cat, St. John, named after Kim Philby's father, a celebrated scholar of the Arab world, Mrs. Philby was relaxed and at ease. Encountering a brash radio interviewer who kept trying to draw her into a political discussion of the Middle East (one of Kim Philby's areas of specialization) she showed her claws, told him off and went mute.

A "completely apolitical person" by her own description, Eleanor Philby decided to tell her story of her marriage to Kim Philby, and the time she spent with him in Russia after his defection to Moscow, and to tell it through the *Observer* of London when it became apparent that there was going to be a wave of Philby articles and books. The *Observer*, for which Kim Philby had long been a correspondent, was the only paper Mrs. Philby would consider talking to, and she did, taping part of her story and going over it with an *Observer* staff member, Patrick Seale, who helped her put it in order, first for the newspaper, then in book form. Of the other Philby books on the way, she says she has read only "The Third Man" by E. H. Cookridge, to be published here

By Barbara A. Bannon. From *Publishers Weekly* 193, no. 10 (March 4, 1968), pp. 23–24.

by Putnam, and she calls it "full of complete lies," at least insofar as she herself is concerned. "Nobody can write *my* story but me," she told *PW*, and "nobody can use me in a movie version without my permission." There have been two very interesting film nibbles for "The Spy I Married," one from Richard Burton (whom Eleanor Philby thinks Kim Philby resembles slightly) and one from Trevor Howard. Terence Rattigan has shown interest in doing a screenplay.

"The Spy I Married" was put down on paper only after Eleanor Philby had received Kim Philby's permission to do it. The idea, she says, was to do a non-mudslinging book that would try to be fair to all concerned. The book is, indeed, remarkably free from bitterness, even in the final section dealing with Philby's affair with Melinda Maclean, ex-wife of spy Donald Maclean, for whom Philby left Eleanor.

So far as Eleanor Philby knows, she is still Kim Philby's legal wife. Although one London paper printed that he had divorced her and married Melinda, she has received a cable from Philby saying that there had definitely been no divorce. For her part, she says that when she returned to Moscow in 1964 after a visit with her daughter in this country, it was with every intention of remaining Philby's wife. "I brought back a two-years' supply of art materials for me and clothes for Kim," she says, and reacting as only a woman could to an apartment she had finally got fixed up, she says wistfully of their Moscow flat, "It was the first time I've ever had a place where everything at last was the way I wanted it."

If there is little bitterness in "The Spy I Married," Eleanor Philby is human enough to allow herself some now. Kim Philby, she says, sends her occasional funds, "but not enough to buy a house and settle down as I wanted." Asked if *she* would ever consider divorcing *him*, she snapped back, "I don't intend to spend any money getting a divorce."

As for Kim Philby's own future in Russia, Eleanor Philby thinks "he will still be exceedingly valuable to the Russians so long as we have crises in the Middle East. He knows all the people who will be coming up in the governments and cabinets there. He also knows a great deal about Africa."

Asked whether, if she had it all to do over again, she would do anything different, Mrs. Philby said dryly, "I think I'd ask my next husband if he was a dedicated Communist before marrying him, but then if he was a dedicated Communist, he wouldn't tell me anyway, would he?"

Ishbel Ross

Ishbel Ross was born and grew up in the Highlands of Scotland, north of Inverness. (Ishbel is a Scottish version of Isabelle.) Although she has lived in New York since 1919, there is still a lovely Scots lilt to her voice. Most of her long and highly acclaimed writing career has been devoted to studies of famous 19th century American women ("and sometimes to their husbands, too"), among them, Mary Todd Lincoln, Varina Davis, the wife of Jefferson Davis, Mrs. Ulysses S. Grant, Clara Barton, Lola Montez. In all, she has written 19 works of nonfiction and five novels.

Her new book, "Power with Grace" (*Putnam*), is the life story of Edith Bolling Wilson, the wife of Woodrow Wilson, who came to be called, not always kindly, "our first woman president," when she tried to protect her seriously ailing husband from the demands of his office.

Ishbel Ross's own life story is as interesting in its way as that of any of her subjects, and listening to her one can instantly perceive the natural affinity of this Scottish lady for other women who have taken their lives in hand, sometimes against great odds.

The Highland countryside in which Ishbel Ross was raised contained some of the finest shooting boxes of the British aristocracy in those far-off golden days before World War I. American millionaire Andrew Carnegie had his castle only 10 miles away and the young Ishbel watched the coaches "come right near our home, carrying beautiful American women and such illustrious guests as the Battenbergs, the Duke of Sutherland, Balfour, Lord Cecil, G. B. Shaw, Kipling," and even, later on, Woodrow Wilson who

By Barbara A. Bannon. From *Publishers Weekly* 208, no. 13 (September 29, 1975), pp. 6–7.

wanted Carnegie to back him in his peace plans. "Carnegie did not believe in shooting, himself, but he allowed his guests to do so," she recalls.

"We are very bookish in the Highlands. I was sunk in the classics," she says, looking back to a very happy childhood. "I cannot remember the time I did not want to be a writer. I was hideous in math and the sciences, but my English teacher gave me special privileges and allowed me to devote special time to reading in the heather under a willow tree. Those Highland schools are very good."

However, "Scots are notoriously restless," and, fresh from school, during World War I, when so many men had gone to war and left their jobs, Ishbel Ross left Scotland for Toronto, Canada, in search of a job on a newspaper. "I couldn't type and I didn't know the city, and the managing editor quite rightly said to me, 'What good can you be to us? Go to business school, learn to type.' I did and then I went back to him, only to discover he had forgotten all about me."

He must have been a kindly soul, however, or else very shrewd at playing his hunches, because he gave the young woman a job in the library filing cuts for five or six weeks. Then, just the way it happens in the movies and occasionally in real life, an opportunity arose and Ishbel Ross was ready for it. Mrs. Emmeline Pankhurst, the British suffragist leader, who during the war years put aside the fight for the vote to back the war effort, was coming to Toronto, and the same managing editor dreamed up the idea of sending someone to board her train in Buffalo and get an exclusive interview. "He had no one else handy to send, so he called me out of the library and off I went at three A.M. on a snowy morning, connecting with her train at seven," Ishbel Ross remembers. "I knocked on her drawing room door and asked to see her, but I was told by her secretary, 'Mrs. Pankhurst has laryngitis and cannot see anyone.'

"I went back to my car thinking 'My career is over before it started.' Then I thought it over and wrote a little note to her. I told her this was my first assignment and asked her if she, who had done so much for her fellow women, could possibly turn me down?"

Mrs. Pankhurst, who really did have laryngitis, but who also had a very good sense of publicity, granted "a wonderful interview. I took fast notes. As I got off the train in Toronto I saw all my rivals from the other papers rushing to meet her. The city editor read what I wrote, said, 'My word, this is good,' and gave me a front-page headline and a by-line. It was pure beginner's luck."

That same managing editor in Toronto knew the managing editor of the then *New York Tribune* (afterwards the *Herald Tribune*), and in 1919 he gave Ishbel Ross a letter of introduction and she was off to Park Row in New York. "The *Tribune* was broad minded," she says, "and although they had only one woman in the city room, Emma Bugby, at that time, there was a shortage of men, and women could get good assignments. We did front-page stories and straight news. [In 1928 Ishbel Ross was writing about a trip to the Great Wall of China.] It was Mrs. Ogden Reid who brought in Irita Van Doren. Mrs. Molloney ran the *Herald Tribune* Forum. In the 1920s and 1930s the paper added a number of women in very important executive jobs. The arrival of the tabloids galvanized us all. The more conservative papers cared more about how the story was written, but the girls who worked for the tabloids were quite sensational in their way and it was when they began to get by-lines that we did, too."

Ishbel Ross of the *Herald Tribune* and Bruce Rae of the *New York Times* met while they were both covering the sensational two-year-front-page James A. Stillman divorce case. They were married in Montreal in 1924. As reporters on rival major papers "we had to be so everlastingly careful," she says. "Just by chance we would be assigned to the same story. I remember one day Bruce left home quietly, went off into the wilds on a lead—and scooped me." In her years at the *Tribune*, Ishbel Ross covered everything from flower and fashion shows to the Hall–Mills murder case and the Lindbergh kidnapping. Bruce Rae became a *Times* executive in the early 1930s (he died in 1962) and Ishbel Ross left the *Herald Tribune* in 1933 to write books, the first of which, "Promenade Deck," a novel, was a big best seller and sold to the movies.

It was Stanley Walker, a famous city editor at the *Tribune* of the 30s, who turned Ishbel Ross toward nonfiction with the idea for a book that became "Ladies of the Press," and which covered the country in terms of the famous newspaperwomen of the 1930s, among them Dorothy Thompson, Anne O'Hare McCormick, Dorothy Dix, Adela Rogers St. John.

Looking back at those 19th and early 20th century presidential wives about whom she has written so extensively, Ishbel Ross says: "They all had one thing in common. They were just madly in love with their husbands. They were not ambitious for themselves, but for them. Varina Davis became hysterical when Jefferson Davis had to spend eight months in chains after the Civil War. Edith Bolling Wilson was very elusive with the press. She detested personal limelight and publicity. What she wanted for Woodrow Wilson after his crippling stroke was total quiet and freedom from worry. She thought of herself as carrying out a 'stewardship' for him. And when her memoirs were published in 1939, she was rather unforgiving to some of those men who had ridiculed her and accused her of undue influence over her husband. That book revived old scars.

"Not until Eleanor Roosevelt arrived in the White House could the press really obtain interviews with presidential wives. Eleanor Roosevelt went out of her way to honor Mrs. Wilson in any way she could, and Mrs. Wilson did fare better when the Democrats were in office. She lived long enough to see such women as Oveta Culp Hobby and Frances Perkins in high government office, and her last public appearance was with President John F. Kennedy, who had used Wilson in 'Profiles in Courage.' "

Ishbel Ross knew and interviewed Edith Bolling Wilson in the 1920s and 1930s. She recalls her as "always fashionable, always full of steam, always ready to set off for anything that was going to honor Wilson. Presidential wives do have it so difficult when they come out and express their own opinions, and yet some of those earlier women in the White House had tremendous power of wifely counsel over their husbands. As for Edith Wilson, she really enjoyed the life of being wife to the President of the United States. How many presidential wives these days can say that?"

[We deeply regret that our interview with Ishbel Ross has become instead a memorial tribute. Mrs. Ross died suddenly on September 21.—A.W.E.]

Al Silverman

WHAT DO YOU DO if you are the author of a new book, and at the same time you happen to be the editorial director of the Book-of-the-Month Club? If you're Al Silverman, you deliberately keep your book, "Foster and Laurie" (*Little, Brown*), at arm's length and decline even to consider it. However, as Silverman told *PW* in a recent interview, "Someone managed to smuggle it in anyway, and without my involvement at all, the judges chose it as an alternate." Thus was honor satisfied—but, like most authors who work at something else as well, Silverman would far rather talk about his book than his job.

It is in fact his 10th book in a writing career that goes back nearly 20 years—and his very first on a subject outside of sports. Football and baseball were Silverman's specialties during a busy period as a freelance magazine writer that ended in 1960 when he became editor-in-chief of *Sport* magazine. During his editorship he wrote and edited a number of books with and about such figures as Mickey Mantle, Frank Robinson, Joe DiMaggio and, most notably, Gale Sayers. The book he wrote with Sayers, "I Am Third" (*Viking*), later became the moving (and multi-award-winning) TV movie "Brian's Song."

Finally, however, Silverman got "fed up with jocks," and left *Sport* in 1972 to write a book. His first idea, to get away as far as possible from the heavily masculine world he had known, was to do a book about some of the most celebrated women of our time: Hepburn, Garbo or perhaps Callas. "Then one day I read the story in the *New York Times* of the shooting down of those two cops, Gregory Foster and Roc-

By John F. Baker. From *Publishers Weekly* 205, no. 10 (March 11, 1974), pp. 8–9.

co Laurie, on the Lower East Side, and how they were black and white, patrolling together, and how they'd served in Vietnam together, and I had my theme. It gave me a chance to take another look at the black–white thing, and it also suggested a whole new angle to the usual cop story— what about their family lives, the business of being a police wife?"

Silverman wrote to the two policemen's widows (who had both been approached for TV documentaries after the shooting); Mrs. Foster was receptive, Mrs. Laurie turned him down at first but later agreed. Finally they both spent hours talking to him about their lives with their husbands, their childhoods, their present feelings. "It was almost like being a father confessor—but they both seemed to pick up emotionally as a result of our talks."

He found the police of the precinct where Foster and Laurie were shot to be wary and cautious about him. "I had to work hard to convince everyone I planned to do an honest book, telling it as it really was; and in the course of doing it I think I came to understand cops better, and the way they feel about the world. You know, down there east of Avenue A it's like the DMZ in Vietnam—there's always this heavy feeling of menace in the air."

Silverman made some unusual discoveries in the course of his research in the battered streets where the killings occurred; the group of kids who had admired the dead Foster, and who named themselves The Cool Ones and wrote a letter about him which they left at the funeral home; the boy who had seen the shootings from his window and was the first to reach the bodies; the cops who patrol the same beat today, with the strange mixture of dread and excitement that seems to come with the territory.

It was a hard book to do, Silverman says, because some of the people were difficult to reach, and because it was awkward to organize. "I didn't want to begin with the shooting and work back from there, because then there's no tension. On the other hand, most of the action in the book follows it." And being named as editor-in-chief of BOMC when the writing was already under way didn't help either.

"I shan't write anything else now," Silverman says. "I'm too busy, and anyway it's not suitable for me to be an author with my job at BOMC. In fact, all of us are very sensitive to the problem of books written by BOMC employees or judges."

Silverman reads about 25 books a month himself in search of ones worthy of classification by the club as a main or an alternate selection. His six in-house reader–editors read about 300 between them, and there are also outside experts in various specialized areas who read books in their fields. The editors' choices are passed along to the panel of judges for evaluation and ultimate classification; judges can also introduce books they come across themselves.

He insists that the selections are made purely from the viewpoint of quality, and not sales potential. "I could tell you of several recent books that we knew would have enormous sales, but which we would never consider at all.'' He declines to name them, however. Silverman is a diplomat who is well aware of the power he wields in the publishing industry.

He confirms the trend so apparent in best sellers of recent years, toward nonfiction and away from fiction. ''We sell more of our nonfiction choices than our fiction ones, generally speaking—and our selections seem to work about 3–2 in favor of nonfiction.'' He has not discerned any particular direction in the taste of the judges, though he concedes that they may be rather more serious-minded than they were some years ago. ''The main thing is to try and strike a good balance in each monthly offering.'' Currently he is enthusiastic about BOMC's paperback scheme, now running on a trial basis under Linda Stewart's direction.

All in all, Al Silverman is delighted to be doing what he is, pleased with his book, and glad to be free, finally, of the world of sports. For a man with three teenage sons, however, the quality of the transition isn't always self-evident. ''For years, as editor of *Sport*, I attended the Superbowl game, and made a presentation of some big car to the magazine's choice of the Most Valuable Player,'' he says with a grin. ''This time we didn't go to the Superbowl, but just watched it on TV like anyone else. When the time for the Most Valuable Player award came around, one of my sons asked me: 'What would you do this year—give him a book?' ''

Stanley Weintraub

HOW DO YOU BECOME a biographer? For Stanley Weintraub, whose major study of the painter James Abbott
McNeill Whistler has just been published by Weybright and
Talley (distributed by David McKay), the answer seems to
be "by indirection."

Weintraub, a genial, enthusiastic and voluble man, confessed on a recent visit to New York from his Pennsylvania
eyrie (where he is director of the Institute for the Arts and
Humanistic Studies at Penn State) that his was not a background of glittering academic achievement from the start.
Graduating from a small state college with bad grades ("It
was just after the war, and I was up against all those returning vets on the G.I. Bill"), he found himself whisked into
the Army and sent to Korea before he had even learned to
fire a gun. "I was put in charge of this huge U.N. hospital
for prisoners of war—10,000 beds and 11,000 patients—and
it was that experience that led to my first published book,
which wasn't a biography at all, but an account of the hospital life I called 'War in the Wards.' "

Before the Army, Weintraub's academic interest had
been in Dryden and the Restoration. In Korea he found that
bridge was the chief leisuretime activity of his fellow officers, and since this bored him, he fell with avidity on the
books his brother sent him—which happened to be largely
the Penguin editions of G. B. Shaw. "That was the beginning of a fascination with Shaw that has lasted to this day,"
Weintraub says. He has been editor of the *Shaw Review*
since 1956, has published several books on him ("Private
Shaw and Public Shaw," "Shaw: An Autobiography" and

By John F. Baker. From *Publishers Weekly* 205, no. 5 (February 4, 1974),
pp. 8–9.

"Journey to Heartbreak," about Shaw in World War I, among them). And it was through his Shaw expertise that he found his publisher: Victor Weybright was a friend of the Irish playwright's, and "picked me up."

After that, Weintraub found himself becoming more and more deeply immersed in the artistic world of late Victorian England. He wrote a highly regarded study of Aubrey Beardsley, which was nominated for a National Book Award in 1967, "Reggie," a study of Reginald Turner, a writer who was at the center of the Oscar Wilde circle (published by George Braziller), and now one of Whistler—whom he sees, incidentally, as one of the founding fathers of the esthetic philosophy of the period. As his biography makes clear, Whistler's revolt against the Victorian notion that art should be useful, or morally uplifting, or that pictures should tell a story, or mean something in other than purely visual terms, was a major breakthrough for many of the painters and writers who followed him.

Personally, says Weintraub with a cheerful grin, Whistler was "a son of a bitch," and his book is an exhaustive account of the American-born painter's vanity, quarrelsomeness, occasional cruelty and perpetual financial troubles, which he did his best to evade by failing to pay his bills. Artistically, however, he remained admirably singleminded, well aware that despite the ridicule often heaped upon his pictures during his lifetime, his work would find a place in history. He sold his "The Artist's Mother," perhaps the most famous portrait painted in the 19th century, to Paris' Luxembourg Museum for a pittance, on the condition that it went eventually into the Louvre—for that, he knew, would secure his immortality.

One of the reasons Weintraub finds this period such a rich lode for biographers is that only now can much of the voluminous material about the lives of its often outrageously eccentric writers and painters be published. "There's had to be so much discretion until now," he says. "There's been a constant problem with relatives still living, and holding the threat of lawsuits over you if you go into too much detail about their forebears' private lives." Some of the revelations about such august Victorians as Ruskin, Rossetti and Swinburne may now be safely printed between hard covers, but might still strike readers of PW's chaste pages as a trifle gamey, so some of Weintraub's more fascinating tidbits will have to go unreported here.

But he is indefatigable in pursuit of his quarry; in the course of preparing his new book he journeyed to Glasgow (a younger sister of the painter's widow left a vast quantity of Whistler material to the university library there), the British Museum, where many contemporary newspapers carried blow-by-blow accounts of Whistler's constant feuds and suits, and the Library of Congress. And now that the book is done he finds he cannot extricate himself from the period and the people. One of the crucial chapters in the book concerns a suit Whistler brought against Ruskin for demeaning his works in a published review; in the arguments in court when the case was heard (Whistler won, but only nominally),

Weintraub sees the essential arguments about the nature and purpose of art. Now he is trying to write a play based on the trial, using much of the real dialogue; he realizes it may be too static for the stage, but feels impelled to work on it anyway.

His next book, he has decided, will be on Dante Gabriel Rossetti, most remarkable member of a remarkable family in English literary and artistic life of the time—"Once again, there's so much you couldn't have said before; he had so many mistresses he even tried to marry one of them off, to get rid of her."

One of the reasons there is such a wealth of available material about the great Victorians is that they were vigorous and prolific letter writers—and that, beginning with Whistler, they learned the value of the mass media and became the first artists who were truly public personages, with larger-than-life personalities, faces instantly recognizable to anyone who read a newspaper, and well-publicized views. Whistler, with his dandyism, his enormous cane, his carefully prepared flow of epigrams (only Oscar Wilde was credited with more scintillating *mots*, and some of those may have been stolen from the painter) and his instantly identifiable butterfly signature on his paintings, was a press agent's dream—and received press coverage accordingly.

Weintraub is pleased with his book, and understanding but regretful of what had to be cut for space (though it is still a well-packed 500 pages); and he appreciates the fact that he can now use illustrations that only a few years ago would have been regarded as hazardous. "When I published 'Beardsley' in 1967 I wanted to use some of his erotic Lysistrata drawings, but the publishers declined, telling me: 'Lady librarians won't buy the book if you do.' Now I see Penguin has brought out my Beardsley biography using them. Things have certainly changed quite rapidly."

Currently Weintraub is teaching a course on Shaw at Penn State, and next term he plans to teach one on biographical writing. He feels he learned most from Leon Edel, the great Henry James biographer, Richard Ellman, author of the definitive studies of Joyce and Yeats, and Catherine Drinker Bowen. From Miss Bowen he learned one particularly important thing: "All her life she regretted having made up conversations in her biographies—and that's something I shall tell my students. If you do conversations, you must have good reason to believe in their authenticity. And don't always use a story just because it's a good one, or because it's widely accepted as true. There's a famous story of Oscar Wilde's body being disinterred for reburial, and a former lover leaping into the grave with it; the man was not even in the country at the time."

He couldn't resist an aphoristic summary: "The art of biography is at least partly to be able to resist the temptation to tell a good story." It could have been only modesty that prevented him from adding that a striking life, well told, will make a good story in any case.

4
Autobiography, Letters, Memoirs

Svetlana Alliluyeva

SVETLANA ALLILUYEVA'S precedent-shattering press conference at New York's Hotel Plaza on April 26 has been reported in voluminous detail by the press of the world, more than 300 of whom attended the televised proceedings.

For *PW* readers, however, many of whom will be selling, reviewing, publicizing her book about her life as Joseph Stalin's daughter, there is, we believe, some interesting background material on Mme. Alliluyeva as a writer and a Soviet intellectual that came up in the press conference and that was not always given as much feature space in newspaper accounts of the event as some of the more immediately newsworthy statements she made. This article is based upon the personal observations and notes of a *PW* reporter who attended the press conference and on some additional information we have been able to obtain about her forthcoming Harper & Row book, which Patricia Johnson Mac-Millan is translating.

The aplomb with which Mme. Alliluyeva faced the first press conference she had ever attended was clearly visible to television viewers and drew her a standing ovation from the case-hardened reporters at the end of the nearly hour-long session. The first impression she makes is that of a very womanly woman with lovely coloring (copper-colored hair, pink cheeks). She is feminine enough to have replied rather plaintively when asked a question about freedom of the press in America, "I cannot understand why if they write something about a new person, why it should be mentioned how much pounds he is weighing." The second impression Mme. Alliluyeva makes is that she

By Barbara A. Bannon. From *Publishers Weekly* 191, no. 19 (May 8, 1967), pp. 24–25.

is a woman of formidable intelligence and wit, with a mind of her own.

In introducing her to the press, Edward S. Greenbaum, her counsel, referred to her as having come to America "because she wanted to have the right to believe in God and to publish what she had written." It was the first point that was particularly seized upon at her press conference, but as Mme. Alliluyeva continued to express herself clearly and forcefully in words of her own choosing, it became apparent how galling it must have been for this woman to be denied all these years the right to express herself freely as a writer, never being allowed to take on the task of doing more than translate the words of other writers.

Self-expression, she said at one point, is absolutely essential "for the person who thinks he is a writer. Such a person needs freedom to express what he likes and that person should be sure that his books will be published. This is what I could not—like many other writers—have at home." Reverting to this same theme later on, she said that while she lived by the standards of ordinary Soviet citizens "a privileged life," "as you know, people cannot live only by bread. People need also something else. And I knew exactly that work as a writer would never be possible for me in the Soviet Union."

One of the points Svetlana Alliluyeva made that was not as widely picked up by the press as it might have been, dealt with the influence on her of the trial two years ago of the writers, Sinyavsky and Daniel. She said, specifically, that in addition to the blow dealt her by the Soviet government's refusal to let her formally marry her late Indian husband, Brijesh Singh, and his subsequent death, one of the major factors influencing her decision "that it is impossible for me to return home" was the trial of Sinyavsky and Daniel. This trial, she said, "produced a horrible impression on all the intellectuals in Russia . . . I can say that I lost [then] the hopes which I had before that we are going to become liberal somehow. The way those two writers were treated and sentenced made me absolutely disbelieve in justice [in Russia"].

It was during the winter of the two writers' trial that the manuscript of her book was sent to India for safekeeping via Indian friends. The book had been written in August, 1963. When she arrived in India the manuscript was returned to her.

It had been reported in the *New York Times* that Mme. Alliluyeva was planning to meet soon with American writers and intellectuals. She said that she planned no such formal meetings in the near future and that she wanted to lead "a rather quiet, secluded life. I want to work, I want to write. Big, large meetings with many people," might come later.

In response to another question she said that Hemingway is "still my favorite American writer" and that she likes Salinger's work very much. "We do not know much about modern American writers in Russia," she added. "I hope here I will be able to get acquainted."

Mme. Alliluyeva also expressed a hope that the time will come when all of Boris Pasternak's works will be published in the Soviet Union, saying "it is a great shame that such a great Russian writer is not yet fully published, and 'Dr. Zhivago' is not yet published in Russia." Many, many fine writers writing inside Russia today, she said, "are never printed, and quite a lot of good poetry and short stories and novels we know only in titles, because there is quite a lot of modern literature in Russia which is not printed."

Asked about the situation of the Jews in Soviet Russia today, Mme. Alliluyeva answered: "I do not know much about Jewish religion. All I can say, I always had many friends among Jewish people in Russia and what I know, what I can see, I know about restrictions in universities and in the institutes when very talented Jewish young people sometimes are not adopted, and instead of them people of other nationalities are adopted, who are less talented. . . . This is what I can say as a fact because I know it myself."

Many of the questions about her father which were put to Mme. Alliluyeva at the Hotel Plaza press conference she fielded neatly by referring her questioners back to her forthcoming book where the story of her relationship with him would be told in more detail. A spokesman for Harper & Row described the book as having many passages of "lyrical beauty" and a "poetic" quality. It is said to be basically non-political in tone, yet casting new light on many of the events during Stalin's rule. The book begins with her happy marriage to Brijesh Singh and goes backwards in time to her father's death, including as well much earlier material on her family life and her reactions when she discovered that her mother had committed suicide.

Foreign publishers and news media are currently vying in secret bids for rights to the Alliluyeva manuscript, with one source quoting rights in Germany alone liable to go for a quarter of a million dollars. Mme. Alliluyeva plans to give a substantial portion of the money she receives for the book to establish something like a Brijesh Singh memorial fund in her late husband's Indian village. Other moneys will go to children's homes in Switzerland and to some American charity, as yet undecided upon.

Asked by one reporter at the press conference if all the money she would receive for the book was not going to turn her into a capitalist, she replied with some spirit. "First of all, according to Marx, writers are not capitalists, because it's a different way of labor." She added that in addition to the charities to which she hopes to contribute money from her book, "I am not going to become a very rich woman because, while my children are far away from me and they have a rather more than modest life, it is absolutely impossible for me to become a rich person here. I think you understand this."

David Amram

WHEN DAVID AMRAM conducts a benefit concert of his own music in Houston on November 30, it will mark another "first" in the wonderful world of book publishing; for the concert is being sponsored by a bookseller, the Sam Houston Book Shop, in cooperation with a publisher, Macmillan, and memory does not reveal when a comparable conjunction of effort took place before. For the first half of the concert, Mr. Amram will conduct the Houston Symphony and the University of Houston Choral Group in a chamber piece, a composition for orchestra and a choral work. For the second half, Mr. Amram will play French horn and George Barrow will play saxophone in four original jazz compositions. "An Evening of Music by David Amram" will be held at Jones Hall in Houston, and it has been sold out for more than a month.

"Vibrations," Mr. Amram's autobiography of his life in music, accounts for bookseller's and publisher's interest in sponsoring the concert, which will benefit the Houston Chamber Orchestra Society. The concert's combination of jazz and more formal music is the Amram touch, for the 37-year-old musician believes that all kinds of music, from opera to rock and roll, are related. That is what his career and his book are all about.

David Amram has been called a prodigy and a *wunderkind*. He has written operas, chamber music, scores for theater and films and television and jazz pieces with splendid titles like "Tompkins Square Park Consciousness Expander." He was the New York Philharmonic's composer-in-residence for its 1966–67 season. A lot of people who knew

By Roger H. Smith. From *Publishers Weekly* 194, no. 22 (November 25, 1968), pp. 5–6.

David Amram when he was struggling without money or recognition in Greenwich Village in the 1950s are delighted to see him now so busy in the world of music, for his coming to prominence is in a sense symbolic of a new generation taking over in the arts. But why should he, at age 37, write an autobiography?

It started more than a year ago when Mr. Amram appeared on a Channel 13 (New York City) panel show and, in the course of the program, put forth his theories about the unity among all kinds of music. A fellow panelist was Macmillan editor Al Rinzler, and as in the usual course of such events, the editor got around to asking the composer if he had ever thought of doing a book.

"I'd written articles before," Mr. Amram told *PW* over drinks in a Village bar the other afternoon. "Articles about music are usually pedantic. But musicians feel so much joy in music, and it's the joy that I've tried to capture in the book. Enough negative things have been written about music, like musicians and drug addiction, and I want to get at the joy and the beauty of creating."

In "Vibrations," Mr. Amram makes composing sound like nothing but "joy and beauty." Actually, he told *PW*, he finds it hard work "but something I do naturally." Writing the book was hard work, too—a full year of it—but, he said, no harder than composing music. Since the book came out on October 14, he has been guest of honor at a party thrown by George Plimpton and at a reception–jam session which Macmillan hosted at Max's Kansas City with a roster of guests that included Arthur Miller, Bob Dylan, members of the Philharmonic, Sterling Moss and Gerry Mulligan.

In the near future, he will be making national television appearances, playing with the bands on shows such as "Tonight" and "Merv Griffin." A mobile fellow, he is frequently on tour as guest conductor, university lecturer or founder–member of the Amram–Barrow Quartet, and his current schedule includes Pittsburgh, Washington and Chicago, where he will be making appearances for the book. In January, he will be in Los Angeles and San Francisco. In any of these places, he is likely to cause a stir, because David Amram is now "making it" in the music world.

"We are seeing the coming of age of the musician in America," he says. "We are no longer treated like victims. There's no more patronage system. Musicians are now taking their destiny in their own hands. This is true of jazz and rock and roll and of the young composers.

"Some, like me, learn the music business very young and, like boxers, know how to take care of themselves outside the ring. My music is recognized now as a result of 20 years of work, but it's taken an instinct for survival. The book tries to show what a life in music is like and to break down some of the bad impressions. Music and dance are not things apart but are an important way of life, and they are becoming more so all the time." For David Amram, and his autobiography, life in music has clearly been a joy.

Sammy Cahn

THE REALLY POPULAR songwriter is the most successful poet the world has ever seen. His lines may be—and usually
are—extremely simple, but they are memorized by millions,
and are paid for at an extravagant rate. Opportunities to
meet such lyric poets are, however, rare, since their habitat
is at the keyboard of battered upright pianos in the back
rooms of Broadway agents' offices in movie musicals a decade or more old; and it was therefore with more than the
customary anticipation that *PW* went recently to meet Sammy Cahn, one of the most illustrious of that rare breed, who
had temporarily strayed over into publishing territory by
writing an autobiography, "I Should Care," just out from
Arbor House.

Cahn was already seated at the lunch table when the *PW*
interviewer arrived and launched at once, in the most
friendly way in the world, into a wry and low-keyed account
of how he had offered to share his cab with a pretty girl, and
reassured her by stressing that he was a happily married
man. Cahn seems almost compulsively friendly, with a directness and frankness that can be disconcerting, but which
are sweetened by a very genuine interest in other people,
and by what seems, for someone who has spent his life
among highly sophisticated people, a remarkable naïvete.
"I talk to everyone I meet," he explains, "even cab drivers.
Everyone has their hangups—they aren't the domain only of
the talented."

There is something about the dry, Lower East Side voice,
the insinuating phrasing, that carries a strong suggestion of
Groucho Marx; but Cahn draws back, horrified, from the

By John F. Baker. From *Publishers Weekly* 206, no. 21 (November 18,
1974), pp. 10–11.

comparison. "Can't stand the man," he says. "First time I met him he did this," and he takes the interviewer's hand, and with a leer, tickles his palm with a lascivious finger.

The story of Cahn's life could be the script for almost any Broadway musical—the Lower East Side childhood, the start in vaudeville, the struggles up the ladder, the early encounters with such as Phil Silvers, Milton Berle, Jack Benny, Frank Sinatra, the broken first marriage, the ulcers, the blissful second marriage—even climaxing with something almost unknown for a songwriter, the one-man hit show on Broadway. At the time of the interview Cahn was just closing in "Words and Music" and taking it on what turned out to be a highly successful tour, and he still couldn't quite believe it all.

"Little Sammy Cahn, up there on the stage, and everyone paying to come and see him," he marveled. "If you knew how many people I've known who just wanted to be *in* a Broadway show, and there I am, the whole show." Most of his old colleagues had been to see him, he added, with one exception that saddened and troubled him: Frank Sinatra, for whom he wrote some of the songs that made Sinatra famous: "All the Way," "The Second Time Around," "I'll Walk Alone." (And now that some songs have been mentioned, any reader who still wonders how many of Cahn's songs he or she knows should be reminded: "Love and Marriage," "I've Heard that Song Before," "Call Me Irresponsible," "Three Coins in the Fountain," "The Things We Did Last Summer" and the English words for "Bei Mir Bist Du Schein," to name only a handful.)

Cahn writes the lyrics, and his most successful collaborators as tune-smiths have been Jule Styne and Jimmy van Heusen. Cahn loves music with a passion ("If I'm driving, and music comes on the radio, I have to pull over to the side of the road") and he is impossible to keep away from a piano, but he doesn't actually *think* music. What he has is an uncanny ability to fit shapely, singable words to almost any tune written, however devious the melodic line, and make them sound inevitable. It's a gift he doesn't quite understand himself: "I don't know where it comes from. I just see the words in my head as soon as I hear the tune." Sometimes it involves what seem to be impossible repetitions, unlikely words, awkward sequences; but once Cahn has written the words to a song, no other words could be imagined.

And though the process sounds suspiciously like inspiration by a real longhair muse, Cahn remains utterly calm and professional about it all. "Professional" in fact is his favorite tribute, and he will have no truck with artistic temperament that obstructs a job to be done. "Someone has to open the store. It's not given to us all to be talented, but at least we can be on time." He writes his lyrics on an IBM Executive typewriter, and figures that they must be the neatest in the business. He has written an entire lyric in less than 10 minutes, and his pay per word is enough to make more conventional poets, and even best-selling novelists, swoon.

He was once paid $75,000 for a song called "It's Been a Long, Long Time," and since the entire song contains only 75 words, artfully repeated, Cahn was paid at the rate of $1000 a word.

Curiously enough, until he made it on his own, Cahn had never been associated with a Broadway hit musical, although it was not for lack of trying. And although he has written title songs that have often been better remembered than the movie they adorned ("A Touch of Class" was the latest), and would love to do a movie musical, it just doesn't happen. "There are a lot of us who would love to do movie musicals," he says, mentioning several top songwriters, "But nobody wants to do that kind of picture any more. The only musicals now are rock, or revivals that go back even before me."

There is no "As Told To" indication of collaboration on his book, and Cahn is proud of the fact that he wrote it himself. How did he happen to publish through Don Fine at Arbor House? It happened apparently through Phil Silvers, whose agent for *his* autobiography was Arthur Pine, who in turn is a friend of Fine's. "Don Fine said, 'We're going to have to take this book," Cahn beamed, adding: "He also said we're going to have to make some changes. But, like I say, I'm a professional, I make the changes." At this point the urge to sing overcomes him, and in an indescribable light, husky baritone that seems nowhere near on pitch but that phrases with unfailing musicality, he improvises the slam-bang finish of "Three Coins in the Fountain":

> "Make it mine
> Pine and Fine
> Make it mine!"

"That's what you call a vaudeville finish," he continues quietly as the startled diners at nearby tables resume their lunch. "People want to applaud, so the thing to do is end on a high note. Aalll the waaay!" he sings and "I should care . . . aaand I DOOO!"

"I'll tell you," Cahn concludes, subsiding instantly from his curtain-call finishes to his normal, gentle *sotto voce*. "For me, selling a book will be just like singing a song. I went to a sales meeting for the book at McKay [which distributes Arbor House titles] and I challenged those salesmen to sell more books than I do." And indeed, his tour with "Words and Music" over, Cahn was launching this month into a vigorous talk-show schedule that will obviously include music as well as words.

"We'll get the word out," he said cheerfully. "Come blow your horn. Sound your A. Right?"

Lynn Caine

FOR THE BEST PART of 20 years Lynn Caine, publicity manager at Little, Brown, has been promoting the books of others. Now, suddenly, it is her turn to beat her own drum. She will be going out shortly on a coast-to-coast promotion tour on behalf of "Widow," published this week by William Morrow, and, she says, "I intend to enjoy it."

Publishers and editors occasionally write books, publicists hardly ever; but for Lynn, whose husband Martin died in the spring of 1971 of cancer ("In fact today is the third anniversary of his death," she told the *PW* interviewer), a book about her harrowing experience of widowhood came to seem inevitable. She recalled how for the first year after Martin's death she had been in a mental and emotional fog. She moved with her two children from a Manhattan apartment to a house in suburban Hackensack, New Jersey, then back again after only a few months: "I only functioned in my job—that's what kept me going. Maybe if I'd had more money, so I didn't have to work, I could have had a nervous breakdown."

After a year of this strange limbo, however, the Barbara Walters TV program, "Not For Women Only" decided to do a program on the impact of death—"and they wanted a woman who could talk about widowhood, and they asked me." Lynn didn't know at first whether she should do it, "but it seemed as if a door had opened for me, so I decided to go ahead and talk about how I felt. It turned out that I was the only person on the show who had actually experienced a death recently, and at first hand, and it became very easy to talk."

By John F. Baker. From *Publishers Weekly* 205, no. 21 (May 27, 1974), pp. 10–11.

The Walters show comes on after the "Today" show in the morning, and, says Lynn, "It's amazing how many publishers watch it." Enough, anyway, for her to receive calls from four different publishers. One was from an old friend, Sherry Arden, Lynn's counterpart at William Morrow, who became what Lynn calls the "godmother" to the book (and who shared in the *PW* interview like a very proud parent). A long lunch followed, with Morrow editor Joni Evans as a third party, and the seeds for "Widow" were sown.

Lynn had plenty of material to draw on. For the first year of anguish, often awaking in the pre-dawn hours, she had covered yellow legal pads with "scribblings about what I was feeling from day to day—I called it my paper psychiatrist. I wrote hundreds of pages of the stuff, some of it so vile and bitter I was afraid that the children might find it. But it was helpful when I came to do the book, because it enabled me to keep track of how I felt through that time." Some of this material is directly quoted in the book, but Lynn taped most of the narrative, then worked at it with Ms. Evans. "I got worried at one stage, that I was being too frank, making myself too vulnerable, but Joni said people would believe in it and trust me far more if I really told everything, just the way it was."

And the book's frankness did cause her some problems. Her 12-year-old son Jon refused to read it at first ("He was blocking it"), but finally relented, read a chapter "and then came and hugged me." She could never be sure how friends and colleagues would react, and got some "extraordinary" comments. But she shrugs off the more personally critical ones: "I think everyone reveals themselves in the sort of things they say." She still wonders whether the public is ready for a book that faces the problems of widowhood squarely. "We're all so afraid to talk about death—but if only we could accept our mortality, that's what whets our appetite for life." And she hopes it can be therapeutic for the millions of American widows who have no idea what problems lie in store for them: "Knowing what to expect might soften their grief, and help them to know what traps to avoid—like don't decide on *anything* in a hurry."

Now that "Widow" is on its way ("and writing the book was *not* a catharsis, as people keep saying—it was more a sorting out of the emotions"), Lynn finds herself "scribbling again." She is deliberately vague about writing plans, but will only say, "I'm fascinated by the subject of jealousy," and that in her writing she is determined to be affirmative.

But whatever turn her new writing career takes, she remains a devoted publicist—and one who was particularly grateful to her firm that they allowed her to take time out to promote her own book outside of her vacation time. Lynn has in fact been a part of the publicity scene in New York publishing for as long as most people can remember. She actually began as an editorial secretary to Marc Jaffe (now editorial director at Bantam) at New American Library, then decided to go into the publicity side because "I saw women doing well there." She explains: "I always wanted to work with either books or music, and it turned out to be books." Later Lynn worked for a time in publicity as an assistant to Eleanor Friede at World, then went to Farrar, Straus & Giroux for nine years, and finally to Little, Brown in 1969.

She and Martin were in at the beginning of the Publishers' Publicity Association—in fact it was Martin who wrote its charter, while she was one of its founders. And Lynn has seen many changes in the field in her years in publishing. "Selling and merchandising techniques are so much better now—on the other hand, there are many fewer outlets; there were so many more newspapers then, and more magazines that reviewed books. Still, I think publishers are much closer now to what's going on in American life—they used to be quite isolated. And I still think it's the best field to be in; it's clean, and honest and worthwhile."

For a time, when her children were younger, Lynn left publishing for a while to devote herself to motherhood. "It was a terrible mistake—two of the unhappiest years of my life. Really, I'm so much happier working; I would never have gotten through all this without my job to turn to."

Does she find any awkwardness with the authors she works for, now that she is one of them? "Certainly not. Some writers want to talk about it, but I just tell them, 'Let's talk about your book instead.' "

Henri Charrière

LE GRAND CHARRIÈRE, Papillon. A face like a bowl of lumpy mashed potatoes. A deep, gravelly voice, a basso Bankhead in French. Big, brusque, overwhelming. Padding lightly and quickly across the Plaza's thick carpets, talking rapidly, gesticulating, grabbing your arm to stress a point. Most un-butterfly-like.

Henri Charrière doesn't speak a word of English. The front people for Cavett, Carson and Griffin were wary. Nix, they said, despite the presence of the lithe and winning Sylvia Panijel, translator *extraordinaire*.

The author of a sensational international best seller, "Papillon" (over three-million copies in print and doing well here in the Morrow editions), nonetheless manages to make himself understood, and he has very definite opinions on everything. He is given to grandiose, sweeping statements, as befits the author of a grandiose, sweeping story, the authenticity of which has been seriously questioned. It is about his astonishing imprisonment on and escape (*twice*) from Devil's Island, the notorious French penal colony off the coast of South America. He vehemently argues that the book is authentic, though he admits to minor inaccuracies, noting that he did not travel with a typewriter around his neck.

And when you read the book (once you get beyond the first 30 pages or so of polemics), you don't really give a damn whether it is true or not. It is hair-raising entertainment, a great adventure book in the old style.

Papillon himself, at 64, is very much in the old style—shrewd, melodramatic, warm, threatening. He has fought

By Doulgas N. Mount. From *Publishers Weekly* 198, no. 25 (December 28, 1970), pp. 19–21.

hard all of his life, and now he is immensely rich, smooth-shaven and scented, sporting expensive but casual clothes and boots. A fat diamond adorns the pinkie of one hand; the thumb is missing from the other.

He has just completed shooting a film in Venezuela, starring himself, Stanley Baker and Claudia Cardinale. Called "Popsy-Pop," it is a romantic adventure (written by Charrière and directed by Jean Herman) about an old roué (naturally) who falls in love with a young girl and gets into all sorts of scrapes. He delights in showing off the stills: Charrière menacing his enemies with a pistol, Charrière in a life-and-death struggle with a great brute of an Indian (a non-actor and old friend of his), Charrière making love to Miss Cardinale. In many of the photos he is naked to the waist, and in addition to the famous "papillon" on his chest, his upper body is covered with unusual and colorful tattoos.

He also talked about the film version of the book, which has been sold to the Walter Reade Organization. "Papi," as Sylvia often refers to him (he had the unnerving habit during our interview of rubbing her leg or back every time he became excited), is under contract to work on the script and plans, he explained, to "protect my moral right, and in order that the truth may not escape." Naturally, he envisions *three* films from the book, costing about $8-million each, and "as big as 'Gone with the Wind.' " He has talked to Roman Polanski about directing, and wants only Jean-Paul Belmondo or Warren Beatty to star. It will be a surprise if he does not get his way.

He is anxious for the film to be made because, he says, throwing modesty to the winds, "Papillon belongs to everyone; they suffer with him, fight with him, make love with him, reject the society he rejects. Papillon is not a message, he is a protest. He is better than the people who attack him, the French justice and the police. He is proof that every man has the right to be saved, to be rehabilitated."

He also talked about the United States, and about New York City, which was enjoying fine weather at the time of his visit. He found the city beautiful and exciting, and was looking forward to a walking tour of Fifth Avenue bookstores which Morrow had planned as part of its promotion.

But he also missed Caracas—his adopted home—and the political struggles there with which he has identified.

"Life does not move at the speed of an elevator," he said. "To find real civilization you must go back to the Indians. America has become a huge machine where every man is a wheel, and no one even has the time to get dressed or to make love. To have your soul refreshed, you must come to Caracas.

"Man has disappeared," he continued. "He built the machine to get freedom, but he now finds himself a slave to the machine."

The American presence in South America is also a favorite subject. "America thinks that it is the fireman of the world. Very often it puts the fire out, but when it does the people suffer. It is indisputable that the

American technology has created resources of worldwide importance, but it is also true that the politics of the U.S. are the politics of Coca-Cola, especially in South America. If the American technician drank and made love with the people, he would be America's best ambassador, but he does not; he lives with the other Americans in a little separate community, frightened of the people. This is no good."

Papillon was in business for himself in Venezuela for many years before he wrote his book. He lost "a fortune" running a fleet of shrimp boats, then had a restaurant and was given a large tract of land in the bush, but could not get anyone to work it. He took off for Israel to study the kibbutz experiment. Then he went to France, where until recently he was considered an undesirable because of his murder conviction.

Then disaster struck at home. An earthquake destroyed his business, the cook died "and left me with his wife and three children—I was in despair, I did not know what to do." He happened around this time to read Albertine Sarazin's immensely successful (and notoriously gossipy) autobiography.

"I said to myself, 'This is what I need!' It was very well written, but you know there was really nothing in it. I told myself I had a far more interesting life than this woman, and she has made a fortune."

After some wrangling with publishers, he sold the book to André Deutsch in England. It has been a best seller in France, Germany and Italy. *Paris-Match*, the picture-and-text magazine, retraced the entire escape route with Charrière in a big picture story which *Life* used here. After New York, Charrière was off to Chicago and San Francisco, where he was anxious to visit Alcatraz to talk to the Indians who have seized the old prison.

Our visit was followed by a press conference, at which Papi held forth at great length on a wide range of subjects—prison reform (prisoners were rioting at two local jails during his visit), law, justice, sex, the importance of his book, and his hope that it will mean as much to youth as it seems to mean to his own generation. He loves to tell the story of the woman who told him that she was on the verge of suicide until she read his book and "it changed her whole life," or of the man who was mute for seven years, but regained his voice after reading "Papillon." He has a lot of stories like these. You tell yourself he is a consummate charlatan, an engaging fraud who has written a fraud of a book. But he makes you want to strike out alone for the remote bush jungles.

The bookstore tour was on the following day. High fashion stores like Bergdorf-Goodman and Lord & Taylor had windows with "butterfly fashions" tied in with displays of the book. At Doubleday's and Brentano's, Papillon composed dramatic dedications, often over a page long.

At Rizzoli, he autographed French, German, Italian and Spanish editions of his book. At Scribners, where the window featured editions from many countries, Charrière drew a large crowd on the sidewalk, chattering away in French and Spanish with all sorts of people, signing any little scrap of paper (since books were not available).

The last time we saw Papi, he was beaming and sweating, surrounded by admirers at a party in his honor at the St. Regis. He was babbling away, inscribing books, obviously pleased with his American reception. We said good-bye, he dropped everything and delivered a bone-crushing hug and said, it has been one of the most wonderful experiences of his entire life. He returned to his admirers and we limped out.

Michael Collins

PROBABLY EVERYONE has his own idea of what one of the lunar astronauts is like, but Michael Collins doesn't really fit any preconception. He is quite slight, with a large head and a rather nervous expression. Far from being either hearty or monosyllabic, he is soft-spoken, rather intense, and with a remarkably wide-ranging and thoughtful view of the space program—and the world. He also thinks of himself as "basically lazy," but has just published (with Farrar, Straus & Giroux) what seems to be the most careful, exhaustive and—inevitably—fascinating account of an astronaut's life and journeyings, called "Carrying the Fire."

Resisting the temptation to inquire earnestly: "What was it *really* like up there?" (Collins makes it resoundingly clear in his book that this is a question that he is sick and tired of being asked), *PW* instead asked him when he first thought of writing his book. "Right after the Apollo II flight," he said. That was the one on which Collins navigated the command module, orbiting the moon all by himself while Neil Armstrong and Buzz Aldrin walked the lunar surface. Collins decided he wanted to describe in detail the training and the life of an astronaut, "tell people honestly what the space program was like—and communicate it without going through a PR filter." And, since Collins admits he is a reticent man who really dislikes reporters, photographers and TV appearances, "I thought I'd rather do it by writing than orally."

There is no way to become an astronaut without being highly organized, and Collins was an assiduous collector of notes and memos about the space program. After he left it

By John F. Baker. From *Publishers Weekly* 206, no. 6 (August 5, 1974), pp. 8–9.

(he worked for a time in an administrative post in the State Department, and is now the director of the National Air and Space Museum at the Smithsonian Institution in Washington) he kept "writing on pieces of paper and throwing them in shoeboxes." After a time he had a lot of paper and shoeboxes, and two years ago he began to put it all together, writing in the evenings and on weekends.

Like most of the astronauts, who signed a joint contract with *Life* magazine for their personal stories of the various space flights, Collins acquired an agent, and when he had completed two chapters and an outline of the rest, he turned it over to him. The agent took it to Farrar, Straus, where Collins was promptly given a contract, and where Roger Straus III became his enthusiastic editor.

"You know, I've been buying books for years without noticing who published them," Collins says. "Now I notice, though—and I have the feeling that a book like mine will come with an element of surprise from a house like Farrar, Straus. It's a small house, and mostly a literary one, and perhaps this surprise element will get it more attention from reviewers."

With such a sophisticated view of publishing, it's hardly surprising that Collins was not difficult to edit. He pays tribute in the book to his English teacher, and according to Straus it was well-deserved tribute. "It's been a very easy and pleasant relationship," he says, and Collins concurs: "My wife kept telling me that when I got to New York they'd want me to cut all that stuff, and change everything around. But it was only a bit of minor surgery."

His fellow moon astronauts, he says, have not seen the book, although only a few days after the interview he was reunited with them for the fifth anniversary of their flight from Cape Kennedy. "We talk on the phone sometimes but don't see much of each other," he says. Aldrin has published a book, "Return to Earth" ("A great title!" enthuses Collins), but that deals with as much with his troubles on the ground after the flight as the occasion itself. Armstrong has yet to be heard from.

Collins seems to have settled down extremely well after what for many astronauts was the climax of their lives, making everything else anticlimatic. "I guess the space program wasn't my whole life the way it was for some of the other guys. That's when I mean what I say I'm really lazy. My wife thinks I'm very active, always flinging myself into something, working hard on this book for instance, but I don't tend to fling myself 100 percent into anything: I've always got a bit in reserve."

Coffee is brought, and Collins struggles to get the lid from his plastic cup. "I'm not really too handy as an engineer," he says. "My wife's a lot handier." And, the coffee drunk, he compulsively gathers up the fragments of sugar packets and sweeps them into a bag. "I still find myself picking things up all the time, because when you're in space, things like this would just drift around and keep getting in your way." He grins briefly. "I'm not really much tidier at home, though—there's been no useful residue of that sort."

Collins is somewhat saddened by the current lack of public interest in the space program. "When it was popular it was probably *too* popular. Now people don't think about it enough. The American public is really rather faddish about such things." He is grateful, though, for the comparative anonymity into which he has been able to retire in his job at the Smithsonian. "I love to walk, and I can walk around Washington now and only one person in ten recognizes me." For this reason he is deeply reluctant, though resigned, to making one or two TV appearances on behalf of his book. "I want the book to sell well, but at the same time I really hate that tube. . . ."

Collins still worries whether he's succeeded in saying in the book everything he wanted to say. He was the first astronaut to make a prolonged space walk, and for him that was the high point of the program. "I don't know if I really succeeded in getting across the strangeness of it. There's just you, hanging there in that deep dark space, with the world going by your shoulder. And I wanted to get across a sense of the fragility of everything—of men's little pink bodies carried in all that fire and metal; of all that complicated machinery, which has to work just right; and of the whole world itself, just that little blue and white globe hanging there in space and that thin envelope of air around it."

"Carrying the Fire" has an eloquent introduction by Charles Lindbergh, who writes of the sympathy he felt toward Collins on his solitary journey around the moon, reminding him of his own solo Atlantic flight so long ago. "We sent him a copy of the manuscript, and he called up to offer to do anything he could to help the book," Collins said. Does he know Lindbergh? "Not really. I've met him briefly at a social function or two. But I see him occasionally. Every now and again he comes into the museum and spends a few minutes looking up at the *Spirit of St. Louis*." Collins was obviously touched by that. Amid all the problems of getting out a first book, that was a feeling he understood.

Loren Eiseley

LOREN EISELEY is (as Eliot said of John Webster) "much obsessed with death." As a literary anthropologist, his matter is often a sad musing upon the transience of human existence, a fascination with the ravages wrought by time on man and landscape. And his life, as starkly revealed in his latest book, "All the Strange Hours" (out in mid-November from Scribners) has been in many ways a hard and difficult one. The *PW* interviewer therefore expected his encounter with Dr. Eiseley to be a predominantly somber occasion, with long and thoughtful silences punctuated by occasional resounding declarations of mortality.

His expectations were not fulfilled. Dr. Eiseley bustled up from Philadelphia, where he holds a special chair in anthropology at the University of Pennsylvania, settled himself at the lunch table with a bourbon and water at his elbow and proceeded, as he noted ruefully himself after an hour or so, to "chatter like a magpie."

His "chatter," which was certainly thoughtful but not generally gloomy, ranged over such disparate subjects as the academic lecture circuit, the birthplaces of famous literary figures, the habits of the Sphex wasp, the slang used by hoboes during the Depression, and his unlikely legacy as a former provost of his university—eradicating a campus traffic hazard. Many of these subjects are touched on also in his new book, which is subtitled "The Excavation of a Life," and which is as close as Eiseley has come to writing a formal autobiography. (He recalled that one distinguished academic colleague had asked him what he was writing, and when he replied "An autobiography," told him: "You've been doing that ever since you began writing.")

By John F. Baker. From *Publishers Weekly* 208, no. 18 (November 3, 1975), pp. 10, 12.

It is a tale of a tragic boyhood, scarred by the early death of his father, the deafness of a neurotic mother, an upbringing in the windswept bleakness of Nebraska in which one of the epochal events was a bloody jail escape in a snowstorm by some desperate convicts with whom Eiseley mysteriously identifies to this day.

At a parting dinner with W. H. Auden just before the poet moved to Austria (they mutually admired each other's work), Eiseley recalls a discussion of what was the first public event each recalled from his childhood. For Auden it was the sinking of the *Titanic*, for Eiseley that jail break—and he told Auden sadly and revealingly, "We never made it."

Eiseley continued to struggle—with crushing poverty that sent him riding freight trains rootlessly around the country as a young man, later with severe illness and then with transitory total deafness of his own—all the while striving to complete his education and to become the mixture of writer, scientist and humanist he at last achieved.

He had been writing verse since he was in high school and recalls bitterly how one of his university professors suspected him of plagiarism because an essay he had written was thought to be too good to have been written by one of his age. It was as an essayist that he found himself as a writer, however. His poetically conceived visions of man and time, his keen observations of the animal world, began appearing in magazines in the 1950s. In 1957 a collection of these pieces, carefully linked to present an entire vision, was published by Hiram Haydn at Random House as "The Immense Journey." It scored a notable success and has proved durable (like all of Eiseley's books since, it is still in print).

He then wrote a big book, "Darwin's Century," on commission from Doubleday, followed Haydn to Atheneum for "The Firmament of Time," thence to Harcourt Brace Jovanovich for "The Unexpected Universe." Haydn in his autobiography wrote with bitterness over Eiseley's failure to agree on terms for his next book at HBJ, and his departure shortly thereafter for Scribners. Eiseley declines to be drawn out on the matter, beyond saying that he had written an introduction to a book Kenneth Heuer published at Macmillan, and when Heuer went to Scribners (where he is now science editor), he decided to join him there. "No one was stealing anything—this was entirely my own decision," he says firmly—and adds, parenthetically, that he has written nothing in his own autobiography about people with whom he has quarreled, and also that he has been very happy, as well as productive, at Scribners ever since (six books in five years).

He muses over the autobiographical imperative. "I was planning to wait until I retired before I wrote it, but then"—his wary smile—"I've been planning to retire since I was 15 years old, and I haven't managed it yet." He had found it a difficult book to write, some of it painful in the dredging of his unhappy past. "Is it a catharsis? Perhaps at the time but not now, not afterwards. In the end, I suppose you're writing for someone out there you feel may be similar to you. My books seem to appeal mostly to the young, or to people even older than myself—which is very old indeed." (He is in fact 68.) "They apparently find hope in what I've written, even when I've been rather melancholy."

And in fact his vision, of man's brief moment in eons of time, is inevitably a melancholy one. The human mind, as Eiseley sees it, is essentially "a pack rat's collection of odd trifles." In his book he seems to be gazing ahead with stoicism toward his own death—"There are times when I want to be done with life—go back into the Pleistocene." He takes a pessimistic view of human progress: "You might think about Toynbee," he observed (the great historian's death had just been reported).

His life he sees as "wading deeper into leaves and silence—and there are times when I did not always expect to survive the winter." If he lives another 10 years he could imagine another book, called (with his passion for titles, he has thought of one already) "Late in October."

Ask Eiseley about the influences on him, and he will speak of school, library and a lifetime of voracious reading, but names pop up: Jack London, Hart Crane, Poe, but especially H. M. Tomlinson's "The Sea and the Jungle" and a totally obscure book he read in childhood—"The Home Aquarium: How to Care for It," which first got him interested in natural history, and thus radically changed his life.

While geological and anthropological time have been passing in review, pressing terrestrial time has been galloping, and with a start Eiseley realizes he has only 20 minutes to catch a train back to Philadelphia. He dashes for a taxi, leaving the *PW* interviewer gazing somberly into his notebook, wherein is inscribed something Eiseley had found in one of his own youthful archaeological notebooks, and could never place in context. "Life," he had written in some forgotten whim, "she no matter."

Ruth Gordon

YOU DON'T INTERVIEW Ruth Gordon. You just sit back and listen and let one of the Great Ladies tell it her way. The setting is the Belasco Room at Sardi's and Miss Gordon is making her first appearance at a luncheon for critics in connection with "Myself Among Others" (*Atheneum*), her utterly beguiling account of a lifetime of great friendships.

"How long did you work on the book, Miss Gordon?" a young thing asks. "Seventy-five years, honey," she purrs back. "Thornton Wilder says I have a thing about being 75 years old. He says every time I get into a taxi I tell the driver, 'Hello, I'm Ruth Gordon and I want to go to such and such a place and I'm 75 years old.' "

A little later, *PW* asked Miss Gordon if, happy as she is with life at 75, she had felt a few qualms at reaching 40 or 50?

"When Garson [Kanin] and I got married in 1942, there was a story in the *Washington Post* headlined, 'Actress, 46, marries director, 30,' " she says. "That's when I knew I'd married the right guy. He said, 'Look at it this way, Ruth. If they wrote "Actress, 45" everybody would think you were really 50. But "actress, *46?*"—you've got to believe it.'

"If anyone knows of any more book luncheons," Miss Gordon tell her guests, "let me know. I'd like to hang in there. I've acquired a new accomplishment—just talking. When I asked Thornton how it would be talking about my book, he said, 'Whether or not you can do it depends on your gregariousness quotient.' Well, my gregarious and solitude quotients are both okay. I define my gregariousness quotient as being measured by any assembly I show up at

By Barbara A. Bannon. From *Publishers Weekly* 199, no. 22 (May 31, 1971), pp. 63–65.

and do not get paid for. But I think an author should go out and talk to people and be proud to have something to say and of having people to say it to. My book is a record of 75 years worth of people being helpful to me." (Among the "people"—Alexander Woollcott, Alfred Lunt and Lynn Fontanne, the Barrymores, Somerset Maugham, Robert E. Sherwood, George Bernard Shaw and dozens more.)

There is, deliberately, no index to "Myself Among Others" because Ruth Gordon doesn't want anyone looking up famous names and reading only bits and pieces about them. "I don't want anyone hunting for the bits about Kit or Larry or Noel. I believe there is a continuity to the book," she says. "It's what I choose to remember.

"The thing that, I guess, made me think I would really write some day was a letter from Edith Wharton when I was playing in 'Ethan Frome.' This had been a very unhappy period in my life and she wrote me, 'Miss Gordon, I have the impression that in addition to being able to play Mattie Silver, well, you could be a writer.' Well, after that, what else could I do but write?

"Garson and I never read each other's work while we're writing," she says. "Up to now (publication day) Mr. Garson Kanin has not read any of 'Myself Among Others.' I enjoy writing it all in longhand and I have two secretaries, who are geniuses, who can read my handwriting. Most actresses have terrific memories. I really have total recall. I suppose some of it stems from having interesting things happen to you. I got to meet them all.

"I'm a great believer in intention. Too many people give up. When I left home (Wollaston, Mass.) in 1914 I had one great intention. I was going to be an actress. Anybody can do anything if he never under any circumstances faces the facts. Rise above the facts. Facts are ridiculous. I'm in love with the past, but I'm having an affair with the future."

As for the way she writes, Miss Gordon says, "I think it comes from being an actress. I go over and over it for weeks until I think I know what I'm doing. I'm used to rehearsals. There are several houses full of my writings, draft upon draft. Then the time comes when I say, 'This is it,' and just hand it in. As for criticism, I go along with what Robert E. Sherwood said, 'I'll take criticism so long as it isn't constructive.' "

Summing it all up, Ruth Gordon puts it this way, "I am my very dearest and oldest friend, somebody I can count on. I know what I've gone through to get here. Never give up. I've had a damn hard life in many ways, or so I've always thought. But when I read my book I was struck by what a perfectly radiant, glorious life I've had in retrospect. The remark that has made me happiest about the book is something Thornton Wilder said, 'There's no malice on any page.' "

Martin Gray

THE INTERVIEWER KNOWS that he had better write this only once in his career. So he hesitates before saying that Martin Gray's life story is the most remarkable he has ever read. And then he knows that he is going to say it all the same. The young-old man he has come to see—he is wearing boxing trunks in the sunshine, he has a bad eye and rugged features and looks like a fighter—has lived a number of life stories, as a smuggler of food and combatant in the Warsaw ghetto, as a victim and escapee of the Gestapo, as the only man to have found his own way out of the inferno of Treblinka concentration camp. Then (after a succession of near-fatal escapes from other jails and camps) he joined the Polish partisans, later the Soviet secret police, the NKVD. While serving with the Russians in Berlin he boarded a subway train going west, and managed to get to the United States.

That wasn't the end of his saga. In postwar America he made enough money, quickly, to retire at age 35 to a hillside estate in southern France with his wife Dina, a beautiful Dutch-born model, and there they began to raise their four children. On October 3, 1970, fire roared over the hillside, killing his wife and all their children. Martin Gray had lost his first family in Warsaw and Treblinka. "For Those I Loved," which Little, Brown will publish on November 8, is the story of these losses. And of a fierce resolution to continue: Gray has set up a Dina Gray Foundation to arouse public concern over the dangers of forest fires. His book royalties go to the Foundation, and they should be tremendous.

By Herbert R. Lottman. From *Publishers Weekly* 202, no. 12 (September 18, 1972), pp. 18–20. Reprinted by permission of Herbert R. Lottman.

In the original Robert Laffont edition, and through a French book club, sales of "For Those I Loved" are approaching 250,000. In the United States the book is the main December selection of the Book-of-the-Month Club, and NAL has purchased paperback rights. It is being translated everywhere in the world, in remote countries as well as big ones (into Hebrew, for George Weidenfeld's Israeli company). In Germany it will be published by Econ-Verlag, and Gray is hoping that it will also be a success there. "I was surprised that my book has been sold everywhere except in the Eastern Bloc. Even the Poles wanted it but they couldn't choke down the chapters on my success in America."

The drive up to the Gray estate from the Riviera coast provided warning signs. A criss-cross of slopes with sparse pine forest, the countryside is scarred with what seem to be bent black wires set upright in the ground, actually the remains of the abundant woodland destroyed in the tragic fire. I knew that Gray's young wife and little children had been caught on this road driving down to Mandelieu, while Gray stayed behind organizing help for neighbors on the hill. When I made the trip recently there were new fires in the area (the mayor of Gray's village was blaming electric power lines which run through the woods).

Martin Gray receives at the wrought-iron gate of the 20-acre estate. His bathing costume, his tan, suggest that he has been living on the sun terrace where we are sitting now, adjoining the 17th-century stone house, restored and decorated by Martin and Dina Gray, which survived the fire. I see that Martin Gray has also survived once more, having chosen to go on living.

Early in our talk he hands me a few of the remarkable letters from readers (he received nearly 5000), who usually inform the author that "For Those I Loved" has transformed their lives.

What kind of book do you have to write to get such response, what kind of a man do you have to be? Martin Gray was born 47 years ago and began fighting for bread and water at age 14. At 17 he had organized a vast net to smuggle provisions into the ghetto isolated by the Nazis, and he had survived and escaped Treblinka. He was 20 when he arrived in Berlin with the Russians. "I believe one should use any means to survive. I killed men with my own hands, despite my own sensitivity. But my book is a testimonial to life, and readers take it as an encouragement to live. No matter what life becomes, one has to be faithful to it. Courage seems to be missing from the lives of many people and they think they can get it from me. I'm happy that I can give it. A psychiatrist wrote me that he considers the book the best medicine for his patients.

"I must tell you that never once did I think that I would be killed during an escape. If I had thought so I'd never have survived. My father told me. 'You'll do everything you can to live.' After my recent tragedy I was sitting here on the terrace and I wanted to kill myself, and then I remembered what my father had said and what I had done once before to stay alive."

Under the sun of Provence, my back turned to the burnt-out peach orchard, it was hard to conjure up tragedy, especially in the company of this man so obviously attached to life. Somewhere in the garden a concealed loudspeaker emitted stereophonic music. "But if you survive when thousands of people just like you die," he went on, "you feel guilty, just as today I feel guilty because I survived and my family died. I had pushed to have the road built on which my wife and children were driving when they were caught by the fire.

"Guilt can't be explained. A couple came to my gate the other day because they wanted to shake my hand. When I invited them to come in to go through the house they confessed that they had three children waiting for them in their car outside—they had felt guilty about letting me see them, because I had lost my own children.

"In the war I knew that not everybody could have done what I did. Some people couldn't escape because they feared to endanger their families. Others were blinded by German propaganda. The commandant of a concentration camp would say that we were going to be exchanged for German prisoners of war, that he needed us Jews more than we could imagine, because for each Jew he would get two prisoners in exchange.

"And Jews still believe in miracles. In the camps they were waiting for something to happen. They had always lived in situations of submission, revolt being out of the question. There weren't many like me—and those that survived *are* like me. I didn't know it at the time, but when I was in Treblinka a mass escape was being organized. That may have been why the inmates didn't try to get out as individuals.

"All the Jews who survived the war became more Jewish than anyone else. This is why it was so difficult for me to support the anti-Semitism of the other NKVD officers.

"Jewish collaborators? If I had heen made a *kapo* in camp I think I'd have taken the job. If you have a chance to survive you'll take it."

If Martin Gray was able to retire at an age when most men are just beginning, it was thanks to an elaborate scheme involving the importing of antiques, especially old porcelain, to New York's Third Avenue dealers. He continues to keep active with a small-scale manufacturing enterprise, making copies of antique chandeliers in Paris.

Early next month, Gray returns to the U.S. for the first time since the fire to tour the country in connection with Little, Brown's publication of "For Those I Loved." He is proud of the fact that he remains an American citizen, as were his wife and their children.

After this trip, well, he doesn't know. He is certain he won't stay in this big empty house, planned stone by stone with his wife. "Leaving is no good, but staying is absolutely no good either." At present, he isn't even sure he'll remain in France, where his extraordinarily successful book has made him something of a celebrity.

"I won't return to business—if I retired when I had four children and my wife, do you think I'd go back now? I want to reorganize my life, to find a meaning, some cause. I'm working on another book just now. I feel compelled to answer all the people who have been writing to me. 'For Those I Loved,' it would seem, gave something to a lot of people. I believe I owe them something more . . ."

Verta Mae Grosvenor

WHITE SOUTHERNERS emigrating to New York City find it virtually impossible to order anything recognizably Southern to eat in the city's restaurants. Historian C. Vann Woodward calls them the "other" great unassimilated minority group, and they are as tribalistic a bunch as one can imagine. At the first drawl, they fall all over each other.

One of the first things two good old boys discuss when they come together in the big city is Southern cooking and how much they miss it. Eventually, they discover "soul food" restaurants, and delight for a time in the double novelty of high-priced down-home food served up in declaredly "Knee-Grow" restaurants.

Unfortunately, many of these restaurants have lately been casualties of the fashion to patronize all things "black": theater, books, movies—and restaurants. As soon as the limousines begin to line up outside, the prices double and the food and service deteriorate. This is a disaster for Southern expatriates, black and white, for however strongly they may have felt about one another down South, they all grew up on the same greasy over-cooked, over-spiced, delicious food. And they miss it.

However, Southerners (and Northerners who are daring) have been rescued from this dilemma by a self-styled "culinary anthropologist," Verta Mae Grosvenor, who has written an autobiography-*qua*-cookbook called "Vibration Cooking, or the travel notes of a geechee girl" (*Doubleday*). In it she tells you how to cook that fine Southern food yourself and where to buy many of the ingredients.

"Miss Mae," as she is called by many of her readers, has

By Douglas N. Mount. From *Publishers Weekly* 197, no. 26 (June 29, 1970), pp. 49–50.

been around, and everywhere she has been, she has cooked a little something. She comes from Beaufort County, South Carolina, where blacks are called Geechees and speak a dialect that is incomprehensible to the outsider.

Having moved around Europe and the U.S. for a few years, working as actress, designer and cook, Verta Mae Grosvenor now lives in a garden apartment on the Lower East Side of Manhattan with her two daughters, Chandra, seven, and Kali, nine (Doubleday has also just published "Poems by Kali"). *PW* talked to her in her kitchen over oxtail soup and a bottle of muscadine wine.

Her "cookbook" is that in name only. Julius Lester called it "a cookbook the likes of which the world has never before seen." It is a long rap about Verta Mae's life, the people she loves, the things that make her mad (she can get very mad very quickly). It is a book about black people, and is written in straightforward down-home language. The narrative is frequently interrupted by recipes because Mrs. Grosvenor, like most country people, grew up in the kitchen and food—what you eat, what you do with it and whom you eat it with—is very important to her.

She vehemently despises the prepackaged, flash-frozen, portion-controlled "garbage that people call food today." She cannot understand how anyone can take cooking and eating that casually, and she thinks it says something important about the contemporary American mentality. Her book includes a recipe for "Cracker Stew": "Take a can of any kind of soup and add 1 box of any kind of frozen vegetables and then add 1 cup of Minute Rice. Heat and serve with toasted crackers on top."

"Black folks spend more money for food than white folks," she says. "White folks can take a can of tuna fish and feed multitudes."

Ingredients in her book are casually listed, amounts almost never are. She says she relies on her "vibrations" to judge when a dish is done, and that no dish ever turns out the same way twice.

She has strong opinions about many things. "I dislike plastic flowers, instant coffee, gossip, subways, hospitals, working from nine to five, people who point their finger in your face, Con Ed, opera, elevators, bank tellers, the jet set, dogs with jeweled collars, Cadillacs and I can't stand people with shiny cars and dingy children," she states flatly.

She has done a lot of research on the origins of black Southern foodstuffs. Collard greens, she says, are "prehistoric"; watermelon and okra (properly called "gombo") date back to Africa, and she traces other foods to India and Egypt. On chitterlings: "People think chitterlings is something only the Southern nigras eat, but let me tell you about the time I was in this fancy restaurant in Paris and the people said, 'Let us order, we know this place.' . . . So these people order for me and they are just on pins and needles, dying, really, for me to taste this enjoyable rare dish. Well, thank you, Jesus, the food arrives and it ain't nothing but CHITTERLINGS in the form of sausage. They call it *andouillette*."

Verta Mae Grosvenor seems to know everybody who is anybody in the worlds of black theater, literature, music, fashion, dance. She has given readings from her cookbook at Liberty House in Harlem and at the Countee Cullen branch of the New York Public Library; she has appeared on "Soul," the NET show on black arts which is nationally distributed; she says that the manager of a prominent Greenwich Village bookstore told her that her book has replaced Eldridge Cleaver's "Soul on Ice" as the most frequently stolen book; she says that it can be purchased "hot" in Harlem bars. After her appearance on "Soul" with soul singer Wilson Pickett, she says, she was recognized on the streets of New York and at the airport in Atlanta. She has had reports of demands for her book from Cambridge to California—demands, her informers report, from people who do not normally buy books, much less read them.

Mrs. Grosvenor's book, published in both hardcover and paperback, seems to have been well received by that segment of the black community that has heard about it, despite the fact that Doubleday has not specifically made an effort to sell it to black people through the black media. (The firm has taken ads in the *New York Times Book Review* and *Saturday Review*; it also arranged a demonstration at Abraham & Straus during the department store's recent "Soul Week.") Mrs. Grosvenor's appearance on "Soul," she says, was through personal contacts. At one point a group of her friends had decided to chip in and take an advertisement in the *Amsterdam News*, New York's leading black newspaper, in the name of "The *Ad Hoc* Committee to Get 'Vibration Cooking' Out of the Bookstore and into the Home."

"Vibration Cooking" is an unusual book; not every publisher would have accepted it. Black writers are finding it easier (but not yet easy) to have their works published, but, they complain bitterly, they are finding it impossible to get their works *sold* unless they are written for white people and therefore can be promoted through the white media, which white publishers naturally know best. "The failure is really one of ignorance," another black writer told *PW*. "When it comes to black people, they just don't know what they're doing." Mrs. Grosvenor agrees with this view; and is perplexed and disappointed. Her book, however, continues to sell itself. She has done a piece for *McCall's* which will appear in the fall. She recently planned the menu for a meeting of the NAACP Legal Defense Fund in New York. It included Shabazz bean pie, "Chicken cooked in George Washington Carver's discovery with natural brown rice," sassafras tea and "Third World Coffee."

She showed us a short review of her book which appeared in a Southern metropolitan newspaper. "But then, this is not so much a cookbook," the review concluded, "as it is a chance for the author to relieve her frustrations concerning the world in which she must live."

Verta Mae gave a loud laugh. "Right on," she said.

August Heckscher

THE IDEA OF NAMING literary men to positions of high public office is not uncommon in Europe, though until President Kennedy brought men like Arthur Schlesinger, Jr., and John Kenneth Galbraith to Washington it was virtually unknown in this country (and keen observers of the political scene will note that in recent years it has relapsed into its customary rarity). Mayor John Lindsay's appointment of August Heckscher as New York's Parks Commissioner in 1967 therefore raised some eyebrows. His background, after all, was that of a newspaper editorial writer, author (of "The Politics of Woodrow Wilson" and "The Public Happiness," among others), adviser on the arts to President Kennedy and chairman of the Twentieth Century Fund. What did he know about parks?

A great deal, as it turned out—and as he explained to *PW* in a recent interview about his book "Alive in the City: Memoir of an Ex-Commissioner," which is published by Scribners this week. "During the New Deal I traveled all over the country, and stayed in dozens of American cities," he says. "They're all so different—and so many of them radiate out from a central park area of some kind—a town green in New England or a courthouse square in the Midwest. It's important in looking at the future of American cities to see how they relate now, and how they will relate, to their open spaces."

Now that he is no longer Parks Commissioner (and the role of his successor seems to be embroiled in controversy), he is in the happy position of being able to draw together the three strands of his life into one. He has resumed his jour-

By John F. Baker. From *Publishers Weekly* 205, no. 11 (March 18, 1974), pp. 8–9.

nalism, as a columnist for the *Christian Science Monitor*, he is traveling about the country studying the role of parks and open spaces in American cities; and he is doing it on a grant from his professional alma mater, the Twentieth Century Fund. "I'm going to take two years at it—maybe more if I need it," he said. "Someone has to look into some questions. Who is decreeing the future shape of American cities—builders and developers, highway engineers, city planners, zoning boards? And what provision are they making for green spaces? What about some of the big highways and expressways that were never finished, that got stopped cold halfway through a city by citizen action, as in Boston and San Francisco? What can be done with them now?"

The talk was interrupted by the arrival of the first finished copy of Mr. Heckscher's book, and he immediately pounced upon it with more than the customary eagerness of an author greeting his newborn. He ran a highly professional eye over the binding, examined the type minutely and pointed out some obscure but apparently highly satisfactory design touches. "This is a hobby of mine," he confessed. "I've always been enthralled by printing, and I have a press in the basement in my house. The trouble is, I've just been too busy to do much in the last few years, and my wife keeps piling things on top of the press. Of course I wanted very much to see what Scribners was going to do with the book, but I've been very careful not to butt in on the design. They've done very well, though."

About some of the lively times he had as Parks Commissioner, including his controversial Central Park "Love-Ins" and his mass wedding ceremony in Brooklyn's Prospect Park, he is still somewhat wistful—and not at all apologetic. "The whole idea was to let people really enjoy the parks again. Of course not everything we did worked, and we trod on some toes, but it was an exhilarating time." Mr. Heckscher remains the public official more than the newspaperman when it comes to behind-the-scenes anecdotes of his incumbency: some lively tales and observations are placed firmly off the record—but enough still come through in his book to give an unusually detailed picture of how a big bureaucracy works.

"There are certain cardinal principles to civic administration," he says, his faintly Mephistophelian look enhanced by a mischievous glint to the eye. "Always put the blame on someone else for anything that goes wrong; and when you're trying to do something, always try to make sure you end up by giving someone else the responsibility for the next step."

As someone who has been involved for a long time with the question of public support for the arts, how does he account for the fact that under President Nixon, rather surprisingly, federal funds have been flowing more generously than usual in this direction? "It seems to me that the less involvement a public figure has in the arts, the more he is inclined to give them. It's the reverse of another principle: that people who already have a powerful and obvious constituency will usually lean over backwards to avoid seeming to play favorites.''

Would he consider serving in public office again? ''I'd rather not repeat *anything* I've done before,'' he says. ''I can't imagine having another editorial page to fill, serving another president, or another mayor. What I'm doing now is what I've always hoped to do—pull everything in my life together; like the poet says, 'I'm rolling all my strength and sweetness up into one ball.' ''

City commissioners who can quote Andrew Marvell will never grow on trees.

Sir Edmund Hillary

SIR EDMUND HILLARY is not, as he puts it, "one of those authors who feel the world is waiting breathlessly to hear what they've got to say." Writing, in fact, is by no means among his principal pleasures—and, he cheerfully admits, one of the main reasons he wrote his autobiography, "Nothing Venture, Nothing Win," just out from Coward, McCann & Geoghegan, is because "my agent kept after me about it."

Hillary is a bronzed and powerful man with a visionary eye, an air of enormously cheerful self-deprecation, and the ability to make any companion feel they would much rather be halfway up a mountain or shooting the rapids of a wild river with him than wherever they happen to be at the moment. He gives off so strong a sense of energy held in check that the effect of talking to him across a sedate New York breakfast table is roughly that of trying to entertain a tiger in an overstuffed living room.

For the conqueror of Everest, leader of a fantastically underequipped (by American standards) dash to the South Pole, hero and survivor of a thousand dramatic escapes in the world's wildest territories, confesses that what has driven him throughout his life—and continues to do so as he moves into his fifties—is sheer restlessness: "I just don't like being bored." An intense urge to "*make* things happen"—coupled with what he acknowledges with a grin as "a kind of Victorian upbringing, in which hard work has a strange virtue all its own" has fueled an almost unbelievably strenuous and competitive life. "Even today, if I lie down for a brief rest during the day I feel guilty."

By John F. Baker. From *Publishers Weekly* 207, no. 23 (June 9, 1975), pp. 16–17.

But although Hillary claims that he envies people who can relax in the middle of a busy life, he has no doubt that it is his compulsiveness that has transformed him from what he frankly describes as "just a country hick" who began adult life as a beekeeper in a rural New Zealand backwater into a world celebrity. "There've always been plenty of people around who can think three times as fast as I can. But when you've got a mind that churns away, like mine does, it works up a lot of plans in advance for everything that can happen the next day. Then when something happens you're ready. Fellows I've climbed with would make a joke of it— 'Which plan is this, Ed—74A or 74B?' " And in the interviewer's mind is a sudden picture of a tent perched on a narrow ice ledge on the brink of some unfathomable gulf at a temperature of 35 below and a height of 25,000 feet, and Hillary lying there in the darkness planning his way through the next day's climb.

After Everest in 1953, and the South Pole expedition four years later, Hillary's life took on many new dimensions. While on a visit to the U.S. he won some funding for an expedition from Field Enterprises in Chicago, later became a director of their World Book Encyclopedia program and helped it to prosper in Australia ("We were last on the scene there, but it's been a very successful operation"). He also made the first of a number of reluctant forays into authorship, beginning with "High Adventure," an account of the Everest undertaking, including an account of his Antarctic dash, and ending, until recently, with "Schoolhouse in the Clouds," which deals with a subject especially dear to his heart: his efforts on behalf of the Sherpas in the Himalayan corner of Nepal, one of whom stood with him on the summit of Everest and who, he feels, have been shamefully neglected both by their own government and by subsequent climbers in the area. He has lent his prestige to raise money to build bridges, schools and a hospital for the Sherpas, still travels regularly to their lofty valleys to supervise the work and to see that new development (the Japanese have built a hotel at the foot of Everest) takes place with a minimum of disturbance to their peaceful ways of life.

And there is one more association that still gives him an opportunity to do what he enjoys best—traveling in the wilderness, preferably in conditions of some ruggedness, and sleeping under canvas. For many years now he has been a consultant to Sears Roebuck on their tents and camping equipment, and this role gives him ample opportunity for field testing, along with a welcome dash of occasional danger. Not long ago he and several senior Sears sales executives were nearly swept to their deaths when they embarked on the Salmon River in Idaho when it was in full spring flood and their boats overturned. A few days after the *PW* interview—and after a hasty two days in New York for Coward, McCann to promote his autobiography—he was off on a similar trip along the wild Buffalo River in Arkansas. "I usually end up paddling something, pushing something or walking something."

Although his life—and his new book—are full of color and adventure, Hillary remains the least typical of authors, in that he has "a constant sense of astonishment that anyone should want to read about me." As to writing methods, he has always, since his earliest climbing days, kept a diary, "and my mother kept all the letters I ever wrote her." As a result, detailed material on his early life was ready to hand when he started, thus avoiding "a desperate search in old cupboards." He wrote snatches of the book in between his other activities, finally settled down to "grind it out" for about six months. "I suppose that's the easiest kind of writing, just describing what happens to you. You don't really have to be creative. Mind you, I sometimes feel I've failed to bring out my philosophy."

And there really is a philosophy underlying the struggle and endurance of his life. When he lectures, as he often does, he dwells on such themes as what he calls "racialism," conservation, aid to the poorer countries— "The vociferous minority, they call us, but we keep going." Concepts of duty and obligation to others remain paramount, but there is no sense of self-sacrifice about his good works. "I admire people who make sacrifices—really I only do what I enjoy, though it might seem like hardship to other people."

Hillary has been terrified many times in his life—and with good reason—but the conquest of fear, he feels, can be one of life's most rewarding experiences. "It's a challenge, and overcoming it can make you more alive." But after surviving the worst that nature can throw at an adventurous man, one of his lowest moments came at a publishing party given here by Dutton some years ago to launch "High Adventure." About halfway through the festivities, a waiter brought him the bill. "It was for thousands of dollars. Luckily Macrae was at my side, and he grabbed it and told the man off. But it was a terrible moment." And with a firm handshake the man who has stood on the roof of the world stepped off determinedly along West 44th Street in search of new adventure.

Chet Huntley

CHET HUNTLEY's strong ties to his Montana boyhood are implicit in every line of his happy memoir, "The Generous Years: Remembrances of a Frontier Boyhood" (*Random House*). That link with a now vanished American way of life finds tangible expression in several ways in the NBC television newscaster's otherwise ultra modern NBC office. Reproductions of 19th century Western Americana share wall space with a map of street lots in the ghost town of Virginia City. Mr. Huntley owns one of those lots and pays 50 cents a year taxes on it. And the office is so arranged that Chet Huntley can turn directly to a large old-fashioned rolltop desk from an electric typewriter and an electronic push button system that puts him in instant communication with his partner, David Brinkley. The desk is the one that Chet Huntley's father used as a railroad telegrapher in the West, during part of the time covered in "The Generous Years."

A few years ago, when he was on vacation in Mexico, Mr. Huntley says he "just started writing one day" out of what seemed to be almost "total recall" of those boyhood Montana years beginning with 1913. The book was written over a three-year period and Mr. Huntley was about to sign with a literary agent who had got wind of the manuscript, when Mrs. Huntley said, in effect, "Let me see what I can do." What she did was to go right down to Random House with predictably happy results for all concerned.

Chet Huntley's maternal grandfather was a warm and important figure in his grandson's life and he figures prominently in "The Generous Years." "He was a young grandfather," Mr. Huntley recalls, "only about 44 when I

By Barbara A. Bannon. From *Publishers Weekly* 194, no. 10 (September 2, 1968), pp. 19–21.

was born. In those days it was taken for granted that grandparents lived with a family and they were in final authority.''

"The Generous Years" closes with Chet Huntley in his teens. Those were the years, he reports, when he was discovering books: James Oliver Curwood, Mark Twain, Jack London and "all the trash I could get my hands on: westerns, Nick Carter, the Rover Boys, Zane Grey."

In his schooling after the period covered in the book, he had been thinking vaguely of going in for medicine when he found "English becoming a lot easier than science." He won a scholarship in a national forensic tournament, and switched to speech, going on to the University of Washington. Mr. Huntley's broadcasting career began in 1934 when he was just out of college, "trying my best to make some imprint on the local radio industry in Seattle." He wrote his own commercials and other program copy. Now, he says, he is "thinking a little bit" of writing next about those early days of radio.

Involved in TV to some extent in its beginning years in Los Angeles, he came East to NBC, and the first "Huntley–Brinkley Report" went on the air, live, for 15 minutes the night of October 30, 1956. The two-man team had three major developments to cover: the Hungarian revolt, the invasion of Suez, an American presidential election two weeks away.

These days Huntley and Brinkley make extensive use of film material prepared by other newsmen, but the two men still handle their personal commentary themselves. Mr. Huntley says he "lives with it constantly all day long," starts whipping things into final shape about 5 P.M. From 6:30 to 7 P.M. the show is taped so that NBC stations can use it either right in that time spot or from 7 to 7:30 P.M.

Chet Huntley still keeps roots down in Montana. His parents live there in Billings and he has a small herd of cattle in Montana. When he goes back he finds himself saddened by what has happened to many of the towns and much of the farmland he knew as a boy. The towns have dried up and the farms have blown away, as is the case with his own family's. "The early farmers just did not know enough scientifically to understand that this land should never have been put to the plough, that it was really grazing land," he says.

"It used to be you could say anything in defense of agriculture and you'd have 99 percent of Congress behind you," Mr. Huntley says. He thinks the farmer's cause today does not always fare so well. Asked to sum up his reactions to the way things are "now" as opposed to the way they were "then" in "The Generous Years," with all their problems, Mr. Huntley put it this way: "It is very difficult to be unorthodox these days and to take your lumps. Being a maverick isn't easy." In his own maverick way Mr. Huntley has in the past tangled with a powerful labor union, with members of Congress and governmental agencies. The background for his way of thinking and acting is right there in "The Generous Years."

Hildegard Knef

OF HILDEGARD KNEF an astrologer once predicted, "You will always have to fight and you will always be impatient." Miss Knef's autobiography, "The Gift Horse" (*McGraw-Hill*) attests to the accuracy of his analysis. Most Americans knew Hildegard "Neff" (her name was changed for Hollywood films) for her postwar acting success in "Decision Before Dawn" and "Silk Stockings." Yet as a young girl she lived in wartime Germany and was held captive in a Russian prison camp.

Miss Knef and her husband, David Cameron Palastanga, who translated "The Gift Horse" into English, were in New York recently, and *PW* spoke with them about the book. (The couple and their three-year-old daughter, Christina, live part of the time in Salzburg, Austria and part in St. Moritz, Switzerland.)

"I started writing six years ago," Miss Knef told us, "wrote one chapter and put it down. I looked for excuses because I was petrified to write about the war. I knew I would have to relive the war in order to capture the utter chaos, absurdity and insanity of the last days of Berlin before and after the capitulation of Germany." After she had put aside the manuscript she and her husband embarked as a team on what is currently their major interest: Hildegard's songs. She writes the lyrics and sings them; he finds the composer and produces the songs and the concerts. In March, 1969, Miss Knef interrupted her singing career to finish "The Gift Horse." It took her a year and a half.

By the time she was halfway through the book, Hildegard Knef said she had decided upon its title. One of her favorite

By Lila P. Freilicher. From *Publishers Weekly* 200, no. 2 (July 12, 1971), pp. 39–41.

short stories, by J. D. Salinger, supplied it. In "Teddy" Salinger wrote, "In my opinion life is nothing but a gift horse." Miss Knef said, "I thought this was a good title for the story of a generation whose primary concern had been survival. Life has to be accepted as a 'gift horse' without being fatalistic about it. In other words, one has to deal with life as a challenge, not only as a matter of good or bad luck." Miss Knef told us she subtitled her autobiography, "Report on a Life," because "I was not interested in getting emotionally involved in telling the story. I wanted to use myself as a camera."

A major portion of Hildegard Knef's "report on a life" deals with World War II. It paints a picture of indoctrinated youngsters who did not think to question conditions in Germany. "During the war," Miss Knef explained, "there was no way of comparing. The first time I saw the difference was right after the war when I went to Zurich. I stood in the sunlight on its main street and I couldn't stop crying. No houses were destroyed; people were dressed in a way I had never seen before and I saw no one suddenly race off the streets because of an attack of dysentery."

It was especially gratifying, Miss Knef told us, to have heard from her editor, Anne Murphy, that a young Jewish girl had liked the book. The girl told Anne Murphy that she now understood what it was like to have lived in Germany under Hitler and had now stopped thinking of the Germans as a nation of people guarding only concentration camps.

As the astrologer had predicted, life continued to be a struggle for Hildegard Knef even after the war. Though she married an American G.I. she did not gain American citizenship for three years. Yet under German military law she had lost her German citizenship and was, therefore, "stateless."

She told *PW*, "I found myself in a position where I had to carry more papers than if I had been a citizen of only one country." (Miss Knef is now a British citizen like her husband.) Even after she had received her American citizenship, she felt she was regarded as a second-class citizen in this country. Travel restrictions placed on naturalized citizens hindered her from spending time out of the country to make films. In addition she was frequently questioned about her political background because of her German origin.

In her film career she was both praised and damned. In the early fifties in Germany she was called "the sinner" because of a film with that title in which she had played a "scandalous" role. In America work was hard to get; being a German was held against her. After refusing David Selznick's suggestion to change her name to Gilda Christian and her nationality to Austrian, she finally achieved recognition for her performances in "Decision Before Dawn" and "Silk Stockings."

In "Silk Stockings" she was compared to Greta Garbo who had starred in the original "Ninotchka." "I thought the comparison was ridiculous," Miss Knef told us. "Nobody was more beautiful than Garbo on the screen. She had her own mystique and her own unforgettable aura. Why should anybody come trouping in from Germany and be compared to Garbo just because of similar hair color?"

"Filmmaking can be rewarding if you have a good director and a good story," Miss Knef said. Then she added, "but it really is a bad profession because you get praised and criticized for things you are not responsible for. It is actually the script writer and director who make the film. Yet if the film is a flop the actor suffers most because he is judged by his decision to be in the film. The actor, you see, may not know that the good script he reads will turn into a bad film. During my career there was one seven-year period in which I had a contract with a studio and had no choice over my films. I was like a sheep being brought either to the slaughter or to win the first prize at the fair."

Acting, Hildegard Knef said, is no longer a thing she longs for. "I needed a long time in an extrovert profession to be strong enough to work in an isolated one like writing. Yet 15 years ago if you had told me that I would enjoy writing more than acting I would not have believed you. At certain times I have a need for a new outlet for my tensions, and writing now appeals to me much more than acting."

The fact that "The Gift Horse" has sold 400,000 copies in Germany both overwhelms and worries Hildegard Knef. "It took me months to grasp what was happening with the book. Now I am trying not to worry about it too much because I don't want to become caught up in a centrifugal turmoil of excitement. I want to go on writing and I want to take my time about it."

Anita Loos

THE DIMINUTIVE but perfectly shaped body that might have made her a movie star, the wit and enthusiasm that did make her an essential part of the smart set for most of her adult life, and the passion for books and writers that won her the company and friendship of people like H. G. Wells, Aldous Huxley, Christopher Isherwood and W. H. Auden—all are still alive and well in the person of Anita Loos, who holds sway from an apartment across the street from Carnegie Hall in New York, and who has just published her umpteenth book.

A slight deafness is her only concession to age (about which she is playful, but which ungallant reference books give as an unbelievable 83); otherwise she continues to live as she always has, keeping what she calls "the hours of a farmhand—I get up at 4 A.M. and go to bed at 9, which I guess is a strange way to live in the heart of New York," and reading omnivorously. The table in her living room is piled high with books, many of them sent by publishers who hope she will send them publishable quotes. "But I think publishers who send books and don't ask for permission to quote you don't deserve quotes. And anyway, they send me all the wrong sort of books."

The "wrong sort of books," as far as she is concerned, are show business histories and ghost-written movie memoirs, genres for which she has little tolerance—though in the case of a recent arrival, a lavishly illustrated memoir by an old friend, Douglas Fairbanks, Jr., she has found something of real interest. "Look, it's a picture of Robert Sherwood's wedding, and there's me—and I don't remember even being there. I didn't like his wife, anyway."

By John F. Baker. From *Publishers Weekly* 210, no. 23 (December 6, 1976), pp. 6–8.

Her own latest excursion into print is itself lavishly illustrated, but *certainly* not ghost-written. It is "Cast of Thousands," which was suggested to her by Grosset & Dunlap's editor-in-chief Robert Markel, and which is a swift-moving, affectionate once-over, heavily spiced with anecdote, of her own life and times as seen from her position as a Hollywood and Broadway insider ever since she wrote her first screenplay while still in her teens. (She sent it to a movie company on 14th Street in New York, having copied the name off a can of film, and without revealing her age or sex. It was accepted, and became an early D. W. Griffith two-reeler.)

The pictures in "Cast of Thousands" range from portraits and caricatures of Loos herself to remarkable stills and studio shots from the early days of the movies, many of them never seen before. "I never realized I had this collection until recently. I've moved a lot in my life, and usually I never kept things, but at MGM for 18 years I had a secretary who kept and filed everything. When I came East I left it all at my brother's house in packing cases, then one day he sent it on over here. I looked out the window and there it all was, standing on 57th Street." She now has a young movie buff at work organizing and filing it all.

The Loos archive could be a valuable resource because, as she points out, all too few of the old studios kept their material in any methodical way. "Then when they'd go out of business, as a lot of them did, all that stuff went with them." She wishes some provision could be made for collecting historical film material, "like those colleges that collect writers. They do the silliest things, emptying wastebaskets, then building special wings to house the paper." Her next mining of her collection will be for a book on the Talmadge sisters she is doing for Viking, which will contain, she promises, "hundreds of pictures never seen before."

These books represent her latest outburst of activity, but in fact her typewriter has seldom been idle since the time she was taken to meet Mr. Griffith by her mother, and he promptly assumed it was her mother who had written the scripts he had been shooting. Few authors have one book in a lifetime to equal the world success of "Gentlemen Prefer Blondes" which Loos wrote in 1925, irritated by the attention her idol H. L. Mencken paid to a very blonde blonde. Her Lorelei Lee's adventures were translated into 14 languages and formed the basis of a highly successful musical and movie, as well as innumerable advertising campaigns and jokes. George Santayana once described it as the major American novel of the century, and it made its author, until then an only moderately successful screenwriter, famous overnight. Does the fact that this is the only writing of hers that everyone automatically remembers ever irritate her? "How can it when my royalties are still coming in to this day?" But she confesses she was very much surprised by it—and that her own favorites among her writing are "A Mouse Is Born," about a Lorelei-like creature in Hollywood, and the screenplays for "San Francisco" (Clark Gable) and "Red-Headed Woman" (Jean Harlow). Her work is nearly always on view somewhere. "They did 'Gigi' in Berlin last week, and soon they're bringing back 'Happy Birthday,' which I wrote for Helen Hayes, and gave her the chance to play a drunk."

But although she is proud of her ability to entertain, she sees it as no more than craftsmanship. "My taste in literature prevented me from ever thinking of myself as a real writer," she smiles. "I'm just out there hustling." What *are* her own tastes in literature? It turns out that Goethe is probably her favorite writer—"but I like Heine too. Mostly I just read the classics, which I get from the library." Recent favorite books have included "a wonderful biography of the Earl of Essex," Robert Craft's series of books enshrining his conversations with Stravinsky ("They're just the wittiest books I know") and, among movie memoirs, one by Raoul Walsh: "He was such a civilized man, and his book is just like him. I was so sorry it never really clicked."

Loos's conversation is like her new book, darting around without many wasted words, but always shedding fresh light on some famous names. Paulette Goddard, for instance, is her best surviving friend—"the only star I've ever known who really likes to walk. We'd often go out together and walk for miles, all the way round Central Park, for instance." Didn't anyone ever recognize them? "Me they wouldn't, and Paulette always said the best way to avoid being recognized was to wear a dark dress." The best parties in the old Hollywood she remembers from the 30s were the ones given by Cole Porter. "He was always so witty and his friends were so intelligent. At most Hollywood parties they'd just have a drink and then run a movie—they had to run a movie quick, before conversation died." W. H. Auden she recalls affectionately as the dirtiest man she ever met. "That apartment of his down on St. Mark's Place, it was so filthy you wouldn't believe. When you went to a party you didn't even want to drink out of the cups, they were so dirty. But as soon as he started talking. . . . Why would a man as intelligent as that always choose to live in such discomfort? When he lived in Austria the railroad ran right by his house and you couldn't hear yourself speak when a train passed."

She has lived in New York for 12 years now, thinks of herself as a New Yorker. "Yes, I was born in California, but I was brought up in San Francisco. I never thought of Los Angeles as anything but a place to work." She was last back there five years ago, but returned quickly, and shudders delicately at the recollection. "It all seems to be diabolism there now— like a miasma over everything, it's terrifying. In my day the most evil thing we had around was Aimée Semple McPherson."

She starts work as soon as she gets up in the morning—and "Cast of Thousands" turned out to be harder than she expected. "When Bob Markel came to persuade me, I had the impression the book would be 60 percent pictures, and only 40 percent text and caption. Maybe it was, but they got Irwin Glusker to design it, and you know what designers are. I found I had to write exactly 10 lines here, another 20 there. It's a good job. I'm a professional and used to deadlines!''

She is frequently invited to parties, but seldom goes, "because I always want to be home by 9, you know." Reminded that publishing parties are usually earlier than that, she agrees, but "aren't they usually pretty dull too?"

She goes occasionally to the movies, "and if I find a good one I'll see it two or three times rather than press my luck." A current favorite is "The Clockmaker," from the book by Georges Simenon, which she thinks of as "the best movie version of a book I ever saw." At the theater, "I generally find I'm thinking of something else, so it's a good opportunity to sit and meditate."

From her living room windows she can look down on the scene outside Carnegie Hall, across the street, and often does so: "It's better than the show inside, most of the time." All her surviving friends live nearby— Paulette Goddard, Lillian Gish, Leo Lerman (to whom the new book is dedicated). And there's only one thing that dims her irrepressible spirit. "I still feel great, but I'm at that age when suddenly everyone you know is dying around you." Loos will last a good while longer yet.

Jan Morris

JAN MORRIS, the author of "Conundrum," is 15 minutes late arriving for lunch, and she acknowledges it with a playful smile. James Morris, on the other hand, the author of "The World of Venice," "Pax Britannica," "The Great Port" and several other admired books as well as countless newspaper stories and magazine articles, was *never* late for lunch, and was frequently found seated at the table first, his head probably buried in a book. This was the first conundrum faced by the *PW* interviewer, who had known James as an exceptionally charming and sensitive man, and who now encountered Jan for the first time as the woman James had always wanted to become.

There have been transsexuals before, of course, even transsexuals who have written books about their transformation (Christine Jorgensen, a highly successful lecturer on the campus circuit, springs immediately to mind). But Jan Morris's experience is unique in several ways; because of her virtually lifelong conviction, despite physical evidence to the contrary, that she was a woman, with a feminine— *soul* is the only possible word; because of the degree of eminence she achieved in life as a man, with a career that included a dashing military interlude and a climb of Everest; and because of the extraordinary felicity of her style, which has enabled her to make an ordeal that is almost incomprehensible to most people (including, apparently, some reviewers) into a candid, graceful and poignant account of self-discovery.

Although the transformation was achieved with remarkable tact, drawing on large reservoirs of English reticence in

By John F. Baker. From *Publishers Weekly* 205, no. 17 (April 29, 1974), pp. 10–11.

such matters and of goodwill built up among journalistic colleagues by years of skillful practice in that profession, Ms. Morris faced the impending publication of her book in the U.S., with some trepidation. There was a feeling that Americans might be rather brash about it all, and ask all sorts of embarrassing questions; and the reaction to the publication in the *New York Times Magazine* of a long and sympathetic account of the transformation by English journalist David Holden, an old friend, was not reassuring. Crank letters began to come in to Ms. Morris's publishers, and instead of staying in a hotel, as originally planned, she went to the New York home of her agent and long-time friend Julian Bach for the duration of her U.S. stay.

And there is no doubt that even among the more sophisticated members of New York's literary and publishing community, there was an almost febrile undercurrent of gossip and conjecture about her. She was judiciously assessed as a woman: Were her shoulders broader than they should be? Was her voice too deep? An editor who had not seen her since she was James was apologetic, but still could not resist demanding insistently of the *PW* interviewer: "But how did it *seem*, talking to her? Was it awkward, difficult—embarrassing?"

The answer to all these questions, for this interviewer, has to be no, not at all. James always seemed delicate, almost fragile, and with a special quickness of intuition that to admirers of the sex seems a peculiarly feminine quality. He was profoundly tolerant, except of cruelty and stupidity, perpetually self-amused, deeply attentive, eternally curious. Jan retains these characteristics in full measure—and despite her anxieties about America, there seems a new confidence about her, as if what was tentative in James has now come to full fruition in Jan.

That confidence particularly embraces her work, and "Conundrum" is very close to her at present. "I wouldn't have believed I could do it," she says, and in a person naturally modest the assertion has extra impact. "Usually I've thought of myself as a very conscious writer, but there were times in the writing when I honestly just seemed to be taken over. It's by far the best thing I've ever done. In fact, I like to think it will still be read 100 years from now."

She had been worried that with the final change of sex—after years of hormone treatment that altered James Morris's secondary sexual characteristics, creating toward the end a rather hermaphroditic figure, he had the ultimate sex-change operation in Casablanca two years ago—might come a change in her writing style, which had been justly admired. (In fact, even an otherwise rather hostile review of "Conundrum" spoke of James as "perhaps the finest descriptive writer in our time, of the watercolor kind." "Quite right," says Jan. "I *am* a watercolorist; nothing wrong with that.")

But the style seems to have survived intact, and with it a sharper sense of personal involvement, of interest in her fellow beings. She confesses freely in the book that the genre of writing for which James was most celebrated—what in a charming misprint is described as "the specious [for spacious] topographical essay"—was underpopulated. She attributes this to her former sense of isolation in her curious sexual wilderness, and welcomes the intimacy of feeling that has arrived with her new gender. It is probably significant that after years of writing about places, organizations and historical movements, her next book after "Conundrum" is to be a biography. Jan is a passionate Welsh nationalist, despite a background that is at least equally English, and has chosen as her subject Owen Glendower. Not much known to Americans, other than as a character who appears fleetingly in Shakespeare's "Henry IV," he was a celebrated Welsh chieftain of the Middle Ages, whose end was uncertain. Jan is eager to supply him with a speculative ending. She has also decided that she might even turn to fiction ultimately; and with her finely wrought prose, and her remarkable insight into both male and female psyches, as well as the borderland between them, she could make a formidably equipped novelist.

Whichever way she turns, her work will continue to be lovingly cherished by Helen Wolff, who has brought out every Morris book in the United States. She recalled for *PW* recently, in the course of a party she gave in Jan's honor, how she and Kurt had been in London "in one of those freezing winters just after the war," and had called on Faber & Faber— then, as now, Morris's sole publisher in Britain—to see what they had. "We got this extraordinary book about traveling in America, and I sat up all night reading it—it was too cold to sleep, anyway—and I thought it was the most remarkable writing about this country I'd ever read." The book was "As I Saw the U.S.A." ("Coast to Coast" in Britain) and it marked the beginning of a relationship of mutual affection and admiration that has never wavered. When Kurt Wolff died, and Helen moved her list from Pantheon to Harcourt Brace Jovanovich, James moved right along.

Helen Wolff does not think in terms of best sellers, but it is possible that in "Conundrum" she may have one. Reviews have been extensive even before publication, and it is already clear from their wide variations in tone that it is a book, and a subject, that passionately divides people.

Not its least controversial aspect is the sort of woman Jan is. James Morris was a warm romantic, and Jan is no less so. She delights in what her sterner sisters of the Women's Lib movement regard as the fripperies of her sex. She finds it a relief to be no longer as much concerned with public events as she was as a man; she finds herself flirtatious, quickly emotional, highly susceptible to flattery, and prone to accept masculine judgments of women's inferiority in such matters as parking cars. She loves the notion of being a part of what she really does see as the weaker sex. "Women who like to feel cherished by a stronger man have every right to their feelings. Perhaps they are being closer to their true nature than women who insist on complete independence. Have you ever met a really happy Women's Libber? I haven't."

And unlike many women (but like, perhaps, most men), Jan has her ideal of what a woman should be. In "Conundrum" she writes of her conviction that "the nearest humanity approaches to perfection is in the persons of good women—and especially perhaps in the persons of kind, intelligent, and healthy women of a certain age, no longer shackled by the mechanisms of sex but creative still in other kinds, aware still in their love and sensuality, graceful in experience, past ambition but never beyond aspiration. In all countries, among all races, on the whole these are the people I most admire; and it is into their ranks, I flatter myself, if only in the rear file, if only on the flank, that I have now admitted myself."

Willie Morris

THIRTY-TWO is generally regarded as a tender age for writing autobiography. Nevertheless, Willie Morris, editor of *Harper's* magazine, has written his autobiography at the age of 32, and Houghton Mifflin will publish it, "North toward Home," on October 23. Already it is one of the most talked-about nonfiction books of the season (*Saturday Evening Post* ran a 10,000-word chunk of it in its October 7 issue), and John Kenneth Galbraith seems to have summed up the general pre-publication reaction: "No one at 32," he said, "should write his memoirs; Willie Morris is the only exception."

Fiction is the expected medium for 32-year-old writers. "For a long time, I worked on this material in fictional form," Mr. Morris told *PW* in an interview the other day. "Then I decided: Why not tell it like it really was?"

The result—"like it really was"—is a book about three places: Mississippi (Yazoo City, where Mr. Morris was born, grew up, was a "big wheel" in high school); Texas (Austin and the University, where he was a splendidly controversial editor of the student newspaper); and New York City (where, like so many literary outlanders before him, he was initially rebuffed by the literary "establishment" and subsequently became one of its ornaments).

What's so unusual about growing up in Mississippi? "Small town life in the Mississippi Delta upsets me and probably always will," Mr. Morris said. "There's the heaviness of nature, the overwhelming sense of the past, the emphasis on storytelling, the courtliness and violence. Once you have it, it's always with you. The older I get, the more it

By Roger H. Smith. From *Publishers Weekly* 192, no. 15 (October 9, 1967), pp. 21–22.

talks to me." Mr. Morris said he had no idea how the book would be received in Mississippi. "I hope," he said, "that a few people there will see the book for what it is: an act of love." He had no comment about whether Mississippi now is a better or a worse place than it was when he was growing up there in the 1940s and '50s. "After the Supreme Court's school desegregation decision in 1954, Mississippi went through an almost criminal period," he said. "More recently, there has been recognition that racial sickness is a national thing; it belongs to us all. The South, at its best, could lead the country out of this social madness."

Mr. Morris said that his next major writing project probably will be fiction ("though not any time soon") and that he plans to write, probably a long essay, about the fourth major place in his life, not covered in "North toward Home": Oxford, where for four years he studied as a Rhodes Scholar. "Oxford," he said, "is a great place. It gave me four years to think. But in this book, I skipped it consciously; I wanted this to be a book about America."

Meanwhile, except for a book promotional trip or two, Mr. Morris' basic concerns these days are with the editorial direction of *Harper's*, where he has been editor since July 1. "We're going to be doing a lot more with book material," he said, pointing to the current issue, which excerpts 50,000 words of William Styron's "The Confessions of Nat Turner" (*Random House*). "And we're going to be looking conscientiously for opportunities to publish new, good writers."

David Niven

DAVID NIVEN has to be one of the more indestructible actors of our time. He is 65, but as the *PW* interviewer set out to meet him recently he was followed by sighs of envy from his wife and most of his female colleagues at *PW*. "He's so—debonair," explained one of them. "So suave and gentlemanly."

He is indeed all these things, to an astonishing degree. The qualities of gentleness, humor and slightly quizzical skepticism that have served him so well in dozens of movie performances over the past 40 years come across just as strongly in person—perhaps more strongly, since Niven the person can often produce dialogue a great deal sharper and wittier than many screenwriters have managed to write for Niven the actor.

He is in fact a magnificent raconteur, a fact well known to the large number of people who read "The Moon's a Balloon" four years ago, and which will be proved all over again to those who pick up his new book. "Bring on the Empty Horses," which Putnam is bringing out here next month. The first book was largely autobiographical; the second is basically a portrait of Hollywood from 1935, when Niven arrived on the scene as an eager young extra, to 1960, when the movie industry began to move decisively away from the old studio setup and yield the field to TV. It's at once a portrait of the old Hollywood in its palmiest days and a collection of profiles of some of the stars Niven has been closest to over the years: Clark Gable, Humphrey Bogart, Errol Flynn, Fred Astaire, Cary Grant, Robert Newton, and many others. It also contains one or two telling cautionary

By John F. Baker. From *Publishers Weekly* 208, no. 8 (August 25, 1975), pp. 216–218.

tales about anonymous Hollywood personalities—and ends with a frank and unflattering anecdote at the author's own expense (which involves a carefully rehearsed piece of typography, which Niven was particularly anxious should go right in the finished book, as it hadn't in the galleys).

"I didn't want it to be an 'in' sort of book about Hollywood," Niven said, crinkling his brow with that hint of comic worry that has stood him in such good stead through nearly 80 movies. "It's really intended for people who want to have an idea of what Hollywood was like, but who don't really know the difference between a producer and a director. At least it's written by someone who was there, and who knew things from the inside," he goes on, warming to his theme. "So many books about Hollywood and the stars seem to be written by newspapermen, and they weren't really the best of sources. In the heyday of the old studios, there used to be 300 or 400 correspondents from around the world covering the Hollywood beat. And whenever they did an interview with a star they had to send their copy in to be vetoed by the studio; if someone was quoted as saying something the studio didn't want them to say, out it came, and a new quote was substituted."

It was in many ways a hypocritical time—"I remember the parties, where the photographers would take shots of us all sitting around talking politely, with never a glass in sight, then once the photographers had gone the liquor would come out and the real party would begin." About the time he ceased to be a Hollywood fixture, however, things began to change. "You had all these exposés and things, and the confession magazines, and that made it all seem actually *worse* than it was. I don't really know which was more dishonest."

He has tried to maintain a balance in his own account, and thinks he has been fair—"I didn't write about anyone I really didn't like, what's the point?"—but is still anxious about the reception of the new book. "It's funny, I've made 80 movies, but I'm far more anxious about what people think of the book than I was about any of them. Oh dear, perhaps I shouldn't have done it—what do you think?" It soon becomes clear that Niven is suffering from a syndrome common among writers who have scored a major success and who then wonder if they can repeat it; and it emerges that he had taken the popularity of "The Moon's a Balloon" very much for granted. "I'm afraid the first time out I just didn't realize how lucky I was. When I was told that my book had hit the best-seller list, I thought: 'Of course—what did they expect?' After all, I'd spent a year at it, therefore I deserved it. I'm afraid I never thought enough about writers who work much harder and *don't* get on the best-seller list. After that I suddenly got frightfully nervous, and began to feel like a crab, all exposed. And all the time I was carrying on like a maniac, preening myself all over the joint, because I'd written a book."

Niven utterly astonished the book world by writing personally to any critic who had praised his book. "I thanked them from the bottom of my heart, and some of them wrote back and said, 'Look here, you're not supposed to do this.' " (He also endeared himself to the staff at Putnam by touring the publishing house and thanking each staff member, down to the lowliest secretary, for helping to make the book a success.)

Although "Moon" is the only book most people remember, it was not in fact Niven's very first essay into print. Before that, in the early 1950s (while on suspension by Samuel Goldwyn for some infraction of the Hollywood rules) he wrote a novel, called "Round the Rugged Rocks" in England and "Once Over Lightly" in this country. "It was partly based on me, and was all about a man who wanted to be an actor, and who owned a bulldog which eventually became a star in TV commercials instead of him." The novel did not enjoy vast sales—he recalls them as about 10,000, "probably mostly out of curiosity, because people wanted to see if I could do it." But it gave rise to one of those delicious "if only" footnotes that stud publishing. The novel had been published here, says Niven, by Prentice-Hall, and when his agent was selling American rights for "Moon," it was discovered that the publisher had an option on his next book. The rights were accordingly offered, but Prentice-Hall, deciding apparently that an actor's memoirs were not very hot box-office, declined to exercise its option. The book then went to Putnam, and on to a paperback sale that ultimately exceeded 4-million copies.

Niven tells stories effortlessly, with superb timing, and with irresistible sound effects and mime thrown in, and it is not hard to believe, as he claims, that the writing comes easily to him, though he polishes away at it all the same. The chief difficulty, to hear Niven tell it, is getting the material on paper. "I started off by trying to dictate into a machine, but the sound of my own voice going on and on bored me; then I hired a lady from Nice [he lives on the Riviera when he is not in Switzerland for the winter skiing] but she objected to the four-letter words. Then I got another lady, who laughed so hard at my jokes all the time that I found myself playing up to her, and throwing in extra little bits just for an extra laugh, and that wouldn't do. Finally, I wrote it all myself, in kids' school notebooks, and it's all typed up for me, very beautifully, by the secretary of the manager of the Connaught Hotel in London, who does it in her spare time."

Niven does not claim total recall of conversations, "but the harder I think about it all, the more I found that all sorts of things were wriggling out from under the rocks." He made a few notes of some of his Hollywood encounters, a habit he began when he was once asked, many years ago, to write a Hollywood column for a London newspaper. He wouldn't dream, however, of making constant notes like his friend Garson Kanin, who fills file cabinets with Hollywood anecdotes and talk: "Everyone's terrified to talk to Gar any more."

These days Niven tries to make no more than one film a year, just to pay the bills. When *PW* saw him he was just back from a spell in Hollywood making a movie for Walt Disney, but showed considerably more enthusiasm for a forthcoming project, "Murder by Death," a screenplay by Neil Simon in which a group of famous fictional detectives attempt to solve the murder of one of them. There is an all-star cast, including Orson Welles as Mr. Moto, and Niven himself as Nick Charles, the Thin Man, the role originally created by William Powell. "And guess who's playing Myrna Loy," he says delightedly. "Myrna Loy!"

Ninety minutes passes much more swiftly than a movie in Niven's presence, as he recounts a hilarious confrontation with Otto Preminger in Paris, the encounter of Olivier with a Method actor (when Olivier forgot a line and muttered to the other man to give it to him, the Method man snarled, "We don't do it that way"), his horror in the Bel Air Hotel swimming pool last week as he saw a long, dark shape moving along the bottom (he had just seen "Jaws") and it turned out to be a man with a snorkel cleaning the pool.

Despite the occasional complaints of some old ladies about the racy language in some of Niven's anecdotes, it would be hard to have to do without such stories as the one, in "Bring on the Empty Horses," about Hungarian director Michael Curtiz and his struggles with English. "You think I know f—— nothing!" he once screamed at Flynn and Niven during the making of "Charge of the Light Brigade." "Well, let me tell you— I know F——ALL!"

William A. Nolen

Bill Nolen is not the kind of doctor that the American Medical Association would ever trot out as a spokesman. He is immodest, opinionated, candid to a fault, and he would be delighted to see the mystique taken out of medicine. His first book, "The Making of a Surgeon" (*Random*), describing his training years at Bellevue Hospital in New York, was a tough, illuminating picture of what happens in the surgical wards of a metropolitan hospital, and it did not exactly endear him to the pooh-bahs of medicine. His new book, "A Surgeon's World" (also *Random*), will hardly enhance his popularity among doctors, but since patients are his true concern, it is a good bet that the audience that made his initial literary effort a major success will be considerably widened and even more informed about surgery, medical practice, and the doctor–patient relationship.

Dr. Nolen's new book picks up where "The Making of a Surgeon" left off. He has moved to the small town of Litchfield, Minnesota, 65 miles west of Minneapolis, a "Main Street" type of town, where he has practiced surgery since 1960. With an Irish flair for the illustrative anecdote, Dr. Nolen describes his working life, operations he has performed, medical triumphs and misfortunes, mundane happenings and stop-your-heart crises. But he doesn't stop at the routine stuff. Audaciously, he tackles such subjects as doctors and extramarital sex (not as much as you'd think), doctors' wives, doctors and nurses, malpractice, fee-splitting, unjustifiable surgery, and other matters most doctors would just as soon leave undiscussed and mysterious.

"A lot of doctors thought I was a traitor to the profession

By Arnold W. Ehrlich. From *Publishers Weekly* 202, no. 20 (November 13, 1972), pp. 16–17.

when 'The Making of a Surgeon' was published," Dr. Nolen told *PW* in a recent talk in New York. "There was a lot of heat and a lot of static, but, as you can see they didn't drum me out of the profession. I just don't see why there has to be so much mystery to medicine. Of course, I took some kidding, too." With almost hysterical candor, Dr. Nolen had described, in that book, his first fumbling attempts to perform an appendectomy, with results both ludicrous and ghastly. "In Litchfield, a man who had read the book said to me, 'I hope you'll do a better job on my appendix than the one you described botching in your book.' " In the sequel, Dr. Nolen, recounts an incident in which a clamp is left behind in a patient's insides after surgery. The situation is resolved satisfactorily, but "there aren't many secrets kept in a small town. A friend of mine said, 'I hear you're not much of a carpenter—you don't pick up tools when you finish a job.' " It's that kind of candor which can give the profession the willies, readers a chilling tickle.

Doctor–patient relationships loom large in Dr. Nolen's thinking, to the extent that "I've learned to be very careful what I say in front of a patient coming out of anaesthesia," for example, as well as "what may be trite, trivial and mundane to me" may not be to the patient on the table. "What upsets patients can bore the hell out of us doctors, but we've got to be conscious always of how patients feel. Through their eyes I've come to see myself better," he commented, "and writing itself has made me a better doctor." Dr. Nolen's writing, apart from his two major books, includes a medical column in *McCall's*, and on his future writing program he foresees a book for young people on the order of "So You Want to Be a Doctor," which will explain to potential M.D.'s precisely what a doctor goes through to win his coveted standing. Like many concerned doctors, he frets about the possible shortage of doctors, their ignorance of what medical training demands, and their almost total lack of preparation for the economics of medicine—a point he hammers home in "A Surgeon's World." His interest in writing also surfaces in summer when he lectures and attends a writers' conference in Bemidji, Minnesota. "It was there, last summer," he recalled, "that a visiting Irish poet lectured me—a doctor—on why people fear death," a point which led to a protracted discussion with the *PW* interviewer on the possibility of introducing LSD into the medication of terminal patients: "Tell me more, what do you think of it, have you tried it?" Dr. Nolen asked, with all the eager curiosity of an interne. "Where can I read more about it?" The interviewer referred him to the article in *Harper's* some years ago that had triggered the question.

Curious, humane, confident of himself in the best sense of the word (his new book is bound to provoke all sorts of long-distance calls from would-be patients), Dr. Nolen makes a winning score in his new book. He's as scared of having another surgeon operate on him as he is of flying.

"Well, then, tell me, Bill, do you have a physical examination every year? After all, the medical profession insists on it; so does every corporation. What about you?"

"Good God, no. I haven't had a physical in ten years. I feel great. You don't want to go looking under any rocks when you don't have to, do you?"

Dusko Popov

THE SECRET AGENT has fixed the rendezvous for 1300 hours at Paris' Left-Bank Brasserie Lipp. A bit nervous, the *PW* interviewer arrives five minutes early, for he remembers that Lipp has closed every Monday for at least the past 20 years. The secret agent is supposed to be a long-time resident of France—shouldn't he have known about Lipp's closing? Fearing a trap, *PW*-I gingerly steps up to the closed café and finds a note taped to the door—from the *inside*:

I am at the Café de Flore across the street.—Popov

They find each other, secret agent and interviewer, at an obscure table. As promised, the agent's black briefcase contains galleys of his book, "Spy/Counterspy," published today by Grosset & Dunlap and already reprinted following heavy advance orders. Popov also brings along a note just received from a Riviera neighbor and one-time intelligence colleague, Graham Greene: "Mr. Popov, who as Tricycle was the most important and successful double agent working for the British during the war, has written a book which deserves to become a classic of espionage."

Dusko Popov has established his credentials, as far as the interviewer is concerned. Sir John Masterman, who after a long struggle had got Her Majesty's Government to allow him to publish "The Double-Cross System," described how the British managed to turn every spy Germany sent them over to a double agent called Tricycle—"one of the chief figures of the double-cross world." Actually Tricycle's first loyalty had never been in doubt. Tapped by the Germans to become a master spy against the Allies, he volunteered his services to the British to deceive the Germans with false information.

By Herbert R. Lottman. From *Publishers Weekly* 205, no. 16 (April 22, 1974), pp. 12–13. Reprinted by permission of Herbert R. Lottman.

Evidently the Masterman revelations aroused curiosity about the identity of Tricycle. One of the curious was Ladislas Farago, who had been coming across various code names such as Tricycle, Scout, Ivan-1 and Ivan-2, and then discovered they were all the same person. "Farago got my name from one of his contacts and traveled all over Europe to find me. He told me that my story would require him to revise 'The Game of the Foxes' and he hoped that I'd write my own book."

Until the Masterman book came out Popov, a loyal officer who received the Order of the British Empire for his wartime services, felt bound by the Official Secrets Act. Now he was free to put on tape his version of events. "I gave the tape to a secretary to transcribe," he recalls, "but to my errors of syntax she added her spelling errors." He tried using a journalist as coauthor, but he painted in too much background. "Finally my publisher told me to write it in my own words and let them do the editing."

The result is a sober, absorbing narrative of a nonconforming Yugoslav of good family whose friends in Germany—where he had gotten a doctorate in law and political science—recruited him into the Abwehr. Popov was attached to MI-5 under Sir John Masterman and the so-called Committee XX (from which the name "Double-Cross" was derived). He also worked for Sir Stewart Menzies, the famous "C," head of MI-6 (Popov is the godfather of Menzies' first child). On one or another of his 14 trips to Lisbon he met MI-6's Iberian desk chief Kim Philby, who later took up residence in Moscow (but he never actually encountered Philby's deputy, Graham Greene). He had a nodding acquaintanceship with a young Naval Intelligence officer named Ian Fleming, who later let it be known that Tricycle was one of the models for James Bond.

Indeed, some of Dusko Popov's exploits under his playboy cover, including a seemingly reckless casino scene at Estoril which Fleming observed from the wings, have a Bondian flair. "But just between us," Popov tells *PW*-I, "I wouldn't want to be Bond because I find him quite stupid." (If James Bond had aged like the rest of us, a British reporter once concluded, he would have looked like Dusko Popov.) Popov's well-to-do family allowed him to play the big-money game convincingly, and at one time he managed to get the Germans to use him to channel funds to their agents in Britain. "But my playboy days ended when the war was over," he sighs. "They gave me the OBE, two civilian suits, and said goodbye." Actually as an acting lieutenant colonel, Popov was never officially demobilized, but put "on leave."

Bond may have played around with women, but Popov has been strictly monogamous. When he found a beautiful Swedish girl he married her, and they now live with their three young sons in a hillside villa above Cannes which was once the summer residence of the bishops of Grasse. He works as an adviser to a number of international companies, but (if the tan on his leathery features is any indication) without letting it interfere with his poolside life, or his mountain retreat in a new winter resort north of Nice.

He looks the way a retired James Bond might look, in his three-piece tweed suit, striped shirt and polka-dot tie. He might also be a successful Cicero—but that valet-spy in the British Embassy in Ankara was paid off by the Nazis in counterfeit money, as moviegoers remember from "Five Fingers" starring James Mason. In fact Popov-Tricycle was in on the Cicero affair, having provided a tip on leaks from that embassy which pointed to Cicero, just as he helped confirm the success of "Operation Mincemeat," in which the British outfitted a corpse as an officer carrying secret documents to deceive the Germans as to where the Allies would open a southern beachhead (the movie "The Man Who Never Was" dramatized that episode).

Of more direct relevance to American readers, Popov was sent to the United States by the Nazis (with MI-6 encouragement) armed with a questionnaire reduced to microdots—apparently the first example of this German technique of miniaturizing messages to the size of full stops on a typewriter to fall into Allied hands. Not only did Tricycle hand microdots to the FBI "on a silver platter," but the information requested by the Germans pointed clearly to a Japanese attack on Pearl Harbor. Instead of sending it to the U.S. Navy for action J. Edgar Hoover sat on the information—something Popov feels the British services, with all their traditional rivalries, would not have done. "Spy/Counterspy" reproduces the microdot questionnaire, and it is said that the FBI wishes he hadn't raised the issue now. "My point is that people have the right to know what really happened," he explains, "and I'm only asking questions." Actually Popov's book also supplies the answers. It is a day-by-day account of what a real spy does, and so it is likely to please readers both of James Bond and of contemporary history—for it also names names.

Will life ever be the same again for Tricycle? Until a few years ago even his code name was unknown to the world. Release of "Spy/Counterspy" by Grosset & Dunlap will be the world's introduction to the man behind the name, and then publication will follow in London (Weidenfeld), Paris (Laffont), Milan (Bompiani). In Yugoslavia, Naprijed in Zagreb will be doing the book. (Although his family's interests were taken over by the Tito regime, Popov can visit Yugoslavia—where his father lives—and indeed the disclosure of Tricycle's exploits has made him a celebrity there.) Germany? If his prewar friend Johann Jebsen, who brought him into the Abwehr but remained as good a German as you could find in those times, is more or less the hero of the book, no German publisher had been lined up at the time of writing. Most Germans who might remember Tricycle as their man in London still don't know the truth. They are in for a surprise.

"The Germans had a good espionage system, but each chief derived his prestige from his agents. Mine boasted about me as the best agent in London. So he was always my best defender, and I'm not sure he wouldn't have closed his eyes if he had felt there was something suspicious about me.

"That was part of the American problem too. Hoover would also have kept it to himself."

V. S. Pritchett

"MIDNIGHT OIL," the second and concluding volume of V. S. Pritchett's autobiography (*Random House*), sees young Pritchett clear of his flighty, godly, ruinous parents, and in Paris. There he met neither Hemingway nor Fitzgerald, who were in residence; he sold glue. Then he fell about among a lot of other countries. The sense of mishap in his travels is delightful. In Paris he landed among the pious, in Spain among agnostics, and in Tennessee among hillbillies. He walked right into the Irish Troubles; but he did manage to meet Sean O'Casey. The playwright had a notice in his room saying, "GET ON WITH THE BLOODY PLAY!" And so to the present.

The present is touched on but lightly in "Midnight Oil." It occupies less than a fifth of the book. The audience who rolled upon and relished the Edwardiana of "A Cab at the Door," the first volume, may be surprised by Pritchett's swift passage through his later years; surprised if not actually dismayed. For he is a writer who inspires love; and in the maturing of his reputation, those who love him feel intimately concerned.

Modesty is partly the cause; since much of that reputation, especially as a literary critic, was made by his friends. But there is also something in it, happily, the reverse of modesty. Pritchett knows he is good, as good as he ever was. To write of one's recent past might somehow suggest the concluding of it. Besides, he does not write as an old man, but with a young man's anguish and rejections, as if every new thing is his first. This in a writer must be the only definition of the writer's only essential—enthusiasm.

By Philip Norman. From *Publishers Weekly* 201, no. 15 Part I (April 10, 1972), pp. 22–23. Reprinted by permission of Philip Norman.

The opening lines of "Midnight Oil" discover him, in fact, staring with perplexity at his 70-year-old reflection with its "exclaiming eyebrows and loosely grinning mouth." He had a wretched childhood and has felt younger every year since. This is the spring of his gift for autobiography. He has no sense of passing time in the literary sense—the passing of time into quaintness. "I still go to Dulwich, where I spent time as a boy," he says, "and stand on the bridge, as I used to, and watch the engines coming out of Sydenham Tunnel; but I always expect it to be the sort of engine that used to come out."

"Midnight Oil" deals also with the things that were kind to him. America is one of these. It is a relationship befitting one of the abiding masters of the short story and the last place on earth where realistic prices are paid for the work; but Pritchett gives thanks also for American editors in an emotional sense. His benefit from their encouragement dates from his early days as a not very apt correspondent of the *Christian Science Monitor*. No writer, he says, ever grows out of the need for reassurance. "Only 2 percent of something may be any good, but that is what an American editor will single out to praise," he said in a recent interview. "There is this wonderful attitude of 'let us see what good can be discovered in this man.' "

On that first visit to Tennessee, Pritchett reports, he was drunk with the dialect and wrote down whole chapters of it. As a lecturer and writer in residence since, at Princeton, Brandeis and Smith, he has suffered the common dilemma of recoiling from American life as an Englishman but responding to it as a writer with all his heart. "I got pulled up very sharply in New York once for remarking that, after midnight, every American male bursts into tears," V.S.P. told *PW*. Pritchett began to chuckle uproariously. "It's *true*. Not actually start crying, but they'll suddenly begin attacking each other—'you're nothing but a failure . . . look what you've done to your wife'—as if it's been the decision of a town council meeting inside them."

For all this fascination and large affection, none of his novels was ever set in America, nor any of the short stories. His explanation is that he did not think it right, through fiction, to broach a national temperament other than his own. Pritchett says this almost as if it had been a matter of good taste and propriety. Besides, he points out, look how Henry James slipped up on trying to broach the English from outside. V.S.P. has written of New York beautifully in nonfiction, ["New York Proclaimed"] and of Spain ["The Spanish Temper" and "Marching Spain"], Ireland ["Dublin: A Portrait"], and many other countries. He brings the thrill of literature to travel, as he does the grip of narrative to literary criticism. In fiction, however, his life's study has been what the English say and do and, above all, what the English insinuate. In illumination of this he will even transmute to an English setting material he has gathered abroad. He still, in America, makes notes of dialogue. But if a story occurred to him there, for its point of crystallization he would probably set it in England.

Since the past is not a foreign country to him, V.S.P. has never written self-consciously "period" stories. The wonderful one about the Edwardian evangelist falling from the punt first appeared when Edwardiana was not chic, it was living memory. Indeed, the praise heaped upon "A Cab at the Door" for its atmosphere—its mingling scents of fried fish and ladies' bloomers—rather astonished him. The past does not represent to him what is lost. "One can understand," he says, "the upper classes feeling like that, when whole chunks of their past have been swept away, but not someone brought up in the lower classes as I was, sometimes in poverty. There's an old lady living down the road who's 92 and says the most *extraordinary* things. I think her husband was a colonial servant. She'll say, 'It never rained like this in Khartoum.' But if I wrote about her, I couldn't write about her in the past. As she is now, here, she's very much hot from real life."

V.S.P. describes himself as stoical by temperament, fond of a good laugh, with the consequent leaning to melancholia. He begins new writing with an overwhelming despair, a feeling of having to learn to write all over again, but he still begins. In a moment it feels better. Though everything he finishes is the residue of countless discarded words, he still enjoys the action of writing rather than the state of having written. "If I've done something I'm really pleased with, I can't bear to show it to anyone. I don't want to look at it myself. Then when I do read it, I think it's wonderful. When I read it again, I still think it's wonderful. When I read it still again, I think it's bloody awful."

Stoicism triumphs, as it must. V.S.P. can contemplate without terror the millions of discarded words that lie behind him, and in front. There are other stories he wants to do. There are his literary articles for the *New Statesman* and *New York Review of Books*, and few other critics have arisen with Pritchett's qualities in that forensic art. He is ice-clear yet warm-natured. His American admirers have steadily grown over the years and he has formed lasting friendships with many American writers and editors.

He preserves some of the adventuring sense of his self-education. And he may do another novel. He has written four, as opposed to seven volumes of stories, but, he says, he has always felt himself dogged over the longer course by faulty construction. All the same, the novels included one tour de force, "Dead Man Leading," a story of the Amazon which he entirely looked up in books. "There was one last thing I needed to know—if a house in a certain place was lit by gas or electricity. Then, fortunately, I met a drunk man in a train who'd just got back from there, and he was just sober enough to be able to tell me."

"I write to find out what I think and feel," V.S.P. says. Thus, the auto-biography, which some have called his greatest accomplishment, is a final assessment of the disturbed early life which for years has vibrated through his fiction. His recovery from bitterness is also what makes him a young writer. "When I was doing it, I kept wishing my father was still alive so that I could take him out to a restaurant for a really good feed-up."

David Roberts

DAVID ROBERTS, a modest but determined young man from Colorado, experienced at 22 a peak of adventure and physical endurance which few men ever reach. He climbed Mt. Huntington in Alaska, a very difficult mountain, on its western face, a supremely difficult route. In his opinion, firmly stated to *PW* the other day, even the Himalayas would not be as dangerous to climb as Huntington was because of its jagged steepness, its storms, and "incredible snow and ice features." The only way to climb it, Roberts and his three friends knew as they started out, was to devote to it emotion, spirit and body in every respect. It was "the equivalent of a religious experience."

What he and his friends accomplished, what he felt and thought about it, and what it did to him he has recorded in a fine book which has won much pre-publication praise for its good writing, taut excitement and intense narrative. Vanguard is publishing the book, "The Mountain of My Fear."

Mt. Huntington, 12,240 feet high, is near Mt. McKinley. The west-face climb was pioneered in June–August, 1965, by Roberts and three friends who had all met in the Harvard Mountaineering Club: Ed Bernd, Don Jensen (now a graduate student in mathematics in California and a winter guide for mountain tours in the Sierra), and Matt Hale (a University of Maryland graduate student in history). Roberts is now earning his Ph.D. in creative writing at the University of Denver.

The most common question people ask Roberts about his climb, he says, is "Why?" This he tackles in his book with a self-analysis which is moving, unsparing and utterly sincere.

From *Publishers Weekly* 193, no. 14 (April 1, 1968), pp. 5–7.

He doesn't claim that the "why" is reasoned, thinks perhaps that it cannot be, and admits that his friends on the expedition don't agree with him on the reasons for climbing Huntington.

Just to pitch a tent on the mountain they had to spend five hours chopping a platform in the ice. Then pitons were driven into the rock wall above the platform and ropes tied from the pitons around the tent and to the flaps. So securely fastened, the tent would stay on the ledge even if the sleepers hurled themselves outward—but whenever they emerged they had to clip life ropes to a safe anchor.

The last climb, to the summit, after 20 days of effort, took "a 25-hour day—maybe nobody ever climbed a block of ice for so long a consecutive time." Keenly aware of the danger of relaxing, the climbers were tense, their adrenalin output high, constantly forced, so that if they had been hurt they would have had no reserves and might have collapsed. Roberts banged his elbow in rappelling down, after the summit. It was a very minor accident, yet it almost made him faint.

During the early part of the descent, one of the party, Ed Bernd, slipped loose from his rope and fell, probably because of a failure of equipment while rappelling. He probably fell 4000 feet; there was no hope of saving him, nor even of recovering his body. The loss of their friend cast a deep shadow over the expedition's ending.

Roberts does not think he would ever do a climb like that again. He is "more convinced of the inescapability of danger and more involved in other people." He is now married—his pretty, dark-haired wife, Sharon, is also earning a degree, her M.A., at the University of Denver, in creative writing (short stories in her case).

Roberts' next summer's expedition, to Mt. Igikpak in the Brooks Range, Alaska, will not be as "intense." However, he is a member of a tentative K-2 expedition to the Himalayas in 1969, everything hanging on whether Pakistan will allow climbers in. Roberts cannot imagine a summer without mountain climbing.

Meanwhile, he keeps in shape for climbing not by skiing, but by taking freshman physical education. This is "embarrassing," because the participants are the students he teaches in freshman English. They "take out all their hostilities" on him and love to be able to call him by his first name.

What next for him as a writer? At 25, he has this book, his first, about to be published, another book, a "more personal, introspective" book about an earlier mountain-climbing adventure with Don Jensen in Alaska, ready—it was his master's thesis in creative writing—and a third book surfacing in his imagination. The third, inspired by "Gulliver's Travels," will be a baroque satire on America.

He thinks of "Gulliver" as satire, not fiction. He told us he is more interested in nonfiction than novels. "Nonfiction has a certain kind of relevance that the novel doesn't. Journalism is more exciting than fiction writing." At Harvard he switched toward writing from his major, mathematics. "All the exciting courses I had were in the humanities and social sciences." A great influence on him was James Rieger, who then taught creative writing at Harvard and is now at the University of California at Berkeley.

The third book will have a four-part structure, as "Gulliver's Travels" does and as do symphonies and quartets. Roberts plays the cello and the piano. "The highest form of art is music and I wish I could somehow make art that approximates music," he said. "The kind of writing I would like to do is unfashionable. The best writing today tends to be amoral. I think it should be moral. The 18th century was the best time in literary history. I would like to write an 18th-century book."

Dalton Trumbo

DALTON TRUMBO, Dalton Trumbo, what ever happened to Dalton Trumbo?

He's alive and well and living in Los Angeles. He has just written and directed his own film. (He describes himself as "the oldest new director in Hollywood.") It's based on his 1939 novel, "Johnny Got His Gun," which will be reissued this year by Bantam in paper and Lyle Stuart in hard covers.

Dalton Trumbo, screenwriter, novelist, pamphleteer, was one of the original Hollywood Ten—the first victims of a blacklist that finally marked and in many cases ruined over 200 writers, actors, directors and producers. He is easily the best known of the ten; the most vocal, the most prolific, and probably the most successful.

The occasion for this revival of interest in Trumbo is the publication of his letters, by M. Evans, under the title "Additional Dialogue: Letters of Dalton Trumbo, 1942–1962."

Mr. Trumbo's collected correspondence—skillfully edited by Helen Manfull, who discovered them untouched at the University of Wisconsin Center for Theater Research—makes an extraordinary document. In 1947, he commanded $75,000 a picture. After his indictment for contempt of Congress (for refusing to testify before the House Un-American Activities Committee about possible Communist affiliation—that standard question which always began, "Are you now or have you ever been . . .") he got as little as $3000 per screenplay on the black market. When he could get more, it was usually under a pseudonym or under someone else's name, in which case he split with the name, keeping two-thirds for himself.

By Douglas N. Mount. From *Publishers Weekly* 198, no. 14 (October 5, 1970), pp. 21–23.

The letters make astonishing reading for one who, though aware of the blacklist and its evils, never really understood what it meant. This man was a politically active liberal who was terrifically successful even by today's inflated economic standards. (He notes that he and his wife "ran through $300,000 the first five years of our marriage.") He liked to live well, and still does. He has always sported a gold cigarette case, lighter and holder from Dunhill. These things make him feel good. He likes good food and liquor. He does things with great style and wit.

The letters are therefore understandably boring at times—petty, frivolous, and inordinately concerned with money, money, money. Trumbo was reduced from a truly flush member of the Hollywood Establishment at its apex—the forties—to imprisonment, penury, exile, humiliation, lying, cheating. Though he managed throughout—at least in his letters—to remain civilized and to keep his sense of humor, there is an edge of bitterness in him now that cannot be denied.

In his pre-blacklist days he authored such commercial successes as "Kitty Foyle," "A Guy Named Joe," and "Thirty Seconds over Tokyo." Under the blacklist, he "received" an Oscar for "The Brave One" (under the pseudonym "Robert Rich"; Trumbo never got the statuette, and his friend and fellow blacklistee, Michael Wilson, was denied a nomination the same year for "Friendly Persuasion").

Trumbo spent a year in federal prison, a horrible period of exile and financial madness in Mexico City, and then became so successful on the black market that he was actually in a position to act as broker for other blacklistees.

In 1960, Otto Preminger broke the blacklist (which by then was something of a monstrous joke) by announcing that he had hired Dalton Trumbo to write the screenplay for "Exodus" and that Mr. Trumbo would receive screen credit. Trumbo has since worked on "Spartacus," "Hawaii," "Lonely Are the Brave," and currently his own film.

He has mellowed over the years. When we talked to him over the telephone from Los Angeles he spoke very slowly, chose his words carefully, and sounded like John Huston. We talked about "Johnny Got His Gun," which is his consuming passion right now. Published at a time when, as he has put it, "pacifism was anathema to the American Left," the novel dealt with a basket case, a limbless, youthful war veteran who reminisces about his childhood in a series of flashbacks.

It is really a "family picture": Trumbo directed, his son-in-law Bruce Campbell produced, son Christopher was the assistant director, daughter Melissa did the still photography and wife Cleo—who is a professional photographer—developed the prints. He says he brought it in "for under a million" with private financing, has no distribution, but has had two offers from major studios based on a partial rough cut. It stars Donald Sutherland, Jason Robards, Jr., and two young unknowns—Timothy Bottoms and Cathy Fields—in the leads. It has received no advance publicity—by design. Trumbo says it will "make it on its merits or not at all."

Dalton Trumbo doesn't really know what to think about this collection of his letters. "People have always asked me to write about those times," he says. "But I lived those times so thoroughly and so intensely, and they led so inevitably to other times, that any book I might write about them would be boring." He says he is "embarrassed" by some of the letters. He also claims that he is "not bitter." "I guess I have the capacity to adjust to—not accept, you understand—what has happened."

But Dalton Trumbo, despite his extraordinary cool, comes through in letters and in conversation as a very bitter man who was abused almost beyond bearing. It is amazing that he survived at all, and his letters document the myopic political witch-hunting that continues to victimize many who stand up for their causes.

5

Current Social Concerns and Social Commentary

Daniel Berrigan

IT'S NOT USUAL for a Catholic priest to address anti-war rallies, conduct teach-ins in east Harlem, arrange beg-ins on New York's Fifth Avenue, join Alabama civil rights marches, write poetry that wins major prizes *and* be the subject of angry advertisements in the *New York Times*. But the Rev. Daniel Berrigan, S.J., as we learned in an interview with him last week, is not a usual Catholic priest.

Father Berrigan first burst into the public consciousness about a year ago when an ad appeared in the *Times*, carrying thousands of signatures, protesting that Father Berrigan had been "exiled" to Latin America because of his civil rights and anti-war activities. His next appearance in public prints was when he returned from his four-month exile with assurances from his superiors that he could continue his peace activities. After that, he was in the papers for picketing the Chancery in New York City to protest warlike statements made in Vietnam by Francis Cardinal Spellman.

Then there was a furor in Chicago, where Father Berrigan went to give a poetry reading in a church. In the discussion period which followed, he answered a question about Vietnam, and the church's priest threatened to throw him out; another priest in the audience invited Father Berrigan to come to *his* church. As the first priest cried "Stick to poetry! Stick to poetry!" the meeting packed up and moved down the street to the second priest's church.

Father Berrigan is likely to continue generating this kind of furor as, from his post as a roving editor of *Jesuit Missions*, he continues to address various groups on public questions. The day after the *PW* interview, he was off to address student groups in Berkeley and Los Angeles.

By Roger H. Smith. From *Publishers Weekly* 191, no. 9 (February 27, 1967), p. 43.

Father Berrigan finds nothing unusual in this pattern of agitated activity; rather, he regards it as a natural development in his life and his career in the clergy. "In my family, we were brought up in a tradition of social action," he said the other day. "My father was a socialist, a union organizer. We lived on a farm in upstate New York and we were poor, and we always kept a table for the poor. There's a tradition of priests in the family—currently, my brother Philip and myself—good priests, in the immigrant tradition.

"My father was a poet. He'd broadcast his poetry orally and in every other way possible. He'd yell Shakespeare until it seemed the house would fall down. I became a poet in high school. I published my first poem in *America* in 1942." His first book of poetry, "Time Without Number," published by Macmillan in 1957, was the Lamont Poetry Selection for that year.

Father Berrigan has done a lot of travel, most of it voluntary. In South Africa, tape recordings of talks that he made there circulate as part of the underground. In the early 1950s, he was involved with the worker-priest movement in France, which, until it was terminated by Pope Pius XII, sent small teams of priests to live with and help the poor.

He was back in France in 1963–64, when the hangover from France's Vietnam and Algerian wars was still a depressant. "The church's role in those wars had been mixed," Father Berrigan recalled, "but all the respected European Catholics were pacifists. When I got back home, it was obvious to me that we would have the same experience from the American Vietnam War, and I felt there was no sense in repeating it. . . .

"In the fall of 1964, my brother and I signed a declaration of civil disobedience, and there was hell to pay. Maybe I should have asked permission, but I didn't because it was a matter of my own conscience." What followed were anti-war rallies, organization of the interdenominational Clergy Concerned about Vietnam—and exile for four months.

"They said it was an assignment to get background material about Latin America for the magazine," Father Berrigan told *PW*. "Actually, what they were saying was: 'Get lost.' I'm not ungrateful. I had a good time in Latin America." Father Berrigan's new book, "Consequences: Truth and . . .," which Macmillan will publish on April 3, he described as "journal jottings" written during his exile. "I'd been so involved in teaching that I needed to put down what I think now." Sparked by the *Times* ad, the church ended Father Berrigan's exile, and since then he has been on the anti-warpath. (Out of the *Times* ad came the organization of the Institute for Freedom in the Church, which, Father Berrigan said, is composed of lay Catholics who protest "if someone gets kicked around.")

If Father Berrigan had an audience at the White House, what would he say to the president? "I'd try to convey to the president," Father Berrigan said, "something about the world reaction to his policies. I don't know his mind, but I'd hope he'd understand that we are hated for our policies, that we are delaying the course of real world revolution and that we are ruining our name in the world." What kind of reaction would such a statement get? "I don't have any hopes about the high levels of the U.S. government," Father Berrigan said. "The Establishment—forget it. I place my hopes with the young people."

Since he was clearly at odds with much of the church Establishment, would he be more effective if he left the clergy? "I'd never leave it," he said. "Oh, there are dioceses where I don't go to lecture because they would make it too tough for me at home. But there is a more liberal attitude in the church right now than there used to be, and the clergy are freer to move around as they want to. I stay in it because it's a way of celebrating life, and it's better to do that in a community than alone."

Murray Teigh Bloom

"THE TROUBLE WITH LAWYERS" by Murray Teigh Bloom is a book that bids fair to have some of the same impact on the legal profession that Jessica Mitford's "The American Way of Death" had on undertakers. A whole battery of Simon and Schuster lawyers carefully scanned each line of the book in advance of publication and gave their approval with one proviso—there could be no index. After Simon and Schuster sent out advance paperback copies (pub date is January 20) three threats of libel suits came in (never followed up), one telegram announcing "suit for defamation follows" (it never did) was received, and a prominent jurist who had first given the publishers a quote that the Bloom book was "superb and really needed," called back a half hour later to say that on reflection he would rather they didn't use it. On January 25 in Chicago a public relations adjunct of the American Bar Association is having a one-day seminar, part of which "will cover methods of dealing with adverse publicity and pitfalls to be avoided" in response to a portion of Mr. Bloom's book which appeared in the *Ladies' Home Journal*. (Reader response to the same article was a number of calls from people who wanted to use it in their own cases against lawyers.)

Mr. Bloom, a professional journalist of considerable experience, who wrote "The Man Who Stole Portugal" (*Scribners*) and has contributed to *Harper's* and the *Readers' Digest* among many other media, talked to *PW* the other day about "The Trouble with Lawyers." He got interested in the special problems the middle class faces in its dealings with the legal profession back in 1959 when a

By Barbara A. Bannon. From *Publishers Weekly* 195, no. 2 (January 13, 1969), pp. 43–44.

friend of his died and his widow and children were faced with enormous probate fees. Several magazine pieces on the law followed and then about three years ago Mr. Bloom began to plan a book that would incorporate a great many of his detailed findings about the way in which certain lawyers can, and sometimes do, take advantage of their clients. He discovered in his research that "almost everybody has a gripe against lawyers, if not for himself, on behalf of someone in his family."

"The middle class," Mr. Bloom claims, "has become the number one victim and target of the legal profession because it has money and property and lacks group power to protect itself." And "middle class" to most lawyers means anyone who has an income of $6000 a year or $500 in the bank.

For several years Mr. Bloom accumulated files of material on legal cases, traveled around the country and attended the last four conventions of the American Bar Association. Lawyers, "many of whom do not see themselves as doing any wrong," talked freely to him, he says (although it is doubtful if they do so in the future after the book comes out). One group of lawyers who were especially responsive to many of the points he was trying to make were those who teach in university law schools.

Although he has some hair-raising tales of legal chicanery to tell in "The Trouble with Lawyers," it is not Mr. Bloom's contention that most lawyers are crooks. Most of the trouble comes from plain incompetence, he believes, or from the evils of fee fixing on a contingency-percentage basis. He quotes "one of the top estate lawyers in the country" as answering the question, "What percentage of lawyers in this country would you trust to draw up good, simple wills?" with "Not 10 percent of them." And he makes the point that whereas in their dealings with businesses, lawyers' legal fees are generally fixed by the amount of time the lawyer spends, based on an hourly rate of pay, in meeting basic middle class legal needs "the percentage arrangement is often the only one the lawyer will accept." This means that even if the service the lawyer is performing calls for very little in the way of special legal knowledge or technique and requires him to spend very litle time on the matter he can charge on the basis of a percentage of the amount of money involved. "Yet, in most law offices," Mr. Bloom says, "the bulk of the probate work, for example, is done by secretaries. Most probate work is routine bookkeeping."

The best the average person in need of a lawyer can do, Mr. Bloom suggests, is to ask friends whose judgment he trusts if they can recommend one *they* trust. "Find out in advance what it is going to cost you," Mr. Bloom advises. "The great problem is that people are afraid to ask lawyers in advance about fees. They have a perfect right to do so. People who live in large cities can perhaps 'shop around' and might even find a lawyer who will handle their work on an hourly basis."

Specifically, Mr. Bloom suggests, these are some of the things that can help effect legal reforms: The press can do much more than it does now to publicize legal injustices; federal judges, who sit for life and are subject to very little if any political pressure, could do more than they are doing now to set a top example; fees should be taken out of the partnership level and based on how much time and legal skill is expended; the state should examine at regular intervals the relationship between the people and the courts to see what the situation really is; bar associations in general could do much more than they are doing now to police their own membership. (The Association of the Bar of New York does an outstanding job in this respect, as Mr. Bloom documents in his book.) "Basically," Mr. Bloom told *PW*, "it is time for a reexamination of the whole client–lawyer relationship. We've settled for tossing meaningless insults back and forth. All this has done is help cover up something that is basically wrong in itself. What's wrong has to be brought out into the open."

Malcolm Boyd

"PRAYER IS ACTION. It's your attitudes. Asking God for miracles is not really dealing with God at all." That is the way Father Malcolm Boyd talks, in coffee houses, on college campuses, even in night clubs, and his message is getting across to a lot of people who will have nothing to do with organized religion as such. The Episcopal priest whose "Are You Running with Me, Jesus?" is now in an 11th printing for Holt, making a total of 110,000 copies, has just had the paperback edition published by Avon Books. On March 20 his new book of meditations, "Free to Live, Free to Die" will be published by Holt, and the advance is already 26,000 copies. The second week in March he'll record a second album of readings for Columbia, these from the new book.

In person Father Boyd comes across in an interview as cool, candid, very much with it. Brought up as an Episcopalian, he turned away from the church in his college days, went on to a successful Hollywood career in public relations, advertising, television. It was not until 1951 that he began to see something more to religion than the smug piety he had come to despise. That year he decided to enroll in divinity school.

Father Boyd told *PW* that he had for years been jotting down just for himself the kind of "prayers," mature reflections on any and all aspects of life, that make up "Are You Running with Me, Jesus?" He started putting them on paper while he was on Cyprus during the height of the conflict there among religious and ethnic groups. The first inkling he had of the kind of reception his book might have came in

By Barbara A. Bannon. From *Publishers Weekly* 191, no. 9 (February 27, 1967), pp. 42–43.

October, 1966, when he received galley proofs of the Holt edition while making one of his campus tours. He had never read any prayers to his audiences before but he started, choosing at random from the galleys, and found that before he could even get back to where he was staying his phone was ringing with requests from students for copies. "My whole motivation with that book," he says, "was to keep it out of the religious shelves in bookstores, and get it in with the straight nonfiction where people who ordinarily never look at a religious book could see it."

From his first parish, in Indianapolis slums, Father Boyd went directly into work with students on college campuses. He wasn't always popular with the higher-ups. (Colorado State College asked him, politely but firmly, to leave.) Wayne State was more receptive, and it was there through the writings of plays, in some of which he also acted, that Father Boyd became involved with the newly emerging coffee house ministry.

Peter Yarrow of "Peter, Paul and Mary" folk song fame, wrote some background music for Father Boyd, the noted jazz guitarist, Charlie Byrd, asked to appear with him, and Father Boyd started his night club career in Washington, D.C. Although he regularly travels throughout the country, Father Boyd is now under the jurisdiction of the Episcopal Bishop of Washington.

"I have no pat answers," Father Boyd says of his coffee house and night club appearances. "I usually start by asking my audience, 'what's on your mind?' " What happens next may run the gamut from a basic discussion of the nature of faith ("everyone has faith in *something*, even if it has nothing to do with religion. I try to show people that you can have a faith and not be dishonest in it") to a discussion of "the pill," sex, including homosexuality, Vietnam. The people with whom Father Boyd comes in contact in these situations are, he says, essentially people "who have no metaphysical belief in life. I acknowledge to them that we must all grope for the answers in life. I am speaking to them perhaps not so much verbally as by just being there in my symbolic stance as a priest . . . what binds us together is respect for each other's honesty." When it comes to questions on Vietnam Father Boyd says, "I'm no pacifist, but I'm fed up with people blessing people going off to kill each other."

On the college campuses the questions Father Boyd most frequently encounters, especially from coeds, have to do with whether or not they should have sexual relations with their boy friends. He gives no pat answers here, either, but he does have one direct and jazzy answer to pass along to the girl who really doesn't want to "make out" on a date. It is: "I like you very much, but you just don't turn me on."

Father Boyd has been active in the civil rights movement for years, going on marches, living and working with Negroes in the deep South. When *PW* asked him about the Roman collar he always wears, even in his night club appearances, he told us he wore it deliberately as a visible sign of what he is, "like a Negro's negritude. It's a uniform," he said, "a deliberate symbol of tension and paradox. In effect I'm saying, 'if I can't make it this way, forget it, and if that collar is a hang-up for you, then maybe we should go through the hang-up together.' " A Roman collar, he has found, intimidates a lot of people into not wanting to sit next to him on a plane, just as some people will still try to avoid sitting next to a Negro. "Dick Gregory and I," he says of the Negro comedian-civil rights worker, "once figured out that between us we could change the whole seating pattern of a plane."

Robert F. Capon

FATHER ROBERT F. Capon, whose new book is "The Supper of the Lamb" (*Doubleday*), is an Episcopal priest, a husband and father of six, a gourmet cook, a skilled amateur musician—and a happy man. This last is by no means least. In an age in which clerics of all persuasions, to say nothing of laymen, are often tormented by doubts, Father Capon impresses one as a man as completely at home with the world he believes God created as he is with his own role as a priest. It is this happy balance between an appreciation of the good things of this world—particularly good food and wine, and good talk—and their underlying spiritual relevance that makes "The Supper of the Lamb" such an unusual book.

One Sunday recently a *PW* editor visited the Capons in their home in Port Jefferson, Long Island, to find out first hand how good a cook Father Capon is. The answer is— he's marvelous, although cooking, like almost everything else in the Capon household is very much a cooperative venture. "She was converted to cooking by me," Father Capon says of his wife, Peggy, and like all good converts she is an enthusiast. In cooking as in just about everything else the Capons complement each other very well and most menus end up a joint venture. One of the Capon sons served our dinner deftly, only occasionally summoned by a piercing whistle from his father.

Father Capon and his family have lived for 20 years in an old manse in Port Jefferson near Long Island Sound. At current count, it has 18 rooms, is full of comfortable old furniture, children, animals (two cats and one old dog) and a

By Barbara A. Bannon. From *Publishers Weekly* 195, no. 6 (February 10, 1969), p. 30.

collection of musical instruments on which Father Capon and several of his children regularly harmonize. His specialty is the recorder and on one memorable occasion the Capon Renaissance and Baroque Consort (including one priest–musician friend) played Carnegie Hall when the regularly scheduled concert was cancelled suddenly.

In a household with six children the kitchen is apt to be a focal point even if the father is not a gourmet. The Capons solved the stove problem for a family of this size by importing a six-burner restaurant stove complete with grill and two ovens.

The menu served for *PW*'s benefit was indeed something special and had been in preparation for several days. It started off with terrine of goose (part of a leftover from the New Year's feast) consommé with liver dumplings, chicken and sweetbreads boned and filleted, homemade noodles, spinach served in a delicate sauce that contained mayonnaise and Parmesan cheese, zabaglioni for dessert, with appropriate wines along the way, and coffee. Father Capon makes his own beef and chicken stock and the latter had been prepared while a photographer–interviewer team from *Life* looked on, recording Capon in the kitchen for possible magazine use.

There can't be many priests who can cook like Father Capon, but his background is an unusual one. Born and raised in Queens, where he lived in the same house in Jackson Heights off Roosevelt Avenue until he married and was assigned to a Port Jefferson church, Robert Farrar Capon comes from a family in which his grandfather was a butler and his grandmother "a good Swedish cook." As a youth, he told *PW*, he worked for a time as an office boy in the American Bureau of Shipping. "Very early in high school I half thought of the priesthood and half of becoming a naval architect," he says, but there doesn't seem to have been much doubt which would win out.

Although some Long Islanders may be a little startled to hear it, Port Jefferson ranks as a mission area in the Episcopal Church and Father Capon serves his parish there at the special directive of the bishop. He is also chaplain to the Stony Brook, L.I., Fire Department, teaches theology and Greek at the George Mercer, Jr. Memorial School of Theology in Port Jefferson, and does a special job of working with a group of candidates for the Episcopal priesthood who have a late vocation (men over 30 who work at a regular job while studying for the priesthood Saturdays and nights).

Much as he may enjoy cooking as an avocation, "my real work is a whole series of things," Father Capon says, "prayers, writing, the Mass, parish calling. I say Mass every day of the week." His two books before "The Supper of the Lamb" were "Bed and Board" (*Simon and Schuster*) and "An Offering of Uncles" (*Sheed and Ward*). Next, he hopes to write about the doctrine of creation, a subject he's still thinking through and is exploring in a series of lectures this spring at General Theological Seminary in New York.

As the particular kind of a priest he is ("every priesthood is different") Father Capon is well aware that he has the best of several worlds—writing, teaching, counseling, the celebration of the liturgy. "I've had 20 years of the vocation of the priesthood," he told *PW*. "You have to be a workman in everything you do. I knock myself out at things, but I am at ease in what I am doing. I'm a priest because I *have* to be. That is my life and the way I'm called." And everything else aside, it is as a priest that Robert Farrar Capon really finds his answers.

Pierre Chevigny

"POLICE POWER: Police Abuses in New York City" by Pierre Chevigny (*Pantheon*) is a study sponsored by the New York Civil Liberties Union, where Mr. Chevigny, the son of the late Hector Chevigny, is a staff attorney. The new book is a detailed analysis of specific instances in which police power in New York City was abused during a two-year period, 1966 and 1967, in the view of the NYCLU. This does not mean, however, that Mr. Chevigny is violently anti-all police or that he sees the men in blue as secret inborn sadists. One of the strongest points he makes in the new book is that the police respond to a given situation as they think society wants them to respond. Their ambivalences and contradictions reflect our own.

Talking to *PW* the other day, Mr. Chivigny proved to be a sensible, no-nonsense type, who is realist enough to believe that "society's attitude won't change much in the near future," and that the civilian review board which many well-intentioned people have sought "isn't the answer" to problems of police abuse.

If real reform is to come within the New York City or any other police department, Mr. Chevigny sees "no alternative" to it coming in at the middle level of police authority, with the full support of the top brass. The problem is that the police tend to abide by an unwritten law that says every policeman supports every other policeman, even if it means lying.

"The same thing doesn't happen in the army," Mr. Chevigny points out. "You don't find army sergeants covering up for privates."

By Barbara A. Bannon. From *Publishers Weekly* 195, no. 5 (February 3, 1969), pp. 25–26.

What Pierre Chevigny would like to see in the New York City Police Department is "lateral recruiting," such as you have in federal or state civil service, whereby people specially trained could enter the department at various levels and bring their expertise to bear on specific problems. "But in the police, you just don't take men in from outside." They are all supposed to come up from the ranks.

The kind of training Mr. Chevigny wants to see the police give their own men would stress their not "getting automatically into a threatening attitude" with the public, including minority groups.

"It is possible to train cops to contribute to community understanding," he believes and he cited to *PW*, as an example of the kind of training the department should give to more of its men, the work being done by one special squad on the upper West Side of Manhattan, ordinary cops, who have been taught to go out and break up family quarrels before they can mushroom into violence.

If you think you see a police abuse of power taking place, Mr. Chevigny advised, "report it and stay with the case. People who try to personally intervene can get arrested," (as brought out in some cases in his book). One of the strongest weapons the police have against the average citizen in such a case is an arrest for disorderly conduct. "The built-in escape hatch" for the police in such an arrest is that most people would rather plead guilty and pay a $10 fine, than fight and run the risk of going to jail.

Many people are convinced they have the right to resist an unlawful arrest and, indeed, according to the common law since 1666, they have had a right to do so. Since March of this year, however, the situation has been quite different in New York, Pierre Chevigny told *PW*. A rider in the "shoot-to-kill bill," Mr. Chevigny reports, has made it unlawful to resist even what you honestly believe to be an unlawful arrest. Mr. Chevigny would like to have the public made more aware of this important change in the law, which he believes is a denial of the due process of law and ought to be challenged in court.

As for police claims that recent Supreme Court decisions have made their operations against criminals more difficult, Mr. Chevigny had a pithy answer. "The process of search has been hampered mostly," he said, "because the police do not understand that they really have much more freedom to search than they think they have. They believe their own damn propaganda."

Vine Deloria, Jr.

VINE DELORIA, JR., wants to be the red man's Ralph Nader. He is big, young (35), articulate and very militant. When we met him he was wearing spectacles, a white shirt and tie, a plain business suit, very long hair and heavy, decorated western boots. He'd like nothing better than to kick the white man right off the reservation.

To that end, he is studying law in Denver, Colorado, where he lives with his wife and two children. Recently he has been promoting his first book, "Custer Died for Your Sins" (*Macmillan*), a scathing indictment of whites and their treatment of Indians.

Talking to Vine Deloria is like talking to an older, calmer version of a black separatist or a student militant. Two of his favorite targets are the "Indian-grandmother complex" among whites and the hordes of white anthropologists and ethnologists who every summer descend upon Indian reservations with fat research grants. ("If we had all the money they've spent since 1948, we'd be sitting pretty.")

"The problem now is that they [whites] have always had the right to exclude us, and they suddenly can't take the idea that we might want to exclude them," he says. "The situation among militant tribes in Minneapolis, the Northwest coast and California had been one step away from violence for years."

Vine Deloria, Jr. is a Standing Rock Sioux, the son of an Episcopal minister and educator. He went to prep school in the East, joined the Marines ("a bunch of guitar-picking hillbillies"), and went on to seminary after studies at Iowa State University. Today, he is no longer a practicing minister, and he says of the church on the reservation: "They gotta go."

By Douglas N. Mount. From *Publishers Weekly* 196, no. 22 (December 1, 1969), pp. 7–9.

"To keep your tribes together," he continues, "you must establish a new religious base. Besides, they [the white church] have a lot of our land, which the government gave them so they could civilize us. We have revisionary title on that land, and we're going to get it back." There is, he says, a discernible return to Indian religion, centering on the Native American Church, which now has court protection for its controversial use of mescaline and peyote.

Mr. Deloria sees tribalism as the key to the whole Indian struggle, but says that it may also be the Indians' greatest liability. "You have to understand that it is a way of life, a way of thinking," he told us. "It is essentially a great tradition which is timeless, which has nothing to do with the sequence of events. This creates a wonderful relaxing atmosphere, a tremendous sense of invulnerability."

He added, however, that it also encourages the conviction that the white man will eventually go away just as everything else has through the centuries. "Tribalism also leaves the Indian tied to the chief concept," he added. "The day of the Battle of the Little Big Horn, Crazy Horse went through the camp and said, 'I am going to war today; all of you who think you are worthy, come with me.' That kind of leadership will work today."

The early civil rights movement made no sense to Indians at all, says Mr. Deloria. "We couldn't understand why they [blacks] would ever *want* to assimilate or integrate with whites. Now they seem to be coming around to our point of view." He is an admirer of the Black Panthers, and of Carl Foreman and Roy Innis, whose minority economic programs he would like to adapt to the red struggle. "You know, tribalism creates as many Quislings as it does de Gaulles," he continued, blaming white proponents of "Ethnic Studies" for encouraging the worst aspects of tribalism. "They love to write about the 'plight' of the Indian," he said frowning. "We are always 'between two worlds,' which is why we sit around the campfire and drink too much."

Mr. Deloria hopes that one day tribalism will work for the Indian: that the government can—through the courts—be forced to withdraw entirely from most reservations, settling an annual lump sum on each tribe to be administered internally. He is opposed to violence of any kind. But he expects there will be a good deal of violence in some areas before the struggle is finished.

Mr. Deloria is already at work on a second book, on "the idea of tribalism." When he finishes his legal studies, he plans to work with small tribes, helping them to clarify their positions with the government. He also plans to continue writing and speaking, trying to encourage greater militancy among more of his brothers. ("Besides the civil rights problems, you've got a helluva lot of lazy Indians," he says.) He had high praise for Buffy St. Marie, and for N. Scott Momaday, a Kiowa whose first novel, "House Made of Dawn" (*Harper*), has just won a Pulitzer Prize. He also admires Carlos Castaneda's "The Teachings of Don Juan" (*U. of Calif./Ballantine*) and Stan Steiner's "The New Indians" (*Harper*).

Walter Gellhorn

THE WORD "OMBUDSMAN" picked up a lot of currency after New York City's voters decided, last November, against a civilian board to review the actions of the police department, and it was in search of enlightenment that we had lunch, a few weeks after that election, with America's leading authority on the "ombudsman" concept, Walter Gellhorn, who is Betts Professor of Law at Columbia University.

The day of our luncheon was also the day on which Harvard University Press published two books by Mr. Gellhorn, "Ombudsmen and Others," which examines how the "ombudsman" system or variations of it operate in nine countries; and "When Americans Complain," the Oliver Wendell Holmes Lectures which Mr. Gellhorn delivered at the Harvard University Law School in March of last year.

What had bothered us most about the word "ombudsman" was its etymology. Mr. Gellhorn assured us that confusion on this point is not unusual; the word's roots go back to Old Norse, and there aren't too many experts on Old Norse around these days. Besides, he continued, the "ombudsman" concept is a rather new one for Americans. "Really," he said, "it was only eight or nine years ago that I became aware of it."

The "ombudsman" system is currently operative in the four Scandinavian countries and New Zealand, and four other countries—Japan, Poland, the U.S.S.R. and Yugoslavia—have somewhat comparable systems. Mr. Gellhorn visited all nine of these countries in preparation for writing "Ombudsmen and Others."

By Roger H. Smith. From *Publishers Weekly* 191, no. 2 (January 9, 1967), p. 25.

Who—and what—is an "ombudsman"? Mr. Gellhorn said that typically he is a lawyer or a law professor or a retired judge—or a combination of all three—who is appointed by the executive or legislative part of the government to listen to citizens' complaints about the way in which governmental agencies function or fail to function.

"He's the fellow," Mr. Gellhorn said, "who gets governmental agencies to explain their shortcomings. If he is efficient, he may make the agencies so sick of explaining their shortcomings that they may actually do something about correcting them. He looks at a situation after the events have taken place, which gives him a great advantage. Moral suasion is his only power, but it can be a lot."

Would the "ombudsman" concept be practical for the United States? Mr. Gellhorn said he thought it would work at the city or county or even the state level, but that an "ombudsman" for the entire country probably would face a task of insurmountable magnitude. "But I see no reason why it wouldn't work at a lower level," he said. "Rhode Island, California, Massachusetts and St. Louis, for example, are going ahead with plans for 'ombudsman' systems." And, he added, a *Time-Life* reporter told him that a few days after the defeat of New York City's civilian review board proposal, Mayor John V. Lindsay was observed carrying two books about "ombudsmen," both of them written, of course, by Mr. Gellhorn.

Euell Gibbons

ABOUT AN hour-and-a-half's drive from Harrisburg, in the rolling Pennsylvania countryside, is the home of Euell and Freda Gibbons. As the author of "Stalking the Wild Asparagus," "Stalking the Blue-Eyed Scallop," "Stalking the Healthful Herbs" and the forthcoming "Euell Gibbons' Beachcomber's Handbook" (all *McKay*), Mr. Gibbons is one of this country's top experts on "living off the land."

A *PW* interviewer paid a visit to the Gibbons, not long ago, to sample for herself "a wild food party" and to talk to Mr. Gibbons about his interest in the natural health foods that grow wild, and which he has managed to tame into some very tasty recipes.

The menu consisted of: wild frost grape juice; a cocktail of poached bluegill fillets; chilled wild cherry soup; braised venison in coconut-wild mushroom sauce; as vegetables, steamed cattail hearts, buttered milkweek buds, cattail bloom spikes à la trivet, day lily buds in soya sauce; a salad made up of wild watercress, sheep sorrel, sour grass, purslane, live-forever, with wild garlic dressing; a dark bread made out of persimmons, hickory nuts, black walnuts, home-made maple sugar; a choice of wild strawberry, wild blueberry, wild red raspberry and wild elderberry jams; sassafras tea; a chiffon pie of wild dewberries; candied fresh wild mint leaves. The only non-"wild" ingredients were the seasonings of salt, pepper, butter, a little oil in the salad dressing, and the crust for the dewberry pie.

We can report unequivocally that not only was it one of the most lavish feasts we've been exposed to in some time, it was also one of the most delicious. The cattail bloom

By Barbara A. Bannon. From *Publishers Weekly* 192, no. 11 (September 11, 1967), pp. 25–27.

357

spikes turned out to taste rather like artichokes. The buttered milkweed buds, which look like broccoli florets, tasted a little like asparagus, and the day lily buds rather resembled braised endive. All the wild ingredients had come from the Gibbons' property or nearby countryside, with the exception of the venison, bagged by a neighbor in the hunting season and stowed away in a freezer. Even the bluegill trout Mr. Gibbons caught in his own pond. Before buying the property, which goes under the pleasant Pennsylvania Dutch name of "It Wonders Me," Euell Gibbons took a good, long look "at the foraging possibilities." They are still holding up well and the only "gardening change" over nature the Gibbons have effected consists of moving a few handfuls of wild watercress from one location to another.

There is nothing faddish or cranky about Euell Gibbons' interest in wild foods. He has no illusion that they and they alone are the right foods from the standpoint of health. Most of the time the Gibbons eat much like the rest of us, although they have learned some real gourmet touches in their use of wild foods. Euell Gibbons also knows the value of wild foods as a way of survival and has taught it to boys and girls at the rugged Outward Bound schools in Maine and Minnesota, where children are trained in the techniques of survival. After training by Mr. Gibbons, they go alone on three-day living-off-the-land trips, with a minimum of equipment, including a knife, a small tarpaulin, only four matches.

"I cannot remember a time when I wasn't interested in wild foods," Mr. Gibbons says. "My mother and grandmother were good at wild foods." His grandmother's people were Union adherents in Tennessee during the Civil War, and during some of the darkest days of the war it was a question of eating from the wild or not eating at all. The same experience befell Euell and his immediate family when he was a boy of 12. The Gibbons were living in a remote part of New Mexico after a series of disasters that left Euell the man of the house. To survive, they were dependent on what he could forage, trap or shoot.

Over the years Mr. Gibbons has traveled through almost every part of this country. (His Hawaiian years are the subject of the new book, out October 2, "Euell Gibbons' Beachcomber's Handbook.") Wherever possible, he has made it a point to learn what the Indians or earliest known inhabitants of each area lived on and to track down the types of wild food still there.

After a lifetime of this, he now describes his interest in wild foods as "a way of having a creative encounter with nature. I don't want to be a 'nature tourist,' " he told PW. "Eating wild foods is a passport to getting involved with nature in the same way other creatures do. It gives you a better understanding of what ecology really is, and of the inter-relationships of various life forms with each other." All life forms depend on one another in some way, and, as Mr. Gibbons sees it, nature, properly understood, "is full of mercies and kindnesses and cooperation. In order to exist we must cooperate with many species. Man is a part of nature."

Judging by the success of the Euell Gibbons' books and by the letters he receives, there are a great many people in this country who are beginning to share his interest in wild foods. The letters, he reports, come from all walks of life, the poor and uneducated and the more sophisticated. The one thing his writers have in common is simply a love of the land. Perhaps surprisingly, however, there is no central organization of wild food fanciers in this country, although Mr. Gibbons is hoping to establish a branch of the international society of wild food lovers that does exist. That group has its headquarters in Argentina.

It was while Euell and Freda Gibbons, who are both Quakers, were living at the Quaker center, Pendle Hill, that his writing career began seriously. He had been contributing poetry and other material to various Friends' publications when the agent, Mavis McIntosh, saw some of his work. "I had a novel with a terrible amount of wild food in it," he recalls. "She showed it to Eleanor Rawson at McKay, who sent back word, 'Take the novel out. Leave the wild food in.' " Mr. Gibbons did just that, and "Stalking the Wild Asparagus" came into being.

Germaine Greer

GERMAINE GREER, Australian-born author of "The Female Eunuch" (*McGraw-Hill*), is a professor–actress–journalist and women's liberationist who likes men. "It isn't the men who are castrating us," she told *PW* recently. "it's the whole society today." Miss Greer has a Ph.D. for research on Shakespeare, teaches literature at Warwick University in England, acts on television and in films and contributes editorials to *Suck*, a European sex magazine.

In her book she talks candidly, often relying on four-letter sexual terms, about the differences between the sexes, woman's role and the relationship of men and women to each other. Published April 19, "The Female Eunuch" has received very enthusiastic reviews. McGraw-Hill has given it a big push—a large advertising budget and a 50,000-copy first printing.

Most women, Germaine Greer told *PW*, are "eunuchs," castrated creatures who have been deprived during their education in "femininity" of their true individuality and sexuality. This education, Miss Greer said, works by a system of rewards. "If you come up to your uncle and look at him from under your eyelashes, he'll say how cute you are and give you a Mars Bar or something." Girls trained like this, she says, grow up and marry and become housewives because they were taught to do so. If they are unhappy in their marriages they think it is their own fault, that they have done something wrong.

Miss Greer says, "I wrote the book for these women. They read it and it works like a shock of recognition. I also wrote the book for the girl who wants to get married so bad-

By Lila P. Freilicher. From *Publishers Weekly* 199, no. 19 (May 10, 1971), pp. 13–14.

ly that she can't get it all together. She overcompensates in her work and is generally unhappy.''

Being extremely clever in school and beating the boys, she said, helped her escape this castration process, herself. "And then, of course," she added, "I was so inconsiderate as to grow to be six feet tall. In Australia people think it's terrible if you go out with a guy who is smaller than you. I met a 5′ 2″ musician who decided I was what he wanted. He was proud of me and proud that he came up to my elbows. I began to realize that the 'normal' feminine role wasn't for me. If I had worn ribbons and lace, the entire populace might have had a fit of the giggles. So I learned to stand straight and pull my shoulders back.''

PW asked Germaine Greer how she went from teaching literature to writing a book about women's liberation. "I'm not through teaching," she explained. "I'm away temporarily to promote the book and to write two other books about women, but I'll go back to teaching because it is the most stimulating thing I have. My students keep me in touch with real problems because they are coping with growing up and sorting out their roles in life. I've learned more while teaching than ever before in my life, including things like humility and gentleness and patience.''

It was when Germaine Greer's English TV series was ending that her agent, Diana Crawford, suggested she write a book about the failure of women's emancipation. Said Miss Greer, "I told her 'What do you mean the failure of women's emancipation? There has never been any bloody emancipation.' I went away angry, but later I told a friend about the incident and he asked me why I couldn't write a book about the fact that there has been no emancipation. And that's how I came to write 'The Female Eunuch.' ''

It didn't faze McGraw-Hill or MacGibbon & Kee, her English publisher, that she has frequently used four-letter words in "The Female Eunuch." Miss Greer told us, however, that MacGibbon & Kee decided they would have to censor the book for the Australian public. "You know I have a large excerpt from 'Last Exit to Brooklyn' in my book, and 'Last Exit' is banned in Australia. But I told MacGibbon that they simply would not be able to anticipate what the Australians would find indecent. I said they could cut the book to smithereens and Australians would still find something which would be offensive to them.''

Germaine Greer believes that women must adopt what she calls "a conscious revolutionary attitude" if they are to achieve their potential. "This does not mean," she explained, "flinging Molotov cocktails at the Chase Manhattan Bank. But by all means do raid a men's club and protest to grant Medicaid to women seeking abortions. You probably won't be admitted to the club or change Rockefeller's mind but it's all part of the process of harassment.''

Things will improve gradually for American women, Germaine Greer thinks, if women's lib groups adopt the "vertical structure" (breaking up after 10 meetings into pairs which form new groups). "The women's revolution when it comes," she said, "will happen in households all over this country as the quality of life changes. The women's revolution will be the first great mass movement in America."

Gilbert Highet

GILBERT HIGHET could best be described by a word from his native Scotland: "dominie," which strictly speaking means schoolmaster, but with the extra sense of a lord of learning. For Highet, in his more than 40 years as a teacher at Oxford and Columbia universities, has thought long and hard about university teaching. Twenty-five years ago his thinking produced a minor best seller in "The Art of Teaching," and his further reflections will appear at the end of this month in "The Immortal Profession," published by Weybright and Talley (a division of David McKay).

The book is a collection of essays on various aspects of teaching and learning, on the continuity (and importance) of culture, on the very prevalent illusion of perpetual human progress, on the perspectives of history and on such revered teachers as Albert Schweitzer and Jesus Christ.

It grew out of a meeting between Highet and his publisher, Truman Talley, at a party in East Hampton some summers ago, at a time when Highet was retiring from Columbia and thinking of recording some of his reflections on his time there. The two withdrew to a back room where they had what Talley describes as "the most fascinating conversation in my 28 years in publishing." Highet himself recalls that he was in a philosophical frame of mine at the time. "I was thinking 'What good has it all been?' " he says. "The events of the 1960s in the academic world made you think over your whole life very carefully. I wondered whether teaching wasn't after all a rather useless profession, like, say, astrology. In the end I decided it wasn't and that I'd write about what it had meant to me, and what it *could* mean to teachers and students alike."

Highet reads constantly, both for his own pleasure and in

By John F. Baker. From *Publishers Weekly* 209, no. 15 (April 12, 1976), pp. 6–7.

his capacity as a long-time judge for the Book-of-the-Month Club, and at any moment in conversation with him, something he has recently read will pop up as an illustration to his discourse. He has just been reading a big forthcoming Putnam study of Edward Teller and recalls someone saying of Teller that he was an excellent teacher for someone who knew nothing about the subject, or everything about it, but not so good for anyone in between. "I like to think I was good with the in-betweens," Highet smiles—and adds that the best times he had at Columbia were in his last 20 years there, with the graduate students rather than the undergraduates. "Older professors can have a difficult time with arrogant young undergraduates. I gave up teaching them myself when I was 50 [he is 70 now] because I had begun to find that when a good undergraduate asked an interesting question I was taking the rest of the afternoon to answer it, and that wouldn't do."

Even teaching one graduate seminar a year, however, as he had been doing until his recent retirement, "kept me jumping," Highet notes ruefully. He has always practiced what he preaches in his new book—the necessity of keeping up with all developments in one's field; and in his case this would involve making a précis of important new books (even seeking them out on interlibrary loan where necessary), pursuing current research efforts through scholarly seminars and papers in journals, talking constantly to colleagues about new theories and developments. Highet's specialty, of course, has always been Greek and Roman literature and history, and more recently he has come to be more deeply interested in "the continuity of world history," a fascination he first discovered when he read Oswald Spengler. "The whole spread of world history is one of the hardest things for a classicist to learn," he says. "But it's a wonderful feeling when you make the connections—and when you're able to pass them along to your students. I remember how in the early days of the atomic bomb the students were worried about it, and that civilization could come to an end, and I was able to tell them about the Dark Ages and how people had to learn all over again how to read and write books and teach."

His own favorite piece in his new book, he says, is based on a talk he gave at West Point, in which he outlined first the problems and tribulations of that year (1964) and then gave his audience thumbnail sketches of all the triumphs and tragedies of the same year in other centuries—1564, 1764 and so on. He is proud of his abilities as a public speaker—"When you have an audience like that at West Point, thoroughly homogenized, all sitting there at attention dressed in identical uniforms, you have to break them up, make them give you their individual attention. They're used to having generals stand stiffly behind a lectern and lecture them, so I'd walk all around the stage, talking to different parts of the audience, looking them right in the eye. I think one of my most successful talks was on modern oratory, in which I'd imitate the various styles of contemporary public speakers. I called it 'How to Start Wars and Influence People.' "

He has in fact been doing research for a history of Greek and Roman oratory, though after recent illness, followed by an operation, he feels now that "I've run out of gas for another large book. The effort of putting it all together would be just too much." He retains his passionate interest in odd byways of cultural history, however, and talks with enthusiasm of his recent discovery of the work of Dio Chrysostom, Greek intellectual of the first century AD ("rather an Aldous Huxley type") who worked as a tutor for a wealthy Roman nobleman until his patron was killed, who then wandered the Roman Empire as a slave laborer until the Emperor Domitian was assassinated, and who then came back into favor and was appointed a sort of cultural ambassador to the Greek colonial cities. Chrysostom made many speeches that were models of classical oratory, many of which have been preserved.

At this point Highet's publisher chimes in eagerly, "Would you do a novel about him, Gilbert?" "No, no," Highet demurs. "I'm married to a fictioneer, and more than one in the household would be impossible." His fictioneer wife is, of course, his fellow countrywoman Helen MacInnes, and by the happiest of coincidences her own latest thriller, "Agent in Place," is coming out from Harcourt Brace Jovanovich on the same day as Highet's own book.

His wife's is not the only fiction Highet reads, however. He has been a judge for the Book-of-the-Month Club for 20 years, keeps his ear to the ground on promising new books of any kind ("I asked to see 'Jaws' when I first heard about it, very early on, and we were all very keen on it," he notes). But despite his continuing interest in novels, Highet complains that "in the past 10 years we older judges have become more and more afflicted with nausea at some of the stuff we have read. There are books that seem intended to make you throw up—I don't know if this is worse than having your mouth stuffed with lavender-flavored cachous, as used to be the case."

Highet, as a man who loves debate (throughout the conversation with Talley and *PW* he would nod with obvious approval and mutter "good, good," whenever he felt a particularly effective point had been made), can see both sides even to this question. "Despite their shocking nature, some of the novels published today cover whole new areas of human experience. And although the effect is often nauseating, I'm glad they're being written. When I was growing up in Scotland in the 1920s the sort of popular novels being written were like Jello set in concrete—ghastly books, utterly remote from any sort of life."

He sees this above all as a period of "vivid, energetic nonfiction" and adds: "I think TV has helped here—people think much more about current issues than they used to, about social trends, about politicians, and they have far more awareness of history.''

But he is not as enthusiastic about current publishing standards. ''We older BOMC judges all notice the deterioration of editorial quality in recent years. The constant misuse of foreign words in particular is very bad. I've never been able to read a book without a pencil in my hand, and sometimes, after reading galley proofs, I've sent five pages of corrections back to the publisher. Half the time they were simply ignored.''

He sighs. ''Helen's now persuaded me to stop doing it. Since I've been ill I'm supposed to just read the books and not do anything about their mistakes.'' It is obviously hard to renounce a lifetime of enthusiastic pedagogy.

J. Anthony Lukas

"TODAY'S YOUNG people are as richly variegated, as stubbornly idiosyncratic, as their elders, and can only be understood in highly personal terms," J. Anthony Lukas says in the conclusion of "Don't Shoot, We Are Your Children," to be published April 12 by Random House.

When *PW* interviewed Mr. Lukas recently, he told us he had originally contemplated doing a spectrum of the youth movement as it existed in the fall of 1967, when he started the book. But it soon became evident to him that the movement was changing month by month, making it difficult to arrive at any genuine spectrum.

Mr. Lukas says his book was founded on the belief that "one will not know the general unless one knows the particular." The danger he tried to avoid was unfounded generalizations, falling into the trap of dealing with a whole generation as if it were one phenomenon. What he produced instead were 10 profiles of alienated or radicalized youths.

Mr. Lukas won a Pulitzer Prize for his 1967 story, "The Two Worlds of Linda Fitzpatrick." It was from this story of Linda, who was found brutally murdered in a Greenwich Village basement with Jim "Groovy" Hutchinson, that Mr. Lukas began his book. The other portraits came from personal contacts—interviews with approximately 150 people. From those he selected eight other young people whose personal stories interested him. Of these, only Jerry Rubin, one of the Chicago Seven, has reached national prominence.

In retrospect, Mr. Lukas thinks it might have been better to select some other yippy less well known. "Nobody can come to the Jerry Rubin chapter without having his mind

By Pamela Bragg. From *Publishers Weekly* 199, no. 10 (March 8, 1971), pp. 27–28.

already made up about Jerry," he said. "I wanted the reader to come to all of these people with something of an open mind and I think that is impossible with Jerry."

The 10 stories form the core of the book, with only an introduction and conclusion containing brief summations by the author. Mr. Lukas thinks there may be criticism of this. However, he feels there is entirely too much judgment on both sides about American youth: "We have been so bombarded with people's subjective reactions to American youth—they hate them or they love them; they feel they are going to destroy the American heritage or they are the salvation to come," he told *PW*.

It is his hope that his book presents facts about those we are talking about when we use the term, "disaffected youth." Most important, he felt, was the need to get to know 10 individuals well, and to present them as vividly as possible.

Mr. Lukas was born in New York City of Hungarian–German background. Members of his family were active in the theater, but, after expressing an interest in it during his teen years, he turned to government and journalism at Harvard University. There he became an editor and associate managing editor for the *Crimson*, covering the McCarthy period for the magazine. A fellowship at the Free University of Berlin followed, combined with travel to East Germany, Yugoslavia and Czechoslovakia. Returning to this country in 1956, Mr. Lukas was drafted into the army and served most of his time with a psychological warfare unit in Tokyo, writing 15-minute radio news commentaries for converting the Chinese and Koreans to the "democratic way of life."

After working for four years for the *Baltimore Sun*, Mr. Lukas was hired by the *New York Times* as a foreign correspondent in the Congo and West Africa and then India.

Returning to the United States in 1967 for a year, Mr. Lukas was given the Linda Fitzpatrick story to do and found "there were things happening in this country which were infinitely more interesting and compelling than abroad."

Following a Nieman Fellowship at Harvard, Mr. Lukas went to Chicago as roving national correspondent for the *Times*, a job that allowed him to rove anywhere and everywhere around the country doing stories largely of his own choosing. While there he quickly decided the conspiracy trial was *the* story he wanted to cover, and after some bitter battles with the *Times* over whether he should cover the trial, and how it was to be covered, Mr. Lukas left the staff of the daily paper. He recently returned to New York as a staff writer for the *Times Sunday Magazine*. In between he managed to write "The Barnyard Epithet and Other Obscenities: Notes on the Chicago Conspiracy Trial."

Without trying to put forth any grand pattern of history, or falling prey to the easy generalization which he abhors, Mr. Lukas gave *PW* some conclusions he had reached about the youth movement after writing

"Don't Shoot, We Are Your Children." He quoted a statement by Erik Erikson, professor of human development at Harvard, that seems to him to clarify some of the young lives he encountered: " 'The generation gap is just another way of saying that the younger generation makes overt what is covert in the older generation; the child expresses openly what the parent represses.' "

We tend to treat these young people's lives and views as though they bear no relation to the past, but they must be viewed in the context of their parents' lives and the community in which they grew up.

Following through Professor Erikson's logic, Mr. Lukas thinks that parents inevitably get caught up in their own hypocrisies, in saying one thing but doing something else. "But I'm just as convinced that this is going to happen to this generation, too. I can see it already," he says. "This generation, which has so scathingly exposed the hypocrisies of the older generation, is already beginning to live its own hypocrisies, and, in turn, will inflict those hypocrisies upon their children."

Mr. Lukas told *PW* that while writing the book he went through two cycles of change within himself. During the first year of writing it, his contacts with thoughtful young people caused him to confront his own assumptions about the world. To write about this country and its people, he felt the need to be continually alive—to have some convictions, some certain ways of viewing the world. But, he added, "one must remain flexible enough so that one can absorb the new insights and new perspectives which come along—not rigidify and not seize up in some sort of outmoded view of the world."

Then came a reverse cycle, he found, a cycle of disillusionment. He had the feeling that some of the people he was writing about were partially fraudulent and that the freshness inside the movement, the idealism, the openness of the New Left when it began had turned inward, grown sour, bitter and desperate. Jerry Rubin, was, Mr. Lukas felt, the focus of that feeling. He became very distrustful of Jerry's motivation.

As for the present, Mr. Lukas said, there is no simple answer. "I haven't merely shifted from an old position to a new position. I guess, if anything, the book has left me very skeptical about any ideological position." He is particularly skeptical about colleagues and editors, on his own and other major publications, who seem never to have questioned or seriously examined their own beliefs and assumptions. But, he stated, "I'm equally skeptical of ideologists on the left who are not examining their assumptions either—who have, without realizing it, grown rigid in their own assumptions about reality."

Maybe the best answer for all lies in the conclusion of "Don't Shoot, We Are Your Children," where Mr. Lukas states: "Perhaps we should spend more time asking ourselves whether the unspoken values and assumptions we all carry around with us still adequately reflect the kind of world we live in."

Malachi Martin

MALACHI MARTIN has assisted in his time at 11 exorcisms, once had to take over when the officiating priest collapsed, but "I'd be terrified to actually conduct one myself—I'm afraid the direct clash with evil might destroy an essential element in me: what I can only call my sensuality." He goes on to explain that he does not mean sexuality, but his rich awareness of life, a sense of love and joy that have come to him late in a life that has been mostly lived close to the center of religious power and politics.

Dr. Martin is in fact an extraordinary bundle of contradictions: a former Jesuit, a scholar deeply versed in biblical languages and lore and in Middle Eastern archaeology, a priest who once stood high in the councils of the Vatican and was an intimate of Pope John—who 10 years ago gave up his Vatican post ("an honorable discharge," he calls it wryly) and came to this country penniless and spiritually bewildered. He washed dishes and waited tables in Schrafft's, drove a cab in the Bronx, New York, finally began writing what turned out to be a series of increasingly well-received studies of contemporary religious consciousness. Now he has published, through Reader's Digest Press, a serious and at the same time sensational study of exorcism, "Hostage to the Devil."

In it Dr. Martin examines the nature of exorcism, the hideous struggle the exorcising priest has to undergo in order to free a possessed human being from the powers of evil (literally offering himself as a hostage for the victim, with only his faith and moral courage to sustain him), and the insidious ways in which the powers of darkness have

By John F. Baker. From *Publishers Weekly* 209, no. 7 (February 16, 1976), pp. 14, 16.

learned to work on some of the most cherished tenets of modern philosophy. At the heart of the book are long, frequently harrowing and sometimes terrifying accounts of possession, and of the exorcisms that drove out the demons of five Americans living today.

At the time William Peter Blatty's "The Exorcist" came out, to be followed by the highly successful movie, Dr. Martin wanted to do his book, to try to show the real spiritual dimensions of the struggle, but his editor, Lila Karpf, persuaded him to wait, that any serious book about exorcism at that time would be buried by Blatty's fiction. It certainly seems likely to have more impact now that the sensation has receded somewhat—yet "Hostage to the Devil" yields nothing to Blatty in terms of power, terror, or even sex and scatology.

Dr. Martin himself took part in his first exorcism 10 years ago, soon after he arrived in this country; an assistant had collapsed during the proceedings, and a friend called him in to substitute. (Although the exorcist himself is invariably a practicing priest, the assistants may all be lay persons, the only necessary qualifications being physical strength, in order to hold down the exorcee at climactic moments, a strong stomach and a degree of determination.) Since then he has witnessed 17 such occasions, mostly in the New York area, has another coming up next month, an interruption to a planned tour for his book. Once, as noted, he had to take over and complete the rite, "but at a point where the real confrontation was over." On other occasions he has tried to take over—"Once I was struck by the exorcist to keep me back"—but at present would be afraid to conduct the rite himself. "Perhaps when I'm older, and have a greater light. . . ."

The genesis of the book lay in the remark one day of a man who had just been exorcised, and who told Dr. Martin: "Someone should come out and talk about this, about what it means." Dr. Martin set to work to ferret out some notable cases of American exorcisms—not the ones he had been involved in himself. "Some I knew about, others I sought out." Eventually he had 11 case histories, including such startling ones as a former presidential candidate, a would-be astronaut, a parish priest, even an Irish–American bishop, who underwent the only deathbed exorcism he has ever heard of.

He realized, however, that 11 such histories, with the detail he wanted to give them, would have made the book far too long, and he eventually settled on the five it now contains. These were carefully chosen, Dr. Martin says, because for him they represent the ways in which the forces of evil have been able to work through currently fashionable ways of thinking to enlist the victims to their cause. There is Marianne, who believes that there are no values other than those of personal preference; Father Jonathan, a hip young priest to whom religion was simply a matter of rationality, and identification with nature; Richard/Rita, a transsexual who became the victim of a confusion between gender and sexuality; Jamsie, a radio announcer led into unbridled individualism by a "familiar" who sat behind him as he drove his car; and Carl, a brilliant archaeologist who believed that in his psychic experiments he had triumphed over human limitations.

In each case Dr. Martin had long talks with the subjects and with their exorcists, tracing the development of possession sometimes from childhood, and the ways in which the priest was formed for his fearful task. One of the standard items at a modern exorcism is a tape recorder, and in each case the tapes of the actual exorcism were made available to the author, so that the dialogue of priest and possessed—confused, manic, frequently obscene but always horrifying in its implications—is as authentic as only transcription can make it.

The identities of both exorcist and exorcee have, of course, been carefully disguised in each case, and even the backgrounds have been changed where it was felt they might give them away. All the subjects read the manuscript before publication, Dr. Martin says, and confirmed his accounts as accurate—and sufficiently anonymous.

Dr. Martin in person is for the most part disconcertingly incongruous with his somber subject. A mercurial figure, with lively, darting eyes and slightly breathless speech full of beautiful Irish modulations, it is difficult to imagine him as part of the Vatican hierarchy—and, in fact, he sees his life having essentially broken in two the year he left and came to the U.S. "I've never had such joy as I feel now, the sweet experience of being human. America gave me a home, and I owe it a great deal."

Dr. Martin was born in Ireland in 1921 ("Daddy claimed he got my name, Malachi, by opening the Bible at random, but I think he cheated—it's a traditional Irish name too") into a family that was "half Protestant, half Catholic, with a strain of Jewish, and always fighting." Educated by the Jesuits ("A Jesuit education is not brainwashing—they don't work on your brain at all at first, just your will; it's will-forming"), he continued formal education at Trinity College, Dublin and the National University, studying philosophy and languages, then to Louvain, Belgium, for theological training. He specialized in the Dead Sea Scrolls and testamentary studies, finally received his doctorate in Semitic languages, archaeology and Oriental history. He was appointed to the Vatican in 1958, and quickly became part of the circle of advisers close to Pope John, whom he recalls with the warmest affection. His frequent archaeological trips throughout the Middle East also gave him a role as a sort of roving Vatican intelligence agent in the biblical lands, and what with the reports he had to write and his work on helping to shape papal pronouncements on various theological issues, "I found I had no time for my studies, or for lecturing, anymore."

He also found life at the Vatican changing him in ways he did not welcome. Once he recalls having to dismiss someone from the papal staff, and the man asking him: "Have you no compassion?" "I realized that no, I hadn't. When I told John about it, he told me I should leave—that power was corrupting me. The pope said [here Dr. Martin lapses into Italian], 'When I die, you must leave, or you might become a cardinal!' He feared for me, because *he* had compassion."

He found himself, says Dr. Martin, "full of hate and anger—I thought you could experience *holy* hate and anger—but there was no love."

Meanwhile he had begun to write, under a pseudonym ("I'd do it during the siesta"), and in 1962 he met Rabbi Abraham Heschel, who is a friend of publisher Roger Straus, Jr. Through this connection he published a pseudonymous book, "The Pilgrim," with Farrar, Straus in 1964 and began to think of leaving the Vatican. "I wanted a new life, but I didn't know what it would be—my family thought I was mad." Straus sponsored him as an immigrant and, having acquired his discharge papers, he arrived in this country early in 1965.

Straus wanted him to write a book about the inner workings of the Vatican, but at that time he felt he couldn't do it. "I had to go off on my own." With no money, and no prospects, he went to work in Schrafft's, then as a cab driver. A chance meeting led to a Guggenheim grant, on which he wrote "The Encounter," a critique of modern religions, which Straus published in 1970 to enthusiastic reviews. Two years later came "Three Popes and a Cardinal," an examination of the workings of the Vatican Council. Meanwhile Dr. Martin had met Lila Karpf, then subsidiary rights director at FS&G, and when she went to Dutton he went along. "She helped me write the truth—it's difficult to get back to it when for so long you have been instructed *not* to tell it." Two more books followed at Dutton, "Jesus Now" (1973) and "The New Castle" (1974), and when Ms. Karpf was appointed to Reader's Digest Press, this time as senior editor, the long-simmering exorcism book was ready to proceed.

The writing in "Hostage to the Devil" is dramatic and highly colored, a kind of writing Dr. Martin has never tried before. "Ten years ago I coundn't have written about love or nature, run the risk of exposing myself this way." And he feels that he has not emerged entirely unscathed from writing about the repeated humiliation and expulsion of Satan and his demons. He found while he was working on the book that he became highly irritable, his emotions were disordered, he conceived an odd and entirely uncharacteristic hatred for children and women. Dr. Martin speaks with passionate conviction, and it is difficult not to believe him when he adds quietly: "I'm afraid that while I was doing that book something got at me in my essential nature. There was a *presence*, I don't know. . . . You could certainly say there is an interested party that doesn't like me."

Lee Metcalf and Vic Reinemer

"WE JUST HAD to write this book," Sen. Lee Metcalf (D., Montana) and Vic Reinemer, the senator's executive secretary, told *PW*'s interviewer, over a hearty, western-style breakfast in New York's Biltmore Hotel. The two men were in New York for a series of personal radio and TV interviews in connection with their new book, "Overcharge" (*David McKay*).

"People are being overcharged and they don't know it. They think the investor-owned utilities—what we call the IOU's—are tightly regulated by the government, but they aren't. Overcharges are common, and cost the consumer thousands of dollars they shouldn't be paying if the IOU's were regulated as Congress intended them to be. There hasn't been a definitive book in the field of utilities' regulation since the thirties."

According to the authors, the book is an outgrowth, in part, of the senator's successful campaign for re-election last year. Since the senator had been a foe of Montana utilities both on and off the Senate floor, he expected a bitter fight. He decided to have Mr. Reinemer gather ammunition on public utilities from the files of the Federal Power Commission. Mr. Reinemer, who has written articles for national magazines, and was formerly the associate editor of the Charlotte (N.C.) *News*, spent so much time going through the FPC files FPC people thought he worked there. He soon realized, he says, that the problem of utility regulation went far beyond one state. The book, which criticizes the entire privately owned utility industry, is one result of the investigation.

By Sylvia Auerbach. From *Publishers Weekly* 191, no. 7 (February 13, 1967), p. 41.

Mr. Reinemer added that a stockholder wrote in and said he had 10,000 shares of Montana Power and was indignant at how much the company was taking from him unfairly. Another Montana legislator called the senator's office, said he had read the book, and had wanted to appropriate money to buy copies for the commissioners responsible for regulating power in the state—since the book points out how state commissioners are hampered by lack of funds and staff. The legislator was astonished when the commissioner replied, "Don't give us the money. We're doing all right. Don't rock the boat."

One chapter of the book, The Schools—Guess Who Teacher Is," points up the acute shortage of texts and supplementary material for the teaching of economics in elementary and high schools, and the lack of trained teachers. It's a gap, said the senator, which is being filled by tax-exempt, so-called educational groups sponsored by the utility industry, which give the schools extremely distorted right-wing material. These same groups pressure school trustees, and maintain very close ties with school administrators.

In the senator's opinion the industry's campaign has been so clever that anyone can be misled. "My own son," he said, "went to some annual event sponsored by the Montana Power Company for business administration majors—and came home and said maybe I was too harsh on them. Even *he* had been brainwashed!"

As part of the "educating process" he hopes the book will accomplish, the senator has sent out a questionnaire to state regulatory agencies, asking them the size of their staffs, how many industries they have jurisdiction over, and what kind of specialized training the staff has, since their work is highly technical. (The book cites many states which have not had rate investigations for scores of years, are very understaffed, and must supervise hundreds, sometimes even thousands, of carriers, building operations, utility companies, etc.) The questionnaire is now being tabulated and should provide additional material for possible Senate hearings, and for informing the public on the problem.

"As I point out in the book," said Senator Metcalf, "we have the technology, through computers, of economically comparing rates and keeping informed on the state of the industry throughout the United States. We can push buttons now and get the answers to problems of uniformity and regulation. We hope the book will educate the public to find out what can be done to stop cheating them of the savings they should have from the technological advances of the industry."

Senator Metcalf also hopes to schedule hearings, through the government operations committee of the Senate finance committee, on the many problems the book raises. "Not punitive hearings," said the senator, "but informative, since there is so little knowledge about the industry, not only among the public, but also among business executives, government officials, etc. We have a statement in the book from the Investment Bankers Association that even institutional investors can't follow and compare utilities' accounting practices.''

The book examines the rate structure, regulatory practices and accounting methods of the industry and analyzes the discrepancies in consumers' bills because of different power situations prevailing in different sections of the country. It also describes the public information campaign the industry runs, which the authors state is heavily biased in favor of right-wing groups such as the John Birch Society. Their charges, all of them extensively documented, include excessive consumer rates; intimidation of the press; inaccurate and deceptive allocation of costs to the benefit of utility company officers and stockholders, and the detriment of consumers; pressure on school trustees and administrators; and completely inadequate government regulation. We asked the authors what kind of reaction they had gotten from the industry.

"They are trying to keep it quiet," Senator Metcalf replied. "They are advising their members not to buy the book and not to contribute to our royalties. But we are getting interesting reactions. In Georgia one legislator got copies for all the members of the legislature and said he was buying some for libraries in the state.''

Merle Miller

LAST JANUARY, the writer, Merle Miller, in an extraordinarily honest and moving article in the *New York Times Magazine*, described "What It Means to Be a Homosexual." Without indulging in sensationalism or special pleading but making it clear that he was writing directly from his own experience, he bridged the gap between the "straights" and the "gays" in a way that few recent writers on the subject have done. He also put himself on the line as a well-known writer who was not afraid to publicly acknowledge his homosexuality.

Now Random House is publishing this month Merle Miller's "On Being Different: What It Means to Be a Homosexual," the *Times* piece, plus an afterword in which Mr. Miller describes how the article came to be written, what the effect has been on his own life, and some of the reactions he has had from readers of the *Times* article. All told, he received about 2500 letters, a number of them from men in the armed forces in Vietnam, the overwhelming majority of them sympathetic.

"One of the interesting things about the homosexual minority," Mr. Miller told *PW* recently, "is that it is really the only minority group that has a choice of 'coming out.' If you're black, you're black. You can't evade that. Of course, now, a lot of the homosexual kids have never been 'in' in the sense of trying to hide what they are. After the *Times* article I discovered that people over 30 thought it was great. The kids thought it was a real middle-aged sob story. Yet, when I went to a meeting of the Gay Activists' Alliance I received a standing ovation. There must have been 350 people there, most of them guys, only a sprinkling of them my age.

By Barbara A. Bannon. From *Publishers Weekly* 200, no. 14 (October 4, 1971), pp. 17–18.

"Homosexuals all have had problems of what to tell about themselves and whether to tell their parents (most of whom probably know anyway). Even some of the leaders of the Gay Liberation movement do not appear publicly under their own names, but use a pseudonym.

"No, I don't see any great rush of people lining up to declare themselves as homosexuals. Who is to say they should do so? I think, however, it is rather important. For one thing, you cannot demand your rights, civil or otherwise, if you are unwilling to say what you are. People in the small towns are just as hung up and lonely about their feelings as they were when I was growing up in Iowa. Last July some 5000 people marched in New York in the Gay Lib movement, just about as many as the year before. The interesting and depressing thing about that is that there were at least about three times as many people standing on the sidewalk, watching, and wanting to march, and not being able to do so.

"It isn't so much a question of permissiveness. It is the openness of being able to acknowledge what you are that is very healthy. I think that if we have learned anything from the lesson of the Pentagon Papers it is that candor in all walks of life is a good thing."

Ideally, *PW* asked, what kind of attitude toward homosexuality would Mr. Miller like to see?" "There ought to be an area in which hetero- and homosexuals can coexist quite happily," he says. "I'd like to see a world in which the description of people's sex lives would come after the description of the color of their eyes. 'He's 5 feet, 9 ½ inches, has gray eyes—and is a homosexual.' The important questions are: Is he kind, intelligent, sympathetic, good at his job? I don't think, however, that any drastic change in attitude towards homosexuality in America will come in our lifetime."

Merle Miller has two books coming up in the next year or so. One, "Marshalltown, Iowa," to be published by Holt, Rinehart & Winston, he thinks "will be a very surprising book, a heartening one." Marshalltown is his home town, in which he grew up, lonely and none too happy. "I do not think it is now the way I remembered it," he says of Marshalltown. "Sweeping generalizations don't apply to the Middle West any more. The people are not so insular. They are more sophisticated.

"I haven't been to Marshalltown since last January and the *Times* article, but before that I spent four months there, interviewing people for a cross-section of what their lives are like today. I hope my book will be on the order of 'Akenfield' (*Pantheon*). The one area about which we never talked was homosexuality. Now I plan to go back and do so. I think some Marshalltown people's attitudes toward me will now be different, but I am not sure.

"One of the more heartening letters I received after the *Times* article came from a woman who had been in my high school class. She was great. She wrote that she had raised five children and hoped people were more broad-minded today than in our Marshalltown days. The people who are able to talk about homosexuality are not the ones you have to worry about. It's the ones who do not say anything—until after you are gone—who have their own problems."

Merle Miller's next novel, "What Happened," will be published by Harper & Row in 1972. It is, he says, "about three people who went to school together and then made the long journey we all make into later life. I guess what it says is that it's rough for everybody. One of the characters is a homosexual, but he does not get it from life any more than anyone else in the novel. He only gets it differently. Life has its go at all three of these people. To survive is all. I used to think that some people were lucky, golden, the anointed of the gods. The only thing I have learned in life, as I have grown older, is that there isn't anybody who doesn't get it one time or another, and it hurts internally, really unbearably. I like to think intelligent people make intelligent decisions, but in the emotional area, we're still in the finger-painting stage."

Jessica Mitford

RELAXING in a captain's chair at the country home of some Long Island friends, Jessica Mitford, author of a formidable book on the American funerary business, "The American Way of Death" (*Simon and Schuster*, 1963), and now of a formidable book on the American prison business, "Kind and Usual Punishment" (*Knopf*), gives an initial impression of gentle amiability. The impression is not dispelled as she warms to the *PW* interviewer's questions, but her eyes, which are of striking shape and an almost alarming blue, begin to hint of steely qualities within—along with a mordant and highly developed sense of humor.

Moral commitment, biting wit, spectacular tenacity and no doubt a touch of cunning—these are at least some of the qualities that Miss Mitford, sweeping aside whatever pious, legalistic or other obstructions may be laid in her path, brings to her chosen task of exposing fraud, injustice and sometimes cruelty in high (or at least highly organized) places.

"I wasn't remotely interested in prisons till I began to read about the Soledad Brothers and the California prisons. The prisoners got me hooked on the subject." Now, she confides, her social crowd consists mainly of ex-convicts. This can give rise to embarrassment, as when, in company, she asked a man what he did before he went to prison and got the reply: "I was a professional thief."

Being hooked—and being Jessica Mitford—she swiftly set about turning thoughts and feelings into action. She wrote an article for the *Atlantic Monthly* attacking California's much-touted indeterminate sentence and asked the ed-

By Peter Gardner. From *Publishers Weekly* 204, no. 14 (October 1, 1973), pp. 32–33.

itor to distribute copies of it to as many prisoners as possible. The result was a flood of letters from convicts, often astonishing for both content and style. This marked the beginning of a correspondence which, maintained over several years with some 100 convicts and conducted through the intermediary services of her lawyer-husband (California's Penal Code grants prisoners the right to correspond with lawyers and public persons), helped her greatly in writing "Kind and Usual Punishment."

Prison authorities, on the other hand, tend to be far less forthcoming than inmates on what goes on inside prison. "Some of those in the corrections racket are very mixed-up people," she says with the air of someone making an understatement,"—also very political." She is in a good position to know, having met so many of them in the past few years. "Yet there are decent people in the field," she adds with Mitford fairness, and begins to talk about the Director of Corrections in California, whom she describes as a "torn soul."

Miss Mitford displays the same ready gift for the trenchant phrase in conversation as in print. "The only healthy thing that goes on in prison," she declares firmly, "is rebellion." Then she adds its logical corollary: "The people who should be on trial are the prison administrators." Anyone who has followed her through the pages of "Kind and Usual Punishment"—where the indeterminate sentence, the inmate welfare fund, the work furlough system and the parole board system are roundly and efficiently damned, the helplessness of the prisoner (legal and physical) is poignantly underlined, and the horrors of prison life in both its day-to-day and its more Orwellian aspects are glaringly exposed—is likely to agree with both statements.

She also seems to have a good memory for statistics. "Out of every 100 crimes committed in this country," she says, "only 1 ½ percent are punished." This touches on a central point in her book, which is that the prison population reflects not justice but the structure and prejudices of society. It's the "lower-class" crimes that tend to get punished, those chiefly committed by poorer blacks and Puerto Ricans and the underprivileged generally, while "upper-class" crimes—embezzlement, food adulteration, fraudulent advertising and the like—tend to go unpunished. The ironic implication is that crime tends to be where you want it to be (if *you* happen to be a member of the social establishment, that is).

Recently, Miss Mitford relates with a chuckle, two black teenagers were apprehended for stealing her car. But since she estimated that she would suffer far less through the loss of the car than the teenagers would in going to prison for stealing it, she refused to prefer charges against them. The dutiful officer who had caught the delinquents was most upset. Advancing another statistic, Miss Mitford says that 88% of murders are committed within the family; she does not, therefore, see that fearful picture, so often painted by police officials, politicians and other ready statistical reckoners, of murderers roaming at large within our society seeking whomsoever they may devour.

"Kind and Usual Punishment," however, may leave the reader with some nagging questions. Granting the author has given a most convincing demonstration of the evils of prison, what alternative to it does she propose? In the first place, she says, her book was primarily aimed at exposing the injustice, cruelty and ineffectiveness of prison; counter-schemes lie beyond its scope. However, she continues, her thoughts go in the direction of community control at all levels, resident neighborhood police (positions adopted, incidentally, by the Black Panther party) and the total abolition of the prison system as it now exists.

What were the reactions to some of her earlier writings, especially "The American Way of Death" and her 1969 article in the *Atlantic Monthly* attacking the Famous Writers' School? Reactions to the first, she says, were strongly mixed. It would seem, however, that the mixture was of simple composition: those in the mortuary business were con (in fact they were outraged), their clients were pro. *"All* the letters I got (from the latter) said that the way I described the involved and expensive procedure of getting buried was exactly the way it happened." She attributes the great and quite unexpected success of the book (it was on the best seller list for months) to the fact that it was taken up by the media. Reporters were assigned to ferreting out the secrets of the mortuary scene in different parts of the country; a CBS special, based on the book, was viewed by 40-million people and had the undertakers "squirming."

The thought of squirming undertakers seems to fill Miss Mitford with amusement. "I screamed with pleasure," she says, when she read in the mortuary magazine *Casket and Sunnyside* things like "the Mitford storms are howling through the Midwest." The magazine, however, was not content with the rhetoric of rebuttal; it hired a Madison Avenue PR agency to do what she called a hatchet job on her character. The agency leapt on her autobiography, which had been subpoenaed by the House Un-American Activities Committee, and when she appeared on a TV program it used the press to "heap garbage" on both herself and the interviewer. Congressman James B. Utt of Santa Ana, California, read some pages of the book into the Congressional record, but Miss Mitford ("I don't like loyalty oaths") refused to reply to his charges. The *New York Times*, in an editorial titled "How Not to Read a Book," blasted Utt and in its obituary of him, which had to be written shortly thereafter, gave him the unkindest cut of all by saying that he would be best remembered for his attack on "The American Way of Death." All such publicity, says Miss Mitford, was grist to the mill for her book. (It looks as though her present book is not wanting for grist either.)

As for the reactions to her article on the Famous Writers' School, subsequently reprinted in the *Washington Post* and the *Des Moines Register*, she received a "barrage" of letters from dissatisfied students who had signed on the dotted line without realizing that the total charges for their course amounted to something like $900. What should they do now, they asked her? "Don't pay a cent, and say I advised you not to." The Famous Writers' School has since gone bankrupt.

Jessica Mitford is clearly an investigator to be feared in her special realm of moral knight errantry—by those who have something to fear.

Her own education may have been "nil," as she charmingly puts it, but Miss Mitford, who is already a member of the San Quentin Six Committee, is about to become a Distinguished Professor of Sociology at San José, her lecture course to be titled "The American Way." She keenly looks forward to taking up her professional duties, and her students-to-be are no doubt agog to learn of further oddities and ironies lying concealed within this once-proud "way."

One final question: Did she *enjoy* writing her book on prisons? "Alas," says Miss Mitford, "funerals were far jollier."

Vance Packard

VANCE PACKARD's five books published to date (all by McKay in this country) have sold a combined total of 590,000 copies in hard covers in various editions, exclusive of book clubs. None, however, has required so much research as the new "The Sexual Wilderness," and it is entirely possible that the new book, on which Mr. Packard spent four years instead of his accustomed two per title, may outsell any of the others. McKay has set a 75,000-copy first printing and an initial ad budget of $25,000 for the new book. *McCall's* is running two excerpts from "The Sexual Wilderness," and Longman's, Mr. Packard's British publisher, has paid five times as much as it ever did before for the rights to a Packard book for "The Sexual Wilderness."

The man behind all this, the author of such earlier best sellers as "The Hidden Persuaders," "The Status Seekers," "The Waste Makers," is a pleasantly low-key as they come. If Mr. Packard has a "hard sell" cell in his body, it certainly doesn't come through in an interview. Talking to *PW* recently about the research he did for "The Sexual Wilderness" and some of the findings he uncovered, he was objective, candid, very much the reporter, not the polemicist.

"The Sexual Wilderness" began as an attempt to find out what the generation of kids born after World War II was thinking and doing, but it expanded as Mr. Packard realized that you could not talk about these young people without talking as well about what was happening to an older generation. The word "sexual" in the title of his book definitely does not refer solely to the physical aspects of sex, but to

By Barbara A. Bannon. From *Publishers Weekly* 194, no. 6 (August 5, 1968), pp. 13–15.

courtship and marriage and life adjustment seen in the context of the total male–female relationship. "Sexual is the only word that describes it all," Mr. Packard says.

"I had assumed a lot of information on the subject would be readily available," he told *PW*. "Instead, I discovered how much argument and confusion there was among the experts themselves. I did not plan to do an extensive survey of my own, but after doing research on the book for two years I found it was necessary."

Accordingly, Mr. Packard devised a questionnaire of his own, all on male–female relationships, which went to some 21 different colleges and universities in the United States and to students in England, Germany, Canada, Norway, and Italy. This is the first research for any of his books he has done outside the United States. He also visited 10 foreign countries.

Anonymity of response to the college survey was assured, and the questions asked ranged all the way from "Do you support the idea that individuals and society function best if male and female roles in life remain essentially different though equal?" to "If coitus was achieved, circle age of first experience" (the possible answers ranging from 14 or under to 24 or more). There was room for amplifying comments and these as received, ran to about 110,000 words.

The overall rate of return to the college sampling was 67%. Mr. Packard found a definite correlation between the return rate and the intelligence of the students, based on the admission standards of the colleges. The best returns (more than 75% response) came from schools with the highest academic standard, the poorest from schools with the lowest standing. Patterns of response in the United States and Canada were quite similar. Analyzing the European returns, Mr. Packard was impressed by the "extreme sexual liberality of the English mods." The Italian response was small, conservative, but interesting, and came only from women students. Italian males, Mr. Packard discovered, were outraged at the mere idea of being asked any questions about their sexual life.

A University of Connecticut team has made arrangements with Mr. Packard to present the results of his college-age survey in more formal sociological terms.

The research for "The Sexual Wilderness" involved a great deal more than the college level survey. Mr. Packard estimates that he read a stack of material "35 feet high" (much of it books bought from the New Canaan Bookshop in Connecticut), and personally talked to and interviewed hundreds of people. Unlike any of his other books, this one in its entirety was first "talked into a dictating machine in terms of the research material compiled," then condensed into text form and transcribed as the basis for a first draft. Vance Packard's 23-year-old son and 20-year-old daughter helped with the research, with Mrs. Packard pointing the way to relevant articles in women's magazines.

Mr. Packard told us he was "quite impressed by the liberality of viewpoint expressed by professional marriage counselors and ministers" he met. Young people, he found, are bewildered by sex. They want some kind of standards to go by, but don't know what those standards should be. "The whole damn complex of what is going on in our society today is that so many kids want independence without responsibility."

Women, Mr. Packard reports, do not have so much of a sense of failure as men if they are not strong in sexuality. "They can fake it as men cannot." Many young women today are not as career-minded as they might be. Only 50% of those replying to the Packard questionnaire at college level said they could imagine themselves being willing to pursue a career for 20 years. In answering the questionnaire, women turned out to be much more articulate than men, more matter-of-fact in their approach. A great many of the women interviewed for "The Sexual Wilderness" reported that one of the sexual problems they encountered was that men were so shy.

Asked about his own reactions after four years of research, Mr. Packard admitted his personal views on sex had undergone quite a liberalization process. This does not mean, however, that he or "The Sexual Wilderness" come out in favor of sexual promiscuity. In a final summary in the book, he comments, ". . . the case of sexual freedom as it is commonly understood—where every male and every female is free to behave sexually as he or she sees fit, as long as no one is hurt—seems to be a dubious goal. This, of course, does not necessarily mean that in our new kind of world we should strive to reinforce the traditional norm under which the bride and groom have been expected to confront each other as virgins."

What Mr. Packard proposes instead makes up the final three chapters of his book. It is, indeed, reasonably "liberalized" in its approach towards premarital sex under certain specific conditions. Perhaps the part most apt to arouse comment, however, concerns Mr. Packard's view that the first two years of marriage be regarded by society as "a confirmation period." At the end of that time, the marriage papers would become final and the couple would receive a "certificate of confirmation" if they wanted to go on together. If, however, one or both parties want a dissolution of the marriage, it could be achieved by a formal request two months before the confirmation period was up. No dissolution, without specific proof of extraordinary hardship, would be permitted before the two-year married period had been completed. Mr. Packard is convinced if such a "confirmation period" existed, the marital breakup ratio, which is now at about 50%, would go down to 10%.

C. P. Snow

C. P. SNOW's profoundly disturbing new book, "The State of Siege" (*Scribners*), the John Findley Green Foundation Lectures he delivered at Westminster College last November, is a grim delineation of the "food-population collision" facing the world. It would be good to be able to say that in the months since he spoke out so vehemently on a subject that has brought him "nearer to despair . . . than ever in my life," Lord Snow has seen some cause to change his mind. Such is not the case.

"I still see a bleak outlook. There has been no sign of improvement, I am sorry to say," he told *PW* in a recent interview. If the rising population flood continues and there is no revolutionary break-through in new sources of food supply, no massive cooperation to meet the situation between the U.S.A. and the U.S.S.R., Lord Snow foresees many more local famines by 1975–80 and major world disaster by 1990. Farming the sea and new methods of growing grain hold out some promise, but not nearly enough as yet. "It is partly because the idea of famine is so abstract to people like ourselves that we do nothing," Lord Snow observed. "Our capacity for bearing other people's misfortunes is almost infinite."

One of the few encouraging signs he sees in the world today is the willingness of young people from the more prosperous countries to go out to work in the underdeveloped countries. His own sixteen-and-a-half-year-old son is working in a hospital in Africa between school and university. "I would not be very happy to be my son's age now," Lord Snow says of the world that lies ahead.

By Barbara A. Bannon. From *Publishers Weekly* 195, no. 15 (April 14, 1969), pp. 25–27.

"The John F. Kennedy assassination was a kind of watershed," Lord Snow told *PW*. "Since then all the signs point the wrong way." In the Victorian era, "when people were quite callous about the poor, believing the poor were a separate race, poor because they were wicked, the stakes were not quite so high," Lord Snow said. There was not so much potential power loose in the world as there is today, with all the danger that implies of conflict between the rich and the poor.

Although he intends from now on to devote himself wholly to writing, the teaching of science is still a subject of major interest to Lord Snow. He thinks science is being very much better taught in general these days, especially in America. Both Britain and America are experimenting with a freer curriculum and this is all to the good, he believes. "There has been an improvement in bridging the gap between science and the humanities," he told *PW*, again emphasizing that this is especially so in the United States. At the high school level he thinks there should be an educational component of science throughout the years of study. At the university level, he believes there should be some sort of course in comprehensive science for art students and science students ought to learn their own literature and history and a language. "At the next level down from the best, you are much better than we are," Lord Snow said of American education. "Some of your small liberal arts colleges are magnificent."

The final novel in the notable Strangers and Brothers sequence of fiction Lord Snow has been writing for many years is under way now, he told *PW*. It will be called, appropriately enough, "Last Things," and it will pick up immediately after the ending of the last novel, "A Sleep of Reason," continuing into the year 1968.

The series, as it nears completion, is substantially the same as he conceived of it in the beginning, Lord Snow says. He has never kept formal notes on the project, although he has jotted down some comments. "One gets fonder of some of them as one goes on," he said of the many characters who have peopled the novels, "Your views about them change. Some of their virtues you begin to admire more as you get older." There is talk in England of possibly making a television series out of the Strangers and Brothers sequence of novels, after the fashion of the television dramatization of "The Forsyte Saga," which was an enormous critical and popular success in Britain.

A visitor to Russia on several occasions, Lord Snow observed that being there "is a bit more like being in America than most Americans would realize." One of the major themes in "The State of Siege" is the urgent need for cooperation and some sort of understanding between Russia and the United States on behalf of peace and the food needs of the world. The Russian birth rate is now much lower than ours, Lord Snow said. "A family of more than two children in Russia is rare today." He suggested that in a certain sense both the governments of the U.S.S.R.

and the U.S.A. want "passionately" to end the arms race, "but do not know how to achieve it. They really cannot afford their big military budget," he said, "and you can only just afford yours."

Violence and cruelty are important plot elements in Lord Snow's most recent novel, "The Sleep of Reason," but not permissively so by any means. If you reach the point where anything goes in literature and on the stage, he believes, "there is just one other step left to take. In Rome in the second century it was possible to see an actual execution on the stage."

In Russia there is strict control over violence and sex in writing and on television. In Denmark there is virtually none. Lord Snow thinks it will be interesting to observe in 20 years' time what the effects, if any, have been on the population of Denmark and an area of somewhat comparable size, Soviet Georgia, places where two diametrically opposing views about total freedom of expression have prevailed.

Lord Snow, who was knighted in 1957, and entered public affairs at the outbreak of World War II, has had a long and illustrious career in science at Cambridge and elsewhere and his first published work was scientific papers. It might be supposed all of this would indicate some deep-seated fascination with scientific subjects from earliest boyhood on. Lord Snow, however, gave us a refreshingly candid answer to the question, "How did you become interested in science?"

"It was sheerly through poverty," he told *PW*. "I came from a very poor home and I had to earn a living. Science was the easiest way for me to get comfortably established. If I had been well off, I might have become a lawyer for a time, or a professional writer right away."

James A. Pike

THE DAY THAT the Right Reverend James A. Pike talked to us at lunch immediately following his appearance on Mimi Benzell's NBC radio show wasn't an entirely typical day in the Episcopal bishop's life. On the other hand, it wasn't entirely untypical. He was in New York for not quite two days, en route from his office at the Center for the Study of Democratic Institutions, Santa Barbara, to several points in Europe.

The previous night, the retired bishop of California had been up 'til 12:15 correcting galleys of "The Bishop Pike Affair," the book by William Stringfellow and Anthony Towne, which recounts his disputes with conservative colleagues and reviews the issues leading to his possible forthcoming trial for heresy. (Harper & Row expects to publish the book about the time the Episcopal Church's House of Bishops meets in Seattle in September.)

In the morning, Bishop Pike was up very early to appear on NBC-TV's "Today" show. Then he hurried on to ABC to appear on one network program and one local show; and then to the Mimi Benzell interview, live, at noon. After lunch he was to record for the "Long John Nebbel Show" and the "Barry Gray Show," and somehow he was going to squeeze in time to write a jacket blurb for Harper and finish a foreword for a small publisher, and, possibly, look at some more proofs—before flying that night to England.

One of his first appointments there, he told us, would be with a scholar in Manchester, a biblical expert who may have turned up evidence about use of psychedelic drugs in the Middle East in New Testament times—with possible

By Chandler B. Grannis. From *Publishers Weekly* 191, no. 26 (June 26, 1967), pp. 28–29.

bearing on the insights and imagery of the Book of Revelation! A day or two later, Bishop Pike was to meet with a famous Dead Sea Scrolls expert in France. Then he was to join, at Geneva, with fellow members of the Center for the Study of Democratic Institutions, and with scholars and famous churchmen from all over the world, for "Pacem in Terris II." That conference, Bishop Pike said, would be aimed at some of the urgent issues involving East and West Germany, Vietnam, Rhodesia, Israel, the new stirrings of Communist–Christian dialog, and so on. (The conference took place May 28–31. Whether it will have some impact, directly or in personal, indirect ways, remains to be seen. But it was important to make the effort, Bishop Pike indicated, because it was a continued discussion in the spirit of the late Pope John's "Pacem in Terris" encyclical.)

The occasion for Bishop Pike's appearance on radio and TV, arranged by Harper & Row, was first of all the publication of his "You and the New Morality: 74 Cases." It also afforded an opportunity for mention of "The Bishop Pike Affair," and for the Bishop's own "If This Be Heresy," which Harper will publish Sept. 13.

In "You and the New Morality," the bishop explained, he takes up some of the kinds of ethical decisions that people have to make, with reference to real situations. What he is trying to show, he told us—and this is clear from the book—is that "*you* are finally responsible for all aspects of your life," and that this demand of responsibility has a higher ethical claim than any fixed code, since a code doesn't necessarily cover everything—though it may offer some valuable generalizations. The conclusion of the book calls for responsible, loving decisions about ethical dilemmas, "the rating of persons above things" and a recognition that there are no "ready-made answers for particular decisions."

Bishop Pike is, of course, no stranger to case studies. As a former federal attorney, he is the author of "Cases and Other Materials on the New Federal and Code Procedure." His religious book of a few years ago, "Doing the Truth," used a similar approach. We asked him whether all the "cases" in "You and the New Morality" are actual ones. A few are contrived, he said—some are obviously absurd, and so intended to make a point; but most are real, based on publicly reported events or on incidents that come to his attention in very extensive pastoral counseling. "If your emphasis in the ministry is on counseling," he said, "you see patterns of behavior repeating." Except for the mention of the late Rev. James Reeb, killed in Selma, Alabama, identities of the persons involved are concealed.

It was an allegation that he showed "lack of pastoral concern" which particularly aroused Bishop Pike in last year's vote of "censure" against him by the House of Bishops. He has even counseled some Episcopalians who couldn't get appointments with their own bishops, he remarked. He has insisted that, if he is tried, pastoral concern be one of the issues. He reminded us he had demanded a heresy trial because the censure vote gave no opportunity for a proper hearing. The vote, his mail has shown, "outraged thousands of people" in the church. He resigned, meanwhile, as Bishop of California in order to take up studies at the Center in Santa Barbara. He retains his rank of bishop, but at the moment, he told us, he is "a bishop out on bail." When he demanded a heresy trial, under an old canon of church law, the presiding bishop appointed a committee to examine the issues. The committee has asked people from various denominations including the Rev. John Courtney Murray; S.J., Rev. John MacQuarrie of Union Theological Seminary, the Rt. Rev. John A. T. Robinson, Bishop of Woolwich in England, to present papers on theological and legal issues involved. If the committee adopts an "adequate" report, and the House of Bishops in September ratifies it, Bishop Pike told us, he will be content to withdraw his application for a trial.

Meanwhile, the "bishop out on bail" keeps busy at the Center in Santa Barbara, where, as he explained, his typical day involves private study, dictation or research, seminars with the scholars in other disciplines who belong to the Center, and frequent talks with visiting scholars. Cross-disciplinary study is the key, he pointed out; the results of the studies and discussions may be quite unpredictable. But the Center has been a contributing factor to the antipoverty program, the movement for organization among Catholic priests, the use of weather satellites and a variety of other developments. And, Bishop Pike remarked, there's more discussion of theology at the Center than at the House of Bishops, where "theology is out of order."

The continuing development of his own theological thinking, the bishop said, is the subject matter of his September book, "If This Be Heresy." It is logically a sequel to "A Time for Christian Candor" and "What Is This Treasure?" (*Harper & Row*). This sequence, he said, is a study of belief— "an analysis of what you can believe on the basis of available data *plus faith*."

Though he appears often fascinated with innovations, Bishop Pike's view of innovation is within the traditions. We recalled the summer Chapel of St. James the Fisherman which he established some years ago at Wellfleet, Massachusetts, on Cape Cod—an apparently radical design, a chapel-in-the-round which actually, as he explained, revived a form of structure used by some of the early Christians. He considers his efforts at reform to be essentially conservative, to arrive at "fewer beliefs" and "more belief," as he kept saying in weekday sermons at St. Thomas's, New York last winter.

But he does enjoy refreshing innovations. We remembered how he had hurried away from Harper & Row's anniversary party before the National Book Awards in March. He explained that he had had to go to a dinner at Fordham University. Equal numbers of men and women had been invited, and the "date" assigned to him, he said, was an attractive young woman in a polka-dot dress. It turned out she was a Sister of Charity— "out of uniform" for the occasion.

Colin M. Turnbull

WITH HIS BOTTOM snug on a soft plush seat in a Broadway theater, it is difficult, sometimes even dizzying, for a play-goer to become oriented to the work of Samuel Beckett. Do the Nobel Laureate's characters, typically bereft of all hope and every shred of self-pity, wander through the mists that antedate civilization? Has some unknowable catastrophe wiped out mankind, leaving only the doomed survivors we see before us?

Colin Turnbull, a distinguished anthropologist, found just such beings not on the stage, but in the inhospitable uplands of Uganda and lived among them for two years. The result is "The Mountain People," published by Simon and Schuster last month.

The Ik (as the people Turnbull stayed with call themselves) once were hunters and gatherers who ranged unchecked through their corner of East Africa. Then closing borders and rising nationalism effectively boxed them in and they are dying off. The 2000 or so who remain travel light: They live without love, without God, without sympathy, without pity—all of the attributes most people would call human have dropped away. Children are kicked out of the house to fend for themselves at the age of three. Old people are abandoned to die, their death struggles a cause of amusement to the kin who left them behind.

Turnbull, a lanky Scotsman who has spent much of his life living in places the rest of us have never heard of, admits he wasn't ready for the Ik: "However he tries, a field worker can't really be objective," he told *PW*. "Everyone has a viewpoint which colors what he sees. In the notes I wrote

By Michael Mok. From *Publishers Weekly* 202, no. 19 (November 6, 1972), p. 14.

immediately afterwards, I described them not as they are, but as I thought they should be, or perhaps as I imagined they once had been."

But as he came to know the Ik better, Turnbull's attitude shifts radically. Toward the end of the book, the anthropologist describes giving food to an old woman who had been dying on her back like an injured beetle, her plight the source of merriment to fellow tribesmen:

"Perhaps if we had left Lo'ono, she would have died laughing, happy that she was at least providing her children with amusement. But what did we do? We prolonged her misery for no more than a few brief days. . . . She was already dead, and we made her unhappy as well. At the time I was sure we were right, doing the only 'human' thing. In a way we *were*—we were making life more comfortable for ourselves, confirming our own sense of superiority.

"But now I wonder. In the end I had a greater respect for the Ik, and I wonder if their way was not right, if I too should not have stood with the little crowd at the top of the rise and laughed as she flapped about like a withered old tortoise on its back, then left her to die, perhaps laughing at herself, instead of crying."

For the last 12 years, Turnbull has kept a *pied à terre* in the Chelsea section of Manhattan, and, walking west from this elegant district, often has to step over the derelicts who sprawl on the pavements along Ninth Avenue.

"I am convinced, for myself at least," Turnbull admitted, "that indifference is an emotional necessity. To survive, to keep from having a nervous breakdown, I have to seal off whole portions of my mind. Bums flop in the streets, and I don't care; I hear that one of my neighbors has been shot and I am unmoved.

"We and the Ik are heading in the same direction. Many will read the book and dismiss it saying they wouldn't do that kind of thing 'unless we were starving.' Yet the point at issue is not starvation but interpersonal relationships within a society. What keeps us together is the necessity for cooperation; without it we revert to animality. For the Ik, all legitimate reasons for cooperation have been removed."

Turnbull thinks the very sort of alienation that characterizes the Ik is taking hold in more civilized parts of the world.

"The same kind of thing is happening in our society, but here excessive technological development is the cause," Turnbull told *PW*. "We share the same services, the same apartment buildings, but that's about all. Our technology removes the necessity for cooperation between humans—instead we depend on machines and institutions."

Surprisingly, Turnbull was not "turned off" by his stint with these ultra-dispassionate people. "Living among the Ik one can be absolutely honest. With us, deceit, hypocrisy and diplomacy are standard ways of dealing with alienation.

"Until encountering the Ik, I thought there were basic human values, a universal 'good.' Now I have come to a contrary conclusion. I believe there is potential disaster in the cozy belief that everything will be all right, that we are all good people. Now I know and understand that goodness is a luxury, something each person must divine for himself and work toward fiercely."

Jane van Lawick-Goodall

DURING THE LAST 11 years Jane van Lawick–Goodall has spent at least as much time in Africa with "man's closest living relative" (the chimpanzee) as she has with man. Dr. Goodall's experience living among chimpanzees is the subject of "In the Shadow of Man," her new Houghton Mifflin book.

Dr. Goodall recently talked to *PW* about her background, her work and her book. British by birth, Jane Goodall first went to Africa when she was 18, hoping to study wild animals, something she had wanted to do since the age of eight. Even before that, however, animals had fascinated her. "When I was very young I hid in the henhouse for five hours to see how a hen laid an egg," she recalled. "At age five I was watching animals and dictating stories about them to my mother."

Jane Goodall's intense interest in animals convinced Dr. L. S. B. Leakey, the famous anthropologist, that a young girl just out of high school could tackle a scientific study of chimpanzees in the wild. Only one other person, Professor Henry W. Nissen, had previously studied wild chimpanzees, spending a mere two-and-a-half months in the field. In 1960 Jane Goodall set up the Gombe Stream Chimpanzee Reserve in Tanzania with the help of her mother. "The government officials of the area would not hear of a young English girl working by herself in the bush," she told *PW*.

Dr. Goodall worked on her Ph.D. part-time while living at Gombe, having enrolled at Cambridge in a doctoral program without first attending a university. "Cambridge permits

By Lila P. Freilicher. From *Publishers Weekly* 200, no. 21 (November 22, 1971), pp. 7–9.

this once in a while," she said. "Dr. Leakey's recommendation certainly helped. . . . I stretched my length of study to its utmost, continually asking for extensions so that I could go back to Gombe." (Today Jane Goodall, her husband Hugo van Lawick—the photographer sent to Gombe by Dr. Leakey—and their four-year-old son, make their home at Gombe. Mr. van Lawick's photographs appear in "In the Shadow of Man.")

In the early stages her work was discouraging, Jane Goodall said. "It took me nearly half a year until the chimps would even let me get into their range of vision without fleeing. Breaking down this barrier of distrust was certainly my most rewarding experience with the chimps."

In "In the Shadow of Man" Jane Goodall writes of her first close contact with the chimps: "Now two males were sitting so close that I could almost hear them breathing. I knew them both—David Graybeard, who had always been the least afraid of me, was one and the other was Goliath. . . . For more than ten minutes David Graybeard and Goliath sat grooming each other, and then, just before the sun vanished over the horizon behind me, David got up. And it so happened that my elongated evening shadow fell across him. . . . Later it acquired an almost allegorical significance, for of all living creatures today only man, with his superior brain, his superior intellect, overshadows the chimpanzee."

"Today new students at Gombe are accepted because the chimps have learned to trust people," she said. "Before I left this last time, one of the students reported an incident that occurred when he was following a male chimpanzee. The chimp and the student both stopped. Then the chimp lay down to sleep, and in the process of finding himself a comfortable position he wound up with his head on the student's foot."

Discussing some of the behavioral similarities between chimp and man, she explained, "Chimp and man share the same kinds of emotional communication. Some of the chimp gestures such as embracing in greeting, kissing, holding hands, we can understand without having studied the chimp. If you meet a chimp for the first time in your life and he takes your hand when it is offered, you will understand. . . . I am quite sure we share a common ancestor. The similarities are too striking to contemplate parallel evolution."

By studying the chimpanzee we can get at the basics of human behavior, Dr. Goodall believes. "Chimp behavior is not as complicated as human behavior because far less cultural tradition is passed down from one generation to another. This makes it easy to see the essentials."

Before Jane Goodall's work at Gombe, most scientists believed that man was the only animal that could modify objects for use as tools. Jane Goodall, however, observed chimps stripping the leaves from a stem and using the finished product as a tool to poke out termites from their nests. (Termites are a chimp delicacy.) "We also saw chimps using leaves as tools to sop up drinking water in exactly the same manner as the Kalahari Bushman."

She has also found chimp family behavior to resemble that of man. "Chimp babies are completely dependent upon their mothers until the age of seven, and they are watched over through adolescence. Even a son of 25 may be seen moving about with his mother, helping her out when she is in trouble. . . . Adult male siblings seem to favor each other's company over that of other males."

What did she hope to accomplish by writing "In the Shadow of Man" in the language of the layman? "I feel strongly that the public deserves to know what the scientists are doing. For one thing the scientist's work is largely supported by the public. For another, we owe it to the chimp. We want to conserve him in his natural habitat, but if people know nothing about the chimp, why should they help conserve him? Scientists can read the scientific publications. You can't expect the average businessman to bother spending long hours delving into learned scientific journals."

What has man to learn from chimp behavior? Perhaps something about the biological nature of aggression and the influence of culture on aggressive behavior, Dr. Goodall suggests. "Our experience with banana feeding has shown that with the crowding of many chimps into a small area aggression rocketed. Chimps can be extremely aggressive, but the aggression is mostly bluffing—throwing rocks and swinging branches. . . . The chimp hasn't yet discovered lethal weapons. If he had things might be different. A wild animal doesn't want to endanger his own life so he doesn't get into risky fights. But if a chimp had a gun and could shoot it without causing any damage to himself, I couldn't swear he would not pull the trigger."

A study of Western man figures in Jane Goodall's future plans ("because we need it so badly"). She believes it is up to the scientists to show us convincing evidence of our mistakes. "The question," Jane Goodall says, "is: 'Will we see our mistakes in time?' " Pointing to changes being made in the areas of overpopulation and pollution, she told us she is optimistic, and added, "We must never say it's too late to try."

Esther Vilar

THE MOST OUTSPOKEN opponent of the ideology of Women's Lib we have yet had has got to be Esther Vilar, author of "The Manipulated Man" (*Farrar, Straus & Giroux*). Dr. Vilar (she is an M.D.) and her thesis that "men have been trained and conditioned by women not unlike the way Pavlov conditioned his dogs, into becoming their slaves" are currently making the round of the talk shows across the country.

In person Esther Vilar is an attractive, mid-thirtyish woman of German parentage, born and raised in Buenos Aires, soft-spoken but unwilling to give one inch in her view of the relationship between the sexes. "A woman will make use of a man whenever there is an opportunity. A woman is a human being who does not work," she says, and she means it.

"The Manipulated Man" is Esther Vilar's fourth book and first success, although it took nine months for it to catch on in Germany where it was first published. Half a million copies have now been sold. The book has been translated into 21 languages and published in countries as different as Turkey and Iceland.

The reactions from women readers "are either very positive or very negative," Ms. Vilar says. "Men are more in between in their reactions, more cautious. I do get a certain number of letters from men who say, 'of course, it's all true what you write about men being manipulated by women—but I'm the exception.'

"I wrote the book very quickly, much of it in the United States where I spent about a year in all, gathering material

By Barbara A. Bannon. From *Publishers Weekly* 203, no. 6 (January 29, 1973), pp. 202–203.

that convinced me American men are the most manipulated of all by their women. What I put into the book is what I have thought all my life. Ever since Simone de Beauvoir and 'The Second Sex' it has been popular to say women are suppressed by men, but I never saw any signs of it. When I studied medicine in Buenos Aries only 10 percent of the medical students were women and I always felt we were being treated better than the men. I think I am not any better than the rest of women. There have been many times when I took advantage of being a woman. If you're writing a book like this you must know what you're talking about.

"Do I enjoy being a woman? I feel guilty at being part of the exploiter's sex, but it is a much greater joy than being a man would be. They have a terrible time of it. Maybe I'm lucky in that I did not have too much of an opportunity personally to exploit men."

Esther Vilar was married for two years to a German writer, Klaus Wagn, and they have a seven-year-old son.

"In my eyes married women have a very bad image," she says. "They are exploiters of the male labor force. That is why I decided to get a divorce. Now, my ex-husband and I are on very good terms. He loves my ideas. Of course, a man can be just as exploited by a woman who lives with him without being married to him. He may even feel more guilty and more under her control because of that."

Esther Vilar's most difficult problem now is "trying to raise my son," she says. "All the other children are being manipulated, the girls to their advantage, the boys to their disadvantage. I cannot quite make my son the first non-manipulated boy as I would like, because I do not want him to be an outsider in society. I tell him things like, 'it is best not to cry because it is not good to show your feelings too openly,' but I leave his sex out of my education of him. I never say, 'don't do this or do that because you are a boy.' "

Some criticism has been made of "The Manipulated Man" on the grounds that no footnotes are included, no specific statistics to support Esther Vilar's sometimes sweeping claims about how women use men and let their own intelligence atrophy. "This book is generalizing, I know," she admits. "I would call it a kind of pamphlet, and a very rude one, but I had to be rude to be heard. I had to put things as strongly as I did to be heard above the loud Women's Libbers. Women's Libbers are just imitating the male ideas of women from Freud and Lenin on. My book is the first *real* Women's Lib book because it makes it clear to women that they can liberate themselves if they want to, but they have to do it from within themselves."

Many women can work well when they have to do so to support themselves, Esther Vilar admits, "and women did a fantastic job of replacing men in a work situation during the war, but afterwards most of them retreated immediately.

"As for the term 'male chauvinist,' no such thing really exists. Men love to be called that by women because it makes them feel big and strong, which women have always told them they must be. Its use by women is just another kind of a trick to make men do what they want them to do. Women get so many advantages out of the system as it works for them today that I do not have much hope for many of them wanting to change things and really liberate themselves from the manipulation of men.

"It would take a lot of character for a man to be emancipated enough to stay home and do the housework or take care of young children. Not many men would dare to do that. And as for married women who work, how many of them would be willing to go out to work to support a perfectly healthy non-working husband every day of their life until retirement at 65? And yet that is what women expect men to do for them."

There is, however, one area in which Esther Vilar is sister under the skin to Germaine Greer, Gloria Steinem and every stenographer in an office pool. She is a firm believer in women making every bit as much money as men in the same job situation.

Dan Wakefield

"PEOPLE WHO WATCH today's soap operas are enjoying some of the best storytelling of our time." This surprising statement comes from Dan Wakefield, author of "All Her Children," a new book about contemporary soap operas due shortly from Doubleday. And his views deserve a hearing: he is a man with two best-selling novels and five nonfiction books behind him and a contributing editor of the *Atlantic Monthly*. His articles have appeared in virtually every major magazine and newspaper.

"Lots of people are in on them," Wakefield told a *PW* interviewer recently in his fashionable townhouse on Boston's Beacon Hill. " 'All My Children' [the soap on which his book is based] alone has a daily following of more than 10 million." And he reeled off the names of some prominent addicts—such varied people as Van Cliburn, Maurice Sendak and Carol Burnett, noting that men were now coming out of "the soap opera closet." In New York, in fact, Norman Lear's tongue-in-cheek contribution to the genre, "Mary Hartman, Mary Hartman," is becoming something of a fad among the intelligentsia.

Wakefield was first drawn to soap opera during the holiday season that followed his divorce. "Soaps, I found, were the only programs that presented the kinds of problems and anguish that the holiday season brings to many people. I remember one showing a woman whose boy friend was a married man. He had gone home to his wife and kids and she was left sitting alone in a bar while 'White Christmas' played on the jukebox. In another, the parents were all upset because Junior wouldn't come home. Every other pro-

By Joan Norris. From *Publishers Weekly* 209, no. 6 (February 9, 1976), pp. 14–15. Reprinted by permission of Joan Norris.

gram was just one big smiling Santa Claus. It impressed me that the soaps included, and dealt with, people's lives as I think they are.

"Then when I was reporting around the country, I used to go back to my motel after interviews and turn on the soaps, and I often found that they were very good reflections of what people were thinking."

Wakefield decided to follow up on his interest by writing an article. (He admits that half the reason was that he wanted to meet the cast.) He had no intention of writing a full-length book, in fact was in the midst of his third novel. However, he found the subject absorbing, a book took shape, and Doubleday snapped it up at auction.

The range of the book should give it an appeal beyond the soap fan. There's a full confession from Wakefield of his long addiction to soaps. There's a discussion that draws parallels between the daytime writers of today and the 19th-century serial writers like Dickens and Trollope. Another section details the grueling work that goes into the production of each day's episode. There are many amusing anecdotes about the show and its characters, onstage and off.

And Wakefield comes up with some surprises—that soaps are taught in contemporary culture courses on many college campuses; that professors report that all other activities stop from Princeton to Stanford when certain soaps come on; that some psychologists use them in therapy; that videotapes of most serials are destroyed by the networks, who see storing them as wasting space. For Wakefield, this last information is devastating news, for he sees Agnes Nixon (creator of his favorite "All My Children") as the Charles Dickens of our day.

"When 'The Old Curiosity Shop' was being serialized in America, it came over by boat," he reminds the interviewer. "One installment ended with Little Nell on her deathbed. When the next one was due, fans gathered on the docks and as the boat drew near, shouted out: 'Is Little Nell dead?' Look at that involvement! The same kind of intensity exists today as people gather for each new segment of their favorite story.

"Another story I heard was told by the historian Henry Bragdon, who said that when new installments of 'Uncle Tom's Cabin' would arrive, his great aunt Melissa would ring the bell to call everyone in from the fields on their farm in upstate New York. It was the big event of the week—entertainment for an entire community of people."

Such audiences, notes Wakefield, have a long history of influencing the stories and characters of their favorite authors. If Dickens saw sales weren't going well, he threw in a new story line. When "The Bostonians" was serialized in the *Atlantic Monthly*, even Henry James changed Miss Birdseye's character after suffragettes complained his portrayal was unfair to women. Just as 19th-century writers changed their stories or characters in response to readers' comments, daytime serial writers do the same if ratings falter.

Mention of the recent TV series "Beacon Hill" brings a grimace from Wakefield. "It was too much like modern movies. Everything was done for the photographer or the director. The concern was with appearance, not with storytelling.'' He went on to talk about the characters not being authentic, the sets wrong; then he stopped, leaned back, sipped on his drink and smiled: ''Well, it's my prejudice, but really they just should have hired Agnes Nixon.''

Wakefield's writing career began at the age of nine when he wrote his first 10-page ''novel,'' ''Lateral Pass,'' which he describes as ''a football drama.'' No adults took his career plans seriously, but he always knew he would be a writer. ''You know,'' he says, ''I remember guys in college who were anguished because they were talented in architecture and music and writing and painting. I didn't have that problem. I wasn't any good at anything else. I had no choice whatsoever.''

His first job after graduating from Columbia was on a weekly newspaper in Princeton, New Jersey. Soon he was writing regularly for the *Nation* and went to Israel for six months. ''I was very anxious to travel, see the world and get shot at—to do all those things I figured were necessary to being a good journalist. I'd read Hemingway and I believed all that stuff.''

From the journalism came five books of nonfiction: ''Island in the City,'' ''Revolt in the South,'' ''The Addict,'' ''Supernation at Peace and War,'' and ''Between the Lines.'' Then, with a growing reputation as a journalist, he turned to fiction, finding it ''more emotionally satisfying.'' His first novel was ''Going All the Way,'' the second ''Starting Over.'' Both made the best seller lists and were Literary Guild selections. ''Starting Over'' was the first of a three-book contract for fiction with Seymour Lawrence/Delacorte Press.

Wakefield has lived in Boston since 1963, when he left New York to take a Neiman Fellowship. He does not miss the New York scene. ''It became difficult for me to go to cocktail parties and hear what other people were doing and how much money they were making. There comes at some point a lot of talking about writing instead of actually doing it. Some people are immune to this problem. I'm not.''

Boston is certainly a more habitable a place for Wakefield, who can walk from his home on Beacon Hill to Seymour Lawrence's office on Beacon Street, to the *Atlantic* on Arlington, to the Boston Public Library on Boylston, and then to lunch at Copley's. Everything is within walking distance—and when all else palls, his television set is just upstairs.

Tom Wicker

THE DAY *PW* went to the offices of the *New York Times* to interview Tom Wicker about his book on the 1971 Attica prison rebellion, "A Time to Die," the story was still alive—three and a half years after it happened. That very day the *Times* carried a story on the trial of two former Attica inmates charged with the killing of a correction officer during the revolt that took 43 lives.

Partly because it remains such a remarkable story—and partly because during the rebellion Wicker, who was chosen as one of the mediators, was forced to confront himself, and has written about it in unusually frank terms—the book has stirred considerable advance interest. Even before publication this week, Quadrangle/New York Times Book Company had decided its first printing of 35,000 would not be enough and had ordered a large second one. The book got the cover of the March issue of *Esquire*, *Book Digest* picked up second serial rights, BOMC made it a main April selection, and Arthur Penn reportedly took a "very fancy option" for a movie. So as *PW* tackled Wicker (who had been awakened early that morning by Secretary of Defense James Schlesinger, calling to complain about a column), the first question was whether he thought the interest in the book arose from Attica itself or from his intensive self-examination in it.

A: I don't think anyone is interested any more in the raw episode. It is a very personal book and I planned it that way. I decided to write only the story that I knew, with only the necessary additional material to make what I'd seen and taken part in comprehensible. The second decision I made

By Joyce Illig. From *Publishers Weekly* 207, no. 10 (March 10, 1975), pp. 14–15.

was that it was a matter of interest to me as to how I came to be there. Why did they call me? What was it about a small-town Southern boy that injected him into this episode?

Q: Why did you decide to write the book in the third person?

A: Since I was a participant in this story and intended to question myself, I thought it would be easier for me to look at myself objectively. Having read Mailer's books, I also thought that it could be an effective literary device.

Q: Did you come out of that Attica experience with a zealous attitude toward what it meant in your life?

A: I think I did. I just didn't come out originally with the notion of writing a book. I was approached several weeks after Attica by another publisher, who made a pre-emptive offer. I thought it was a wonderful offer. I knew the people and was willing to do it. However I'd made a gentleman's agreement with Sydney Gruson, the *Times* vice-president in charge of subsidiaries, that if I ever did a nonfiction book I would give Quadrangle the right to bid on it. To my astonishment he matched the offer. That was 1971, and Quadrangle was just starting. When I agreed to do the book I was then engaged in a substantial rewrite of my novel that came out in 1973, "Facing the Lions." It was not until the summer of '72 that I thought about his prison book, much less got to work on it. By that time it was almost a year after the event. Many a time I regretted that I'd agreed to do it. But you know how book contracts are. They bind you right away by giving you money, which you spend, and then there's nothing to do but go ahead and write the damn book.

Q: When you finished, did you feel that you found things about yourself that you hadn't known?

A: I wouldn't say that I found out very much about myself in the broadest terms, because I have always been introspective. I was forced to analyze more nearly what I had done and not done at Attica. And I do think I see that more clearly now. I both feel better about what I did there and worse about what I didn't do.

I got a very acute reading of the manuscript from Roger Wilkins, who really helped the book an enormous amount. On one particular point in my conversation with him, there came a very important insight that I didn't have time to develop, so I had to stick it in the Afterword. In the long run, those inmates trusted and believed in the state and society more than the state and society did in them—including me. We all believed they were going to kill those hostages. They could have. But they didn't. And you have to concede that these guys—didn't really believe the state was going to kill them.

Q: Has Rockefeller read your book yet? [Vice-President Rockefeller, at the time governor of New York, declined to meet with the rebellious Attica convicts in a mediation effort.]

A: I doubt it. I didn't send him a copy. I have some reason to believe, but I'm not in a position to prove it, that Rockefeller would have been pleased if that grand jury had indicted some of those state troopers. It would have made everything look better. I don't believe any of the explanations that Rockefeller was acting politically. But I do think that Rockefeller did not believe that the governor of the great state of New York ought to negotiate with a lot of black cons. He would have looked at those people as failures in the free enterprise system—to which he gives great adherence.

Q: At some point, didn't it occur to you to ask some of your influential friends in politics and at the *Times* to intercede with Rockefeller?

A: In retrospect it's a very good idea, for people like me, Herman Badillo and Clarence Jones, who have some contacts. We ought to have been on that phone saying call Rockefeller, bring pressure on him. We should have been doing that and we didn't. But it didn't occur to me.

Q: What else do you think you should have done that you didn't do at Attica?

A: I should have gotten up on Sunday afternoon and told those guys that the state was getting ready to blow them down. I believed then, and it's clear now, that it was the cold absolute truth. I'm not entirely clear why I didn't do it.

Q: You thought a lot about death, about dying at Attica, didn't you?

A: You're damn right I did. But there again, I assumed that those were the kind of guys that might kill me. And looking back on it, I don't think there was any possibility that they were going to do anything like that.

Q: Have you reached the point yet where you feel you may have fulfilled the youthful dream that you speak about in your book: to be a famous author?

A: No. It's going to be ironic. I can already see it happening, you know. The world being what it is, people are going to say, 'This is his finest book.'

Q: I think you'd better be ready for it.

A: Oh, I'm ready for it. I know it's going to happen. And they're going to say it's so much better than that bad novel. But you know, that novel is my child. This is something that was forced on me. But that's the way it goes, so what the hell.

Q: Do you expect to make a lot of money from this book?

A: I don't think I'll make a lot more. They paid me a substantial advance, all of which came up front, and they would have to sell a hell of a lot of books for me to earn more out of the hardcover. And to anticipate the question, I have quite rigorously assigned at least 10 percent of everything I've gotten out of this to the Attica Brothers Defense and will continue to do so. I'm very sensitive to the likelihood that someone would think I was trying to exploit this situation.

Q: Are you writing another novel?

A: As soon as I get this promotion tour over with I'm going to start another novel (under contract to Viking). It's going to be a war novel with the setting in the Civil War. I have a high regard for myself as a novelist, which nobody else does.

Q: If there's a similar prison riot tomorrow, and you're called up again, would you go?

A: I would do that, but I would have a whole different approach to it. I would announce to both sides: 'Look here, I'm not here trying to negotiate your goddamn problems. I'm going to stand here and if either of you shoot the other, you've got to shoot me first because I'm in between.'

Peter Wyden

WHEN PETER WYDEN learned about the Institute of Group Psychotherapy in Beverly Hills, and its successful program for improving rocky marriages by teaching the partners how to fight and fight fair, it wasn't surprising that he became fascinated with the subject. Nor was it surprising that before long he had written about it in "The Intimate Enemy: How to Fight Fair in Love and Marriage," prepared in collaboration with Dr. George R. Bach, inventor of the technique and head of the Institute of Group Psychotherapy. Morrow is publishing the book February 10.

The subject—marriage problems and an intensive, tested technique for dealing with many of them—was within Mr. Wyden's range of lively concerns as executive editor of the *Ladies' Home Journal* since 1965, and formerly a senior editor of *McCall's*. And it was in line with the broad social and family themes of five other well-researched books he has written—"Suburbia's Coddled Kids" (*Doubleday*, 1962), "The Hired Killers" (*Morrow*, 1963), "The Overweight Society" (*Morrow*, 1965; *Pocket Books*), "How the Doctors Diet" (*Trident*, 1968), and "Growing up Straight: What Every Thoughtful Parent Should Know About Homosexuality" (*Stein & Day*, 1968; also a Literary Guild alternate selection)—the last two written with his wife, Barbara Woodman Wyden—who is women's editor of the *New York Times Magazine*, formerly an editor at *Newsweek*. Mr. Wyden has two teenaged sons.

"I think of these books," Peter Wyden told *PW* recently, "as Wyden's Five-Foot Shelf of Contemporary Worries. I'm interested in being a successful writer, but I'm inter-

By Chandler B. Grannis. From *Publishers Weekly* 195, no. 6 (February 10, 1969), pp. 30–32.

ested also in helping to show people how to cope with this complex world.''

The books don't add up to five feet, literally—but considering Mr. Wyden's exuberant energy, his expansive enthusiasm both for solutions to family problems, and for a worthy commercial project, his eventual output may well fill the proverbial shelf.

"These books are not about strictly female problems," he explains. "They're about family problems; the family is where it's at." He adds, "I have become impressed with the information gap between research in the behavioral sciences and the enormous number of people who are looking for solutions."

One-time writer for the *Wichita Eagle* and *St. Louis Post-Dispatch*, Chicago editorial chief for the *Saturday Evening Post* and a Washington correspondent for *Newsweek*, Mr. Wyden is a compulsive writer, prolific, and gifted at putting things clearly. "I don't write exclusively to entertain" he says, "though no one will read what I write if I'm not entertaining. I see myself as a sort of U.N. interpreter, a translator, trying to present technical material so that the public can use it." Some critics, he observes, think a piece of writing "can't be important if it's comprehensible—and that's where I get upset."

Considering the accelerating pressures that assail family life from all sides today—the pressures of affluence, of high mobility, of increasingly sophisticated facts and situations to be mastered—"people need help in learning to live with each other more cooperatively," Mr. Wyden argues. If they don't get help, "we'll have a real breakdown of the American family."

That's what "The Intimate Enemy" is all about. It's not a book that can be summed up in a nutshell—and, in fact, an oversimplified statement of its recommendations for constructive, properly planned "fights" between intimates may arouse initial skepticism. But when the training given successfully to thousands of couples through Dr. Bach's institute is examined closely, it seems mightily persuasive. Dr. Bach doesn't claim absolute success; there are couples that just can't bring their aggressions into a creative and mutually helpful pattern—but the doctor claims genuine success with 85% of the couples he has counseled—or, to use his preferred term, trained.

The Bach techniques of making something loving and constructive out of the inevitable family disputes first came to wide public attention through a long article in the May 17, 1963, issue of *Life*, by Shana Alexander. It was she who later introduced Dr. Bach to Mr. Wyden; the book was an eventual result of this three-way friendship.

Mr. Wyden wrote the body of the book; Dr. Bach, a technical appendix and a concluding essay, "The Impact Theory of Aggression: A Conceptual and Semantic Clarification." The body of the text includes "122 actual fight excerpts," condensed from millions of words recorded in Dr. Bach's group therapy sessions—excerpts chosen to illustrate the successive points in the 405-page book.

"The Intimate Enemy," Mr. Wyden points out, starts pretty much where "The Games People Play" leaves off—it shows how couples can stop playing self-justifying games with their relationship, and start "leveling" with each other.

Mr. Wyden pays high tribute to Howard Cady, editor, and Larry Hughes, president, at Wm. Morrow, for their editorial and promotional backing for the book, and to his wife, "probably the world's most creative copy-editor." (The Wydens say they themselves have benefited by the Bach techniques.)

"The Intimate Enemy" provides more than enough ammunition for one of half a dozen lecture subjects which Mr. Wyden has contracted to offer through W. Colstein Leigh, Inc.—subjects based both on his books and his editorship. Meanwhile he has been promoting the new book with an appearance January 24–25 for Higbee's (Cleveland) Bridal Week, with book department cooperation; and he will give other talks during the winter and spring at AMC stores and elsewhere.

About 10% (16,000 words) of the book has run in five installments of the *Ladies' Home Journal*, concluding with the current issue and giving the book "front cover exposure on 35-million copies"; there was a piece based on the book in the *New York Times Magazine* in January; there will be a short excerpt in the April *True*; Newsday Syndicate will begin circulating excerpts to newspapers April 15; letters from prominent psychologists endorsing the book are going to marriage counselors and clinical psychologists throughout the country; booksellers some weeks ago got leaflets ("A Self-Training Program") based on the book; co-op ads have been arranged with Doubleday Book Shops, Brentano's and Pickwick; and demonstrations of marital fights—the wrong kind vs. the right kind— are being arranged for broadcast. Booksellers are invited to encourage a double sale of the book by displaying two copies, each with a red heart-shaped cut-out for Valentine's Day, one labeled "His," the other, "Hers"—so that couples won't have to fight over the book (page 57).

As a sort of subtle guarantee, the dedication of the book reads: "To Peggy and Barbara." That is, to Mrs. George R. Bach and Mrs. Peter Wyden.

6

History and Political Commentary

Dean Acheson

DEAN ACHESON's big new September book, a record of his State Department years, 1941–1952, bears an intriguing title: "Present at the Creation." During the ABA Convention in Washington, his publisher, W. W. Norton & Co., and his editor, Eric Swenson, made it possible for members of the press to meet with Mr. Acheson. As trim and erect as ever, looking the very model of a statesman, Mr. Acheson talked about the book and the political scene, at times with considerable candor.

Richard M. Nixon, Mr. Acheson believes, "is much brighter and abler" than many people give him credit for being. One of the problems he faces as president, however, is that his advisors are too weak. "There is a very great gap between Nixon and his advisors" Mr. Acheson said. "He is better than they are. A serious president is likely to be better than his advisors. Nixon is going to have trouble because he *is* better than his associates. I would not say Eisenhower was a serious President."

Dwight D. Eisenhower is not one of Mr. Acheson's most revered political figures. In the final chapter of "Present at the Creation," he describes Eisenhower as "wary, withdrawn, and taciturn to the point of surliness" when invited to meet with Truman and Acheson on the orderly transferral of the administration. Speaking more bluntly in Washington the other day, he put it this way, "That S.O.B. Eisenhower never invited Truman or me to the White House once while he was there."

By contrast, Mr. Acheson believes, Harry S Truman is "a great hero. This is the subject of my book. I believe Truman

By Barbara A. Bannon. From *Publishers Weekly* 195, no. 26 (June 30, 1969), pp. 25–27.

as president was one of the greatest we have ever known." The last part of "Present at the Creation" is devoted to an analysis of Truman's essential nature. He is, Mr. Acheson said in Washington, "a very complicated and a very simple man, a man of integrity, of energy, of orderly mind, a man who always as president conducted himself fairly, so that perhaps in the last analysis he is really a very, very simple man after all." Typical of the essential Truman, Mr. Acheson believes, was the much-quoted motto he kept on his desk as president—the one that read, "The buck stops here."

LBJ, by contrast, "is so complex, he could meet himself coming around four corners, before you could get around one," Mr. Acheson said.

"Present at the Creation" is dedicated to Harry S Truman, "The captain with the mighty heart." Mr. Acheson's other great hero in the book is George C. Marshall, under whom he served in the State Department.

The book's arresting title is taken from a quotation attributed to Alphonso X of Spain: "Had I been present at the creation I would have given some useful hints for the better ordering of the universe." In a sense, Mr. Acheson believes, the war and immediate postwar years that are covered in the book were a time of creation, a reordering of the universe as we had known it.

In addition to his own voluminous papers, and memory of events, Mr. Acheson was able to draw upon the material he and several colleagues in the State Department recorded in 1953 and 1954 for the late Dr. J. Robert Oppenheimer, at the Institute for Advanced Study at Princeton, setting down their recollections of how the major foreign policies of the Truman administration took shape. One source Mr. Acheson did not have was diaries. He never keeps them.

"Present at the Creation" was written in the West Indies and at Mr. Acheson's home in Maryland. "Writing is not easy," he says, "when what one has to do is to overcome the old Adam of laziness."

The book came into being because Mr. Acheson decided that with the country today, and especially so many young people, affected by moods of depression, disillusion and withdrawal from action, it was time to "tell a tale of large conceptions, great achievements, and some failures, the product of enormous will and effort." Originally, he had intended to close his memoirs with the earlier volume, "Morning and Noon" (*Houghton Mifflin*), because he thought he could not be objective about the period of larger events in his life. Over the intervening years, however, he decided to set aside detachment in favor of speaking out.

Mr. Acheson "reads a good deal, but outside of my own period," he told *PW*. One of the most fascinating periods in history, he believes, is the Tudor and Elizabethan, and he likes to turn to it often, "to see the same kind of problems we face being dealt with by other people. No one ever thinks anything ever happened before," Mr. Acheson said, "but if you read history you can see your own problems evolving." The Elizabethan period and the 20th century have much in common, he believes. "No one can understand our dealings with the Russians" without a knowledge of the complicated intrigues that involved Henry VIII, Elizabeth, the Pope and the King of Spain in their time.

Summing up the view of history he has attempted to achieve in "Present at the Creation," Mr. Acheson quoted from the historian C. V. Wedgwood, who in her life of William the Silent wrote, "History is lived forward but it is written in retrospect. We know the end before we consider the beginning and we can never wholly recapture the beginning only." "Present at the Creation," Mr. Acheson said, "is the discussion of the beginning of the greatest changes wrought in life since the Roman Empire. It is a biography of my experience of an epoch in this modern world."

Russell Baker

THE BIOGRAPHICAL note on the jacket of Russell Baker's new book, "Poor Russell's Almanac" (*Doubleday*), describes the author, in part, in these words: "Russell Baker was born in 1853 aboard a schooner in the Malay Straits, served as a bag man for the railroad during the administration of Ulysses S. Grant, and graduated eight years later from the University of Heidelberg . . ." and concludes, "Mr. Baker holds many leading prizes and has made a fool of himself on many distinguished occasions. He has been dead for a number of years and has two cats."

Now, of course, any reader of Mr. Baker's *New York Times* column, "The Observer," knows immediately that either: (1) S. J. Perelman and Woody Allen have teamed up and taken a job writing jacket blurbs for Doubleday, or; (2) the words are the work of the author himself.

"I wanted something different from the usual notes you read about authors on book jackets," Mr. Baker said, in a recent interview at the offices of his publisher, admitting that he himself penned the lines. What he didn't say was that these few brief words contain the essence of the Russell Baker style; in this case reflecting gentle, yet perceptive, bemusement at the foibles of publishing, authors—and himself.

The book is a collection of Mr. Baker's *Times* columns and comments, "many of them rewritten and reworked," he explains, "so they wouldn't all be the same length, which gets monotonous. They are purposely arranged in the style of an almanac so that they can be read a piece at a time on a given day in the year." This is the fifth collection of Mr.

By Thomas Chastain. From *Publishers Weekly* 201, no. 4 (January 24, 1972), pp. 28–30. Reprinted by permission of Thomas Chastain.

Baker's columns to appear in book form and he said that he had devised the almanac format in the hope that it would head off those reviewers who have complained that the problem with such collections is that it's difficult to read them through in one sitting. (Wouldn't you know, within hours of the *PW* interview, a leading weekly news magazine appeared with a review of Mr. Baker's new book, a most laudatory review, which still concluded: "But to read 212 pages of him at a sitting is a mistake." Alas, Poor Russell, foiled again.)

Although his "Observer" column is frequently devoted to political humor, Mr. Baker selected only a few such examples for inclusion in "Poor Russell's Almanac." "Most of the political stuff was purposely left out," he told *PW*, "because it ages and because some of it is sometimes sharp-tempered."

He concedes, in answer to a question, that he does on occasion write in anger and then rewrites "to achieve more control, to create a constant identity for the column, a created expression of me." What he tries for, ideally, is to vary the pace of the column, "sometimes to be me in high dudgeon, sometimes to carry on a casual, convivial conversation with my reader." Even when his political columns are, as he puts it, "sharp-tempered," there have been no reverberations from political circles. "But," he points out, "I don't get invited to the White House, either."

On the other hand, "The Observer" column does draw mail from its readers; in fact, Mr. Baker was obviously amused to report, he had just recently discovered that he shares with Thomas Jefferson "this insufferable burden of letters." Smiling whimsically, he explained that after he had come across a remark made by Thomas Jefferson to John Adams, complaining of receiving 1200 to 1300 letters a year and calling it, "this insufferable burden of letters," he had done a check of mail to "The Observer" and found that he, too, was receiving 1200 to 1300 letters a year.

In writing his column, which appears three times a week opposite the editorial page in the *Times*, Mr. Baker follows a systematic routine, writing at specific hours on specific days, either at his home in Washington or in an office at the Washington Bureau of the *Times*: the Tuesday column is written on Sunday, the Thursday column on Tuesday, and the Sunday column on Friday. "There is always only a one-day lag between," he points out, and he has no backlog of columns to draw upon. He does not attend press conferences or briefings, but in coming months he plans to spend more time outside since it's a presidential election year; he feels it's important to observe the candidates first-hand before writing about them. "In a way, writing political humor is like cartooning. You have to do it with quick character sketches and bold strokes."

As for the state of humor in the country today, Russell Baker feels very strongly that it is not dying out, as some say, but that it has become quite different. "Those who say humor is dying," he muses, "are talking about the old humor of gaiety, a limited humor, when the country was more isolated than it is today. Now we have a sophisticated humor, a worldly humor that comes out of an awareness that ours is a country with global responsibilities.'' He mentions some of his own favorite writers of today's humor, Art Buchwald, Woody Allen, Donald Barthelme, Roger Angell, Art Hoppe, "and, of course, Perelman—S. J. Perelman.''

When he is not writing his column, Mr. Baker spends most of his days reading newspapers, magazines, and books on the best seller list (his personal taste runs to 19th-century novels), to gather material for his column and to spot trends in politics, the news, fashion, and the mores of the country. "The kind of material the *Times* often doesn't report in the paper until later on,'' he says. There *is* one subject he would like to write about in his column but which he has never attempted: sex. "There's so much being written about sex and discussed on TV that I'd like to comment on, but it's a matter of language, of the words themselves, which restrict me from writing about it pungently. I just don't see how it can be discussed in a newspaper like the *Times*.''

A subject that does recur frequently in "The Observer'' is Mr. Baker's fondness for trains and train travel—is there a particular reason? "I'm basically a guy with a yearning for the past,'' he says candidly. "A time when things were better. Life was better when there were trains. It's probably a sign of the hardening of the mental arteries, this yearning for boyhood, the kind of thing I dislike when I hear it from other people.'' But, he adds, he did grow up in Loudoun County, in northern Virginia, which was then a railroad center of the nation, and trains were, for many years, part of his life. "When my own boys were younger, I took them on cross-country train trips. I felt it was important for them to get the feel of the country in their bones in a way that never happens in an airplane but does on a train.''

Mr. Baker seemed startled when asked why, since his column could be written anywhere, he lived in Washington. "Inertia as much as anything,'' he finally answered with a smile. He added, "Washington is not really a writer's town. Buchwald and I are lonely there. We have lunch together once a week.''

Still, Washington has been home for Russell Baker and his family ever since he went there as White House correspondent for the *Baltimore Sun* in the early 1950s. He had first joined the *Sun* after graduating from Johns Hopkins University in 1947. He switched from the *Sun* to the *New York Times* in 1954 and for the next seven or eight years worked in the Washington Bureau, on the political beat, and covering the White House. He started writing "The Observer'' in the *Times* in 1962.

"Before that time,'' he recalls, "there was a regular feature on the paper's editorial page called 'The Topics of the Times.' Some years before a very good writer named Simeon Strunsky had written the 'Topics,' but by then just about anybody on the *Times* was working on it, possibly including some of the copy boys." Mr. Baker wanted a new name for the column and John Oakes, who's in charge of the *Times* editorial page, suggested "The Observer." Russell Baker, "The Observer," and the *Times* have been together ever since.

It was while he was still in Baltimore, that he and his wife, Miriam, who is known as Mimi, were married in 1950. They have three children, Kathleen, 20, Allen, 19, and Michael, 17. The children are at the age where they are leaving home—the two oldest are already gone—and Mr. Baker says, "I'm going to miss them for more than the usual reasons. They put me in touch with ideas and what's going on in the world." He is most optimistic about the intelligence of today's young people.

Will "Poor Russell's Almanac" be published annually from now on, like "The Farmer's Almanac?" "I doubt it," Mr. Baker laughs. "This one came from seven years of columns."

Cedric Belfrage

CEDRIC BELFRAGE is a courtly, elderly Englishman with bright blue eyes and heavy freckles. He could easily be a country lawyer living an uneventful life in a cathedral city. Instead he is a deportee from the United States, living in Mexican exile from his chosen country—and allowed into the United States only for a scanty 30-day visit during which his time and his activities are checked as carefully as a Chinese diplomat's.

Mr. Belfrage is also the author of "The American Inquisition: 1945–1960" (*Bobbs-Merrill*), an exhaustive account of the reign of terror for leftist intellectuals in this country that began before Senator Joseph McCarthy came to power and survived his disgrace and death by some years.

He is here to promote his book, to make a number of speeches at various colleges—and to renew acquaintance with a country he has not seen since he was expelled from it in 1955. Even now he is only here because the Emergency Civil Liberties Committee and about 40 senators and congressmen (including Mike Mansfield and Jacob Javits) brought pressure on the State Department to relax the ban on admitting him even temporarily to the U.S.

"I believe this is something of a record," Mr. Belfrage said quietly, at lunch with *PW* recently with his American wife Mary. "No deportee from that period has ever been allowed to return before, to my knowledge."

He was deported under the infamous McCarran–Walter Act, adopted at the height of the McCarthy scare, which branded him an undesirable alien because of his interest in

By John F. Baker. From *Publishers Weekly* 203, no. 22 (May 28, 1973), pp. 14–16.

left-wing causes and his coeditorship, with James Aaronson, of the now defunct *National Guardian*. "Many of the younger congressmen who spoke up for me were amazed that I was still excluded because of what happened during that period," Mr. Belfrage said. "They said, 'We thought that was all over years ago,' but no, the law is still on the books, and it's still being enforced, as you can see."

He doesn't know how many people were deported for political reasons during that period—but McCarran–Walter is still keeping out of this country many notable intellectuals, particularly from Latin America, who would like at least to visit this country and accept speaking engagements or participate in international conferences held here. "Every now and then they'll let someone in, if enough fuss is made," Mr. Belfrage said. "But they do it just as an example, so they can pretend the law is not rigidly enforced." Thus the poet Pablo Neruda has been to the U.S. but the great painters Orozco and Siqueiros have been kept out for the past 20 years. "Some just don't know whether or not they can get in, others have long ago stopped trying."

Mr. Belfrage himself was finally given his visa—"stamped with all sorts of threatening hieroglyphics"—after a two-month delay, when he had about given up hope. The U.S. Consul in Mexico City who issued it had an enormous file on Mr. Belfrage by his elbow—"He kept looking through it and sighing deeply, and at one stage he actually asked me, in exactly these words: 'Is it true that you ever advocated the overthrow of the United States, either by force or by the ballot?' "

Mr. Belfrage smiled. "I don't know to this day whether they really think I'm a Communist or not. But all this is a long hangover of something that ought to have finished many years ago."

But for the accidents of war Mr. Belfrage might have become an American citizen long ago—and then his views, although they would undoubtedly have gotten him into severe trouble, would at least have been unable to get him deported.

Born in London nearly 69 years ago, he came to the U.S. in the mid-1920s and began working as a writer about movies in Hollywood. He took out his first U.S. citizenship papers in 1937, but before the procedure could be completed the war intervened. As a British citizen still, he served in British intelligence in New York, thus making it impossible to become a U.S. citizen and continue his work. At the end of the war he went to Germany and took part in the denazification of the German press—and by the time he was able to return to the U.S. the cold war was under way, and loyalty oaths and informers had become the political order of the day. "It was all very unfortunate," he says now, not having forgotten the knack of understatement.

As coeditor of the *Guardian* Mr. Belfrage was in the thick of the fight with such virtually forgotten groups as the House Un-American Activities Committee, the Subversive Activities Control Board, the Internal Security Subcommittee and the various loyalty boards. Finally, in 1953, he was called to testify and declined to do so. He spent some time in jail in New York before he became convinced that his cause was hopeless, and accepted deportation. For the last 10 years he has lived in Cuernavaca with his wife, writing and entertaining friends—for the last several of those years compiling the impressively documented "American Inquisition."

He sent it initially to Grove Press and understood they would publish it, "but then I couldn't get an answer out of them, and each time I'd be given a different secretary to talk to. I learned later, of course, that they were publishing mostly pornography at that time, and had became involved in all sorts of lawsuits."

Eventually Bobbs-Merrill took the book, "provided it was heavily cut." Altogether Mr. Belfrage took 100,000 words out (though the book is still 300 closely printed pages), and looks upon the amount of cutting philosophically. "You know, the Left always goes on too long. If you try and cut all the jargon you get to the point much quicker."

In its present form, he feels, the book "provides at least an outline—it can't be more than that—of an extraordinary period. But there are still enormous areas of this period that should be explored, and I just didn't have the research facilities there in Cuernavaca." Actually he has a well-stocked library, and the complete files of the *National Guardian*, which printed the news day by day as it was made, for the years in question.

"My book is only a sketch for what should be written about that time. But when the definitive study is done, the writer will have to take an overall view of the whole thing. There's still a tendency, in the few books written about aspects of the Inquisition, to suggest that this was something that had to be done, but which simply wasn't done very genteelly. My contention is that it was not something to be done at all. The whole idea of political trials, of being penalized for one's beliefs, is deeply alien to the American ideal."

Mr. Belfrage brought up a host of bizarre memories of those years, in his book and in his conversation. Scattered through the book are a series of what he calls "Fever Charts," one for each year, encapsulating some of the ludicrous things that were said and done during the period following World War II. And in his talk he recalls the book burnings, when intellectuals who had proscribed books on their shelves quietly burned them because they could be evidence, to FBI informers, of radical tendencies. "And there were actual 'arrests,' too, of books that were taken from libraries and placed under lock and key. There was a movie, with Bette Davis as a liberal librarian—do you remember?

"And there were the informers—people who actually made a living out of turning people in and testifying against them. Harvey Matusow, for instance—he turned in hundreds of people, then he repented and said it had all been lies. What could they do? They couldn't pretend all those cases built on his lies hadn't happened. So they indicted him for perjury for saying that he'd lied, and he was jailed for five years!" Mr. Belfrage shook his head in disbelief at the strangeness of the memories of that time.

"Somebody should compile a sort of Bibliography of Lost Books for those years," Mr. Belfrage said. "After Angus Cameron was fired from Little, Brown all the publishers were scared—librarians, too. People like Howard Fast and Albert Maltz had to publish their own books themselves; nobody would touch them. And if a book was contracted for, and a publisher had to go through with it, it would be printed in a few copies, and then instantly buried—no advertising, no reviews, no library sale."

How did America seem now, revisiting it after nearly 20 years? Mr. Belfrage puffed reflectively on his pipe. "After a while you get to see everything. In nearly every way America is a better place to live today for anyone with radical political views. In our day leftists were just talking to themselves, and afraid all the time of being overheard and reported. Now the air is much clearer, and everyone talks up. And the blacks have made an extraordinary advance. Back then, if you had any black friends you were automatically suspect as a subversive—why else would you be friends with a black? And if one came into a restaurant like this, he'd either be told it was full, or seated way in the back out of sight. And you can see how different they feel now, from the way they walk in the street."

He smiled again. "One of the things the consul told me in Mexico City when he was doubtful whether I'd be allowed in was: 'After all, we have plenty of people in the U.S. right now expressing your sort of views. Why should we import them?' "

Allan R. Bosworth

THE SEARCH for the right author to tell the story of "America's Concentration Camps" occupied nearly a year of editor Merrill Pollack's time. He finally found him in the person of former Naval Intelligence officer Allan R. Bosworth, through the suggestion of Captain Bosworth's literary agent, Marie Rodell, who brought the two men together. Now "America's Concentration Camps" is about to be published by Norton, on February 20, and the advance reviews, including one in the *PW* of December 12, 1966, are very good. Bantam has bought paperback rights.

Mr. Pollack had served in the 10th Mountain Division in World War II. Like all veterans of the Italian campaign, he knew of the extraordinary war record racked up in Italy and later in France by the Nisei "Go for Broke" 100th Infantry Battalion and 442nd Regimental Combat Team. It was not until he returned from the war, however, that Mr. Pollack heard for the first time of the mass evacuation on brutally short notice of all West Coast Japanese to lonely and remote "relocation" camps, under Executive Order No. 9066, signed by President Roosevelt. While the "Go for Broke" young Japanese were fighting and dying in Europe and other Japanese Americans were serving as intelligence men or interpreters with the army in the Far East, their families were forced to stay in the camps.

The story behind all of this, as told in "America's Concentration Camps," is one that involves a massive violation of civil rights and the fomentation of race hatred. At the time only a few American voices spoke out against the tide of wartime hatred and panic directed at anything Japanese.

By Barbara A. Bannon. From *Publishers Weekly* 191, no. 6 (February 6, 1967), p. 39.

The American Civil Liberties Union was a notable voice of sanity. The then Attorney General of California, Earl Warren, was one of those most vehemently demanding evacuation of the West Coast Japanese. He declined to give Captain Bosworth any statement on the matter for his book in the light of events since 1942.

PW talked with Mr. Pollack and Captain Bosworth about "America's Concentration Camps." Captain Bosworth enlisted in the navy in 1922, eventually working his way into Naval Intelligence and continuing undercover work of this sort while he also acted as a newspaperman. (His journalistic employers were aware of his double role.)

One of the factors that interested the captain in writing a book for Norton about what had happened to Japanese Americans in World War II, he told *PW*, was that he had been working before the war with the FBI to police *known* foreign agents and spies. He was personally aware the Japanese Americans presented no great threat to wartime America. Naval Intelligence even in 1942 took the strong position that there was no need to assume that *all* Japanese Americans were potential spies and saboteurs, but protection of the West Coast was officially assigned to Army Intelligence which took an entirely opposite point of view. Interestingly enough, in Hawaii, where the attack on Pearl Harbor occurred, there *never* was throughout the war years any forced round-up of all Nisei. The situation was handled there with far less panic than on the mainland.

While the Nisei have come through their ordeal well, the fact remains that the United States Supreme Court in upholding the constitutionality of the 1942 Evacuation Act has, in the opinion of Captain Bosworth, set a dangerous precedent which could potentially be turned against any minority group, Cubans, perhaps, if another and worse missile crisis arose; or Chinese if the situation in Vietnam brought the United States into open conflict with Red China.

The United States Supreme Court in the Korematsu case decided after the war upheld the constitutionality of the Evacuation. It was not a unanimous decision, however, and Captain Bosworth quotes from Justice Robert M. Jackson's dissenting opinion to show the danger that his research into this book convinces him still exists. Justice Jackson wrote that "a military order, however unconstitutional, is not apt to last longer than the military emergency. . . . But once a judicial opinion rationalizes such an order to show that it conforms to the Constitution . . . the Court for all time has validated the principle of racial discrimination in criminal procedure and of transplanting American citizens. *The principle then lies about like a loaded weapon ready for the hand of any authority that can bring forward a plausible claim of an urgent need.*" The italics are Captain Bosworth's.

Archibald Cox

ARCHIBALD COX, whose insistence on getting the Watergate tapes from President Nixon led to his dismissal as Special Prosecutor, and then to the "fire-storm" that helped hasten Nixon's departure from office, never wrote a book on his Watergate experiences; sometimes, in fact, it feels as if he was almost alone among the participants in that bizarre episode in not doing so.

It's not that he wasn't asked, as the genial Harvard law professor told *PW* recently. "Several people approached me for a narrative account of my Watergate experiences, a sort of Watergate diary of my time as Special Prosecutor. But I turned away from anything like that—I don't think it's important. Now if someone had come to me and said never mind about the narrative, give us your thoughts about American government, about the White House and the power of the presidency in relation to the whole affair, I'd probably have been interested. And, of course, they'd have wound up with *some* personal narrative anyway, but introduced in my own way."

As it is, however, nobody did, and Archibald Cox is currently far too busy doing three things at once to think of a new book for some time to come. What *has* just appeared under his name, from Oxford University Press, is a thoughtful and learned small book called "The Role of the Supreme Court in American Government," which is based on a series of lectures he gave last year at All Souls College, Oxford—and in which, sure enough, he includes his own observations of the significance of the Watergate business in illustrating the power and influence of the High Court in political matters.

By John F. Baker. From *Publishers Weekly* 209, no. 9 (March 1, 1976), pp. 8–9.

Cox gave his lectures at Oxford while spending some time in England as a visiting Fellow in Cambridge, and recalls with amusement the attitude of the legendary John Sparrow, Warden of All Souls, toward the journalistic notoriety of his guest. "The editors of the university student magazine wanted to interview me, and Sparrow just couldn't understand why I'd bother to talk to them; he sat through the interview muttering about how ignorant they were." Another possible problem was more smoothly resolved. As part of his discussion of the Supreme Court handling of censorship cases, Cox had to cite one in which a young man had a vulgar four-letter word printed on his T-shirt. "Could I actually say the word to my Oxford audience? I put it to Sparrow, and he ruled that since the word was actually part of the Court's judgment, I could quote from it, and that would be all right."

Cox gives his hearty booming laugh; he is somewhat deaf in one ear, and like many deaf people tends to talk loudly, but his conversation is so full of zest that it seems totally suited to a high-volume delivery.

One of the lectures—and therefore chapters—in his book is about the Court's role in safeguarding individual liberty, and deals with most of the major cases in recent years involving freedom of the press. He feels highly encouraged by current developments in this area, and although he comments in his book that the Court's *Gertz* decision suggests some cooling of the libertarian enthusiasm of the Warren Court, "the freedom from risk of liability which the Berger Court has accepted is more significant than what little is left of the law of libel." He feels, in fact, that the American press now has very wide latitude indeed in reporting evidence of corruption in office, and adds: "I don't really think Watergate would have been uncovered in England, with the press subject to the sort of restraints it is there."

Unlike some civil libertarians, however, he thinks there must be some restraints on freedom to report *everything* at any time; "You should be able to publish anything except what will clearly cause overwhelming harm," he comments and suggests that a newspaper should be prevented for instance, from publishing such information as, during WW II, that the British had broken the Nazi command codes. He sees press freedom as being "constantly enlarged," and adds: "You may differ about where you think it has been enlarged to, but the process of enlargement is continuous." On questions like the gag rule on pre-trail publicity he is a bit more ambivalent: "I'm not particularly in favor of the gag, but the press can be so shrill on some of these issues, acting as if they were being gagged for the first time ever, whereas in fact their ability to report in such detail on an accused is still very new. One of the ways you could certainly cut down on pretrial publicity is to clamp down on public prosecutors leaking material to the press—that's the best way to get at a lot of the abuses."

Cox, as noted, is a busy man on three fronts currently (or four, if you count the efforts he is making for Oxford on behalf of his new book). He continues to maintain a busy teaching schedule at Harvard, he is chairman of a commission set up to reform court procedures in Massachusetts (which, he says, suffers trial delays greater than any other state in the country) and he is extremely active in Congressman Morris Udall's presidential campaign. The day *PW* saw him he had, in fact, introduced Udall at a Boston rally the previous night, and was still glowing about the enthusiastic turnout. Cox has also starred as Udall's chief supporter in a series of newspaper ads, and *PW* could not resist asking whether he had in fact written the copy for these ads himself. "Yes, indeed," he cries, "I *always* write my own material. Even if someone supplied me with a text of the quality of a Shakespearean sonnet, I'd throw it away and do it over in my own words."

Cox has some unusual reflections on the subject of lawyers and how they write. "When I write anything, it's always for the ear, not the eye. I have to hear it in my head first of all, as if I'm delivering a brief. And I have to wait until the last minute, when I'm all charged up. When I was Watergating, for instance," (this appears to be a coinage of his own, but he rolls it off the tongue as if it were common usage) "and I had to have something for the press, I would never prepare it much in advance. I had to leave it to the last minute, and then I'd get my charge, and be able to deliver." And he says he never keeps notes, or a diary, on anything, even though he has been through one of the most extraordinary experiences of the decade. "One of the penalties of being a lawyer is that you don't remember things, and you don't particularly *want* to remember them. As a lawyer you have to force-feed your mind for your hour in court with all sorts of material you'll never ever need again, and somehow there's no room for anything else. So you get into the habit of letting everything else slide."

A publisher, he said, had approached him with the idea of a book covering his various experiences in government: in his time he has been Solicitor General, in addition to Watergate Special Prosecutor, and has frequently represented the government in cases before the Supreme Court. He was also a member of the wartime Wage Stabilization Board; but although he can see that he has been a participant in many important matters, the thought of involving himself in what he calls his own "life research project" leaves him dubious: "I doubt that it's worth it."

Yet, as an academic, he cannot resist the temptation to leave behind him "something major" in terms of published work. He is already the author, with Derek Bok, of one of the basic texts on labor law, but his interest now has shifted toward constitutional law. He plans a new series of lectures on the subject at Northwestern a year from now which, he says, might form the basis of a new book. "Like all academics, I want to prove that I really *can* do scholarly work, and stop being so busy on other things."

Usually, as a Harvard professor, he has dutifully published through the Harvard University Press, feeling, as he puts it, that "one should support home industries." He is on the board of directors of the Press, helped to choose present Press director Arthur Rosenthal, whom he warmly praises for "turning the whole operation around." Asked to compare Harvard's efforts with those of Oxford, he becomes the soul of diplomacy. "Well, when you go to another university, I think their Press has first call on what you say there. . . . Comparisons are odious, but let's just say that Oxford has been very active in promotion, and there have been times I have felt that Harvard could be stronger in this area."

Has he read many of the post-Watergate books himself? "I've dipped in here and there, but not much really." His assistant in the Special Prosecutor's office, James Doyle, has been writing his own account of that stirring time, and Cox notes with a wry twinkle that his manuscript includes a dramatic account of how, on the day of the final press conference in which Cox insisted that the president must hand over the tapes, immediately followed by his dismissal, an important call came into the office and his staff was unable to find him. In the end he was discovered in a nearby Brentano's bookstore, browsing. "Jim has it that this is an example of how calm I was at this time of crisis, but I'm afraid he hasn't got it quite right.

"I wasn't really calm at all; it was just that tension in the office was so high that I couldn't stand it, and I felt I had to go out and do something—and I felt that a bookstore was a peaceful place where no one would notice me."

Walter Cronkite

AT THE AGE of 54, CBS-TV's prestigious news editor and evening newscast anchorman, Walter Cronkite, is rated the newsman's newsman by most of the professionals in his business. Much of the authority, zest and conviction that make Mr. Cronkite so totally credible on TV also comes through in his first book, "Eye on the World."

PW visited Mr. Cronkite recently in his office at the CBS Broadcast Center on New York's West Side. Teletypes were humming and a vigilant air of you-never-know-what's-coming-in filled the big newsroom as we walked through it.

Mr. Cronkite's office reminded us of a space capsule, with its ceiling-high window affording a view of the news team outside monitoring the world. "Eye on the World" was the right title for the first book Mr. Cronkite had written. A first book? Hadn't Mr. Cronkite considered writing one earlier? Of course we would have his memoirs in time. . . .

"I've had offers—many offers," he said. But finding time in his busy schedule has always been the problem. Aside from his duties as managing editor of the CBS News, Mr. Cronkite gets around a lot, makes speeches, keeps himself informed—on politics, world affairs, science (he devoured volumes preparing for the moon-landing telecasts). "Actually, although I did a lot of writing, my book was a joint effort—a lot of hard work and time put in by myself and others—" the professional in him gestured toward the newsroom outside.

"Eye on the World" contains some eloquent writing by Mr. Cronkite, expressing his deeply felt convictions about ecology, population growth, politics, war—all closely inter-

By Albert H. Johnston. From *Publishers Weekly* 199, no. 18 (May 3, 1971), pp. 15–17.

related matters. But the book is also an in-depth presentation of the total CBS News effort in 1970—an accurate, absorbing picture of the year's news big and small, Nasser's funeral, Cambodia and its aftermath, the election campaigns, human interest footnotes, Eric Sevareid's masterly commentary.

PW asked whether the book, in view of its timing, was in any sense an answer to Spiro Agnew's criticism of the news media, especially network newscasting, which had begun late in 1969. Mr. Cronkite smiled, not noticeably feeling any pain.

"No," he said, "the book was conceived as something else—actually a yearly record which would become an annual." Television viewers, Mr. Cronkite stressed, have both a right and a need to know what is happening—in our democracy, in the world—but in the kind of depth that only the printed word can bring at the present time. His book, he feels, answers that need.

"Everything—" he spread his hands, gazing out toward the busy newsroom, "*everything* we do here is an answer to Mr. Agnew."

His meaning was perfectly clear: CBS News and Mr. Cronkite are giving millions of Americans as complete, balanced, fair and accurate a picture of "the way it is" as TV can manage within its limitations. But how to explain those limitations? Mr. Cronkite nodded. "For years I've been saying—in speeches, over the air—that people should really try to understand the meaning of news. Television can only bring highlights, headlines, glimpses—at least during the regular newscasts. I've urged people to read newspapers, magazines, books. . . ."

A wide-ranging discussion was spurred on by Mr. Cronkite's stated conviction—which went contrary to the direction of Agnew's thrust—that TV news coverage does not, and can hardly (because of the average TV viewer's short attention span) be expected to do more than passing justice to the multidimensional world of events and issues. TV's strength, Mr. Cronkite feels, is eyewitness immediacy; but by its nature TV can only supplement the printed media, never supplant the written word. "That could happen only in a totally new society. But I don't have a crystal ball. . . ."

Mr. Cronkite, although he has been associated with CBS's excellent "The 21st Century" sci-tech series, doesn't manage such CBS documentaries as the controversial "Migrants" and "The Selling of the Pentagon." He cannot quite conceive TV developing, as literature has, an electronic Tolstoy or Dickens. "Tape has stifled creativity in that direction. But fellows like Mike Douglas, Morley Safer, David Wolper, Jerry Wolf, others—they're showing the way, and who knows?" He glanced out into the news room. "A lot of the boys," he said, "would like to work live again."

We quoted Rutherford Platt: "Just imagine what a field day TV commentators would have if . . . life is ever discovered other than on planet earth." Would Mr. Cronkite give his right arm to make *that* broadcast?

Mr. Cronkite chuckled, leaned forward, then became serious. He had a faraway look in his eyes. "Peace," he said, "that would be the greatest story of all. . ." Suddenly he smiled, his eyes eager: "Space flight," he said, "Space flight would be it!"

Mr. Cronkite had already acknowledged that much of his TV career has been "pale" compared to his experiences as a correspondent covering D-Day in the air over Normandy, dropping into Holland with the 101st Airborne (although his "free fall" in a Westinghouse saucer-shaped submarine to the sea bottom at 2600 feet was unforgettable—it happened around 1965). But the thought of sailing "out there" in a space capsule seemed to sum up his vital, future-oriented personality.

That, and one other thing: If TV ever were to become an arm of Big Brother, if 1984 were to come true as Orwell had described it? "I'd lose my taste for the business," Mr. Cronkite said soberly. "I'd get out. Well, most of my career is behind me—" he glanced at the busy newsroom. "But those young men out there, I think most of them wouldn't stay."

Will and Ariel Durant

MEETING WILL AND ARIEL DURANT, it seems that the tiny, frail pair could hardly outweigh their own latest huge history. But they make up in spirit and an insatiable appetite for work what they lack in size and weight: they produced "The Age of Napoleon," just published by Simon and Schuster, at the ages respectively of 90 and 77, the latest (who is to say the last?) volume in a series that began in 1935 and has now attained its 11th volume.

The Story of Civilization, as they call their series of wide-ranging histories, has grown infinitely beyond their expectations. Durant (whose speech still retains a trace of his French-Canadian background, as his wife's does of her Russian childhood) recalls that when they published the first volume, in 1935, "We thought we'd be able to do the whole thing in five books." In fact it extended to seven, finally, by 1968, to 10, "and at that stage we'd only reached 1789." (The volume, "Rousseau and Revolution," in which they did so won a Pulitzer Prize that year.)

"After that we were exhausted, and felt it was about as far as we could go," Durant says. "But around then I had one of my regular physical checkups and the doctor said I was still in perfect health." "So I asked him: 'What are you going to do with yourself for the next five years?' " puts in Mrs. Durant. The answer was, of course, back to work for the prolific pair. Five more years of reading, research, argument and eventual writing, and The Story of Civilization was up to 1815. In their introduction the Durants describe it as "a book too long in total, too short and inadequate in every part" and add: "Only the fear of that lurking Reaper made us call a halt."

By John F. Baker. From *Publishers Weekly* 208, no. 21 (November 24, 1975), pp. 6–7.

There is little doubt, however, that their hundreds of thousands of readers will not find it a bit too long or inadequate—just as professional historians (like Professor J. H. Plumb, who recently gave the book the back of his hand in a scathing *N.Y. Times Book Review* notice) will deplore its looseness, its emotionalism and its refusal to take account of the most recent scholarship. The Durants have come to cheerful terms with the fact that their many readers (the books sell, including BOMC, about 300,000 per volume) are not academics.

"We're amateurs, and I think we've learned to speak to people," Durant says. "We want to make history meaningful for ordinary readers, say intelligent high school graduates. We need specialists who devote their time to research, and who work from first-hand materials, sure, but I reject the notion that only university professors can write history. There's room for an integral view, which looks at every aspect of an age—its art, its manners and morals, its philosophy, even its architecture—and shows how they all interrelate. That's how history works—it's not all in separate compartments."

The Durants agree on their approach to history, but on hardly anything else, and it is clear that they speak true when they assert that the books are born out of constant argument. Most of The Story of Civilization is about European history, and their temperaments incline them toward different civilizations. Durant leans toward the Latin, with its combination—especially in France—of flamboyance and rationality. Mrs. Durant is strongly Anglophile. Instantly they are arguing, almost as if demonstrating their work methods (Mrs. Durant: "We differ about everything—I guess that's why we're great collaborators").

Will: French women have always played a more powerful role in history than those of any other nation.

Ariel: Nonsense. English women may not have been as showy, but they've been much more influential.

Will: There's no comparison. The elegance, the wit of the Frenchwoman created a milieu in which rational discourse could. . .

Ariel: They're brittle, superficial. The British may be clumsy, but they take the large view, and there's no doubt which country had the more lasting political influence.

Will: Well, it's true that there's no comparison between the Assembly and Parliament. . .

Ariel: That's how it goes, you see. We discuss it back and forth all day.

Will: And I'm writing it, so I usually have the last word.

Ariel: Unless I persuade him otherwise.

Will: Well. . . . I guess. Being half French, as I am, and brought up as a Catholic, I found it very difficult to give a square deal, for instance, to Martin Luther.

Ariel: (with great satisfaction): I put him right on that.

The Durants have been married for 62 years, and a little quick arith-
metic will indicate that for Ariel Durant it was a *very* early marriage. She
was in fact his pupil when he was teaching, in 1912, at a progressive school
in New York. "He had a much stronger French accent then, and I used to
mock him for the other kids," she recalls. "One day he made me stay
after class, and pointed out that I was making it very difficult for him. He
spoke to me so nicely I felt guilty about it, and after that I was on his
side." They were married shortly thereafter, when Durant was 28 and she
was 15. They set up house together and went to Columbia University
together, where they sat at the feet of such giants as Santayana, Dewey,
William James.

Then Durant began to lecture (at $5 a time) at New York's Labor
Temple. For 14 years he delivered two lectures a week, covering a huge
gamut of subjects: philosophy, history, music. "I was learning myself, all
the time. I just had to keep a jump ahead of my audiences," he smiles. "It
was during those years that I formed this amateurish outlook on history,
and learned what interested people."

One of the people who came to hear him during those years was Emmanuel Haldeman-Julius, Kansas publisher of the celebrated Little Blue
Books. He heard Durant talk on Plato and suggested it might make a little
book. "I said I was too busy, but after he went back to Kansas he sent me
a check for $150 and asked me again to write it. How could I refuse when I
had the money?" Durant wrote 11 of the Little Blue Books over the next
few years.

On to 1925, when Max Schuster and Richard Simon were just starting
out as publishers. Schuster was a keen reader of the Little Blue Books,
and suggested to Durant one day that he might rewrite the ones on philoso-
phers into one big book. "He asked me how many I thought it might sell,
and I said maybe 1100. He said he had to sell 1700 to break even." In fact
"The Story of Philosophy," as it was called, sold over two million copies
in the next few years, and became one of S&S's first huge sellers. It still
sells today (in four different editions, cloth and paper) and, says Ariel,
"We could live on the proceeds of that book alone."

Simon and Schuster, says Will, "became our best friends. They were
beautiful people. I remember Max used to sign himself in his letters to us
'Your publisher but friend.' To me he was always more like a poet than a
publisher. We'd go for walks, and whistle bits of symphonies to each
other, asking: 'Who wrote that?' He always got more right than I did."

"They were younger than us, too," sighs Ariel. "And now they're both
gone. Only Leon Shimkin is still around from that time."

The Durants moved out to California in 1943 ("It didn't seem fair to
leave Ariel here in the cold while I was traveling around in the sun lecturing") and on the seventh volume of The Story of Civilization, Ariel, who
had long collaborated on the extensive research that goes into each book,

finally got a joint byline with her husband. He still does the actual writing, but only, as has been seen, after running the gamut of a host of contrary views from his wife.

They have, however, collaborated in the writing of a joint autobiography, which is locked in a safe for posthumous publication. Being very old, the Durants are on cheerfully unafraid terms with "the Reaper," and as the *PW* interviewer rises to take his leave (towering over both of them as he does so), an impish thought strikes Ariel Durant. "You know, if Will dies first, I could rewrite the whole thing!" she exclaims. "And don't think she wouldn't!" is the rejoinder.

Bernard B. Fall

"I'M PROBABLY the only Frenchman who speaks English with a Southern Illinois accent," Dr. Bernard B. Fall says cheerfully, and a startled interviewer has to agree. The author of the new Lippincott book about the siege of Dien Bien Phu, "Hell in a Very Small Place," is a French citizen who learned English from G.I.'s after seeing service as a teenager with the Maquis in World War II.

A scholar who has made Indochina and Vietnam his special field of study, author of several books, professor of international relations at Howard University, Dr. Fall is now on a combined sabbatical and Guggenheim grant in the Far East. He talked with a *PW* interviewer shortly before leaving.

"Hell in a Very Small Place" is an enormously detailed and very interesting study of the 56-day siege of the French garrison at Dien Bien Phu, then Indochina, in 1954. In addition to research in both South Vietnam and Hanoi (where a scale model of the Dien Bien Phu battlefield is a major display), Dr. Fall interviewed many survivors of the battle in Algeria soon after that country obtained its independence from France. Approximately 70% of the garrison at Dien Bien Phu were not French, but colonials.

"It was a little like being a German doing research in France right after V-E Day," Dr. Fall recalls of his trip to Algeria, but the men talked freely, often telling him proudly how they had put to use against France the guerrilla tactics they had first seen used against them by the Vietnamese at Dien Bien Phu.

Dr. Fall was also able to persuade the French Defense

By Barbara A. Bannon. From *Publishers Weekly* 191, no. 1 (January 2, 1967), p. 21.

Minister to give him access to France's still-secret military files on Dien Bien Phu, access which had never before been granted to anyone. He told *PW* he obtained permission by persuading the minister that while Dien Bien Phu would always be a bitter defeat for France, a balanced appraisal of all the facts might demonstrate that there were more factors involved than just a French military error.

One of those factors that emerges in "Hell in a Very Small Place" is the disclosure of the key role played by the then Senate Majority Leader Lyndon B. Johnson in keeping the United States from giving the hard-pressed French garrison at Dien Bien Phu the air support it was desperately pleading for.

It is Dr. Fall's contention that massive air power given to the French in time could have kept Dien Bien Phu alive long enough for the Geneva Conference then going on to have brought about a cease-fire in Indochina on terms less devastating to the West than the total French collapse which occurred.

"If the French had not lost Dien Bien Phu *so badly*," Dr. Fall told *PW*, "perhaps the present Vietnam War could have been avoided. The North Vietnamese would have been less confident, the South Vietnamese less crushed." He believes that their tremendous victory over the French gave the North Vietnamese the idea that they could accomplish the same thing in battle with the United States and has had a profound effect on the present conflict.

The United States, Dr. Fall says, got into the war in Vietnam "piecemeal and in fits of absentmindedness. You can't just say you'll opt for just 10 percent of a war. It's like talking about 10 percent of virginity. There's no such thing." The real problem now, he thinks, is "how much further you can go with military force and not get the Russians more involved. They have their hawks, too."

In a war like the one in Vietnam he thinks, "you come to the point of exhaustion. You get to the point where you've got to prove to yourself that the other side is worse than we are, and we are better just because we are winning."

When his book comes out this month Dr. Fall will be in Vietnam again. He is engaged now in a study of the Vietcong, what makes them tick, what they are really thinking.

Frances FitzGerald

LIKE MOST OF HIS GENERATION, the *PW* interviewer did his stint in Vietnam, and one unlovely incident that lodges in memory like a flake of soot in the eye has to do with some fishermen who hid from an American search-and-destroy mission by taking refuge in underwater caves. The hollow bamboo pipes through which they gulped oxygen somehow were spotted from the air by a Cobra gunship which greased them. The dead men subsequently were listed as confirmed Vietcong casualties.

"Do you figure those guys were fishermen or VC?" an American Marine wondered.

"Enemy," replied his friend without hesitation. "You know the drill: if they're dead they're confirmed, and if they get away, we call them suspects. . ."

To those thousands of Americans who have been to Indochina and to the uncounted millions more who by now merely switch channels, or flip to the sports pages rather than heed the latest news from that battered peninsula, Vietnam is as real, persistent, aggravating (and about as interesting) as a case of athlete's foot that just won't go away.

If this is the case, then how does one explain the brushfire popularity of Frances FitzGerald's "Fire in the Lake" (*Atlantic-Little, Brown*), a book on Vietnam priced at $12.50 which has melted off the shelves since its publication last month?

Perhaps it is because Miss FitzGerald's book somehow manages to get under the skin of this ugly war which has left so many Americans feeling bewildered and morally bankrupt. In clear, often poetic language, the author illumines

By Michael Mok. From *Publishers Weekly* 202, no. 16 (October 16, 1972), pp. 16–17.

the cultural incongruences which reduce most attempts at communication between the Vietnamese and ourselves to something bizarre, like a dog trying to talk to a duck.

Here she describes a U.S. sweep through enemy-held terrain:

"For the Americans to discern the enemy within the world of the Vietnamese village was to attempt to make out figures within a landscape indefinite and vague—under water, as it were. Landing from helicopters in a village controlled by the NFL, the soldiers would at first see nothing, having no criteria with which to judge what they saw. As they searched the village, they would find only old men, women and children, a collection of wooden tools whose purpose they did not know; altars with scrolls in Chinese characters, paths that led nowhere: an economy, a geography, an architecture totally alien to them. . . . Clumsy as astronauts, they would bend under the eaves of the huts, knock over the cooking pots, and poke about at the smooth earth floor with their bayonets. . . ."

If the notion of a book on Vietnam being catapulted onto the best-seller list is surprising these days, the appearance of the author is no less so: she is a tawny, extremely comely blond, who looks much younger than her 30 years and affects neither elephant hair bracelets nor Army wristwatches other women have used to hint they've been to the war.

But cover it she did, and the articles which appeared in U.S. magazines, including the *Atlantic* and the *New York Times Magazine* earned her the 1967 Overseas Press Club Award for best interpretation of foreign affairs.

In an interview with *PW*, Miss FitzGerald speculated about the ultimate denouement of the seemingly endless war.

"Nixon is hoping that the North is going to cave in, but unless we are willing to fight on the ground, that is never going to happen; and the idea which is prevalent in some quarters that we can transform the South into a client state with light industry, seems equally illusory. It is true," she went on, "that certain areas of the country are benefiting from a (false) prosperity but this is dependent on aid, rather than trade. I just don't think it's going to work."

One example of the futility of our efforts in Vietnam, Miss FitzGerald told *PW*, is the monster port scheme at Camranh Bay: "We poured millions of dollars into the project, dredging out a deep water port, but the Vietnamese themselves have no need of a place to berth large ships, and the whole area is barren of drinking water. Americans brought it in from the outside at ruinous expense, but the likelihood of a new sponsor with an ever-filled purse is fairly remote. . ."

When she went back to Vietnam this year to cover the elections, she took a side trip to the abandoned facility for old time's sake and encountered two journalist colleagues who had just returned from a swim.

"What's it like out there?" asked Frankie, as she is known to her friends.

"The water's fine," said one of the reporters, "but the habor entrance is choked with drifting sand."

Everywhere she went, Frankie said, she encountered evidences of the U.S. withdrawal, some of them sad, others ironically amusing.

"We Americans hate to take things down," Miss FitzGerald said. "At the same time we were dismantling military installations, other groups of engineers were compulsively building swimming pools."

She also visited Kontum, which had been planned as a permanent U.S. Army base in the Central Highlands. "When I was in Vietnam the first time, this was a must stop on the itinerary of any visiting journalist; a place where you could always depend on getting very dry martinis and a charcoal-broiled steak after overflying some operation or other. Well, this time there was no sign of the American 'presence' except rusty barbed wire and, lying in a ditch, a water-logged fielder's mitt."

Miss FitzGerald said this state of affairs might strike many of us as melancholy, but it doesn't have quite the same effect on citizens of the ravaged country. "To the Vietnamese, nothing is impossible as long as this war finally comes to an end."

Before she left Saigon, she ran into a Catholic priest she remembered from her first trip. "What's going to happen now?" Frankie asked. "Never mind," was the reply. "Just leave and we will settle things for ourselves."

Frank Gervasi

ACCORDING TO a certain stereotype, the international correspondent is supposed to be a very cool customer: covering a revolution one day, a fashion show another day and finding little to choose between them in the way of importance. Frank Gervasi does not fit the stereotype. He *cares*. Evidence of this is his new book, "The Case for Israel," which Viking Press has just published. It is no more—or less—cool than a prosecuting attorney's address to a jury.

The Mediterranean has been Mr. Gervasi's "beat" since the 1930s. He was chief of International News Service's Rome bureau, then a war correspondent for *Collier's* covering the Desert War and the Middle East fronts, then an executive for the Marshall Plan in Italy. His work took him to Palestine many times, and in due course he became a convert to the cause of a Jewish homeland. "I became a non-member Zionist," is the way he now describes it.

The book had its beginnings in 1956, when Mr. Gervasi was covering the Sinai War. He was thinking of a book about the Mediterranean as an area and the need for an American policy toward the area. "We've never had one, you know," he commented the other day. "The whole thing is dictated by the oil companies." But nothing came of the book idea until this year, when the June War broke out. "I turned on the television," Mr. Gervasi said, "and there was Federenko calling the Israelis 'Nazis,' and I heard the flow of Arab rhetoric at the U.N. go largely unanswered. Abba Eban did a good job when he got here, but I still felt there was a need for a book to put it all in historical perspective. This isn't a book about war. It's not a *what* book but a *why* book."

By Roger H. Smith. From *Publishers Weekly* 192, no. 19 (November 6, 1967), pp. 13–14.

Having reached the decision to write, Mr. Gervasi started the kind of schedule to which the final phrase, "hot off the press," frequently is appropriate: a journalistic drive applied to the writing of a book. Starting June 29, he wrote the first five chapters in three weeks. Then he went to Israel for a couple of weeks, looked up old acquaintances and visited places he had seen during the 1956 war. "I'd been away for a long time," Mr. Gervasi said, "and I wanted to see the changes first-hand." Back in New York, he finished up the book and delivered the manuscript on September 27. Publication date was October 29. Total elapsed time: four months.

Having written "The Case for Israel," did Mr. Gervasi think that there was a convincing case for the Arabs? "Sure there is," he said, "and I'd love to write it. I'd like to say to Nasser, 'Look, I've written the Israeli side, and now I'd like to write yours.' It's impossible, of course, because they wouldn't cooperate, and I couldn't write such a book just from clippings. Some of the less militant Arab countries might cooperate, though, and if I could find a publisher to finance the project, I'd love to do it."

Mr. Gervasi soon hopes to get back to a long-deferred book, a full-scale biography of Garibaldi, for which he has dug up a lot of new research material. Meanwhile, he is enjoying the publication of the book on Israel. Not the least of his enjoyment comes from his fondness for the book's principal bell-ringer, his son, Tom Gervasi, publicity director of Viking Press.

Stephane Groueff

STEPHANE GROUEFF is American bureau chief for Paris *Match*. His March 27 Little, Brown book, "Manhattan Project," about the making of the first atomic bomb in this country during World War II, is to be serialized by *Reader's Digest*. International publication is planned in France, England, Italy, Japan, West Germany.

M. Groueff spent a considerable amount of time interviewing engineers, scientists and military men about the Manhattan Project, code name for the development of the atomic bomb, and he came to believe that this particularly extraordinary collaboration of the industrial, military, labor efforts of a whole nation was a peculiar product of "the American System." He has tried to explain in his book the intellectual, political, free enterprise climate that made this kind of collaboration possible in the America of the 1940s.

Paradoxically, he believes, "most of those people, practically all of them," involved in the Manhattan Project "wished that all of this effort was done for some much nobler goal." The majority of the Manhattan Project workers, while knowing they were working on a secret wartime project, did not know during the war years the actual details of what they were working on.

Some of the most interesting, previously untold stories in the book are those dealing with individuals who *never* knew, until Mr. Groueff interviewed them, that they had taken part in the making of the first atomic bomb. This happened to a group of people working for the Chiclets Company, making gum, who only knew during 1942 and 1943 that some strange things were going on in their New York factories, that mili-

From *Publishers Weekly* 191, no. 3 (January 16, 1967), p. 41.

tary people were coming and going using a particular machine of theirs, which ostensibly made cardboard boxes.

Work on the Manhattan Project was going on from 1942 to 1945 in places as far apart as Berkeley and Oak Ridge, New York and Los Alamos.

Although Stephane Groueff never asked for or received any official clearance paper from the Atomic Energy Commission in his research, he did receive help. "There were," he says of his investigations, "a lot of cool and cautious voices on the telephone when I would ask for a first interview. They would say no. I would ask if I could call back in two or three days. I knew in the meantime they would check with the AEC and when I called back the voices would be completely different and they would say yes to an interview."

The emphasis in "Manhattan Project," M. Groueff says, is on "how materially the bomb was made, by whom, what companies, what people, why they did it, how they did it, what their names were." The human element involved is M. Groueff's concern.

Alex Haley

In his dedication of "Roots" Alex Haley writes: "It wasn't planned that 'Roots' research and writing would finally take 12 years"; and there were obviously times when both he and Doubleday despaired of his ever finishing. Now that he has, however, neither the slight, scholarly author nor his publisher is likely to regret the time spent; for "Roots" bids fair to be one of the year's biggest books, and even before its publication October 1 has earned Haley a million dollars, with a hefty assist from a $6-million, 10-installment TV version that will begin showing shortly after the book reaches the stores.

"I had always wondered what a million-dollar author was like," the soft-spoken Haley mused over lunch recently. "Now I've met two of them, Arthur Hailey and Harold Robbins, and it seems I'll be one myself. I shan't exactly make whoopee with the money," he adds, rather unnecessarily. "It just means I'll have the funds to finance the travel and research for the writing I want to do. And in future I'd like not to have to have advances any more. If they're small, they're not enough, and then if you get a track record, they're too big, and that pressures you. The main thing is to be free, and that's something I've always wanted to be. If you're working for someone, that someone is determining what you're worth—and no matter what they decide you're worth, it has to be that someone is making money off you."

The status of a millionaire must have seemed impossibly remote to Haley when he left the U.S. Coast Guard in 1959 after a 20-year career there in which he had created for himself the rank of Chief Journalist. Beginning by writing letters

By John F. Baker. From *Publishers Weekly* 210, no. 10 (September 6, 1976), pp. 8, 9, & 12.

for his fellow ratings, he painstakingly taught himself the rudiments of journalism and finally began placing articles about naval life in magazines. On his release from the service, "I went straight to Greenwich Village, rented myself a basement room and prepared to starve." He came close enough. "One day I was down to 18 cents and a couple of cans of sardines, and that was *it*." A friend bought him a meal, the next day a small check came, and he struggled on. "In my new home in California I've framed that 18 cents and those sardines, as the emblems of my determination to be independent."

He resolutely refused to take a job, but it was a bad time for him. "One time I felt so low I wrote to six other black writers living in Greenwich Village, just for some companionship. None of them ever replied, but Jimmy Baldwin, who didn't know me from Adam, came right over, and spent hours talking to me, cheering me up. I've never forgotten that."

Eventually Haley began to work for *Playboy*, doing some of their first *Playboy* Interviews, and it was one he did with Malcom X that began to change his fortunes. The interview led to a commission to do the "Autobiography of Malcom X" and when Malcolm was assassinated shortly after the book was completed, it was sold to the movies and Haley began to see his first real money.

"Roots" had its genesis in a lunch Haley had with his agent Paul Reynolds and Doubleday's Kenneth McCormick and Lisa Drew in 1966—"in this very restaurant, as a matter of fact, which is one reason I wanted to meet you here today," he told *PW*. At that time he had only what he calls "a rather nebulous idea" of trying to trace his family back, through tales of his grandmother he heard as a child growing up in Tennessee, and the legends of a man the family called "the African," who had been seized by slavers in the dim past as he chopped wood to make a drum. Haley just thought there might be a book in the search for his past, but at that time he hadn't been to Africa, and "wasn't all that fired up about it." If he couldn't trace any African angle, he was prepared just to make the book a black American family saga. Doubleday gave him an advance of $5000, enabling him to go to Africa to see if he could pursue the trail of his past into the remote rural villages of Gambia—and it would be easy to say that the rest is history, except that it involved years of agonizingly hard work, financial problems and bitter feelings for Haley.

He tells the story of his search in the closing chapters of "Roots"—how with a bare handful of clues he pinpointed the African language of his forebear Kunta Kinte, eventually even found the Gambian village where his ancestor had been seized by slavers, then ransacked British and American naval records for the very ship on which Kinte was brought to colonial American in 1767. What he doesn't indicate there is the despair he sometimes experienced that he would ever finish. He piled up material obsessively, spending long months talking to the old *griots*—verbal historians—of the African villages, poring over missionary records, naval records, the history of the slave trade. He even crossed the Atlantic on a freighter, deliberately incarcerating himself in a dark hold day after day, so as to experience as nearly as possible what the crossing felt like to a slave. "That was the hardest part, writing about the slave ship. There were times on that boat I felt like jumping off. I was deep in debt by then, felt I'd never finish the damn book. One time I must have been almost mad with despair, because I went into a sort of dream, and I really thought I heard the dead voices of my family talking to me, encouraging me. That was what kept me going in the end. After that I felt I really had to do it, for them."

Haley seems always able to see the humorous side of even his own more dramatic pronouncements. "Yeah, you could say this book was a long time aborning," he grins suddenly. "I'd keep telling Doubleday I'd finish any day now, but I never did. I worked on it solidly for the last two and a half years in Jamaica, then in February they sent me my last draft for what was meant to be a final read-through. It was supposed to take me no more than a couple of days, but I knew when I saw it I'd have to do more work on it. I hid out in the Hotel Commodore so that Doubleday wouldn't know where I was, and I did a whole new chapter and a lot of rewriting. It took me two weeks, and for last 48 hours I worked around the clock. Then I sent it off by messenger, and got on a plane for Indiana, where I was supposed to give a lecture, and the next thing I remember is when I woke up there, knowing it was all over."

Long before it was all over, however, word of "Roots" had spread, partly by way of Haley's indefatigable lecturing—"I figure I must have talked to over a million people about the book in the last six years, and if they all buy a copy we're in"—and partly by way of the Hollywood grapevine, which he describes as "even yakkier than the publishing one." Even before he had finished, last fall, representatives of David Merrick and David Wolper were bidding for the movie rights. Wolper won, with an ABC-TV special serialization in mind (hot on the heels of the enormous success of the Irwin Shaw "Rich Man, Poor Man" series) and the company went right into production. "They were actually writing their scripts direct from my ms. I was scared at one time they'd catch up with me from behind, and want a script for a section I hadn't written yet."

ABC spent $6-million on the filming, a record for a TV production, and in recent weeks Haley has been on hand in Georgia and Hollywood to observe the shooting. "They reconstructed the African village in Georgia, and it looked so incredibly authentic to me that I actually bought the house where they had Kinte being born." He found, too, that the black actors identified so strongly with their roles that during the filming of a slave ship sequence one "slave" got so carried away that he hurled the white actor playing the shipmaster overboard.

In a book that reads so much like an exciting novel—until the closing chapters in which Haley describes his detective work—how much is verifiable fact and how much is made up? "I call it 'faction,' " Haley says. "All the major incidents are true, the details are as accurate as very heavy research can make them, the names and dates are real, but obviously when it comes to dialogue, and people's emotions and thoughts, I had to make things up. It's heightened history, or fiction based on real people's lives."

His next project is already nearing completion. It is a strictly nonfiction account of the details of his long odyssey, a huge expansion of the material only sketched in the closing pages of "Roots." "It's called 'My Search for 'Roots,' and it's supposed to be ready in October," Haley says. "Of course, I can't *promise*, what with the tour for 'Roots' and all. Then after that there'll be a detailed study of Henning, Tennessee, where I was born and grew up. I've done all the research for that, and it'll be a pleasure to be able to complete a book in under 12 years."

Haley is a dedicated writer—"There's nothing I'd rather do, except perhaps be a surgeon. In many ways it's similar delicate, careful work, and I *act* like a surgeon. When I'm writing I take six showers a day, and wash my hands maybe 20 times. And it's a physical thing with me. When it's going well, I find myself tapping my foot in rhythm with the keys, as if there's a cadence going. I like to do first drafts at night, when I'm tired, and then do the surgical work in the morning when I'm sharp—and I love writing on a ship at sea. In fact, if I had my druthers, I'd spend half the year at sea."

He paused, with the slow grin that has been winning his lecture audiences for years. "You've got me talking about writing. Most people want me to talk about being black, and that's OK too, but I do love to talk about writing!"

Lee Lockwood

TALK ABOUT CUBA with photographer-journalist Lee Lockwood, whose "Castro's Cuba, Cuba's Fidel" was published last month by Macmillan, was preceded in an interview—by talk about North Vietnam. Mr. Lockwood was the first American photographer to be admitted to North Vietnam since 1954, and *Life* magazine, in its April 7 issue, devoted its cover plus 16 pages to Mr. Lockwood's North Vietnam report.

Mr. Lockwood's trip to North Vietnam began in Cuba, where in May, 1966, he requested a visa from the North Vietnam Embassy. In September, he was told the visa would be coming through in a few weeks, and finally it came through in January. He went down to get it.

"To go to Cuba now," Mr. Lockwood said, "you go to the New York passport office and apply for permission. You must do this for each trip. I can now go to North Vietnam any time I want to, but I have to get permission for Cuba each time. Then you go to Mexico City, where you wait around a couple of days for the documents that will enable you to get back into Mexico. Then you wait for the plane. Cubana Airlines has service twice a week between Mexico City and Havana, when the planes run."

In Havana, Fidel Castro came around to the hotel for a drink with Mr. Lockwood, and the gist of what the Cuban leader told him about North Vietnam was this: "You will see how determined those people are to fight to the end, and no amount of U.S. bombing will make any difference. Any guerilla revolutionary movement fighting on its home ground can never lose as long as the leaders make no mis-

By Roger H. Smith. From *Publishers Weekly* 191, no. 18 (May 1, 1967), p. 21.

takes. Eventually the U.S. has to lose that war, though it may take 50 years. You may render the U.S. a service by showing the wisdom of getting out. We'd just as soon see the U.S. waste its energies in Vietnam, but the North Vietnamese are our friends and they are being victimized.''

"The Cubans," Mr. Lockwood added, "feel very militant about the Vietnam War, and Cuba is the staunchest and least opportunist of North Vietnam's allies."

Mr. Lockwood's association with Fidel Castro dates from December 31, 1958, when as a free-lance photo-journalist for a West German magazine, he arrived to cover the Castro takeover and the fall of Batista. He went back to Cuba several times on assignments in 1959–60, and in 1964 he represented *Newsweek* when Castro invited 30-odd American newspapers and three magazines to cover the July 26 independence celebrations. At the end of that visit, Mr. Lockwood mentioned to Castro that he might do a book about him. Castro was enthusiastic. In May, 1965, Mr. Lockwood went back to Cuba for three months of photography and research, during which he had a week-long interview with the Cuban leader.

"The only part of the book that Fidel edited was the interview itself," Mr. Lockwood said. "I'd expected some kind of strong reaction from him, but the changes he made were minor and some of them I changed back. He liked the interview very much and thought he hadn't been misinterpreted. He asked what would be in the rest of the book, and I read him the chapter titles. Then he said, 'My part of the book is the interview. The rest of the book is Lee's, and I will look at that when it comes out.' "

Castro has now seen the book, Mr. Lockwood added, but has not expressed any opinion of it.

Mr. Lockwood's immediate future plans include writing some magazine articles based on his North Vietnam observations "but not a book yet," he said, "not on the basis of a limited, one-month initial visit. But I hope to go back to North Vietnam later this year and after that, if I feel I know enough, I might do a book about it."

Norman Mailer

As NORMAN MAILER sees it, "the next Apollo shot (Apollo 14, January 31) is particularly frightening because they're going up without quite knowing what went wrong on the last one [when the moon landing was aborted]."

The author of "Of a Fire on the Moon" (*Little, Brown*) was in New York the other day, talking with characteristic candor about the book and the problems he faced in writing it, not the least of which was the frustrating fact that never at any time before or after the moon landing was he permitted to meet with astronauts Armstrong, Aldrin and Collins.

"I actually wrote them a letter at one time, saying 'you wouldn't let a commercial pilot fly Apollo, why not let someone who is recognized as one of the better journalists in the world meet you in order to write about you?" he said. "Armstrong replied with 'your argument is lucid and convincing, but the answer is no.' After the book was written I did talk to Aldrin on the phone and he allowed as how he would like to get together with me, but then somehow he seemed to get a hint that there might be girls in the offing and he withdrew and wasn't interested. He sounded like a strong and virile liar to me." As for a reaction to the book from NASA, it has been "zero," Mailer said.

Mr. Mailer sees America's astronauts as "very complicated fellows, extraordinarily shielded, maybe for the best reasons or the worst. All I did meet had a presence you respected. I think they embody the peculiar schizophrenia of our time. They all have two personalities, a public one and a private one."

By Barbara A. Bannon. From *Publishers Weekly* 199, no. 4 (January 25, 1971), pp. 177–179.

In the "totalitarian bag" that is big-time government bureaucracy, in order to get advanced by NASA to the point where you can actually fly a mission, the astronauts, Mr. Mailer said, "have to play a tough, mean game and occasionally they have to make an imaginative move."

Given the restrictions imposed by NASA and the tremendous volume of technological data which no layman could entirely absorb, Mailer found himself in a very difficult position when he tackled "Of a Fire on the Moon." "How do you go at understanding a large modern phenomenon like this with partial information?" he asked. "This book was written by way of dramatizing that particular problem. What is interesting about it is that it's the first time I know of that a writer who takes himself fairly seriously got himself into a position where it was almost impossible to come back with a kill if you went at it straight and didn't cheat.

"I had a moment of extraordinary woe when I realized that there was no way to cover this thing journalistically and come back with a book I could accept. Then I really began to recognize the moon landing as an event no man could ever dominate with his ego, and I realized I was going to have to work 20 times harder on the book than I had thought I would."

An interviewer suggested that he had gotten the impression from "Of a Fire on the Moon" that Mailer "had come to bury Wernher von Braun, but then did not."

"A man tries to look for a pattern to a story like this," he answered. "One pattern is to hope for a sensational villain. I went to Huntsville, Alabama, to meet von Braun with this idea in mind, but then I discovered he had sort of lost touch with the world and the Mephistophelian powers he had helped unleash. It would not have been fair to cast him as a villain and the 22 percent of me that considers itself a gentleman decided it would not be at all gentlemanly."

"There are areas of ambiguity about the landing on the moon at least as large as when Columbus came back from the discovery of the New World," he continued. "The way the NASA program is set up a man is absolutely geared to fulfill his mission, but it may get to the point sometime in the future when, as ground control begins to relax, then the men up there may, also." It's not impossible to conceive of some future astronaut out in space, Mailer believes, deciding to ignore some of the "subtle suggestions" being beamed at him by NASA and do something completely on his own.

"Would you have liked to make the moon trip yourself?" an interviewer asked Mailer. "Sure I would," he shot back. "If I could have gone up it would have been a better book. I keep thinking I'm going to spend all my life pleading with NASA to send me to the moon, and then they'll finally decide to send John Updike.

William Manchester

WILLIAM MANCHESTER, whose "The Arms of Krupp" was published by Little, Brown on November 25, works in a large, quiet office on the second floor of the Wesleyan University Library in Middletown, Conn. There is no name on the office door. The first floor receptionist carefully screens Mr. Manchester's visitors to make sure they are *really* expected.

The security measures may seem a bit overdone, but probably they can be traced to two things: Mr. Manchester's reluctant appearance as a figure of public controversy two years ago during the "battle of the book"—Jacqueline Kennedy's effort to censor his "The Death of a President"; and his experiences as a one-man counterespionage force against the Krupp empire as he conducted his research for the new book.

Inside the office at Wesleyan, the writer's tools are arrayed on flat surfaces within easy reach of a swivel chair on wheels: pens, pads, typewriter, reference books. On the wall above the work table are maps of Germany, the Ruhr and Essen, home of Krupp. The visitor is shown some Kennedy memorabilia: a snapshot of JFK, an inscribed photo of Jacqueline, copies of "The Death of a President" in 16 different foreign languages (it has just become the number-one best seller in Rumania, Mr. Manchester says, with some amazement) and the Dag Hammarskjöld International Medal for Literature, which the book won in 1967. Mr. Manchester and the Kennedys are still friends, he says, and ultimately the Kennedy Library will get between $4- and $5-million in royalties from the book. "It's ironic," Mr. Man-

By Roger H. Smith. From *Publishers Weekly* 194, no. 22 (November 25, 1968), pp. 6–7.

chester said to a visitor just before Election Day, "that all they wanted to cut from the book were things that might reflect badly on LBJ. They weren't things about Jackie at all."

Mr. Manchester interrupted his Krupp research and writing for two years in order to write "The Death of a President." When he finished it, he rushed right back to the Krupp project. "It was exhilarating to be back writing about the Franco-Prussian War and not have to care who won," he said.

"The Arms of Krupp, 1587-1968" is a unique book in that it is not only the definitive chronicle of a dynasty but is published in the year that the dynasty ended. Alfried, the last Krupp to head the giant industrial complex, died last year, and the firm is now a public company, producing a vast range of civilian and paramilitary products. Much of Krupp's postwar return to eminence has come from business with developing countries.

When Mr. Manchester talks about Krupp, he tends to use political metaphors (state-within-a-state). When he talks about his research, there are overtones of espionage. "In the U.S. there has never been a business like Krupp," he told *PW*. "It's as though General Motors had always been owned by one individual." At the beginning, Krupp agents were not enthusiastic about Mr. Manchester's project. A stranger photographed him as he got off the plane in the Ruhr to do research. He was shadowed, and his rooms were searched. A Krupp agent—who was "just checking"—tracked him to an unmarked office deep in the National Archives, where he was working on "The Death of a President."

But security cannot be total in an organization as large as Krupp. Someone knocked on Mr. Manchester's door in Essen one night and left a portfolio of Krupp family letters of the 1930s. Repeated calls on public relations men eventually led to interviews with executives in the organization and members of the Krupp family, including Alfried. He gained access to the family archive and though this was limited, feels that, "In one way or another, I got everything I needed." In an earlier effort to gain Krupp cooperation, he had sent copies of two of his earlier books, "A Rockefeller Family Portrait" and "Portrait of a President," which showed that Mr. Manchester was not anti-capitalism or anti-big business. What the Krupps did not know was that Mr. Manchester, as preparation for his researches, had read the complete 14,000-page transcript of Alfried's Nuremberg trial as a major Nazi war criminal, and this enabled him to put his subsequent findings in context. Included in the transcript were addresses of witnesses against Krupp. Mr. Manchester sent out hundreds of letters to these people and got some replies that are incorporated in the book, with names changed, as examples of slave labor conditions under Krupp.

"I had wanted to write a history of Germany for some time," Mr. Manchester told *PW*, "and Krupp provided the handle. The story of Krupp, everything good and everything bad, is really the story of Germany, which is what makes the book so long." Toward the end of the long book comes the horror of slave labor and the concentration camps, and the author's sense of outrage, up to that point pretty well held in check, rises to the surface. Mr. Manchester makes no apology for this. "Krupp ran 138 concentration camps, including one for little children," he told *PW*. "A historian can't say something like, 'Many people think this unfortunate.'

"I believe there is such a thing as national character. The German national character is brutish, but it is also idealistic. But I'm not anti-German any more than I'm anti-Dallas. I couldn't have written this book without the cooperation of some Germans. Remember, Krupp was convicted on the testimony of some Germans, who knew what might happen to them in reprisal."

The anti-German charge already has been aired in the press in Germany, where Kindler Verlag will publish the book late this year or early next. A more explosive issue for the American press is likely to be the book's account of how in 1951 Alfried Krupp, after serving six years of his sentence, was released and had his property restored by John J. McCloy, American Commissioner to Germany. He was released when the cold war was at its coldest, when the U.S. needed a committed Germany and Krupp steel.

"It was wrong to release Alfried," Mr. Manchester commented. "But McCloy thought Alfried was a playboy and not really responsible. He hadn't read the 14,000 pages of testimony. Was Alfried responsible? Eichmann said he never killed anybody, he was just in the transportation business. Alfried said the same thing. Responsibility in these circumstances poses a moral dilemma and one that I wrestled with for a long time while I was working on the book."

Robert K. Massie

WHEN ROBERT AND SUE MASSIE's son, Bobby, was six months old, they discovered he had hemophilia. Bobby is now 11. And some 10½ years after his parents first had to face up to what it means to have a child with this dread blood disease, his father, Robert K. Massie, a journalist who has worked for *Collier's*, *Newsweek*, and the *Saturday Evening Post*, has produced one of the most fascinating historical studies of the fall, "Nicholas and Alexandra: An Intimate Account of the Last of the Romanovs and the Fall of Imperial Russia" (*Atheneum*). It is already on *PW*'s best seller list only a few weeks after publication. There is a direct connection between Bobby Massie's hemophilia and the book. It was his research into all that is now known about hemophilia (much has been discovered just in the last 15 or 20 years) that drew Robert Massie's attention to one of the most famous hemophiliacs in history, the boy Alexis, last czarevitch of Russia. The author's study of Nicholas and Alexandra, Alexis' loving and tragic parents, makes very clear that during one of the most fateful periods in modern history, the last 16 months before the final outbreak of the Russian Revolution, Alexis' hemophilia played an indirect but decisive role in what was to come. It was because the czarina placed such faith in the corrupt self-styled monk, Rasputin, who could at times relieve Alexis of excruciating pain, that he was permitted to become the power behind the throne, capriciously and arrogantly dictating policy and dismissing ministers. If this final débacle had not occurred, it is possible that Russia might have turned to some form of constitutional monarchy without going all the way to violent revolution.

By Barbara A. Bannon. From *Publishers Weekly* 192, no. 12 (September 18, 1967), p. 39.

Hemophilia is carried through the woman's line, but affects only men, except in the rarest combination of circumstances. It was Queen Victoria who spread it through her offspring to the Romanoffs and royal families in Germany and Spain. It can lie dormant for many generations, then reappear (technically it could still reappear in the British royal family, although the likelihood of its ever doing so seems increasingly remote). It can also erupt suddenly as a mutation of the chromosomes. This appears to have been the case with the Massies. Mrs. Massie, who is Swiss, can trace her family back for nine generations and through 42 male relatives without ever finding the slightest sign of any hint of hemophilia before it struck young Bobby. A writer and researcher herself, she helped her husband with much of the background data and final editing of "Nicholas and Alexandra." The chapter "A Mother's Agony," which describes very movingly the czarina's concern for her son, was written only after Robert and Sue Massie sat down and talked very frankly together as parents of a hemophiliac child about what this means to the mother in particular. "Nicholas and Alexandra" is dedicated to Suzanne Massie.

Sue Massie's Swiss mother had been marooned in Russia on a girlhood visit at the time of the Revolution and forced to remain there for six years, and she passed on to her daughter some vivid impressions of what that period was like to live through.

Most of the research for "Nicholas and Alexandra" was done right in New York, at the main public library and at Columbia University. Mr. Massie says he wrote the book for two reasons. First, to set the record straight about Nicholas and Alexandra, to express what he found to be the truth about them as human beings caught in a terrible dilemma; and second, to explain to some degree to the general reading public something about hemophilia and what it involves. The writer on history whose work he most admires is Barbara Tuchman, and he tried to keep her in mind as a model.

One of the most interesting sources of information for him proved to be the voluminous correspondence of Alexandra to Nicholas which was carefully kept by her, then dumped by the revolutionaries into a storeroom at Ekaterinburg where the last of the Romanoffs were murdered. It was later found and published *in toto* in the early 1920s. The czarina had never imagined that her intimate letters would be published. "They are almost Joycean in tone," Mr. Massie reports, "she didn't keep any secrets back. There was constant talk back and forth between her and Nicholas about Alexis." These letters, interestingly enough, were written in English. Alexandra, a German princess, never learned to speak Russian very well, and Nicholas, a first cousin to George V, was fluent in English and very much at home in it.

After completing "Nicholas and Alexandra" this past spring, Mr. Massie and his wife paid their first visit to Russia. Although both had become deeply involved personally in the lives of the last of the Romanoffs and had come to think of them sympathetically as a family they knew well, they were very much impressed by what they saw in Soviet Russia today of regard for the beauties of the past. Many of the royal palaces were destroyed, not by rampaging revolutionaries in 1917, but by the Germans in World War II, and these palaces are being painstakingly and exquisitely restored now in exact duplication of what they were like under the Romanoffs. The difference is that they are now open to all the people of Russia, who take a deep pride of ownership in this aspect of their past.

Eleven-year-old Bobby Massie is now reading "Nicholas and Alexandra," his father reports, and has already become fascinated by the character of Alexis, so many of whose harrowing agonies he has shared. "He keeps asking me questions about Alexis," says Mr. Massie, "and some of them I can't answer despite all my research. He wants to know such things as, 'Did Alexis like ice cream? Did he know how to swim?' "

One of the things the Massies have learned about hemophiliac children from their own experience is that when they are happy and the adults around them can manage to control their fright if serious bleeding starts, the children will bleed less. This, he thinks, may be one clue to Rasputin's ability to soothe Alexis. Quite apart from any hypnotic powers Rasputin may have possessed (and modern doctors are somewhat dubious about hypnotism's ability to completely control bleeding), he was a marvelous storyteller. He would keep Alexis enthralled for hours. He was boisterous and loud and full of life, and this must have seemed a magic contrast to the little Russian prince, whose parents showed their worries so openly and poignantly.

Samuel Eliot Morison

SAMUEL ELIOT MORISON is a profoundly contented man. Seated at a desk at the Oxford University Press, busily inscribing copies of his just-published "The European Discovery of America: The Southern Voyages," he exudes the calm relief of one who knows that a long life has been well spent, and who has achieved a lifelong ambition with some time to spare.

Sipping a glass of Campari ("I take it as a medicine—the quinine helps my heart fibrillations") and seeming only slightly daunted by a round of interviews and celebratory meals during a two-day visit to New York from his Maine retreat, Admiral Morison bears his 87 years lightly. It feels inevitable to call him "Admiral"—as the people at Oxford do. His life, as man and historian, has been intimately bound to the sea, his seamed and weather-beaten face is just such a face as might have been worn by one of his favorite 15th- and 16th-century explorers. And his manner—downright, spare and salty—is very much that of the old Yankee sea dog.

"This book may be considered the signoff on my career," he says flatly of "The Southern Voyages," which with its companion volume "The Northern Voyages," published three years earlier, makes for a massively detailed and richly readable account—already being hailed by some fellow historians as definitive—of all that is known about those who discovered the New World.

"All my life I have wanted to write the full history of the discovery of America, and now I've done it. And I'm so grateful I've been able to retain my faculties to finish it. It's

By John F. Baker. From *Publishers Weekly* 206, no. 19 (November 4, 1974), pp. 6–7.

good that the reviewers didn't have to say: 'Poor old Morison—he's a bit past it.' "

Now the grand work is completed, he will write no more: "I'm too old and tired now, and I've finished everything I promised myself I would do 50 years ago. Why should I jeopardize my reputation by going on, like one of those ancient historians who fall into decline and finally receive only pitying reviews?"

It is a proud conclusion to a professional life of remarkable productivity that has been garlanded with innumerable prizes and awards (including two Pulitzers) and countless medals and honorary degrees. He has written the official history of U.S. naval operations in World War II (in 15 volumes; he joined the Navy especially to write it, soon after Pearl Harbor, was in "two or three naval battles and enjoyed every minute"); a history of Harvard, his alma mater, where he has been on the faculty since 1915 (in five volumes); the classic history "The Growth of the American Republic" (with Henry Steele Commager) and his own later "Oxford History of the American People"; books on Columbus, John Paul Jones, Boston, Maine, Massachusetts maritime history, and many more. He is in fact what fellow historian Daniel Boorstin recently described as an American historic monument all by himself.

How does it feel to be a historic monument? A wintry smile. "Just the same as being Professor Samuel Eliot Morison."

Morison talks with animation and dry humor of his start as a historian. "I entered Harvard to become a mathematician, but failed in calculus, so I had to turn to something easy, like history." He had been fond of sailing since his earliest youth, and after a history professor suggested to him the subject of his first book, Harrison Gray Otis ("the only time a book was ever suggested to me—all the rest have been my own idea"), he decided to specialize in maritime history. "It seemed like a good way to combine a hobby with a profession." He wrote his maritime history of Massachusetts in 1922, "and I've been at it ever since."

He has managed to produce all his books—enough to fill several shelves—by working "always within reason and within my powers." He actually writes fast, but spends the bulk of the time on each book studying and thinking. "I've always been able to think about whatever I'm working on at the same time as I'm doing something else—watching a boring play, perhaps. And I make notes whenever I have a spare moment—in that gap, for instance, between the time when I was ready to go out for the evening, and when my wife was." (His wife Priscilla died during the writing of "The Southern Voyages," and he is deeply saddened that she never saw its completion.)

"I've been a quick worker, but, I hope, an accurate one," adds the admiral. "I've had some errata when I trusted too much to memory—but not many." As a great traveler and sailor, it has always been one of his great contributions to the history of exploration that he went over the actual scenes himself, and had a working sailor's knowledge of speeds, winds, shoals and distances. "I've seen all the major landfalls of the explorers in the New World," he says. He crossed the Atlantic before World War II in a schooner, which he had specially square-rigged so that he could understand the problems of Columbus, Drake and Magellan. "It was an eye-opener." He has cruised the Caribbean islands and the shores of Central America, flown down the coasts of Brazil and Argentina and over the Strait of Magellan, comparing what he could see now with descriptions in the logs and journals of mariners 400 years dead.

As a result he has often been in conflict with other authorities on who landed where, and when—and has generally been proven right in the end. "I rather enjoy a little set-to with other historians," he says with a gleam in his eye, "especially with those who sat on their bottoms in the library and tried to decide where everyone went." He knows, for instance, that Sebastian Cabot—"one of the greatest liars among the explorers"—never went to Cape Breton Island, as he claimed, because "he just didn't have the time. Accepting his word for it is the sort of mistake many historians make because they don't know how fast the ships of the time could go. And others have expressed amazement that Drake could capture Valparaiso with one ship. That's because they think of Valparaiso as a big city, like today. Actually Drake had more men in his one ship than the whole town of Valparaiso contained then; it was just half-a-dozen huts."

Admiral Morison has had a variety of publishers over the years—Little, Brown and Houghton Mifflin for most of the works with a New England interest, Knopf occasionally, Oxford for the big general histories ("I think Oxford, with its worldwide distribution, is probably most effective with these sort of books"). His relations with publishers, he says, have always been cordial. "I'd never fight with them, like that Red—what's his name, man who did 'Main Street' and won the prize, and quarreled with his publishers—Lewis, Sinclair Lewis, that's right. I always figure that if a publisher didn't do more with a book, it's because perhaps it didn't deserve more."

He recalls with a chuckle the time he wrote first for Oxford, "The Oxford History of the American People," and the executive editor, Sheldon Meyer, came to lunch to discuss the project. "We gave him a very good lunch, and then my wife took him aside and told him that these Boston publishers just regarded me as a hometown boy who made good. Actually, she told him, I was a great historian, and should be made much of, and the book would be a tremendous success.

"Meyer looked polite, but rather incredulous. So Oxford went ahead and published and, of course, it turned out she was right!"

It is an immodest moment, but a warming one, because of course Mrs. Morison *was* right; and as the spare figure climbs painfully to his feet to bid a courtly farewell to the *PW* interviewer, it seems that more than a man is being taken leave of: a whole generation, a way of seeing . . . in fact, yes, a historic monument.

Orville Prescott

ORVILLE PRESCOTT retired from a long and impressive career as daily book critic for the *New York Times* in 1966. One of the chief reasons behind his retirement, he told *PW* in a recent interview, was to find time for research and writing he had long wanted to do, particularly in the fields of Renaissance and Medieval history. Released from the chore of compulsory reviewing, he also enjoys being able to read "only the books I want to read." "Critics," he says with candor, "make a mistake if they try to remain active critics too long."

Mr. Prescott's first book since retirement is "Princes of the Renaissance," just published by Random House, a colorful and exciting history of the great ruling families of Italy in the 15th century. Sforzas, d'Estes, Gonzagas, Baglioni, members of the House of Aragon, Dukes of Urbino, and many more, they march through these pages as men, and a few exceptional women, who wielded absolute power and possessed strong and striking personalities.

Mr. Prescott has deliberately excluded two famous Renaissance families of Italy, the Medici and the Borgias from his book, except as their lives impinged on his princes, because both have been so extensively written about before. The Medici, he points out, were not themselves independent sovereign rulers. They were "political bosses who ruled by political machinery." The title "prince," as used in his book, takes on the connotation it had in the Middle Ages and Renaissance, meaning a ruler of a state.

Mr. Prescott's enthusiasm for the Renaissance period of Italian history goes back to the summer when, 18 and al-

By Barbara A. Bannon. From *Publishers Weekly* 195, no. 11 (March 17, 1969), pp. 19–21.

465

ready an "omnivorous reader," he found in his grandfather's library a little blue book that was a chronicle of the stormy intrigue and warfare of Perugia. Some of the quaint flavor of that early chronicle he has tried to capture in his own writing about Perugia.

"Before that summer was over," he told *PW*, "I had devoured a dozen books on the Renaissance. For the next 10 years I thought I would write a novel on the period. By the time I was sufficiently mature to know I was not a novelist, I knew I would write a history on the period some day."

In his long years as *Times'* book reviewer, Mr. Prescott assiduously kept every book that came in on the Renaissance, haunted second-hand bookstores, and some of the research, material which he drew on in the 1960s for "Princes of the Renaissance" was originally translated for him by a young Italian student back in 1935 when he still thought he would write that novel.

"Princes of the Renaissance," Mr. Prescott says, "was written to fill a niche." His book is, he believes, the only one in English which makes available some of the material he has included on these dramatic figures. There is hardly anything in English on the House of Aragon, or the Baglioni of Perugia, or even about Pope Julius II as a separate figure, he told *PW*—material on Julius, the extraordinary churchman-warrior, he found in books on other characters.

Although he has traveled extensively over the years through just about every part of Italy, Mr. Prescott does not speak Italian. He can, he says, translate a paragraph with the aid of an Italian dictionary, but in much of his research he was aided by an Italian professor who translated for him the source material Mr. Prescott himself found. Much of the research was done in libraries in this country. Useful information turned up in an unpublished thesis in a manuscript found in the Bodleian Library of Oxford. The Bodleian, Mr. Prescott learned, would not permit him to withdraw books from its collection for his use in London, but would send them to him in this country if they were requested through the New York Public Library.

The fascination of the Renaissance, Mr. Prescott says, "is its blazing color. The Middle Ages could be drab, but by the time the Renaissance came along, you had great art, a great revolution in thought, a tremendous explosion of genius going on." His "Princes of the Renaissance" were the men who were profoundly molding that new society.

While medieval monks kept the chronicle of history alive, it was men like Machiavelli, Mr. Prescott points out, who brought into usage the art of writing history as history. These Renaissance chroniclers had a notion of what was important, of what to include in terms of the political and military aspects of history. They recognized the influence of human character and some of them are fascinating mines of information even today. To read Machiavelli on Florence can be a "blazing revelation."

However cruel and vindictive they were (and "Princes of the Renaissance" includes some bloodcurdling examples), many of these Italian rulers were enormously talented men, consumed with a love of beauty and admiring the ideal of the cultivated man. There have been no other rulers quite like them in this respect, Mr. Prescott believes, except in England where the ideal of cultivating Latin and Greek and personal scholarship also flourished for a time.

"Teddy Roosevelt was the last truly cultivated President we had," he says of America. "Wilson was a scholar, but narrow-minded."

In his years at the *Times* Mr. Prescott did much to bring to critical notice a number of fine historical novels. Most critics, he says, ignore the historical novel because there are so many bad examples of it around. At its best, "good and strong," outstanding historical fiction of the past several years would include, Mr. Prescott believes, "The Golden Warrior," "The Golden Hand," "The Man on a Donkey," the writing of Alfred Duggan and some of Zöe Oldenbourg, and now Cecelia Holland.

Next on Orville Prescott's own agenda is the choice of material for an anthology of history as literature, selections from the great history written from antiquity on. All of the material will be chosen for its dramatic interest, entertainment value and literary qualities, he says. And all of it will be nonfiction, making it a companion volume to a book Mr. Prescott edited some time back, which contains outstanding examples of good historical fiction.

Arthur Schlesinger, Jr.

"IT SEEMS TO HAVE come at a propitious time for what is
essentially a scholarly study," says Arthur Schlesinger, Jr.
He is speaking of his new book "The Imperial Presidency,"
published last month by Houghton Mifflin; and no one is
likely to quarrel with his assessment of his timing. The book
is a full choice of the Book-of-the-Month Club for January,
and is already climbing some best-seller lists.

"I had intended to do a slenderer book," the author adds,
perched on a desk in the sleek book-lined office he occupies
as Albert Schweitzer Professor of Humanities at the City
University of New York. "But one of the beneficial side
effects of Watergate is to make you take a fresh look at the
Constitution and the philosophy of the Founding Fathers.
When such a crisis comes, you can go back—as I wish the
president's advisers would do—and see just what they said
and thought."

Mr. Schlesinger, as a former presidential adviser himself,
in the Kennedy era, is accustomed to being interviewed,
and seldom has to pause in search of the right word. His
spoken thoughts, like his book, are crisply and clearly ordered; he answers each question concisely and waits atten-
tively for the next, his rather puckish face watchful above
the inevitable bow tie.

One of the early reviews of his book, while praising its
careful overview of the progress of presidential power, had
suggested that in fact such tampering with administrative
processes as Schlesinger suggests is irrelevant, since the
electorate had voted overwhelmingly for Mr. Nixon knowing very well the sort of man he was. "But was there really

By John F. Baker. From *Publishers Weekly* 204, no. 25 (December 17,
1973), pp. 10–11.

such a mandate?'' he says quickly when asked about this. ''A Republican president with a Democratic Congress—the voters wanted Nixon as president, but obviously not with unlimited power.''

He is quick to scotch the idea that Mr. Nixon has sought to enrich himself personally out of the presidency. ''It's just that he sees power as carrying with it imperial trappings—that's why you get these heavy expenditures on his houses. He talks of respect for the presidency as if this was something that came automatically, unearned.

''When President Kennedy used to fly to Hyannisport for the weekend,'' he continues, ''some of us, if we were going to Boston or up to the Cape, used to hitch rides on the presidential plane; but President Kennedy became unhappy about this, and let us know that he didn't regard it as appropriate. Now you get Kissinger using *Air Force One* just to fly up to New York for a party dinner. It's all a question of sensitivity. A more sensitive man wouldn't feel the need constantly to exercise all his special privilege.''

A touch of nostalgia in the way he describes this time prompts an obvious question: Would he return to government service if the occasion arose? ''Well, Washington is a most agreeable place to live, but I have no great desire to return there in government service. We were there, all of us in the Kennedy administration, under the best of circumstances and at an exhilarating time. Even so, it was frustrating at times, and I don't see how you could remain in an administration if you didn't agree with 90 percent of what it was doing—you could afford to differ with 10 percent, I guess. But now there seems to be such a sense of shame and disgust about so many of the people who worked for the White House—this is something there has never been in previous administrations.''

Schlesinger's book, which traces the steady growth of presidential power in foreign and domestic affairs in the course of American history, has a chapter that is strongly critical of Mr. Nixon's approach, and has been cited as a scholarly (but merely implicit) case for the impeachment of the president. Does he think Mr. Nixon is impeachable?

''An impeachable offense doesn't have to be indictable in normal legal terms. It's his behavior in office that is at stake, and in that sense it seems to me he is impeachable.''

With its careful tracing of the various precedents for exercise of presidential power, could his book not be a useful reference work for lawyers working on the president's various constitutional presentations? The wide-mouthed, skeptical grin: ''There is no indication that 'The Imperial Presidency' has been read at the White House. However, my taxes have not been investigated, though no doubt I have fortified my position on the 'Enemies List.' ''

Schlesinger produced his closely packed work in an astoundingly short space of time. ''I wrote a long article for *Foreign Affairs* about Congress and the war-making power, and my publishers suggested I expand it into a book. Essentially I had all the research" (in his outer office are file cabinets loaded with the results of voluminous reading in history, magazines and newspapers) "and I began writing in March." Seven months later a 400-page book, with index and extensive notes, is in the stores.

Schlesinger, who taught at Harvard before being brought to Washington by President Kennedy, has always been published in Boston. He published originally with Little, Brown, but was persuaded by Bernard de Voto to move to Houghton Mifflin and has never regretted it. Have there been other offers? The smile is positively sphinxlike. "Attempts have been made to lure me away, but Houghton Mifflin has always been very efficient and I never saw any good reason to change."

He has ventured outside on occasion, however, notably to compile and write an introduction for the "History of American Political Parties," just published jointly by Chelsea House and the R. R. Bowker Company. Schlesinger found this, and companion volumes such as an anthology of Presidential Inaugural Addresses, "extremely useful reference works," and enjoyed helping to choose the various statements and manifestos that went into it.

Schlesinger has twice won the Pulitzer Prize, for "The Age of Jackson" in 1946 and his book about the Kennedy administration, "A Thousand Days," in 1966. Currently he is working on a big book about Robert Kennedy; he dislikes the term "authorized biography," but he has special access to papers that have been made exclusively available to him by Kennedy's widow Ethel. He aims to finish this about a year from now, and feels it will be the most complete examination of the late president's assassinated younger brother to date.

Until two years ago Schlesinger continued to write movie reviews for *Vogue* (having begun with *Show*), and he still enjoys movies above all other forms of entertainment—"but I just don't have time to write about them any more." He spends all his time writing, and teaching at CUNY, where he conducts seminars in American history with graduate students.

He is clearly delighted at the prospects of strong sales for "The Imperial Presidency," and has enjoyed the reviews so far, even when they did not praise without qualification. "But, you know," he adds musingly as he steers his visitor to the door, "in my youth a pub date used to be sacred, and reviews would coincide. Now they just seem to come out all over the place at any old time." Not very methodical, in fact.

Jean-François Steiner

His book touched off one of the more heated controversies of the past season in France, but one finds it hard to connect the polemics with this lean young man with the inquiring eyes, dressed in the casual attire of St. Germain des Prés. "Treblinka," published in Paris in March, 1966, when the author was 28, has already sold over 100,000 copies, allowing its author, Jean-François Steiner, to give up day-to-day journalism, let his hair grow a little, and begin the more withdrawn life he has always wanted. He is, however, looking forward to one return visit to society, when he travels to New York for the first time in May for American publication of his book by Simon and Schuster.

From the moment of publication, "Treblinka" was on the firing line. It is the moving story, told in reconstructed dialog, of the deportation of hundreds of thousands of Jews to the camp of that name, of their life and death there, and above all of their climactic attempt at resistance and escape. But was the resistance general? Was it sufficient to redeem those who died without apparent revolt? This is the crux of the stormy debate which raged in the French press last year, and which helped push "Treblinka" to the top of French best-seller lists. (60,000 copies were sold the first month, and translations will be published in England, Holland, Germany, Italy and other countries. In the United States it will be an alternate selection of the Literary Guild and a full selection of the Mainstream Book Club.)

The reaction seemed to have been ignited by an unfortunate expression used by Simone de Beauvoir in her introduction to "Treblinka." She repeated the question

By Herbert R. Lottman. From *Publishers Weekly* 191, no. 16 (April 17, 1967), pp. 22–23. Reprinted by permission of Herbert R. Lottman.

voiced by young Israelis: "Why did the Jews allow themselves to be led to the slaughterhouse as sheep?" The question was reiterated by Monsieur Steiner himself, who was quoted in the Gaullist weekly *Candide* last June: "If I wrote this book it was because, more than the indignation or the emotion . . . I felt the shame of being one of the sons of this people, six million of whom allowed themselves to be led to the slaughterhouse, as sheep."

The critics did not always bother to go beyond these statements to the book itself, which detailed the preparations of the underground resistance at Treblinka. "The book is full of racist formulas," a professional polemicist snapped in *Candide*. Jewish historian Leon Poliakov wrote: "The essential of M. Steiner's thesis can be summed up: 'The behavior of Jews, that is the sheeplike passivity attributed to them, is specifically Jewish.' " The organ of the International League Against Anti-Semitism criticized "Treblinka" and wondered why the "generally more serious" Simone de Beauvoir and the left-wing press had endorsed it. Steiner's interview in *Candide*—not the book—was attacked by a veteran of Auschwitz in these terms: "Rarely have I met statements as irresponsible, affirmations as gratuitous as they are unjust."

The book had its ardent defenders—President de Gaulle, first of all, who called it deeply moving and noted its resistance theme; François Mauriac; but also the *Jerusalem Post* and the French Jewish periodical *L'Arche*, which called "Treblinka" a reply to Hannah Arendt's "Eichmann in Jerusalem" (the subject of controversy for similar reasons). Most significantly, Jean-François Steiner's volume won the Prix de la Résistance for 1966, awarded by a large French resistance organization.

"There shouldn't have been any polemic," the author says now. "I was in agreement with my adversaries. Many Jews today, particularly of the younger generation, are ashamed because of the failure of heroism during that period. I wrote my book to show they were mistaken, that Jews weren't cowards. But I had to begin with the question as to why Jews died like sheep, as a working hypothesis. Then I could show that what was taken for submission was actually revolt." His book makes the point in these words (p. 70 of the French edition): "Certainly there was a degree of cowardice in the attitude of the Jewish masses who preferred to accept the worst degradation rather than revolt. But cowardice is more apparent than real, as the tragic end of this story will demonstrate sufficiently."

"Historians would like the Jews to have suffered their martyrdom in white gloves," M. Steiner told *PW*'s interviewer. "But the ignominy of the Nazi system was that it attacked souls as well as bodies. Everyone agrees, but when you start showing *how* the Nazis destroyed souls, no one agrees any more. For the truth you have to read John Hersey's 'The Wall,' Hannah Arendt, and, of course, the documentary evidence."

Steiner's own father died in a concentration camp. His mother remarried a Jewish doctor, and the young man grew up in the Paris suburbs where he was born. At 17 he spent a year and a half on a kibbutz in Israel, returning to philosophy studies at the Sorbonne. He was a paratrooper in Algeria during the liberation war there and described his experience laconically in an article, "The Making of a Parachutist," published in Sartre's magazine *Temps Modernes*. As a professional journalist, he worked for the daily *Combat*, then *Réalités*, *L'Express*, *Candide*, specializing in Algerian and German affairs.

"Then I became bored with journalism," he recalls. "Constantin Melnik, an editor at Fayard, gave me the opportunity to write a book. Haunted by the subject of Jewish resistance, I wanted to find out what it really was. I went to Israel in November, 1964, for a month, realized I couldn't possibly deal with the subject in general, so I decided to investigate the revolt at Treblinka. Living on advances from my publisher, I spent six months in Israel in all, reading the testimony taken by a Polish commission in 1945, then the more complete records of the Yad Vashem Institute, and I talked with 14 of the 21 survivors of Treblinka living in Israel."

In March, 1965, he returned to France, completing the book during the summer. He says he had advance warning of the storm to come when one of Fayard's advisers laced into the book. As a form of insurance he asked Madame de Beauvoir, whom he knew, to write the preface.

"I didn't expect commercial success," Monsieur Steiner says, smiling tentatively. "But I knew the book wouldn't leave people indifferent. I wrote it with passion, not sleeping much during that period, working in my parents' country home in the middle of a field. I went to Paris weekends to let off steam. There was very little rewriting."

Now country life is a necessity for Steiner. He is giving up his Paris apartment this spring and moving into a rented 17th-century house on the frontiers of Normandy, close to Château Gaillard, the fort Richard the Lion-Hearted built to keep the French from coming up the Seine valley toward Rouen. Steiner, who is not married, would like to buy the house eventually. "I spend my days in Paris doing nothing, and yet I have no time for myself." Soon he'll be able to group his Paris appointments on a one-day visit each week. He is working on a new book, which seems to be taking the shape of an autobiographical novel à la Céline. "But I can't really describe it yet," he confesses. "It's a journalist's hunt for the grail, the grail being the mystery of the extermination of the Jews."

John Stoessinger

PRESIDENT NIXON, everyone seems to have agreed whether they liked it or not, pulled off quite a diplomatic and political coup when he announced that he would visit Mainland China in the spring of next year. Since that announcement, we have witnessed sweeping changes in the media's (and therefore the Establishment's) attitude toward what is often referred to as "a quarter of the world's population." It is as if those who determine these things have abandoned the rhetoric of the Luces and the Dulleses with relief.

Telephone service has been restored. Trade missions are being planned. The American Management Association has announced a seminar on how to make money in China. Taiwan has become, finally, the offshore, island republic that it is. American journalists have visited the land mass, made enthusiastic pronouncements, dispatched pictures of Ping-Pong matches, described elaborate, mouth-watering dinner parties and even undergone acupuncture. In what may have been the last gasp of cold war idiocy and ignorance, China has become real again. The favorite foreign language course at American universities in the 1970s—rushed into curricula in response to student demands—will no doubt be Chinese. Exploring China is going to be far more exciting for most of us than exploring the moon, if only because the moon is already old hat, while China—China is new and mysterious and full of people.

But before those students plunge into the bewilderment and delight of ideograms, and before those businessmen are informed of the mechanics of selling small appliances to what in the 1950s was still referred to as "The Yellow Per-

By Douglas N. Mount. From *Publishers Weekly* 200, no. 12 (September 20, 1971), pp. 15–17.

il," they ought to read John Stoessinger's book, "Nations in Darkness" (*Random House*). As Mr. Stoessinger, who teaches political science at Hunter College and is acting director of the political affairs division of the United Nations, told *PW* in a recent interview, the attitude of each country toward the other has traditionally been "a mixture of benign contempt and avuncular concern." He also points out that indeed until quite recently, "more Americans had visited the moon than Mainland China."

John Stoessinger's book is a study in the sort of super-paranoia that characterizes relations between nations—specifically Soviet–American relations and Sino–Soviet relations—and he makes his point through a series of case studies that trace this nation's interactions with the other two super-powers from their origins to the present. He is perhaps uniquely qualified: Imagine an Austrian Jew who fled to Prague in 1938 just ahead of the Nazi onslaught, tarried until the Mediterranean route was closed ("We thought, like a lot of Jews, that Hitler would be satisfied; that's why six million of us were killed"), caught a ride to Vladivostok in Siberia and ended up in Shanghai just in time for Pearl Harbor. He was stuck there for the duration, going to "a British public school with British instructors, under Japanese occupation and in the British Extraterritorial Zone." He was not alone. A ghetto of some 20,000 Jews weathered the war in Shanghai, and a German contingent which lasted—under Japanese protection—longer than the Reich itself. When this country dropped its atomic bombs on Japan, the residents of Shanghai were certain they would be next.

John Stoessinger finally came to the U.S. in 1947, attending Grinnell College and Harvard University, where one of his many distinguished classmates was Henry M. Kissinger.

"The seed of this book is the very confusing life I have lived," he told us over lunch at the U.N. "Vienna, Prague, China—all of those people could not be right. It wasn't until I came to this country that I was able to learn the truth." We talked about the Pentagon Papers, and he referred to the "intellectual shabbiness" of the foreign policy thinking represented there. "I was attuned, from my own work, to look for key words: Comparisons of Mao to Hitler, to Stalin, and so forth. Most of these people got their formative political experience in the Second World War and the cold war. They obviously simply transferred their European experience to Asia. I was not so much impressed with the deception as with the sheer intellectual shoddiness. Nobody bothered to study the other side except the CIA. That was their job, and they come out looking better than anyone else.

"I've had incredibly enthusiastic responses to the book. It's been a long drought for me—three years of work—but I thought all along that some day this sort of analysis would be accepted. You know, many of these guys hide their intellectual bankruptcy behind political science jargon. I'll tell you, it's the first time I haven't felt lonely about this business. For the first time, I feel a sense of intellectual camaraderie."

Stoessinger, whose job at the U.N. is to write political analyses for the Secretary General at his request on whatever situation attracts him, is an intense, athletic (tennis) man—at times almost melancholy about the sad state of the world—with prematurely steel-gray hair. He took us into the rose garden of the U.N., with its fine view of the East River and its refreshing calm after the bustle of midtown Manhattan. We talked of Kissinger.

"The key to Henry's thinking is his doctoral thesis, 'A World Restored,' about the Congress of Vienna, which managed to keep the peace in Europe for a long time. At the heart of it is the idea of the balance of power, and this is his thing: that you strengthen your hand by having relations with both of the other powers, by being equidistant from both so that neither of them knows what you are going to do.

"I think that Nixon was deeply influenced by Kissinger in this regard. And of course, only a President with impeccable Republican credentials could do it without getting blasted by the opposition for selling out."

As for Peking, "The fact that a foreign president visits China is very much in the Chinese tradition: The barbarian leader has always visited China. [Well up into the twentieth century, he had told us earlier, the Chinese had always had an office of Barbarian Affairs.] Washington goes to Peking; Peking does not go to Washington. It is clear that Chou En-lai will do most of the talking, but the old man [Mao] will still have the final say in any policy decision."

Of the Russians, he said, "They now realize that the Chinese will have a sphere of influence in Asia. The Russians are suddenly saying, O.K., but where is ours? Eastern Europe, of course. You have this really Machiavellian triangle operating."

He gave us the text of his remarks for a television broadcast, the last sentences of which sum up his view of our changing relations with China: "Talks alone, of course, will not dissolve objective problems. Beasts will not change into beauties over night. Reality will be difficult enough. But at last statesmen in both China and America will have the opportunity to fashion policies less on fears and more on facts. Angels and devils have no place in foreign policy."

Theodore H. White

THEODORE H. WHITE calls himself "embattled, desperate and determined"—and somehow, out of fierce pressure, deadlines almost like those of a daily newspaper, and constant infusions of fresh material, he has wrapped up "The Making of the President 1972" and Atheneum will publish it on schedule early in August.

Chain-smoking, and pacing the living room of his East 60s townhouse in New York as if to stretch muscles cramped by long hours at the typewriter, "Teddy" took a couple of hours off one recent afternoon to talk to *PW* about the book, President Nixon, Watergate, the state of the country and whatever else was on a lively and teeming brain.

White had 11 chapters of the book's 14 already written, and was envisaging an orderly finish when the Watergate scandal began to come apart at the seams three months ago; since then, in a wearing battle with the clock, typists, editors, proofreaders and the ever-mounting material, he has written a special prologue to the book and two new chapters incorporating Watergate details and their significance.

"But it's not a book about Watergate," he insists. "You have to see what happened there in the context of Nixon's whole presidency—you have to start back in 1968 or 1969, when he was first elected, and trying to get a grip on affairs."

Basically, White believes, the attitudes that eventually culminated in the scandal were given birth by Mr. Nixon's long antipathy toward the press. "You get these secret details being published, and he sends up the cry: 'Find the leaks!' And as it goes down through the chain of command it

By John F. Baker. From *Publishers Weekly* 203, no. 24 (June 11, 1973), pp. 96–98.

reaches guys who don't know what the law is. It's like King Henry II, saying 'Who will rid me of this troublesome priest?' and you end up with some hired assassin killing Becket on the altar.''

He sees the president as having surrounded himself with ''a group of arrogant young men determined to be more loyal than the king himself. Drunk with power, they defiled the whole process of American politics.'' And he is afraid that now the scandal, and its intimate link with the election, may have stolen all meaning from the Nixon victory. ''The mythology will be that Nixon stole the election, and that all politics are crooked,'' he said. ''Neither of these is true, but I'm afraid too many people are going to think so.''

Although a lifelong Democrat, White is not personally hostile to Mr. Nixon, and feels none of the glee common in liberal circles at the president's current agony. He has met all of the last six American presidents, and, like Will Rogers in another context, ''never met one I didn't like.'' He is keenly aware of the president's dilemma, and urges human sympathy for it. ''He may turn out to be the man most betrayed. There is real tragedy here—human anguish—the man is going to have to face up to it; he will have to put some of his friends in jail for what they thought they were doing for him.''

As for the widespread popular belief that Watergate was merely typical dirty politics, unworthy of the current furor, White, who has been a close student of American politics for 20 years and probably knows as much about them as any man alive, will have none of it. ''Of course there've been dirty tricks, always—even in Pompeii they found writing on the walls, 'Vote for Vatius the Wife-Beater'; and there's always been smearing, and vote-buying—but this carries it all one giant step beyond dirty tricks into the area of actual crime. It's somehow a nerve that's gone dead. Always before there had been rules that were mutually understood by both parties—and there has never been burglarizing or wiretapping before.''

Did he think that the extent of the corruption by the Nixon campaign staff might actually have influenced the outcome of the election, by swinging the Democratic choice to George McGovern as an easy opponent? ''Certainly not. McGovern won by the fairest and squarest means, and by one of the most brilliant and romantic strategies in American political history. Muskie was already on the decline before that 'Canuck' letter came out.'' (This was a letter attributed to Nixon campaign aides that was said to have damaged Muskie in an early primary.)

Both the 1972 candidates, he feels, ran intensely personal campaigns, ignoring the regular party machines—and both ran into disaster, though the enormity of President Nixon's disaster was not apparent until after the returns were in. Senator McGovern's disaster was the Eagleton affair, in which his ineptitude over picking a vice-presidential candidate (''one of the most serious political exercises possible") made party politics look ridiculous. The excesses of Mr. Nixon's aides, however, showed that they despised party politics.

"And this was the year when all the national problems that had been building for years converged on the campaign," White said. "That's the real theme of the book—that this was the end of an era, the end of the postwar world that the guys of my generation put together; it's all finished, with the dollar declining, the Common Market rising, the end of American rule of the world. And at home everything is changing—the cities, the suburbs, civil rights, the revolution in education, the way TV has changed our way of looking. No one is willing to look at the consequences of all these revolutions; in the election, neither candidate faced these issues, neither party really made any response to what people need."

What did he really think of President Nixon? The round face broke into one of its fleeting, quizzical grins. "A lot of people don't understand him. He's an old American type: the tinkerer—the guy who wants to know how things work, and then how to make them work himself. He knows the details of American politics down to his fingertips. And above all he wants to make peace work and he wants to make the country work."

White was pacing again, his head wreathed in cigarette smoke. "You know, when you interview presidents they all sound the same; what they talk about is peace and parks—peace and parks!" He discounted the notion that power or money drives a man any longer by the time he becomes president. "When they get that far up all they want to do is write their name in history, to leave a mark. It's an exercise in identity. And by making peace and creating parks, they can do it."

"The Making of the President 1972" will be White's fourth essay in the genre which, he claims proudly and without fear of contradiction, "I invented." He began as a Harvard specialist in Chinese history, and on a visit to China in the 1930s found himself under bombardment and filed newspaper dispatches about it; "I found it a lot more fun writing about history as a newspaper correspondent." After the war he went to Europe as a correspondent, writing extensively about the Marshall Plan. He also wrote a couple of novels during this period, including "The View from the Fortieth Floor," which he sold to Hollywood.

He had become increasingly fascinated with American politics over the years, and tried to interest a number of publishers in a book that would cover the 1960 presidential election campaign in detail, from earliest hat-in-ring to Inauguration. "I wanted to show how a campaign was run, but for a long time no one was interested. Finally Mike Bessie took it, but I had to pay my own expenses—I did it with the Hollywood money."

Paying his own way, he followed the candidates around: "Kennedy was amused at the idea of a book about presidential politics, but Nixon couldn't see why a novelist should want to follow him around, and I was never in the regular press plane, only the backup one."

He delights to remember the success the book achieved—"It was like playing the tuba while it's raining gold"—with the Pulitzer Prize to cap his efforts. After that, the pattern was set: every four years Theodore White, with a remarkable combination of sweep and precision, would show the country how it had chosen its last president. Each book takes three years' work, he says: two to follow the candidates around, then a year to write. "And in the intervals I do silly things, like trying to write the history of the world; my project is called 'The Castle on the Hill,' and right now I've got to Oliver Cromwell and I'm stuck."

After the last galley of "President 1972" has been corrected and White's typewriter has cooled, he plans to spend publication month relaxing and calming down. But probably not for long. "I've been asked to do a Watergate book," he says. "And I just might consider it."

Appendix

Published Works of Authors Interviewed

ACHESON, DEAN 1893–

The Pattern of Responsibility (ed. by McGeorge Bundy), Houghton Mifflin, 1952; Kelley, 1975. *A Democrat Looks at His Party*, Harper, 1955. *An American Vista*, Hamish Hamilton, 1956. *A Citizen Looks at Congress*, Harper, 1957; Greenwood, 1974. *Power and Diplomacy*, Harvard Univ., 1958; Atheneum, 1962. *Meetings at the Summit: A Study in Diplomatic Method*, Univ. of New Hampshire, 1958. *Sketches from Life of Men I Have Known*, Harper, 1961; Greenwood, 1974. *Fifty Years After*, Overbrook Press, 1961. *Real and Imagined Handicaps of Our Democracy in the Conduct of Its Foreign Relations*, Institute for National and International Affairs, 1962. *The Dilemmas of Our Times*, Univ. of Connecticut, 1963. *Morning and Noon*, Houghton Mifflin, 1965. *Private Thoughts on Public Affairs*, Harcourt, 1967. *Present at the Creation: My Years in the State Department*, Norton, 1969. *Korean War*, Norton, 1971. *Struggle for a Free Europe*, Norton, 1971. *This Vast External Realm*, new ed., Norton, 1973.

Also, numerous addresses, lectures, and statements published by the U.S. Department of State or the U.S. Government Printing Office.

ALLILUYEVA, SVETLANA 1926–

Dvadsat pisem k druga, pub. as *Twenty Letters to a Friend* (trans. by P. J. McMillan), Harper, 1967. *Tol'ko odin god*, pub. as *Only One Year* (trans. by Paul Chavchavadze), Harper, 1969, 1970.

Also, author of a pamphlet, *Borisu Leonidovichu Pasternaku*.

AMRAM, DAVID 1930–

Vibrations: The Adventures and Musical Times of David Amram, Macmillan, 1968; Viking, 1971.

Also, composer of numerous orchestral works, wind symphonies, pieces of chamber music, choral works, keyboard music, incidental music, film scores and television scores.

ANDERSON, ROBERT W. 1917–

Tea and Sympathy, Random House, 1954. *All Summer Long* (adapted from the novel *A Wreath and a Curse*, by Donald Wetzel), Samuel French, 1955. *Silent Night, Lonely Night*, Random House, 1960. *The Days Between*, Random House, 1965. *You Know I Can't Hear You When the Water's Running*, Random House, 1967. *I Never Sang for My Father*, Random House, 1968. *Solitaire/Double Solitaire*, Random House, 1972. *After*, Random House, 1973; Fawcett, 1974.

Also, author of numerous adaptations for film, television, and radio.

ARLEN, MICHAEL J. 1930–

Living Room War, Viking, 1969. *Exiles*, Farrar, 1970; Ballantine, 1976. *An American Verdict*, Doubleday, 1973. *Passage to Ararat*, Farrar, 1975; Ballantine, 1976. *The View from Highway 1*, Farrar, 1976.

Also contributor of articles to *The New Yorker*.

BAINBRIDGE, BERYL 1934–

A Weekend with Claude, Hutchinson, 1967. *Another Part of the Wood*, Hutchinson, 1968. *Harriet Said*, Duckworth, 1972; Braziller, 1973; NAL, 1974. *The Dressmaker*, Duckworth, 1973; pub. as *The Secret Glass*, Braziller, 1974; NAL, 1975. *The Bottle Factory Outing*, Duckworth, 1974; Braziller, 1975, 1976. *Sweet William*, Duckworth, 1975; Braziller, 1976. *A Quiet Life*, Braziller, 1976. *Injury Time*, Braziller, 1977.

BAKER, CARLOS 1909–

American Issues (editor; with Willard Thorp and Merle Curti), Lippincott, 1941. *The American Looks at the World* (editor), Harcourt, 1944. *Shelley's Major Poetry*, Princeton Univ., 1948; Russell, 1961. *Hemingway: The Writer as Artist*, Princeton Univ., 1952; rev. ed., 1972. *A Friend in Power*, Scribner, 1958. *Hemingway and His Critics* (editor), Hill & Wang, 1961. *Ernest Hemingway: Critiques of Four Major Novels* (editor), Scribner, 1962. *A Year and a Day*, Vanderbilt Univ., 1963. *The Land of Rumbelow*, Scribner, 1963. *Ernest Hemingway*, Scribner, 1969. *The Gay Head Conspiracy*, Scribner, 1973. *The Talismans and Other Stories*, Scribner, 1976.

Also, editor of eight books on English literature.

BAKER, RUSSELL 1925–

Washington: City on the Potomac (author of text), Arts, 1958. *An American in Washington*, Knopf, 1961. *No Cause for Panic*, Lippincott, 1964. *Baker's Dozen*, New York Times Co., 1964. *All Things Considered*, Lippincott, 1965. *Our Next President: The Incredible Story of What Happened in the 1968 Elections*, Atheneum, 1968. *Poor Russell's Almanac*, Doubleday, 1972. *The Upside-Down Man*, McGraw-Hill, 1977.

Also, author of newspaper column "Observer," published continuously since 1962; and contributor to numerous periodicals.

BEDFORD, SYBILLE 1911–

The Sudden View: A Mexican Journey, Gollancz, 1953; Harper, 1954; rev. ed., Atheneum, 1963; pub. as *A Visit to Don Otavio: A Traveller's Tale from Mexico*, Collins, 1960. *A Legacy*, Weidenfeld and Nicolson, 1956; Simon & Schuster, 1957; Ecco, 1976. *The Best We Can Do: An Account of the Trial of John Bodkin Adams*, Collins, 1958; pub. as *The Trial of Dr. Adams*, Simon & Schuster, 1959. *The Faces of Justice: A Traveler's Report*, Collins, 1961; Simon & Schuster, 1963. "Compassionata at Hyde Park Corner," in *23 Modern Stories*, Knopf, 1963. *A Favourite of the Gods*, Collins, Simon & Schuster, 1963. *A Compass Error*, Collins, 1968; Knopf, 1969. *Aldous Huxley, A Biography*, Chatto and Windus, Collins, 2 vols., 1973, 1974; Knopf, 1974.

Also, contributor to numerous magazines.

BELFRAGE, CEDRIC 1904–

Away from It All, Simon & Schuster, 1937. *Promised Land*, Gollancz, 1938. *Let My People Go*, Gollancz, 1940; pub. as *South of God*, Modern Age, 1941. *They All Hold Swords*, Modern Age, 1941. *A Faith to Free the People*, Dryden, 1944. *Abide with Me*, Sloane, 1948. *Seeds of Destruction*, Cameron & Kahn, 1954. *The Frightened Giant*, Secker & Warburg, 1957. *My Master Columbus*, Doubleday, 1961. *The Man at the Door with the Gun*, Monthly Review Pr., 1963. *The American Inquisition*, Bobbs, 1973. *Something to Guard* (with James Aronson), Columbia Univ., 1978.

Also, translator of books from Spanish for Monthly Review Pr.

BENES, JAN 1936–

Do Vrabcu jako kdyz streli, Nase Vojsko, 1963. *Disproporce* ("Disproportions"), 1964. *Az Se se mnou vyspis budes plakat* ("If You Sleep with Me, You Will Cry"), 1968. *Na miste* ("On the Spot"), 1968. *Situace* ("Situations") Ceskoslovenky Spisovatel, 1969. *Second Breath* (trans. by Michael Montgomery), Orion, 1969. *Trojuhelnik s madonou* ("Triangle with Madonna"), 1970. *Blind Mirror* (trans. by Jan Hertzfeld), Orion,

1971. *Banana Dreams*, Konfren Lah'en, 1974. *Kiss Me I Am Bohemian*, Publishers 68, 1977.

Also, author of plays for television.

BERRIGAN, DANIEL 1921–

Time without Number, Macmillan, 1957. *The Bride: Essays in the Church*, Macmillan, 1959. *Encounter*, World, 1960; new ed., Assoc. Artists, 1965. *The Bow in the Clouds: Man's Covenant with God*, Coward, 1961. *The World for Wedding Ring*, Macmillan, 1962. *No One Walks Waters*, Macmillan, 1966. *They Call Us Dead Men: Reflections on Life and Conscience*, Macmillan, 1966, 1968. *Consequences: Truth and . . . .*, Macmillan, 1967. *Love, Love at the End: Parables, Prayers, and Meditations*, Macmillan, 1968. *Night Flight to Hanoi: War Diary with 11 Poems*, Macmillan, 1968. *Go From Here: A Prison Diary*, Open Space Action Committee, 1968. *False Gods, Real Men: New Poems*, Macmillan, 1969. *The Trial of the Catonsville Nine*, Beacon, 1970; Bantam, 1971. *No Bars to Manhood*, Doubleday, 1970. *Trial Poems: A Poet, A Painter* (with Tom Lewis), Beacon, 1970. *Selected Poetry of Daniel Berrigan S.J.*, Anchor, 1970. *Prison Journals of a Priest Revolutionary*, Holt, 1970. *The Dark Night of Resistance*, Doubleday, 1971. *The Geography of Faith: Conversations Between Daniel Berrigan, When Underground, and Robert Coles* (with Robert Coles), Beacon, 1971. *America Is Hard to Find*, Doubleday, 1972. *Prison Poems*, Unicorn, 1973; Viking, 1974. *Selected & New Poems*, Doubleday, 1973. *Absurd Convictions, Modest Hopes* (with Lee Lockwood), Random House, 1973. *Lights On in the House of the Dead: A Prison Diary*, Doubleday, 1974. *The Raft is Not the Shore* (with Thich N. Hanh), Beacon, 1975. *A Season in Jail and Other Felonious Conversations*, Random House, in press.

Also poems included in the following anthologies: *From One Word*, Devin, 1950. *Anthology of Catholic Poets* (ed. by Joyce Kilmer, new supplement by James E. Tobin), Doubleday, 1955. *Sealed Unto the Day*, Catholic Poetry Society of America, 1955. *Twentieth Century American Poetry* (ed. by Conrad Aiken), Modern Library, 1963.

Also, contributor to periodicals.

BERTEAUT, SIMONE 1923–

Piaf: A Biography, Harper, 1972.

BLOOM, MURRAY TEIGH 1916–

Money of Their Own, Scribner, 1957. *The Man Who Stole Portugal*, Scribner, 1966. *The Trouble with Lawyers*, Simon & Schuster, 1969. *Rogues to Riches*, Putnam, 1972. *Lawyers, Clients & Ethics*, Council on Legal Education, 1974. *The 13th Man*, Macmillan, 1977.

Also, contributor of more than six hundred articles to magazines.

BLOTNER, JOSEPH 1923–

The Political Novel, Doubleday, 1955. *Faulkner in the University* (with F. L. Gwynn), Univ. of Virginia, 1959. *The Fiction of J. D. Salinger* (with F. L. Gwynn), Univ. of Pittsburgh, 1959. *William Faulkner's Library: A Catalogue*, Univ. of Virginia, 1964. *The Modern American Political Novel: 1900–1960*, Univ. of Texas, 1966. *Man and the Movies* (contributor; ed. by W. R. Robinson), Louisiana State Univ., 1967. *Themes and Directions in American Literature* (contributor; ed. by Ray B. Browne and Donald Pizer), Purdue Univ., 1969. *William Faulkner/Eugene O'Neill/ John Steinbeck* (contributor), CRM, 1971. *Faulkner: A Biography*, Random House, 1974. *Faulkner: Fifty Years After "The Marble Faun"* (contributor; ed. by George Wolfe), Univ. of Atlanta, 1976. *Romantic and Modern: Reevaluations of Literary Tradition; Selected Letters of William Faulkner* (contributor; ed. by George Bornstein), Random House, 1977.

BOLTON, ISABEL 1883–1975

(Isabel Bolton is the pseudonym of Mary Britton Miller)
Songs of Infancy, Macmillan, 1923. *Menagerie*, Macmillan, 1928. *Without Sanctuary*, Macmillan, 1932. *Intrepid Bird*, Macmillan, 1934. *In the Days of Thy Youth*, Scribner, 1943. *The Crucifixion*, Scribner, 1944. *Do I Wake or Sleep* (under pseud.), Scribner, 1946. *The Christmas Tree* (under pseud.), Scribner, 1949. *Many Mansions* (under pseud.), Scribner, 1952. *Give a Guess*, Pantheon, 1957. *All Aboard*, Pantheon, 1958. *A Handful of Flowers*, Pantheon, 1958. *Jungle Journey*, Pantheon, 1959. *Listen the Birds* (under pseud.), Pantheon, 1961. *Under Gemini: A Memoir*, Harcourt, 1967. *The Whirligig of Time*, Crown, 1971.
   Also, contributor of short stories to magazines.

BOSWORTH, ALLAN R. 1901–

Lovely World of Richi-San, Harper, 1960. *America's Concentration Camps*, Norton, 1967.

BOURJAILY, VANCE 1922–

The End of My Life, Scribner, 1947; W. H. Allen, 1963. *The Girl in the Abstract Bed*, Tiber, 1954. *The Hound of Earth*, Scribner, 1955; Spearman, 1956; Dial, 1964. *The Violated*, Dial, 1958. *Confessions of a Spent Youth*, Dial, 1960; W. H. Allen, 1961. *The Unnatural Enemy*, Dial, 1963. *The Man Who Knew Kennedy*, Dial, 1967. *Brill among the Ruins*, Dial, 1970; W. H. Allen, 1971. *Country Matters: Collected Reports from Fields and Streams of Iowa and Other Places*, Dial, 1973. *Now Playing at Canterbury*, Dial, 1976.
   Also, editor, *Discovery 1–6*, Pocket, 1953–55; and contributor of short stories to periodicals.

BOYD, MALCOLM 1923–

Crisis in Communication, Doubleday, 1957. *Christ and Celebrity Gods*, Seaburg, 1958. *Focus*, Morehouse, 1960. *If I Go Down to Hell*, Morehouse, 1962. *Christianity and the Contemporary Arts* (contributor), Abingdon, 1962. *The Hunger, the Thirst*, Morehouse, 1964. *On the Battle Lines* (editor), Morehouse, 1964. *Are You Running with Me, Jesus?*, Holt, 1965. *Free to Live, Free to Die*, Holt, 1967. *Witness to a Generation* (contributor; ed. by Edward Fiske), Bobbs, 1967. *Book of Days*, Random House, 1968. *Fantasy Worlds of Peter Stone*, Harper, 1968. *As I Live and Breathe*, Random House, 1970. *The Lover*, Word, 1972. *Human Like Me, Jesus*, Simon & Schuster, 1972; Pyramid, 1973. *Palestrina's Style: A Practical Introduction*, Oxford Univ., 1973. *The Runner*, Word, 1974. *Christian*, Hawthorn, 1975. *The Alleluia Affair*, Word, 1975. *Am I Running with You, God?*, Doubleday, 1977. *Take Off the Masks*, Doubleday, 1978.

Also, author of five plays and their adaptations for television and film.

Also, columnist for the *Pittsburgh Courier* and several church-affairs magazines. Contributing editor to *Renewal*. Contributor of articles to *Wall Street Journal*.

BRALY, MALCOLM 1925–

Felon Tank, Fawcett, 1961; Pocket, 1976. *Shake Him Till He Rattles*, Fawcett, 1963; Belmont–Towers, 1971; Pocket, 1976. *It's Cold Out There*, Fawcett, 1966; Pocket, 1976. *On the Yard*, Little, 1967; pub. as *False Starts: A Memoir of San Quentin & Other Prisons*, Little, 1976. *And Into the Fire*, Playboy, 1978. *Buddies*, Little (forthcoming).

Also, contributor to several periodicals.

CAHN, SAMMY 1913–

I Should Care, Arbor, 1974; Pyramid, 1975.

CAINE, LYNN

Widow, Morrow, 1974; Bantam, 1975. *Lifelines, Living Alone without Being Lonely*, Doubleday, 1978.

CALISHER, HORTENSE 1911–

In the Absence of Angels: Stories, Little, 1952; Heinemann, 1953. *False Entry*, Little, Secker and Warburg, 1962. *Tale for the Mirror: A Novella and Other Stories*, Little, Secker and Warburg, 1964. *Extreme Magic: A Novella and Other Stories*, Little, Secker and Warburg, 1964. *Journal from Ellipsia*, Little, 1965; Secker and Warburg, 1966. *The Railway Police and the Last Trolley Ride*, Little, 1966. *The New Yorkers*, Little, Cape,

1964. *Queenie*, Cape, 1969; Arbor House, 1971. *Standard Dreaming*, Arbor House, 1972; Dell, 1974. *Herself*, Arbor House, 1972; Dell, 1974. *Collected Stories of Hortense Calisher*, Arbor House, 1975. *Eagle Eye*, St. Martin, 1975.

Also, contributor to magazines; and to *Works in Progress*, Doubleday, 1973.

CAPON, ROBERT F.

Bed & Board: Plain Talk About Marriage, Simon & Schuster, 1965. *An Offering of Uncles*, Sheed & Ward. *Supper of the Lamb*, Doubleday, 1969; Pocket, 1970; Doubleday, 1974. *The Third Peacock*, Doubleday, 1972. *Hunting the Divine Fox: Images & Mystery in Christian Faith*, Seabury, 1974. *Exit 36: A Fictional Chronicle*, Seabury, 1975; Bantam, 1976.

CHARRIÈRE, HENRI 1907–1973

Papillon, Morrow, 1970; Pocket, 1973. *Banco: The Further Adventures of Papillon* (trans. by Patrick O'Brian), Morrow, 1973; Pocket, 1974.

CHEVIGNY, PIERRE

Police Power: Police Abuses in New York City, Pantheon, 1969. *Cops and Rebels: A Study of Provocation*, Pantheon, Irvington, 1972. *Criminal Mischief, a Novel*, Pantheon, 1977.

COHEN, ARTHUR A. 1928–

Martin Buber, Hillary House, 1957. *Anatomy of Faith* (editor), Harcourt, 1958. *American Catholics: A Protestant-Jewish View* (contributor), Sheed & Ward, 1959. *The Natural and the Supernatural Jew*, Pantheon, 1963. *Religion and Contemporary Society* (contributor), Macmillan, 1963. *Christianity: Some Non-Christian Appraisals* (contributor), McGraw-Hill, 1964. *Humanistic Education and Western Civilization* (editor), Holt, 1964; Bks. for Libs. *The Communism of Mao Tse-Tung*, Univ. of Chicago, 1964. *What's Ahead for the Churches?* (contributor), Sheed & Ward, 1964. *The Carpenter Years*, NAL, 1967. *Myth of the Judeo-Christian Tradition: And Other Dissenting Essays*, Schocken, 1971. *In the Days of Simon Stern*, Dell, 1974. *Osip Emilievich Manelstam: An Essay in Antiphon*, Ardis, 1974. *Sonia Delaunay*, Abrams, 1975. *A Hero in His Time*, Random House, 1976.

COLLINS, MICHAEL 1930–

Brass Rainbow, Dodd, 1969. *First on the Moon: The Astronauts' Own Story* (with others), Little, 1970. *Path to Freedom*, British Bk. Ctr., 1971.

The Silent Scream, Dodd, 1973. *Carrying the Fire*, Farrar, 1974; Ballantine, 1975. *Blue Death*, Dodd, 1974. *Flying to the Moon and Other Strange Places*, Farrar, 1976.

COX, ARCHIBALD 1912–

Cases on Labor Law; Law and National Law or Policy, Harvard Univ., 1960. *Civil Rights, the Constitution and the Courts*, Harvard Univ., 1967. *The Warren Court*, Harvard Univ., 1968.

CRONKITE, WALTER 1916–

Eye on the World, Regnery, 1971. *Challenges of Change*, Public Affairs Pr., 1971.

DANNAY, FREDERIC 1905—

Ellery Queen, Ellery Queen, Jr., and Barnaby Ross are all joint pseudonyms of co-authors Frederic Dannay and Manfred B. Lee. Except as noted, the Ellery Queen books were published by Stokes and Lippincott to 1940, and by Little, Simon and Schuster, Random House, 1940–66, by NAL, 1966–68, by World, 1969–.

Novels with M. B. Lee under joint pseudonym Ellery Queen: *The Roman Hat Mystery*, 1929. *The French Powder Mystery*, 1930. *The Dutch Shoe Mystery*, 1931. *The Greek Coffin Mystery*, 1932. *The Egyptian Cross Mystery*, 1932. *The American Gun Mystery*, 1933. *The Siamese Twin Mystery*, 1933. *The Chinese Orange Mystery*, 1934. *The Spanish Cape Mystery*, 1935. *Halfway House*, 1936. *The Door Between*, 1937. *The Devil to Pay*, 1938. *The Four of Hearts*, 1938. *The Dragon's Teeth*, 1939. *Calamity Town*, 1942. *There Was an Old Woman*, 1943. *The Murderer is a Fox*, 1945. *Ten Days' Wonder*, 1948. *Cat of Many Tails*, 1949. *Double, Double*, 1950. *The Origins of Evil*, 1951. *The King is Dead*, 1952. *The Scarlet Letters*, 1953. *The Glass Village*, 1954. *Inspector Queen's Own Case*, 1956. *The Finishing Stroke*, 1958. *The Player on the Other Side*, 1962. *And on the Eighth Day*, 1964. *The Fourth Side of the Triangle*, 1965. *A Study in Terror*, 1966. *Face to Face*, 1967. *The House of Brass*, 1968. *The Last Woman in His Life*, 1970. *A Fine and Private Place*, 1971.

Also, novels with M. B. Lee under joint pseudonym Barnaby Ross: *The Tragedy of X*, Viking, 1932 (reissued as by Ellery Queen, 1940). *The Tragedy of Y*, Viking, 1932 (reissued as by Ellery Queen, 1941). *The Tragedy of Z*, Viking, 1933 (reissued as by Ellery Queen, 1942). *Drury Lane's Last Case*, Viking, 1933 (reissued as by Ellery Queen, 1946).

Also, story collections with Lee under joint pseudonym Ellery Queen: *The Adventures of Ellery Queen*, 1934. *The New Adventures of Ellery Queen*, 1940. *The Case Book of Ellery Queen*, 1945. *Calendar of Crime*, 1952. *Q.B.I.: Queen's Bureau of Investigation*, 1955. *Queens Full*, 1965. *QED: Queen's Experiment in Detection*, 1968.

Also, anthologies and bibliography with Lee under joint pseudonym Ellery Queen: *Challenge to the Reader*, 1938. *101 Years' Entertainment*, 1941. *The Detective Short Story*, 1942. *Sporting Blood*, 1942. *The Female of the Species*, 1943. *The Misadventures of Sherlock Holmes*, 1944. *Best Stories from Ellery Queen's Mystery Magazine*, 1944. *Rogues' Gallery*, 1945. *The Queen's Awards: First Series*, 1946. *To the Queen's Taste*, 1946. *The Queen's Awards: Second Series*, 1947. *Murder by Experts*, 1947. *20th Century Detective Stories*, 1948. *The Queen's Awards: Third Series*, 1948. *The Queen's Awards: Fourth Series*, 1949. *The Queen's Awards: Fifth Series*, 1950. *The Literature of Crime*, 1950. *The Queen's Awards: Sixth Series*, 1951. *The Queen's Awards: Seventh Series*, 1952. *The Queen's Awards: Eighth Series*, 1953. *Ellery Queen's Awards: Ninth Series*, 1954. *Ellery Queen's Awards: Tenth Series*, 1955. *Ellery Queen's Awards: Eleventh Series*, 1956. *Ellery Queen's Awards: Twelfth Series*, 1957. *Ellery Queen's 13th Mystery Annual*, 1958. *Ellery Queen's 1960 Anthology*, 1959. *Ellery Queen's 14th Mystery Annual*, 1959. *Ellery Queen's 1961 Anthology*, 1960. *Ellery Queen's 15th Mystery Annual*, 1960. *Ellery Queen's 1962 Anthology*, 1961. *Ellery Queen's 16th Mystery Annual*, 1961. *The Quintessence of Queen* (ed. by Anthony Boucher), 1962. *To Be Read Before Midnight*, 1962. *Ellery Queen's 1963 Anthology*, 1962. *Ellery Queen's Mystery Mix #18*, 1963. *Ellery Queen's 1964 Anthology*, 1963. *Ellery Queen's Double Dozen*, 1964. *Ellery Queen's 1965 Anthology*, 1964. *Ellery Queen's 20th Anniversary Annual*, 1965. *Ellery Queen's 1966 Annual*, 1965. *Ellery Queen's Crime Carousel*, 1966. *Ellery Queen's 1967 Anthology*, 1967. *Poetic Justice*, 1967. *Ellery Queen's All-Star Lineup*, 1968. *Ellery Queen's 1968 Anthology*, 1968. *Ellery Queen's Mystery Parade*, 1969. *Minimysteries*, 1969. *Ellery Queen's 1969 Anthology*, 1969. *Ellery Queen's Murder Menu*, 1969. *Ellery Queen's Grand Slam*, 1970. *Ellery Queen's 1970 Anthology*, 1970. *Ellery Queen's Headliners*, 1971. *Ellery Queen's 1971 Anthology*, 1971. *Ellery Queen's Mystery Bag*, 1972. *Ellery Queen's 1972 Anthology*, 1972. *Ellery Queen's 1973 Anthology*, 1973. *Ellery Queen's Crookbook*, 1974. *Ellery Queen's 1974 Anthology*, 1974. *Ellery Queen's Murdercade*, 1975. *Ellery Queen's 1975 Anthology*, 1975. *Ellery Queen's Crime Wave*, 1976. *Ellery Queen's 1976 Anthology*, 1976. *Masterpieces of Mystery*, 1976. *Ellery Queen's 1977 Anthology*, 1977. *Ellery Queen's Searches and Seizures*, 1977. *Ellery Queen's Cops and Capers*, 1977. *Ellery Queen's X Marks the Plot*, 1977. *Ellery Queen's Crimes and Consequence*, 1977.

Also, history of the genre and criticism with Lee under joint pseudonym Ellery Queen: *Queen's Quorum*, 1951; *In the Queen's Parlor*, 1957.

Also, with Lee under pseudonym Ellery Queen—Books of True Crime: *Ellery Queen's International Case Book*, 1964; *The Woman in the Case*, 1966.

Also, juvenile books with Lee under joint pseudonym Ellery Queen, Jr.: *The Black Dog Mystery*, 1941. *The Golden Eagle Mystery*, 1942. *The*

Green Turtle Mystery, 1942. *The Red Chipmunk Mystery*, 1946. *The Brown Fox Mystery*, 1948. *The White Elephant Mystery*, 1950. *The Yellow Cat Mystery*, 1952. *The Blue Herring Mystery*, 1954. *The Mystery of the Merry Magician*, 1961. *The Mystery of the Vanished Victim*, 1962. *The Purple Bind Mystery*, 1965. *The Silver Llama Mystery*, 1966.

Also, author with Lee of more than 100 true-crime articles (nonfiction) in *American Weekly* and more than 50 short stories in magazines. Editor of fifteen collections of short stories with Lee and six collections by himself.

DECKER, WILLIAM B.   1926–

To Be a Man, Little, 1967; Pocket, 1975.

DELDERFIELD, R. F.   1912–1972

Napoleon's Marshals, Chilton, 1966. *A Horseman Riding By*, Simon & Schuster, 1967; included in *Post of Honor*, vol. 2, Ballantine, 1974. *Green Gauntlet*, Simon & Schuster, 1968; Ballantine, 1974; Pocket, 1975. *Give Us This Day*, Simon & Schuster, 1968; Pocket, 1975. *The Avenue Goes to War*, Simon & Schuster, 1969; Ballantine, 1975; Pocket, 1976. *Mr. Sermon*, Simon & Schuster, 1969; G. K. Hall, 1972; Pocket, 1975. *Too Few for Drums*, Simon & Schuster, 1971; Pocket, 1974, 1975. *To Serve Them All My Days*, Simon & Schuster, 1972; Pocket, 1975. *Farewell the Tranquil Mind*, Pocket, 1973, 1975. *Long Summer Day*, Pocket, 1974. *Return Journey*, Simon & Schuster, G. K. Hall, 1974. *God is an Englishman*, Pocket, 1975. *Diana*, Pocket, 1975. *Theirs was the Kingdom*, Pocket, 1975. *Seven Men of Gascony*, Simon & Schuster, 1975; Pocket, 1976. *Charlie, Come Home*, Simon & Schuster, 1976.

DELORIA, VINE (VICTOR), JR.   1933–

Custer Died for Your Sins, Macmillan, 1969; Avon, 1970. *We Talk, You Listen: New Tribes, New Turf*, Macmillan, 1970; Dell, 1972, 1974. *The Red Man in the New World Drama* (editor, and author of introduction to the work by Jennings C. Wise), Macmillan, 1971. *Of Utmost Good Faith* (compiler), Straight Arrow, 1971. *God is Red*, Grosset, 1973; Dell, 1975. *Behind the Trail of Broken Treaties*, Delacorte, Dell, 1974. *The Indian Affair*, Friendship, 1974. *Indians of the Pacific Northwest*, Doubleday, 1977. *Planetary Man: The Metaphysics of Modern Existence*, Harper, 1977.

DIMENT, ADAM

The Dolly, Dolly Spy, Dutton, 1967.

DISNEY, DORIS MILES 1907–

A Compound for Death, Doubleday, 1943. *Murder on a Tangent*, Double-day, 1945. *Who Rides the Tiger*, Doubleday, 1946; Ace, 1974. *Dark Road*, Doubleday, 1946. *Appointment at Nine*, Doubleday, 1947. *Enduring Old Charms*, Doubleday, 1947. *Testimony by Silence*, Doubleday, 1948; NAL, 1974. *That Which Is Crooked*, Doubleday, 1948. *Family Skeleton*, Doubleday, 1949. *Count the Ways*, Doubleday, 1949. *Fire at Will*, Dou-bleday, 1950; Manor, 1976. *Look Back on Murder*, Doubleday, 1951. *Straw Man*, Doubleday, 1951. *Heavy, Heavy Hangs*, Doubleday, 1952; Ace, 1976. *Do Unto Others*, Doubleday, 1953. *Prescription: Murder*, Doubleday, 1953. *The Last Straw*, Doubleday, 1954. *Room for Murder*, Doubleday, 1955. *Trick or Treat*, Doubleday, 1955. *Unappointed Rounds*, Doubleday, 1956. *Method in Madness*, Doubleday, 1957. *My Neighbor's Wife*, Doubleday, 1957; NAL, 1974. *Dead Stop*, Dell, 1957. *Too Innocent to Kill*, Avon, 1957. *Black Mail*, Doubleday, 1958. *Quiet Violence*, Foul-sham, 1959. *No Next of Kin*, Doubleday, 1959. *Did She Fall or Was She Pushed?*, Doubleday, 1959. *Dark Lady*, Doubleday, 1960; pub. as *Sinister Lady*, Hale, 1962. *Mrs. Meeker's Money*, Doubleday, 1961. *Should Auld Acquaintance*, Doubleday, 1962. *Find the Woman*, Doubleday, 1962. *Here Lies*, Doubleday, 1963. *The Departure of Mr. Gaudette*, Doubleday, 1964; pub. as *Fateful Departure*, Hale, 1965. *The Hospitality of the House*, Doubleday, 1965. *Unsuspected Evil*, Hale, 1965. *Shadow of a Man*, Doubleday, 1965. *At Some Forgotten Door*, Doubleday, 1966; Man-or, 1975. *The Magic Grandfather*, Doubleday, 1966; Manor, 1975. *Money for the Taking*, Doubleday, 1967. *Night of Clear Choice*, Doubleday, 1967. *Only Couples Need Apply*, NAL, 1974. *Don't Go into the Woods*, NAL, 1975. *Look Back on Murder*, Ace, 1976; *Winifred*, Doubleday, 1976.

DOCTOROW, E. L. 1931–

Welcome to Hard Times, Simon & Schuster, 1960; Random House, 1975; Bantam, 1976. *Big as Life*, Simon & Schuster, 1966. *The Book of Daniel*, Random House, 1971. *Ragtime*, Random House, G. K. Hall, 1975; Ban-tam, 1976.

DURANT, ARIEL K. 1898–

For writings, *see* Will Durant and Ariel Durant, joint authors, below.

DURANT, WILL 1885–

Philosophy and the Social Problem, Macmillan, 1917. *The Story of Phi-losophy*, Simon & Schuster, 1926; rev. ed., 1933. *Transition: A Sentimen-tal Story of One Mind and One Era*, Simon & Schuster, 1927. *Arthur*

Schopenhauer, Works (editor), Simon & Schuster, 1928; rev. ed., Ungar, 1962. *Mansions of Philosophy: A Survey of Human Life and Destiny*, Simon & Schuster, 1929; reissued as *The Pleasures of Philosophy: A Survey of Human Life and Destiny*, Simon & Schuster, 1953. *The Case for India*, Simon & Schuster, 1930. *Adventures in Genius*, Simon & Schuster, 1931; excerpted as *100 Best Books for an Education*, 1933; excerpted as *Great Men of Literature*, 1936. *A Program for America*, Simon & Schuster, 1931. *On the Meaning of Life*, R. R. Smith, 1932. *Tragedy of Russia: Impressions from a Brief Visit*, Simon & Schuster, 1933. *The Story of Civilization*, Simon & Schuster (vol. 1: *Our Oriental Heritage*, 1935. vol. 2: *The Life of Greece*, 1939. vol. 3: *Caesar and Christ*, 1944. vol. 4: *The Age of Faith*, 1950. vol. 5: *The Renaissance*, 1953. vol. 6: *The Reformation*, 1957).

Will Durant and Ariel Durant, joint authors. *The Story of Civilization*, Simon & Schuster (vol. 7: *The Age of Reason Begins*, 1961. vol. 8: *The Age of Louis XIV*, 1963. vol. 9: *The Age of Voltaire*, 1965. vol. 10: *Rousseau and Revolution*, 1967). *The Lessons of History*, Simon & Schuster, 1968. *Interpretations of Life*, Simon & Schuster, 1970. *The Age of Napoleon*, Simon & Schuster, 1975.

DURRELL, LAWRENCE 1912–

Pied Piper of Lovers, Cassell, 1935. *Panic Spring* (under pseud. Charles Norden), Faber, Covici Friede, 1937. *The Black Book: An Agon*, Obelisk, 1938; Dutton, 1960; Faber, 1973. *Prospero's Cell: A Guide to the Landscape and Manners of the Island of Corcyra*, Faber, 1945; Dutton, 1960. *Cefalû*, Editions Poetry, 1947; pub. as *The Dark Labyrinth*, Ace, 1958. *A Landmark Gone*, privately printed, 1949. *Key to Modern Poetry*, Peter Nevill, 1952; pub. as *A Key to Modern British Poetry*, Univ. of Oklahoma, 1952, 1971. *Reflections on a Marine Venus: A Companion to the Landscape of Rhodes*, Faber, 1953; Dutton, 1960. *Esprit de Corps: Sketches from Diplomatic Life*, Faber, 1957; Dutton, 1958. *Bitter Lemons*, Faber, 1957; Dutton, 1958, 1959. *White Eagles over Serbia*, Faber, Criterion, 1957; S. G. Phillips, 1958. Alexandria Quartet: *Justine*, Faber; Dutton, 1957; Pocket, 1975. *Balthazar*, Faber; Dutton, 1958; Pocket, 1975. *Mountolive*, Faber, 1958; Dutton, 1959; Pocket, 1975. *Clea*, Faber; Dutton, 1960; Pocket, 1975. *Stiff Upper Lip: Life among the Diplomats*, Faber, 1958; Dutton, 1959. *Art and Outrage: A Correspondence about Henry Miller Between Perles and Lawrence Durrell, with an Intermission by Henry Miller*, Putnam, 1959; Dutton, 1960. *Lawrence Durrell and Henry Miller: A Private Correspondence* (ed. by George Wickes), Faber; Dutton, 1963. *Sauve Qui Peut*, Faber, 1966; Dutton, 1967; Pocket, 1969. *Tunc*, Faber; Dutton, 1968; Pocket, 1969. *Spirit of Place: Letters and Essays on Travel* (ed. by Alan G. Thomas), Faber; Dutton, 1969; Dutton, 1971. *Nunquam*, Faber; Dutton, 1970; Pocket, 1971. *The Happy Rock*,

Village, 1973. *Le Grand Suppositoire*, Editions Pierre Belfond, 1972; pub. as *The Big Supposer*, Grove, 1974. *The Revolt of Aphrodite*, Faber, 1974. *The Best of Antrobus*, Faber, 1974. *Blue Thirst*, Capra, 1975. *Monsieur; or the Prince of Darkness*, Faber; Viking, 1975; Pocket, 1976.

Also, the following verse: *Quaint Fragment: Poems Written Between the Ages of Sixteen and Nineteen*, Cecil, 1931. *Ten Poems*, Caduseus, 1932. *Bromo Bombastes*, Caduseus, 1933. *Transition: Poems*, Caduseus, 1934. *Poems: An Anthology of Poems* (with others), Fortune, 1938. *A Private Country*, Faber, 1943. *Cities, Plains and People*, Faber, 1946. *Zero, and Asylum in the Snow: Two Excursions into Reality*, privately printed, 1946; Circle, 1947. *On Seeming to Presume*, Faber, 1948. *Deus Loci*, Di Mato Vito, 1950. *Private Drafts*, Proodos, 1955. *The Tree of Idleness and Other Poems*, Faber, 1955. *Selected Poems*, Faber, Grove, 1956. *Collected Poems*, Faber, Dutton, 1960; rev. ed., 1968. *Penguin Modern Poets 1* (with Elizabeth Hennings and R. S. Thomas), Penguin, 1962. *Beccafico Le Becfigue* (trans. by F. J. Temple), La Licorne, 1963. *La Descente du Styx* (trans. by F. J. Temple), La Murene, 1964. *Selected Poems 1935–63*, Faber, 1964, 1974. *The Ikons: New Poems*, Faber, 1966; Dutton, 1967. *The Red Limbo Lingo: A Poetry Notebook for 1968–70*, Faber, Dutton, 1971. *On the Suchness of the Old Boy*, Turret, 1972. *Vega and Other Poems*, Faber, Random House, 1973; Faber, 1974. *Plant-Magic Man*, Capra, 1973.

Also, the following plays: *Sappho: A Play in Verse*, Faber, 1950; Dutton, 1966; Faber, 1967. *An Irish Faustus: A Morality in Nine Scenes*, Faber, 1963; Dutton, 1964. *Acte*, Faber, 1965; Dutton, 1966.

Also, editor, *Personal Landscape: An Anthology of Exile* (with others), Editions Poetry, 1945. *A Henry Miller Reader*, New Directions, 1959; pub. as *The Best of Henry Miller*, Heinemann, 1960. *New Poems, 1963: A P.E.N. Anthology of Contemporary Poetry*, Hutchinson, 1963. *Lears Corfu: An Anthology Drawn from the Painter's Letters*, Corfu Travel, 1965. *Wordsworth*, Penguin, 1973.

Also, translator, *Six Poems from the Greek of Sekilanos and Seferis*, privately printed, 1946. *The Kings of Asine and Other Poems* (by George Seferis), Lehmann, 1948. *The Curious History of Pope Joan* (by Emmanuel Royidas), Verschoyle, 1954; revised as *Pope Joan: A Personal Bibliography*, Deutsch, 1960; Dutton, 1961; Penguin, 1974.

Also, author of a script for television, and music and text for a recording.

EBERHART, MIGNON 1899–

The Patient in Room 18, 1929; Popular, 1972; Aeonian, 1976. *While the Patient Slept*, 1930; Popular, 1973; Aeonian, 1976. *The Mystery of Huntings End*, 1930; Popular, 1972; Aeonian, 1976. *From This Dark Stairway*, 1931; Popular, 1972; Aeonian, 1976. *Murder by an Aristocrat*, 1932; Popular, 1972; Aeonian, 1976. *The White Cockatoo*, 1932; Popular, 1972; Aeonian, 1976. *The Dark Garden*, 1933; Popular, 1973; Aeonian, 1975. *Cases of Susan Dare*, 1934; Popular, 1971; Aeonian, 1975; Popular, 1975. *The House on the Roof*, 1935; Popular, 1972; Aeonian, 1976. *Fair Warning*, 1936; Popular, 1970; Aeonian, Popular, 1975. *Danger in the Dark*, 1936; Popular, 1973; Aeonian, 1975. *The Pattern*, 1937; Popular, 1975; Aeonian, 1976. *Hasty Wedding*, 1938; Popular, 1968; Aeonian, 1976. *The Glass Slipper*, 1938; Popular, 1971; Aeonian, 1976. *The Chiffon Scarf*, 1939; Popular, 1971; Aeonian, Popular; 1975. *Hangman's Whip*, 1940; Popular, 1971; Aeonian, 1976. *Speak No Evil*, 1941; Popular, 1973. *With This Ring*, 1941; Popular, 1970, 1976. *Wolf in Man's Clothing*, 1942; Popular, 1969, 1974. *The Man Next Door*, 1943; Popular, 1970, 1976. *The Unidentified Woman*, 1943; Popular, 1969, 1975. *Escape the Night*, 1944; Popular, 1969. *Wings of Fear*, 1945; Popular, 1969. *The White Dress*, 1946; Popular, 1970, 1976. *Another Woman's House*, 1947; Popular, 1973. *House of Storm*, 1949; Popular, 1969. *Hunt With the Hounds*, 1950; Popular, 1968, 1974. *Never Look Back*, 1951; Popular, 1973. *Dead Men's Plans*, 1952; Popular, 1968, 1974. *Unknown Quantity*, 1953; Popular, 1968, 1974. *Man Missing*, 1954; Popular, 1969, 1974. *Jury of One*, Popular, 1968, 1974. *Woman on the Roof*, Popular, 1969, 1974. *Deadly Is the Diamond*, Popular, 1969, 1974. *Postmark Murder*, Popular, 1969, 1974. *Run Scared*, Popular, 1969, 1974. *The Cup, the Blade or the Gun*, Popular, 1973. *Witness at Large*, Popular, 1973. *Another Man's Murder*, Popular, 1973. *R.S.V.P. Murder*, Popular, 1973. *Danger Money*, Random House, 1974; Popular, 1976. *Family Fortune*, Random House, 1976.

EISELEY, LOREN 1907–

The Immense Journey, Random House, 1957. *Darwin's Century*, Doubleday, 1958. *Firmament of Time*, Atheneum, 1960. *The Mind as Nature*, Harper, 1962. *Francis Bacon and the Modern Dilemma*, Univ. of Nebraska, 1963. *The Unexpected Universe*, Harcourt, 1969, 1972. *The Invisible Pyramid*, Scribner, 1970, 1972. *The Night Country*, Scribner, 1971. *Notes of an Alchemist*, Scribner, 1972, 1974. *The Man Who Saw Through Time*, Scribner, 1973. *The Innocent Assassins*, Scribner, 1973. *All the Strange Hours*, Scribner, 1975. *Another Kind of Autumn*, Scribner, 1977.

ELLISON, JAMES WHITFIELD 1929–

I'm Owen Harrison Harding, Doubleday, 1955; Pocket, 1975. *The Freest Man on Earth*, Doubleday, 1958. *The Summer After the War*, Dodd, 1972. *Proud Rachel*, Stein, 1975.

Also, screenwriter for Columbia Pictures, and editor at several publishing firms.

FALL, BERNARD B. 1926–1967

The Viet-Minh Regime, Southeast Asia Program, Cornell Univ., 1954; 2nd rev. ed., Cornell Univ. and Institute of Pacific Relations, 1956; Greenwood, 1975. *Street Without Joy: Indochina at War, 1946–54*, Stackpole, 1961; pub. as *Insurgency in Indochina*, 4th rev. ed., 1964; Schocken, 1972. *Two Viet-Nams: A Political and Military Analysis*, Praeger, 1963; 2nd rev. ed., 1966. *Viet-Nam Witness, 1953–66*, Praeger, 1966. *Hell in a Very Small Place*, Lippincott, 1966. *Ho Chi Minh on Revolution: Selected Writings, 1920–66* (editor, and author of introduction), Praeger, 1967. *Last Reflections on a War* (ed. by Dorothy Fall), Schocken, 1972.

Also, author of over two hundred articles on politics, military affairs and Indochinese problems.

FARRELL, JAMES T. 1904–

Studs Lonigan: A Trilogy, Vanguard, 1935; Constable, 1936; pub. separately as *Young Lonigan: A Boyhood in Chicago Streets*, Vanguard, 1932; *The Young Manhood of Studs Lonigan*, Vanguard, 1934; *Judgment Day*, Vanguard, 1935. *Gas - Mouse McGinty*, Vanguard, 1933; United Anglo-American Bk. Co., 1948; rev. ed., Avon, 1950. Danny O'Neill Pentalogy: *A World I Never Made*, Vanguard, 1936; Constable, 1938. *No Star Is Lost*, Vanguard, 1938; Constable, 1939. *Father and Son*, Vanguard, 1940; pub. as *A Father and His Son*, Routledge, 1943. *My Days of Anger*, Vanguard, 1943; Routledge, 1945. *The Face of Time*, Vanguard, 1953; Spearman, 1954. *Ellen Rogers*, Vanguard, 1941; Routledge, 1942. Bernard Carr Trilogy: *Bernard Clare*, Vanguard, 1946; pub. as *Bernard Clayre*, Routledge, 1948; pub. as *Bernard Carr*, NAL, 1952. *The Road Between*, Vanguard, Routledge, 1949. *Yet Other Waters*, Vanguard, 1952; Panther, 1960. *The Name Is Fogarty: Private Papers on Public Matters* (under pseud. J. T. Fogarty, Esq.), Vanguard, 1950. *Poet of the People: An Evaluation of James Whitcomb Riley* (with others), Indiana Univ., 1951. *This Man and This Woman*, Vanguard, 1951. *Reflections at Fifty and Other Essays*, Vanguard, 1954; Spearman, 1956. *French Girls Are Vicious and Other Stories*, Vanguard, 1955; Panther, 1958. *An Omnibus of Short Stories*, Vanguard, 1956. *A Dangerous Woman and Other Stories*, NAL, 1957; Panther, 1959. *My Baseball Diary: A Famed Author Recalls the Wonderful World of Baseball, Yesterday and Today*, A. S. Barnes, 1957. *Saturday Night and Other Stories*, Panther, 1958. *It Has Come to Pass*, Herzl, 1958. *Dialogue with John Dewey* (with others), Horizon, 1959. *The Girls at the Sphinx*, Panther, 1959. *Looking 'em Over*, Panther, 1959. *Boarding House Blues*, Paperback Library, 1961; Panther, 1962. *Side Street and Other Stories*, Paperback Library, 1961; Panther, 1962. *Sound of a City*, Paperback Library, 1961. *Selected Essays*, McGraw-Hill, 1964. *A Universe of Time: The Silence of History*, Doubleday, 1963; W. H.

Allen, 1964. *What Time Collects*, Doubleday, 1964; W. H. Allen, 1965. *When Time Was Born*, Horizon, 1966. *Lonely for the Future*, Doubleday; W. H. Allen, 1966. *New Year's Eve/1929*, Horizon, 1967. *A Brand New Life*, Doubleday, 1968. *Judith*, Duane Schneider, 1969. *Invisible Swords*, Doubleday, 1971. *Childhood is Not Forever and Other Stories*, Doubleday, 1969. *Judith and Other Stories*, Doubleday, 1973.

Also, the following poems: *Collected Poems of James T. Farrell*, Fleet, 1965.

Also, editor, *Prejudices* (by H. L. Mencken), Knopf, 1958. *A Dreiser Reader*, Dell, 1962.

FITZGERALD, FRANCES 1940–

Fire in the Lake: The Vietnamese and Americans in Vietnam (excerpts first pub. in the *New Yorker*, 1972), Little, 1972; rev. ed., Random House, 1973.

Also, contributor to newspapers and magazines.

FOWLES, JOHN 1926–

The Collector, Cape, Little, 1958, 1963; Dell, 1975. *The Aristos: A Self-Portrait in Ideas*, Little, 1964; rev. ed., 1970; Cape, 1965; NAL, 1975. *The Magus*, Cape, Little, 1966; Dell, 1973. *The French Lieutenant's Woman*, Cape, Little, 1969; NAL, 1971. *Poems*, Ecco, 1973. *The Ebony Tower: Collected Novellas*, Cape, Little, 1974; NAL, 1975. *Shipwreck*, Cape, 1974; Little, 1975. *Cinderella* (trans. from Perrault), Cape, Little, 1975.

FRANCIS, DICK 1920–

The Sport of Queens: the Autobiography of Dick Francis, Joseph, 1957; rev. ed., Joseph, 1968; Harper, 1969. *Dead Cert*, Joseph, Holt, 1962; Pocket, 1975. *Nerve*, Joseph, Harper, 1964; Pocket, 1975. *For Kicks*, Joseph, Harper, 1965; Pocket, 1975. *Odds Against*, Joseph, 1965; Harper, 1966; Pocket, 1975. *Flying Finish*, Joseph, 1966; Harper, 1967; Pocket, 1975. *Blood Sport*, Joseph, 1967; Harper, 1968; Pocket, 1975. *Forfeit*, Joseph, 1968; Harper, 1969; Pocket, 1975. *Three to Show*, Harper, 1969. *Enquiry*, Joseph, Harper, 1969; Pocket, 1975. *Rat Race*, Joseph, 1970; Harper, 1971. *Bonecrack*, Joseph, 1971; Harper, 1972. *Smokescreen*, Joseph, Harper, 1973; G. K. Hall, 1973. *Slay-Ride*, Joseph, 1973; Harper, 1974; Pocket, 1975. *Knock-Down*, Joseph, 1974; Harper, 1975; Pocket, 1976. *Across the Board*, Harper, 1975. *High Stakes*, Joseph, 1975; Harper, 1976. *In the Frame*, Joseph, 1976; Harper, 1977. *Risk*, Joseph, 1977; Harper, 1978.

Also, the following short stories: "A Carrot for a Chestnut," *Sports Illustrated*, January 1970. "A Day of Wine and Roses," *Sports Illustrated*, May 1973. "The Rape of Kingdom Hill" and "Nightmare," in numerous publications, including the *London Times*.

Also, editor, *Racing Man's Bedside Book* (with John Welcome), *Transatlantic*, 1970.

Also, author of a screenplay and a television series.

FREELING, NICOLAS 1927–

Love in Amsterdam, Gollancz, Harper, 1962; Penguin, 1975. *Because of the Cats*, Gollancz, 1963; Harper, 1964; Penguin, 1975. *Gun before Butter*, Gollancz, 1963; pub. as *Question of Loyalty*, Harper, 1963. *Valparaiso* (under pseud. F. R. E. Nicholas), Gollancz, 1964; pub. as *Nicolas Freeling*, Harper, 1965. *Double Barrel*, Gollancz, Harper; 1964; Penguin, 1975. *Criminal Conversation*, Gollancz, 1965; Harper, 1966. *The King of the Rainy Country*, Gollancz, Harper, 1966. *The Dresden Green*, Gollancz, Harper, 1966. *Strike Out Where Not Applicable*, Gollancz, Harper, 1967. *This Is the Castle*, Gollancz, Harper, 1968. *Tsing-Boum*, Hamish Hamilton, 1969; pub. as *Tsing-Boom!*, Harper, 1970. *Kitchen Book*, Hamish Hamilton, Harper, 1970. *Cook Book*, Hamish Hamilton, 1971. *Over the High Side*, Hamish Hamilton, 1971; pub. as *The Lovely Ladies*, Harper, 1971; Ballantine, 1973. *A Long Silence*, Hamish Hamilton, 1972; pub. as *Auprès de ma blonde*, Harper, 1972. *Dressing of Diamond*, Hamish Hamilton, Harper; 1974; Penguin, 1976. *The Bugles Blowing*, Harper, 1976. *Lake Isle*, Heinemann, 1976; pub. as *Sabine*, Harper, 1978. *Gadget*, Heinemann, Coward; 1977.

GALLICO, PAUL 1897–1976

The Adventures of Hiram Holiday, Knopf, Joseph, 1939. *The Secret Front*, Knopf, 1940. *The Snow Goose*, Knopf, Joseph, 1941. *Confessions of a Story Writer*, Knopf, 1946. *The Lonely*, Joseph, 1947; Knopf, 1949; Avon, 1972. *The Abandoned*, Knopf, 1950; pub. as *Jennie*, Joseph, 1950. *Trial by Terror*, Knopf, Joseph, 1952. *Snowflake*, Joseph, 1952; Doubleday, 1953. *The Foolish Immortals*, Doubleday, Joseph, 1953. *Love of Seven Dolls*, Doubleday, Joseph, 1954. *Ludmila: A Legend of Liechtenstein*, Joseph, 1955; pub. as *Ludmila*, Doubleday, 1959. *The Steadfast Man: A Biography of St. Patrick*, Joseph, 1958. *Thomasina: The Cat Who Thought She Was God*, Doubleday, 1958; pub. as *Thomasina*, Joseph, 1957. *Mrs. 'Arris Goes to Paris*, Doubleday, 1958; pub. as *Flowers for Mrs. Harris*, Joseph, 1958. *Too Many Ghosts*, Doubleday, 1959; Joseph, 1961. *The Hurricane Story* (on World War II), Doubleday, 1960. *Mrs. 'Arris Goes to New York*, Doubleday, 1960; pub. as *Mrs. Harris Goes to New York*, Joseph, 1960. *Further Confessions of a Story Writer: Stories Old and New*, Doubleday, 1961. *Confessions of a Storyteller*, Joseph, 1961. *Scruffy: A Diversion*, Doubleday, Joseph, 1962. *Coronation*, Doubleday, Heinemann, 1962. *Love, Let Me Not Hunger*, Doubleday, Heinemann, 1963. *The Hand of Mary Constable*, Doubleday, Heinemann, 1964; Popular, 1974. *The Silent Miaow: A Manual for Kittens, Strays and*

Homeless Cats, Crown, Heinemann, 1964. *The Golden People*, Double-day, 1965. *Mrs. 'Arris Goes to Parliament*, Doubleday, 1965; pub. as *Mrs. Harris, M.P.*, Heinemann, 1965. *The Man Who Was Magic: A Fable of Innocence*, Doubleday, Heinemann, 1966. *The Story of Silent Night*, Crown, Heinemann, 1967. *The Revealing Eye: Personalities of the 1920's*, Atheneum, 1967. *The Poseidon Adventure*, Coward, Heinemann, 1969; Dell, 1972. *Matilda*, Coward, Heinemann, 1970. *The Zoo Gang*, Coward, Heinemann, 1971; Dell, 1973. *Honorable Cat*, Crown, Heinemann, 1972. *The Boy Who Invented the Bubble Gun: An Odyssey of Innocence*, Dela-corte, Heinemann, 1974; Dell, 1975. *Mrs. Harris Goes to Moscow*, Heine-mann, 1974; pub. as *Mrs. 'Arris Goes to Moscow*, Delacorte, 1975; Dell, 1976. *Miracle in the Wilderness; A Christmas Story of Colonial America*, Delacorte, 1975.

Also, the following juvenile books: *The Small Miracle*, Joseph, 1951; Doubleday, 1952. *The Day the Guinea Pig Talked*, Heinemann, 1963; Doubleday, 1964. *The Day Jean-Pierre Was Pignapped*, Heinemann, 1964; Doubleday, 1965. *The Day Jean-Pierre Went Round the World*, Heinemann, 1965; Doubleday, 1966. *Manxmouse*, Coward, Heinemann, 1968. *The Day Jean-Pierre Joined the Circus*, Heinemann, 1969; Double-day, 1970.

Also, author of numerous plays and adaptations for the stage and film.

GELLHORN, WALTER 1906–

Federal Administrative Proceedings, John Hopkins Univ., 1941; Green-wood, 1972. *Security, Loyalty, and Science*, Cornell Univ., 1950. *The States and Subversion* (coauthor), Cornell Univ., 1952; Greenwood, 1976. *Children and Families in the Courts*, Dodd, 1954. *Individual Freedom and Governmental Restraints*, Louisiana State Univ., 1956; Greenwood, 1968. *The Freedom to Read* (coauthor), Bowker, 1957. *Administrative Law–Cases and Comments*, Foundation, 1940; 6th ed., 1974. *American Rights*, Macmillan, 1960. *Kihonteki Jinken*, Yuhikaku, 1960. *Ombudsmen and Others: Citizens' Protectors in Nine Countries*, Harvard Univ., 1966. *When Americans Complain: Governmental Griev-ance Procedures*, Harvard Univ., 1966. *The Sectarian College and the Public Purse: Fordham—A Case Study*, Oceana, 1970.

Also, member of editorial board, *American Scholar*, 1951–55.

GERVASI, FRANK H. 1908–

War Has Seven Faces, Doubleday, 1942. *But Soldiers Wondered Why*, Doubleday, 1943. *To Whom Palestine?*, Appleton, 1945. *Big Government*, Whittlesey, 1949. *The Real Rockefeller*, Atheneum, 1964. *The Case for Israel*, Viking, 1967. *Adolf Hitler: a Biography*, Hawthorn, 1973. *Thunder Over the Mediterranean*, McKay, 1975.

Also, writer and narrator for television films and programs; contributor to national magazines.

GIBBONS, EUELL 1911-1975

Stalking the Blue-Eyed Scallop, McKay, 1964. *Euell Gibbons' Beachcombers' Handbook*, McKay, 1967. *Stalking the Wild Asparagus*, McKay, 1970. *Stalking the Healthful Herbs*, McKay, 1970. *Stalking the Good Life*, McKay, 1971. *Stalking the Far Away Places*, McKay, 1973. *The Euell Gibbons Stalking Library*, McKay, 1975. *Feast on a Diabetic Diet* (with Joe Gibbons), Fawcett, 1975.

GODDEN, RUMER 1907-

Chinese Puzzle, Davies, 1936. *The Lady and the Unicorn*, Davies, 1938. *Black Narcissus*, Davies, Little, 1939. *Gypsy, Gypsy*, Davies, Little, 1940. *Breakfast with the Nikolides*, Davies, Brown, 1942; Viking, 1964; Avon, 1975. *Runglis–Rungliot* ("Thus Far and No Further"), Davies, 1944; pub. as *Rungli–Rungliot Means in Paharia, Thus Far and No Further*, Little, 1946. *Bengal Journey: A Story of the Part Played by Women in the Province, 1939-1945*, Longman, 1945. *A Fugue in Time*, Joseph, 1945; pub. as *Take Three Tenses: A Fugue in Time*, Little, 1945; Avon, 1976. *The River*, Joseph, Little, 1946; Viking, 1959; Avon, 1975. *A Candle for St. Jude*, Joseph, Viking, 1948; Avon, 1975. *In Noah's Ark*, Joseph, Viking, 1949. *A Breath of Air*, Joseph, 1950; Viking, 1951. *Kingfishers Catch Fire*, Macmillan, Viking, 1953; Avon, 1975. *Hans Christian Andersen: A Great Life in Brief*, Hutchinson, Knopf, 1955. *An Episode of Sparrows*, Viking, 1955; Macmillan, 1956; Avon, 1975. *Mooltiki: Stories and Poems from India*, Macmillan, Viking, 1957. *The Greengage Summer*, Macmillan, Viking, 1958; Avon, 1974. *China Court: The Hours of a Country House*, Macmillan, Viking, 1961; Avon, 1974. *The Battle of the Villa Fiorita*, Macmillan, Viking, 1963; Avon, 1975. *Two Under the Indian Sun* (with Jon Godden), Macmillan, Viking, 1966. *Swans and Turtles: Stories*, Macmillan, 1968; pub. as *Gone: A Thread of Stories*, Viking, 1968; Avon, 1976. *In This House of Brede*, Macmillan, Viking, 1969; Fawcett, 1976. *The Raphael Bible*, Macmillan, Viking, 1970. *The Tale of the Tales*, Warne, 1971. *Shiva's Pigeons: An Experience of India* (with Jon Godden), Chatto and Windus, Viking, 1972. *The Peacock Spring*, Macmillan, 1975; Viking, 1976. *The Butterfly-Lions*, 1977.

Also, the following juvenile books: *The Doll's House*, Joseph, 1947; Viking, 1948, 1962, 1970. *The Mousewife*, Macmillan, Viking, 1951; Viking, 1971. *Impunity Jane: The Story of a Pocket Doll*, Viking, 1954; Macmillan, 1955. *The Fairy Doll*, Macmillan, Viking, 1956. *Mouse House*, Viking, 1957, 1968; Macmillan, 1958. *The Story of Holly and Ivy*, Macmillan, Viking, 1958. *Candy Floss*, Macmillan, Viking, 1960. *Miss Happiness and Miss Flower*, Macmillan, Viking, 1961. *Little Plum*, Macmillan, Viking, 1963. *Home Is the Sailor*, Macmillan, Viking, 1964. *The Kitchen Madonna*, Macmillan, Viking, 1967. *Operation Sippacik*, Macmillan, Viking, 1969. *The Old Woman Who Lived in a Vinegar Bottle*, Macmillan, Viking, 1972; Viking, 1974. *The Diddakoi*, Macmillan, Viking, 1972; G. K. Hall, 1973. *Mr. MacFadden's Hallowe'en*, 1976.

Also, editor, *A Letter to the World: Poems for Young People* (by Emily Dickinson), Bodley Head, 1968. *Mrs. Mander's Cookbook* (by Olga Manders), Macmillan, Viking, 1968.

Also, translator, *Prayers from the Ark* (by Carmen de Gasztold), Macmillan, Viking, 1962.

GORDON, RUTH   1896–

Myself Among Others, Atheneum, 1971. *My Side*, Harper, 1976.

GRAY, FRANCINE du PLESSIX

Divine Disobedience: Profiles in Catholic Radicalism, Knopf, 1970. *Hawaii: The Sugar-Coated Fortress*, Random House, 1972. *Lovers and Tyrants*, Simon & Schuster, 1976.

GRAY, MARTIN

For Those I Loved (with M. Gallo), Little, 1972; NAL, 1974. *A Book of Life*, G. K. Hall, Seabury, 1975.

GREEN, GERALD   1922–

His Majesty O'Keefe (with L. Kingman), Scribner, 1948; Rivercity Pr., 1976. *The Sword and the Sun*, Scribner, 1950. *The Last Angry Man*, Scribner, 1957; Pocket, 1974; Rivercity Pr., 1976. *The Lotus Eaters*, Scribner, 1959; Rivercity Pr., 1976. *The Heartless Light*, Scribner, 1961; Rivercity Pr., 1976. *The Portofino PTA*, Scribner, 1962; Rivercity Pr., 1976. *The Legion of Noble Christians; or, the Sweeney Survey*, Trident, 1965. *The Senator* (with Drew Pearson), Doubleday, 1968. *To Brooklyn with Love*, Trident, 1968. *The Artists of Terezin*, Hawthorn, 1969. *Faking It; or, The Wrong Hungarian*, Trident, 1971; Pocket, 1972. *The Stones of Zion: A Novelist's Journal in Israel*, Hawthorn, 1971. *Blockbuster*, Doubleday, 1972. *Tourist*, Doubleday, 1973; Popular, 1975. *My Son the Jock*, Praeger, 1975. *The Hostage Heart*, Playboy, 1976.

Also, author of an adaptation for film.

GREER, GERMAINE   1939–

The Female Eunuch, McGraw-Hill, 1971; Bantam, 1972.

GROSVENOR, VERTA MAE   1939–

Vibration Cooking, or the travel notes of a geechee girl, Doubleday, 1970. *Thursdays and every sundays off, a domestic rap*, Doubleday, 1972. *And if i show you my tenderness . . .*, Doubleday, 1978.

GROUEFF, STEPHANE

Manhattan Project, Little, 1967. *L'Homme et la Mer*, Larousse, 1973. *L'Homme et la Terre*, Larousse, 1974. *L'Homme et le Cosmos*, Larousse, 1975.

HALEY, ALEX   1921–

Autobiography of Malcolm X (editor), Grove, 1965. *Roots*, Doubleday, 1976.

HASLIP, JOAN

Out of Focus, 1931. *Grandfathers Steps*, 1932. *Lady Hester Stanhope*, 1934. *Parnell*, 1936; Folcroft, 1937. *Portrait of Pamela*, 1940, 1948. *Lucrezia Borgia*, 1953. *The Sultan*, 1958; Holt, 1973. *The Lonely Empress*, 1963, 1965; Avon, 1973. *The Crown of Mexico*, Holt, 1972; Avon, 1973. *Catherine the Great*, Putnam, 1977.

HECKSCHER, AUGUST   1913–

These Are the Days, Yale Daily News, 1936. *A Pattern of Politics*, Reynal, 1947. *The Politics of Woodrow Wilson* (editor), Harper, 1956. *Diversity of Worlds* (with Raymond Aron), Reynal, 1957. *The Public Happiness*, Atheneum, 1962.
Also, frequent contributor to magazines.

HIGHET, GILBERT   1906–

The Classical Tradition: Greek and Roman Influences on Western Literature, Oxford Univ., 1949, 1957. *The Art of Teaching*, Knopf, 1950; Random House, 1954. *People, Places, and Books*, Oxford Univ., 1953. *Man's Unconquerable Mind*, Columbia Univ., 1954. *The Migration of Ideas*, Oxford Univ., 1954. *Juvenal the Satirist*, Oxford Univ., 1954, 1961. *A Clerk of Oxenford*, Oxford Univ., 1954. *Poets in a Landscape*, Knopf, 1957. *Talents and Geniuses*, Oxford Univ., 1957. *The Power of Poetry*, Oxford Univ., 1960. *The Anatomy of Satire*, Princeton Univ., 1962. *Explorations*, Oxford Univ., 1971. *The Speeches in Vergil's "Aeneid,"* Princeton Univ., 1972. *The Immortal Profession: The Joys of Teaching and Learning*, Weybright, 1976.

HILLARY, SIR EDMUND 1919–

Crossing of Antarctica the Commonwealth Trans-Antarctic Expedition, 1955–1958 (with Vivian Fuchs), Greenwood, 1959. *Nothing Venture, Nothing Win*, Coward, 1975.

HOLLAND, CECELIA 1943–

The Firedrake, Atheneum, 1966. *Rakossy*, Atheneum, 1967. *The Kings in Winter*, Atheneum, 1968; Pocket, 1969. *Until the Sun Falls*, Atheneum, 1969; Pocket, 1970. *Antichrist*, Atheneum, 1970. *The Earl*, Knopf, 1971. *Death of Attila*, Knopf, 1973; Ballantine, 1974. *Great Maria*, Knopf, 1974; Warner, 1975. *Floating Worlds*, Knopf, 1976.

 Also, the following juvenile books: *Ghost on the Steppe*, Atheneum, 1970. *The King's Road*, Atheneum, 1971.

HUIE, WILLIAM BRADFORD 1910–

The Fight for Air Power, Fischer, 1942. *Mud on the Stars*, Fischer, 1942; Hutchinson, 1944. *Seabee Roads to Victory*, Dutton, 1944. *Can Do! The Story of the Seabees*, Dutton, 1944. *From Omaha to Okinawa: The Story of the Seabees*, Dutton, 1946. *The Case against the Admirals: Why We Must Have a Unified Command*, Dutton, 1946. *The Revolt of Mamie Stover*, Duell, 1951; W. H. Allen, 1953; Dell, 1972. *The Execution of Private Slovik: The Hitherto Secret Story of the Only American Soldier since 1864 to Be Shot for Desertion*, Duell, 1954; Delacorte, 1970; Dell. *Ruby McCollum: Woman in the Suwanee Jail*, Dutton, 1956; pub. as *The Crime of Ruby McCollum*, Jarolds, 1957. *Wolf Whistle and Other Stories*, NAL, 1959. *The Americanization of Emily*, Dutton, 1959; W. H. Allen, 1960. *The Hero of Iwo Jima and Other Stories*, NAL, 1962. *Hotel Mamie Stover*, W. H. Allen, 1962; Potter, 1963. *The Hiroshima Pilot*, Putnam, Heinemann, 1964. *Three Lives for Mississippi*, Whitney Communication Corp., Heinemann, 1965. *The Klansman*, Dial, 1967; W. H. Allen, 1968. *He Slew the Dreamer: My Search with James Earl Ray for Truth about the Murder of Martin Luther King*, Delacorte, W. H. Allen, 1970. *In the Hours of the Night*, Delacorte, 1971. *A New Life to Live*, Thomas Nelson, 1977. *Did the F.B.I. Kill Martin Luther King?*, Thomas Nelson, 1977.

HUNTLEY, CHET 1911–1974

The Generous Years, Random House, 1968.

JAMES, P. D. 1920–

Cover Her Face, Faber, 1962; Scribner, 1966. *A Mind to Murder*, Faber, 1963; Popular, 1976. *Unnatural Causes*, Scribner, Faber, 1967; Popular, 1975. *Shroud for a Nightingale*, Scribner, Faber, 1971; Popular, 1976. *The*

Maal and the Pear Tree (with T. A. Critchey), Constable, 1971. *An Unsuitable Job for a Woman*, Faber, 1972; Popular, 1975. *The Black Tower*, Scribner, Faber, 1975; Popular, 1976. *Death of an Expert Witness*, Scribner, Faber, 1977.

KALB, BERNARD 1932–

Kissinger (with Marvin Kalb), Little, 1974. Also, contributor to newspapers and magazines.

KALB, MARVIN L. 1930–

Eastern Exposure, Farrar, 1958. *Dragon in the Kremlin*, Dutton, 1961. *The Volga: A Political Journey through Russia*, Macmillan, 1967. *Roots of Involvement* (with Elie Abel), Norton, 1971. *Kissinger* (with Bernard Kalb), Little, 1974. *In the National Interest*, Simon & Schuster, 1977.

Also, author of introduction to *One Day in the Life of Ivan Denisovich*, Dutton, 1963.

Also, contributor to various magazines.

KANTOR, MACKINLAY 1904–

Diversey, Coward, 1928. *El Goes South*, Coward, 1930. *The Jaybird*, Coward, 1932. *Long Remember*, Coward, 1934. *Turkey in the Straw*, Coward, 1935. *The Voice of Bugle Ann*, Coward, 1935; school edition by F. H. Law, Globe, 1953. *Arouse and Beware*, Coward, 1936. *The Romance of Rosy Ridge*, Coward, 1937. *The Boy in the Dark*, International Mark Twain Society, 1937. *The Noise of Their Wings*, Coward, 1938. *Valedictory*, Coward, 1939. *Cuba Libre: A Story*, Coward, 1940. *Angleworms on Toast*, Coward, 1942. *Gentle Annie*, Coward, 1942. *Happy Land*, Coward, 1943. *Author's Choice*, Coward, 1944. *Happy Land and Gentle Annie*, Dial, 1944. *Glory for Me*, Coward, 1945. *But Look the Morn*, Coward, 1947. *Midnight Lace*, Random House, 1948. *Wicked Water: An American Primitive*, Random House, 1948. *The Good Family*, Coward, 1949. *One Wild Oat*, Fawcett, 1950. *Signal Thirty-Two*, Random House, 1950. *Lee and Grant at Appomattox*, Random House, 1951. *Don't Touch Me*, Random House, 1951. *Gettysburg*, Random House, 1952. *Warhoop*, Random House, 1952. *The Daughter of Bugle Ann*, Random House, 1953. *God and My Country*, World Publishing, 1954. *Andersonville*, World Publishing, 1955; abridged edition, W. H. Allen, 1956. *Lobo*, World Publishing, 1957. *Silent Grow the Guns, and Other Tales of the American Civil War*, NAL, 1959. *Frontier: Tales of the American Adventure*, NAL, 1959. *The Work of St. Francis*, World Publishing, 1959; pub. as *The Unseen Witness*, W. H. Allen, 1959. *It's about Crime*, NAL, 1960. *If the South Had Won the Civil War*, Bantam, 1961. *Spirit Lake*, World Publishing, 1961. *Three: Happy Land, Lobo, Cuba Libre*, Paperback Library, 1962. *The Gun-Toter and Other Stories of the Missouri Hills*, NAL, 1963. *Mission with LeMay: My Story* (with Curtis E. LeMay), Doubleday, 1965. *Story Teller*, Doubleday, 1967. *Beauty Beast*, Putnam, 1968. *The Day I Met a Lion*, Doubleday, 1968. *Missouri Bittersweet*, Doubleday, 1969. *Hamilton County* (with Tim Kantor), Macmillan, 1970. *I Love You, Irene*, Doubleday, 1972. *The Children Sing*, Hawthorn, 1973. *Valley Forge*, M. Evans, 1975.

KAZAN, ELIA 1909–

America, America, Stein, 1962, 1974. *The Arrangement*, Stein, 1966, 1974; Warner, 1976. *The Assassins*, Stein, 1972. *The Understudy*, Stein, 1974, 1975.

Also, author of an adaptation for film; contributor to several magazines.

KEMELMAN, HARRY 1908–

Friday the Rabbi Slept Late, Crown, 1964; Lanewood, 1972; Fawcett, 1975. *Saturday the Rabbi Went Hungry*, Crown, 1966; rev. ed., Fawcett, 1976. *The Nine Mile Walk: The Nicky Welt Stories of Harry Kemelman*, Putnam, 1967; Fawcett, 1972. *Sunday the Rabbi Stayed Home*, Putnam, Lanewood, 1969; Fawcett, 1975. *Common Sense in Education*, Crown, 1970. *Monday the Rabbi Took Off*, Putnam, 1972; Fawcett, 1975. *Tuesday the Rabbi Saw Red*, Arthur Fields' Bks., 1973; G. K. Hall, 1974; Fawcett, 1976. *Wednesday the Rabbi Got Wet*, Morrow, 1976.

Also, author of "Nicky Welt" series in *Ellery Queen's Mystery Magazine*. Contributor to *Bookman*.

KENEALLY, THOMAS 1935–

The Place at Whitton, Cassell, 1964; Walker, 1965. *The Fear*, Cassell, 1965; Soccer, 1976. *Bring Larks and Heroes*, Cassell, 1967, 1968; Viking, 1968; Belmont-Tower, 1972. *Three Cheers for the Paraclete*, Angus and Robertson, 1968, 1969; Viking, 1969; Belmont-Tower, 1972. *The Survivor*, Angus and Robertson, 1969, 1970; Belmont-Tower, 1972. *A Dutiful Daughter*, Angus and Robertson, Viking, 1971. *The Chant of Jimmie Blacksmith*, Angus and Robertson, Viking, 1972. *Blood Red, Sister Rose*, Collins, 1974; pub. as *Blood Red, Sister Rose: A Novel of the Maid of Orleans*, Viking, 1975; Ballantine, 1976. *Moses the Lawgiver*, Harper, 1975. *Gossip from the Forest*, Harcourt, 1976.

Also, author of plays for the stage and television.

KIRST, HANS HELLMUT 1914–

Night of the Generals, Harcourt, 1964. *The Wolves*, Coward, 1968. *Damned to Success* (trans. by J. Maxwell), Coward, 1973; Berkley, 1975. *A Time for Truth*, Coward, 1974. *Revolt of Gunner Ashe*, Pyramid, 1975.

Everything Has Its Price (trans. by J. Maxwell), Coward, 1976. *Forward, Gunner Ashe*, Pyramid, 1976. *The Night of the Long Knives* (trans. by J. Maxwell), Coward, 1976. *The Return of Gunner Ashe*, Pyramid, 1976.

KNEF, HILDEGARD 1925–

Der geschenkte Gaul: Bericht aus einem Leben, Verlag Fritz Molden, 1970; pub. as *The Gift Horse: Report on Life* (trans. by David Palastanga), McGraw-Hill, 1971; Dell, 1972. *The Verdict*, Farrar, 1976.

KOESTLER, ARTHUR 1905–

Von Weissen Nachten und Roten Tage, Ukrainian State Pubs. for National Minorities, 1933. *Menschenopfer Unerhort*, Carrefour, 1937. *Spanish Testament*, Gollancz, 1937; abridged as *Dialogue with Death*, Macmillan, 1942. *The Gladiators* (trans. by Edith Simon), Cape, 1939; Macmillan, 1939, 1967. *Darkness at Noon* (trans. by Daphne Hardy), Cape, 1940; Macmillan, 1941; Bantam, 1970; Modern Lib. *Scum of the Earth*, Cape, 1941; Macmillan; 1968. *Arrival and Departure*, Cape, 1943; Macmillan, 1943, 1967. *The Yogi and the Commissar and Other Essays*, Cape, 1945; Macmillan 1945, 1967. *Thieves in the Night: Chronicle of an Experiment*, Macmillan, 1946, 1967. *Les Temps Heroiques*, Occident, 1948. *Insight and Outlook: An Inquiry into the Common Foundations of Science, Art, and Social Ethics*, Macmillan, 1949. *Promise and Fulfillment: Palestine 1917–1949*, Macmillan, 1949. *The Age of Longing*, Collins, Macmillan, 1951. *Arrow in the Blue*, Collins-Hamish Hamilton, 1952; Macmillan, 1952, 1967, 1970. *The Trail of the Dinosaur and Other Essays*, Collins, Macmillan, 1955. *Reflections on Hanging*, Gollancz, Macmillan, 1957. *The Sleepwalkers: A History of Man's Changing Vision of the Universe*, Hutchinson, Macmillan, 1959; Grosset, 1963; section published as *The Watershed: A Biography of Johannes Kepler*, Doubleday, 1960. *The Lotus and the Robot*, Hutchinson, 1960; Macmillan, 1961; Harcourt. *Hanged by the Neck: An Exposure of Capital Punishment in England* (with C. H. Rolph), Penguin, 1961. *The Act of Creation*, Hutchinson, Macmillan, 1964; Dell, 1966. *Dialogue with Death*, Macmillan, 1967. *Ghost in the Machine*, Hutchinson, 1967; Macmillan, 1968; Regnery. *Drinkers of Infinity: Essays 1955–1967*, Hutchinson, 1968; Macmillan, 1969. *Beyond Reductionism: New Perspectives in the Life of Sciences* (with J. R. Smythies), Macmillan, 1970. *The Call-Girls: A Tragi-Comedy with Prologue and Epilogue*, Hutchinson, 1972; Random House, 1973; Dell, 1974. *The Case of the Midwife Toad*, Hutchinson, 1971; Random House, 1972, 1973. *The Roots of Coincidence*, Hutchinson, 1972; Random House, 1972, 1973. *The Lion and the Ostrich*, Oxford Univ., 1973. *The Challenge of Chance: Experiments and Speculations*, Hutchinson, 1973; pub. as *The Challenge of Chance: A Mass Experiment in Telepathy and Its Unexpected Outcome*, Random House, 1975. *The Heel of Achil-*

les: Essays 1968–1973, Hutchinson, 1974; Random House, 1975. *The Thirteenth Tribe: The Kazer Empire & Its Heritage*, Hutchinson, Random House, 1976.

Also, the play *Twilight Bar: An Escapade in Four Acts*, Cape, Macmillan, 1945; and a screenplay for a documentary.

Also, editor, *Suicide of a Nation: An Enquiry into the State of Britain Today*, Macmillan, 1964; Hutchinson, Random House, 1976.

KOSINSKI, JERZY 1933–

The Future Is Ours, Comrade (under pseud. Joseph Novak), Doubleday, 1960; Reinhardth, 1961; Dutton, 1964. *No Third Path* (under pseud. Joseph Novak), Doubleday, 1962. *Notes of the Author on "The Painted Bird" 1965*, Scientia Factum, 1965. *The Painted Bird*, Houghton Mifflin, 1965, 1975; W. H. Allen, 1966; rev. ed., Modern Library, 1970; Bantam, 1972. *The Art of the Self: Essays à propos "Steps"*, Scientia Factum, 1968. *Steps*, Random House, 1968; Bodley Head, Bantam, 1969. *The Time of Life: A Time of Art*, De Bezige Bij, 1970. *Being There*, Harcourt, Bodley Head, 1971; Bantam, 1972. *The Devil Tree*, Harcourt, Hart Davis MacGibbon, 1973; Bantam, 1974. *Cockpit*, Houghton Mifflin, Hutchinson, 1975; Bantam, 1976. *Blind Date*, Houghton Mifflin, 1977; Hutchinson, 1978.

Also, editor, *Socjologia Amerykanska: Wybor Prac 1950–1960*, Polish Inst. Arts, 1962.

KOTLOWITZ, ROBERT 1924–

Somewhere Else, Charterhouse, 1972; Dell, 1974. *The Boardwalk*, Knopf, 1977.

Also, contributor to various periodicals, and Contributing Editor, *Atlantic Monthly*, 1971–1976.

LEE, MANFRED B. 1905–1971

Ellery Queen, Ellery Queen, Jr., and Barnaby Ross are all joint pseudonyms of coauthors Manfred B. Lee and Frederic Dannay. Except as noted, the Ellery Queen books were published by Stokes and Lippincott to 1940, and by Little, Simon & Schuster, Random House, 1940–1966, by NAL, 1966–68, by World, 1969–.

Novels with Frederic Dannay under joint pseudonym Ellery Queen: *The Roman Hat Mystery*, 1929. *The French Powder Mystery*, 1930. *The Dutch Shoe Mystery*, 1931. *The Greek Coffin Mystery*, 1932. *The Egyptian Cross Mystery*, 1932. *The American Gun Mystery*, 1933. *The Siamese Twin Mystery*, 1933. *The Chinese Orange Mystery*, 1934. *The Spanish Cape Mystery*, 1935. *Halfway House*, 1936. *The Door Between*, 1937. *The Devil to Pay*, 1938. *The Four of Hearts*, 1938. *The Dragon's Teeth*, 1939.

Calamity Town, 1942. *There Was an Old Woman*, 1943. *The Murderer is a Fox*, 1945. *Ten Days' Wonder*, 1948. *Cat of Many Tails*, 1949. *Double, Double*, 1950. *The Origins of Evil*, 1951. *The King is Dead*, 1952. *The Scarlet Letters*, 1953. *The Glass Village*, 1954. *Inspector Queen's Own Case*, 1956. *The Finishing Stroke*, 1958. *The Player on the Other Side*, 1962. *And on the Eighth Day*, 1964. *The Fourth Side of the Triangle*, 1965. *A Study in Terror*, 1966. *Face to Face*, 1967. *The House of Brass*, 1968. *The Last Woman in His Life*, 1970. *A Fine and Private Place*, 1971.

Also, novels with Frederic Dannay under joint pseudonym Barnaby Ross: *The Tragedy of X*, Viking, 1932 (reissued as by Ellery Queen, 1940). *The Tragedy of Y*, Viking, 1932 (reissued as by Ellery Queen, 1941). *The Tragedy of Z*, Viking, 1933 (reissued as by Ellery Queen, 1942). *Drury Lane's Last Case*, Viking, 1933 (reissued as by Ellery Queen, 1946).

Also, story collections with Dannay under joint pseudonym Ellery Queen: *The Adventures of Ellery Queen*, 1934. *The New Adventures of Ellery Queen*, 1940. *The Case Book of Ellery Queen*, 1945. *Calendar of Crime*, 1952. *Q.B.I.: Queen's Bureau of Investigation*, 1955. *Queens Full*, 1965. *QED: Queen's Experiment in Detection*, 1968.

Also, anthologies and bibliography with Dannay under joint pseudonym Ellery Queen: *Challenge to the Reader*, 1938. *101 Years' Entertainment*, 1941. *The Detective Short Story*, 1942. *Sporting Blood*, 1942. *The Female of the Species*, 1943. *The Misadventures of Sherlock Holmes*, 1944. *Best Stories from Ellery Queen's Mystery Magazine*, 1944. *Rogues' Gallery*, 1945. *The Queen's Awards: First Series*, 1946. *To the Queen's Taste*, 1946. *The Queen's Awards: Second Series*, 1947. *Murder by Experts*, 1947. *20th Century Detective Stories*, 1948. *The Queen's Awards: Third Series*, 1948. *The Queen's Awards: Fourth Series*, 1949. *The Queen's Awards: Fifth Series*, 1950. *The Literature of Crime*, 1950. *The Queen's Awards: Sixth Series*, 1951. *The Queen's Awards: Seventh Series*, 1952. *The Queen's Awards: Eighth Series*, 1953. *Ellery Queen's Awards: Ninth Series*, 1954. *Ellery Queen's Awards: Tenth Series*, 1955. *Ellery Queen's Awards: Eleventh Series*, 1956. *Ellery Queen's Awards: Twelfth Series*, 1957. *Ellery Queen's 13th Mystery Annual*, 1958. *Ellery Queen's 1960 Anthology*, 1959. *Ellery Queen's 14th Mystery Annual*, 1959. *Ellery Queen's 1961 Anthology*, 1960. *Ellery Queen's 15th Mystery Annual*, 1960. *Ellery Queen's 1962 Anthology*, 1961. *Ellery Queen's 16th Mystery Annual*, 1961. *The Quintessence of Queen* (ed. by Anthony Boucher), 1962. *To Be Read Before Midnight*, 1962. *Ellery Queen's 1963 Anthology*, 1962. *Ellery Queen's Mystery Mix #18*, 1963. *Ellery Queen's 1964 Anthology*, 1963. *Ellery Queen's Double Dozen*, 1964. *Ellery Queen's 1965 Anthology*, 1964. *Ellery Queen's 20th Anniversary Annual*, 1965. *Ellery Queen's 1966 Annual*, 1965. *Ellery Queen's Crime Carousel*, 1966. *Ellery Queen's 1967 Anthology*, 1967. *Poetic Justice*, 1967. *Ellery Queen's All-Star Lineup*, 1968. *Ellery Queen's 1968 Anthology*, 1968. *El-*

lery Queen's Mystery Parade, 1969. *Minimysteries*, 1969. *Ellery Queen's 1969 Anthology*, 1969. *Ellery Queen's Murder Menu*, 1969. *Ellery Queen's Grand Slam*, 1970. *Ellery Queen's 1970 Anthology*, 1970. *Ellery Queen's Headliners*, 1971. *Ellery Queen's 1971 Anthology*,1971. *Ellery Queen's Mystery Bag*, 1972. *Ellery Queen's 1972 Anthology*, 1972. *Ellery Queen's 1973 Anthology*, 1973. *Ellery Queen's Crookbook*, 1974. *Ellery Queen's 1974 Anthology*, 1974. *Ellery Queen's Murdercade*, 1975. *Ellery Queen's 1975 Anthology*, 1975. *Ellery Queen's Crime Wave*, 1976. *Ellery Queen's 1976 Anthology,* 1976. *Masterpieces of Mystery,* 1976. *Ellery Queen's 1977 Anthology*, 1977. *Ellery Queen's Searches and Seizures*, 1977. *Ellery Queen's Cops and Capers*, 1977. *Ellery Queen's X Marks the Plot*, 1977. *Ellery Queen's Crimes and Consequence*, 1977.

Also, history of the genre and criticism with Dannay under joint pseudonym Ellery Queen: *Queen's Quorum*, 1951; *In the Queen's Parlor*, 1957.

Also, with Dannay under pseudonym Ellery Queen—Books of True Crime: *Ellery Queen's International Case Book*, 1964; *The Woman in the Case*, 1966.

Also, juvenile books with Dannay under joint pseudonym Ellery Queen, Jr.: *The Black Dog Mystery*, 1941. *The Golden Eagle Mystery*, 1942. *The Green Turtle Mystery*, 1942. *The Red Chipmunk Mystery*, 1946. *The Brown Fox Mystery*, 1948. *The White Elephant Mystery*, 1950. *The Yellow Cat Mystery*, 1952. *The Blue Herring Mystery*, 1954. *The Mystery of the Merry Magician*, 1961. *The Mystery of the Vanished Victim*, 1962. *The Purple Bind Mystery*, 1965. *The Silver Llama Mystery*, 1966.

Also, author with Dannay of more than 100 true-crime articles in *American Weekly* and more than 50 short stories in magazines. Editor of fifteen collections of short stories with Dannay.

LESSING, DORIS 1919–

The Grass Is Singing, Joseph, 1950; Crowell, 1950, 1975; NAL, Popular, 1976. *This Was the Old Chief's Country: Stories*, Joseph, 1951; Crowell, 1952. *Martha Quest* (Children of Violence), Joseph, 1952; NAL, 1970. *Five: Short Novels*, Joseph, 1953. *A Proper Marriage*, Joseph, 1954; with *Martha Quest*, Simon & Schuster, 1964; NAL, 1970. *Going Home*, Joseph, 1957; Ballantine, 1968; Popular, 1975. *The Habit of Loving*, MacGibbon & Kee, 1957; Crowell, 1958, 1974; Popular, 1973, 1976; NAL, 1976. *A Ripple from the Storm* (Children of Violence), Joseph, 1958; NAL, 1970. *Fourteen Poems*, Scorpion, 1959. *In Pursuit of the English: A Documentary*, Joseph, 1960; pub. as *Portrait of the English*, Simon & Schuster, 1961; Popular, 1975. *The Golden Notebook*, Simon & Schuster, 1962; NAL, 1970; Bantam, 1973. *A Man and Two Women: Stories*, MacGibbon & Kee, Simon & Schuster, 1963; Popular, 1975. *Landlocked*

(Children of Violence), MacGibbon & Kee, 1965; with *A Ripple from the Storm*, Simon & Schuster, 1966. *African Stories*, Joseph, 1964; Simon & Schuster, 1965; Popular, 1975. *Particularly Cats*, Joseph, Simon & Schuster, 1967; NAL, 1971. *Nine African Stories*, Longman, 1968. *The Four-Gated City* (Children of Violence), MacGibbon & Kee, Knopf, 1969; Bantam, 1970; NAL, 1976. *Briefing for a Descent into Hell*, Cape, Knopf, 1971; Bantam, 1972. *The Story of a Non-Marrying Man and Other Stories*, Knopf, 1972. *The Temptation of Jack Orkney and Other Stories*, Knopf, 1972; Bantam, 1974. *The Summer Before the Dark*, Cape, Knopf, 1973. *The Sun Between Their Feet*, Joseph, 1973. *This Was the Old Chief's Country*, Joseph, 1973. *A Small Personal Voice: Essays, Reviews, Interviews* (ed. by Peter Schlueter), Knopf, 1974; Random House, 1975. *The Memoirs of a Survivor*, Octagon, 1974; Knopf, 1975; Bantam, 1976.

Also, the following plays: "Each His Own Wilderness," included in *New English Dramatists*, Penguin, 1959. *Play with a Tiger*, Joseph, 1962. *The Singing Door* (ed. by Alan Durband), Hutchinson, 1973. And other works for the stage and television.

LEVIN, IRA 1929–

A Kiss Before Dying, Simon & Schuster, 1953; Joseph, 1954. *Rosemary's Baby*, Random House, Joseph, 1967. *This Perfect Day*, Random House, Joseph, 1970; Fawcett, 1976. *The Stepford Wives*, Random House, Joseph, 1972.

Also, the following plays: *No Time for Sergeants* (adaptation of the novel by Marc Hyman), Random House, 1956. *Interlock*, Dramatists Play Service, 1962. *Critics Choice*, Random House, 1961. *Veronica's Room*, Random House, 1974. And other works, including those for the stage and film.

LOCKWOOD, LEE 1932–

Castro's Cuba, Cuba's Fidel, Macmillan, 1967; Random House, 1969. *Conversations with Eldridge Cleaver/Algiers*, McGraw-Hill, Dell, 1970. *Absurd Convictions, Modest Hopes* (with Daniel Berrigan), Random House, 1972.

Also, editor, *Contemporary Photographer Quarterly*, 1963–1967.

LOOS, ANITA 1893–

Gentlemen Prefer Blondes: The Illuminating Diary of a Professional Lady, Boni & Liveright, 1926. *But Gentlemen Marry Brunettes*, Boni & Liveright, 1928. *A Mouse Is Born*, Doubleday, 1951. *No Mother to Guide Her*, McGraw-Hill, 1961. *A Girl Like I*, Viking, 1966; Ballantine, 1975. *The King's Mare* (trans. and adapt. of the work by Jean Canolle), Evans, 1967. *Twice Over Lightly* (with Helen Hayes), Harcourt, 1972. *Kiss Holly-*

wood Goodbye, Viking, 1974; Ballantine; G. K. Hall, 1975. *The Anita Loos Scrapbook*, Grosset, 1976. *Breaking into the Movies* (with John Emerson).

Also, author of foreword, *Women, Women, Women* (by Dody Goodman), Dutton, 1966.

Also, the plays: *Happy Birthday*, French, 1948. *Gigi* (adapted from the novel by Colette), Random House, 1952; rev. ed., 1956.

Also, author of numerous plays, screenplays, and books for musicals.

LUCAS, J. ANTHONY 1933–

The Barnyard Epithet and Other Obscenities: Notes on the Chicago Conspiracy Trial, Harper, 1970. *Don't Shoot We are Your Children!*, Random House, 1971. Also, contributor to magazines.

McCARTHY, MARY 1912–

The Company She Keeps, Simon & Schuster, 1942; Weidenfeld and Nicolson, 1957. *The Oasis*, Random House, 1949; pub. as *A Source of Embarrassment*, Heinemann, 1950. *Cast a Cold Eye*, Harcourt, 1950; Heinemann, 1952. *The Groves of Academe*, Harcourt, 1952; Heinemann, 1953. *A Charmed Life*, Harcourt, 1955; Weidenfeld and Nicolson, 1956. *Sights and Spectacles, 1937–56*, Farrar, 1956; pub. as *Sights and Spectacles: Theatre Chronicles, 1937–58*, Heinemann, 1959; pub. as *Mary McCarthy's Theatre Chronicles, 1937–62*, Farrar, 1963. *Venice Observed: Comments on Venetian Civilization*, Reynal, Zwemmer, 1956; Harcourt, 1963. *Memories of a Catholic Girlhood*, Harcourt, Heinemann, 1957; Harcourt, 1972. *The Stones of Florence*, Harcourt, Heinemann, 1959; Harcourt, 1963, 1976. *On the Contrary*, Farrar, 1961; Heinemann, 1962; Octagon, 1976. *The Group*, Harcourt, Weidenfeld and Nicolson, 1963. *Vietnam*, Harcourt, Weidenfeld and Nicolson, 1967. *Hanoi*, Harcourt, Weidenfeld and Nicolson, 1968. *The Writing on the Wall*, Harcourt, Weidenfeld and Nicolson, 1970; Harcourt, 1971. *Birds of America*, Harcourt, Weidenfeld and Nicolson, 1971. *Medina*, Harcourt, 1972; Wildwood House, 1973. *The Mask of State: Watergate Portraits*, Harcourt, 1974, 1975. *The Seventeenth Degree*, Harcourt, 1974; Weidenfeld and Nicolson, 1975.

Also, the following uncollected short stories: "The Company Is Not Responsible," *New Yorker*, 22 April 1944. "The Unspoiled Reaction," *Atlantic Monthly*, March 1946. "The Appalachian Revolution," *New Yorker*, 11 September 1954. "The Hounds of Summer," *New Yorker*, 14 September 1963.

MACDONALD, JOHN D. 1916–

The Brass Cupcake, Fawcett, 1950, 1971. *Murder for the Bride*, Fawcett, 1951. *Judge Me Not*, Fawcett, 1951, 1972, 1974, 1976. *Weep for Me*, Fawcett, 1951. *Wine of the Dreamers*, Greenberg, 1951; Fawcett, 1973, 1975. *The Damned*, Fawcett, 1952, 1971, 1976. *Ballroom of the Skies*, Greenberg, 1952; Fawcett, 1971, 1973, 1975. *The Neon Jungle*, Fawcett, 1953, 1970, 1973, 1975, 1976. *Dead Low Tide*, Fawcett, 1953, 1971, 1976. *Cancel All Our Vows*, Appleton, 1953; Fawcett, 1972, 1976. *All These Condemned*, Fawcett, 1954, 1972, 1976. *Area of Suspicion*, Dell, 1954; Fawcett, 1972, 1975. *Contrary Pleasure*, Appleton, 1954; Fawcett, 1971, 1975. *A Bullet for Cinderella*, Dell, 1955; Fawcett, 1972, 1976. *Cry Hard, Cry Fast*, Popular, 1955. Fawcett, 1971, 1973. *You Live Once*, Popular, 1955. Fawcett, 1973. *April Evil*, Dell, 1956; Fawcett, 1972, 1974, 1976. *Border Town Girl*, Popular, 1956; Fawcett, 1974. *Murder in the Wind*, Dell, 1956; Fawcett, 1972, 1976. *Death Trap*, Dell, 1957; Fawcett, 1972, 1976. *The Price of Murder*, Dell, 1957; Fawcett, 1972, 1976. *The Enemy Trap*, Popular, 1957. *A Man of Affairs*, Dell, 1957; Fawcett, 1972, 1974. *The Deceivers*, Dell, 1958; Fawcett, 1974; *The Soft Touch*, Dell, 1958; Fawcett, 1972, 1976. *The Executioners*, Simon & Schuster, 1958; Fawcett, 1971, 1973, 1976. *Clemmie*, Fawcett, 1958, 1971, 1974. *Deadly Welcome*, Dell, 1959; Fawcett, 1970, 1975. *Please Write for Details*, Simon & Schuster, 1959; Fawcett, 1973, 1975, 1976. *The Crossroads*, Simon & Schuster, 1959; Fawcett, 1971, 1974, 1976. *The Beach Girls*, Fawcett, 1959, 1972, 1976. *Mystery Writers of America Anthology* (editor), Dell, 1959. *Slam the Big Door*, Fawcett, 1960, 1972, 1975. *The End of the Night*, Simon & Schuster, 1960; Fawcett, 1970, 1971, 1973. *The Only Girl in the Game*, Fawcett, 1960, 1970, 1973, 1975. *Where is Janice Gantry?*, Fawcett, 1961, 1970, 1976. *One Monday We Killed Them All*, Fawcett, 1961, 1972, 1973, 1976. *A Key to the Suite*, Fawcett, 1962, 1971, 1976. *A Flash of Green*, Simon & Schuster, 1962; Fawcett, 1972. *The Girl, the Gold Watch & Everything*, Fawcett, 1962, 1970, 1976. *On the Run*, Fawcett, 1963, 1973, 1976. *I Could Go On Singing*, Fawcett, 1963. *The Drowner*, Fawcett, 1963, 1970, 1976. *The Deep Blue Good-bye*, Fawcett, 1963, 1964, 1968, 1976; Lippincott, 1974. *Nightmare in Pink*, Fawcett, 1964, 1971, 1976; Lippincott, 1976. *A Purple Place for Dying*, Fawcett, 1964, 1971, 1975. *The Quick Red Fox*, Fawcett, 1964, 1970, 1975; Lippincott, 1974. *A Deadly Shade of Gold*, Fawcett, 1965, 1972; rev. ed., 1976; Lippincott, 1974. *Bright Orange for the Shroud*, Fawcett, 1965, 1972, 1976; Lippincott, 1972. *The House Guests*, Doubleday, 1965; Fawcett, 1973. *Darker Than Amber*, Fawcett, 1966, 1971, 1976; Lippincott, 1970. *One Fearful Yellow Eye*, Fawcett, 1966, 1969, 1976. *The Last One Left*, Doubleday, 1967; Fawcett, 1970, 1976. *Pale Gray for Guilt*, Fawcett, 1968, 1971; Lippincott, 1971. *Three for McGee*, Doubleday, 1968. *No Deadly Drug*, Doubleday, 1968. *The Girl in the Plain Brown Wrapper*, Fawcett, 1968, 1971, 1976; Lippincott, 1973. *Dress Her in Indigo*, Fawcett, 1969, 1972, 1976; Lippincott, 1971. *The Long Lavender Look*, Fawcett, 1970, 1973, 1976; Lippincott, 1972. *End of the Tiger and Other Stories*, Fawcett, 1971. *S*E*V*E*N*, Fawcett, 1971, 1976. *A Tan and Sandy Silence*,

Fawcett, 1971, 1975. *The Scarlet Ruse*, Fawcett, 1973, 1976. *The Turquoise Lament*, Lippincott, 1973; Fawcett, 1975. *The Dreadful Lemon Sky*, Lippincott, 1975; Fawcett, 1976; G. K. Hall. *Condominium*, Lippincott, 1977.

Also, author of over five hundred pieces of fiction in major periodicals.

MACDONALD, ROSS 1915–

(Ross MacDonald is the pseudonym for Kenneth Millar)
The Dark Tunnel (under pseud. Kenneth Millar), Dodd, 1946. *Trouble Follows Me* (under pseud. Kenneth Millar), Dodd, 1946. *Blue City* (under pseud. Kenneth Millar), Knopf, 1947; Cassell, 1948. *The Three Roads* (under pseud. Kenneth Millar), Knopf, 1948; Cassell, 1949. *The Moving Target*, Knopf, 1949; Cassell, 1950; Bantam, 1970. *The Drowning Pool*, Knopf, 1950; Cassell, 1951; Bantam, 1975; Garland, 1976. *The Way Some People Die*, Knopf, 1951; Cassell, 1952; Bantam, 1971. *The Ivory Grin*, Knopf, 1952; Cassell, 1953; Bantam, 1971. *Meet Me at the Morgue*, Knopf, 1953; Bantam, 1972; pub. as *Experience with Evil*, Cassell, 1954. *Find a Victim*, Knopf, 1954; Cassell, 1955; Bantam, 1972. *The Barbarous Coast*, Knopf, 1956; Cassell, 1957; Bantam, 1975. *The Doomsters*, Knopf, Cassell, 1958, Bantam, 1972. *The Name is Archer*, Bantam, 1958, 1971. *The Galton Case*, Knopf, 1959; Cassell, 1960; Bantam, 1967. *The Ferguson Affair*, Knopf, 1960; Cassell, 1961. *The Wycherly Woman*, Knopf, 1961; Collins, 1962; Bantam, 1973. *The Zebra-Striped Hearse*, Knopf, 1962; Collins, 1963; Bantam, 1970. *The Chill*, Knopf, 1964; Collins, 1965; Bantam, 1970. *The Far Side of the Dollar*, Knopf, 1965; Collins, 1966; Bantam, 1967. *Black Money*, Knopf, 1966; Collins, 1967; Bantam, 1972. *The Instant Enemy*, Knopf, 1968; Bantam, Collins, 1969. *The Goodbye Look*, Knopf, Collins, 1969; Bantam, 1970; G. K. Hall, 1972. *The Underground Man*, Knopf, Collins, G. K. Hall, 1971; Bantam, 1972. *On Crime Writing*, Capra, 1973. *Sleeping Beauty*, Knopf, Collins, 1973; G. K. Hall, 1973. *Great Stories of Suspense*, Knopf, 1974. *The Blue Hammer*, Knopf, Collins, 1976. *Lew Archer, Private Investigator*, The Mysterious Pr., 1977.

MACINNES, HELEN 1907–

Sexual Life in Ancient Rome (trans. with Gilbert Highet, from the work by Otto Kiefer), Routledge, 1934; Dutton, 1935. *Friedrich Engels: A Biography* (trans., with Gilbert Highet, from the work by Gustav Mayer), Chapman and Hall, 1936. *Above Suspicion*, Little, Harrap, 1941; Harcourt, 1954; Fawcett, 1976. *Assignment in Brittany*, Little, Harrap, 1942; Harcourt, 1971; Fawcett, 1976. *While Still We Live*, Little, 1944; Harcourt, 1971; pub. as *The Unconquerable*, Harrap, 1944. *Horizon*, Harrap,

1945; Little, 1946; Harcourt, 1971; Fawcett, 1975. *Friends and Lovers*, Little, Harrap, 1948; Harcourt, 1971; Fawcett, 1975. *Rest and Be Thankful*, Little, Harrap, 1949; Harcourt, Fawcett, 1976. *Neither Five Nor Three*, Harcourt, Collins, 1951; Fawcett, 1976. *I and My True Love*, Harcourt, Collins, 1953; Fawcett, 1976. *Pray for a Brave Heart*, Harcourt, Collins, 1955; Fawcett, 1976; Dell. *North from Rome*, Harcourt, Collins, 1958; Fawcett, 1975. *Decision at Delphi*, Harcourt, Collins, 1961. *Assignment: Suspense*, Harcourt, 1960; Fawcett, 1975; Watts. *The Venetian Affair*, Harcourt, 1963; Collins, 1964; Fawcett, 1975. *Home is the Hunter*, Harcourt, 1964. *The Double Image*, Harcourt, Collins, 1966; Fawcett, 1975. *The Salzburg Connection*, Harcourt, 1968; Collins, 1969; Fawcett, 1976. *Message from Málaga*, Collins, Harcourt, 1971; rev. ed., Fawcett, 1975. *Triple Threat: Three Novels*, Harcourt, 1973. *The Snare of the Hunter*, Collins, Harcourt, 1974; G. K. Hall, 1975; Fawcett, 1976. *Agent in Place*, Collins, Harcourt, 1976.

MAILER, NORMAN 1923–

The Naked and the Dead, Rinehart, 1948. *Barkary Shore*, Rinehart, 1952. *The Deer Park*, Putnam, 1955. *The White Negro*, City Lights, 1959. *The Presidential Papers*, Putnam, Deutsch, 1964. *An American Dream*, Dial, Deutsch, 1965. *Cannibals and Christians*, Dial, 1966; Deutsch, 1967. *The Bullfight*, Macmillan, 1967. *The Armies of the Night: History as a Novel, the Novel as History*, Weidenfeld and Nicolson, 1968. *The Idol and the Octopus: Political Writings on the Kennedy and Johnson Administrations*, Dell, 1968. *Miami and the Siege of Chicago: An Informal History of the Republican and Democratic Conventions of 1968*, World, 1969; pub. as *Miami and the Siege of Chicago, An Informal History of the American Political Conventions of 1968*, Weidenfeld and Nicolson, 1969. *Why Are We in Vietnam?*, Putnam, Weidenfeld and Nicolson, 1969. *Of a Fire on the Moon*, Little, Weidenfeld and Nicolson, 1970. *The Prisoner of Sex*, Little, Weidenfeld and Nicolson, 1971. *The Long Patrol, 25 Years of Writing from the Works of Norman Mailer* (ed. by Robert Lucid), World, 1971. *Existential Errands*, Little, 1972. *St. George and the Godfather*, NAL, 1972. *Marilyn*, Grosset & Dunlap, Hodder and Stoughton, 1973; Warner, 1975. *The Faith of Graffiti* (with Mervyn Kurlanksy and Jon Naar), Praeger, 1974; pub. as *Watching My Name Go By*, Mathews Miller Dunbar, 1974. *The Fight*, Little, 1975; Bantam, 1976. *Some Honorable Men: Political Conventions 1960–1972*, Little, 1976.

Also (with others), *New Short Novels 2*, Ballantine, 1956. *Advertisements for Myself*, Putnam, 1959; Deutsch, 1961. *Death for the Ladies and Other Disasters*, Putnam, Deutsch, 1962. *The Deer Park: A Play*, Dial, 1967; screenplay, *Maidstone: A Mystery*, NAL, 1971, and several films.

MANCHESTER, WILLIAM   1922–

Disturber of the Peace: The Life of H. L. Mencken, Harper, 1951. *The City of Anger*, Ballantine, 1953, 1967. *Shadow of the Monsoon*, Doubleday, 1956. *Beard the Lion*, Morrow, 1958. *A Rockefeller Family Portrait*, Little, 1959. *The Long Gainer*, Little, 1961. *Portrait of a President*, Little, 1962, 1967. *The Death of a President*, Harper, 1967. *The Arms of Krupp*, Little, 1968; Bantam, 1970. *The Glory and the Dream*, Little, 1974. *Controversy and Other Essays in Journalism*, Little, 1976. *American Caesar*, Little, in press.

Also, contributor: *Social Problems in America* (ed. by Bedemier and Tobey), Wiley, 1960. *Combat World War I* (ed. by Don Congdon), Dial, 1964. *Securities Exchanges, and the SEC* (ed. by Poyntz Tyler), Wilson, 1965. *The Girl in the Black Raincoat* (ed. by George Garrett), Duell, Sloan and Pearce, 1966. *The Writers Voice*, Morrow, 1973. *Where Speed is King*, Morrow, 1972.

Also, contributor to numerous magazines, and editor, *Encyclopedia Britannica*, 15th edition, 1974.

MAREK, GEORGE R.   1902–

Puccini, Simon & Schuster, 1957. *Opera as Theater*, Simon & Schuster, 1958. *R. Strauss*, Simon & Schuster, 1965. *Beethoven*, Crowell, 1967. *Beethoven: The Biography of a Genius*, Funk, 1970; Apollo, 1972. *Mendelssohn: Gentle Genius*, Funk, 1972. *The Eagles Die*, Harper, 1974. *Toscanini*, Atheneum, 1975. *The Bed and the Throne*, Harper, 1976.

MARTIN, MALACHI

Encounter, Farrar, 1970. *Three Popes & the Cardinal*, Farrar, 1972; Popular, 1973. *Jesus Now*, Dutton, 1973; Popular, 1974. *New Castle*, Dutton, 1974; Dell, 1975. *Hostage to the Devil*, Reader's Digest Pr., 1976.

MARTIN, RALPH G.   1920–

Boy from Nebraska, Harper, 1946. *The Best Is None Too Good*, Farrar, 1948. *Front Runner, Dark Horse* (with Ed Plaut), Doubleday, 1960. *Money, Money, Money* (with Morton Stone), Rand McNally, 1961. *Ballots and Bandwagons*, Rand McNally, 1964. *The Bosses*, Putnam, 1964. *President from Missouri: Harry S. Truman*, Messner, 1964; rev. ed., 1973. *Skin Deep*, McKay, 1964. *World War II: Pearl Harbor to V–J Day*, Fawcett, 1965. *Wizard of Wall Street*, Morrow, 1965. *The GI War: 1941–1945*, Little, 1967. *Jennie: The Life of Lady Randolph Churchill*, Prentice-Hall, vol. 1, 1968; NAL, 1970. *The Woman He Loved*, Simon & Schuster, 1974; NAL, 1975.

Also, with Richard Harrity: *Eleanor Roosevelt: Her Life in Pictures*, Duell, Sloan & Pearce, 1962. *Man of the Century: Winston Churchill*,

Duell, Sloan & Pearce, 1962. *World War II: From D-Day to VE-Day*, Fawcett, 1962. *The Three Lives of Helen Keller*, Doubleday, 1962.

Also, contributor: *The GI Story of the War*, Duell, Sloan & Pearce, 1946. *Stevenson Speeches*, Random House, 1952. *Social Problems in America*, Holt, 1955. *The Stars and Stripes*, McKay, 1962. *Democracy in Action*, Macmillan, 1963. Work has appeared in various magazines.

MASSIE, ROBERT K. 1929–

Nicholas and Alexandra, Atheneum, 1967. *Journey* (with Suzanne Massie), Knopf, 1975.

METCALF, LEE 1911–

Overcharge (with Vic Reinemer), McKay, 1967.

MILLER, MARY BRITTON. *See* BOLTON, ISABEL

MILLER, MERLE 1919–

Island 49, Crowell, 1945. *We Dropped the A-Bomb* (with Abe Spitzer), Crowell, 1946. *That Winter*, Sloane, 1948. *The Sure Thing*, Sloane, 1949. *The Judges and the Judged*, Doubleday, 1952. *Reunion*, Viking, 1954. *A Secret Understanding*, Viking, 1956. *A Gay and Melancholy Sound*, Sloane, 1961. *A Day in Late September*, Sloane, 1963. *Only You Dick Darling; or How to Write One Television Script, and Make $50,000,000* (with Evan Rhodes), Sloane, 1964. *On Being Different: What It Means to Be a Homosexual*, Random House, 1971. *What Happened*, Harper, 1972. *Plain Speaking: An Oral Biography of Harry S. Truman*, Putnam, 1974.

Contributor. *The Best from Yank*, Dutton, 1945. *Yank: The G.I. Story of the War* (ed. by Del Myers and others), Duell, Sloan & Pearce, 1947. *A Treasury of Great Reporting* (ed. by L. L. Snyder and R. B. Morris), Simon & Schuster, 1949. *Highlights from Yank*, Dell, 1953. *Women Today: Their Conflicts, Their Frustrations and Their Fulfillments* (ed. by Elizabeth Brogdon), Bobbs, 1953. *Writers Roundtable*, Harper, 1955. *Writing in America* (ed. by John Fischer and R. B. Silvers), Rutgers, 1960.

Also, author of several screenplays, film scripts, and television plays, and contributor to numerous magazines.

MILLS, JAMES

Panic in Needle Park, Farrar, 1966; NAL, 1971. *The Prosecutor*, Farrar, 1969; Pocket, 1970. *Report to the Commissioner*, Farrar, 1972; Pocket, 1975. *On the Edge*, Doubleday, 1975. *Just One Man*, Simon & Schuster, 1975; Pocket, 1976. *The Seventh Power*, Dutton, 1976.

MITFORD, JESSICA 1917–

Lifeitselfmanship, privately published, 1956. *Daughters and Rebels*, Houghton Mifflin, 1960; pub. as *Hans and Rebels*, Gollancz, 1960. *The American Way of Death*, Simon & Schuster, 1963; Fawcett, 1975. *The Trial of Dr. Spock*, Knopf, 1969. *Kind & Unusual Punishment: The American Prison Business*, Knopf, 1973; Random House, 1974. *A Fine Old Conflict*, Knopf, 1977.

Also, contributor of articles to magazines.

MOORE, BRIAN 1921–

Revolution Script, Pocket, 1972, 1973. *Judith Hearne*, Collins, Deutsch, 1955; pub. as *The Lonely Passion of Judith Hearne*, Little, 1956. *The Feast of Lupercal*, Little, 1957; Deutsch, 1958. *The Luck of Ginger Coffey*, Little, Deutsch, 1960. *An Answer from Limb*, Little, 1962, Deutsch, 1963. *Canada* (with editors of *Life*), Time, 1963. *The Emperor of Ice-Cream*, Viking, 1965; Deutsch, 1966. *I Am Mary Dunne*, Viking, Cape, 1968; Penguin, 1976. *Fergus*, Holt, 1970; Cape, 1971. *Catholics*, Cape, 1972; Harcourt, 1973. *The Great Victorian Collection*, Cape, Farrar, 1975; Ballantine, 1976.

Also, the following short stories: "Sassenach," *Atlantic Monthly*, March 1957. "Lion of the Afternoon," *Atlantic Monthly*, November 1957. "Next Thing Was Kansas City," *Atlantic Monthly*, February 1959. "Grieve for the Dear Departed," *Atlantic Monthly*, August 1959. "A Vocation," *The Irish Genius*, NAL, 1960. "The Apartment Hunter," *Best American Short Stories 1967* (ed. by Martha Foley and David Burnett), Houghton Mifflin, 1967. "Preliminary Paces for a Work in Revenge," *Canadian Writing Today*, Penguin, 1970.

Also, the screenplay: *Catholics*, Holt, 1973; and others.

MORISON, SAMUEL ELIOT 1887–1976

The Life and Letters of Harrison Gray Otis, 2 vols., Houghton Mifflin, 1913. *A History of the Constitution of Massachusetts*, Wright and Potter, 1917. *Maritime History of Massachusetts, 1783–1860*, Houghton Mifflin, 1921, 1961. *Prologue to American History*, Oxford Univ., 1922. *Oxford History of the United States*, 2 vols., Oxford Univ., 1927; pub. as *The Growth of the American Republic* (new ed. with Henry Steele Commager), 2 vols., Oxford, 1933, 1962. *Hour of American History, from Columbus to Coolidge*, Lippincott, 1930; rev. ed., Beacon, 1960. *The Proprietors of Peterborough*, Peterborough (N.H.) Hist. Soc., 1930. *Builders of the Bay Colony*, Houghton Mifflin, 1930; rev. ed., 1964. *Puritan Proanos*, New York Univ. Pr., 1936; pub. as *Intellectual Life of Colonial New England*, New York Univ. Pr., 1956. *Tercentennial History of*

Harvard University, 1636–1936, 4 vols., Harvard (*Development of Harvard University Since the Inauguration of President Eliot*, 1930; *Founding of Harvard College*, 1935; and *Harvard College in the Seventeenth Century*, 2 vols., 1936); also, *Three Centuries of Harvard, 1636–1936*, 1 vol., 1936. *The Pilgrim Fathers, Their Significance in History*, Merrymount, 1937. *Second Voyage of Columbus*, Clarendon, 1939. *Route of Columbus along the North Coast of Haiti*, Amer. Philosophical Society, 1940. *Portuguese Voyages to America in the Fifteenth Century*, Harvard, 1940. *Admiral of the Ocean Sea: A Life of Christopher Columbus*, 2 vols., Little, 1942; 1 vol., 1942. *History of United States Naval Operations in World War II*, 14 vols. and Supplement Index, Little, 1948–1962. *Ropemakers of Plymouth*, Houghton Mifflin, 1950; reprint, Arno, 1976. *By Hand and By Sea*, Knopf, 1953. *Christopher Columbus, Mariner*, Little, 1955. *The Story of the "Old Colony" of New Plymouth*, Knopf, 1956. *Freedom in Contemporary Society*, Little, 1956. *Strategy and Compromise*, Little, 1958. *William Hickling Prescott, 1796–1859*, Mass. Hist. Soc., 1958. *John Paul Jones, a Sailor's Biography*, Little, 1959. *Story of Mount Desert Island, Maine*, Little, 1960. *The Scholar in America: Past, Present, and Future*, Oxford, 1961. *One Boy's Boston*, Houghton Mifflin, 1962. *The Two-Ocean War: A Short History of the United States Navy in the Second World War*, Little, 1963. *Vistas of History*, Knopf, 1964. *The Caribbean as Columbus Saw It* (with Mauricio Obregon), Little, 1964. *Oxford History of the American People*, Oxford, 1965; 3 vols., NAL. *Spring Tides*, Houghton Mifflin, 1965. *Samuel De Champlain: Father of New France*, Little, 1972. *The European Discovery of America: the Northern & Southern Voyages*, 2 vols., Oxford, 1974.

Also, editor of numerous volumes on American history.

MORRIS, JAN 1926–

(Also JAMES MORRIS)

As James Morris: *As I Saw the U.S.A.*, Pantheon, 1956. *Sultan in Oman*, Pantheon, 1957. *Islam Inflamed*, Pantheon, 1957. *Coronation Everist*, 1958. *South African Winter*, Pantheon, 1958. *The Hashemite Kings*, Pantheon, 1959. *The World of Venice*, Pantheon, 1960; rev. ed., Harcourt, 1973, 1974. *The Road to Huddersfield*, Pantheon, 1963. *Outriders—a Liberal View of Britain*, Verry, 1963. *Cities*, Harcourt, 1963. *The Presence of Spain*, Harcourt, 1964. *Oxford*, Harcourt, 1965. *Pax Britannica*, Harcourt, 1968. *The Great Port: Passage through New York*, Harcourt, 1969. *Places*, Harcourt, 1973. *Heaven's Command: An Imperial Progress*, Harcourt, 1973. *Farewell the Trumpets*, Harcourt, 1978.

As Jan Morris: *Conundrum*, Harcourt, 1974; NAL, 1975. *Travels*, Harcourt, 1976. *The Oxford Book of Oxford*, Oxford Univ., rev. ed., 1978. *Oxford* (new ed.), Oxford Univ., 1978.

MORRIS, WILLIE   1934–

The South Today: 100 Years After Appomattox (editor and author of foreword), Harper, 1965. *North toward Home*, Houghton Mifflin, 1967; Dell, 1970. *Yazoo*, Harper, 1971. *Good Old Boy*, Harper, 1971; Avon, 1974. *The Last of the Southern Girls*, Knopf, 1973; Avon, 1974.

   Also, contributor of stories and articles to various magazines.

NIVEN, DAVID   1910–

Once Over Lightly, Prentice-Hall, 1951. *The Moon's a Balloon*, Putnam, 1971; Dell, 1973. *Bring on the Empty Horses*, Putnam, 1975; Dell, 1976.

NOLEN, WILLIAM A.

The Making of a Surgeon, Random House, 1970; Pocket, 1972, 1976. *Spare Parts for the Human Body*, Random House, 1971. *A Surgeon's World*, Random House, 1972; Fawcett, 1974. *Healing: A Doctor in Search of a Miracle*, Random House, 1975; Fawcett, 1976. *A Surgeon under the Knife*, Coward, 1976.

   Also, author of a medical column in *McCall's*.

O'BRIEN, EDNA

The Country Girls, Hutchinson, Knopf, 1960. *The Lonely Girl*, Cape, Random House, 1962. *Girls in Their Married Bliss*, Cape, 1964; Houghton Mifflin, 1968; Penguin, 1975. *August Is a Wicked Month*, Cape, Simon & Schuster, 1965. *Casualties of Peace*, Cape, 1966; Simon & Schuster, 1967. *The Love Object*, Cape, 1968; Knopf, 1969; Penguin, 1975. *A Pagan Place*, Weidenfeld and Nicolson, Knopf, 1970. *Night*, Weidenfeld and Nicolson, Knopf, 1972; Bantam, 1976. *A Scandalous Woman and Other Stories*, Weidenfeld and Nicolson, Harcourt, 1974; Ballantine, 1976. *Mother Ireland*, Harcourt, 1976. *Johnny I Hardly Knew You*, Weidenfeld and Nicolson, 1977.

   Also, the following screenplays: *The Girl with Green Eyes*, Penguin, 1964. *Zee and Co.*, Weidenfeld and Nicolson, 1971. And others.

   Also, the following plays: *A Cheap Bunch of Nice Flowers*; included in *Plays of the Year 1962–1963*, Elek, 1963. *A Pagan Place* (adaptation of her own novel), Faber, 1973. And others.

O'CASEY, EILEEN   1924–

Sean, Coward, 1972.

OË, KENZABURO

Personal Matter (trans. by John Nathan), Grove, 1968. *The Silent Cry* (trans. by John Bester), Kodansha, 1975; orig. title *Football in the First Year of Mannen*.

O'HIGGINS, PATRICK

Madame: An Intimate Biography of Helena Rubenstein, Viking, 1971; Dell, 1972.

OZ, AMOS 1939–

Artzot ha'tan ("Where the Jackals Howl"), Massada, 1965; Am Oved, 1976. *Ma'Kom a'her* (trans. by Nicholas de Lange), Sifriat Poalim, 1966; pub. as *Elsewhere, Perhaps*, Harcourt, 1973; Bantam, 1974. *Michael Sheli* (trans. by Nicholas de Lange in collaboration with Oz), pub. as *My Michael*, Knopf, 1972; Lancer, 1973; Bantam, 1976. *Ad m'avet* ("Unto Death"), Sifriat Poalim, 1971; trans. pub. in *Commentary*, August 1971; Harcourt, 1975. *Lagaut Bamayin Laga'at Ba'ruach* ("Touch the Water, Touch the Wind"), Am Oved, 1973; Harcourt, 1974. *Har Hàetsa Ha'raah* ("The Hill of Evil Counsel"), Am Oved, 1976.

PACKARD, VANCE 1914–

How to Pick a Mate: the Guide to a Happy Marriage (with Clifford R. Adams), Dutton, 1946; pub. as *How to Pick a Mate: A Guidebook to Love, Sex and Marriage*, Blue Ribbon Bks., 1947. *Animal I.Q.: the Human Side of Animals*, Dial, 1950; pub. as *The Human Side of Animals*, rev. ed., Pocket, 1961. *The Hidden Persuaders*, McKay, 1957; Pocket, 1976. *Books and Culture as Status Symbols: Comments at the 1959 ABA Convention*, McKay, 1959. *The Status Seekers*, McKay, 1959; Pocket, 1961. *Do Your Dreams Match Your Talents?*, Science Research Associates, 1960. *The Waste Makers*, McKay, 1960; Pocket, 1975. *The Pyramid Climbers*, McGraw-Hill, 1962. *Your Goals and You: A Guidance Handbook* (with others), Science Research Associates, 1962. *The Naked Society* (excerpt, "Invasion of Privacy," pub. in the *Atlantic Monthly*, March 1964), McKay, 1964; Pocket, 1974. *The Sexual Wilderness: the Contemporary Upheaval in Male–Female Relationships* (excerpts, "Sex on Campus," pub. in *McCall's*, August, September 1968; excerpt, "Some Contemporary Styles in Wedlock," pub. in *PTA Magazine*, October 1968), McKay, 1968; pub. as *The Sexual Wilderness: the Upheaval in Male–Female Relationships, the Break-Up of Traditional Morality, New Trends in Sexual Behavior among the Young*, Pan, Pocket, 1970. *A Nation of Strangers* (excerpts pub. in *Ladies Home Journal*, September, November 1972), McKay, 1972.

Also, contributor to various periodicals.

PHILBY, ELEANOR

The Spy I Married, Ballantine, 1968.

PIKE, JAMES A. 1913–1969

Cases and Other Materials on the New Federal Code Procedure, Callaghan, 1938. *The Faith of the Church* (with W. Norman Pittenger), Seabury, 1951. *Beyond Anxiety*, Scribner, 1953. *If You Marry Outside Your Faith*, Harper, 1954; rev. ed., 1962. *Roadblocks to Faith* (with John M. Krumm), Morehouse, 1954. *The Church, Politics and Society* (with John W. Pyle), Morehouse, 1955. *Doing the Truth*, Doubleday, 1955; rev. ed., Macmillan, 1965. *Man in the Middle* (with Howard A. Johnson), Seabury, 1956. *Modern Canterbury Pilgrims* (ed. and contributor), Morehouse, 1956; abridged ed., 1959. *The Next Day*, Doubleday, 1957. *A Roman Catholic in the White House* (with Richard E. Byfield), Doubleday, 1960; Greenwood, 1973. *A New Look at Preaching*, Scribner, 1961. *Our Christmas Challenge*, Sterling, 1961. *Beyond the Law*, Doubleday, 1963; Greenwood, 1974. *A Time for Christian Candor*, Harper, 1964. *Teen-agers and Sex*, Prentice-Hall, 1965. *What Is This Treasure?*, Harper, 1966. *You and the New Morality*, Harper, 1967.

POLITE, CARLENE HATCHER 1932–

The Flagellants, Editions Julliard, 1966; Farrar, 1967. *Sister X and the Victims of Foul Play . . .*, Farrar, 1975.

Also, contributor to *Mademoiselle*.

POPOV, DUSKO

Spy/Counterspy, Grosset, 1974; Fawcett, 1975.

POTOK, CHAIM 1929–

The Chosen, Simon & Schuster, 1967; Fawcett, 1976. *The Promise*, Knopf, 1969; Fawcett, 1976. *My Name Is Asher Lev*, Knopf, 1972; Fawcett, 1976. *In the Beginning*, Knopf, 1975; Fawcett, 1976.

Also, contributor of articles and short stories to numerous magazines.

PRESCOTT, ORVILLE 1906–

In My Opinion: An Inquiry into the Contemporary Novel, Bobbs, 1952. *The Five-Dollar Gold Piece: The Development of a Point of View*, Random House, 1956. *Mid-Century: An Anthology of Distinguished Contemporary Short Stories* (editor), Pocket, 1958; Washington Square Press, 1971. *The Undying Past* (editor), Doubleday, 1961. *A Father Reads to His Children: An Anthology of Prose and Poetry* (editor), Dutton, 1965. *Princes of the Renaissance*, Random House, 1969. *History as Literature* (editor), Harper, 1971. *Lords of Italy*, Harper, 1972.

PRITCHETT, V. S. 1900–

Marching Spain, Benn, 1928. *In My Good Books*, Chatto & Windus, 1942; Kennikat, 1970. *The Living Novel*, Chatto & Windus, 1946; Reynal, 1947; pub. as *The Living Novel, and Later Appreciations*, rev. ed., Random House, 1964. *Why Do I Write?* (with Elizabeth Bowen and Graham Greene), Percival Marshall, Folcroft, 1948; Haskell, 1975. *Books in General*, Harcourt, 1953; Greenwood. *The Spanish Temper*, Knopf, 1954; Greenwood, 1976. *London Perceived*, Harcourt, 1962, 1963, 1966. *Foreign Faces*, Chatto & Windus, 1964; pub. as *The Offensive Traveller*, Knopf, 1964. *New York Proclaimed*, Harcourt, 1965. *The Working Novelist*, Chatto & Windus, 1965. *Dublin: A Portrait*, Harper, 1967. *A Cab at the Door: A Memoir*, Random House, 1968, 1971; pub. as *A Cab at the Door: An Autobiography, Early Years*, Chatto & Windus, 1968. *George Meredith and English Comedy*, Random House, 1970. *Midnight Oil*, Chatto & Windus, 1971; Random House, 1972, 1973. *Balzac*, Knopf, 1973; Random House, 1974. *The Gentle Barbarian—Turgenev*, Chatto & Windus, Random House, 1977.

Also, the novels: *Clare Drummer*, Benn, 1929. *Shirley Sanz*, Gollancz, 1932; pub. as *Elopement into Exile*, Little, 1932. *Nothing Like Leather*, Macmillan, 1935. *Dead Man Leading*, Macmillan, 1937. *Mr. Beluncle*, Harcourt, 1951.

Also, the short stories: *The Spanish Virgin and Other Stories*, Benn, 1930. *You Make Your Own Life*, Chatto & Windus, 1938. *It May Never Happen and Other Stories*, Chatto & Windus, 1945; Reynal, 1947. *Collected Stories*, Chatto & Windus, 1956; pub. as *The Sailor, Sense of Humor, and Other Stories*, Knopf, 1956; pub. as *The Saint and Other Stories*, Penguin, 1966. *When My Girl Comes Home*, Knopf, 1961. *The Key to My Heart: A Comedy in Three Parts*, Chatto & Windus, 1963; Random House, 1964. *Blind Love and Other Stories*, Chatto & Windus, 1969; Random House, 1970. *The Camberwell Beauty & Other Stories*, Random House, 1974.

Also, editor: *Robert Louis Stevenson, Selected Novels and Stories*, Duell, Sloan, 1946. *Robert Southey, the Chronicle of the Cid*, J. Enschede en Zonen for Limited Editions Club, 1958.

Also, writer for a weekly column in the *New Statesman*; author of works for television; contributor to magazines and periodicals.

QUEEN, ELLERY. *See* DANNAY, FREDERIC; *See also* LEE, MANFRED B.

REINEMER, VIC 1923–

Overcharge (with Lee Metcalf), McKay, 1967. Also, contributor to magazines.

ROBBE-GRILLET, ALAIN 1922–

Les Gommes, Editions de Minuit, 1953; pub. as *The Erasers* (trans. by Richard Howard), Grove, 1964; (ed. by J. S. Wood), Prentice-Hall, 1970.

Le Voyeur, Editions de Minuit, 1955; pub. as *The Voyeur* (trans. by Richard Howard), Grove, 1958; pub. original title (ed. and intro. by Oreste F. Pucciani), Ginn-Blaisdell, 1970. *La Jalousie*, Editions de Minuit, 1957; pub. as *Jealousy* (trans. by Richard Howard), Grove, 1959; pub. as *Jealousy: Rhythmic Themes by Alain Robbe-Grillet*, Allen, 1971; pub. original title (ed. by Germaine Bree and Eric Schoenfeld), Macmillan, 1963; (ed. by B. G. Garnham), Methuen, 1969. *Dans le labyrinthe*, Editions de Minuit, 1959; pub. as *In the Labyrinth* (trans. by Richard Howard), Grove, 1960; (trans. by Christine Brook-Rose), Calder & Boyars, 1967; pub. as *Dans le labyrinthe* [and] *Dans les couloirs du Metropolitain* [and] *Le Chambre secrete*, Union Generale D'Editions, 1964. *L'Année dernière à Marienbad: cine-roman*, Editions de Minuit, 1961; pub. as *Last Year at Marienbad* (trans. by Richard Howard), Grove, 1962; pub. as *Last Year at Marienbad: A Cine-Novel*, Calder & Boyars, 1962. *Instantanes*, Editions de Minuit, 1962; pub. as *Snapshots* (trans. by Bruce Morissette), Grove, 1968; new ed., 1972. *L'immortelle: cine-roman*, Editions de Minuit, 1963; pub. as *The Immortal One* (trans. by A. M. Sheridan Smith), Calder & Boyars, 1971. *Pour un nouveau roman*, Edition de Minuit, 1963; new ed., Gallimard, 1970; pub. as *Snapshots* [and] *Towards a New Novel* (trans. by Barbara Wright), Calder & Boyars, 1965; pub. as *For a New Novel: Essays on Fiction* (trans. by Richard Howard), Grove, 1966. *La Maison de Rendez-vous*, Editions de Minuit, 1965; pub. under original title (trans. by Richard Howard), Grove, 1966; pub. as *The House of Assignation: A Novel* (trans. by Sheridan Smith), Calder & Boyars, 1970. *Two Novels* (contains *Jealousy* and *In the Labyrinth*, trans. by Richard Howard), Grove, 1965. *Projet pour une revolution à New York*, Editions de Minuit, 1970; pub. as *Project for a Revolution in New York* (trans. by Richard Howard), Grove, 1972. *Rêves de jeunes filles* (with David Hamilton), Montel, 1971; pub. as *Dreams of a Young Girl* (trans. by Elizabeth Walter), Morrow, 1971; pub. as *Dreams of Young Girls*, Collins, 1971. *Les Desmoiselles d'Hamilton* (with David Hamilton), Laffont, 1972. *Glissements progressifs du plaisir: ciné-roman*, Editions de Minuit, 1974. *Topologie d'une cité fantôme*, Editions de Minuit, 1976.

Also, author of screenplays and contributor to numerous magazines.

ROBERTS, DAVID S.   1943–

Mountain of My Fear, Vanguard, 1968. *Deborah: A Wilderness Narrative*, Vanguard, 1970. *Earth and the Great Weather* (contributor), Friends of the Earth, 1971. *The Mountains of America* (contributor; ed. by Franklin Russell), Abrams, 1976.

Also, contributor of articles and reviews to various national journals and periodicals.

Also, on editorial board, *Mountain Gazette* and *American Alpine Journal*.

ROSS, ISHBEL 1897–1975

Ladies of the Press: The Story of Women in Journalism by an Insider, 1936; Arno, 1974. *First Lady of the South*, 1958; Greenwood, 1973. *Silhouette in Diamonds: The Life of Mrs. Potter Palmer*, 1960; Arno, 1975. *Son of Adam, Daughters of Eve: The Role of Women in American History*, Harper, 1969. *Rebel Rose*, Mockingbird, 1973. *Power with Grace: The Life Story of Mrs. Woodrow Wilson*, Putnam, 1975.

SANDERS, LAWRENCE 1920–

The Anderson Tapes, Putnam, 1970. *The Pleasures of Helen*, Putnam, 1971. *Love Songs*, Putnam, 1972. *The First Deadly Sin*, Putnam, 1973. *The Tomorrow File*, Putnam, 1975. *The Tangent Objective*, Putnam, 1976. *The Marlow Chronicles*, Putnam, 1977. *The Second Deadly Sin*, Putnam, 1977.

SCHLESINGER, ARTHUR, JR. 1917–

Orestes A. Browns On: A Pilgrim's Progress, Little, 1939. *The Age of Jackson*, Little, 1945. *The Vital Center: The Politics of Freedom*, Houghton Mifflin, 1949. *The General and the President* (with R. H. Rovere), Farrar, 1951; rev. ed. pub. as *The MacArthur Controversy and American Foreign Policy, 1965. Harvard Guide To American History* (coeditor), Harvard, 1954. *Guide to Politics* (editor, with Quincy Howe), Dial, 1954. *The Age of Roosevelt* (vol. 1, *The Crises of the Old Order, 1919–1933*, Houghton Mifflin, 1957; vol. 2, *The Coming of the New Deal*, Houghton Mifflin, 1959; vol. 3, *The Politics of Upheaval*, Houghton Mifflin, 1960). *Kennedy or Nixon: Does It Make Any Difference?*, MacMillan, 1960. *The Politics of Hope*, Houghton Mifflin, 1963. *Four Portraits and One Subject: Bernard DeVoto* (contributor), Houghton Mifflin, 1963. *A Thousand Days: John F. Kennedy in the White House*, Houghton Mifflin, 1965. *The Bitter Heritage*, Houghton Mifflin, 1967. *The Promise of American Life* (editor of the work by Herbert Croly), Belknap, 1967. *The Crisis of Confidence*, Houghton Mifflin, 1969. *The Imperial Presidency*, Houghton Mifflin, 1973. *Robert Kennedy and His Times*, Houghton Mifflin, 1978.

Also, contributor to numerous scholarly and popular magazines; and motion picture reviewer for several magazines.

SEGAL, ERICH 1937–

Euripides: A Collection of Critical Essays, Prentice-Hall, 1968. *Roman Laughter: The Comedy of Plautus*, Harvard Univ. Pr., 1968. *Plautus: Three Comedies* (editor and translator), Harper, 1969. *Love Story*, Harper, 1970; NAL, 1970. *Fairy Tale*, 1973. "Dr. Fastest," *Playboy*, December 1977. *Oliver's Story*, Harper, 1977.

Also, contributor of articles and reviews to *American Journal of Philology, Greek, Roman & Byzantine Studies, Comparative Literature, Yale Review, The New Republic, New York Times Book Review, Le Monde, Le Nouvel Observateur*, and others. Contributing editor, *Diacritics: A Review of Contemporary Criticism, 1974–*.

Also, author of adaptations for film and stage productions. Book and lyrics for several stage works.

SHEDD, MARGARET

Hurricane Caye, Harper, 1942. *Inherit the Earth*, Harper, 1944. *Return to the Beach*, Doubleday, 1950. *Run*, Doubleday, 1955; Gollancz, 1956; pub. as *Sauve qui Peut*, Presses de la Cité, 1957. *Hosannah Tree*, Doubleday, 1967. *Malinche and Cortes*, Doubleday, 1971; pub. as *La Malinche y Cortes*, Editorial Diana, 1974. *A Silence in Bilbao*, Doubleday, 1974.

Also stories included in magazines and anthologies.

SILVERMAN, AL   1926–

Sports Titans of the Twentieth Century, Putnam, 1968. *More Sports Titans of the Twentieth Century*, Putnam, 1969. *I Am Third* (with Gale Sayers), Viking, 1970; Bantam. *Foster & Laurie*, Little, 1974; Popular, 1975.

SINGER, ISAAC BASHEVIS   1904–

The Family Moskat (trans. by A. H. Gross), Knopf, 1950; Farrar, 1965; Secker and Warburg, 1966. *Satan in Goray* (trans. by Jacob Sloan), Farrar, 1955; Peter Owen, 1958; Avon, 1966. *Gimpel the Fool and Other Stories* (trans. by Saul Bellow and others), Farrar, 1957; Peter Owen, 1958. *The Magician of Lubin* (trans. by Elaine Gottlieb and Joseph Singer), Farrar, 1960; Secker and Warburg, 1961. *Spinoza of Market Street and Other Stories* (trans. by Elaine Gottlieb and others), Farrar, 1961; Secker and Warburg, 1962; Avon, 1966. *The Slave* (trans. by the author and Cecil Hemley), Farrar, 1962; Secker and Warburg, 1963; Avon, 1971. *Short Friday and Other Stories* (trans. by Ruth Whitman and others), Farrar, 1964; Secker and Warburg, 1967. *Selected Short Stories*, Modern Library, 1966. *In My Father's Court* (trans. by Channah Kleinerman-Goldstein and others), Farrar, 1966; Secker and Warburg, 1967. *The Manor* (trans. by Elaine Gottlieb and Joseph Singer), Farrar, 1967; Secker and Warburg, 1968; Dell, 1969. *The Seance and Other Stories* (trans. by Ruth Whitman and others), Farrar, 1968; Cape, 1970; pub. as *Seance*, Avon, 1969. *Isaac Bashevis Singer Reader*, Farrar, 1971. *A Friend of Kafka and Other Stories*, Farrar, 1970; Cape, 1972. *The Estate* (trans. by Joseph Singer, Elaine Gottlieb, and Elizabeth Shub), Farrar, Cape, 1969; Dell, 1971. *Enemies: A Love Story* (trans. by Alizah Shevrin and Elizabeth Shub), Farrar, 1972. *The Hasidim: Paintings, Drawings and Etchings* (with Ira Moscowitz), Crown, 1973. *A Crown of Feathers and Other Stories*, Farrar, 1973; Cape, Fawcett, 1974. *A Little Boy in Search of God: Mysticism in a Personal Light* (trans. by Joseph Singer), Doubleday, 1976. *Naftali the Storyteller and His Horse Sus*, Farrar, 1976. *A Tale of Three Wishes*, Farrar, 1976.

Also, the following juvenile books: *Zlateh the Goat and Other Stories* (trans. by the author and Elizabeth Shub), Harper, 1966; Secker and Warburg, 1967. *Mazel and Schimazel; or, The Milk of a Lioness* (trans. by the author and Elizabeth Shub), Harper, 1966; Farrar, 1967. *The Fearsome Inn* (trans. by the author and Elizabeth Shub), Scribner, 1967; Collins, 1970. *When Schlemiel Went to Warsaw and Other Stories* (trans. by the author and Elizabeth Shub), Farrar, 1968. *A Day of Pleasure: Stories of a Boy Growing Up in Warsaw* (trans. by the author and Elizabeth Shub), Farrar, 1969. *Elijah the Slave* (trans. by the author and Elizabeth Shub), Farrar, 1970. *Joseph and Korza; or, The Sacrifice to the Vistula* (trans. by the author and Elizabeth Shub), Farrar, 1970. *Alone in the Wild Forest* (trans. by the author and Elizabeth Shub), Farrar, 1971. *The Topsy-Turvy Emperor of China* (trans. by the author and Elizabeth Shub), Harper, 1971. *The Wicked City* (trans. by the author and Elizabeth Shub), Farrar, 1972. *The Fools of Chelm and Their History* (trans. by the author and Elizabeth Shub), Farrar, 1973. *Why Noah Chose the Dove* (trans. by Elizabeth Shub), Farrar, 1974.

Also, author of two plays.

SNOW, C. P.   1905–

Death Under Sail, Doubleday, 1932; Garland, 1976; rev. ed., Heinemann, 1959. *New Lives for Old* (pub. anon.), Gollancz, 1933. *The Search*, Gollancz, 1934; Bobbs, 1935; rev. ed., Scribner, 1958. *Richard Aldington: An Appreciation*, Heinemann, 1938. *Writers and Readers of the Soviet Union*, Farleigh, 1943. *The Two Cultures and the Scientific Revolution* (the Rede Lecture), Cambridge Univ., 1959; pub. as *The Two Cultures and a Second Look*, rev. ed., Cambridge Univ., 1963; NAL, 1964. *The Moral Un-Neutrality of Science*, 1961. *Science and Government* (the Godkin Lectures), Harvard Univ., 1961. *A Postscript to "Science and Government,"* Harvard Univ. and Oxford Univ., 1962. *Magnanimity* (the Rector's address), Univ. of St. Andrews, 1962. *C. P. Snow: A Spectrum: Science, Criticism, Fiction* (ed. by Stanley Weintraub), Scribner, 1963. *A London Childhood* (author of introduction of the work by John Holloway), Routledge, 1966; Scribner, 1967. *A Mathematician's Apology* (author of the foreword of the work by G. H. Hardy), Cambridge Univ., 1967. *Variety of Men*, Scribner, 1967. *State of Siege*, Scribner, 1969; Oxfam, 1970. *Public Affairs*, Macmillan, Scribner, 1971. *The Malcontents*,

Macmillan, Scribner, 1972. *In Their Wisdom*, Macmillan, Scribner, 1974. *Trollope: His Life and Art*, Macmillan, Scribner, 1975.

Also, novels in *The Strangers and Brothers* series: *Strangers and Brothers*, Faber, 1940; Macmillan, 1958; Scribner, 1960; pub. as *George Passant*, Penguin, 1973. *The Light and the Dark*, Faber, 1947; Macmillan, 1948; Scribner, 1961. *Time of Hope*, Faber, 1949; Macmillan, 1950; Scribner, 1961. *The Masters*, Macmillan, 1951; Scribner, 1960. *The New Men*, Macmillan, Scribner, 1954. *Homecomings*, Macmillan, 1956; pub. as *Homecoming*, Scribner, 1956. *The Conscience of the Rich*, Macmillan, Scribner, 1958. *The Affair*, Macmillan, Scribner, 1960. *Corridors of Power*, Macmillan, Scribner, 1964. *The Sleep of Reason*, Macmillan, 1968; Scribner, 1969. *Last Things*, Macmillan, Scribner, 1970.

Also, the play, *The Public Prosecutor* (with Pamela H. Johnson, adapted from the play by George Dzhagarov, trans. by Marguerite Alexieva), Peter Owen, 1969; and others.

Also, editor: *Winter's Tales 7* (with Pamela H. Johnson), Macmillan, 1961; pub. as *Stories from Modern Russia*, St. Martins, 1962. *Discovery*, 1938–40. *Cambridge Library of Modern Science*, 1938–1940s.

Also, published many scientific papers between 1929 and 1935.

Also, contributor to *Sunday Times*.

STEINER, JEAN-FRANÇOIS 1938–

Treblinka, Fayard, 1966; Simon & Schuster, 1967; Lib. Gen. France, 1968. *Les Meteques*, Fayard, 1970. *Chaplain*, Balland, 1970.

STEWART, RAMONA 1922–

Desert Town, Morrow, 1945. *The Stars Abide*, Morrow, 1961. *The Surprise Party Complex*, Morrow, 1963. *Professor Descending*, Doubleday, 1964. *Confidence in Magic*, Doubleday, 1965. *Kit Larkin*, Doubleday, 1966. *Casey*, Little, 1968. *The Possession of Joel Delaney*, Little, 1970. *The Apparition*, Little, 1972. *Age of Consent*, Dutton, 1975; NAL, 1976.

Also, stories included in *Best Short Stories of 1950*, and *Two and Twenty*, St. Martins, 1962.

STOESSINGER, JOHN G. 1927–

The Refugee and the World Community, Minnesota, 1956. *The Might of Nations: World Politics in Our Time*, Random House, 1962, 1965, 1969, 1973, 1975. *Financing The United Nations System* (with others), Brookings, 1964. *Power and Order* (editor, with A. F. Westin), Harcourt, 1964. *The United Nations and the Superpowers*, Random House, 1965, 1970, 1973, 1976. *Nations in Darkness: China, Russia, America*, Random House, 1971, 1975. *Why Nations Go to War*, St. Martins, 1974. *Henry Kissinger: The Anguish of Power*, Norton, 1976, 1977.

Also, Chief Book Review Editor, *Foreign Affairs*, for five years.

SUSANN, JACQUELINE 1921–1974

Valley of the Dolls, Bantam, 1970. *Love Machine*, Simon & Schuster, 1969; Bantam, 1971. *Every Night Josephine*, Bantam, 1972; Morrow, 1974. *Once Is Not Enough*, Morrow, 1973; Bantam, 1974. *Dolores*, Morrow, 1976.

TRUMBO, DALTON 1905–

Eclipse, Dickson and Thompson, 1935. *Washington Jitters*, Knopf, 1936. *Johnny Got His Gun*, Lippincott, 1939; Bantam, Lyle Stuart, 1970. *The Remarkable Andrew: Being the Chronicle of a Literal Man*, Lippincott, 1941; pub. as *The Remarkable Andrew: The Chronicle of a Literary Man*, Lane, 1941. *Harry Bridges*, League of American Writers, 1941. *An Appeal to the People*, privately printed, 1942. *The Time of the Toad: A Study of Inquisition in America, by One of the Ten*, Hollywood, Ten, 1948; Harper, 1972. *The Devil in the Book*, Emergency Defense Committee, 1956. *Additional Dialogue: Letters of Dalton Trumbo* (ed. by Helen Manfull), M. Evans, 1970.

Also, the play, *The Biggest Thief in Town*, Dramatists Play Service, 1949; English Theater Guild, 1952.

Also, numerous screenplays.

TRYON, THOMAS 1926–

The Other, Knopf, 1971; Fawcett, 1976. *Harvest Home*, Knopf, 1973. *Crowned Heads*, Knopf, 1976. *Lady*, Knopf, 1974; G. K. Hall, 1975; Fawcett, 1976.

TURNBULL, COLIN M. 1924–

The Forest People, Simon & Schuster, 1961. *The Lonely African*, Simon & Schuster, 1962. *The People of Africa*, World, 1962. *Wayward Servants*, American Museum of Natural History, 1965. *The Mbuti Pygmies: an Ethnographic Survey*, American Museum of Natural History, 1965. *Peoples of Africa* (contributor; ed. by James Gibbs), Holt, 1965. *Tradition and Change in African Tribal Life*, World, 1966. *Tibet* (with Thubten Jigme Norbu), Simon & Schuster, 1968. *The Mountain People*, Simon & Schuster, 1972. *Africa and Change* (editor), Knopf, 1973. *Man in Africa*, Doubleday, 1976.

URIS, LEON 1924–

Battle Cry, Putnam, Wingate, 1953; Bantam. *The Angry Hills*, Random House, 1955; Wingate, 1956; Bantam, 1972. *Exodus*, Doubleday, 1958; Wingate, 1959; Bantam, 1975. *Exodus Revisited*, Doubleday, 1960; pub. as *In the Steps of Exodus*, Heinemann, 1962. *Mila 18*, Doubleday, Heinemann, 1961; Bantam, 1970. *Armageddon: A Novel of Berlin*, Doubleday,

Kimber, 1964; Dell. *The Third Temple* (with *Strike Zion*, by William Ste-venson), Bantam, 1967. *Topaz*, McGraw-Hill, 1967; Kimber, 1968; Ban-tam, 1969. *Q.B. VII*, Doubleday, 1970; Kimber, 1971; Bantam, 1972. *Ireland, A Terrible Beauty: The Story of Ireland Today* (with Jill Uris), Doubleday, 1975. *Trinity*, Doubleday, 1976.

Also, author of a play and two screenplays.

USTINOV, PETER 1921–

Krumnagel, Lippincott, 1975.

VAN LAWICK–GOODALL, JANE 1934–

(Jane Goodall)

Primate Behavior (contributor, ed. by Irven DeVore), Holt, 1965. *My Friends, the Wild Chimpanzees*, National Geographic Society, 1967. *Pri-mate Ethology* (contributor, ed. by Desmond Morris), Aldine, 1967. *The Behavior of Free-Living Chimpanzees in the Gombe Stream Reserve*, Tindall & Cassell, 1968. *Innocent Killers* (with Hugo van Lawick), Col-lins, 1970; Houghton Mifflin, 1971. *In the Shadow of Man*, Houghton Mifflin, 1971; Dell, 1972, 1974. *Grub: the Bush Baby* (with Hugo van Law-ick), Houghton Mifflin, 1972.

Also, contributor to journals.

VIDAL, GORE 1925–

Williwaw, Dutton, 1946; Heinemann, 1970. *In a Yellow Wood*, Dutton, 1947. *The City and the Pillar*, Dutton, 1948; Lehman, 1949; rev. ed., Dut-ton, 1965; Heinemann, 1966; NAL. *The Season of Comfort*, Dutton, 1949. *A Search for the King: A Twelfth Century Legend*, Dutton, 1950. *Dark Green, Bright Red*, Dutton, Lehman, 1950. *The Judgment of Paris*, Dut-ton, 1952; Heinemann, 1953. *Death in the Fifth Position* (under pseud. Edgar Box), Dutton, 1952; Heinemann, 1954. *Death before Bedtime* (un-der pseud. Edgar Box), Dutton, 1953; Heinemann, 1954. *Death Likes It Hot* (under pseud. Edgar Box), Dutton, 1954; Heinemann, 1955. *Messiah*, Dutton, 1954; Heinemann, 1955; rev. ed., Little, 1965. *A Thirsty Evil: 7 Short Stories*, Zero, 1956; Heinemann, 1958. *Rocking the Boat*, Little, 1962; Heinemann, 1963. *Three: Williwaw, A Thirsty Evil, Julian the Apos-tate*, NAL, 1962. *Julian*, Little, Heinemann, 1964; Modern Library, 1970; NAL; Random House, 1977. *Washington, D.C.*, Little, Heinemann, 1967; NAL, 1968; Random, Ballantine, 1976. *Myra Breckinridge*, Little, Blond, 1968; Bantam, 1974. *Reflections upon a Sinking Ship*, Little, Heinemann, 1969. *Two Sisters: A Novel in the Form of a Memoir*, Little, Heinemann, 1970. *Homage to Daniel Shays: Collected Essays, 1952–1972*, Random House, 1972; pub. as *Collected Essays, 1952–1972*, Heine-mann, 1974; Random House, 1972. *Burr*, Random House, 1973; Heinemann, 1974; Bantam, 1976. *Myron*, Random House, 1974; Heinemann, Ballantine, 1975. *Eighteen Seventy-Six*, Random House, 1976.

Also, the following plays: *Honor*, in *Television Plays for Writers: Eight Television Plays* (ed. by A. S. Burack), The Writer, 1957; pub. as *On the March to the Sea: A Southern Comedy* (rev. version), in *Three Plays*, 1962. *Visit to a Small Planet and Other Television Plays*, Little, 1957. *The Best Man: A Play of Politics*, Little, 1960; in *Three Plays*, 1962. *Three Plays (Visit to a Small Planet, The Best Man, On the March to the Sea)*, Heinemann, 1962. *Romulus: A New Comedy* (adaptation of the play by Friedrich Dürrenmatt), Dramatist Play Service, 1962. *Weekend*, Dramatist Play Service, 1968. *An Evening with Richard Nixon*, Random House, 1972.

Also, author of numerous plays for film and television.

VILAR, ESTHER   1935–

Der Dressierte Mann, Caann Verlag, 1971; pub. as *The Manipulated Man*, Farrar, 1973.

VONNEGUT, KURT, JR.   1922–

Player Piano, Scribner, 1952; Macmillan, 1953; Delacorte, 1971; Dell, 1972, 1974. *The Sirens of Titan*, Fawcett, 1959; Gollancz, 1962; Delacorte, 1971; Dell, 1971, 1974. *Canary in a Cathouse*, Fawcett, 1961. *Mother Night*, Fawcett, 1961; Cape, 1968; Delacorte, 1971; Dell, 1972, 1974. *Cat's Cradle*, Holt, Gollancz, 1963; Delacorte, 1971; Dell, 1974. *God Bless You, Mr. Rosewater; or, Pearls Before Swine*, Holt, Cape, 1965; Delacorte, 1971; Dell, 1974. *Welcome to the Monkey House: A Collection of Short Works*, Delacorte, 1968; Dell, 1970, 1974. *Slaughterhouse-Five; or, The Children's Crusade*, Delacorte, 1969; Cape, 1970; Dell, 1971, 1974. *Happy Birthday, Wanda June*, Delacorte, 1971; Cape, 1973; Dell, 1974. *Between Time and Timbuktu; or, Prometheus-5: A Space Fantasy*, Delacorte, 1972; Dell, 1974. *Breakfast of Champions; or Goodbye Blue Monday*, Delacorte, Cape, 1973; Dell, 1974, 1975. *Wampeters, Foma, and Granfalloons*, Delacorte, 1974; Dell, 1975, 1976. *Slapstick, or Lonesome No More*, Delacorte, Cape, 1976.

Also, author of "The Very First Christmas Morning," *Better Homes and Gardens*, December 1962. "Fortitude," *Playboy*, September 1968.

Also, author of the play, *Welcome to the Monkey House*, Dell, 1970.

WAKEFIELD, DAN   1932–

Island in the City: The World of Spanish Harlem, Houghton Mifflin, 1959; Arno, 1975. *Revolt in the South*, Grove, 1961. *The Addict: An Anthology* (editor), Fawcett, 1963, 1974. *Between the Lines*, NAL, 1967. *Supernation at Peace and War*, Atlantic Monthly Pr., 1968. *Going All the Way*,

Delacorte, 1970; Dell, 1971. *Starting Over*, Delacorte, 1973; Dell, 1974. *All Her Children*, Doubleday, 1976.

Also, contributor, *Who We Are: An Atlantic Chronicle of the United States and Vietnam* (ed. by Robert Manning and Michael Janeway), Atlantic Monthly Pr., 1969; and contributor of articles, essays, reviews, and short stories to numerous periodicals and several anthologies.

WALKER, ALICE 1944–

Once, Harcourt, 1968. *The Third Life of Grange Copeland*, Harcourt, 1970. *Revolutionary Petunias*, Harcourt, 1973. *Langston Hughes*, Crowell, 1973. *In Love and Trouble: Stories of Black Women*, Harcourt, 1973. *Meridian*, Harcourt, 1976.

WALLACE, IRVING 1916–

The Fabulous Originals, Knopf, 1955. *The Square Pegs*, Knopf, 1957. *The Sins of Philip Fleming*, Fell, 1954; NAL, 1968. *The Fabulous Showman*, Knopf, 1959; NAL, 1973. *The Chapman Report*, Simon & Schuster, 1960; NAL. *The Twenty-Seventh Wife*, Simon & Schuster, 1961; NAL, 1971. *The Prize*, Simon & Schuster, 1962; NAL. *The Three Sirens*, Simon & Schuster, 1963; NAL, 1971. *The Man*, Simon & Schuster, 1964; Fawcett, 1971; Bantam, 1974. *The Sunday Gentlemen*, Simon & Schuster, 1965; Bantam, 1976; Pocket. *The Plot*, Simon & Schuster, 1967; Pocket, 1973. *The Writing of One Novel*, Simon & Schuster, 1968, 1969; Pocket, 1969, 1971. *The Seven Minutes*, Simon & Schuster, 1969, Pocket, 1973. *The Nympho and Other Maniacs*, Simon & Schuster, 1971; Pocket, 1972. *The Word*, Simon & Schuster, 1972; Pocket, 1973. *The Fan Club*, Simon & Schuster, 1974; Bantam, 1975. *The People's Almanac* (with David Wallechinsky), Doubleday, 1975. *The R Document*, Simon & Schuster, 1976, Bantam. *The Book of Lists* (with David Wallechinsky and Amy Wallace), Morrow, 1977. *The Two* (wth Amy Wallace), Simon & Schuster, 1978. *The People's Almanac 2* (with David Wallechinsky), Morrow, Bantam, 1978.

WAMBAUGH, JOSEPH 1937–

The New Centurions, Little, 1971; Dell, 1972. *The Blue Knight*, Little, 1972; Dell, 1973. *The Onion Field: A True Story*, Delacrote, 1973; Dell, 1974. *The Choirboys*, Delacorte, 1975; Dell, 1976. *The Black Marble*, Delacorte, 1978.

WEIDMAN, JEROME 1913–

I Can Get It for You Wholesale, Simon & Schuster, 1937; Heinemann, 1938. *What's in It for Me?*, Simon & Schuster, 1938; Heinemann, 1939. *The Horse That Could Whistle "Dixie" and Other Stories*, Simon &

Schuster, 1939; Heinemann, 1941. *Letter of Credit*, Simon & Schuster, 1940. *I'll Never Go There Anymore*, Simon & Schuster, 1941; Heinemann, 1942. *The Lights around the Shore*, Simon & Schuster, 1943; Hale, 1948. *Too Early to Tell*, Reynal, 1946. *The Captain's Tiger*, Reynal, 1949. *The Price Is Right*, Harcourt, 1949; Hammond, 1950; Manor, 1973, 1976. *The Hand of the Hunter*, Harcourt, 1951; Cape, 1952. *The Third Angel*, Doubleday, 1953; Cape, 1954. *Give Me Your Love*, Eton, 1954. *Your Daughter Iris*, Doubleday, 1955; Cape, 1956. *A Dime a Throw*, Doubleday, 1957. *The Enemy Camp*, Random House, 1958; Heinemann, 1959. *Before You Go*, Random House, 1960; Heinemann, 1963. *My Father Sits in the Dark and Other Selected Stories*, Random House, 1961; Heinemann, 1963. *Back Talk*, Random House, 1963. *The Sound of Bow Bells*, Random House, 1962; Heinemann, 1963. *Word of Mouth*, Random House, 1964; Bodley Head, 1965. *Where the Sun Never Sets and Other Stories*, Heinemann, 1964. *The Death of Dickie Draper and Nine Other Stories*, Random House, 1965. *Other People's Money*, Random House, Bodley Head, 1967. *The Center of the Action*, Random House, 1969; Bodley Head, 1970. *Fourth Street East*, Random House, Bodley Head, Pinnacle, 1971; Lanewood, 1972. *Last Respects*, Random House, Bodley Head, 1972. *Tiffany Street*, Random House, Bodley Head, 1974; Pinnacle, 1975. *The Temple*, Simon & Schuster, 1976.

Also, the following plays: *Fiorello* (with George Abbott), Random House, 1960. *Tenderloin* (with George Abbott, adaptation of the work by Samuel Hopkins Adams), Random House, 1961. *I Can Get It for You Wholesale*, Random House, 1963. *Ivory Tower* (with James Yaffe), Dramatists Play Service, 1969. *Asterisk! A Comedy of Terrors*, Dramatists Play Service, 1969.

Also, the following short stories: "Absolutely Darlings," *McCall's*, July 1965. "Friend of Mary Fowler," *Redbook*, July 1965. "The Wife of the Man Who Suddenly Loved Women," *Ladies Home Journal*, June 1966. "Good Man, Bad Man," *Saturday Evening Post*, July 1967.

Also, editor: *A Somerset Maugham Sampler*, Garden City Bks., 1943. *Traveler's Cheque*, Doubleday, 1954. *The First College Bowl Question Book*, Random House, 1961.

Also, author of plays for stage, film, and television.

WEINTRAUB, STANLEY 1929–

An Unfinished Novel by Bernard Shaw, Dodd, 1958. *C. P. Snow: A Spectrum*, Scribner, 1963. *Private Shaw and Public Shaw*, Braziller, 1963. *The War in the Wards: Korea's Forgotten Battle*, Doubleday, 1964; rev. ed., 1977. *The Yellow Book: Quintessence of the Nineties*, Anchor, 1964. *Reggie: A Portrait of Reginald Turner*, Braziller, 1965. *The Art of William Golding* (with B. S. Oldsey), Harcourt, 1965; Indiana Univ., 1968. *The Savoy: Nineties Experiment*, Penn. State Univ., 1966. *Aubrey Beardsley*,

Penn State Univ., 1967; rev. ed., 1977. *Biography and Truth*, Bobbs, 1967. *The Last Great Cause; The Intellectuals and the Spanish Civil War*, 1968. *Journey to Heartbreak: Crucible Years of Bernard Shaw, 1914–1918*, Weybright, 1971. *Whistler: A Biography*, Weybright, 1974. *Lawrence of Arabia: The Literary Impulse*, Louisiana State Univ., 1975. *Four Rossettis: A Victorian Biography*, Weybright, 1977.

Also, editor: *Shaw Review, 1956–*. *The Court Theater 1904–07* (with Desmond McCarthy), American Theater Assoc., Univ. of Miami, 1966. *The Literary Criticism of Oscar Wilde*, Univ. of Nebraska, 1968. *Shaw: An Autobiography 1856–1898*, Weybright, 1969. *Evolution of Revolt: Early Postwar Writings of T. E. Lawrence*, Penn. State Univ., 1968. *Shaw: An Autobiography 1898–1950*, Weybright, 1970. *Green Carnation* (with Robert Hichens), Univ. of Nebraska, 1970. *Saint Joan*, Bobbs, 1971. *Bernard Shaw's Nondramatic Literary Criticism*, Univ. of Nebraska, 1972. *Directions in Literary Criticism* (with Philip Young), Penn. State Univ., 1973. *Saint Joan: Fifty Years After, 1923–24 to 1973–74*, Louisiana State Univ., 1973. *The Portable Bernard Shaw*, Viking, 1977.

Also, contributor to various magazines and journals.

WEST, JESSAMYN 1907–

The Friendly Persuasion, Harcourt, 1945, 1956; Hodder and Stoughton, 1946; Avon, 1970. *The Witch Diggers*, Harcourt, 1951; Heinemann, 1952. *Cress Delahanty*, Harcourt, 1953, 1954; Hodder and Stoughton, 1954; Avon, 1970. *Love, Death, and the Ladies' Drill Team*, Harcourt, 1955, 1968; pub. as *Learn to Say Goodbye*, Hodder and Stoughton, 1957. *To See the Dream*, Harcourt, 1957; Hodder and Stoughton, 1958; Avon, 1974. *Love Is Not What You Think*, Harcourt, 1959; pub. as *A Woman's Love*, Hodder and Stoughton, 1960. *South of the Angels*, Harcourt, 1960; Hodder and Stoughton, 1961. *A Matter of Time*, Harcourt, 1966; Macmillan, 1967. *Leafy Rivers*, Harcourt, 1967; Macmillan, 1968; Avon, 1974. *Except for Me and Thee: A Companion to The Friendly Persuasion*, Harcourt, Macmillan, 1969; Avon, 1971, 1974. *Crimson Ramblers of the World, Farewell*, Harcourt, 1970; Macmillan, 1971. *Hide and Seek: A Continuing Journey*, Harcourt, Macmillan, 1973. *The Secret Look: Poems*, Harcourt, 1974. *The Massacre at Fall Creek*, Harcourt, G. K. Hall, 1975. *The Woman Said Yes*, Harcourt, 1976. *A Story of Life and Death*, Gollancz, 1977.

Also, the following uncollected short stories: "Search for Tommorrow," *Good Housekeeping*, June 1962. "Last Laugh," *Redbook*, July 1962. "In Search of a Kiss," *Good Housekeeping*, June 1963 "For One Golden Moment," *Good Housekeeping*, November 1963. "Good-bye, Bossy," *Ladies' Home Journal*, June 1965. And others.

Also, editor, *A Quaker Reader*, Viking, 1962. Author of works for the stage and film.

WESTLAKE, DONALD 1933–

The Mercenaries, Random House, 1960. *Killing Time*, Random House, 1961. *361*, Random House, 1962. *Killy*, Random House, 1963. *Pity Him Afterwards*, Random House, 1964. *The Fugitive Pigeon*, Random House, 1965. *The Busy Body*, Random House, 1966. *The Spy in the Ointment*, Random House, 1966. *God Save the Mark*, Random House, 1967. *Philip*, Crowell, 1967. *Once Against The Law* (compiled with Philip Klass), Macmillan, 1968. *Who Stole Sassi Manoon?*, Random House, 1968. *Somebody Owes Me Money*, Random House, 1969. *Up Your Banners*, Macmillan, 1969. *The Hot Rock*, Simon & Schuster, 1970. *Adios, Scheherezade*, Simon & Schuster, 1970. *I Gave at the Office*, Simon & Schuster, 1971. *Under an English Heaven*, Simon & Schuster, 1971; Pocket, 1972. *Bank Shot*, Simon & Schuster, 1972; Pocket, 1973. *Cops and Robbers*, M. Evans, 1972; NAL, 1973. *Gangway!* (with Brian Garfield), M. Evans, 1973. *Help I'm Being Held Prisoner*, M. Evans, 1974; Ballantine, 1975. *Jimmy the Kid*, M. Evans, 1974; Ballantine, 1976. *Too Much*, M. Evans, 1975; Fawcett, 1976. *Brother's Keeper*, M. Evans, 1975; Fawcett, 1976. *Dancing Aztecs*, M. Evans, 1976. *Enough*, M. Evans, 1977. *Nobody's Perfect*, M. Evans, 1977.

Also, under the pseudonym Tucker Coe: *Kinds of Love, Kinds of Death*, Random House, 1966. *Murder Among Children*, Random House, 1968. *Wax Apple*, Random House, 1970. *A Jade in Aries*, Random House, 1971. *Don't Lie to Me*, Random House, 1972.

Also, under the pseudonym Richard Stark: *The Hunter*, Pocket, 1963. *The Man With the Getaway Face*, Pocket, 1963. *The Outfit*, Pocket, 1963. *The Mourner*, Pocket, 1963. *The Score*, Pocket, 1964. *The Jugger*, Pocket, 1965. *The Seventh*, Pocket, 1966. *The Handle*, Pocket, 1966. *The Rare Coin Score*, Gold Medal, 1967. *The Green Eagle Score*, Gold Medal, 1967. *The Damsel*, Macmillan, 1967. *The Dame*, Macmillan, 1967. *The Black Ice Score*, Gold Medal, 1968. *The Sour Lemon Score*, Gold Medal, 1969. *The Blackbird*, Macmillan, 1969. *Deadly Edge*, Random House, 1971. *Lemons Never Lie*, World, 1971. *Slayground*, Random House, 1971. *Plunder Squad*, Random House, 1972. *Butcher's Moon*, Random House, 1974.

WHITE, THEODORE H. 1915–

Thunder Out of China (with Annalee Jacoby), Sloane, 1946; Da Capo, 1975. *Fire in the Ashes*, Sloane, 1953. *The Mountain Road*, Sloane, 1953. *The View from the Fortieth Floor*, Sloane, 1960. *The Making of the President—1960*, Atheneum, 1961; NAL, 1967. *The Making of the President—1964*, Atheneum, 1965; NAL, 1966. *The Making of the President—1968*, Atheneum, 1969. *The Making of the President—1972*, Atheneum, Bantam, 1973. *Breach of Faith: Fall of Richard Nixon*, Atheneum, 1975; Dell, 1976.

Also, editor, *The Stillwell Papers*, Sloane, 1948; and contributor to numerous magazines and newspapers.

WICKER, THOMAS GREY 1926–

Tom Wicker also writes under pseudonym Paul Connolly.
Kennedy Without Tears: The Man Behind the Myth, Morrow, 1964. *JFK and LBJ: The Influence of Personality Upon Politics*, Morrow, 1968. *A Time to Die*, Quadrangle, 1975. *On Press*, Viking, 1978.

Also, novels: *The Kingpin*, Sloane, 1953. *The Devil Must*, Harper, 1957. *The Judgment*, Morrow, 1961. *Facing the Lions*, Viking, 1973.

Novels under pseudonym Paul Connolly: *Get Out of Town*, Gold Medal, 1951. *Tears Are for Angels*, Gold Medal, 1952. *So Fair So Evil*, Gold Medal, 1955.

Also, author of introduction, *U.S. Kerner Commission Report*, Dutton, 1968; foreword, *The People's President: The Electoral College in American History and the Direct Vote*, Simon & Schuster, 1968; and contributor of numerous articles to periodicals.

WILLIAMS, JOHN A. 1925–

The Angry Ones, Ace, 1960; Pocket, 1970; pub. as *One for New York*, The Chatham Bkseller. *Night Song*, Farrar, 1961; Pocket, 1970; The Chatham Bkseller, 1975. *Sissie*, Farrar, 1963; Anchor; The Chatham Bkseller, 1975. *Africa: Her History, Lands and People*, Cooper Sq., 1963. *The Protectors*, Farrar, 1964. *This Is My Country, Too*, NAL, 1965. *The Man Who Cried I Am*, Little, 1967; NAL, 1972. *Sons of Darkness, Sons of Light*, Little, 1969; Pocket, 1970. *The Most Native of Sons: A Bibliography of Richard Wright*, Doubleday, 1970. *The King God Didn't Save*, Coward, 1970; Pocket, 1971. *Captain Blackman*, Doubleday, 1971; Bantam, 1974. *Flashbacks*, Doubleday, 1973; Anchor. *Minorities in the City*, Harper, 1975. *Mothersill and the Foxes*, Doubleday, 1975. *The Junior Bachelor Society*, Doubleday, 1976.

Also, contributor to the following anthologies: *Harlem: A Community in Transition*, Citadel, 1964. *Best Short Stories of Negro Writers*, Little 1967. *Black on Black*, Macmillan, 1968. *34 x Schwartze Lieb*, Barmier & Nickel, 1968. *How We Live*, Macmillan, 1968. *Dark Symphony*, Free Press, 1968. *Nat Turner: 10 Black Writers Respond*, Beacon, 1968. *The Now Reader*, Scott Foresman, 1969. *The New Black Poetry*, International, 1969. *Black Literature in America*, Crowell, 1970. *The Black Novelist*, Merrill, 1970. *Black Identity*, Holt, 1970. *A Native Sons Reader*, Lippincott, 1970. *The New Lively Rhetoric*, Holt, 1970. *Brothers and Sisters*, Macmillan, 1970. *19 Necromancers from Now*, Doubleday, 1970. *Black Insights*, Ginn, 1971. *The Immigrant Experience*, Dial, 1971. *Cavalcade*, Houghton Mifflin, 1971. *Racism*, Crowell, 1971. *Black Literature in America*, McGraw-Hill, 1971. *An Introduction to Poetry*, St. Martin's, 1972. *The Age of Anxiety*, Allyn & Bacon, 1972. *The Fact of Fiction*, Canfield, 1972. *Different Drummers*, Random House, 1973. *Three for Show*, Random House, 1973. *The Choice of Fiction*, Winthrop, 1974. *Giant Talk*, Random House, 1975. *Okike, No. 7*, Univ. of Massachusetts, 1975.

Also, editor of the following anthologies: *The Angry Black*, Lancer Books, 1962. *Beyond the Angry Black*, Cooper Sq., 1966, 1967; NAL, 1971. *Amistad I*, Vintage, 1970, *Amistad II*, Vintage, 1971. *Yardbird VII*, Yardbird, 1977.

Also, contributor of articles to the following magazines: "Subject: Charlie Parker," *Swank*, July 1961. "Dick Gregory: Desegrated Comic," *Swank*, September 1961. "We Regret To Inform You," *Nugget*, December 1962. "Glad Song of the A-Train," *Cavalier*, March 1963. "The Literary Ghetto," *Saturday Review*, April 1963. "Neither Life Enough or Time," *New Leader*, May 1963. "Sex in Black and White," *Cavalier*, September 1963. "The Negro in American Literature," *Ebony*, September 1963. "Small Paradise," *Cavalier*, September 1963. "This Is My Country Too," *Holiday*, August & September 1964. "Never Before or Since," *New York Magazine*, May 1965. "Don't Look Down Your Nose," *Negro Digest*, October 1965. "Black Man in Europe," *Holiday*, March 1967. "Chicago: Three Negro Families," *Holiday*, January 1967. "Pessimistic Postscript," *Holiday*, June 1967. "Race, War and Politics," *Negro Digest*, August 1967. "Juifs et Noirs en Conflit," *Les Nouveaux Cahiers*, 1968. "An Afro-American Looks at South Africa," *Vista*, 1969. "Doing It Ourselves," *Essence*, October 1971. "Grenada: Their Country Too," *Yardbird Reader I*, 1972. "Lourdes Is on Mott Street," *Yardbird Reader II*, 1973. "Crisis in American Letters," *The Black Scholar*, June 1975. And others.

Also, editor: *Negro Market Newsletter*, 1956–57; *Audience Magazine*, 1970–72; *American Journal* (contributor), 1972–73.

Also, author of several introductions to published works. Contributor to numerous newspapers, magazines, and television programs.

WOODHOUSE, MARTIN 1932–

Tree Frog, Coward, 1966. *Bush Baby*, Coward, 1968; pub. as *Rock Baby*, Heinemann, 1968. *Phil and Me*, Coward, 1970. *Mama Doll*, Coward, 1972. *Blue Bone*, Coward, 1973. *The Medici Guns* (with Robert Ross), Dutton, 1974; Ballantine, 1976. *Moon Hill*, Coward, 1976. *The Medici Emerald* (with Robert Ross), Dutton, 1976. *The Medici Hawks* (with Robert Ross), Dutton, 1978.

Also, under the pseudonym John Charlton, crime fiction: *The Remington Set*.

WYDEN, PETER

Suburbia's Coddled Kids, Doubleday, 1961. *The Hired Killers*, Morrow, 1962. *The Overweight Society*, Morrow, 1965. *How the Doctors Diet* (with Barbara Wyden), Trident, 1968. *The Intimate Enemy: How to Fight Fair in Love and Marriage*, Morrow, 1969. *Inside the Sex Clinic* (with Barbara Wyden), World, 1971.

Name Index